This modern text is designed to prepare you for your future professional career. While theories, ideas, techniques, and data are dynamic, the information contained in this volume will provide you a quick and useful reference as well as a guide for future learning for many years to come. Your familiarity with the contents of this book will make it an important volume in your professional library.

EX LIBRIS

Foundations of Personnel/
Human Resource Management

Foundations of Personnel/
Human Resource Management

Revised Edition

John M. Ivancevich
Cullen Professor of
Organizational Behavior
and Management
University of Houston

William F. Glueck
Late Professor of
University of Georgia

1983

BUSINESS PUBLICATIONS, INC.
Plano, Texas   75075

ISBN 0-256-02694-7

Library of Congress Catalog Card No. 82–71973

Printed in the United States of America

1 2 3 4 5 6 7 8 9 0 V 0 9 8 7 6 5 4 3

Preface

The first edition of this text, by Bill Glueck, was entitled *Foundations of Personnel*. It was Bill's belief that many faculty members wanted an uncluttered, straightforward, practically oriented text for their personnel course. He provided a text that appealed to instructors and students both, and this accomplishment is a tribute to his ability to communicate his knowledge in a clear, intelligible way.

Bill's untimely passing prevented his further development and refinement of the text. This revised edition incorporates Bill Glueck's idea, orientation, and basic text structure in its examination of personnel/human resource management (P/HRM).

Personnel/human resource management is a necessary activity in all organizations. Its focal point is *people*. People are the lifeblood of organizations. Without them, there is no need for P/HRM systems, programs, or procedures. Because they involve people, P/HRM activities have to be fine-tuned and properly implemented in order to achieve desired outcomes. The uniqueness of P/HRM lies in its emphasis on people in work settings and its concern for the well-being and comfort of the human resources in an organization. This text focuses upon people who work directly in P/HRM as specialists, and those who, as employees (e.g., engineers, clerks, typists, machinists, chemists, teachers, nurses), are influenced by it.

In order to make the book interesting, scholarly, and practical, a number of pedagogical procedures were adopted:

1. Each chapter begins with a brief list of behavioral objectives and an outline.
2. Each chapter is introduced by a short case emphasizing applied P/HRM techniques and issues. At various points in the chapter, and at its conclusion, the case is further developed. They highlight the chapter's content.
3. Most chapters contain the diagnostic model which serves as the integrative framework of this book.
4. In most chapters, the role played by a P/HRM manager, specialist, or operating manager is described.
5. Most chapters include a "P/HRM Managers Close-Up". These real-life personal viewpoints of P/HRM managers or specialists answer the question: "What does someone actually working in this function do?"
6. Most chapters conclude with recommendations for the most effective use of P/HRM in seven kinds of organizations, which differ on the basis of size (number or employees), complexity of products or services, and degree to which products or services change over time.
7. Each chapter summary provides students with a handy, concise reference to the chapter's main points of interest.

8. The application cases and experiential exercises at the end of each of the six parts reflect the successes and failures of real firms such as Honeywell, General Foods, IBM, Nucor, AT&T, Hooker Chemical, Bechtel Power, DuPont, and Firestone Tire and Rubber.
9. A comprehensive glossary of key terms is provided at the end of each chapter.

The Parts

The revised edition consists of six parts. Part One "Introduction to Personnel/Human Resource Management and the Environment," contains three chapters. Chapter 1 defines the role of P/HRM in organizations. Chapter 2 provides the integrative model that is used throughout the book. Chapter 3 is a comprehensive treatment of equal employment opportunity laws and programs.

Part Two, "Analysis, Planning, and Staffing," contains four chapters covering: job analysis and design, Chapter 4; planning, Chapter 5; recruitment, Chapter 6; and selection, Chapter 7.

Part Three examines performance evaluation and development. Chapter 8 covers performance evaluation; Chapter 9, orientation and training; Chapter 10, development of personnel; and Chapter 11, career planning and development.

Part Four, "Motivation, Rewards, and Discipline," contains five chapters. Chapter 12 discusses motivation. Compensation is covered in Chapters 13 and 14. Employee benefits, services, and pensions are presented in Chapter 15. Discipline and the difficult employee is covered in Chapter 16.

Part Five, "Labor Relations and Safety and Health," includes Chapters 17 and 18, on labor unions, and Chapter 19, on employee safety and health.

Part Six, "Work Scheduling and Evaluation," covers work scheduling, Chapter 20; and procedures for evaluating the P/HRM function, Chapter 21.

New Features

The dynamic changes in personnel/human resource management required some alteration, deletion, and expansion of material presented in the first edition. User and nonuser comments were reviewed and carefully considered in the course of this revision. In addition, personnel/human resource experts in organizations were interviewed. These endeavors resulted in some new features which add to Bill Glueck's original ideas and views about P/HRM:

- A totally revised diagnostic framework used throughout the book. The model is first presented in Exhibit 2–1.
- A totally updated and revised Chapter 3, "Equal Employment Opportunity Programs." In the previous edition this chapter was at the back of the book. The increasing importance of laws, regulations, and court rulings to P/HRM demands more prominence for this topic.
- Four totally new chapters on extremely important subjects: Chapter 4, "Job Analysis and Design"; Chapter 11, "Career Planning and Development"; Chapter 12, "Motivation"; and Chapter 20, "Work Scheduling and Evaluation". Each chapter presents the most relevant information and up-to-date data.

- The first edition contained only one chapter on labor relations. This was insufficient, considering the influence which organized labor has had on P/HRM activities. Consequently, two chapters, 17 and 18, now cover labor unions and relations.
- A new section appearing in many chapters is the "P/HRM Manager Close-Up." Because they describe actual P/HRM specialists, they add a realism difficult to capture with hypothetical vignettes or cases.
- Actual company forms, materials, and charts are used throughout this book. They were furnished by P/HRM managers who wanted to share them with students and instructors.
- Actual company cases rather than hypothetical cases are used to examine P/HRM issues, problems, and successes. The thoughts, actions, and decisions of the people involved are presented for students to review and consider. These realistic cases create a better understanding of what P/HRM entails within organizations.
- A total of eight experiential exercises appear at the end of the various parts. They are streamlined and suited for short time periods.

Each of these new features was designed to (1) stimulate student interest in P/HRM as a field of study and as a set of programs and procedures that influence people within organizations; (2) clearly illustrate that P/HRM is a dynamic, changing field; (3) show by example that what is being discussed has both a theoretical rationale (often a research base) and offers practical useful applications in the "real world"—the organization; and (4) provide instructors with material, statistics, and illustrations that can help make the classroom experience more exciting. In essence, the revised edition was written for students and instructors alike.

Acknowledgments

A textbook in its final form is the result of the efforts of numerous people. Special thanks are due to the following P/HRM managers and specialists who willingly provided ideas, information, and data:

David M. Aultfather
Manager—Personnel Services
Miller-Dwan Hospital
and Medical Center

John F. Baggaley
Director of Personnel
Doctors Medical Center

John F. Barrows
Director—Training and Development
Packaging Corporation of America

Christian K. Bement
Vice President
Director of Industrial Relations
Thrifty Corporation

Paul S. Bernius
Director, Manpower
Planning and Development
Hilti Corporation

Robert L. Berra
Vice President—Personnel
Monsanto Company

Betty Bessler
Director of Personnel
Mary Kay Cosmetics

Louis J. Bibri
Vice President and Director
of Employee Relations
Armstrong World Industries, Inc.

John D. Blodger
Group Director of
Employee Relations
Bendix Corporation

William J. Danos
Safety Engineer
New Wales Chemicals, Inc.

Eileen M. DeCoursey
Vice President
Employee Relations
Johns-Manville

Howard Falberg
Vice President—Personnel
Associated Dry Good Corporation

Adrianne H. Geiger
Manager, Human Resource Systems
Owens-Illinois, Inc.

Ernest J. E. Griffes
Director of Employee Benefits
Levi Strauss & Co.

Richard W. Hucke
Vice President—Human Resources
Weston Company

Audrey Johnson
Employee Relations
Manager
Gillette Company

Mary Kale
Senior College Relations
Representative
Bethlehem Steel Company

David A. Miron
Director of Management Development
and Human Resource Systems
Owens-Illinois, Inc.

Henry Oliver
Manager of Compensation
and Benefits
University Computing Company

Andrew J. Porter
Manager—Communications and
Development
Honeywell Information Systems

James H. Pou
Staff Vice President
Employee Relations
University Computing Company

James Quigley
Vice President for
Human Resources
Dr Pepper

William M. Read
Senior Vice President
Atlantic Richfield Company

William J. Streidl
Director of Management Education
and Development
Tenneco, Inc.

Denise Wilkerson
Assistant Director of Industrial
Relations
Dailey Oil Tools, Inc.

The revised manuscript was reviewed and critiqued by some outstanding reviewers, many of whose ideas and recommendations were used. Their promptness, tactfulness, and knowledge about P/HRM were certainly appreciated. They were:

Ron Beaulieu
Central Michigan University

Michael Gallagher
University of Arkansas Little Rock

Peter Hechler
California State University
Los Angeles

Bobby K. Marks
Sam Houston State University

Cynthia Pavett
University of San Diego

Hussein M. Shatshat
Western Illinois University

Robert L. Trosper
S. Oklahoma City
Junior College

Dorothy A. Wentorf
University of Wisconsin-Oshkosh

Some of the photography was done professionally by Tom Billups of Houston, Texas, who coordinated the details and provided what was needed.

The Business Publications, Inc. team of Cliff Francis and Jimmy Neal had the patience to discuss this revision with me and were willing to support the effort necessary to complete such a project. Specific editorial and organizational support was provided by Cindy Carrel, who, as developmental editor, offered many good suggestions.

Another important contributor to this revision was Carol Geisler, revision editor at Business Publications, Inc., who coordinated the important details of the entire project. Without her efforts the revision would still be on my desk.

I also want to personally recognize my secretary, Erin Mandolare, who pleasantly tolerated my questions and requests, handwritten reams of copy, the retyping of repeated drafts, and even malfunctioning word-processing equipment. Despite all crises, Erin was able to provide the finished book on time.

Finally, I want to dedicate this revision to Bill Glueck. Bill was a hard worker whose contributions will endure long beyond his passing. This edition of *Foundations of Personnel/Human Resource Management* was made possible only because he took the necessary, pioneering step of developing an idea and converting it into an educationally sound text.

John M. Ivancevich

Contents

Foundations of Personnel/
Human Resource Management

Part One

H. Armstrong Roberts

Personnel/human resource management (P/HRM) is concerned with the effective management of people at work. P/HRM examines what can or should be done to make people both more productive and more satisfied with their working lives.

This book has been written for all those interested in people working within organizations. Its goal is to help develop more effective managers and staff specialists who work directly with the human resource of organizations. Their function is called personnel, employee relations, or human resource management. In this book the term *personnel/human resource management* (P/HRM) will be used.

Part One consists of three chapters. Chapter 1 is an introduction to P/HRM. The diagnostic approach to P/HRM is introduced in Chapter 2, which also reviews some behavioral science perspectives on people and how this knowledge affects employee effectiveness at work. The ways managers use knowledge of environmental factors—such as the work setting, government regulations, and union restrictions—to influence the performance of people at work are also discussed in Chapter 2. Chapter 3 describes the legal environmental influences on P/HRM. A number of major laws and regulations are discussed in this chapter.

Introduction to Personnel/Human Resource Management and the Environment

H. Armstrong Roberts

H. Armstrong Roberts

Chapter One

Personnel/Human Resource Management: Its Role in Organizations

Learning Objectives

After studying this chapter, you should be able to:

- Define what is meant by the term *personnel/ human resource management.*

- Describe the personnel/human resource management activities performed in organizations.

- Explain why human resources are the key ingredient in any organization's success.

- Discuss the role that specialists and operating managers play in performing personnel/human resource management activities.

- Illustrate the relationships among objectives, policies, and rules.

Chapter Outline

Case

Don Brokop

For the past nine years, Don Brokop has proven himself to be an outstanding shift supervisor at the Melody Machine Products Corp. plant in South Chicago. He has worked every shift, likes people, and recently was the winner of the Outstanding Plant Manager Award. Don is now 34 years old and is beginning to look closely at his career plans. He believes that if he is going to be in the right place at the right time he will have to gain some experience in jobs other than production.

Last week a position opened at the plant requiring an assistant director of personnel/human resources. At first Don forgot about the position but later asked his boss, Marty Fogestrom, about it. Marty encouraged Don to really think his plans through and to consider whether the personnel/ human resource area was where he wanted to work.

Don talked further with plant colleagues about the new position, looked over the want ads in the *Chicago Tribune,* read *The Wall Street Journal,* and found a number of interesting news items. He noted that many different careers existed in the personnel/ human resource area. He realized that there was a lot of misunderstanding about the job being done by Melody's department of personnel/human resources. He figured his experience in supervisory management would be helpful if he was fortunate enough to land the new job. What struck him the most was that issues and problems concerning people are what personnel/human resources are about.

Highlighted here are a few of the news items that caught his eye:

- There is a videotape circulating through Xerox Corporation in which President David T. Kearns candidly sets forth the company's key strategies, its capital investments, the priorities it places on each of its divisions, and the competition it faces. He ends by saying, "I pledge to you that management of this company at (all levels) will listen to you and put your ideas to work."[1]

- The management philosophies and business principles that have made Matsushita Electric Japan's largest consumer electronics company now flourish in 33 countries on six continents (over 117,000 employees and over $10 billion sales). The reason for this international success is Matsushita's realization that companies alone don't make great products, people do.

- Dow Chemical Company and American Airlines open pages of their company publications to employee criticisms and questions. Embarrassing letters—accusations of management featherbedding, poor labor relations, stupid supervisory practices—are published.

- Brown and Williamson set in motion a three-year plan to close its large tobacco facility in Louisville, Kentucky, employing 3,000 employees. The company was required by terms of its contracts with the Tobacco Workers and the Machinists to give 18 months advance notice. It chose to conduct the phase out over a three-year period. Managers and workers joined together to implement this ambitious readjustment program.

- There are employees bringing legal suits against their employers for supposedly job-related personal, physical, and mental problems. Job pressure, stress, and having to

---

[1]"A New Way of Managing People," *Business Week,* May 11, 1981, p. 89.

work irregular hours were being blamed for marital dissatisfaction, bowel and bladder disorders, heart attack, and sexual dysfunction. The accused parties included Chase Manhattan Bank, U.S. Steel, the U.S. Army, and the City of Chicago.

Don thought about his recent conversations, his career plans, the news stories, and the challenges of moving from production to personnel/human resource management. He wondered if he was qualified for this kind of job, but he had always been confident and he considered his college education and experience invaluable. He wanted new challenges. Then he learned through the grapevine that the job was his if he wanted to make the move. (Don's decision will be presented at the end of this chapter.)

People; human resources; making organizations more aware of human resources; being in the people business—these words and thoughts are common in our modern society. Today bromides and panaceas for solving people problems are being replaced by a total, professional approach to personnel/human resource management (P/HRM). Don Brokop is considering the challenges associated with this new wave of professional treatment and concern for people within organizations. Organizations are definitely in the people business—Don certainly saw this, after only a quick review of a few news stories.

This book will focus on people in organizational settings. The entire book will be concerned with the employees of organizations—the clerks, technicians, supervisors, managers, and executives. Large, medium, and small organizations, such as IBM, Procter & Gamble, Safeway, Medco, Greensway Pharmacies, Tenneco, and TRW Systems understand clearly that to grow, prosper, and remain healthy they must optimize the return on investment of all resources, financial and human.

When an organization is really concerned about people, its total philosophy, climate, and tone will reflect this belief. The orientation of an organization can be determined from its personnel/human resource management philosophy and practices. In this book personnel/human resource management is used to describe the function that is concerned with people—the employees.

 Personnel/human resource management is that function performed in organizations which facilitates the most effective use of people (employees) to achieve organizational and individual goals. *(Fiedler)*

← want to align indiv's goals & orgs goals
(Fiedler)

Terms such as *personnel, human resource management, industrial relations,* and *employee development* are used by different individuals to describe the unit, department, or group concerned about people. The term *human resource management* is now widely used, though many people still refer to a *personnel department*. In order to keep contact with history the more modern term, *personnel/human resource management (P/HRM)* will be used throughout the book. It is a term that reflects the increased concern both society and organizations have in people. Today employees—the human resource—demand more of their jobs and respond favorably to management activities that give them greater control of their lives.

Personnel/human resource management consists of numerous activities, including:

- Equal employment opportunity programs.
- Job analysis.

- Employee planning.
- Employee recruitment, selection, and orientation.
- Career development and counseling, performance evaluation, and training and devlopment.
- Compensation and benefits.
- Safety and health.
- Labor relations.
- Discipline, control, and evaluation of the personnel function.
- Work scheduling.

These activities are the topics of the various chapters in this book. They also appear as elements in the diagnostic model of the P/HRM function which is employed throughout the text. (This model is described in Chapter 2). These items are also the topics of the news stories Don Brokop was considering at the start of the chapter.

Three things should be stressed about P/HRM at the outset.

Action oriented. Effective P/HRM is *action* oriented. It is not focused on record-keeping, written procedures, or rules. P/HRM emphasizes the solution of employment problems to help achieve organizational objectives and facilitate employee development and satisfaction.

Individually oriented. Whenever possible P/HRM treats each employee as an *individual* and offers services and programs to meet the individual's needs. McDonald's, the fast-food chain, has gone so far as to give its chief personnel executive the title of vice president of individuality.

Future oriented. Effective P/HRM is *future* oriented. It is concerned with helping an organization achieve its objectives in the future by providing for competent, well-motivated employees.

The Legacy of Personnel/Human Resources Management (P/HRM)

The field of personnel/human resource management can be traced back to the organized guilds of craftsmen in England. Masons, carpenters, and leather workers organized themselves into guilds. They were able to use a united front to better their conditions of work.[2] These guilds became the forerunners of trade unions.

The Industrial Revolution in the latter part of the 18th century laid the basis for a new and complex industrial society. In simple terms, the Industrial Revolution began with the substitution of steam power and machinery for time-consuming hand labor. Working conditions, social patterns, and the division of labor were significantly altered. A new kind of employee, the boss, became a power broker in the new factory system. With these changes also came a widening gap between workers and owners.

The drastic changes in technology, the growth of organizations, the rise of unions, and government concern and intervention concerning working people resulted in the development of personnel departments. There is no specific date to the appearance of the first personnel department but around the 1920s more and more organizations seemed to take note of and do something about the conflict between employees and management.[3]

---

[2]Henry S. Gilbertson, *Personnel Policies and Unionism* (Boston: Ginn and Co., 1950), p. 17.

[3]Henry Eilbert, "The Development of Personnel Management in the United States," *Business History Review,* Autumn 1959, pp. 345–64.

Early personnel administrators were called welfare secretaries. Their job was to bridge the gap between management and operator (worker); in other words, to speak to workers in their language and then recommend to management what had to be done to get the best results from employees.

The early history of personnel still obscures the importance of the P/HRM function to management. Until the 1960s, the personnel function was considered to be concerned only with blue-collar or operating employees. It was viewed as a record-keeping unit that handed out 25-year tenure pins and coordinated the annual company picnic. Peter Drucker's often quoted comment about personnel management as "partly a file clerk's job, partly a housekeeping job, partly a social worker's job, and partly fire fighting, heading off union trouble," reflects a distinct blue-collar orientation.[4]

The P/HRM function is today concerned with much more than simple filing, housekeeping, and record-keeping. When it is integrated within the organization it plays a major role in clarifying the firm's P/HRM problems and works on solutions to solve them. It is *action, individually,* and *future* oriented. In the 1980s, it would be difficult to imagine any organization achieving and sustaining effectiveness without efficient P/HRM programs and activities. This point will become clear as we move further into the book.

Organizational Effectiveness

Personnel/human resource management activities can help in many ways to ensure that an organization will survive and prosper. Survival is the major long-run objective of any organization. The following case example illustrates how oversight of the P/HRM function can detract from the effectiveness of the organization.

Ted has organized his money, marketing, and machinery problems, but he is disinclined to deal with people problems. Yet a closer analysis of his firm would show that these problems are limiting his growth and his satisfaction with Services Unlimited (SU). What Ted needs is some help with people.

Successful managers recognize that human resources deserve attention because they

---

Ted Byers is the president of a firm with 225 employees, called Services Unlimited (SU), which offers maintenance and repair services to enterprises in its area on a contract or fee basis. The firm is reasonably successful. Ted, who has always been mechanically inclined, is a registered professional engineer in Illinois. He graduated with honors in mechanical engineering from Purdue University 10 years ago. He worked for a similar firm in Chicago, then started his own service company there.

Helen Brooks is in charge of financial and accounting activities, and Ed Webber contacts the accounts and sells SU's services. Ted handles purchasing and oversees the operations of the equipment himself, but whenever he is working on an important mechanical problem or bidding a job he is likely to be interrupted. It may be a dispute between supervisor and worker; or someone quits; or an employee wants a raise or is dissatisfied with the holiday schedule.

---

[4]Fred K. Foulkes, "The Expanding Role of the Personnel Function," *Harvard Business Review,* March–April 1975, pp. 71–72.

are a significant factor in top-management strategic decisions which guide the organization in its future operations. People do the work and create the ideas that allow the organization to survive. Even the most capital-intensive organizations need people to run them.

Managers analyze the objectives, examine the environment for opportunities and threats, evaluate the strengths and weaknesses of the organization, and make strategic decisions based on these analyses. P/HRM considerations contribute significantly in several ways to these decisions. For one thing, people limit or enhance the strengths and weaknesses of the organization. Current changes in the environment are often related to changes in human resources, such as shifts in the composition, education, and work attitudes of employees. The P/HRM function should provide for these changes.

One problem top management has in making strategic planning decisions regarding people is that all other resources are evaluated in terms of money, and at present, in most organizations, people are not. There has been a movement toward human resource accounting, which would place dollar values on the human assets of organizations. Professional sports teams such as the New York Yankees, Boston Celtics, and Cincinnati Reds place a dollar value on athletes. They then depreciate these values over the course of time.

If the objectives of P/HRM are to be accomplished, top managers will have to treat the human resources of the organization as being the *key* to effectiveness. By regarding the development of superior human resources as an essential competitive requirement that needs careful planning, hard work, and evaluation, top managers can begin to accomplish the important objectives of P/HRM.

Objectives of the P/HRM Function

The contributions P/HRM makes to organizational effectiveness are reflected in the objectives pursued by those working in the function, and include the following:

1. To help the organization reach its goals.
2. To employ the skills and abilities of the work force efficiently.
3. To provide the organization with well-trained and well-motivated employees.
4. To increase to the fullest the employee's job satisfaction and self-actualization.
5. To develop and maintain a quality of work life which makes employment in the organization a desirable personal and social situation.
6. To communicate P/HRM policies to all employees.
7. To help maintain ethical policies and behavior.
8. To manage change to the mutual advantage of individuals, groups, the enterprise, and the public.

This is how David Babcock, chairman of the board and chief executive officer of the May Company and formerly its personnel vice president, expresses the first purpose of personnel: "Personnel, like other subunits of the enterprise, exists to achieve the goals of the enterprise first and foremost. If it does not serve that purpose, personnel (or any other subunit) will wither and die."

To Help the Organization Reach Its Goals

To Employ the Skills and Abilities of the Work Force Efficiently

---

Clyde Benedict, the chief personnel officer for Integon Corporation, stated this purpose somewhat differently. He said the purpose is "to make people's strengths productive, and to benefit customers, stockholders, and employees. I believe this is the purpose Walt Disney had in mind when he said his greatest accomplishment was to build the Disney organization with its own people."

To Provide the Organization with Well-Trained and Well-Motivated Employees

---

This is an effectiveness measure for P/HRM. Babcock phrases this purpose as "building and protecting the most valuable assest of the enterprise: people." Pehr Gyllenhammar, president of the Volvo Company in Sweden, has phrased it this way:

> For many years it has been said that capital is the bottleneck for a developing industry. I don't think this any longer holds true. I think it's the work force and the company's inability to recruit and maintain a good work force that does constitute the bottleneck for production. I don't know of any major project backed by good ideas, vigor, and enthusiasm that has been stopped by a shortage of cash. I do know of industries whose growth has been partly stopped or hampered because they can't maintain an efficient and enthusiastic labor force, and I think this will hold true even more in the future. . . .[5]

So the P/HRM effectiveness measure—its chief effectiveness measure, anyway—is to provide the right people at the right phase of performing a job, at the right time for the organization.

To Increase to the Fullest the Employee's Job Satisfaction and Self-Actualization

---

Thus far, the emphasis has been on the organization's needs. But unlike computers or cash balances, employees have feelings of their own. For employees to be productive, they must feel that the job is right for their abilities and that they are being treated equitably. For many employees, the job is a major source of personal identity. Most of us spend the majority of our waking hours at work and getting to and from work. Thus our identity is bound to our job.

Satisfied employees are not *automatically* more productive. However, unsatisfied employees do tend to quit more often, to be absent more frequently, and to produce lower quality work than satisfied workers. Nevertheless, both satisfied and dissatisfied employees may perform equally in quantitative terms, such as processing the same number of insurance claims per hour.

This purpose is closely related to the one above. Quality of work life is a somewhat general concept. Generally speaking, it refers to several aspects of the job experience.

---

[5]Ibid., p. 75.

> To Develop and Maintain a Quality of Work Life Which Makes Employment in the Organization a Desirable Personal and Social Situation

These include: management and supervisory style, freedom and autonomy to make decisions on the job, satisfactory physical surroundings at work, job safety, satisfactory working hours, and meaningful jobs. Not everyone believes that a high quality of life is provided at all workplaces. Jack Golodner, of the AFL-CIO unions for professional employees, has said:

> The satisfactions that come from the job have disappeared. The professional is working in an environment that is more and more dehumanized. He's working in greater and greater masses. You can go to the aerospace industry and see the way an engineer works, in row on row of engineers. He's just one of hundreds of thousands. And in the universities there's less of a one-to-one relationship with the policymakers, so the faculty member feels less and less important. It's no different from what happened to the blue-collar worker who once was a craftsman with dignity, an individual.[6]

> To Communicate P/HRM Policies to All Employees

Clyde Benedict defines the objective this way: It is P/HRM's responsibility "to communicate in the fullest possible sense both in tapping ideas, opinions, and feelings of customers, noncustomers, regulators, and other external publics as well as in understanding the views of internal human resources. The other facet of this responsibility is communicating managerial decisions to relevant publics in their own language."

Closely related to communication within the organization is representation of the organization to those outside. The outside units in contact with an organization include trade unions and local, state, and federal government bodies which pass laws and issue regulations affecting P/HRM. The P/HRM department must also communicate effectively with other top-management people (e.g., marketing, production, research and development) to justify its existence and increase its impact on the organization.

> To Help Maintain Ethical Policies and Behavior

David Babcock feels it is vital for P/HRM to help communicate and monitor the firm's ethical code so that it is more than a piece of paper. P/HRM should develop incentives which reward ethical practices, not the opposite. Clyde Benedict states, "Personnel's purpose is to practice morality in management in preparing people for change, dealing with dissent and conflict, holding high standards of productivity, building acceptance of standards that determine progression, and adhering to the spirit and letter of high professional conduct." Babcock calls this keeping attuned to the times—the social and economic changes affecting working conditions. This relates to both employee satisfaction and organizational efficiency and effectiveness.

[6]Ibid., p. 5–6.

> To Manage Change to the Mutual Advantage of Individuals, Groups, the Organization, and the Public

These eight objectives for P/HRM represent the most significant and most widely accepted ones. There are others and different ways of stating them. But these can serve as the guiding purposes for the P/HRM function in organizations. Effective P/HRM departments set specific, measurable objectives to be accomplished within specified time limits. Chapter 21 will show how this is done. Other chapters discuss cost/benefit analyses to determine whether measurable objectives have been met.

Who Performs P/HRM Activities?

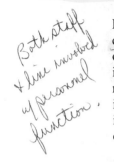

Both staff + line involved in personnel of function.

In most organizations two groups perform P/HRM activities: P/HRM managers and specialists, and operating managers. Delegation of P/HRM duties has changed over time. In organizations, operating managers (supervisors, department heads, vice presidents) are involved in P/HRM activities, since they are responsible for effective utilization of *all* the resources at their disposal. The human resource is a very special kind of resource. If it is improperly managed, effectiveness declines more quickly than with other resources. And in all but the most capital-intensive organizations, the people investment has more effect on organizational effectiveness than resources such as money, materials, and equipment.

Therefore, operating managers must spend some of their time as managers of people. In the same way an operating manager is personally responsible if a machine breaks down and production drops, he or she must see to the training, performance, and satisfaction of employees. Research indicates that a large part of an operating manager's day is spent in unscheduled and scheduled meetings, telephone conversations, and observing other people. The manager, through constant contact with many different people, attempts to improve upon problems and prevent future difficulties.[7]

In smaller organizations, only operating managers are involved in P/HRM work. They have many responsibilities: scheduling work, supervising equipment maintenance, and hiring and paying people. As the organization increases in size, the operating manager's work is divided up and some of it becomes specialized. P/HRM is one such specialized function. Usually the manager of a unit first assigns an assistant to coordinate certain P/HRM matters. P/HRM specialists are employed in organizations with about 100–150 employees, and a P/HRM department is typically created when the number of employees reaches 200–500, depending on the nature of the organization.

The Interaction of Operating and P/HRM Manager

With two sets of employees (operating managers and P/HRM specialists) making P/HRM decisions, there can be conflict. This is partly because operating and P/HRM managers differ on who has authority for what decisions. In addition to role conflict, there may be systemic differences between operating and P/HRM managers. They have different orientations, called *line* and *staff*, which have different objectives.

Miner and Miner argue that operating and personnel managers also have different

---

[7]Henry Mintzberg, *The Nature of Management Work* (Englewood Cliffs, N.Y.: Prentice-Hall, 1980), p. 52.

motivations, if not personalities. In a research study they conducted it was determined that personnel managers are less assertive, less competitive, less interested in administrative detail, and have less positive attitudes toward authority than do operating managers.[8]

The conflict between P/HRM employees and operating managers is most pressing where the decisions must be joint efforts on such issues as discipline, physical working conditions, termination, transfer, promotion, and employment planning. Research indicates that operating managers and P/HRM specialists differ on how much authority personnel should have over job design, labor relations, organization planning, and certain rewards, such as bonuses and promotions.

One way to work out actual or potential conflict of this type so that the employee is not caught in the middle is to try to assign the responsibility for some P/HRM decisions exclusively to operating managers and others exclusively to P/HRM specialists. Some observers feel that this is what is happening, and P/HRM is gaining more power at the expense of the operating managers.[9]

Another approach is to train both sets of managers in how to get along together and how to make better joint decisions. This training is more effective if the organization has a career pattern that rotates its managers through both operating and staff positions such as those in P/HRM. This rotation helps each group understand the other's problems.

The Role of the P/HRM Manager or Specialist

Certain facts are known about the professional in personnel work. In 1981, there were about 250,000 people employed in P/HRM work in the United States. About 60 percent of these work in the private sector, 30 percent in the public sector, and the remaining 10 percent in the third sector (health, education, the arts, libraries, voluntary organizations, and so on). There has been about a 5 percent growth in personnel positions each year since 1970.[10]

When an organization creates specialized positions for the P/HRM function, the primary responsibility for accomplishing the P/HRM objectives described above is assigned to the P/HRM managers. But the chief executive is still responsible for the accomplishment of P/HRM objectives. At all levels in the organization, P/HRM and operating executives must work together to help achieve objectives. The chief P/HRM executive promotes the P/HRM function within the organiztaion to employees and operating executives both.

The ideal P/HRM executive understands the objectives and activities of P/HRM. Ideally, he or she has had some experience as an operating manager, as well as experience in P/HRM. The ideal P/HRM manager has superior interpersonal skills and is creative. It is vital that operating management perceives the P/HRM manager as a manager first, interested in achieving organizational goals, and as a specialist adviser in P/HRM matters secondarily. This makes the P/HRM executive a member of the management team and gives the function a better chance to be effective.

---

[8]John Miner and Mary Miner, "Managerial Characteristics of Personnel Managers," *Industrial Relations,* May 1976, pp. 225–34.

[9]Wickham Skinner, "Big Hat, No Cattle: Managing Human Resources," *Harvard Business Review,* September–October 1981, p. 107.

[10]These are estimates based on data obtained from *Occupational Outlook Handbook*, 1980–81 (Washington, D.C.: U.S. Department of Labor, 1981).

P/HRM's Place in Management

How important is P/HRM in the top-management hierarchy? In the past, the answer clearly was: not very important. As in Drucker's statement, personnel, as it was called, was "work suitable for a file clerk." This view has changed. Recent articles have proclaimed that "Personnel is the fast track to the top" and "Personnel directors are the new corporate heroes."[11] In fact, personnel is advancing rapidly as a vital force in top management. At some firms, such as RCA, United Parcel Service, and Brown and Williamson Tobacco, the top personnel executive is on the board of directors.

A number of presidents and chief operating officers of large firms were promoted to these positions after substantial personnel experience. Examples include the top executives of Colonial Stores, Cummins Engine Company, Delta Airlines, Eli Lilly, and the May Company.

This is not a groundswell trend found in all organizations. However, it does indicate that those who work in the P/HRM function do and can find their way to the top. In the long run it is likely to result in increased opportunities for P/HRM executives in the top jobs.

P/HRM Department Operations

Both the makeup and procedures of P/HRM departments have changed over time. P/HRM units vary by size and sector, but most organizations keep them small. One study found that in the largest headquarters unit there were 150 people.[12]

The number of P/HRM specialists in relation to the number of operating employees, or the personnel ratio, varies in different industries. According to one study national average is one P/HRM specialist per 200 employees. Some industries, such as construction, agriculture, retail and wholesale trade, and services, have fewer personnel specialists than the average. Others, such as public utilities, durable goods manufacturing, banking, insurance, and government, have an above-average ratio.

In one study of the personnel function, the American Society of Personnel Administrators, with Prentice-Hall, surveyed 1,400 P/HRM executives and found both P/HRM staffs and budgets to be growing. Based on this study, Exhibit 1–1 indicates current size and P/HRM ratio variations.

How P/HRM departments allocate their time will be demonstrated in the chapters to follow. An idea of what proportions are devoted to what types of activities can be given here, however. The greatest amount of time, 33 percent, is spent in staffing (recruiting, selection, orientation, evaluation, discipline). Next comes compensation and benefits, 28.5 percent; then training and development, 11 percent; and labor relations, 10 percent. The other activities take 5 percent or less of a P/HRM department's time.[13]

---

[11]Herbert E. Meyer, "Personnel Directors are the New corporate Heroes," *Fortune,* February 1976, pp. 84–88.

[12]David Babcock and John Boyd, "PAIR Department Policy and Organization," in *PAIR Policy and Program Management,* Dale Yoder and Herbert Heneman, Jr. Washington, D.C.: Bureau of National Affairs, 1978).

[13]Dale Yoder, "Personnel Ratios 1970," *The Personnel Administrator,* February 1970, pp. 36–37. Also see Harriet Gorlin, "An Overview of Corporate Personnel Practices," *Personnel Journal,* February 1982, pp. 125–30.

Exhibit 1–1 _____

Size of P/HRM staff

Industry—number reporting	P/HRM staff ratio*	Number on P/HRM staff†
Manufacturing (under 500 persons)—217	1:96	1–12 (300)
Manufacturing (500–999)—136	1:116	1–20 (800)
Manufacturing (1,000–4,999)—142	1:130	2–90 (4,900)
Manufacturing (over 5,000)—26	1:352	7–126 (22,000)
Research and development—15	1:102	1–60 (5,000)
Public utilities—30	1:154	1–110 (22,339)
Hospitals—108	1:180	1–28 (4,000)
Retail stores—47	1:228	1–31 (5,800)
Banks—104	1:98	1–72 (9,000)
Insurance companies—101	1:101	1–142 (30,000)
Transportation and distribution—24	1:272	1–75 (26,000)
Government agencies—41	1:272	2–104 (68,000)
Education—34	1:161	1–46 (11,300)
Nonprofit organizations—28	1:76	1–12 (1,955)
Other firms—328	1:194	1–120 (35,000)

*Average number of employees on payroll for each person on personnel staff.

†Smallest and largest P/HRM staff reported for each industry; numbers in parentheses refer to number of employees on payroll for firms reporting largest personnel staffs. (Firms represented here do not necessarily have the lowest or highest *ratio* of personnel staffers, relative to total work force.)

Source: "The Personnel Executive's Job," *Personnel Management: Policies and Practices,* December 14, 1976, published by Prentice-Hall, Inc., Englewood Cliffs, N.J. Reprinted with permission.

P/HRM Objectives

One major function of the P/HRM executive is the development of P/HRM objectives, procedures, and budgets. As indicated above, the objectives of an organization or department are the ends it seeks to achieve: its reason for existence. Eight objectives of the P/HRM function were also given above. But most of these objectives were stated in very general terms.

To help the organization achieve these objectives, more specific statements are developed in all larger, most middle-sized, and some smaller enterprises. Often, through the use of management by objectives (MBO) programs, the general objective is made more specific. For example, suppose that one of a number of P/HRM objectives is:

- To increase to the fullest the employee's satisfaction with advancement opportunities.

How can this objective be achieved? First, the measurement of these factors can be made specific by designing an attitude survey. This survey would ask employees how satisfied they are. The key issue is to determine what factors contribute to employee satisfaction. Once they are determined, the organization must be geared to increase them in order to raise employee satisfaction—in effect, what the organization does is develop plans to increase these factors. These plans are called *policies* and *procedures/rules*. Exhibit 1–2 which illustrates the relationship between the objectives, policies and rules, indicates that objectives are the most general factor. For example, job satisfaction for employees is an objective. An organization makes an objective more specific by developing policies.

P/HRM Policy

A *policy* is a general guide to decision making. Policies are developed for areas where problems have arisen in the past, or in potential problem areas which management considers important enough to warrant policy development. Policies free managers from having to make decisions in areas in which they have less competence or on matters with which they do not wish to become involved. This assures some consistency in behavior and allows managers to concentrate on decisions in which they have the most experience and knowledge.

After the broadest policies are developed, some organizations develop *procedures* and *rules*. These are more specific plans which limit the choices of managers and employees, as Exhibit 1–2 shows. Procedures and rules are developed for the same reasons as policies.

P/HRM Procedure

A *procedure* or rule is a specific direction to action. It tells a manager how to do a particular activity. In large organizations, procedures are collected and put into manuals, usually called standard operating procedures (SOPs).

Organizations must be careful to have consistent decision making which flows from a well-developed but not excessive, set of policies and procedures. Some organizations in effect eliminate managerial initiative by trying to develop policies and procedures for everything. Procedures should be developed only for the most vital areas.

Exhibit 1–2 _____

Relationship among objectives, policies, and rules

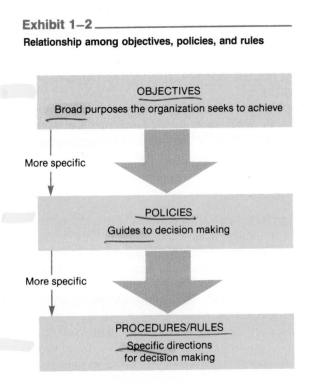

Organization of the P/HRM Department

In most organizations, the chief P/HRM executive reports to the top manager; in the larger firms, perhaps to an executive vice president. Exhibit 1–3 shows one way P/HRM is organized in a large insurance business. Specific attention is given to the employee relations organization and job duties that are presented in Exhibit 1–4. In some other organizations, P/HRM is divided into two departments, personnel and labor relations. In me-

Exhibit 1–3

Organization of large insurance company

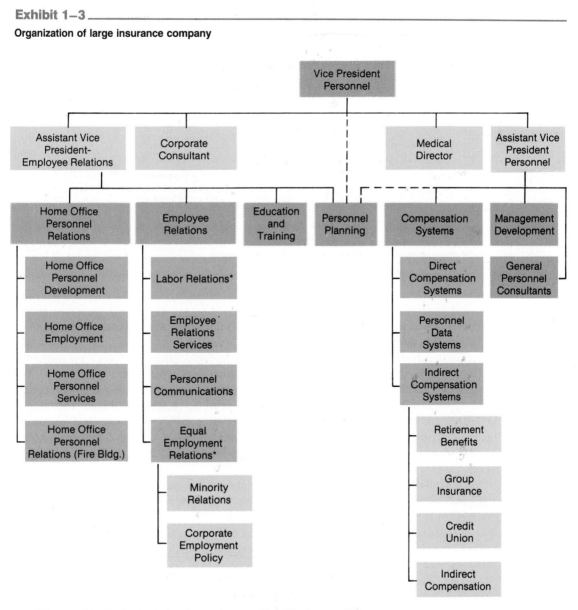

*Manager of function is also assigned general personnel consultant responsibilities

Exhibit 1–4

The organization of the insurance company's employee relations division

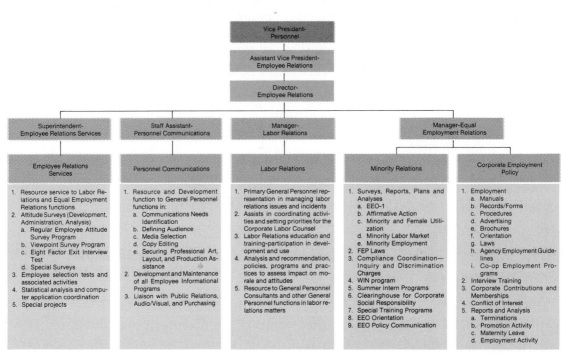

*Manager of function is also assigned general personnel consultant responsibilities

dium-sized and smaller enterprises, however, personnel and other functions such as public relations may be part of a single department.

Thirty percent of all P/HRM managers work for local, state, and federal governments. Exhibit 1–5 is an example of P/HRM organization in a typical state government. The legislature and the governor set policy for departments, subject to review by the courts, and appoint a P/HRM commission which is headed by a P/HRM officer. This central P/HRM unit is a policymaking body which serves a policy, advisory, and regulatory purpose which is similar to that of the home office P/HRM unit of a business. At the federal government level, this personnel commission is called the Civil Service Commission.

In third-sector organizations, such as hospitals and universities, P/HRM typically is a unit in the business office, as shown in Exhibit 1–6. More will be said about differences in P/HRM work in these three settings in Chapter 2.

P/HRM specialists are usually located at the headquarters of an organization, but larger organizations may divide the P/HRM function. Usually the largest group is at headquarters, but P/HRM advisers are also stationed at unit levels (plants for example) and divisional levels. In this case, the headquarters unit consists of specialists or experts on certain topics and advisers to top management, while the unit-level P/HRM people are generalists who serve as advisers to operating managers at their level.

Exhibit 1–5

Personnel organization in a U.S. state government

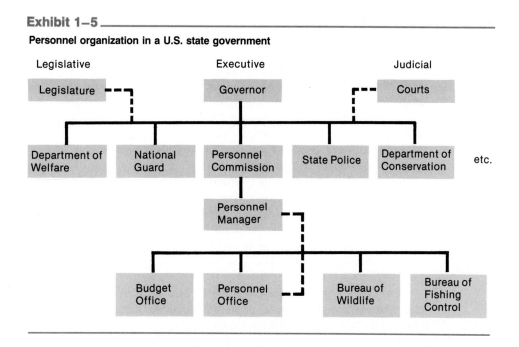

Exhibit 1–6

Organization of a county hospital

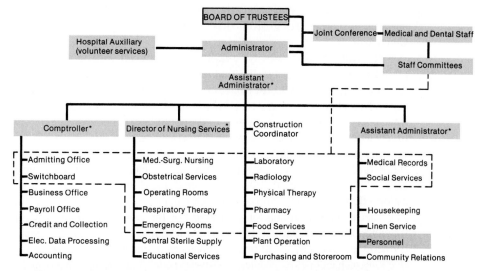

This chart reflects the "line" responsibility and authority in the hospital organization. It should be understood, however, that a great part of the work of the hospital is accomplished through informal interaction between the identified services and functions. These "functional" working relationships are encouraged. Where there is difference in understanding or when changes in procedure are required, the "line" organization should be carefully observed.

*Area directors.

Plan of the Book

This book is designed to show how P/HRM departments work, study the importance of P/HRM activities in organizations of any size, and describe the challenges that exist for P/HRM department employees. The chapters (and many of the sections) begin with a case study from a real organization which describes a *P/HRM* problem currently being confronted. The method by which the problem is solved is a *P/HRM activity*. This activity is defined precisely. Then the people who perform this activity are discussed. The interrelationship between operating and P/HRM managers and the role of top management in the activity is described and analyzed.

In each chapter (or group of chapters, where an activity is described in more than one), the extent to which the activity has been developed is analyzed. Some P/HRM activities are quite well established, while others are just emerging. The activity being considered is assigned to one of four stages through which P/HRM activities seem to evolve. The stage at which an activity is currently located can be assessed by examining the literature on the topic. The stages of activity development are shown in Exhibit 1–7.

Currently, it is most likely that the P/HRM activities of career development, overall organization, and management development approaches would be included in Stage I. Stage II includes systematic evaluation of the total P/HRM function and formal orientation. Typical activities in Stage III are performance evaluation and informal management development. Stage IV functions would include many employment and compensation activities. It appears that historically the P/HRM function begins by focusing on blue-collar employees and then adds white-collar and clerical workers. Only fully developed P/HRM departments focus on management and professional employees as well.

The chapters also include a diagnostic analysis of the activity being discussed. It is assumed that P/HRM activities are affected by many different factors, such as the types of people employed, organized labor, and government. The solution of P/HRM problems depends on consideration of all these factors. This idea will be thoroughly examined in Chapter 2.

For each P/HRM activity, suggestions are given for the techniques, tools, and approaches available to solve the problem, with an evaluation of when each tool is most useful and tips on how to use them well. The various P/HRM activities are evaluated with a cost/benefit approach. Since P/HRM must compete with requests for other resources (machinery, advertising, buildings and so on) the expenditures and investments in the organization's people must be justified in cost/benefit terms.

The chapter summary sections review the major points in each chapter. The organization of the book's chapters is presented in Exhibit 1–8. The six sections and 21 chapters cover P/HRM activities that need to be performed to achieve acceptable levels of organization effectiveness and employee development.

The recommendations for application of the activity are presented as suggestions for the activities use in various types of organizations. Since P/HRM functions are not performed the same way in all organizations, recommendations are given for the most effective way to handle each problem in seven model organizations which differ systematically by size (number of employees), complexity of products or services, and stability or volatility (degree to which the organization's products or services change over time). If you place your focal organization (where you have worked or want to work) on this scale,

Exhibit 1–7_____

Stages of development of a P/HRM activity

Stage I: New, New
   In this stage the experts or originators are exhorting specialists to
   adopt the activity. Panaceas are promised and bromides offered.

Stage II: Early Development
   In this stage, descriptions of organizations perform the activity and
   how happy they are with the results.

Stage III: Conflict
   The doubts begin. The articles warn: it didn't work for us. Multiple
   organization studies are undertaken.

Stage IV: Maturity
   A great deal of empirical data has been gathered, and theories and
   explanations for the conflict in Stage III are established.

Almost
unknown
↓
Well known

you can get an idea of how the P/HRM challenge would be handled there. The seven
model organizations are defined in Exhibit 1–9.

To conclude this introductory section the career histories and job descriptions of several personnel leaders are presented here. First, Robert L. Berra, vice president–personnel
for the Monsanto Company, gives these views of the personnel department there:

> The scope of the personnel function has expanded considerably in recent years, due
> both to greater understanding of its contribution internally and to externalities (govern-
> ment legislation, the rise of dissent, etc.) which have had their impact on all organi-
> zations. There has, therefore, been an increase in the amount of specialized services
> rendered to the line. At the same time, the basic personnel contribution of helping the
> line do its job better has also increased measurably because of the increasing com-
> plexity of interpersonal relationships in our present environment.
>
> At Monsanto we believe that the personnel department exists primarily to enable
> those who create, make, and sell to do their jobs better. We try very hard to keep
> from doing it for them. At Monsanto, nothing has higher priority than the creation of an
> environment in which each individual has the maximum opportunity to realize his full
> potential.
>
> We are blessed with exceptional personnel people at Monsanto. We have an ex-
> cellent mix of seasoned professionals and bright, enthusiastic young people who are
> honing their professional skills. We are also fortunate to have a significant number of
> exceptional beginners in the feeder system. Monsanto has traditionally given much
> attention to its people and, consequently, has considered the personnel department
> as a working partner. However, to who much is given, much is expected, and we are
> constantly challenged to provide policies which anticipate rather than respond to op-
> portunities.
>
> I see the future of the personnel function as being very bright. One of the reasons

Exhibit 1–8 _____

The organization of *Foundations of Personnel/Human Resource Management*

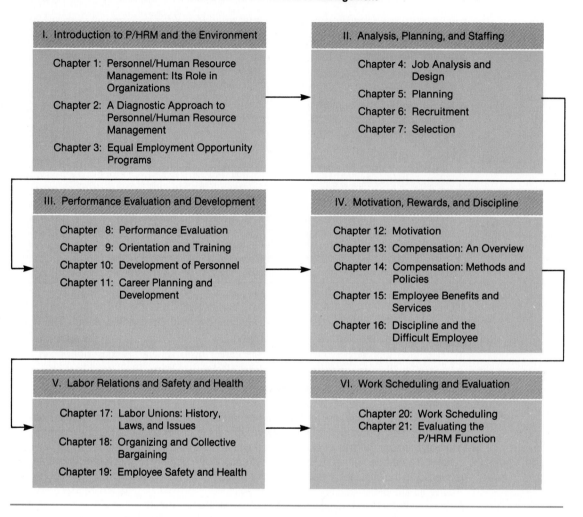

is that our background and training lend themselves to both planning and problem solving in an era where both are essential. More importantly, the future of personnel will be determined primarily by the caliber of people that will be attracted to it. When I review the progress of the professionals who have chosen to work in personnel at Monsanto, as I do on an annual basis, I feel good. We seem now to be attracting more than our share of the best and the brightest. The future should take care of itself.

Eileen DeCoursey, vice president, employee relations, for Johns-Manville Corporation says:

The future of personnel is secure. I think it's going to be the most exciting game in town. And hopefully we are going to attract the best and brightest talent available.

I expect it will become a regular stepping stone to general management such as sales and finance. We are going through enormous changes as we head into "a post-

Exhibit 1–9

Seven model organizations in which various personnel practices might be used

1. Large size, low complexity, high stability.
   Examples: Social security agencies, copper smelter, tuberculosis hospital.
2. Medium size, low complexity, high stability.
   Examples: gym shoe manufacturer, Department of Commerce, state of Indiana.
3. Small size, low complexity, high stability.
   Examples: wooden pencil manufacturer, small insect exterminator.
4. Medium size, moderate complexity, moderate stability.
   Examples: food manufacturer, Memphis city welfare agency.
5. Large size, high complexity, low stability.
   Examples: Mattel Toy Corporation, innovative community general hospital.
6. Medium size, high complexity, low stability.
   Examples: Fashion clothing manufacturer, innovative multiple-purpose hospital.
7. Small size, high complexity, low stability.
   Examples: Solar energy producer, computer manufacturer, elite psychiatric hospital, small media conglomerate.

industrial" society. And the impact on employees, as well as our entire way of doing business, will be greater than anything since the design of the assembly line.

Knowledgeable, prepared employee relations professionals must be able to anticipate the changes before they occur so we are in a position to support and assist the transition—not merely to record its happening.

John Blodger, director of employee relations for Bendix Corporation's Electronics and Engine Control Systems Group, says:

Personnel has come a long way from its initial responsibilities of hiring employees, labor relations, and company picnic planning. Today, the corporation and its employees have high expectations of the personnel professional. This expectation level carries with it a new requirement for individuals occupying positions in the personnel function. Problems of a changing work ethic and the ever-increasing statutory requirements place today's personnel professional at the apex of the management team. EEO, ERISA, OSHA, organizational development, and management development require specialization and a professional approach to problem solving. Understanding the profit-and-loss concept and the contribution that personnel can make to the bottom line will be the key to bringing these expectations to reality.

Summary

This chapter (and all others in the text) concludes with a list of statements summarizing the most important concepts covered in the chapter. You can use this list to review your understanding of the P/HRM process and the P/HRM manager's job.

In your introduction to this field, P/HRM has been defined as the function, in all organizations, which facilitates the most effective utilization of human resources to achieve both the objectives of the organization and the employees. It has described some of the characteristics of today's P/HRM managers and a number of approaches to the organization and operation of P/HRM units. The chapter concludes with a brief description of how the material in this book is organized and the devices we have used to present it. An appendix to the chapter describes careers in P/HRM and P/HRM professionalism, including the literature on the topic and accreditation procedures.

P/HRM Managers Close-Up

Robert L. Berra, Monsanto Company

Job description

Robert L. Berra is responsible for the worldwide direction of the corporate personnel function for Monsanto Company. His areas of responsibility include labor force planning and development, labor and employee relations, salary administration and benefits, professional recruitment and university relations, and corporate headquarters site administration. Berra exercises functional direction of the personnel relations activities in all companies, divisions, and departments of the corporation. He reports to the vice chairman and directly supervises four directors with a total group size of about 350 employees.

Biography

Robert L. Berra, whose title is vice president–personnel for the Monsanto Company, joined that organization as assistant training manager at the former Plastics Division in 1951. Berra was graduated from St. Louis University with a B.S. in commerce and finance. Subsequently he received his M.B.A. degree from the Harvard Graduate School of Business. He has done graduate work in psychology at Washington University, St. Louis.

After holding various positions with Monsanto, Berra became assistant director of the corporate personnel department in June 1967. From October 1970, until June 1974, Berra held the title of corporate vice president of personnel and public relations at Foremost-McKesson, Inc. He rejoined Monsanto Company as vice president–personnel in June 1974.

Berra is the author of several articles in the area of management and motivation. He has served as guest lecturer at Harvard Graduate School of Business, Washington University, St. Louis University, Southern Illinois University, and the University of South Carolina.

Biography

Eileen M. DeCoursey was named to the position of vice president, employee relations for Johns-Manville Corporation upon joining J-M in 1975. Before that,

Eileen DeCoursey
Johns-Mansville Corporation

The statements below highlight the material covered:

1. P/HRM is action and future oriented and focuses on satisfying the needs of individuals at work.
2. P/HRM is a necessary function. Effectively performed, it can make the crucial difference between successful and unsuccessful enterprises.

she served as vice president and executive assistant to the chairman of Squibb Corporation, a position which included extensive work in personnel planning, employee benefits, compensation and personnel policies. DeCoursey has served as a personnel assistant (Warner-Lambert), a research associate (Handy Associate), junior account executive (Johnson & Higgins), employee relations supervisor (Time, Inc.), and manager of employee benefits (Bristol-Myers). She is a native of Livingston, New Jersey, and received her B.S. degree from New Jersey State.

Job description

As vice president, employee relations, of Johns-Manville Corporation, Eileen DeCoursey's responsibilities involve the design and development of corporatewide personnel policies, procedures, and programs. These include recruiting, compensation, benefits, affirmative action, management development, and training.

Biography

John D. Blodger's title is group director of employee relations for the Bendix Corporation, Electronics and Engine Control Systems Group, located at Newport News, Virginia. Prior to moving to Newport News, he was director of employee relations for the Communications Division of the Bendix Corporation in Baltimore. Blodger is a graduate of Wayne State University and has acquired B.S. and M.B.A. degrees. Before joining Bendix, he held a broad range of personnel assignments for several major corporations.

Blodger has been active with the American Society of Personnel Administrators for many years

John D. Blodger
Bendix Corporation

and has held the offices of district director, board member at large, and national treasurer. He was president-elect for 1978 and was president in 1979. He is active in the Industrial Relations Research Association and was formerly a member of the Personnel Association of Greater Baltimore, Inc.

Job description

John Blodger, the group director of employee relations for Bendix (Electronics and Engine Control Systems Group, Newport News, Virginia), is responsible for total employee relations, the safety and security of a two-plant division with employment of 900 salaried and hourly employees, grievance processing through arbitration, wage and salary administration, employee benefits, management development and training programs, and recruitment for both hourly and salaried employees.

3. One of the challenges faced in P/HRM is that many decisions require inputs from both operating managers and P/HRM specialists.
4. This dual purpose can lead to conflict, or it can result in more effective P/HRM decisions.

P/HRM is one of the most challenging and exciting functions in an organization. This book has been written to help you face these challenges more effectively.

Appendix: Careers in P/HRM

This appendix discusses what a P/HRM career is like, describes personnel specialists' positions, and suggests ways personnel specialists can achieve greater professionalism.

P/HRM Careers

Let us begin this section by discussing what current P/HRM professionals are like. At present about 75 percent of P/HRM managers are men. Women P/HRM managers are usually found in medium-sized and smaller organizations. Most P/HRM managers have college degrees. Those who have attended college in recent years have usually majored in business, economics, psychology, or engineering. Their experience is primarily in P/HRM work, especially the younger managers.

P/HRM specialists have been moving toward greater specialization, if not actual professionalism. College training includes courses such as P/HRM, compensation administration, P/HRM problems, labor law and legislation, and collective bargaining. Those who want to become more specialized may join association such as the American Society for Personnel Administrators (ASPA), attend meetings, read professional journals, or seek ASPA accreditation.

P/HRM specialists generally are paid as other graduates of business schools are at the supervisory and middle-management levels. At top-management levels, they sometimes are paid slightly less than operating vice presidents. Current salareis of P/HRM specialists and executives are published yearly by the ASPA in its *Salary Survey*.

A typical career ladder for a P/HRM professional is given in Exhibit 1A–1. A P/HRM professional can enter the field through different types of positions. One way is to become a P/HRM manager for a small unit of a large organization. Remember Don Brokop at the beginning of this chapter? That is what he would be doing if he accepted the Melody Machine Products plant position. When a person enters the small unit of a large organization he or she implements headquarters P/HRM policies at that level and works with local operating managers to help achieve unit goals as well as personnel objectives. This is a very challenging position. The other route is to become a specialized P/HRM professional. Typically, this position is in a large enterprise, and the duties are associated with a single P/HRM function. Examples of this type of position include interviewer and recruiter (employment), and compensation, labor relations, and training and development specialists.

As positions open up, the P/HRM professional can usually move up in the hierarchy. Or the specialist at a large organization can move to a smaller organization as the chief P/HRM executive. Typically, a person with a college degree and P/HRM training will not remain in the bottom two levels ot these positions for long.

What the P/HRM Specialist Does to Professionalize

The P/HRM specialist can advance his or her knowledge of the field by reading specialized journals. These include:

1. Professional journals:
   American Federationist
   Administrative Management
   Employment Benefit Plan Review
   Labor Law Journal

Exhibit 1A–1 _____

Sample career patterns of personnel professionals

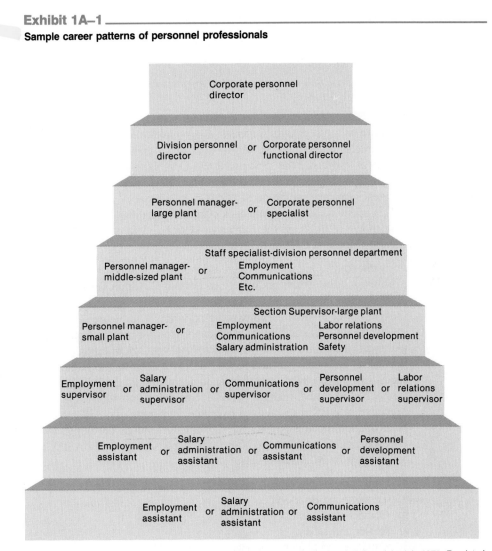

Source: H. H. Mitchell, "Selecting and Developing Personnel Professionals." Copyright July 1970. Reprinted with permission *Personnel Journal*, Costa Mesa, Calif.; all rights reserved.

Monthly Labor Review
The Personnel Administrator
Personnel
Personnel Journal
Public Personnel Management

2. Scholarly journals. The following is a list of publications written for scholars and executives interested in P/HRM management. Reading these requires more technical training than the journals listed above.
Human Relations
Human Organization

Human Resources Management
Industrial Relations
Industrial and Labor Relations Review
Journal of Applied Psychology
Organizational Behavior and Human Performance
Personnel Psychology

3. Abstracts and services. For those wishing to study specialized areas of literature or to get a total overview, *Personnel Management Abstracts* lists most articles in the field and abstracts many of them. *Psychological Abstracts,* especially the "Industrial and Organizational Psychology" section, can suggest leads. And the *Annual Review of Psychology* often has chapters summarizing the latest trends in personnel.

In addition, several companies offer personnel information services. The best known of these are the Bureau of National Affairs (BNA), Commerce Clearing House (CCH), and Prentice-Hall Services.

Accreditation.   One move to increase the professionalism of P/HRM executives is the American Society of Personnel Administrators Accreditation Program. ASPA has set up the ASPA Accreditation Institute (AAI) to offer P/HRM executives the opportunity to be accredited as specialists (in a functional area such as employment, placement and P/HRM planning, or training and development) or generalists (multiple specialisties). Specialists can qualify as accredited P/HRM specialists (accredited personnel specialist—APS) or the more advanced accredited P/HRM diplomates (accredited personnel manager—APM) and the advanced level is accredited executive in P/HRM (accredited executive in personnel—AEP). Accreditation requires passing three-hour examinations developed by the Psychological Corporation of New York. Tests are given by ASPA in the following P/HRM activity areas:

- Employment, placement, and personnel planning.
- Training and development.
- Compensation and benefits.
- Health and safety.
- Employee and labor relations.
- Personnel research.

Questions for Review and Discussion

1. Why would a person conclude that all managers are involved in the personnel/human resource management (P/HRM) function? *P 12*
2. What is meant by the statement that P/HRM is individually oriented? *P 7*
3. Why has the P/HRM function increased in stature and influence in many organizations? *p 8*
4. Do accreditation procedures make the P/HRM field professional? That is, are lawyers, doctors, and P/HRM managers professional? *No p 26-28*
5. Are P/HRM procedures or policies more specific? Explain. *p 16*
6. In your opinions what type of educational background is needed to become an executive in the P/HRM field? *p 26*

Case

Don Brokop

Don Brokop is ready to make an important career decision. He now understands the role that personnel/human resource management plays at Melody. He also can see that P/HRM is important not only to his firm but also to society. The people business is the job of all managers in all organizations. Don has decided to accept the assistant director position and to really become involved on a full-time basis with P/HRM activities.

The activities that Don will learn about firsthand are what this book is about. As you learn more about P/HRM think about Don Brokop and how he stepped from the operating level of management into the P/HRM role in the Melody plant. His on-the-job training will be invaluable in his personal growth and development. However, Don will also have to supplement this firsthand experience with reading and self-learning. Your job is to now dig into the type of reading and self-learning that Don will use to make himself a more successful P/HRM practitioner.

7. Is Peter Drucker correct when he states that work in P/HRM is nothing more than the work of a "file clerk?" *No p 14*
8. Why would a hospital need a P/HRM unit or department? *p 19*
9. What is the difference between the terms *personnel* and *personnel/human resource management?* *p 6*
10. What is the chief or primary P/HRM effectiveness measure? *p 10*

Glossary

Personnel/Human Resource Management (P/HRM). A function performed in organizations which facilitates the most effective use of people (employees) to achieve organizational and individual goals. Terms used interchangeably with P/HRM include *personnel, human resource management,* and *employee development.*

P/HRM Objectives. Objectives are the ends a department such as P/HRM is attempting to accomplish. Some of the specific P/HRM objectives are: (1) to provide the organization with well-trained and well-motivated employees; (2) to communicate P/HRM policies to all employees; and (3) to employ the skills and abilities of the work force efficiently.

P/HRM Policy. A general guide to decision making in important decision areas.

P/HRM Procedure. A procedure is a specific direction to action. It tells a person how to do a particular activity.

Chapter Two

A Diagnostic Approach to Personnel/Human Resource Management

Learning Objectives

After studying this chapter, you should be able to:
- Describe how a diagnostic P/HRM model can be used to examine people problems.

- Explain the difference between external and internal environmental forces that affect P/HRM programs.

- Discuss the role that P/HRM can play in attempts to improve worker productivity.

- Identify some similarities and differences in various jobs.

- List why people act and think in certain ways.

Chapter Outline

Case

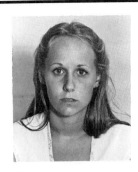

Martha

Lenny

Harry

Martha Winston is the newly appointed manager of the National Pancake House in a major city which is known for its beach area. Officially, the restaurant is known as unit 827. National is a large chain. Martha believes that if she does a good job of managing 827, she has an excellent chance to be promoted at National. She is also thinking about opening up her own restaurant someday.

Martha entered National's management training program after completing college at a small liberal arts school which is well known in her part of the country. The focus of the training program was technical. Martha learned all about the equipment a typical National restaurant has. She also learned about National's finance and accounting system, theft control, and advertising. She was taught a great deal about National's goals for the firm and for unit 827. The topics included sales goals, financial return goals, cleanliness goals, customer service goals, and so on.

She has been at 827 three weeks now and is adjusting pretty well. She is not reaching all the goals National set up for her yet, but she feels she will do so in time. She often wishes the training program had taught her more about the people part of the success equation. Her college courses were not much help to her on this, either.

This problem was in her mind as she sat in her office one morning staring at her paperwork over a cup of coffee. She was thinking of the two cooks on duty, Lenny and Harry. Lenny Melvina is about 24. He's been with National as a cook for almost six years. He finished high school locally. It's the only job he's ever had. He arrives on time, works hard, and leaves on time. He's never absent except for perhaps one day a year for illness. This is what his personnel file shows.

Everyone likes Lenny: the other help, his man-

agers, the customers. It's easy to see why. He does his job well and in a friendly manner. For example, today Martha watched Lenny deal with a customer. National has a policy that second helpings are free. A girl, about 13, came up to Lenny and asked for seconds. He asked her in a friendly manner how many more pancakes she wanted. She said: "Oh, I don't know, one or two."

Instead of having her wait at the serving line, he suggested that she be seated and he'd bring her the pancakes. He delivered a plate with three pancakes on it which looked like this:

The customer and her family were very pleased with his effort to please her and give them a little joke too. They told Martha they'd come back again.

The other cook is Harry Bennis. Harry is about 19. He didn't finish high school. He's worked at National for two years. Harry is tolerated rather than liked. Most of his co-workers tend to ignore him. He rarely says anything beyond the minimum to co-workers, bosses, and customers. He is often late or absent. In about 1 case in 10, his food is sent back. He's not surly but not too pleasant either. He's not bad enough to fire, but not good enough to be pleased with.

Martha wonders why there are these differences in Lenny and Harry. And what, if anything, she can do about it. It affects her now because she must hire a new cook. Business at 827 has been growing faster than usual, even for this busy season. So the staff needs to be expanded to include at least one new cook. Martha wonders how she can be sure to choose a person like Lenny, not another Harry.

And it's raise time. She doesn't have enough money to give everyone a raise. But it's more complicated than that. To hire the new cook she may have to pay close to what she pays Lenny, because few cooks are out of work at present. Yet company policy says you must pay senior people like Lenny more. And as if things weren't complicated enough, the pay must be above the government minimum wage.

Many of the employees at 827 told Martha they wanted more pay because the job wasn't too pleasant: the stove was hot, and you had to deal with the public. What should she do?

To help her make an intelligent, effective decision, she went to visit a friend of hers, Amy Adams, who had taken personnel/human resource management courses at the university. She spent an afternoon with Martha explaining how to deal with the three personnel problems Martha faced (employee satisfaction and performance, selection, and pay) by understanding how three sets of factors affect P/HRM and organizational effectiveness.

These are:

- People.
- The internal and external environment of the organization.
- The organization, task, work group, and leadership.

A Diagnostic P/HRM Model

When you're experiencing pain and must see a physician, you are typically asked a number of questions. Where do you hurt? When did the pain start? What does the pain feel like—is it sharp or dull and aching? The doctor examines you and may also run a number of blood and urine tests. What the doctor is doing is diagnosing the problem. He or she is performing a diagnosis by examination and observation.

The problem faced by Martha at National Pancake House could also be examined through a systematic diagnosis. A personnel/human resource management *diagnostic model* might be of help to her. A diagnostic model in P/HRM is a framework that can be used to help managers focus on a set of relevant factors. The model is a map that aids a person in seeing the whole picture or parts of the picture. The three factors that Martha was concerned about (people, the internal and external environment, and the organization itself) would be included as parts of any P/HRM diagnostic model.

Exhibit 2–1 presents the diagnostic model that will be used throughout the book. The model emphasizes the external and internal environmental influences that directly and/or indirectly affect the match betwen P/HRM activities and people. The people influence such organizational effectiveness factors as individual performance, satisfaction, absenteeism, and turnover. The ultimate outcome of the interaction of environment, activities, people, and effectiveness are products and/or services provided to clients and customers.

Each area of the diagnostic model is important in achieving the eight P/HRM objectives presented in Chapter 1. Again it should be pointed out that the chief effectiveness measure for any P/HRM activity is having the right people at the right phase of performing a job at the right time. The matching of people and activities to accomplish desirable goals is made easier by use of a diagnostic map. Of course, the map shown in Exhibit 2–1 can't include every important environmental influence, P/HRM activity, or effectiveness criteria. Instead it is designed to provide an orderly and manageable picture of how P/HRM diagnosis should proceed.

Exhibit 2–1 _____

A diagnostic model for personnel/human resource management

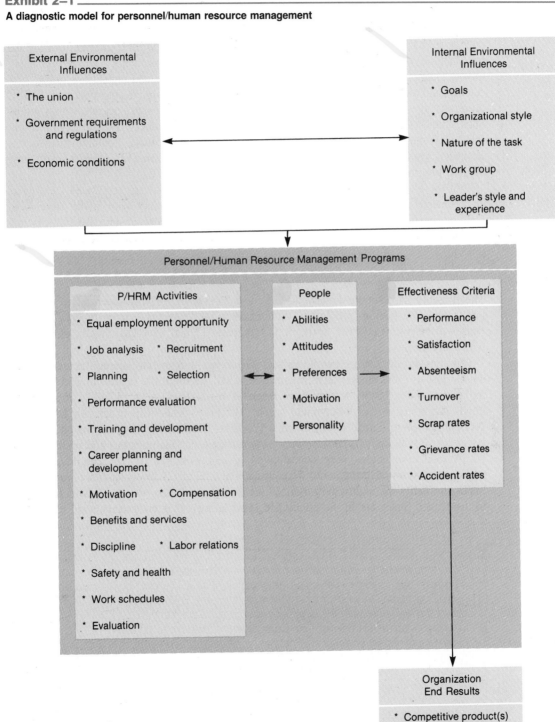

External Environmental Forces

Exhibit 2–1 is intended to show that a P/HRM program in an organization does not operate in a vacuum. It is influenced by and has influence upon the external (outside the organization) and the internal (inside the organization) environments. On the one hand, factors external to the organization—such as government laws and regulations, union procedures and requirements, and economic conditions—have a significant impact on P/HRM programs. On the other hand, the P/HRM program of a firm must operate within guidelines, limits of available resources, and competencies produced by the organization. P/HRM is one important function among other internal functions, including finance, accounting, research and development, marketing, and production. The interaction of these internal programs sets the tone of the entire organizational system.

At the National Pancake House, Martha's P/HRM problems are aggravated by external environmental factors. Remember that Martha is faced with a tight labor market (few cooks who are unemployed) and government wage legislation. Let's look at some external environmental factors.

The Union

The presence of a union directly affects most aspects of P/HRM—recruiting, selection, performance evaluation, promotion, compensation, and benefits, among others. These effects will be discussed later in the book. Chapters 17 and 18 focus directly on relations with labor unions.

Unions differ just as people differ. There are cooperative unions and combative unions just as there are sensitive organizations and irresponsible organizations. Those familiar with union history are aware of the kind of toughness a James Hoffa or a John L. Lewis can bring to the employment scene. The union leadership of the Air Line Pilots Association, State, Local, and Municipal Workers, Baseball Players Association, and others is not so well known, because they have different bargaining styles and philosophies.

At one time unions were concentrated in a few sectors of the economy, such as mining and manufacturing, and were influential in only a few sections of the United States, primarily the highly industrialized areas. But the fastest growing sectors for unions in the United States are in the public and third sectors. It is no longer useful to think of

Mary Agular had been a supervisor at the John Madison Life Insurance Company. At that firm, she could hire her employees, usually with only slight coordination with the personnel/human resource management department. She could hire them on the basis of merit and promote the best ones when they were ready.

When Mary took a new job with Consolidated Electronics, she found that promotion was determined by seniority and that her employees griped about having to pay union dues. She was warned to watch her step by fellow supervisors—to live by the rules, or a grievance would be filed. Pay raises were to follow a schedule, and everyone in a seniority group was to get the same raise. A number of other working conditions were spelled out in the union contract, and there was a steward in her unit who was, in effect, a countervailing force to her leadership. All these conditions existed because CE's employees belonged to the union.

the unionized employee as a blue-collar factory worker. Engineers, nurses, teachers, secretaries, salespersons, college professors, professional football players, and even physicians belong to unions. In sum, unions can be a significant factor in P/HRM programs.[1]

Government Requirements and Regulations

Another powerful, external environmental influence is government law and regulations, which affect many organizations directly. Many federal regulations limit the flexibility of city and state jurisdictions.

The government regulates and influences some aspects of personnel more directly than others. The major areas of legislation and regulation include:

> Equal employment opportunity and human rights legislation, which affects recruiting, selection, evaluation, and promotion directly, and employment planning, orientation, career planning, training and development indirectly.
>
> Compensation regulation, which affects pay, hours of work, unemployment, and similar conditions.
>
> Benefits regulation, which affects pension and retirement.
>
> Workers compensation and safety laws, which affect health and safety.
>
> Labor relations laws and regulations, which affect the conduct of collective bargaining.

Government regulation is increasing substantially. In 1940 the U.S. Department of Labor administered 18 regulatory programs; in 1982 it administered 100.[2] And that's just *one* government agency affecting managers and the activities of the P/HRM department.

John Dunlop lists a number of the problems government regulation imposes on management.[3] All of these make the operating and P/HRM managers' jobs more difficult:

- Regulation encourages simplistic thinking on complicated issues. Small enterprises are treated like large ones. Different industries are regulated the same.
- Designing and administering regulations is an incredibly complex task. This leads to very slow decision making.
- Regulation does not encourage mutual accommodation but rather leads to complicated legal manuevering.
- Many regulations are out of date and serve little social purpose, yet they are not eliminated.
- There is increasing evidence of regulatory overlap and contradictions between different regulatory agencies.

To cope with increasing governmental control, management has tried to influence the passage of relevant legislation and the way it is administered. Managements have sued to

---

[1]Joseph Tomkiewicz and Otto Brenner, "Union Attitudes and the 'Manager' of the Future," *Personnel Administrator,* October 1979, pp. 67–70, 72.

[2]U.S. Department of Labor Office of Information and Public Affairs, Telephone Communication, August 30, 1982.

[3]John Dunlop, "The Limits of Legal Compulsion," *Labor Law Journal,* February 1976, pp. 69–70.

FRANK AND ERNEST

© 1978 by NEA, Inc. Reprinted by permission of NEA.

determine the constitutionality of many of the laws. When such efforts fail to influence the process as management prefers, it has learned to adapt its P/HRM policies.

In sum, there are almost no P/HRM decisions that remain unaffected by government. In what ways and to what degree government affects the P/HRM function will be discussed in each chapter, beginning with Chapter 3.

Economic Conditions

Three aspects of economic conditions affect P/HRM programs: productivity, the nature of competition, and the nature of the labor market.

Productivity • There is growing evidence that the productivity of employees is an important part of a nation's general economic condition. Managers are becoming more concerned with productivity because they feel it is a representative indicator of the overall efficiency of an organization. Productivity is defined as:

> Output of good and services per unit of input of resources used in a production process.[4]

Inputs, as applied in productivity measurement, are expressions of the physical amount or the dollar amount of several elements used in producing a good or a service, including labor, capital, materials, fuel, and energy.

The industrial world's productivity growth passed through three major cycles during the past century.[5]

1. A slow cycle for eight decades (1870–1950), averaging about 1.7 percent a year.
2. Unprecedented growth during the two post-World War II decades, with such rates as Japan's 7.9 percent a year.

---

[4]*Productivity Perspectives* (Houston: American Productivity Center, 1980), p. 61.

[5]Elliott S. Grossman, "Total Factor Productivity Dynamics," in *Productivity Perspectives* (Houston: American Productivity Center, 1980), pp. 2–10.

3. A reduced average rate during 1970–79. During the past few years U.S., Canadian, and British productivity has essentially halted while productivity in Japan, West Germany, and France is advancing at a brisk pace.

Exhibit 2–2 shows the relative productivity story for the 1950–78 period. The increasing disparity of productivity gains in Western economics can be traced in part to:

- The rebuilding of war-torn industry in Japan and Western Europe with modern technology, aided by massive U.S. economic aid and the transfer of technical and managerial knowledge.
- The United States provided a defense umbrella to Japan, Korea, and West Germany. This required a large expenditure for the defense effort.
- Lower investment in industrial renovation and restoring as well as for research and development.
- Legislative controls for pollution and improving occupational safety and health.

These and other factors have contributed to the productivity crises in the United States and in much of the industrialized world.[6] The productivity picture and its consequences must be addressed by P/HRM managers.

Some suggested solutions include the reduction of government controls, more tax incentives to invest in new plants and equipment, and the reindustrialization of the entire

Exhibit 2–2

Real domestic product per employed person, 1950–1978

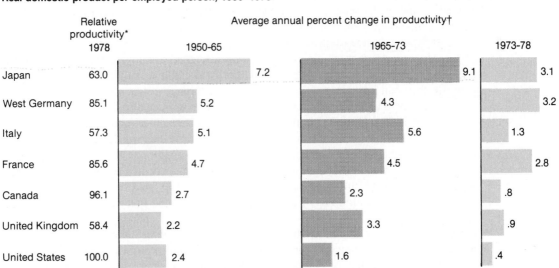

| | Relative productivity* 1978 | Average annual percent change in productivity† | | |
		1950–65	1965–73	1973–78
Japan	63.0	7.2	9.1	3.1
West Germany	85.1	5.2	4.3	3.2
Italy	57.3	5.1	5.6	1.3
France	85.6	4.7	4.5	2.8
Canada	96.1	2.7	2.3	.8
United Kingdom	58.4	2.2	3.3	.9
United States	100.0	2.4	1.6	.4

*Real gross domestic product per employed person using international price weights, relative to the United States.
†Growth in real domestic product per employed person using own country's price weights.
Source: U.S. Bureau of Labor Statistics, 1980.

---

[6]Ralph E. Winter, "Productivity Debate Is Clouded by Problem of Measuring Its Lag," *The Wall Street Journal*, October 13, 1980, pp. 1,19.

business/industrial complex (e.g., plants, equipment). These suggested solutions have both proponents and opponents.[7] For example, there are many citizens who believe that reducing or eliminating legislative controls will have an adverse effect on the quality of life and society for decades to come. Toxic wastes, radiation, air pollution, and other forms of destruction must be carefully controlled. In reality, the P/HRM executive or specialist has little control over the environmental pollution problem. Certainly, he or she is concerned, but has little power to initiate policies or programs in this area.

On the other hand, the P/HRM staff can influence productivity through the utilization of the sound application of P/HRM programs. There are specific activities and practices that can improve individual performance and, consequently, organizational productivity. For example, recruitment and selection techniques can be used to attract and hire high-performers. Motivational and compensation techniques can be used to retain employees and improve job performance. Training and development can be used to improve skill and competency deficiencies which, in turn, increases performance.

Productivity problems will not be solved without concern for the P/HRM function and the activities it performs. Every topic covered in this book can have an effect on productivity. Thus, productivity pressure from the external environment directly and indirectly affects an organization's P/HRM program and vice versa.

The Nature of Competition • The nature of competition is mainly measured by the degree of competition. In industry, competition is considered high when there are many producers competing for the customer's business. The result is usually price pressures. A similar condition can exist in nonprofit or governmental institutions. For example, if there are more dormitory rooms than there are students at universities, competitive pressures operate on tuition charges, extra services offered, and so on. This can happen in hospitals as well. In the public sector, competition for budget increases for an agency can be fierce when the total budget (in real dollars) is stable or declining.

The greater the competitive pressure, the less able the organization is to offer additional inducements, such as higher pay or benefits, to its employees. Effective organizations under economic pressure can compete for good employees by offering nonmonetary rewards: they can provide greater job satisfaction through better reward systems, or job placement, which can facilitate personal fulfillment or self-actualization.

If there is less competitive pressure, the organization has greater flexibility in the variety of P/HRM programs it can offer. For example, the onetime director of the M.B.A. program at Michigan State University interviewed two engineers who wanted to enter the program. They were both employed by a defense contractor in Detroit, 90 miles away. When it was pointed out there was no night program, they said they could come during the day. This was astonishing. Further questioning revealed that they had done nothing for the company for two years except to bring in coffee and do odds and ends. The company was on a cost-plus contract; thus it could "stockpile" them *in case* they were needed and could still recoup their salaries *plus* their built-in profit percentage. Obviously there was no economic or competitive pressure in this situation. The company could afford to be very generous in pay, benefits, and so on. Contrast this with the competitive

---

[7]Burton G. Malkiel, "Productivity—The Problem behind the Headlines," *Harvard Business Review,* May–June 1979, pp. 81–91. Also see Joel Ross, *Productivity, People, and Profits* (Reston, Va.: Reston Publishing 1981).

food industry, in which an additonal five cents on a $10 case of vegetables could lose the order. Firms that have to watch their pennies are concerned with the costs of large wage increases and excessive fringe benefits.

The Nature of the Labor Market • The labor market also directly affects P/HRM programs. When there are more workers than jobs, employers find recruiting costs minimal. Employees apply readily, and selection is less difficult; the employer may be able to choose from five or more qualified applicants for each position. Work attitudes tend to be work-ethic oriented. Martha Winston has significant P/HRM problems at the National Pancake House because this is not the case. When the work ethic predominates in employee attitudes, output increases and performance evaluation can be a motivating experience. A surplus of labor can also reduce employee pressures for compensation and benefit increases. Disciplinary problems, absenteeism, and turnover are likely to decrease, and equal employment opportunity goals may be easier to fill.

The employer must be aware of several labor markets. The primary concern is the local labor market, from which most blue- and white-collar employees are drawn. Managerial, professional, and technical employees may be recruited from a regional, or even a national, market.

It is quite possible that the local labor market is different from the regional or national markets. For example, in the fall of 1982 there was about 10.1 percent unemployment nationwide, but in Flint, Michigan, 23 percent of the workers were unemployed.[8] Recruiting blue-collar workers in Flint was three or four times easier than in Houston that year.

Even though the national and local labor markets differ significantly, there will still be some exchange between them. Thus, if Flint's unemployment rate stays consistently high, those among the unemployed who are younger, have knowledge of jobs elsewhere, and have the money and motivation to move will do so. This movement tends to increase the labor supply in areas with shortages. There also are international labor markets. Illegal aliens who come to the United States to seek work change the labor market balance. It was estimated that there were over 9 million illegal aliens working in the United States in 1980.[9] Currently, some British executives leaving an economy they feel has little future, are trying to emigrate to the United States.[10]

In addition to labor markets determined by geographic differences are markets determined by skill and age considerations. If you are seeking an accountant, a general labor market surplus is not much help if accountants remain scarce. The supply of labor with a particular skill is related to many factors: the number of persons of work age; the attractiveness of the job in pay, benefits, and psychological rewards; the availability of training institutes; and so on. With regard to age the U.S. Department of Labor predicted in 1981 that by 1990 workers aged 25–54 will rise by 22.4 million, while those in the teenage years will decline by almost 2 million.[11] An appendix to this chapter examines in more detail the current composition of the labor force in the United States.

[8]Carol Hymowitz, ''Managers' Malaise,'' *The Wall Street Journal,* July 19, 1982, pp. 1 and 10.

[9]John Erhlichman, ''America's Struggle,'' *Houston Post,* March 14, 1982, p. 9 (Magazine Section).

[10]*The American Economy; Employment, Productivity, and Inflation in the Eighties,* President's Commission for a National Agenda for the Eighties (Washington, D.C.: U.S. Government Printing Office, 1980).

[11]U.S. Department of Labor, *Occupational Outlook Handbook,* (Washington, D.C.: U.S. Government Printing Office, 1980–1981).

In sum, the P/HRM function is affected fundamentally by the state of the labor market not only in the organization's location in the region, but in the nation and the world as well. Also the specific markets for the kinds of employees the enterprise seeks will affect that function.

The Work Sector of the Organization • The diagnostic model presented in Exhibit 2–1 does not take into consideration the work sector in which the organization is located. This was done so that the model could remain relatively simple.

About 60 percent of professional P/HRM specialists work in the *private sector,* consisting of businesses owned by individuals, families, and stockholders, while 30 percent of all P/HRM employees in the United States work in the *public sector,* which is that part of the economy owned and operated by the government. Many economists define other institutions in society that are neither government nor profit oriented as the *third sector.* Examples of these institutions are museums, symphony orchestras, private schools and colleges, not-for-profit hospitals and nursing homes, and voluntary organizations such as churches and social clubs. About 10 percent of P/HRM specialists and employees work in the third sector.

In general, private- and third-sector P/HRM work is structured similarly. Hospitals have different internal organization problems than most businesses, though. For example, the presence of three hierarchies—physicians, administrators, and the board of trustees (representing the public)—can lead to conflicts. Pressures from third-party payees such as Blue Cross or Medicare can lead to other conflicts. Hospitals employ professional groups which zealously guard their ''rights,'' which also leads to conflict. Structurally, P/HRM work in the private and third sectors is similar, but because of organizational differences jobs in the P/HRM function vary.

P/HRM in the public sector is *fundamentally different* from the other two sectors because it varies *structurally.* And the public manager faces a different world. In fact, a manager who moves from the private or third sector to the public sector will find the P/HRM role much more complicated. P/HRM in the public sector generally is much more laden with direct outside pressures. Politicians, the general public, pressure groups, and reporters influence the P/HRM manager much more than in a private business or in the third sector.

For example, most public managers must deal with a central personnel bureau such as the Civil Service Commission. A special problem faced by these managers has always been political appointments. Formerly, politicians always saw to it that their party workers were rewarded with government jobs between elections; this is usually called the spoils system. In an attempt to assure that public jobs are assigned on the basis of merit, not political pull, the Civil Service Commission and equivalent central personnel bureaus were established to set personnel policies for governing public employment. Civil service standardized examinations are not required as part of the selection process for many public-sector jobs. This system was intended to establish merit as the criterion for public employment, but it also increases the system's rigidity and entrenches bureaucracy.

The differences among public-, private-, and third-sector P/HRM activities are largely in the structure of the P/HRM function and the environment of the public manager's job. The P/HRM function does vary by sector, and these differences will be discussed where they are significant.

In sum, P/HRM activities are affected by the external environment, all forces especially union requirements, government regulations, economic conditions, and the work sector of the organization. These forces will become more apparent throughout the rest of the book.

Internal Environmental Influences

The internal environmental influences listed in Exhibit 2–1—goals, organization style, nature of the task, work group, and leader's style and experience—involve occurrences within the organization. Let's examine how each of these influences affects the P/HRM program.

Goals

The goals of organizations differ within and between sectors. All sectors probably include organizations that have goals which include employee satisfaction, survival, and adaptability to change. The differences arise in the *importance* the decision makers place on the different goals. In some organizations, profit is so much more important than employee satisfaction that P/HRM activities are not well developed. In cases like this, employee rewards such as pay and benefits are not high. In other organizations, P/HRM-related goals are highly regarded by decision makers. Thus, how much the P/HRM function is valued and how it is implemented is affected by these goals.

Organization Style

Modern organization theory provides many ways to organize. At one extreme is the *bureaucratic approach*. In this approach, the organization usually centralizes decision making, designs specialized jobs, departmentalizes by function, has standardized policies, uses small spans of control, has clearly defined objectives, and encourages communication through the chain of command.[12] The opposite extreme—the *participative approach*— uses decentralized decision making. It enlarges jobs, departmentalizes by product, uses few detailed policies, has large spans of control, and encourages free flowing, multidirectional communication. These two styles reflect fundamentally different managerial philosophies about the nature of people, the role of work in life, and the most effective ways to supervise. Basic beliefs about how employees are to be treated translate into ideas about the kinds of P/HRM programs that are made available to employees.

Obviously, there are many approaches to organization which fall *between* these two extremes, and most work organizations practice an intermediate approach. Some organizations, for example, are likely to prefer more formalized P/HRM policies, tighter controls on employees, more directly job-related training, compensation policies tied to actual performance, and so on. It seems reasonable to hypothesize that truly bureaucratic and truly participative organizations would have different P/HRM policies. Of course, most organizations are made up of some units that are bureaucratic and some that are participative in outlook, so P/HRM policies would also vary along these dimensions. In these ways, the organization's style influences the P/HRM program.

---

[12]James L. Gibson, John M. Ivancevich, and James H. Donnelly, *Organizations: Behavior, Structure, Processes,* 4th ed. (Plano, Tex.: Business Publications, 1982), p. 353.

Nature of the Task

Many experts believe that the task to be performed is one of the two most vital factors affecting P/HRM. They describe P/HRM as the effective matching of the nature of the task with the nature of the employee performing the task.[13]

There are perhaps unlimited similarities and differences among jobs which attract or repel possible workers and influence the meaning of work for them. Some of the most significant are:

Degree of Physical Exertion Required • Contrast the job of ditch digger with that of a computer programmer. In general, most people prefer work involving minimal amounts of physical exertion. Some companies, like IBM, believe that working with the mind is better for curing productivity problems than working with the back. Exhibit 2–3 captures some of IBM's thinking on this matter.

Degree of Environmental Unpleasantness • Contrast the environment of a coal miner with that of a bank teller. People generally prefer physically pleasant and safe conditions.

Physical Location of Work • Some jobs require outside work; others, inside. Contrast the job of a telephone lineman during the winter in Minnesota with that of a disc jockey. Some jobs require the employee to stay in one place. Others permit moving about. Contrast the job of an employee on an assembly line with that of a traveling sales representative. There are individual differences in preference for physical location.

Time Dimension of Work • Some jobs require short periods of intense effort, others long hours of less taxing work. In some jobs the work is continuous; in others, intermittent.

Human Interaction on the Job • Some jobs require frequent interaction with others. Contrast the position of a radar operator in an isolated location who rarely sees anyone else with that of a receptionist in a busy city hall.

Degree of Variety in the Task • The amount of freedom and responsibility a person has on the job determines the degree of *autonomy* provided for in the work. Contrast the autonomy of a college professor with that of an assembly-line worker.

Task Identity • The degree of wholeness in a job—the feeling of completing a whole job as opposed to contributing to only a portion of a job—is its *task identity*. Contrast the job of an auto assembler with that of a tax accountant.

Task Differences and Job Design • Because jobs are not created by nature, engineers and specialists can create jobs with varying attention to the characteristics described above. There are a number of approaches to those aspects of job design that affect variety, autonomy, task identity, and similar job factors. These approaches will be covered in Chapter 4.

---

[13]"The New Industrial Relations, *U.S. News & World Report,* May 11, 1981, pp. 85–87, 89–90, 92, 94, 96, 98.

Exhibit 2–3 _____

WORKING SMARTER VS. WORKING HARDER.

Japan's productivity keeps improving.
Germany's too.
"So America's going to have to work harder," people say.
But that's not enough anymore.
We also have to work *smarter.*
America's productivity problem isn't caused by lazy workers. It's partly caused by lazy factories, lazy tools, and lazy methods which dilute the efforts of hard-working people.
Working smarter can help change that.
Today, thousands of IBM customers are working smarter by using computers, word processors, and electronic office machines. Insurance companies, retailers, banks, farmers, aerospace companies have all become more productive by making *information* work harder.
In world trade, productivity is a key to success. And America has long been the most productive country on earth.
We can stay that way by working smarter.

How do these task factors affect P/HRM decisions? They obviously affect recruiting and selection, since employees will probably be more satisfied and productive if their preferences are met. As mentioned above, few jobs match all preferences exactly—there are too many of them. With jobs that are difficult, dirty, or in smoky or hot environments, the manager must provide additional incentives (more pay, shorter hours, or priority in vacations) because few people prefer such jobs. Or the manager may try to find employees who can handle the conditions better; for example, people hard of hearing may be hired to work in a noisy environment.

Work Group

> A work group consists of two or more people who consider themselves a group, who are interdependent with one another for the accomplishment of a purpose, and who communicate and interact with one another on a more or less continuous basis. In many cases (but not always), they work next to each other.

An effective group is one whose:

- Members function and act as a team.
- Members participate fully in group discussion.
- Group goals are clearly developed.
- Resources are adequate to accomplish group goals.
- Members furnish many useful suggestions leading to goal achievement.

Most effective work groups are small (research indicates that 7 to 14 members is a good range), and their members have eye contact and work closely together. Effective groups also generally have stability of membership, and their members have similar backgrounds. Their membership is composed of persons who depend on the group to satisfy their needs.[14] An effective work group will help achieve the goals of the organization. Thus, it is in the manager's interest to make the groups effective. It is also in the interest of employees, because effective groups serve their members' social needs.

Although the effective group generally supports management and the organization's goals, it can also work against them. This is usually the case when the group perceives the organization's goals as being in conflict with its own. If the work group is effective and works with management, the manager's job is easier, and objectives are more likely to be achieved. If the group is working against the manager, an effort must be made to change the group's norms and behavior by use of the manager's leadership, discipline, and reward powers, or by the transfer of some group members.

Work groups are directly related to the success of P/HRM activities. If the work group opposes P/HRM programs, it can ruin them. Examples of programs which can be successes or failures depending on work-group support or resistance include incentive compensation, profit sharing, safety, and labor relations. Operational and P/HRM managers who desire success in such programs should at least consider permitting work-group participation in designing and implementing P/HRM.

---

[14]Gibson, et al., *Organizations,* p. 183.

Leader's Style and Experience

The experience and leadership style of the operating manager or leader directly affects P/HRM activities because many, if not most, programs must be implemented at the work-unit level. Thus the operating manager-leader is a crucial link in the P/HRM function. To illustrate how the experience and style of operating management influences the P/HRM function, consider the following case situation.

Case

Claudia

Jenny

The Acme Manufacturing Company has just completed its evaluation of personnel procedures (see Chapter 21). At Acme, this process includes sending the supervisors' reports on the previous period's P/HRM effectiveness measures such as accident rates, turnover (number of persons quitting), amount of absenteeism from the job, and quality reports (number of items that had to be remanufactured because of poor quality). Supervisors were also provided with results of the company attitude survey. Each supervisor was given the average response for all employees in the company for each item on the survey, and the average response for the employees in the supervisor's unit. Those items that differed significantly from the company's average response were circled.

In unit 1 the supervisor is Jenny Argo, who has been a supervisor for less than a year. Her unit's absenteeism, turnover, accident rate, and quality were more than 10 percent worse than the company average. The attitude survey indicated that Jenny's employees were significantly more dissatisfied with Jenny's leadership style, style of communicating, amount of communication, and willingness to discuss work problems with employees.

In unit 2 the supervisor is Claudia Wagner. Claudia has been supervisor for five years. Her unit's ab-

senteeism, turnover, accident rate and quality were 3 percent worse than the company average. The attitude survey indicated about average evaluations of Claudia's supervisory skills.

The day the reports came out, Jenny and Claudia had lunch together and discussed the reports.

Claudia I'm really upset. Those results tell me I'm doing something wrong. I plan to invite Mary Jane Uyalde from the P/HRM Department down. I must be doing something wrong. Maybe my weekly employee meetings are being conducted wrong.

Jenny What weekly meeting?

Claudia I have a meeting on Friday afternoon about coffee break time and we kick around suggestions on how to get the job done better. My gang tells me when I'm leaning too hard on them and about their work problems.

Jenny What a waste of time! You're the supervisor. Why do you give up your authority to the girls like that?

Claudia I don't give up anything. We help each other. Besides, my results are three times better than yours. Why should I listen to your advice?

Jenny Don't worry about results. Mine aren't bad. And if it gets any worse, I plan to really get tough. That'll shape them up.

This case example is designed to point out that the way supervisory and P/HRM decisions are made varies with the leadership style of the managers. Jenny is inexperienced as a leader. She is unconcerned with some rather poor results; she seems to assume that tough disciplinary measures will solve whatever is causing the problems. Claudia is more experienced. She is seeking all the help she can get from the P/HRM specialist and her employees to get at the causes of her problem. Claudia's problem is much less severe, but she considers it seriously. Jenny does not. In addition to differences in experience, there are differences in the leadership style of the two leaders in this example. They see the role of the leader differently. They also perceive the relationship between themselves as leaders and their work groups differently.

Jenny believes the role of the leader involves making the decisions for the work group. She sees communication between herself and the work group primarily as one-way communication downward: from her to the employees. Jenny sees herself as having more formal authority than the employees and having the power to discipline and apply sanctions to the employees if they don't perform well. Note that she didn't discuss her ability to reward positively those who are doing well; she discussed only a plan to "really get tough."

Claudia follows a different leadership style, in which the leader makes decisions only after discussion with the work group. Claudia's communication patterns go two ways, as evidenced by her group meetings. Claudia takes responsibility for results but seeks the help of the work group and of the P/HRM department. Claudia is willing to share her authority with her work group and with P/HRM. She appears willing to take both positive and negative approaches to rewards.

Of course, leadership style is much more complicated than the case implies. Many management experts believe that almost any style can be effective, given the right mix of leader, employees, and task situation. It should be clear that the experience and preferred leadership style of the operating manager-leader will influence how decisions are made and how P/HRM programs are communicated and implemented.[15]

People and the P/HRM Diagnostic Model

People—the human resource element—are the most important concern in the diagnostic model. Simply putting together P/HRM activities without paying attention to people characteristics would be ill advised. The most carefully designed and implemented P/HRM activity may backfire because adjustments for individual differences were not built into the program. In the chapter opening case, Martha is attempting to understand why Lenny and Harry behave differently on the job at the National Pancake House. She will soon discover that people differ in many characteristics. Lenny and Harry differ in their abilities, attitudes, and preferences. They also have different styles, intellectual capacities, and ways of doing the job.

Abilities of Employees

Some employee differences affecting P/HRM programs are due to differences in abilities.

---

[15]Fred E. Fiedler, "The Contingency Model: New Directions for Leadership Utilization," *Journal of Contemporary Business,* Autumn 1974, pp. 65–80.

Abilities Are Skills Which People Possess • Abilities can be classified by mechanical, motor coordination, mental, or creative skills. According to many psychologists, some abilities are caused by genetic factors which are rarely subject to change through training. Examples of these differences are finger dexterity and response time. Other abilities, such as interpersonal skills and leadership, are much more easily subject to change. People learn abilities at home, at school, and at work; their present inventories of abilities are, at least partly, a consequence of this past learning.

Because people differ in abilities, the extent to which they can be trained in a specific skill varies. In most cases an aptitude can be developed into an ability by training and experience. But in other cases it's more sensible to place people with certain abilities in jobs requiring those abilities. Not everyone will have all the abilities necessary to do every job, and a manager does not always have the time or money needed to train people who do not have them.

The importance of a manager's understanding of employee ability differences is emphasized by the example of Harry at National Pancake. Does he lack the abilities to do the job? If it appears that Harry's problem is in fact ability, Martha would have at least two options. One is training, whereby Harry's aptitudes would be developed into the ability needed for the job. The other is placement, whereby Harry could be transferred to another job, such as busboy or cashier.

Do you think Harry's problem is an ability problem?

Employee Attitudes and Preferences

> An attitude is a characteristic and usually long-lasting way of thinking, feeling, and behaving toward an object, idea, person, or group of persons.
>
> A preference is a type of attitude which evaluates an object, idea, or person in a positive or negative way.

How an individual thinks, feels, and behaves toward work and the place of work in his or her life forms one important attitude. People are motivated by powerful emotional forces, and work provides an opportunity for the expression of both aggressive and pleasure-seeking drives. Besides offering a way to channel energy, work also provides the person with income, a justification for existence, and the opportunity to achieve self-esteem and self-worth. The amount of energy directed to work is related to the amount directed to family, interpersonal relations, and recreation. This in turn is partly a consequence of a person's attitudes toward the worth of work in life.

What kind of attitude about work do Lenny and Harry have?

How can an awareness of work attitudes and preferences help managers understand workers and improve their effectiveness? The attitude toward work that an employee has affects most aspects of the P/HRM program. Many P/HRM programs (job enlargement, compensation, leadership, and participation programs) are designed to create a more favorable individual attitude toward work. The assumption is that a positive attitude will result in higher-quality performance and increased production. Recall, however, that performance is also influenced by learning, perception, abilities, and motivation.

Motivation of Employees

> Motivation is that set of attitudes which predisposes a person to act in a specific goal-directed way. Motivation is thus an inner state which energizes, channels, and sustains human behavior to achieve goals.

Work motivation is concerned with those attitudes that channel the person's behavior toward work and away from recreation or other life activity areas. The motivation to work is likely to change as other life activities change.

A number of theories have attempted to explain work motivation. These will be discussed in Chapter 12. The theories differ in their assumptions about how rational persons are and to what degree the conscious and the unconscious mind directs behavior. All of these theories have received some research support, but none has been overwhelmingly substantiated. At the moment, attention is focused on the importance of individual motivation in achieving organizational and individual goals.

How will a knowledge of motivation help a person be a more effective manager of people? As with work attitudes, a manager who can determine what the work motivations of the employees are will make more effective P/HRM decisions. For employees who appear to be work oriented and well motivated toward work, incentive compensation systems will likely lead to more production and higher quality work. Those who are consciously motivated to do a better job benefit from performance evaluation techniques like management by objectives. Managers who can determine or predict which employees are motivated to work harder can select the employees they want. The determination of a person's state of motivation is undoubtedly very difficult. Remember, motivation is *within* a person and a manager must infer the individual's motivational level by his or her behavior. The manager utilizes his or her understanding of individual motivation to select the best possible P/HRM program.

Personality of Employees

> Personality is the characteristic way a person thinks and behaves in adjusting to his or her environment. It includes the person's traits, values, motives, genetic blueprint, attitudes, emotional reactivity, abilities, self-image, and intelligence. It also includes the person's visible behavior patterns.

Each employee has a unique personality. Because of this, it is highly unlikely that a single set of P/HRM activities or leadership approaches will be equally successful for *all* employees. Behavioral scientists have found that:

1. The employee, as a person, is both rational and intuitive-emotional in makeup and behavior. Therefore, his or her choices and behavior are a consequence of rational (conscious) and emotional (unconscious) influences. Choices are occasionally entirely influenced by one or the other, but most behavior is influenced by both.
2. A person acts in response to internal inclinations and choices and environmental influences
3. Each person is unique, and acts and thinks in a certain way because of

- The personality the person develops.
- The abilities the person has or learns.

- The attitudes and preferences the person has or develops.
- The motives the person has or develops.

This section has touched briefly on some relevant concepts from the behavioral sciences which will be developed further in later chapters. They indicate that the nature of the employee has a great influence on P/HRM decisions. The effective manager realizes that the employee's nature is a crucial variable in P/HRM activities and organizational effectiveness. The implications of this knowledge of human behavior for the various P/HRM activities will become more obvious as we move into the book.

How to Use the P/HRM Diagnostic Model

You've now had a chance to learn something about the diagnostic model: this book's way of providing a map of the important factors affecting P/HRM. The model tells you that three sets of factors influence the P/HRM activities used by an organization:

It is reasonable to conclude that managers who must make P/HRM decisions are more effective if they think about the three sets of factors influencing P/RHM activities and effectiveness before they make a decision. Chapters 4–21 tell you **how** each of these factors affects a specific P/HRM decision, such as the selection and pay decisions Martha Winston is considering at the National Pancade House.

Managers concerned with the P/HRM function and activities need some kind of model to guide the way. First, they need to analyze the P/HRM problem—or the person with a problem—by looking at all the data at hand. Then they decide which causes are operating and how the problem can be solved. They do not give up if the most probable cause does not seem to be operating. Rather, they proceed down the list of causes until the underlying source of the problem is found.

Suppose, for example, that a manager notices from the weekly production reports that productivity in the department has been declining over the past few weeks. There could be a number of reasons for this decline. Perhaps the equipment in the department has become defective and is not working properly, or the materials and supplies have been of a comparatively lower quality. Or the cause might be the employees: perhaps some of the more highly skilled employees have been promoted, transferred to other departments, or have quit, and their replacements lack the necessary skills and experience to perform the work effectively. Or, perhaps the problem is one of poor employee morale.

In investigating the problem, the manager using a diagnostic framework may find that turnover in the department has been quite high, that absenteeism has been increasing, and that there have been more complaints and grievances of late. All of these are symptoms

Factors influencing P/HRM:

The People—the employee's abilities, attitudes/preferences, motives, and so on.

The External Environment—how the union, government, and economy affect the P/HRM situation.

The Internal Environment—goals and organization style, tasks to be done, work group, and leaders' experiences and styles.

of low employee satisfaction. They detract from the organization's effectiveness. If the manager concludes that the most likely cause of poor production in the department is the low satisfaction of employees, a solution for this problem will be sought. The manager may consider such solutions as: providing better working conditions, increasing pay and other financial benefits, improving communication between supervisor and employees, redesigning the jobs to make them more interesting and challenging, or modifying the manager's own leadership style.

If, after treating the morale problem, productivity is still low, the manager will turn to the next most probable cause of the problem and continue down the list of causes until the right one is found and corrected.

Summary

The main objective of this chapter has been to introduce you to the diagnostic model of P/HRM. This chapter briefly reviews some concepts from the behavioral sciences to show you how they apply to P/HRM decisions. It also examines two other aspects of the environment of the personnel function: the physical location of the organization in a labor market and the work sector in which it is located. This book has been written with the assumption that effective P/HRM programs will result if the manager or specialist follows a diagnostic approach.

A summary of the major points covered in this chapter follows:

1. A sound P/HRM program can contribute to organizational effectiveness.
2. The diagnostic approach suggests that before you choose a P/HRM program you should examine the nature of the employees, the external and internal environmental influences on the organization, and organizational factors. These factors act as moderating variables in P/HRM decisions, and P/HRM activities are influenced by them.
3. Abilities are skills which people possess.
4. An attitude is a characteristic, and usually a long-lasting, way of thinking, feeling, and behaving. A preference is a type of attitude which evaluates an object, idea, or persons in a positive or negative way.
5. Motivation, the inner state which energizes, channels, and sustains human behavior to achieve goals, is an important concept in P/HRM programs.
6. Various factors in the external environment, such as unionization of employees, government regulations, and competitive pressure, also exert strong influences on the P/HRM function.
7. The work sector in which the organization is operating—public, private or third—determines the complexity and bureaucratic level of the P/HRM function.
8. Organization factors, including goals of organization, style, the nature of the task, makeup of the work group, and leader's style and experience, must all be taken into account to maximize the effectiveness of the P/HRM function.
9. The status of the labor market can also facilitate or impede a company's P/HRM programs.

The appendix to this chapter discusses the labor force and the physical location of the organization in some detail. This type of data and information must be used in conducting a thorough diagnostic analyses before making P/HRM decisions.

Appendix: A Look at the Composition of the Labor Force*

In 1982, the U.S. population was approximately 230 million and the labor force comprised about 100 million persons. By 1990, about 119 million persons will be in the labor force. These figures indicate that about 62 percent of all males 16 years and over were employed. This ranges from about 47 percent for males 16–17 to 25 percent for males over 65; the largest percentage of employed males was about 96 percent of all males 25–44 years of age. Female employment participation was 47 percent, but this is growing. About 34 percent of girls 16–17 were employed. The highest proportion was about 54 percent of women 45–54, and only 9 percent of women over 65 were employed. From 1947 to 1975, the female population increased 52 percent, but the percentage of women working increased 123 percent.

The U.S. labor force is also becoming composed of more single and fewer married persons. One third of all workers are single, and 90 percent of the recent growth in the labor force has been in single workers.

More participation in the labor force has become possible as the life span of the population has lengthened. In the United States, the typical man now lives about 67 years, and the typical woman about 72 years.

In general, the contribution of the U.S. labor force has been growing as productivity has increased. The most productive workers are in (and are expected to be in) the agriculture, forestry, and fishing industries, followed by transportation, communication, public utilities, mining, finance, insurance, and real estate. In the lower productivity category are workers in merchandising, manufacturing, and construction. The least productive workers are in services.

The percentage of the labor force employed by manufacturing, construction, mining, and agriculture has stabilized or declined. It is estimated that by 1990 two times as many persons (78 million) will be employed in service industries such as transportation, utilities, trade, financial, general services, and government as in the stabilized industries (36 million). As far as type of workers are concerned, by 1990 it is predicted that farm workers will represent about 2 to 3 percent; service workers, about 16 percent; blue-collar workers, 31 percent; and the rest—over 50 percent—will be white-collar workers (professional and technical, clerical, sales, and managers). Blue-collar workers, especially unskilled workers, are declining in relative importance. One of the fastest growing segments of employment is state and local government workers. From 1950 to 1982, total employment was up 67 percent, while state and local government employment increased by over 200 percent.

A Closer Look at Some Groups of Employees in the Labor Force

The recent emphasis on equal employment opportunity programs makes analysis of subgroups in the population of special interest. We will look at some statistics on them and will examine the case of temporary and part-time employees, many of whom come from these groups.

---

*Sources: U.S. Department of Labor, "Tomorrow's Jobs" in *Occupational Outlook Handbook, 1980–1981* (Washington, D.C.: U.S. Government Printing Office, 1980), pp. 1–19; John W. Wright, *The American Almanac of Jobs and Salaries* (New York: Avon, 1982); Martin A. Bachler, ed., *The Hammond Almanac of Facts, 1982* (Maplewood, N.J.: Hammond Almanac, Inc., 1982).

Women in the Labor Force • In recent years, about 45 percent of the full-time U.S. work force has been women. The number of married women in the labor force has increased 230 percent since 1947, at the same time that the number of male married employees has increased by 30 percent. In the mid-70s, 52 percent of married women with children aged 6–17 held full-time jobs, and 35 percent of married women with children aged six or under worked. Fifty-one percent of black children and 37 percent of white children 18 and under had mothers in the labor force.

Although it is alleged that everyone has equal job opportunities, it is difficult to argue with the facts of discrimination against women in the workplace. Typically, women hold the lower status, low-pay jobs. For example, one recent study of 163 companies found that 31 percent had 50 percent or more women employees, and 82 percent employed at least 19 percent women. If discrimination were not practiced, at least half of the companies with 50 percent women workers should have a majority of women in higher status, higher paying jobs. This study found, however, that less than 10 percent of the high-pay, high-status jobs were held by women. Similar conditions exist in the public and third sectors.

Minorities in the Labor Force • The situation for women's employment is similar for racial and ethnic minorities in the United States. Large numbers of minority peoples, such as Hispanic Americans, blacks, and American Indians, are employed in low-skill, low-pay jobs, and few are in high-status, high-pay jobs.

Historically, the most recent immigrant group took the lowest level jobs offered. This was true of the Irish, Polish, Yugoslavs, and Jews. One difference between the immigrant groups and other minorities is that most of the minority groups were living in the United States long before the immigrants arrived—the Indians from the beginning, as were many of the Hispanics in the Southwest, and the blacks since the mid-1700s. They have not advanced to the degree that the immigrants have, however. The Indians were kept on reservations, and the Hispanics remained in the areas that once belonged to the Mexican Republic (except for the Cuban and Puerto Rican immigrants, who came much later). Most blacks remained in southern agriculture until relatively recently. These minorities represent about 13 percent of the U.S. population. They have been less well educated than the majority, although recent programs have attempted to improve this situation. Movement to better paying, higher status jobs has been a problem for racial and ethnic minorities, as it has for women.

The Older Employee • The age discrimination legislation defines an older employee as one between the ages of 40 and 70. About 21 percent of the labor force currently is in this category. This portion of the labor force is protected by law because some employers hold negative stereotypes about older workers.

Probably one of the most difficult employment problems today is the older employee who loses his job through no fault of his own. Employers assume that because he is older he is less qualified and less able to adapt. And benefits plans (which may amount to one third of base compensation) are set up in such a way that it costs more to employ older people.

One of the first things to remember about the aging process is that each person ages at a different rate. As we grow older, we lose some of our faculties. But this process is going on all our lives. Rarely is a swimmer better than in his midteens, for example. The key, then, is to match employees with jobs. Older workers may be less efficient on some jobs requiring quick physical response rates. But this is more important for a race driver or airline pilot than for a stock analyst or social worker.

Most studies indicate that even for jobs requiring physical work, employees over 45 have no more accidents than younger employees do. They also have the same or lower rates of absenteeism, at least until age 55. The worst accident rate observed in one study was for employees under 35.[16] When total performance is considered (speed, accuracy, judgment, loyalty, etc.), the older employee has been found to be at least as effective as the younger one. Yet our society tends to assume that the older employee is less effective.

Handicapped Workers in the Labor Force • There are more than 6.5 million handicapped workers in the United States. Studies of handicapped persons indicate that they are of all age-groups, of both sexes, and in many occupations. About 56 percent have been disabled by disease, 30 percent by accident, and 14 percent by congenital diseases. In the latter category, the largest group of people have lost the use of arms or legs, or have back problems. The next largest number are amputees and blind (or partially blind) employees.[17]

Many handicapped persons have had difficulty finding employment of any kind because employers and fellow workers believe that they could not do the job or would cause an excessive number of accidents.

Few people use all their faculties on a job, and there are many jobs for those who do not have all their faculties. When the handicapped are properly matched to jobs, studies show that two thirds of the physically handicapped produce at the same rate as nonhandicapped workers, 24 percent performs at higher levels, and only 10 percent performs at a lower rate. Absenteeism and turnover are normally lower for the handicapped, for two reasons. The handicapped have had their abilities matched to their jobs better, and most handicapped workers seem better adjusted to working and have more favorable attitudes toward work. Thus they are better motivated to do a good job. Most studies indicate that handicapped persons have fewer accidents than nonhandicapped person.[18]

Of course, some handicapped people are physically or psychologically unable to work. Some who are marginally employable can work in training jobs at sheltered workshops and organizations such as Goodwill Industries. But for those able to work, it is most important that the handicapped be treated as normally as other workers. They will respond better to fair treatment than to paternalism. They want a chance.

Veterans in the Labor Force • Veterans are former servicemen realeased from active duty by the military. They are not easily recognized as special employees by employers, but they do have a readjustment to make to civilian life. The government has attempted to ease reentry to civilian life of Vietnam veterans with several programs.

About one fourth of all returning veterans have resumed their interrupted educational careers. But the great majority have entered the civilian labor market, many seeking their first full-time jobs. As of January 1, 1977, there were 558,000 Vietnam veterans aged 20–34 unemployed in this country. The unemployment rate for veterans was 8.6 percent,

---

[16]H. Kahne, et al. "Don't Take the Older Workers for Granted," *Harvard Business Review,* January 1957, pp. 90–94.

[17]Bernard De Lury, "Equal Job Opportunity for the Handicapped Means Positive Thinking and Positive Action," *Labor Law Journal,* November 1975, pp. 679–85.

[18]Ibid.

while the average unemployment rate was 7.8 percent. In the 20–24 age bracket, veterans' unemployment was 18 percent.[19]

Congress has provided specific reentry adjustments for veterans, usually referred to as reemployment rights. In addition to reemployment, Congress has enacted laws making it easier for veterans to enter the federal career service. These include a preference system of points added to test scores for veterans, the Veterans Readjustment Appointment, waivers of physical requirements, the restriction of certain jobs to veterans, preference for retention in case of reduction of force, and similar procedures. The Veterans' Administration also assists veterans who are seeking employment through job marts and apprenticeship training programs. Priority for referral to appropriate training programs and job openings is given to eligible veterans, with first consideration to the disabled veteran. Other federal benefits have also become available to veterans operating their own businesses through the Small Business Administration. Similarly, unemployment compensation for veterans provides a weekly income for a limited period of time, varying with state laws.[20]

Part-Time and Temporary Help Employees • The labor force members considered so far have been full-time employees: those who regularly work about 40 hours weekly. But the labor market includes another group: part-time employees, who regularly (and usually voluntarily) are employed for less than the normal work week. A person who is working part time because she or he cannot get a full-time job is involuntarily a part-time employee. This growing segment of the work force will be discussed in Chapter 20.

The Labor Force and Physical Location of the Organization

The location of the organization influences the kinds of people it hires and the P/HRM activities it conducts. A hospital, plant, university, or government bureau located in a rural area confront different conditions than one located in an urban area. For example, the work force in a rural area might be more willing to accept a bureaucratic organization style. Recruiting and selection in rural areas will be different in that there may be fewer applicants. Yet the organization may find a larger proportion of hirable workers ingrained with the work ethic. It also may be harder to schedule overtime if workers are supplementing farm incomes with an eight-hour shift at a factory. There may be fewer minority "problems," but it also may be difficult to recruit professional/technical personnel, who have shown a preference to work near continuing education and cultural opportunities. While pay may be lower in rural areas, so are costs of living.

An urban location might be advantageous for recruiting and holding professional workers. Urban locations provide a bigger labor force but generally call for higher wages. The late shifts may be a problem here, too, but for different reasons. Workers may not feel safe late at night in the parking lots or going home.

Geographic location therefore influences the kinds of workers available to staff the organization. The location or setting is extremely significant for companies operating in other countries. The employees may speak a different language, abide by the Napoleonic

---

[19]Bureau of National Affairs, *Fair Employment Practices—Summary of Latest Developments, May 21, 1981* (Washington, D.C., 1981).

[20]*Ibid.*

legal code, practice different religions, have different work attitudes and so on. Let's consider some of the major differences between home-based and other-country enterprises.

Educational Factors • Examples include the number of skilled employees available, attitudes toward education, and literacy level. Educational deficiencies in some countries can lead to a scarcity of qualified employees, as well as a lack of educational facilities to upgrade potential employees.

Behavioral Factors • Societies differ in factors such as attitudes toward wealth, the desirability of profits, managerial role, and authority.

Legal-Political Factors • Laws and political structures differ and can encourage or discourage private enterprise. Nations also differ in degree of political stability. Some countries are very nationalistic (even xenophobic). Such countries can require local ownership of organizations or, if they are so inclined, expropriate foreign concerns.

Economic Factors • Economies differ in basic structure, inflation rate, ownership constraints, and the like. The nations of the world can be divided into three economic categories: fully developed, developing, and less developed. The fully developed nations include the United States and Canada, Australia, Israel, Japan, South Africa, and most European countries (the United Kingdom, West Germany, France, the USSR, Belgium, Luxembourg, the Netherlands, Switzerland, Italy, Sweden, Denmark, Norway, Finland). In these countries American and Canadian managers will find fewer differences in educational, behavioral, economic, and legal-political factors than they are likely to encounter in developing or less developed countries.

The developing nations are those that are well along in economic development but cannot yet be said to be fully developed. Examples include Brazil, Mexico, Argentina, Venezuela, Spain, Nigeria, Saudi Arabia, India, and Eastern Europe. These countries provide more constraints in all four factors than developed countries do.

Third-world nations—the less developed countries—are the most difficult to work in because of significant constraints in all four factors. The remaining 90 or so countries in the world are in this group. A sample list would include Egypt, Bolivia, and Upper Volta.

To be successful abroad, P/HRM managers must learn all they can about the countries in which they will be working. There are many sources of this kind of information. Knowledge of differences among nations in educational, behavioral, legal-political and economic factors is essential for managerial success abroad. It is equally important (and more difficult) for the enterprise to obtain managers with proper attitudes toward other countries and their cultures. A manager with the wrong set of attitudes may try to transfer North American ways of doing things directly to the host country, without considering the constraints in these four factors. The more significant the differences, the more likely they are to cause problems for the unperceptive manager.

Effective managers who work abroad must adapt their P/HRM practices to conditions in the host country and learn to understand the new culture. A whole new field is developing for human resource planning in multinational organizations. There are significant challenges in such P/HRM activities. Just as the tools of management science do not work on very unstable problems, leadership styles and P/HRM activities that work for educated, achievement-oriented employees may not do so for uneducated nonachievers.

Case

Martha

Harry

Martha picked up her cup of coffee and thought: Amy helped me a lot. But it is my job to figure out what to do. She wonders what factors could cause the differences between Lenny and Harry. It could be personality differences. Lenny is an outgoing person, and Harry tends to be introverted. There are some differences in abilities. Lenny is more agile. He uses his hands well. Harry seems a bit clumsier. And Lenny is more experienced—he's been on the job four more years than Harry.

Lenny and Harry have the same leader and work group. They do the same task at the same time. The environment is the same. These couldn't cause the differences.

This narrows the option down to motivation and attitude differences. Was there a good match of interests and abilities with the job? Martha decided to discuss the issues informally with Harry. Later that day, she invited Harry to have a chat with her.

Martha: Harry, this is the first chance I've had to chat with you for very long. How do you like it at National by now?

Harry: It's O.K. It's a job.

Martha: Is there anything we can do to make it better than just a job for you?

Harry: Not really. Jobs are jobs. They're all the same.

Martha: All of them? Did you ever have a dream about what you wanted to do?

Harry: Sure. I've always wanted to be a disc jockey, but I hated school. So I quit. Then I got married and I'm locked in. I can't go back to school and make it.

Martha: I didn't know you wanted to go back to school. I'm sure you could go to night school.

Harry: I might be ready for that now.

Martha: If I can help by scheduling you differently, let me know. Everyone should get all the schooling they can. And who knows? You could go on to be assistant manager here—or even a disc jockey.

After talking with Martha, Harry did go back to school. His work improved, as did his willingness to be friendlier with co-workers and customers. Martha's chats became more frequent with all the employees, including Harry. Harry did graduate from high school and now is an assistant manager for National. He's very happy in his job.

What about Lenny? He's chief cook at 827. He's had several opportunities to become assistant manager, but he loves his work and has refused to be transferred. As Lenny put it, "I've found my niche. I do my job, then go to the beach. No worries. And I get to talk to lots of nice people."

What about the new cook? The pay issue had to be settled first. Martha contacted the home office, emphasizing that business had been steadily increasing at 827. When she told them that she needed more money to hire an extra cook to handle the increased business, they gave her more, but not enough to completely satisfy everyone.

Instead of hiding this fact from the rest of her employees, Martha explained the situation and asked them for their suggestions. Their solution was to help her recruit a cook with some experience, but one who would not demand so high a salary that their raises would be eliminated. All of the employees asked their friends for leads to fill the vacancy. Martha called guidance counselors at schools and the state employment service.

Within a week, Martha had hired Fran, a friend of Harry's. Lenny, Harry, and all the other employees liked her very much, and she worked out well as the third cook. Besides that, employee satisfaction improved all around. Not only could Martha pay Fran what she expected as a beginning wage, but all the other employees got a slight increase in pay, too.

In sum, the physical location of the organization (rural or urban, at home or abroad) can have significant impact on how P/HRM programs are used and which activities are conducted. The manager with a diagnostic orientation will understand the complexities involved with physical location differences.

Now that we understand the diagnostic model of P/HRM let's get back to the National Pancake House situation with Martha and Harry.

Questions for Review and Discussion

1. How are people involved in P/HRM programs performing work similar to physicians who must perform a diagnosis before treating a patient?
2. What individual differences play a major role in P/HRM decision making?
3. Can a P/HRM specialist have any impact on productivity?
4. Why must external environmental forces be considered when designing a P/HRM program?
5. What does the term *third sector* mean?
6. What effectiveness criteria are used to examine the success of a P/HRM program?
7. What role does the organization's style play in P/HRM?
8. Someone stated that, "If unemployment in the national and local labor markets differs, there will be a natural movement of people between the markets." What did she mean by this statement?

Glossary

External P/HRM Influences.   These are environmental forces outside the organization such as unions, government, and economic conditions.

Internal P/HRM Influences.   Those internal (inside the organization) environmental forces such as goals, organizational style, tasks, work group, and the leader's style of influencing.

Motivation.   The attitudes which predispose a person to act in a specific goal-directed way. It is an internal state which directs a person's behaviors.

Personality.   The characteristic way a person thinks and behaves in adjusting to his or her environment. It includes the person's traits, values, motives, genetic blueprint, attitudes, abilities, and behavior patterns.

Work Group.   Two or more people who work together to accomplish a goal and who communicate and interact with each other.

Chapter Three

Equal Employment Opportunity Programs

Learning Objectives

After studying this chapter, you should be able to:

- Determine three main influences that led to the development of concern for equal employment opportunity (EEO) programs

- Describe two major criteria used to determine EEO and affirmative action compliance or noncompliance

- Explain the P/HRM implications of five landmark Supreme Court case decisions

- List the enforcement agencies that are responsible for administering Title VII of the Civil Rights Act, Executive Order 11246, and the Age Discrimination Act

- Outline how an organization can implement an affirmative action program

Chapter Outline

I. Introduction

II. How Did EEO Emerge?
 A. Societal Values and EEO
 B. Economic Status of Women and Minorities: Before 1964

III. Government Regulation of EEO Programs
 A. Title VII of the 1964 Civil Rights Act
 B. Discrimination: A Legal Definition

IV. Important Court Decisions
 A. *Griggs* v. *Duke Power* (1971)
 B. *Albermarle Paper Company* v. *J. Moody* (1975)
 C. *Washington* v. *Davis* (1976)
 D. *Bakke* v. *University of California* (1978)
 E. *Weber* v. *Kaiser* (1979)

V. Enforcing the Laws
 A. Equal Employment Opportunity Commission
 B. Office of Federal Contract Compliance Programs (OFCCP)
 C. The Courts

VI. EEO Programs: A Preventive Approach
 A. AT&T's Program for Women Outside-Crafts Workers

VII. Various Groups and EEO
 A. Women
 B. Older Employees
 C. Racial and Ethnic Minorities
 D. Religious Minorities
 E. Physically and Mentally Handicapped Workers
 F. Veterans
 G. White Males

VIII. Mandated Actions in EEO-Affirmative Action Programs

IX. Cost/Benefit Analysis of EEO Programs

X. Summary

Case

Hugo

Gregory

Osanna

Hugo Gerbold, the director of personnel/human resource management at Reliable Insurance, is sitting in his office, thinking. The problem is equal employment opportunity. Reliable is a middle-sized company in the Midwest which specializes in homeowners', auto, and, to a lesser extent, life and health insurance. As is typical of firms of this type, the top-management team members are all white, in their 60s, and have been with the firm all their careers. The work force is mainly composed of:

Salespersons—98 percent white males, the rest white females and black males.

Underwriters—98 percent white males, 2 percent white females.

Claims agents—90 percent white males, 8 percent white females, 2 percent black males.

Clerical staff—90 percent white females, 10 percent black females.

Other administrative personnel: Computer programmers, marketing staff, security, etc.—95 percent white males, 5 percent white females.

Reliable is located in an area where at least 35 percent of the labor force is black.

Hugo knows many firms just like Reliable have been fined back-pay differentials and been ordered to set up affirmative action plans. At a recent conference, Reliable's lawyers had devoted much time to discussing the laws and recent cases. This had prompted Hugo to visit the company president, Gregory Inness. Gregory, 64 years old and a lawyer by training, did not give Hugo much hope that things were going to change at Reliable with regard equal employment opportunities.

It is a few days after this meeting. Hugo has just received a call from a professor at one of the local universities. The professor had encouraged Osanna Kenley to apply at Reliable for a management trainee position which had been advertised. She had been discouraged by the P/HRM department, because, they said, she was a liberal arts major. She'd also been told there were no positions. In fact, the company had just hired a white male for a trainee position. Somehow she'd found out about this.

The professor tells Hugo that Osanna is going to file a complaint against the firm with the Equal Employment Opportunity Commission (EEOC). He suggests Hugo talk with her before she goes to the EEOC. In fact, she is on her way over to see Hugo right now.

Hugo and Osanna have a pleasant talk, but it is clear that she means to open up Reliable to all applicants, even if she personally does not get a job there. He arranges to see Gregory right after Osanna leaves.

Hugo: Gregory, remember how I was just talking about equal employment opportunities? Well, we may have a case on our hands. And remember the insurance company that just paid out $15 million in back pay and had to hire their fair share of minorities as a result?

Gregory: Well, maybe we should hire this young woman. That ought to take care of the problem, won't it?

Hugo: No, it won't. We better get going on an EEO program now.

Gregory: Tell me more about what's behind all this EEO.

Hugo then tells Gregory about EEO, some laws, and affirmative action.

Introduction

> Equal employment opportunity (EEO) programs are implemented by employ-
> ers to prevent employment discrimination in the workplace or to take reme-
> dial action to offset past employment discrimination.

Equal employment opportunities are one of the most significant activities in the P/HRM area today. In a Prentice-Hall/ASPA survey of 1,400 P/HRM executives, the respondents labeled it as one of their top three activities. P/HRM managers and specialists reported spending 14.2 percent of their time on EEO—not just compliance, but full EEO implementation. Of the 1,400 company representatives surveyed, 18 percent reported they had established full-time EOO offices, and 15 percent had hired new employees to handle EEO.[1]

EEO cuts across a number of P/HRM activities, and various P/HRM officials and others are involved. Top managers must get involved in EEO issues and programs to make sure that the organization is in compliance with the law, to avoid fines and to establish a discrimination-free workplace. Operating managers must help by changing their attitudes about protected-category employees and helping all employees to adjust to the changes EEO is bringing to the workplace.

Exhibit 3–1 highlights the key factors in the P/HRM diagnostic model which affect equal employment opportunities. Some of these were noted in the introduction above: union requirements, goals of the organization, and P/HRM activities involved. Others are discussed below: societal values, preferences of workers as reflected in economic status of minorities and women, and government regulations. Knowledge of these factors can contribute to an understanding of why EEO developed and how it operates. To be effective, EEO must influence the entire P/HRM of an organization.

How Did EEO Emerge?

The three main influences on the development of EEO were: (1) changes in societal values; (2) the economic status of women and minorities; and (3) the emerging role of government regulation. The first two are briefly discussed below; information on the third factor is discussed in detail in the next section.

Societal Values and EEO

Throughout history, Western society has accepted the principle that people should be rewarded according to the worth of their contributions. When the United States became a nation, that principle was embodied in the American dream: the idea that any individual, through hard work, could advance from the most humble origins to the highest station, according to the worth of her or his contributions. In America, success did not depend on being born into a privileged family; equal opportunity was everyone's birthright. To this day, the American dream, with its emphasis on merit rather than privilege, is widely accepted by the public.

---

[1]ASPA *The Personal Executive's Job* (Englewood Cliffs, N.J.: Prentice-Hall, 1977).

Exhibit 3–1

Factors affecting equal employment opportunity programs

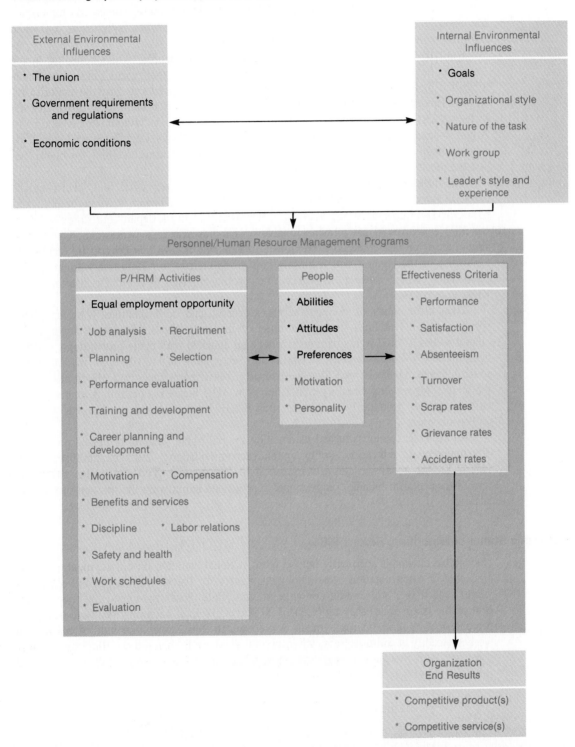

External Environmental
Influences

* The union

* Government requirements
  and regulations

* Economic conditions

Internal Environmental
Influences

* **Goals**

* Organizational style

* Nature of the task

* Work group

* Leader's style and
  experience

Personnel/Human Resource Management Programs

P/HRM Activities

* **Equal employment opportunity**

* Job analysis   * Recruitment

* Planning   * Selection

* Performance evaluation

* Training and development

* Career planning and
  development

* Motivation   * Compensation

* Benefits and services

* Discipline   * Labor relations

* Safety and health

* Work schedules

* Evaluation

People

* **Abilities**

* **Attitudes**

* **Preferences**

* Motivation

* Personality

Effectiveness Criteria

* Performance

* Satisfaction

* Absenteeism

* Turnover

* Scrap rates

* Grievance rates

* Accident rates

Organization
End Results

* Competitive product(s)

* Competitive service(s)

Another value that has encouraged equal opportunity is the profit motive. Nondiscrimination makes good business sense. If a company limits opportunities to white males it cuts itself off from the vast reservoir of human talent comprised of women and minorities. Moreover, it adds to such societal problems as poverty, crime, high taxes, and civic disorder, which also hurt the business community.

Until the early 1960s it was not unusual for many people, while believing in the American dream of rewards based on merit, to also believe that blacks (and other minorities) had their "place"—a place largely cut off from the rewards that the majority received. This apparent contradiction in beliefs was the American dilemma as observed even in the 1940s by the distinguished Swedish economist, Gunnar Myrdal, in his studies of American race relations for the Carnegie Corporation. Blacks were often excluded from schools, public accommodations, jobs, and voting, and economic realities for blacks belied the ideals of the American dream.[2]

The differences between American ideals and American realities lent special significance to the civil rights conflict of the 1960s. The conflict began in Montgomery, Alabama, on December 1, 1955, when Mrs. Rosa Parks, a black department store worker in her 50s, was arrested for refusing to give up her bus seat to a white man. Out of that single act of protest emerged a previously unthinkable act—a bus boycott by blacks. At the center of the boycott was a loosely knit group called the Montgomery Improvement Association, which chose as its leader a new young minister in town, Dr. Martin Luther King, Jr.

Then came years of demonstrations, marches, and confrontations with the police which captured headlines throughout most of the early 1960s. Television accounts included scenes of civil rights demonstrators being attacked with cattle prods, dogs, and fire hoses. These events shocked the public into recognition that civil rights was a serious social problem in the United States. Gradually, overt discrimination declined and recognition of the problems faced by minorities grew. The business community shared in this attitude change, voluntarily supporting such EEO-related efforts as the National Alliance of Businessmen.

As the U.S. Congress turned its attention to civil rights, laws were passed prohibiting discrimination in education, voting, public accommodations, and the administration of federal programs, as well as discrimination in employment. The civil rights movement was instrumental in raising congressional concern and stimulating the passage of this legislation.

Economic Status of Minorities: Before 1964

Undeniable economic inequality helped focus national attention on employment as a specific area of discrimination. Unemployment figures for blacks were twice as high as for whites, and higher still among nonwhite youth. While blacks accounted for only 10 percent of the labor force, they represented 20 percent of total unemployment and nearly 30 percent of *long-term* unemployment. Moreover, in 1961, only one half of black men worked steadily at full-time jobs, while two thirds of white men did so. Blacks were three times as likely as whites to work less than full time. Similar statistical differences existed for other minorities, such as Hispanics and Indians.[3]

---

[2]Gunnar Myrdal, *An American Dilemma: The Negro Problem and American Democracy* (New York: Harper & Row, 1944).

[3]Charles Silberman, *Crises in Black and White* (New York: Random House, 1964).

When they did find work, minorities were relegated to lower status jobs, and consequently their income was far below that of whites. Minorities such as blacks were over three times as likely as whites to be unskilled laboroers. Whites were over three times as likely as blacks to be in professional or managerial positions. While only 9 percent of black men were skilled craftsworkers, 20 percent of white men were. In the tobacco, paper, and trucking industries, blacks were ordinarily segregated into less desirable lines of progression or sections of the company. In the building trades, they were concentrated in the lower paying "trowel trades," such as plastering and bricklaying. Some unions excluded blacks entirely, and others organized separate locals for them.

The inequalities are especially striking in the income comparisons between blacks and whites. In 1962, the average family income for blacks was $3,000, compared with nearly $6,000 for whites. More importantly, the relative position of blacks had been worsening during the preceding 10 years. While black family income was only 52 percent of white family income in 1962, it was 57 percent of white family income in 1952. These inequalities could not be attributed entirely to differences in educational level between blacks and whites. The average income of a black high school graduate was lower than the average income of a white elementary school graduate.[4]

Government Regulation of EEO Programs

In the 1980s, there are many laws and executive orders (issued by presidents) prohibiting employment discrimination. Since it would be impossible to discuss all of them in a single chapter, this chapter will primarily focus on Title VII of the 1964 Civil Rights Act and a few of the presidential executive orders. Considerable understanding of the entire legal framework can be gained by examining how these regulations operate.

Title VII of the 1964 Civil Rights Act

Employers, unions, employment agencies, and joint labor-managment committees controlling apprenticeship or training programs are prohibited from discriminating on the basis of race, color, religion, sex, or national origin by Title VII of the 1964 Civil Rights Act. Other laws protect the aged, the handicapped, and special classes of veterans.[5] Title VII prohibits discrimination with regard to any employment condition, including hiring, firing, promotion, transfer, compensation, and admission to training programs. The Equal Employment Opportunity Act of 1972 amended Title VII by strengthening its enforcement and expanding its coverage to include employees of state and local governments and of educational institutions, as well as private employment of more than 15 persons. However, Indian tribes and private membership clubs are not covered, and religious organizations may discriminate on the basis of religion in some cases. Federal government employees are also covered by Title VII, but enforcement is carried out by the Civil Service Commission with procedures that are unique to federal employees.

---

[4]St. Clair Drake, "The Social and Economic Status of the Negro in the United States," in *The Negro American*, ed. (Boston: Talcott Parsons and Kenneth B. Clark (Boston: Houghton Mifflin, 1966), pp. 3–46.

[5]For an excellent discussion and presentation of the federal laws regarding discrimination, see Lee Modjeska, *Handling Employment Discrimination Cases* (Rochester, (N.J.: The Lawyers Cooperative Publishing Co., 1980).

"Can't those Equal Opportunity people leave well enough alone??"

Reprinted by permission, The Wall Street Journal.

The EEO coverage of government employees is noteworthy. While discrimination has been illegal in government employment since the end of the spoils system and the advent of open competitive examinations in the public service, race and sex inequalities have persisted in the public service. The "merit system" in government employment has had a mixed record. Some of its features have held back minorities over the years. With the 1972 amendments to Title VII, public administrators found themselves subject to the same sorts of EEO burdens that managers in private enterprise had shouldered since the passage of Title VII in 1964.

One clause of Title VII permits employers to discriminate based on sex, religion, or national origin if these attributes are a "bona fide occupational qualification" (BFOQ). This seems like a loophole, but it is a small one indeed. For instance, courts have said that the clause does not allow an employer to discriminate against women simply because they feel that the work is "inappropriate" for them, or because customers might object. The best example of this reasoning was the decision in *Diaz* v. *Pan American Airways* that an airline could not limit its employment of flight attendants to women. At the time, the idea of a male flight attendant was unusual, but that was not a legal justification for Pan American's refusal to hire Diaz in that position.[6]

When is sex a bona fide occupational qualification? One obvious but unusual situation is when one sex is by definition unequipped to do the work—as in the case of a wet nurse. Another is when the position demands one sex for believability—as in the case of a fashion model. A third instance is when one sex is required for a position in order to satisfy basic social mores about modesty—as in the case of a locker room attendant.

Executive Order 11246 was issued by President Lyndon B. Johnson in 1965, superseding President John F. Kennedy's Executive Order 10925. Employment discrimination by federal government contractors, subcontractors, and federally assisted construction contracts is prohibited. While Executive Order 11246 prohibits the same actions as Title VII does, it carries the additional requirement that contractors must develop a written plan of affirmative action and establish numerical integration goals and timetables to achieve equal opportunity. The affirmative action planning requirement is discussed in greater detail later in this chapter.

Virtually every state also has some form of equal employment law. In 41 states, plus the District of Columbia and Puerto Rico, there are comprehensive state "fair employment" laws similar in operation to Title VII. In fact, some of these state laws antedate Title VII. If a state's law is strong enough, charges of discrimination brought under Title VII are turned over by the federal government to the state fair employment practices agency, which has the first chance at investigating it.

Discrimination: A Legal Definition

All the laws discussed above are designed to eliminate discrimination. Would you believe the laws never defined it? It's true; the courts have had to do this when they interpret the laws. The courts arrive at definitions by looking at the history behind a statute, examining the *Congressional Record* to gain insight into the social problems Congress hoped it would solve. Then they define terms like *discrimination* in a way to help solve these problems. For Title VII, the history of the civil rights conflict clearly identifies the problems: economic inequality and the denial of employment opportunities to blacks and other minorities.

The courts have defined discrimination in three different ways since the first days of federal involvement in employment practices.[7] Initially, during World War II, discrimination was defined as *prejudiced treatment:* harmful actions motivated by personal ani-

---

[6]*Diaz* v. *Pan American Airways*, 442 F. 2d 385.

[7]Alfred Blumrosen, "Strangers in Paradise: *Griggs* v. *Duke Power Co.* and The Concept of Employment Discrimination," *Michigan Law Review*, November 1972, pp. 59–110.

mosity toward the group of which the target person was a member. However, that definition was ineffective as a means of solving the problem of economic inequality because it is difficult to prove harmful motives, and that made it difficult to take action against many employment practices that perpetuated inequality.

Then the courts redefined discrimination to mean *unequal treatment*. Under this definition, a practice was unlawful if it applied different standards or different treatment to different groups of employees or applicants. This definition outlawed the practice of keeping minorities in less desirable departments (different treatment), and it also outlawed the practice of rejecting women applicants with preschool-aged children (different standards). The employer was allowed to impose any requirements, so long as they were imposed *on all groups alike*.

To enable Title VII to solve the social problems that Congress wanted it to, the U.S. Supreme Court arrived at the third definition of employment discrimination: *unequal impact*. In the case of *Griggs* v. *Duke Power Co.*, the Court struck down employment tests and educational requirements that screened out a greater proportion of blacks than whites.[8] These practices were prohibited because they had the *consequence* of excluding blacks disproportionately, *and* because they were not *related* to the jobs in question. The practices were apparently not motivated by prejudice against blacks. And they certainly were applied equally: both whites and blacks had to pass the requirements. But they did have an adverse impact on blacks. Today both unequal treatment and unequal impact are considered discrimination.

By way of a summary, the criterion for EEO and affirmative action compliance or noncompliance can theoretically be reduced to two criteria. In question format the criteria are:

> Does an employment practice have unequal or adverse impact on the groups covered by the law? (Race, color, sex, religious, or national origin groups.) Is that practice job-related or otherwise necessary to the organization?

A practice is prohibited *only* if the answers to *both* questions are unfavorable. Even practices that are unnecessary and irrelevant to the job are legal if they have equal impact on the groups covered by the law. This means that employers do not have to validate tests or follow the employee selection regulations if their tests do not exclude one group disproportionately.

This two-question approach does have some exceptions, and getting a straight answer to the second question is especially difficult because of the stringent guidelines that employers must follow. Nevertheless, the two questions are a good place to begin in understanding EEO and affirmative action.

Some believe that, because new cases are constantly being decided and guidelines are undergoing important changes, EEO programs are in a period of total uncertainty. Nevertheless, these two basic questions remain as underlying principles through all the changes.

---

[8]Ibid.

The Discrimination Case Process. • In a discrimination case a person alleges that he or she is being, or has been, discriminated against due to a unlawful employment practice. The person filing the suit is called the plaintiff. The person or organization against whom the charge of discrimination is made is called the defendant. The plaintiff must demonstrate that a prima facie (evidence exists) violation has occurred by gathering evidence showing that the employment practice has had an adverse impact.[9] The *adverse impact* criterion refers to the total employment process that results in a significantly higher percentage of a protected group in the available population being rejected for employment, placement, or promotion.

This means that the minority applicant for a job would have to show that the P/HRM activity (e.g., testing, promotion, selection) had an adverse impact on his or her minority group. For example, a plaintiff might demonstrate that out of 50 black and 50 white applicants for a job who completed a test, no blacks were hired, but 15 whites were placed on the job. This would be evidence of adverse impact and a prima facie violation of Title VII would be established.

Those in P/HRM use what is called the 4/5ths rule for judging adverse impact. This rule notes that discrimination typically occurs if the selection rate for a protected group is less than 80 percent of the selection rate for a majority group. Thus, if 20 out of 100 white applicants are selected (20 percent), at least 16 percent (4/5ths or 80 percent of 20) of minority applicants (e.g., black or Hispanic) should be selected to avoid being accused of adverse impact. It should be pointed out that adverse impact need not be considered for groups which constitute less than 2 percent of the relevant labor force.

Once adverse impact has been demonstrated the burden of proof shifts to the defendant. The defendant must demonstrate that the testing or selection activity at issue is job related or has some business necessity. If the defendant cannot demonstrate the job-relatedness of the testing activity, the judgment will probably be awarded to the plaintiff.

The "shifting burden of proof" model is applied in most suits in which there is a claim of employment discrimination. Exhibit 3–2 presents the model graphically. This model and the adverse impact and job-relatedness criteria are important in understanding most court judgments.

Exhibit 3–2

Shifting burden of proof model

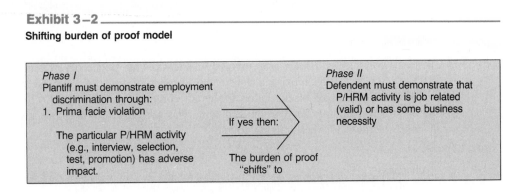

Phase I
Plantiff must demonstrate employment
  discrimination through:
1. Prima facie violation

The particular P/HRM activity
  (e.g., interview, selection,
  test, promotion) has adverse
  impact.

If yes then:

The burden of proof
  "shifts" to

Phase II
Defendent must demonstrate that
  P/HRM activity is job related
  (valid) or has some business
  necessity

[9] Richard D. Arvey, *Fairness in Selecting Employees* (Reading, Mass.: Addison-Wesley Publishing, 1979), pp. 50–52.

Important Court Decisions

Numerous court cases involving employment discrimination laws have become public record.[10] Five of the most publicized court decisions have been selected for special attention in this chapter.

Griggs v. Duke Power (1971)

Willie Griggs was an applicant for a job as a coal handler at the Duke Power Company.[11] Duke required coal handlers to be high school graduates and receive a satisfactory score on two aptitude tests. Griggs claimed that these requirements were unfairly discriminatory in that they were not related to job success. Thus, it resulted in a disproportionate number of blacks being disqualified.

Duke Power Company lost this suit. Supreme Court Chief Justice Burger ruled that (1) discrimination need not be overt; (2) the employment practice must be shown to be job related; and (3) the burden of proof is on the employer to show that the hiring standard is job related.

Perhaps the most important aspect of the *Griggs* decision was the emphasis on the consequences of an employment practice in addition to the examination of the intent involved. It opened the door for giving serious consideration to what the actual consequence of a practice was. The use of statistical methods in reviewing consequences became accepted.

Albermarle Paper Company v. J. Moody (1975)

The *Albermarle* case is important because the courts provided details on how an employer should go about validating a test; that is, how an employer must prove that the test predicts on-the-job performance.

Albermarle had required applicants for employment to pass various tests. The court found that the Albermarle tests were not validated for all jobs for which people were recruited.[12] This court decision indicated that tests or other screening tools that had the effect of screening out a disproportionate number of minorities (i.e., had an adverse impact) or women had to be validated properly. The test had to validly predict performance.

Washington v. Davis (1976)

The *Washington* v. *Davis* case involved a metropolitan police department (Washington, D.C.), which had been using a test for the selection of police recruits. Between 1968 and 1971, 57 percent of blacks failed the exam compared to 13 percent white. The police department demonstrated that the test score was related to examinations given during the police recruits' 17-week training course.[13]

---

[10]For an up-to-date summary of cases, awards, and remedies see *Employment Practices* published twice monthly by Commerce Clearing House, Inc., 4025 W. Petersen Avenue, Chicago, Ill. 60646.

[11]*Griggs* v. *Duke Power Co.,* 401 U.S. 424, 1971.

[12]James Ledvinka and Lyle Schoenfeldt, "Legal Developments in Employment Testing: Albermarle and Beyond," *Personnel Psychology,* Spring 1978, pp. 1–13.

[13]*Washington* v. *Davis,* 12 FEP 1473 (1976).

The Supreme Court ruled that the city of Washington, D.C., did not discriminate unfairly against minority police recruits because the test was job related. This was a departure from previous court decisions. The implication was that a job-related test is not illegal simply because a large percentage of minorities do not successfully pass it. This decision provided test users with hope that testing could still be used as a screening device.[14]

Bakke v. University of California (1978)

The central issue of the now famous *reverse discrimination* case involving Allan Bakke (a white male) was the legality of the admissions policy of the University of California at Davis Medical School. The Davis system set aside 16 or 100 places in its entering classes for "disadvantaged" applicants who were members of racial minority groups. Competitors for these places were evaluated in terms of lower than normal standards. Thus, Bakke sued the university under the "equal protection" clause of the 14th Amendment. The suit claimed that Bakke could compete for only 84 of the 100 places, while minorities could compete for all 100. All individuals were therefore not treated equally.

Justice Lewis Powell writing the key opinion, concluded that the Davis racial quota system was not acceptable because it disregarded Bakke's right to equal protection of the law. However, the Court also stated that affirmative action programs in general are permissible, as long as they consider applicants on an individual basis and do not set aside a rigid number of places.[15]

The *Bakke* case indicated that P/HRM selection decisions must be made on an individual, case-by-case basis. Certainly race can be a key factor in an applicant's favor, but the final decision must be made on the basis of a combination of factors.

Weber v. Kaiser (1979)

Brian Weber, a laboratory analyst at a Kaiser Aluminum plant in Louisiana, brought suit under Title VII of the 1964 Civil Rights Act. He had been bypassed for a crafts-retraining program in which the company and the union jointly agreed to reserve 50 percent of the available training places for blacks.[16]

The company and the union were faced with a dilemma. To eliminate the affirmative action-training plan would risk suits by minority employees. However, to retain the plan would run the risk of reverse discrimination charges by white employees. *Affirmative action* goes beyond equal employment opportunity. It is a systematic plan that specifies goals, timetables, and audit procedures for an employer to make an extra effort to hire, promote, and train those in a protected minority. Kaiser's affirmative action plan focused on giving preference to blacks in the crafts-retraining program.

On June 27, 1979, the U.S. Supreme Court rules that employers can give preference to minorities and women in hiring and promoting for "traditionally segregated job categories." That is, where there has been a societal history of purposeful exclusion of blacks from the job category, resulting in a disparity between the proportion of blacks in the

---

[14]Arvey, *Fairness in Selecting Employees*, p. 76.

[15]"The Bakke Ruling," *The Wall Street Journal*, June 29, 1978, pp. 1, 17 and 18.

[16]Michael J. Phillips, "Paradoxes of Equal Employment Opportunity: Voluntary Racial Preferences and the Weber Case," *Business Horizons*, August 1980, pp. 41–47.

labor force and the proportion of blacks who hold jobs in the category, preference can be given. The Court also noted that the Kaiser plan was a "temporary measure" to eliminate a racial imbalance in a job category.[17] This decision definitely put pressure on employers to establish affirmative action plans.

These five cases are landmarks in discrimination law. They have provided prospective plaintiffs and defendants with insight on the Supreme Court's view of discriminatory practices. Exhibit 3–3 provides a concise summary of these five landmark cases and the outstanding feature(s) of the Court's decision.

Enforcing the Laws

Most employment discrimination laws provide for enforcement agencies, which issue the regulations that affect P/HRM administrators most directly. Exhibit 3–4 provides an overview of the complex agency scene, showing some of the principal laws, the agencies that enforce them, and the guidelines issued by these agencies. The units of government *most* responsible for enforcing the regulations considered here are the U.S. Equal Employment Opportunity Commission (EEOC) and the federal courts, which enforce Title VII; and the Office of Federal Contract Compliance Programs (OFCCP), which enforces Executive Order 11246.

Equal Employment Opportunity Commission

Title VII originally gave EEOC the rather limited powers of resolving charges of discrimination and interpreting the meaning of Title VII. Later, in 1972, Congress gave EEOC the power to bring lawsuits against employers in the federal courts, but the agency still does not have the power to issue directly enforceable orders, as many other federal agencies have. Thus EEOC cannot order an employer to discontinue a discriminatory practice, nor can it direct an employer to give back pay to victims of discrimination. However, EEOC has won these things in out-of-court settlements, and it has made effective use of the limited powers it does have.

Exhibit 3–3 _____

Five important Supreme Court decisions (1971–1979)

Case	Outstanding feature(s) of Court's ruling
Griggs v. Duke Power (1971)	If adverse impact is established defendent must demonstrate that selection practice is valid.
Albermarle v. Moody (1975)	Validation is not proven unless test can predict job success.
Washington v. Davis (1976)	If a test is job related it is not illegal simply because a greater percentage of minorities do not successfully pass it.
Bakke v. University of California (1978)	Reverse discrimination is not allowed; race can be used as a factor in selection decisions.
Weber v. Kaiser (1979)	Employers can give preference to minorities and women in hiring and promoting for "traditionally segregated job categories."

_____

[17]Ibid.

Exhibit 3–4

Partial summary of major employment discrimination laws and orders, enforcement agencies, and regulations

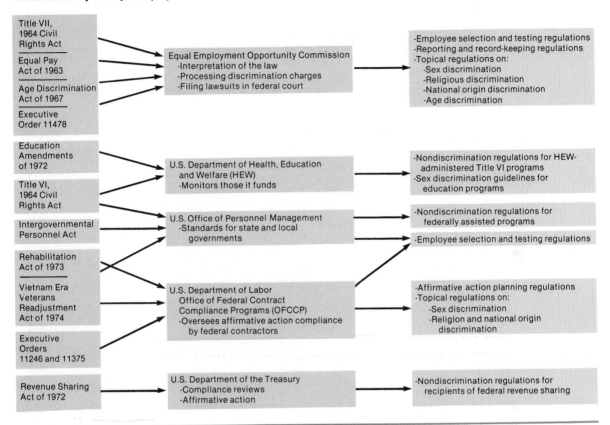

Is the EEOC effective? • One way to find out is to review EEOC's annual report. The 14th annual report, appearing in January 1981, for example, reports on data that were two years old at the time of publication. In 1979 EEOC filed 208 lawsuits—up from 188 lawsuits in 1978. One year later, it had a backlog of over 326 cases.[18] As of June 1982,

EEOC has the power to:

Require employers to report employment statistics. Typically, they do so by completing a form called EEO–1 each year (see Exhibit 3–5).

Process charges of discrimination, as follows:
- The preinvestigation division interviews the complainants.
- The investigation division collects facts from all parties concerned.
- If there seems to be substance to the charge, the EEOC tries to work out an out-of-court settlement through conciliation.
- If conciliation fails, the EEOC can sue the employer.

---

[18]Also, see Robert H. Sheahan, ''Responding to Employment Discrimination Charges,'' *Personnel Journal*, March 1981, pp. 217–20.

Exhibit 3–5 _____

EEO–1 form

Standard Form 100
(Rev. 12-76)
Approved GAO B-180541 (R0077)
Expires 12-31-78

EQUAL EMPLOYMENT OPPORTUNITY
EMPLOYER INFORMATION REPORT EEO-1

Joint Reporting Committee

- Equal Employment Opportunity Commission
- Office of Federal Contract Compliance Programs

Section A — TYPE OF REPORT
Refer to instructions for number and types of reports to be filed.

1. Indicate by marking in the appropriate box the type of reporting unit for which this copy of the form is submitted (MARK ONLY ONE BOX).

(1) ☐ Single-establishment Employer Report

Multi-establishment Employer:
(2) ☐ Consolidated Report
(3) ☐ Headquarters Unit Report
(4) ☐ Individual Establishment Report (submit one for each establishment with 25 or more employees)
(5) ☐ Special Report

2. Total number of reports being filed by this Company (Answer on Consolidated Report only) _____

Section B — COMPANY IDENTIFICATION *(To be answered by all employers)*

OFFICE USE ONLY

1. Parent Company
   a. Name of parent company (owns or controls establishment in item 2) omit if same as label

Name of receiving office | Address (Number and street)

a.

City or town | County | State | ZIP code | b. Employer Identification No.

b.

2. Establishment for which this report is filed. (Omit if same as label)
   a. Name of establishment

Address (Number and street) | City or town | County | State | ZIP code

c.

b. Employer Identification No. | (If same as label, skip.)

d.

3. Parent company affiliation (Multi-establishment Employers Answer on Consolidated Report only)
   a. Name of parent—affiliated company | b. Employer Identification No.

Address (Number and street) | City or town | County | State | ZIP code

Section C — EMPLOYERS WHO ARE REQUIRED TO FILE *(To be answered by all employers)*

☐ Yes ☐ No 1. Does the entire company have at least 100 employees in the payroll period for which you are reporting?

☐ Yes ☐ No 2. Is your company affiliated through common ownership and/or centralized management with other entities in an enterprise with a total employment of 100 or more?

☐ Yes ☐ No 3. Does the company or any of its establishments (a) have 50 or more employees AND (b) is not exempt as provided by 41 CFR 60-1.5, AND either (1) is a prime government contractor or first-tier subcontractor, and has a contract, subcontract, or purchase order amounting to $50,000 or more, or (2) serves as a depository of Government funds in any amount or is a financial institution which is an issuing and paying agent for U.S. Savings Bonds and Savings Notes?

NOTE: If the answer is yes to ANY of these questions, complete the entire form; otherwise skip to Section G.

Section D — EMPLOYMENT DATA

Employment at this establishment--Report all permanent, temporary, or part-time employees including apprentices and on-the-job trainees unless specifically excluded as set forth in the instructions. Enter the appropriate figures on all lines and in all columns. Blank spaces will be considered as zeros.

JOB CATEGORIES	OVERALL TOTALS (SUM OF COL. B THRU K) A	MALE					FEMALE				
		WHITE (NOT OF HISPANIC ORIGIN) B	BLACK (NOT OF HISPANIC ORIGIN) C	HISPANIC D	ASIAN OR PACIFIC ISLANDER E	AMERICAN INDIAN OR ALASKAN NATIVE F	WHITE (NOT OF HISPANIC ORIGIN) G	BLACK (NOT OF HISPANIC ORIGIN) H	HISPANIC I	ASIAN OR PACIFIC ISLANDER J	AMERICAN INDIAN OR ALASKAN NATIVE K
Officials and Managers											
Professionals											
Technicians											
Sales Workers											
Office and Clerical											
Craft Workers (Skilled)											
Operatives (Semi-Skilled)											
Laborers (Unskilled)											
Service Workers											
TOTAL											
Total employment reported in previous EEO-1 report											

(The trainees below should also be included in the figures for the appropriate occupational categories above)

Formal On-the-job trainees	White collar											
	Production											

1. NOTE: On consolidated report, skip questions 2-5 and Section E.
2. How was information as to race or ethnic group in Section D obtained?
   1. ☐ Visual Survey
   2. ☐ Employment Record
   3. ☐ Other — Specify ....
   ....
3. Dates of payroll period used —

4. Pay period of last report submitted for this establishment

5. Does this establishment employ apprentices?
   This year? 1 ☐ Yes 2 ☐ No
   Last year? 1 ☐ Yes 2 ☐ No

Section E — ESTABLISHMENT INFORMATION

1. Is the location of the establishment the same as that reported last year?
   1 ☐ Yes 2 ☐ No 3 ☐ Did not report last year 4 ☐ Reported on combined basis

2. Is the major business activity at this establishment the same as that reported last year?
   1 ☐ Yes 2 ☐ No 3 ☐ No report last year 4 ☐ Reported on combined basis

OFFICE USE ONLY

3. What is the major activity of this establishment? (Be specific, i.e.: manufacturing steel castings, retail grocer, wholesale plumbing supplies, title insurance, etc. Include the specific type of product or type of service provided, as well as the principal business or industrial activity.

e.

Section F — REMARKS

Use this item to give any identification data appearing on last report which differs from that given above, explain major changes in composition or reporting units, and other pertinent information.

Section G — CERTIFICATION (See Instructions G)

Check one
1. ☐ All reports are accurate and were prepared in accordance with the instructions (check on consolidated only)
2. ☐ This report is accurate and was prepared in accordance with the instructions.

Name of Certifying Official	Title	Signature		Date
Name of person to contact regarding this report (Type or print)	Address (Number and street)			
Title	City and State	ZIP code	Telephone Area Code	Number	Extension

there was a backlog of approximately 20,000 discrimination charges filed with the EEOC. When EEOC sought to clear away some of the backlog, its employee union complained this was a speedup and forced employees to violate the law in processing the cases and charges too hastily. Each year, the agency tries to deal with the backlog by requesting sharp increases in its budget. As a result of the backlog, charges take years to be investigated. During that time, records get lost and memories fade, making it hard for investigators to determine how justifiable the original charge was. Besides that problem, critics claim that investigations are often not conducted competently enough to uncover all the information that is available. This leads to selective enforcement of the law.

The result of these problems is that only a very small percentage of charges ever get resolved by EEOC or the courts. Consequently civil rights advocates are not happy with the agency, and of course, many employers are less than enthusiastic about it (or any regulatory agency, for that matter). In spite of this, EEOC has made legal history. It provides individuals and groups with a government contact point to voice their complaints.

Office of Federal Contract Compliance Programs (OFCCP)

This office was originally established to enforce Executive Order 11246. Now it also enforces laws covering employment of veterans and the handicapped. OFCCP has the power to remove a federal contractor's privileges of doing business with the government, but it seldom exercises that power. OFCCP regulations require that all contractors with over $50,000 in contracts and over 50 employees have a written affirmative action plan on file.

Is the OFCCP Effective? • Some data have indicated few positive effects on employment gains for black males; fewer gains for white males; zero or negative effect for other minorities and women; and zero effects on wage and occupational gains on all minority groups. Some experts doubt that OFCCP can alter employment distributions of minorities.[19]

OFCCP has the power to order an employer to:

Survey the labor market and determine the availability of minorities.

Prepare an affirmative action plan to show the jobs minorities are underrepresented in.

Set goals and timetables for making the work force representative of the labor market.

Audit the affirmative action plan to see if the goals are being met.

If the investigator decides that the contractor is not incompliance with Executive Order 11246, he may have a "show cause" order issued against the contractor. This triggers a lengthy sequence of administrative decisions and appeals, which can culminate in the contractor being debarred from government contract work.

---

[19]James Heckman and Kenneth Wolpin, "Does the Contract Compliance Program Work? An Analysis of the Chicago Data," *Industrial and Labor Relations Review,* 1975–1976, pp. 544–64.

One reason for the limited success of OFCCP is the need to delegate its compliance review authority to 13 other agencies. It is no surprise, then, that contractors complain of conflicting agency regulations. Moreover, the 13 agencies are principally in business for some reason other than equal employment. For instance, the Department of Defense had an EEO operation housed in the bureau that was principally responsible for making sure that defense contracting was carried out well, with the right goods and services delivered at the right time. Undue concern with EEO, however, could be seen as impeding contract fulfillment. Thus, EEO was not an overriding concern in some of these agencies. President Carter consolidated these compliance functions as shown in Exhibit 3–4.

The Courts

Besides the agencies (federal and state) the courts are constantly interpreting the laws, and these rulings can conflict. Appellate courts then reconcile any conflicts. All the employment discrimination laws provide for court enforcement, often as a last resort if agency enforcement fails. With regard to Title VII, the federal courts are frequently involved in two ways: settling disputes between EEOC and employers over such things as access to company records, and deciding the merits of discrimination charges when out-of-court conciliation efforts fail. The possible legal routes for complaints against an employer's P/HRM activities are presented in Exhibit 3–6.

Legal maneuvering often makes the court enforcement picture confusing, largely because every step of the process is appealable. And with three parties involved—EEOC, the plaintiff, and the defendant—appeals are commonplace. All these possibilities for trial, appeal, retrial, and even appeal of the retrial can cause several years' delay before the issue is settled. When that delay is added to EEOC's charge-processing delay, the result is discouraging to the parties involved.

Once a final court decision is reached in a Title VII case, it can provide for drastic remedies: back pay, hiring quotas, reinstatement of employees, immediate promotion of employees, abolition of testing programs, creation of special recruitment or training programs, and others. In a class action suit against Georgia Power Company which sought back pay and jobs for black employees and applicants, the court ordered the company to set aside $1.75 million for back pay, and another $388,925 for other purposes. Moreover, the court imposed numerical goals and timetables for black employment in various job classes. If Georgia Power failed to meet the goals, then the court order provided for mandatory hiring ratios: one black was to be hired for each white until the goal percentages were reached. Other courts have ordered companies to give employees seniority credit for the time they have been discriminatorily denied employment.[20]

Many court orders are not so drastic, however. Much depends, of course, on the facts surrounding the case. One important factor is whether the employer is making any voluntary efforts to comply with employment discrimination laws. If the company shows evidence of successfully pursuing an affirmative action plan, the court may decide to impose less stringent measures. This is discussed further in the section on costs and benefits of affirmative action plans, later in this chapter.

---

[20]U.S. Supreme Court, *Teamsters Union*, U.S. 14 EPD (1977), 7579.

Exhibit 3–6 _____

Legal courses for complaints against an employer's P/HRM policies.

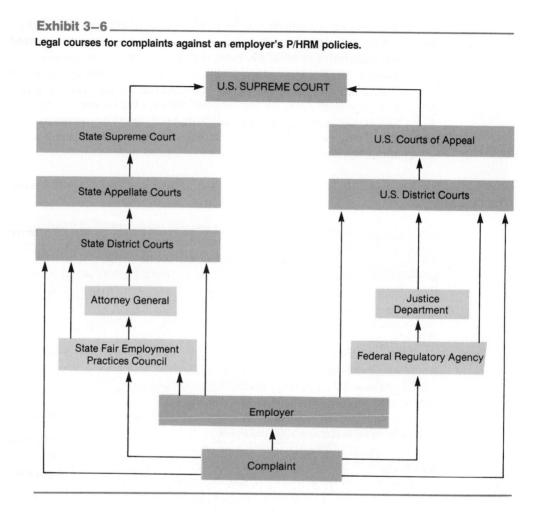

EEO Programs: A Preventive Approach

Many employers face the legal enforcement of EEO regulations with a mixture of resignation and despair, feeling little can be done to minimize the threat of legal action. But a preventive strategy is possible which can reduce the likelihood of employment discrimination charges and assure equal employment opportunities for applicants and employees. Perhaps the best way to gain an initial understanding of such a program, however, is to consider an example: AT&T's program for women in outside crafts.[21]

AT&T's Program for Women Outside-Crafts Workers

Of all employers in the United States, probably none has received more attention for its affirmative action program than the American Telephone and Telegraph Company. AT&T was involved in the largest back-pay settlement in the history of equal employment. As

_____
[21]AT&T, "In the Throes of Equal Employment," *Fortune*, January 15, 1979, pp. 44–57.

part of that settlement, the company was required to make significant strides in increasing employment opportunities for women and minorities. The program that resulted from that settlement exemplifies some of the more advanced EEO efforts in American industry.

The scope of AT&T's affirmative action program is so vast that it is impractical to focus on more than a small segment here. One particularly interesting segment of AT&T's program is its provisions for increasing the employment of women in outside-crafts positions: the various lineworkers, telephone installers, and repair workers whose work is mostly done outdoors. These components are an integral part of affirmative action for any job at any company.

Step 1: Analyzing Underrepresentation and Availability • AT&T found a problem simply by examining the sex composition of their job classes: There were almost no women in outside-crafts positions. But how great was the extent of underrepresentation? Many organizations find the answer to this question in the statistics compiled for affirmative action plans by state labor departments in every state, which show the number of women and minorities in each of 10 or 20 broad occupational groups. Others use the overall population figures compiled by the U.S. Census. Both sets of data are readily available from the appropriate government agencies. In addition, some larger firms are investing in sophisticated labor market studies to arrive at a more accurate estimate of availability. Of course any set of statistics are open to criticism. Many employers strive to collect statistics that put them in the best light. While some may argue that such a strategy is manipulative, it often does succeed in reducing enforcement pressures. Employers are likely to continue using it until such time as there emerges a generally accepted statistical definition of availability.

Step 2: Goal Setting • Once the statistics are agreed upon, the organization sets goals to help achieve greater minority representation in the job in question. EEO goals must be realistic, and they must be attainable without discriminating against those in the majority. Nevertheless, while good availability statistics help make goals realistic, there is no way to be sure that goals will not discriminate in reverse, unless the means by which the company seeks to attain them are carefully planned.

Step 3: Specifying How Goals Are to Be Attained • If the means to goal attainment are to be nondiscriminatory against white males, management should find out the causes of underrepresentation of women and minorities in the company's work force. Otherwise, it will not know what discriminatory employment practices must be changed in order to increase representation without preferential treatment of women and minorities. For example, the underrepresentation of women in a certain job class may be caused by a company's reputation for being rough on women, or by a policy that unnecessarily schedules work shifts so that women workers cannot meet family responsibilities. If management knows the cause, it can attempt to increase the representation of women by working on its public image and by exploring the possibility of retiming the shifts. But if management doesn't know it, it may attempt to increase the representation of women by lowering the requirements for women applying from the outside, or by granting transfers to women employees while refusing to grant them to more qualified men employees. This would not only increase the risk of discrimination charges from white males, it would also contribute to morale problems and foster resentment against women in the company.

"Are you sure you won't quit after a year or two to get married?"

Reprinted by permission, The Wall Street Journal

Identifying discriminatory employment practices calls for a full-scale audit of an organizations P/HRM policies and programs. This audit reviews each step of the P/HRM program, from recruitment to retirement. Ideally, it also examines supervisory practices that might have an unfavorable impact on women or minority employees. If the audit uncovers barriers to the employment of women or minorities, action could be taken to reduce or remove those barriers.

In AT&T's case, the company took the following steps:

- Tried to change the image of craft employees from male to neutral by advertising, public relations, and relationships with guidance counselors.
- Redesigned the jobs so that women could perform them more easily.

Various Groups and EEO

As indicated earlier in the chapter, EEO permeates the P/HRM program. It can require changes in employment planning, recruiting, selecting, evaluation, career planning, training, and other activities. Rather than discuss each P/HRM activity, we will focus on some special features of EEO programs for various groups.

Women

In many companies, EEO for women is more a matter of career design than job design. Women often find themselves locked into their positions with no career path upward; this is especially true of clerical positions. Typists and secretaries usually have little likelihood of promotion to supervisory or managerial positions.

Sometimes the solution to that problem involves training or job rotation for clerical workers. Management training can give them the specific skills they need to assume higher level positions, and job rotation can give them the breadth of experience they need to become effective managers. In other cases, the problem is that the employees of the organization, women included, are unaware of the promotion and transfer opportunities it offers. Larger companies often establish very thorough and elaborate systems to inform employees of job openings in the company. Among other things, these systems may include individual career counseling for employees, which helps identify promising talent at the same time it keeps employees informed.

A second problem area is management attitudes. Ten years ago, resistance to placing blacks in management positions was widespread. Today that resistance seems to have dissipated somewhat. But resistance to women in management positions remains. These attitudes can be changed, too.

A third problem area for women is policies that single them out for unfavorable treatment. For instance, married women may be denied opportunities because the company fears they will leave if their husbands change jobs. This can become a self-fulfilling prophecy. What is the incentive for a couple to remain in an area for the sake of the wife's career if the wife's employer denies her career opportunities?

A fourth problem area for women involves pregnancy. Prior to the Pregnancy Discrimination Act of 1978, women could be forced to resign or take a leave of absence because of pregnancy. Furthermore, employers did not have to provide disability or medical coverage even when coverage was provided for other disabilities and medical problems. This Pregnancy Discrimination amendment to the 1964 Civil Rights Acts now prevents this form of discrimination against women. The act makes it an unfair employment practice to discriminate on the basis of pregnancy, childbirth, or related medical conditions in hiring, promotion, suspension, discharge, or in any other term of employment. The act prohibits an employer from failing to pay medical and hospital costs for childbirth to the same extent that it pays for medical and hospital costs for other conditions.[22]

A fifth problem area involves sexual harassment on the job. One research study of 9,000 women revealed that 90 percent of the respondents had experienced unwanted sexual attention at work, ranging from leers and remarks to overt requests for sexual favors.[23] This and other studies suggest that sexual harassment is a serious problem. Women facing sexual harassment are often subjected to mental anxiety, humiliation, reprimand, loss of job or promotion.

In order for a woman to recover on a claim of sexual harassment under Title VII of

---

[22]Richard Trotler, Susan Rawson Zacur, and Wallace Gatewood, "The Pregnancy Disability Amendment: What the Law Provides: Part I," *Personnel Administrator*, February 1982, pp. 47–54.

[23]Robert W. Schupp, Joyce Windham, and Scott Draugh, "Sexual Harassment under Title VII: The Legal Status," *Labor Law Journal*, (April 1981, p. 239; and Catherine A. MacKinnon, *Sexual Harassemtn of Working Women* (New Haven, Conn.: Yale University Press, 1979). See also Donald J. Peterson and Douglass Massengill, "Sexual Harrassment—A Growing Problem in the Workplace," *Personnel Administrator*, October 1982, pp. 79–89.

the Civil Rights Act, she must allege and establish that submission to the sexual sugges-tion constituted a term or condition of employment. A course of action cannot arise from an isolated incident or a mere flirtation.

Organizations have a duty to establish and communicate a company policy condemn-ing sexual harassment; to establish a grievance procedure which deals with sexual harass-ment in such a way that the employee has the option to remain anonymous; to deal with allegations in a timely fashion; and to communicate to all employees the receptivity of management to all well-founded allegations of sexual harassment.[24]

Older Employees

The Age Discrimination Employment Act of 1967 and the amendment of 1978 protect workers between the ages of 40 and 70 against job discrimination. In the past, the enforce-ment agencies did not press too hard on discrimination against older persons, but recent actions suggest this will no longer be true. The law prevents employers from replacing their staffs with younger workers, whether the purpose is to give the company a more youthful image or to save money in the pension program. While age requirements are illegal in most jobs, the law does not cover all of them. For example, Greyhound was

"Edwards, it's a marvelous face lift but I'm afraid retirement at sixty five is mandatory."

Reprinted by permission The Wall Street Journal.

---

[24]*Heelan* v. *Johns-Manville Corporation,* 451 Federal Supplement (DC Colo., 1978), 16EPD No. 8330; and Donna C. Ledgerwood and Sue Johnson-Dietz, "Sexual Harassment: Implications for Employer Liability," *Monthly Labor Review,* April 1981, pp. 45–47.

allowed to refuse bus driver jobs to applicants over age 40 with the justification that aging brings on slower reaction times, which can adversely affect safety.[25]

A number of barriers face older workers in many organizations. Some are a matter of company economics, others a matter of management attitudes.[26] The economic reasons include the added expense of funding pensions for older workers and the increased premiums necessary for health and life insurance benefit plans. The attitude problems are more difficult to pin down. Perhaps some managers feel that older workers lose their faculties, making them less effective on the job. Yet there is evidence that the intelligence levels of many older employees increase as they near retirement age. Besides, there are other advantages to hiring old workers: lower turnover, greater consciousness of safety matters, and longer work experience.[27]

Racial and Ethnic Minorities

The laws prohibit discrimination against a person because of race, color, and national origin. The specific protected minorities are blacks, Hispanics, American Indians, Asian-Pacific Islanders, and Alaskan natives. These groups historically have had higher unemployment and underemployment and have held the lowest level jobs.

While every ethnic and racial minority is unique, one problem facing them all is adverse P/HRM policies. Examples of such practices are numerous. Height and weight requirements, which have an adverse impact on Asian Americans and Hispanic Americans, were, until recently, commonplace among police departments in the United States. Seniority and experience requirements based on time in a department tend to lock in blacks who move out of segregated departments. They find themselves at the bottom of the seniority lists in their new departments, even though they have had many years with the company. Vague, subjective performance evaluations by supervisors are so subject to bias that many minority group members find they cannot attain high enough ratings to get promotions or merit pay increases. All these practices, along with others, are prime targets for change in the EEO program.

Some barriers are more difficult to change, even though they have an adverse impact on minorities. College degree requirements are common for some jobs, although one study found that 65 percent of the jobs reserved for college graduates could be performed by workers with no more than a high school education.[28] Employers should examine their own job specifications to see if educational requirements can be reduced without sacrificing job performance. Where the requirements cannot be reduced, the organization might consider redesigning or breaking down the job so that people with less education could perform satisfactorily. While job redesign is usually a big step, the resulting increase in opportunities for minorities may make it worthwhile for the enterprise.

---

[25]*Brennan* v. *Greyhound Lines, Inc.*, 9 FED Cases 58 (1975).

[26]Jerome M. Rosow and Robert Zagar, "Work in America Institute's Recommendations Grapple with the Future of the Older Worker," *Personnel Administrator*, October 1981, pp. 47–54, 80.

[27]"Aging and the IQ: The Myth of the Twilight Years," *Psychology Today*, March 1974, pp. 35–40.

[28]Virginia Herwegh, "Compliance in the Real World of Business," presentation at the Equal Employment Opportunity Seminar of the American Society for Personnel Administration, June 29, 1976.

Religious Minorities

The EEO-type laws prohibit discrimination in employment based on religious preference, but there have been few cases thus far charging that employers have discriminated against religious groups in employment and promotion. This is surprising, given the reality that certain employers have had a policy of limited or no hiring of persons who are Jewish, Orthodox Christian, or Roman Catholic, at least for the managerial class. Roman Catholics, for example, are seriously underrepresented in managerial and professional groups in the United States.[29]

The focus of religious discrimination cases has been on hours of work and working conditions. The cases largely concern employers telling employees to work on days or times that conflict with their religious beliefs—at regular times or on overtime. For example, employees who are Orthodox Jews, Seventh-Day Adventists, or Worldwide Church of God members cannot work from sunset Friday through sundown Saturday.

Physically and Mentally Handicapped Workers

As of 1980 about half of the 15.1 million disabled citizens of the United States fit to work cannot find jobs. Tales of crippled, blind, or deaf Americans who send out waves of résumés without success are still quite common.[30] The Rehabilitation Act of 1973 has slowed down but not stopped discrimination in hiring and promoting the disabled. Section 503 of the Vocational Rehabilitation Act of 1973, which is enforced by OFCCP, requires that all employers with government contracts of $2,500 or more must set up affirmative action programs for the handicapped. At present these programs require no numerical goals. They do call for special efforts in recruiting handicapped persons, such as outreach programs; communication of the obligation to hire and promote the handicapped; the development of procedures to seek out and promote handicapped persons presently on the payroll; and making physical changes which allow the handicapped to be employed (e.g., ramps). Employers who are dedicated to improving the handicapped's chances also will set up training programs and partially redesign jobs so the handicapped can perform them effectively.[31]

The biggest hurdle that handicapped persons must face is not their physical (or mental) handicap, but myths and negative attitudes about their ability to do the job. It has been demonstrated that the handicapped can perform successfully. Affirmative action may help give them the chance to use their abilities.

Research has pointed out the contributions that the handicapped make to organizations. DuPont studied over 1,400 employees with various types of handicaps. They found that few disabled workers required special work arrangements and that the handicapped workers had on the average good job performance, excellent safety records, and good job attendance.[32]

There are some tremendous stories of disabled people making it to the top. There are blind judges like Criss Cole of Houston, parapalegic mayors like W. Mitchel of Crested

---

[29]EEOC, "Guidelines on Religious Discrimination," 1977.

[30]"For Disabled, Jobs Few—But Many Make It," *U.S. News & World Report,* September 8, 1980, p. 45.

[31]Gopal C. Pati, "Countdown on Hiring the Handicapped," *Personnel Journal,* March 1978, pp. 144–53.

[32]Robert B. Nathanson, "The Disabled Employee: Separating Myth from Fact", *Harvard Business Review* (May–June 1977), pp. 6–8.

Butte, Colorado, and deaf actresses like Phyllis Frelich, who won the Tony Award as the best Broadway actress in 1980. Max Cleland, who lost his legs and one arm in Vietnam, headed the Veterans Administration in the Carter administration (1976–80), is a visible symbol of hope for over 2.2 million disabled veterans.[33]

Veterans

The Vietnam era Veterans Readjustment Act of 1972 requires federal contractors to take affirmative action for the employment of disabled veterans and veterans of the Vietnam era. This act imposes fewer obligations than the other employment discrimination laws. No numerical goals are required, but the organization must show it makes special efforts to recruit them. In determining a veteran's qualifications, the employer cannot consider any part of the military record that is not directly relevant to the specific qualifications of the job in question.

White Males

If you are a white male, you are by now probably thinking: Women and minorities are getting a better chance for employment and promotion than they used to. But what does this do for me? Will I get a job? Will I get promoted to a better job? Or is *reverse discrimination* likely in my future? This concern is natural. The *Bakke* v. *University of California* and the *Weber* v. *Kaiser* cases show the concern of white males about reverse discrimination. These cases will have a significant impact on future EEO programs. Title VII prohibits discimination based on race and sex, *and that includes* discrimination against white males. The laws that were originally passed to give better opportunities to women and minorities are now being interpreted as protecting the rights of the majority as well.

The obligations of the organization to white males are the same as its obligations to other groups: It must not discriminate for or against any race, sex, religion, or minority group. This presents a problem to employers with numerical affirmative action goals. How are goals to be attained without favoring the disadvantaged groups? The answer is to seek *other* means for satisfying goals which do not in turn discriminate against the advantaged groups. For example, employers could undertake more intensive recruiting efforts for women and minorities, as well as eliminating those employment practices that inhibit their hiring and promotion.

Employers should *never* set numerical goals so high that they can be attained *only* through reverse discrimination. If the goals are already too high, action should be taken to lower them. The courts are increasingly saying that employers cannot use their numerical affirmative action goals as an excuse to discriminate against white males.

At present there appear to be problems in interpreting these rules. For example, the New York Bell Division of AT&T promoted a woman rather than a white male who had greater seniority and better performance evaluation ratings. The judge ruled that the company should have promoted the woman to meet its EEO goals, but the male was discriminated against. The judge ordered the promotion to go through but also ordered the company to pay the white male $100,000 in damages.[34]

---

[33]"For Disabled, Jobs Few," p. 45.

[34]Equal Opportunity Agreement, U.S. Department of Labor, January 18, 1973, Commerce Clearing House *Labor Law Reports,* No. 373, 1973.

The courts themselves may still impose goals that discriminate against white males. But federal agencies may not impose such goals on employers, and employers may not impose them on themselves.

The conclusion that emerges is that employment discrimination laws were passed for the benefit of those groups that have historically been the victims of discrimination; nevertheless, these laws do not allow the employer to bestow such benefits voluntarily by depriving white males of their rights.

Mandated Actions in EEO—Affirmative Action Programs

EEO programs have been presented as a "preventive" approach aimed at ensuring equality of employment opportunity and avoiding charges of discrimination. What happens if charges are made anyway? What requirements are likely to be imposed by an employer if the charging party wins?

Most cases do not proceed further than an EEOC investigation. When EEOC investigates a charge of discrimination, all it can force the employer to do is provide information. But this power is more threatening to employers than one might guess. EEOC's request for information almost inevitably goes beyond the facts and incidents surrounding the original charge. It involves a very extensive investigation into the company's employment practices in an effort to uncover evidence of more systematic discrimination. This evidence might support a more ambitious lawsuit, possibly a class action suit involving a large group of employees or applicants.

As a consequence of EEOC's demand for extensive information, companies that are the subject of discrimination charges often face demands for information that require hundreds of hours of staff time to assemble. Imagine, for instance, a demand that the employer produce information on every applicant interviewed, including the reasons for accepting or rejecting each applicant! This may be but one of dozens of items requested.

In the legal steps beyond investigation, the employer may also be faced with mandates that are part of the settlement of the charges. In the first step beyond investigation (conciliation), EEOC will attempt to gain a voluntary settlement of any charge that the agency's investigation has found. If a voluntary settlement is not forthcoming and the case goes to court, a settlement will come either through mutual agreement among the parties to the suit, or through the judgment of the court if the parties cannot agree.

At a minimum, the employer in these settlements will usually be required to eliminate any practice that evidence indicates is discriminatory. For example, the company could be required to give up its testing program, revise its seniority system, stop using subjective supervisory evaluations as a basis for promotions, or cease doing whatever else is deemed to be illegal. Also, the employer may be required to give back pay or other monetary compensation. If the back pay is awarded to a *class* of people (such as all black employees in certain labor grades during a certain period), it can become expensive. This was certainly true in the *AT&T* and *Georgia Power* cases discussed above.

A third requirement of some settlements is mandatory hiring ratios. The logic is that since discrimination operates against a group (for example, blacks), the relief should be given in a way that restores the group to where it *would be* if the discrimination *had not* occurred. While employers cannot adopt a quota system of hiring blacks and whites as a method for satisfying affirmative action plans, a court can order a company do do so. Usually courts do not do this unless they have reason to believe that an employer will not increase the employment of underutilized groups voluntarily.

Cost/Benefit Analysis of EEO Programs

The cost of an equal employment opportunity plan can be calculated for an employer. They include the added expense of recruitment, special training programs, test validation, job-posting systems, equipment redesign, and whatever other programs the organization includes in its plan. An added cost is for the preparation of reports. The P/HRM manager or specialist may have to compute these costs and justify the expense of such a plan to higher management by citing the benefits to be derived.

Unfortunately, the benefits are difficult to compute. Even if they are computed, they may not outweigh the costs in the short run. Consequently, some top managers may tend to view EEO as a necessary evil, something that must be done because the government requires it, not because of any benefits to be derived by the organization. This can do much to destroy the P/HRM manager's position as the person responsible for the plan, because top-management attitudes are contagious. If higher management does not provide the necessary support and resources, then lower levels of management may be reluctant to cooperate.

Therefore, it is important for managers to be aware of the benefits of EEO programs, even if they are long-range ones that are difficult to quantify. One immediate benefit is that EEO increases the likelihood that the company will stay eligible for government contracts. Another benefit is an increase in the pool of eligible employees that results from providing opportunities to women and minorities. Then there is the obvious benefit of better public relations and increased goodwill among employees that comes from a properly administered EEO program.

One benefit that EEO does not provide is insulation from liability in discrimination court cases. While a good EEO plan may make employees more satisfied and less likely to file charges of discrimination, it provides no presumption of innocence if an employee does take a charge to court. For instance, one General Motors plant had a good record of hiring minorities, but that did not keep a court from finding that it was guilty of discrimination in promoting them.[35] Still, EEO programs can help an employer in court. Some courts have been less stringent when companies seem to be making progress with their affirmative action plans. This alone may make the costs of EEO worth it.

Summary

This chapter has focused on EEO programs designed to eliminate bias in P/HRM programs. The role of EEO and the law as a significant force in shaping P/HRM policies and programs is now an accepted fact in society. The law, executive orders, and the courts' interpretations will continue to have an influence on every phase of P/HRM programs and

---

[35]*Rowe* v. *General Motors Corp.*, 457 F. 2d 348, 5th Cir., 1972.

activities. This influence will become clearer as specific P/HRM activities are discussed in Chapters 4–21. This chapter provides only the general theme of the importance of the law in P/HRM. The remaining chapters will at times spell out specifically how the law impacts P/HRM.

To summarize:

1. Equal employment opportunity is one of the most significant activities in the P/HRM function today.
2. The three main influences on the development of EEO were *(a)* changes in societal values, *(b)* the economic status of women and minorities, and *(c)* the emerging role of government regulation.
3. Laws prohibiting employment discrimination which were discussed in this Chapter are:
   a. Title VII of the 1964 Civil Rights Act.
   b. Executive Order 11246.
   c. The Vocational Rehabilitation Act.
   d. The Age Discrimination Act.
4. Three different definitions of discrimination have been arrived at by the courts over the years:
   a. Prejudiced treatment.
   b. Unequal treatment.
   c. Unequal impact.
5. The criterion for EEO and affirmative action compliance can theoretically be reduced to two questions:
   a. Does an employment practice have unequal or adverse impact on the groups covered by the law? (Race, color, sex, religious, or national origin groups.)
   b. Is that practice job-related or otherwise necessary to the organization?
6. The government units *most* responsible for enforcing EEO regulations are:
   a. U.S. Equal Employment Opportunity Commission (EEOC)—Title VII.
   b. Office of Federal Contract Compliance Programs (OFCCP)—Executive Order 11246.
7. Courts are constantly interpreting the laws governing EEO. Due to numerous appeals, an EEO compliant can be years in reaching ultimate settlement.
8. EEO planning can be used as a preventive action to reduce the likelihood of employment discrimination charges and assure equal employment opportunities for applicants and employees.
9. There are special aspects of EEO planning for each of the groups listed below:
   a. Women.
   b. Older employees.
   c. Racial and ethnic minorities.
   d. Physically and mentally handicapped workers.
   e. Veterans.
   f. White males.
10. A good EEO program is not a guarantee that an employer will not face charges of discrimination.

Exhibit 3–7 lists some recommendations for effective EEO programs using the seven model organizations presented in Chapter 1 (Exhibit 1–8).

Exhibit 3–7

EEO programs for model organizations

Type of organization	Who is responsible for organization's EEO program?			How are women and minorities recruited in EEO program?			Other activities engaged in by organization to encourage EEO		
	Separate department	Separate program director	Part of manager's job	State employment service	Liaison with community groups	Separate offices, etc.	Longer training periods	Transportation to work	Financial counseling
1. Large size, low complexity, high stability	X		X	X	X	X	X	X	X
2. Medium size, low complexity, high stability		X	X	X	X	X	X		X
3. Small size, low complexity, high stability			X	X	X		X		
4. Medium size, moderate complexity, moderate stability		X	X	X	X		X		X
5. Large size, high complexity, low stability	X		X	X	X	X	X	X	X
6. Medium size, high complexity, low stability		X	X	X	X		X		X
7. Small size, high complexity, low stability			X	X			X		

Questions for Review and Discussion

1. What role did societal values play in the evolution of EEO laws?
2. What is the meaning of the term *adverse impact?*
3. Do you feel that "sexual harassment" should be covered by the law? Why?
4. How is goal setting used in an organization's affirmative action program?
5. Why is the *Griggs* v. *Duke Power Company* court decision considered a landmark case?
6. How did the Equal Employment Opportunity Act of 1972 affect Title VII of the 1964 Civil Rights Act?
7. Why are the *Bakke* v. *University of California* and *Weber* v. *Kaiser* rulings considered significant for the P/HRM area of an organization?
8. What is meant by the term a *bona fide occupational qualification* (BFOQ)?
9. What can an employer do to make it easier for handicapped people to be active and contributing employees of an organization?
10. What does unequal treatment mean in terms of discrimination?

Case

Hugo Gerbold has just returned from his discussion with Gregory Inness, company president. Gregory seemed impressed with Hugo's presentation. But he is still doubtful that more women and minorities would "fit in" at Reliable. Hugo had pointed out that the EEOC and the courts wouldn't think much of this reasoning. He wondered if Gregory would take the next step in instituting an EEO plan at Reliable Insurance.

Hugo has decided to be ready, just in case. He prepared an EEO program designed to focus on the areas where he felt Reliable was in the worst shape. He prepared a list of current employees, primarily in the clerical ranks, who could be promoted to underwriters and claims agents. This could increase female representation in better jobs fairly quickly. It would require training, but it could be done.

To get minorities represented fairly in all categories would require special recruiting efforts. Hugo prepared a plan to increase their recruiting efforts in all categories of employment. The plan was drawn up to protect the position of current white male employees and applicants. In no case would a person be hired with fewer qualifications than white male applicants.

Luckily, Reliable was growing and was hiring more people as it expanded. Attrition would also help in most lower managerial, professional, and sales positions.

After spending quite a bit of time on development of the plan, Hugo waited. When he didn't hear from Gregory, he made an appointment to see the president.

Hugo: Gregory, you recall we discussed the EEO issue. We hired Osanna, but that's as far as our effort went. I've prepared an EEO. . . .

Gregory: Hugo, after we discussed it, I checked with the rest of the management team. We feel we're OK as is. We don't want to upset our loyal work force with an EEO plan. Now, about the pay plan for next year. . . .

And that was that. Hugo took his EEO plan and placed it in a folder in his desk drawer.

Six months later, another female employee, Dot Greene, filed a complaint. The EEOC came to investigate, and the investigation is still going on at Reliable.

Glossary

Adverse Impact.   A situation in which a significantly higher percentage of a protected group (women, blacks, Hispanics) in the available population are being rejected for employment, placement, or promotion.

Affirmative Action.   A systematic plan that specifies goals, timetables, and audit procedures for an employer to make an extra effort to hire, promote, and train those in a protected minority.

Age Discrimination Act of 1967 (Amended 1978).   Protects workers between the ages of 40 and 70 against job discrimination.

Civil Rights Act, Title VII 1964.   An important law that prohibits employers, unions, employment agencies, and joint labor-management committees controlling apprenticeship or training programs from discriminating on the basis of race, color, religion, sex, or national origin.

Equal Employment Opportunity Commission (EEOC).   The Civil Rights Act, Title VII, 1964 gave the EEOC limited powers of resolving charges of discrimination and interpreting the meaning of Title VII. Later in 1972, Congress gave EEOC the power to bring lawsuits against employers in the federal courts.

Equal Employment Opportunity Programs (EEO).   Programs implemented by employers to prevent employment discrimination in the workplace or to take remedial action to offset past employment discrimination.

Pregnancy Discrimination Act of 1978.   This law makes it unlawful to discriminate on the basis of pregnancy, childbirth, or related medical conditions in employment-type decisions.

Rehabilitation Act of 1973.   An act that is enforced by the Office of Federal Contract Compliance Programs (OFCCP), requires that all employers with government contracts of $2,500 or more must set up affirmative action programs for the handicapped.

The 4/5ths Rule.   Discrimination is likely to occur if the selection rate for a protected group is less than 4/5ths of the selection rate for a majority group.

Part One

Application Cases and Exercises

Application Case I–1
The Home of Heroes—The Personnel/Human Resource
Management Function

Application Case I–2
The Office Pass: Sexual Harassment!

Exercise I
Dissecting the Diagnostic Model and Its Application

APPLICATION CASE I–1

The Home of Heroes—The Personnel/Human Resource Management Function

The personnel/human resource (P/HRM) department has for years been considered a second-rate department in organizations—an orphan. To many managers, including chief executives, the P/HRM department was staffed with a bunch of drones who created busy work for other people, who handed out baseball bats for the company softball team, and who coordinated all picnics and parties. P/HRM was a one-way ticket to oblivion.

Of course, perceptions are hard to change, especially if they are sometimes accurate. However, the facts of modern organizational life indicate that working in the P/HRM function can be a springboard to bigger and better things. News stories indicate the following:

W. T. Beebe of Delta Airlines became president of the firm. He was once Delta's senior vice president of personnel.

Harold M. Wisely of Eli Lilly had a seat on the company's board of directors. While holding the seat he was also the executive vice president of personnel.

David E. McKinney of IBM became president of the firm's important Information Records Division. Prior to this promotion he was director of personnel resources.

At Chemetron Corp. Melvin Shulman corporate director of human resources worked directly with Chief Executive John P. Gallagher.

These cases point out that a new corporate hero has emerged. The new hero receives experience and training in the P/HRM. The four individuals just cited are certainly not drones: they wield power and achieve results.

It seems that more and more companies are transferring up-and-coming managers into the P/HRM function for a while, en route to greater responsibilities. P/HRM is finally being recognized as an important function totally engaged in the development of human resources. P/HRM has emphasized the need to recognize employees not as spare parts, but as people of value who are essential for the development of a healthy organization.[1] This emphasis is now becoming the philosophy and practice found in most organizations.

Questions for Thought

1. Why has the status and prestige of the P/HRM function increased in the past decade?
2. Why would organizations such as Delta, Eli Lilly, IBM, and Chemetron promote individuals with a P/HRM background to powerful positions?
3. Why do you feel P/HRM department employees were considered drones?

---

[1] For more discussion of the corporate heroes in P/HRM, see Herbert E. Myers, "Personnel Directors Are the New Corporate Heroes," *Fortune*, February 1976, pp. 84–88 and 140.

APPLICATION CASE I–2

The Office Pass: Sexual Harassment!

Paulette Barnes is black, 35 years old, and a mother of three children. She was hired as an administrative assistant by the Environmental Protection Agency (EPA). In fact she worked in the EPA's equal opportunity division. This is her story.

Paulette claimed that the harassment began shortly after she started work. Her boss, who was married and had children, asked her for a date. He was always going to lunch with attractive girls. He told her that she would soon be promoted to a higher grade, provided she granted sexual favors in an after-work affair. After one refusal, her boss told Paulette he would have her job. She ignored this alleged threat.

Paulette was advised to file a complaint with the EPA on the basis of racial discrimination, because her boss (also black) had subsequently eliminated her job and then reinstated her position and hired a white employee. At the EPA hearing on the complaint, a co-worker of Paulette gave testimony that the boss had attempted to seek sexual favors from her, also. The examiner excluded the sex discrimination evidence and rejected the racial discrimination charge.

Paulette went next to the Civil Service Commission, the government agency that oversees Title VII for federal employees. She also hired a lawyer. She asked that her case be reviewed, this time charging sex discrimination. Then she filed the complaint in the U.S. District Court, District of Columbia. Because Title VII suits must be filed against the agency or the company for whom a supervisor works, she pressed charges against the administrator of the Environmental Protection Agency.

At the District Court hearings the judge was not impressed with the case. He denied Paulette's request since it was his opinion that an "after-hours affair" was not the type of discriminatory conduct contemplated under Title VII.

Paulette was still not defeated. She took the case to the U.S. Circuit Court of Appeals for the District of Columbia. Her case was argued before a panel of three judges.[1]

Questions for Thought

1. Do you believe that the study as viewed by Paulette Barnes is a case of sexual harassment? Why?
2. If you were a judge sitting on the panel how would you rule in this case? Explain.

---

[1]This is a true case that is based on *Barnes* v. *Costle*, 561 F2d 983 (CA D of C, 1977), 14 EPD 7755. Also see Shelby White, "The Office Pass—(Continued)," *Across the Board*, March 1978, pp. 48–51.

EXERCISE I

Dissecting the Diagnostic Model and Its Application

Objective: The objective of this exercise is to have students examine in detail the main diagnostic model used in the book (Exhibit 2–1).

Set up the Exercise

1. Each student is to individually examine the various parts of Exhibit 2–1. Note the three main parts of P/HRM programs—activities, people, and effectiveness criteria.
2. Set up groups of four students. Each student is to take a hypothetical organization type—a large manufacturing firm, a medium-sized community hospital (350 beds), a government agency such as the equal employment opportunity commission, and a small mom and pop department store that employs 10 full-time and 15 part-time employees.
3. Each student is to develop an analysis of the type of environmental influences, P/HRM activities, people characteristics, criteria, and end results that pertain to their organization type. Thus, each group will have four separate analyses being prepared. The analyses should use Exhibit 2–1 as the diagnostic model for putting together the analyses.
4. Students will bring their analyses to a group meeting for discussion and to compare similarities and differences.
   a. What are the criteria used in the different organizations?
   b. What are the end result factors?
   c. What environmental forces are important for the various organizations?

A Learning Note

This exercise will require individual and group work. It should show that the diagnostic model (Exhibit 2–1) can be applied to large, medium, and small organizations.

Part Two

H. Armstrong Roberts

Part Two consists of four chapters. Chapter 4 discusses job analysis and design. Techniques of job analysis and design are reviewed and critiqued. Chapter 5 presents the topic of planning as it occurs in organizations of any size. In Chapter 6 recruitment is discussed. The development of an effective recruiting program is vital to the long-term survival of an organization. Chapter 7 covers the selection process. The various steps in the selection process are presented and analyzed.

Analysis, Planning, and Staffing

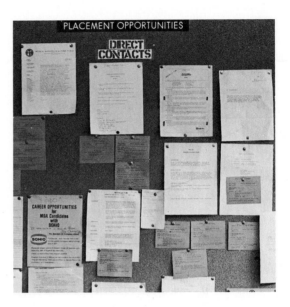

H. Armstrong Roberts

Chapter Four

Job Analysis and Design

Learning Objectives

After studying this chapter, you should be able to:

- Define what is meant by the terms *job analysis, job description,* and *job specification.*

- Illustrate the uses that job analysis information can serve in an organization's P/HRM program.

- Describe four general techniques used to collect job analysis information.

- Interpret what kind of job code and information is found in the *Dictionary of Occupational Titles.*

- List the five core job dimensions used in job enrichment programs.

Chapter Outline

Case

Tim Huggins

Tim Huggins is the new director of human resources of Sprowl Manufacturing, a division of the MBTI corporation. Tim wanted to immediately start a job analysis program. Six weeks after he took over, job analysis questionnaires (six pages each) were given to employees. The results were puzzling. The operating employees' (e.g., machinists, lift operators, technicians, draftspeople, and mechanics) responses were quite different from what their supervisors had responded about the job.

The supervisors viewed the job differently than those doing the work. This is why Tim wanted to do a job analysis. He wanted to study and specifically define the jobs so that misunderstandings, arguments, and false expectations could be kept to a minimum. This is what job analysis attempts to do.

The supervisors listed job duties as simple and routine. The operating employees disagreed and claimed that their jobs were complicated, constrained by limited resources, and located in hot, stuffy, and uncomfortable work areas. This disagreement soon became the basis for some open hostility between supervisors and workers. Finally, Nick Mannis, a machinist, confronted supervisor Rog Wilkes and threatened to punch him out over the "lies" Rog and other supervisors had concocted in the job analysis.

Tim was worried that the job analysis program was getting totally out of hand. He had to do something to keep the lid on. Everyone was getting up in arms over a program Tim felt was necessary.

Introduction

Organizations have evolved because the overall mission and objectives of most institutions are too large for any single person to achieve. The cornerstone of the organization is the jobs performed by employees. The set of jobs is what provides the input needed to accomplish the mission and objectives. These jobs must fit together, coordinate, and link directly to the mission if the organization is to be successful. Thus, studying and understanding jobs is a vital part of any P/HRM program. *Job analysis* involves the formal study of jobs.

Job analysis provides answers to questions such as:

How much time is taken to complete important jobs tasks?

Which tasks are grouped together and are considered a job?

How can a job be designed or structured so that employee performance can be enhanced?

What is done behaviorally on the job?

What kind of person (traits and experience) is best suited for the job?

How can the information acquired via a job analysis be used in the development of P/HRM programs?

In this chapter the contributions made by job analyses to an organization's P/HRM program and specific activities will become clearer. Furthermore, the careful planning needed and various general and specific techniques of a job analysis program will also be highlighted. Finally, the importance of job analysis in the design of jobs will discussed. The chapter will show that job analysis is a necessary part of P/HRM. It is this necessity that is pushing Tim in his drive to institute job analysis at Sprowl Manufacturing.

Job Analysis Vocabulary

The language of job analysis must be learned before the specific process and the techniques are understood. To establish the vocabulary some key terms must be clarified. The following definitions are consistent with those provided by the U.S. Employment Service and the U.S. Office of Personnel Management.[1]

Job analysis. The process of defining a job in terms of tasks or behaviors and specifying the education, training, and responsibilities needed to perform the job successfully.

Job description. The job analysis provides information about the job that results in a description of what the job entails.

Job specification. The job analysis also results in the specification of what kind of traits and experiences are needed to perform the job.

Task. A coordinated and aggregated series of work elements used to produce an output (e.g., units of production of service to a client).

Position. Consists of responsibilities and duties performed by an individual. There are as many positions as there are employees.

Job. A group of positions that are similar in their duties, such as a computer programmer or compensation specialist.

Job family. A group of two or more jobs that have similar job duties.

These terms illustrate that in order to prevent confusion and improper usage the specific meaning of words must be understood. Terms such as *job* and *task* are often used interchangeably. This, however, is technically not correct (as can be seen from the definitions above). Since precision is required by federal and state legislation it is important for the P/HRM manager to be accurate in the use of terms.

The Steps in Job Analysis

There are a number of steps that are performed in the job analysis process.[2] Exhibit 4–1 depicts these steps. The process outlined in Exhibit 4–1 assumes that the job analysis process is occurring in an ongoing organization; in other words, an organization that is

---

[1]Bureau of Intergovernmental Personnel Programs, ''Job Analysis: Developing and Documenting Data'' (Washington, D.C.: U.S. Government Printing Office, 1973).

[2]Jai Ghorpade and Thomas J. Atchison, ''The Concept of Job Analysis: A Review and Some Suggestions,'' *Public Personnel Management Journal,* Summer 1980, pp. 134–144; Ronald A. Ash and Edward L. Levine, ''A Framework for Evaluating Job Analysis Methods,'' *Personnel,* November–December 1980, pp. 53–59.

Exhibit 4–1 _____

Steps in the job analysis process (1–6) and job design (7–8)

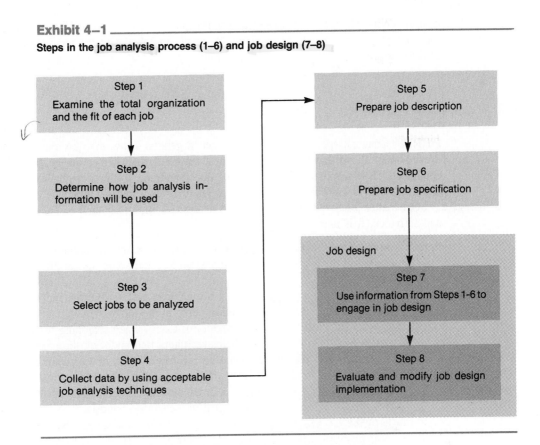

already in operation as opposed to a new venture. Step 1 is important since it provides an overall view of the organization. The fit of each job in the total fabric of the organization is what is being considered. Organization charts and process charts (which will be discussed later) are used to complete Step 1. Step 2 encourages those involved to determine how the job analysis and job design information will be used. More will be said about this step in the next section. Since it is usually too costly and time consuming to analyze every job a representative sample of jobs needs to be selected. In Step 3 attention is called to the selection of jobs that are to be analyzed.

. Step 4 involves the use of acceptable job analysis techniques. The techniques are used to collect data on the characteristics of the job, the required behaviors, and the employee characteristics needed to perform the job. The information collected in Step 4 is then used in Step 5 to develop a job description. Next, in Step 6 a job specification is prepared.

Tim failed to explain these steps at Sprowl. He simply handed out questionnaires. Naturally this resulted in concern among supervisors and operating employees. The people whose jobs were being analyzed and their supervisors simply were not informed on what Tim had in mind. Of course Tim, being an expert in P/HRM, knew all about job analysis. Unfortunately other people at Sprowl were not sure what job analysis was all about.

The knowledge and data collected in Steps 1–6 are then used to engage in Step 7, job design. A job's _design_ is how the elements, duties, and tasks are put together to achieve optimal employee performance and satisfaction. The success or failure of any job design attempt should be evaluated and will probably have to be modified. These actions are spelled out in Step 8. Steps 7 and 8 focus on job design as an output of the job analysis process.

The Uses of Job Analysis

P/HRM managers, specialists, and managers in general know that job analysis has many uses. Some believe that there is no longer a choice about whether job analysis should be conducted. The administrative guidelines accompanying the civil rights/EEO laws now require that organizations conduct a formal job analysis to defend their P/HRM activities.[3]

No matter what reason is given, job analysis is intricately tied to P/HRM programs and activities. It is used in:

1. Preparation of *job descriptions*. A complete description contains a job summary, the job duties and responsibilities, and some indication of the working conditions.
2. Writing *job specifications*. The job specification describes the individual traits and characteristics required to perform the job well.
3. *Recruitment*. Job analysis information is useful when searching for the right person to fill the job. It helps recruiters find and seek the type of people that will contribute to and be comfortable with the organization.
4. *Selection*. The final selection of the most qualified people requires information on what job duties and responsibilities need to be performed. This type of information is provided in the job description.
5. *Performance evaluation*. The evaluation of performance involves comparison of actual versus planned output. Job analysis is used to acquire an idea of acceptable levels of performance for a job.
6. *Training and Development*. Job analysis information is used to design and implement training and development programs. The job description provides information on what skills and competencies are required to perform the job. Training and development work is then conducted to satisfy these skill and competency requirements.
7. *Career planning and development*. The movement of individuals into and out of positions, jobs, and occupations is a common procedure in organizations. Job analysis provides clear and detailed information to those considering such a career movement.
8. *Compensation*. The total job is the basis for estimating its worth. Compensation is usually tied to a job's required skill, competencies, working conditions, safety hazards, and so on. Job analysis is used to compare and properly compensate jobs.
9. *Safety*. The safety on a job depends upon proper layout, standards, equipment, and other physical conditions. What a job entails and the type

---

[3]M. G. Miner and J. B. Miner, *Uniform Guidelines on Employee Selection Procedures* (Washington, D.C.: The Bureau of National Affairs, 1979).

of people needed also contribute information to establish safe procedures. Of course, this information is provided by job analysis.

10. *Job design.* Job analysis information is used to structure and modify the elements, duties, and tasks of specific jobs.

Taken together these uses of job analysis information are comprehensive. They cover the entire domain of P/HRM activities. Exhibit 4–2 provides a sample of the list of activities which benefit from job analysis information. This list is by no means complete. Job analysis is such an important source of information that it transcends P/HRM programs and activities. Managers involved in planning, organizing, controlling, and directing functions also can and do benefit from job analysis information.

Who Does the Job Analysis?

Job analysis is certainly not a job for amateurs. The steps spelled out in Exhibit 4–1 indicate that care and planning are important features of any job analysis effort. Tim really didn't take the care and planning that he should have to start the job analysis program— he started the program too abruptly.

There are managers who do not have enough respect for the work of the job analyst. The following statement presents an interesting message about job analysis.

Although job analysis is an essential feature of almost every activity engaged in by industrial-organizational psychologists, the subject is treated in textbooks in a manner which suggests that any fool can do it and thus it is a task which can be delegated to the lowest level technician. This is quite contradictory to the position taken by Otis

Exhibit 4–2 _____

How job analysis information is used

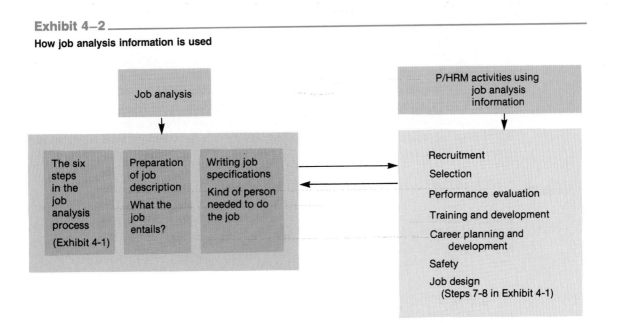

(1953) . . ., and is clearly at variance with the statements in the EEOC Selection Guidelines. . . . Job analysis for these purposes is not accomplished by rummaging around in an organization; it is accomplished by applying highly systematic and precise methods.[4]

The individuals conducting a job analysis should understand people, jobs, and the total organizational system. These individuals would also have to understand how work flows within the organization. An understanding of how P/HRM fits into the overall structure of the organization is also important.

The job analyst could be located in a P/HRM or industrial engineering department or in a unit that is solely responsible for job analysis. Some firms, because of an only occasional need for job analysis information or cost constraints, may hire a temporary job analyst from outside the organization. Whatever the organizational arrangement, the job analyst(s) is not an amateur. He or she is a trained specialist who plays a vital role in P/HRM.

Selecting Methods and Procedures: The Use of Charts

The job analyst has to select the best methods and procedures available to conduct the job analysis. However, even before this selection is made an overview of the organization and jobs is required. An overview provides the job analyst with an informed picture of the total arrangement of departments, units, and jobs.

The Organization Chart

An organization chart presents the relationship among departments and units of the firm. The line functions (the individuals performing work duties) and staff functions (the advisers) are spelled out.

A typical organization chart for a manufacturing firm is presented in Exhibit 4–3. This chart shows the vertical levels in the organization and the various departments. It provides the job analyst with a rough picture of what departments exist and the hierarchy and formal communication networks in the organization. Emphasis is placed on the word *rough*. A chart shows the way the organization is *supposed* to be arranged. The actual arrangement of the organization and the flow of communication is often different from the plan on the chart. However, even an approximate view aids in forming a broad-based conception of the organization.

Process Chart

A process chart is more specific than an organization chart. It displays how jobs are connected to each other. Exhibit 4–4 is a process chart showing how four jobs are related to each other. Specific attention is paid to the technician job. The job analyst would be interested in the flows to and from the technician job.

---

[4]E. P. Prien, ''The Functions of Job Analysis in Content Validation,'' *Personnel Psychology* Summer 1977, pp. 167–74. The ''Otis (1953)'' reference in the quote is in J. L. Otis, ''Whose Criterion?'' presidential address to Division 14 of the American Psychological Association, 1953.

Exhibit 4–3

Organization chart (sample)

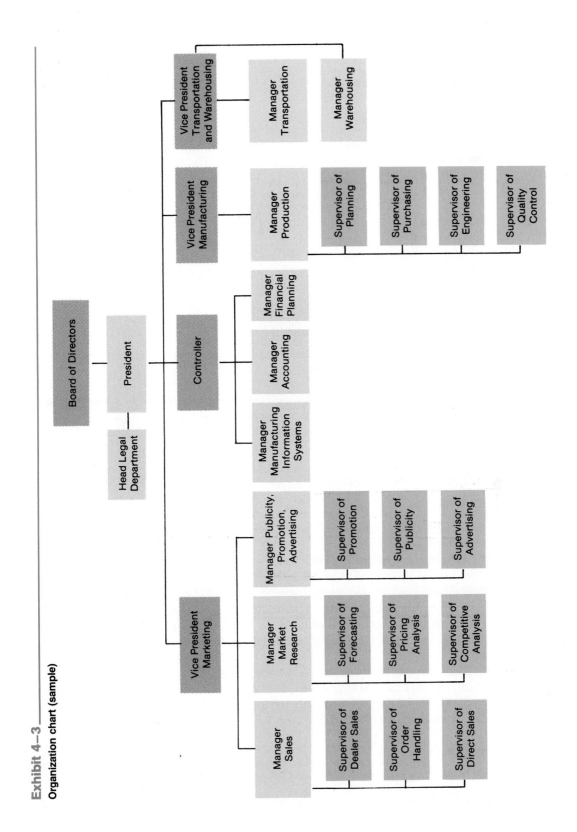

Exhibit 4–4

Process chart of job relationships

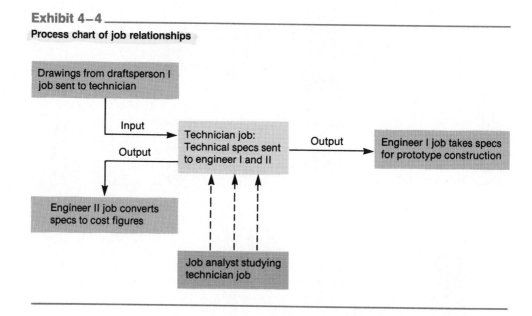

Organization charts provide a broad overview; process charts provide a more detailed analysis of specific jobs. These and other similar sources should be consulted before actual job analysis collection methods are used.

Job Analysis: General Techniques

There are four general techniques used separately or in combination to collect job analysis data—observation, interview, questionnaires, and job incumbent diary/logs. In each of these techniques, information about the job is collected and then the job studied in terms of tasks completed by the job incumbent (person presently working on the job). This type of job analysis is referred to as *job oriented*. On the other hand, a job can be analyzed in terms of behaviors or what the job incumbent does to perform the job (e.g., computing, coordinating, negotiating). This is referred to as *work-oriented* job analysis.[5] Both of these orientations are acceptable under the 1978 Uniform Guidelines on Employee Selection procedures as long as they identify job duties and behaviors that are critical to performing the job.

Thus, the four techniques—or any combination of them—must collect what is called critical information. Since time and cost are considerations, managers need to collect comparable, valid data. Consequently some form of core information is needed no matter what data collection technique(s) is used.[6]

---

[5]E. J. McCormick, *Job Analysis: Uses and Application* (New York: Amacom, 1979), and E. J. McCormick, "Job and Task Analysis," in, ed. *Handbook of Industrial and Organizational Psychology,* ed. M. D. Dunnette (Chicago: Rand McNally, 1976), pp. 652–53.

[6]Richard I. Henderson, *Compensation Management* (Reston, Va.: Reston Publishing, 1979), pp. 146–452.

A questionnaire called the Job Analysis Information Format (JAIF) can provide the basic core information for use of any technique—observation, interview, questionnaire, or job incumbent diary/log. It permits the job analyst to collect job information that provides a thorough picture of the job, job duties, and requirements.

Job incumbents are asked to complete the JAIF. These answers (of course, some questions may not be answered or can't be answered because of a lack of job incumbent knowledge about the question) are then used to specifically structure the data collection technique that will eventually be implemented. Exhibit 4–5 presents a copy of one type of JAIF.

Observation

Direct observation is used for jobs that require manual, standardized, and short-job cycle activities. Jobs performed by an automobile assembly-line worker, an insurance company filing clerk, or an inventory stockroom employee are examples of these. The job analyst must observe a representative sample of individuals performing these jobs.

The use of the observation technique requires that the job analyst be trained to observe *relevant* job behaviors. In conducting an observation the job analyst must remain as unobtrusive as possible. He or she must stay out of the way so that the work can be performed.

But - informal system is used ("By the book" - clogs system)

Interview

Interviewing job incumbents is often used in combination with observation. Interviews are probably the most widely used job analysis data collection technique. They permit the job analyst to talk face to face with job incumbents. The job incumbent can ask questions of the job analyst and this serves as an opportunity to explain how the job analysis information will be used.

Interviews can be conducted with a single job incumbent, a group of individuals, or with a supervisor who is knowledgeable about the job. Usually a structured set of questions will be used in interviews so that answers from individuals or groups can be compared.

One major problem with interviewing is that inaccurate information may be collected. For example, if a job incumbent believes that the job analysis interview will be used to set the job's compensation amount, he or she may provide inaccurate information. Therefore, interviewing more than one person (job incumbents and supervisors), careful planning, good questions, and establishing rapport between the job analyst and interviewees are extremely important guidelines. These guidelines require patience and are time consuming, they improve the quality of information collected. Interview information can be further refined by use of observation and/or questionnaires.

Questionnaires

The use of questionnaires is usually the least costly method for collecting information. It is an efficient way to collect a large amount of information in a short period of time. The JAIF presented in Exhibit 4–5 is a structured questionnaire. It includes specific questions

Exhibit 4–5 _____

JOB ANALYSIS INFORMATION FORMAT

Your Job Title _____ *Code* _____ *Date* _____

Class Title _____ *Department* _____

Your Name _____ *Facility* _____

Superior's Title _____ *Prepared by* _____

Superior's Name _____ *Hours Worked* _____ $\frac{AM}{PM}$ _____ *to* $\frac{AM}{PM}$ _____

---

1. What is the general purpose of your job?

2. What was your last job? If it was in another organization, please name it.

3. To what job would you normally expect to be promoted?

4. If you regularly supervise others, list them by name and job title.

5. If you supervise others, please check those activities that are part of your supervisory duties

   __Hiring   __Coaching   __Promoting

   __Orienting   __Counseling   __Compensating

   __Training   __Budgeting   __Disciplining

   __Scheduling   __Directing   __Terminating

   __Developing   __Measuring Performance __Other_____

6. How would you describe the successful completing and results of your work?

7. *Job Duties*—Please briefly describe WHAT you do and, if possible, HOW you do it. Indicate those duties you consider to be most important and/or most difficult.

   a. *Daily Duties*—

   b. *Periodic Duties*—(Please indicate whether weekly, monthly, quarterly, etc.)—

   c. *Duties Performed at Irregular Intervals*—

   d. How long have you been performing these duties?

   e. Are you now performing unnecessary duties? If yes, please describe.

   f. Should you be performing duties not now included in your job? If yes, please describe

8. *Education.* Please check the blank that indicates the educational *requirements* for the job, not your *own* educational background.

   a. _____ No formal education required.   e. _____ 4-year college degree.

   b. _____ Less than high school diploma.   f. _____ Education beyond under-

   c. _____ High school diploma or   graduate degree and/or
               equivalent.   professional license.

   d. _____ 2-year college certificate or equivalent

   List advanced degrees or specific professional license or certificate required.

   Please indicate the education you had when you were placed on this job.

9. *Experience.* Please check the amount needed to perform your job.

   a. __ None   e. __ More than one year to
                                                         three years

   b. __ Less than one month   f. __ Three to five years

   c. __ One month to less than   g. __ Five to 10 years
           six months

   d. __ Six months to one year   h. __ Over 10 years

   Please indicate the experience you had when you were placed on this job.

10. *Skill.* Please list any skills required in the performance of your job. (For example, amount of accuracy, alertness, precision in working with described tools, methods, systems, etc.)

    Please list skills you possessed when you were placed on this job.

11. *Equipment.* Does your work require the use of any equipment? Yes __ No __. If Yes, please list the equipment and check whether you use it rarely, occasionally, or frequently.

Equipment	Rarely	Occasionally	Frequently
a. _____	_____	_____	_____
b. _____	_____	_____	_____
c. _____	_____	_____	_____
d. _____	_____	_____	_____

12. *Physical Demands.* Please check all undesirable physical demands required on your job and whether you are required to do so rarely, occasionally, or frequently.

	Rarely	Occasionally	Frequently
a. _____ Handling heavy material	_____	_____	_____
b. _____ Awkward or cramped positions	_____	_____	_____
c. _____ Excessive working speeds	_____	_____	_____
d. _____ Excessive sensory require- ments (seeing, hearing, touching, smelling, speaking)	_____	_____	_____
e. _____ Vibrating equipment	_____	_____	_____
f. _____ Others: _____	_____	_____	_____

Exhibit 4–5 *(concluded)* _____

13. *Emotional Demands.* Please check all undesirable emotional demands placed on you by your job and whether it is rarely, occasionally, or frequently

		Rarely	Occasionally	Frequently
a. ____	Contacts with general public	____	____	____
b. ____	Customer contact	____	____	____
c. ____	Close supervision	____	____	____
d. ____	Deadlines under pressure	____	____	____
e. ____	Irregular activity schedules	____	____	____
f. ____	Working alone	____	____	____
g. ____	Excessive traveling	____	____	____
h. ____	*Others:*	____	____	____

14. *Work-place Location.* Check type of location of your job and if you consider it to be unsatisfactory or satisfactory.

		Unsatisfactory	*Satisfactory*
a. ____	Outdoor	____	____
b. ____	Indoor	____	____
c. ____	Underground	____	____
d. ____	Pit	____	____
e. ____	Scaffold	____	____

15. *Physical Surroundings.* Please check whether you consider the following physical conditions of your job to be poor, good, or excellent.

		Poor	Good	Excellent
a. ____	Lighting	____	____	____
b. ____	Ventilation	____	____	____
c. ____	Sudden temperature change	____	____	____
d. ____	Vibration	____	____	____
e. ____	Comfort of furnishings	____	____	____

16. *Environmental Conditions.* Please check the objectionable conditions under which you must perform your job and check whether the condition exists rarely, occasionally, or frequently.

		Rarely	Occasionally	Frequently
a. ____	Dust	____	____	____
b. ____	Dirt	____	____	____
c. ____	Heat	____	____	____

		Rarely	Occasionally	Frequently
d. _____	Cold	_____	_____	_____
e. _____	Fumes	_____	_____	_____
f. _____	Odors	_____	_____	_____
g. _____	Noise	_____	_____	_____
h. _____	Wetness	_____	_____	_____
i. _____	Humidity	_____	_____	_____
j. _____	Others:	_____	_____	_____

17. *Health and Safety.* Please check all undesirable health and safety factors under which you must perform your job and whether you are required to do so rarely, occasionally, or frequently.

		Rarely	Occasionally	Frequently
a. _____	Height of elevated workplace	_____	_____	_____
b. _____	Radiation	_____	_____	_____
c. _____	Mechanical hazards	_____	_____	_____
d. _____	Moving objects	_____	_____	_____
e. _____	Explosives	_____	_____	_____
f. _____	Electrical hazards	_____	_____	_____
g. _____	Fire	_____	_____	_____
h. _____	Others: _____	_____	_____	_____

Signature _____ *Date* _____

Supervisory review

Do the incumbent's responses to the questionnaire accurately describe the work requirements and the work performed in meeting the responsibilities of the job? _____ Yes _____ No. If No, please explain and list any significant omissions or additions.

_____	_____	_____
Date	Title	Signature

about the job, job requirements, working conditions, and equipment. A less structured, more open-ended approach would be to ask job incumbents to "describe their job in their own terms." This open-ended format would permit job incumbents to use their own terms and ideas to describe the job.

The format and degree of structure that a questionnaire should have are debatable issues. Job analysts have their own personal preferences on this matter. There really is no best format for a questionnaire. However, here are a few hints that will make the questionnaire easier to use:

- Keep it as *short as possible*—people do not generally like to complete forms.
- *Explain* what the questionnaire is being used for—people want to know why this must be done. Tim Huggins (in the case at the start of the chapter) failed to explain his job analysis questionnaire. Look again at his problems.
- Keep it *simple*— do not try to impress people with technical language. Use the simplest language to make a point or ask a question.
- *Test* the questionnaire before using it—in order to improve the questionnaire ask some job incumbents to complete it and to comment on its features. This will permit making modifications in the format before using the questionnaire in final form.

Job Incumbent Diary/Log

The diary/log is a recording by job incumbents to job duties, frequency of the duties, and when the duties were accomplished. This technique requires the job incumbent to keep a diary/log on a daily basis. Unfortunately, most individuals are not disciplined enough to keep such a diary/log.

If a diary/log is kept up to date, it can provide good information about the job. Comparisons on a daily, weekly, or monthly basis can be made. This permits an examination of the routineness or nonroutineness of job duties. The diary/log is useful when attempting to analyze jobs that are difficult to observe, such as those performed by engineers, scientists, and senior executives.

Any of these four general techniques can be used in combination. In fact, all four may be used to acquire a comprehensive picture of a job. Of course, using all four would take time and be rather costly. The analyst decides which technique or combination is needed to do a thorough job analysis. Job analysts often use a more specific, widely used technique that incorporates various features of these four general techniques and provides a quantitative score.

Job Analysis: Specific Techniques

The four job analysis techniques just described are presented in general terms. They form the basis for construction of specific techniques that have gained popularity across many types of organizations. These specific techniques provide systematic and quantitative procedures that yield information about what job duties are being accomplished and what

skill, ability, and knowledge is needed to perform the job. Three popular specific techniques are: functional job analysis (FJA); the position analysis questionnaire (PAQ); and
the management position description questionnaire (MPDQ).

*Both just
too long.*

Functional Job Analysis

The U.S. Training and Employment Service (USTES) developed what is called functional
job analysis (FJA).[7] FJA is used to describe the nature of jobs, to prepare job descriptions,
and to provide details on employee job specifications. The end result of FJA is a description of a job in terms of data, people, and things.

FJA assumes that:

- Jobs are concerned with data, people, and things.
- It is important to make a distinction between what gets done and what job
  incumbents do to get things done.
- Mental resources are used to describe data; interpersonal resources are used
  with people; physical resources are applied to people.
- Each function performed on a job draws on a range of worker talents and
  skills to perform job duties.

The job incumbents' activities associated with data, people, and things are listed in
Exhibit 4–6. These activities are used to describe more than 20,000 jobs in the *Dictionary
of Occupational Titles (DOT).*[8]

*Gets used by
state tax
revenue for
forecasting.
+ by researchers*

The DOT classifies jobs on the basis of a nine-digit code. If someone is interested in
a general description of a job, the DOT could be used. Exhibit 4–7 provides DOT descriptions of five jobs. The first three digits of any listing (e.g., Disc Jockey—159) specify
the occupational code, title, and industry. The next three digits (147) designate the degree
to which a job incumbent typically has responsibility and judgment over data, people,

Exhibit 4–6

Activities to be rated: Data, people, and things

Data	*People*	*Things*
0 Synthesizing	0 Mentoring	0 Setting up
1 Coordinating	1 Negotiating	1 Precision working
2 Analyzing	2 Instructing	2 Operating-controlling
3 Compiling	3 Supervising	3 Driving-operating
4 Computing	4 Diverting	4 Manipulating
5 Copying	5 Persuading	5 Tending
6 Comparing	6 Speaking-signaling	6 Feeding-offbearing
	7 Serving	7 Handling
	8 Taking instructions-helping	

Source: Adapted from U.S. Department of Labor, Employment Serivce, Training and Development Administration, *Handbook for Analyzing Jobs* (Washington, D.C.: U.S. Government
Printing Office, 1972), p. 73.

[7]Sidney A. Fine and Wretha W. Wiley, *An Introduction to Functional Job Analysis: A Scaling of Selected Tasks
from the Social Welfare Field* (Methods for Manpower Analysis no. 4.) (Kalamazoo, Mich.: W. E. Upjohn Institute
for Employee Research, 1973).

[8]U.S. Department of Labor, *Dictionary of Occupational Titles,* 4th ed. (Washington, D.C.: U.S. Government
Printing Office, 1977).

Exhibit 4–7

DOT descriptions of jobs

159.147-014   DISC JOCKEY (radio & tv broad.)
Announces radio program of musical selections: Selects phonograph or tape recording to be played based on program specialty and knowledge of audience taste. Comments on music and other matters of interest to audience, such as weather, time, or traffic conditions. May interview music personalities. May specialize in one type of music, such as classical, pop, rock, or country and western. May be designated COMBINATION OPERATOR (radio & tv broad.) when operating transmitter or control console.

159.167-018   MANAGER, STAGE (amuse. & rec.)
Coordinates production plans and directs activities of stage crew and performers during rehearsals and performance: Confers with DIRECTOR, STAGE (amuse. & rec.) concerning production plans. Arranges conference times for cast, crew, and DIRECTOR, STAGE (amuse. & rec.), and disseminates general information about production. Reads script during each performance and gives cues for curtain, lights, sound effects, and prompting performers. Interprets stage-set diagrams to determine stage layout. Supervises stage crew engaged in placing scenery and properties. Devises emergency substitutes for stage equipment or properties. Keeps records to advise PRODUCER (amuse. & rec.) on matters of time, attendance, and welfare benefits. Compiles cue words and phrases to form prompt book. Directs activities of one or more assistants. May instruct understudy, replacement, or extra. May call performers at specified interval before curtain time.

313.381-014   BAKER, PIZZA (hotel & rest)
Prepares and bakes pizza pies: Measures ingredients, such as flour, water, and yeast, using measuring cup, spoon, and scale. Dumps specified ingredients into pan or bowl of mixing machine preparatory to mixing. Starts machine and observes operation until ingredients are mixed to desired consistency. Stops machine and dumps dough into proof box to allow dough to rise. Kneads fermented dough. Cuts out and weighs amount of dough required to produce pizza pies of desired thickness. Shapes dough sections into balls or mounds and sprinkles each section with flour to prevent crust forming until used. Greases pan. Stretches or spreads dough mixture to size of pan. Places dough in pan and adds olive oil and tomato puree, tomato sauce, mozarella cheese, meat, or other garnish on surface of dough, according to kind of pizza ordered. Sets thermostatic controls and inserts pizza into heated oven to bake for specified time. Removes product from oven and observes color to determine when pizza is done.

187.167-094   MANAGER, DUDE RANCH (amuse. & rec.)
Directs operation of dude ranch: Formulates policy on advertising, publicity, guest rates, and credit. Plans recreational and entertainment activities, such as camping, fishing, hunting, horseback riding, and dancing. Directs activities of DUDE WRANGLERS (amuse. & rec.). Directs preparation and maintenance of financial records. Directs other activities, such as breeding, raising, and showing horses, mules, and livestock.

732.684-106   SHAPER, BASEBALL GLOVE (sports equip.) steamer and shaper.
Forms pocket, opens fingers, and smooths seams to shape baseball gloves, using heated forms, mallets, and hammers: Pulls glove over heated hand-shaped form to open and stretch finger linings. Pounds fingers and palm of glove with rubber mallet and ball-shaped hammer to smooth seams and bulges, and form glove pocket. Removes glove from form, inserts hand into glove, and strikes glove pocket with fist while examining glove visually and tactually to insure comfortable fit.

---

things. The lower the numbers' value, the greater the responsibility and judgment. The final three digits (014) are used to calssify the alphabetical order of job titles within the occupational group having the same degree of responsibility and judgment.

The DOT descriptions offer a starting point for learning about a job. The FJA can then be used to clarify and elaborate on the standard DOT listing.

The FJA form of analyzing the job of a dough mixer appears in Exhibit 4–8. The dough mixer's activities in terms of data, people, and things are quantitatively rated a 5, 6, and 2 in item 5. These ratings are based on the analyst's judgment concerning the activities presented in Exhibit 4–6. That is, a dough mixer must be able to copy data (5), speak effectively (6), and control (2) his or her work.

Exhibit 4–8

Sample of end result of job analysis

U.S. Department of Labor
Manpower Administration
(USTES)

JOB ANALYSIS SCHEDULE

1. Established Job Title _____ DOUGH MIXER _____

2. Ind. Assign _____ (bake prod.) _____

3. SIC Code(s) and Title(s) _____ 2051 Bread and other bakery products _____

4. JOB SUMMARY:

Operates mixing machine to mix ingredients for straight and sponge
(yeast) doughs according to established formulas, directs other workers in
fermentation of dough, and cuts dough into pieces with hand cutter.

5. WORK PERFORMED RATINGS:

	D	P	(T)
Worker Functions	Data	People	Things
	5	6	2

Work Field _____ Cooking, Food Preparing _____

6. WORKER TRAITS RATINGS: (To be filled in by analyst)

Training time required

Aptitudes

Temperaments

Interests

Physical Demands

Environment Conditions

If the job analyst were examining the job of an executive secretary the quantitative
score might be 5, 6, 5 (copying, speaking-signaling, tending). On the other hand a research scientist in a laboratory might be rated a 2, 0, 1.

The advantage of the FJA is that each job has a quantitative score. Thus, jobs can
then be arranged for compensation or other P/HRM purposes. For example, all jobs with
5, 6, 2 or 2, 0, 1 scores could be grouped together.[9]

---

[9]Sidney A. Fine, *Functional Job Analysis Scales: A Desk Aid, Methods for Manpower Analysis No. 7* (Kalamazoo, Mich.: W. E. Upjohn Institute for Employment Research, 1973).

Position Analysis Questionnaire (PAQ)

A structured questionnaire for quantitatively assessing jobs was developed by Purdue University researchers and is called the Position Analysis Questionnaire (PAQ).[10] Typically a job analyst completes the PAQ. The PAQ contains 194 items (11 of these are shown in Exhibit 4–9). The job analyst decides whether the item is important in performing the job. For example, measuring devices (item 6) play a very substantial role 5 for the job being analyzed in Exhibit 4–9.

The PAQ's 194 items are placed in six major sections:

1. *Information input.* Where and how does job incumbent get job information?
2. *Mental processes.* What reasoning, decision making, and planning processes are used to perform the job?
3. *Work output.* What physical activities and tools are used to perform the job?
4. *Relationship with other people.* What relationships with others are required to perform the job?
5. *Job contacts.* In what physical and social context is the job performed?
6. *Other job characteristics.* What activities, conditions, or characteristics other than those described in Section 1–5 are relevant?

Computerized programs are available for scoring jobs on the basis of seven dimensions—decision making, communication, social responsibilities, performing skilled activities, being physically active, operating vehicles and/or equipment, and processing information. These scores permit the development of profiles for jobs analyzed and the comparison of jobs.

Like every job analysis technique the PAQ has some advantages and disadvantages. One advantage is that the PAQ has been widely used and researched. The available evidence indicates that it can be and is an effective technique.[11] It is a reliable technique in that there is little variance among job analysts' rating the same jobs. Furthermore, it also seems to be valid in that jobs rated higher with the PAQ prove to be those paying higher compensation rates.

A major problem with the PAQ is its length. It requires time and patience to complete. In addition, since no specific work activities are described, behavioral activities performed in jobs may distort actual task differences in the jobs. For example, a police officer's profile is similar to a homemaker. They both are involved in troubleshooting and crises-handling situations.[12]

Management Positions Description Questionnaire (MPDQ)

Conducting a job analysis for managerial jobs offers a significant challenge to the analyst because of the disparity across positions, levels in the hierarchy, and type of industry (e.g., industrial, medical, government). An attempt to systematically analyze managerial

---

[10]E. J. McCormick, O. R. Jeanneret, and R. C. Mecham, "A Study of Job Characteristics and Job Dimensions as Based on the Position Analysis Questionnaire (PAQ)," *Journal of Applied Psychology,* (August 1972), pp. 347–68 and E. J. McCormick, P. R. Jeanneret, and R. C. Mecham, *User's Manual for the Position Analysis Questionnaire System II* (West Lafayette, Ind.: Purdue University Press, 1978).

[11]E. J. McCormick, A. S. De Nisi, and J. B. Shaw, "Use of the Position Analysis Questionnaire for Establishing the Job Component Validity of Tests," *Journal of Applied Psychology,* February 1979, pp. 51–56.

[12]Wayne F. Cascio and Elias M. Awad, *Human Resource Management* (Reston, Va.: Reston Publishing, 1981), pp. 157–58.

Exhibit 4–9 _____

Portions of a completed page from the Position Analysis Questionnaire

INFORMATION INPUT

1   INFORMATION INPUT

1.1   Sources of Job Information

Rate each of the following items in terms of the extent to which it is used by the worker as a source of information in performing his job.

	Extent of Use (U)
NA	Does not apply
1	Nominal/very infrequent
2	Occasional
3	Moderate
4	Considerable
5	Very substantial

1.1.1   Visual Sources of Job Information

1 | 4   Written materials (books, reports, office notes, articles, job instructions, signs, etc.)

2 | 2   Quantitative materials (materials which deal with quantities or amounts, such as graphs, accounts, specifications, tables of numbers, etc.)

3 | 1   Pictorial materials (pictures or picturelike materials used as *sources* of information, for example, drawings, blueprints, diagrams, maps, tracings, photographic films, x-ray films, TV pictures, etc.)

4 | 1   Patterns/related devices (templates, stencils, patterns, etc., used as *sources* of information when *observed* during use; do *not* include here materials described in item 3 above)

5 | 2   Visual displays (dials, gauges, signal lights, radarscopes, speedometers, clocks, etc.)

6 | 5   Measuring devices (rulers, calipers, tire pressure gauges, scales, thickness gauges, pipettes, thermometers, protractors, etc., used to obtain visual information about physical measurements; do *not* include here devices described in item 5 above)

7 | 4   Mechanical devices (tools, equipment, machinery, and other mechanical devices which are *sources* of information when *observed* during use or operation)

8 | 3   Materials in process (parts, materials, objects, etc., which are *sources* of information when being modified, worked on, or otherwise processed, such as bread dough being mixed, workpiece being turned in a lathe, fabric being cut, shoe being resoled, etc.)

9 | 4   Materials *not* in process (parts, materials, objects, etc., not in the process of being changed or modified, which are *sources* of information when being inspected, handled, packaged, distributed, or selected, etc., such as items or materials in inventory, storage, or distribution channels, items being inspected, etc.)

10 | 3   Features of nature (landscapes, fields, geological samples, vegetation, cloud formations, and other features of nature which are observed or inspected to provide information)

11 | 2   Man-made features of environment (structures, buildings, dams, highways, bridges, docks, railroads, and other "man-made" or altered aspects of the indoor or outdoor environment which are *observed* or *inspected* to provide job information, do not consider equipment, machines, etc., that an individual uses in his work, as covered by item 7).

Note: This exhibits 11 of the "information input" questions or elements. Other PAQ pages contain questions regarding mental processes, work output, relationships with others, job context, and other job characteristics.

jobs was conducted at Control Data Corporation. The result of this work is the Management Position Description Questionnaire (MPDQ).[13]

The MPDQ is a checklist of 208 items related to the concerns and responsibilities of managers. The latest version of the MPDQ is classified into 10 parts:[14]

1. General information.
2. Decision making.
3. Planning and organizing.
4. Supervising and controlling.
5. Consulting and innovating.
6. Contacts.
7. Monitoring business indicators.
8. Overall ratings.
9. Know-how.
10. Organization chart.

Part 6 of the MPDQ is presented in Exhibit 4–10. The job incumbent (manager) responds to the type of questions shown in Exhibit 4–10. These responses are then used to update job descriptions, identify career ladders and facilitate career planning, validate managerial performance appraisal scales, and explore new job evaluation methods.

There are many other specific job analysis techniques available. For the most part the FJA, PAQ, and MPDQ and other specific techniques are behavior oriented. They are designed to describe jobs in terms of standard behaviors. If a job analysis technique provides a reliable and valid quantitative score, jobs can be classified for such purposes as compensation, training, and career development. The quantification feature is an important reason why the FJA and PAQ techniques are so popular.

Instead by using one of the four job analysis techniques Tim Huggins decided to develop a tailor-made, six-page questionnaire for Sprowl. Whether his job analysis will yield reliable or valid data is an issue he should have considered. The opening case suggests that he really didn't do enough thinking about this issue before he started the job analysis program at Sprowl. What do you think? Will his haste to get started cause some problems?

Job Descriptions and Job Specifications

As previously mentioned, the job description (see Exhibit 4–2) is one of the outputs provided by a systematic job analysis. It provides a description of what the job entails. While there is no standard format for a job description, they usually include:

Job title. A title of the job. The *Dictionary of Occupational Titles* contains over 20,000 titles.

Job summary. A brief one- or two-sentence statement of what the job entails.

---

[13]Walter W. Tornow and Patrick R. Pinto, "The Development of a Managerial Job Taxonomy: A System for Describing, Classifying, and Evaluating Executive Positions," *Journal of Applied Psychology,* August 1976, pp. 410–18.

[14]Cascio and Awad, *Human Resource Management,* pp. 158–59.

Job activities. A description of the tasks performed, material used, and extent of supervision given or received.

Working conditions and physical environment. Heat, lighting, noise level, and hazardous conditions are described.

Social environment. Information on size of work group and interpersonal interaction required to perform the job.

Exhibit 4–11 presents a job description for a personnel/human resource manager.

The job specification shown in Exhibit 4–12 evolves from the job description. It addresses the question "What personal traits and experience are needed to perform the job effectively?" The job specification offers guidelines for recruitment and selection. For example, suppose that you were looking for a trained and experienced machinist. The job specification would probably indicate the need for formal training and previous work experience. If certain traits and experience are stated as requirements to perform a job they must be shown to be needed to do the work.

Federal and state legislation has placed new emphasis on job descriptions and job specifications. For example, the Equal Pay Act requires equal pay for all employees performing equal work (in terms of equal effort skill, ability, and working conditions). Therefore, the job description and job specification are consulted to determine compliance with the law. To the extent that job specifications (e.g., height, weight, educational requirements, etc.) are not essential for effective job performance, they may violate Title VII of the 1964 Civil Rights Act.

Job Design

The information provided by job analysis, job descriptions, and job specifications can be very useful in designing jobs; that is, structuring job elements, duties, and tasks in a manner to achieve optimal performance and satisfaction. There is no one best way to design any job. Different situations call for different arrangements of job characteristics. Two of the many available approaches to job design are the rational approach and job enrichment.

The Rational Approach   *Breakdown job for efficiency. Get boredom.*

Job design was central to the view of scientific management by F. W. Taylor. He stated:

> Perhaps the most prominent single element in modern scientific management is the task idea. The work of every workman is fully planned out by the management at least one day in advance, and each man receives in most cases complete written instructions, describing in detail the task which he is to accomplish. . . . This task specifies not only what is to be done but how it is to be done and the exact time allowed for doing it.[15]

The principles offered today by scientific management to job design remain today as follows:

- Work should be scientifically studied (note: this is what job analysis attempts to do).

---

[15]F. W. Taylor, *The Principles of Scientific Management* (New York: Harper & Row, 1911), p. 21.

Exhibit 4—10

Contacts

To achieve organizational goals, managers and consultants may be required to communicate with employees at many levels within the corporation and with influential people outside the corporation.

The purposes of these contacts may include such functions as:

- Informing
- Receiving information
- Influencing
- Promoting
- Selling
- Directing
- Coordinating
- Integrating
- Negotiating

DIRECTIONS:

Describe the nature of your contacts by completing the charts on the opposite page as follows:

STEP 1

Mark an "X" in the box to the left of the kinds of individuals that represent your major contacts internal and external to Control Date Corporation.

Step 2

For each contact checked, print a number between 0 and 4 in *each* column to indicate how significant a part of your position that PURPOSE is. (Remember to consider both its *importance* in light of all other position activities and its *frequency* of occurrence.)

0-**Definitely not** a part of the position.
1-A **minor** part of the position.
2-A **moderate** part of the position.
3-A **substantial** part of the position.
4-A **crucial** and **most significant** part of the position.

- - - - -

STEP 3

If you have any other contacts please elaborate on their nature and purpose below.

226 _____
_____
_____
_____
_____
_____
_____
_____
_____
_____

STEP 1   **STEP 2**

CONTACTS	PURPOSE

INTERNAL	Share information regarding past, present or anticipated activities or decisions	Influence others to act or decide in a manner consistent with my objectives	Direct and/or integrate the plans, activities, or decisions of others
Executive or senior vice president and above 159	167	175	183
Vice president 160	168	176	184
General/regional manager, director, or executive consultant 161	169	177	185
Department/district manager, or senior consultant 162	170	178	186
Section/branch manager or consultant 163	171	179	187
Unit manager 164	172	180	188
Exempt employees 165	173	181	189
Nonexempt employees 166	174	182	190

EXTERNAL	Provide, obtain or exchange information or advice.	Promote the organization or its products/ services.	Sell products/ services.	Negotiate contracts, settlements, etc.
Customers at a level equivalent to or above a Control Data general/regional manager 191	198	205	212	219
Customers at a level lower than a Control Data general/regional manager 192	199	206	213	220
Representatives of major suppliers, for example, joint ventures, subcontractors for major contracts 193	200	207	214	221
Employees of suppliers who provide Control Data with parts or services 194	201	208	215	222
Representatives of influential community organizations 195	202	209	216	223
Individuals such as applicants, stockholders 196	203	210	217	224
Representatives of federal or state governments such as defense contract auditors, government inspectors, etc. 197	204	211	218	225

Exhibit 4–11 _____

Job description of a manager

JOB TITLE: PERSONNEL/HUMAN   Department: P/HRM
            RESOURCE MANAGER   Date: Jan. 1, 1983

General Description of the Job

Performs responsible administrative work managing personnel activities of a large state agency or institution. Work involves responsibility for the planning and administration of a P/HRM program which includes recruitment, examination, selection, evaluation, appointment, promotion, transfer, and recommended change of status of agency employees, and a system of communication for disseminating necessary information to workers. Works under general supervision, exercising initiative and independent judgment in the performance of assigned tasks.

Job Activities

Participates in overall planning and policy making to provide effective and uniform personnel services.

Communicates policy through organization levels by bulletin, meetings, and personal contact.

Interviews applicants, evaluates qualifications, classifies applications

Recruits and screens applicants to fill vacancies and reviews applications of qualified persons

Confers with supervisors on personnel matters, including placement problems, retention or release of probationary employees, transfers, demotions, and dismissals of permanent employees.

Supervises administration of tests.

Initiates personnel training activities and coordinates these activities with work of officials and supervisors.

Establishes effective service rating system, trains unit supervisors in making employee evaluations.

Maintains employee personnel files.

Supervises a group of employees directly and through subordinates.

Performs related work as assigned.

_____

- Work should be arranged so that workers can be efficient.
- Employees selected for work should be matched to the demands of the job (note: job description and job specification used in recruitment and selection).
- Employees should be trained to perform the job.
- Monetary compensation should be used to reward successful performance of the job.

Exhibit 4–12 _____

Job specifications for personnel/human resource manager

General Qualification Requirements

Experience and Training
   Should have considerable experience in area of P/HRM administration. Six-year minimum.

Education
   Graduation from a four-year college or university, with major work in personnel, business administration, or industrial psychology.

Knowledge, Skills, and Abilities
   Considerable knowledge of principles and practices of P/HRM selection and assignment of personnel; job evaluation.

Responsibility
   Supervises a department of three P/HRM professionals, one clerk, and one secretary.

Although these scientific management principles were introduced around the early 1900s they are still significant today. The work of Taylor and scientific management principles initiated interest in research and studying jobs. For example, large research efforts have been devoted to analyzing jobs so that information is available for making rational recruitment, selection, training, compensation, and career development decisions.

Many managers find scientific management principles to job design appealing because they point toward increased organizational performance. Jobs designed according to the principles tend to be specialized (the job incumbent performs only a few duties) and routine (the same duties are repeated again and again). It is assumed that specialization and routineness result in job incumbents' becoming experts rather quickly. This then leads to high levels of output and only minimum training to master the job.

Despite the assumed gains in efficiency behavioral scientists have found that some job incumbents dislike specialized and routine jobs.[16] These workers are not challenged enough to satisfy their need for growth, recognition, and responsibility. When jobs are viewed in this way, workers often attempt to compensate by being absent, resorting to horseplay while on the job, and even quitting.

Thus, although scientific management has introduced important rational guidelines, the bottom line is that the principles do not work for all individuals. Likewise a program of job enrichment is suited for some employees but may be detrimental to other employees.

A Behavioral Approach: Job Enrichment

In the past two decades, much work has been directed to changing jobs so that job incumbents can satisfy their needs for growth, recognition, and responsibility. Herzberg's research popularized the notion of enhancing need satisfaction through what is called *job enrichment*.[17] There are many different approaches to job enrichment, yet all of them attempt to help the job incumbent satisfy personal needs while performing the job.

One widely publicized approach to job enrichment uses what is referred to as the *job characteristics model*.[18] The model is based on the view that three key psychological states of a job incumbent affect motivation and satisfaction on the job. The three states are:

1. *Experienced meaningfulness*. The degree to which the job incumbent experiences work as important, valuable, and worthwhile.
2. *Experiences responsibility*. The extent to which the job incumbent feels personally responsible and accountable for the results of the work performed.
3. *Knowledge of results*. The understanding that a job incumbent receives about how effectively he or she is performing the job.

---

[16]David A. Nadler, J. Richard Hackman, and Edward E. Lawler, III, *Managing Organizational Behavior* (Boston: Little, Brown, 1979), p. 79.

[17]F. Herzberg, B. Mausner, and B. Snyderman, *The Motivation to Work* (New York: John Wiley & Sons, 1959).

[18]J. Richard Hackman, "Work Design," In J. Richard Hackman and J. L. Suttle, *Improving Life at Work* (Santa Monica, Calif.: Goodyear Publishing, 1976), pp. 96–162.

Exhibit 4–13

Key job core dimensions

(handwritten note in left margin: "① meaningfulness", "②", "③", with arrows pointing to dimensions)

Skill variety	The degree to which the job requires a variety of different activities in carrying out the work, which involves the use of a number of an individual's skills and talents.
Task identity	The degree to which the job requires completion of a "whole" and identifiable piece of work—that is, doing a job from beginning to end with a visible outcome.
Task significance	The degree to which the job has a substantial impact on the lives or work of other people—whether in the immediate organization or in the external environment.
Autonomy	The degree to which the job provides substantial freedom, independence, and discretion to the individual in scheduling the work and in determining the procedures to be used in carrying it out.
Feedback	The degree to which carrying out the work activites required by the job results in the individual's obtaining direct and clear information about the effectiveness of his or her performance.

The more these three states are experienced, the more the job incumbent will feel internal work motivation. To the extent that these three states are important for the job incumbent, he or she will be motivated to perform well.

Research has indicated a number of core job dimensions that lead to these psychological states.[19] Exhibit 4–13 presents the five core job dimensions, while Exhibit 4–14 illustrates the job characteristics model.

As presented in Exhibit 4–13 three job dimensions—*skill variety, task identity,* and *task significance* all contribute to a sense of meaningfulness. *Autonomy* is directly related to feelings of responsibility. The more control job incumbents have over the job, the more they feel responsible. *Feedback* is related to knowledge of results.

The job characteristics model presents four sets of factors—core job dimensions, psychological states, personal and work outcomes, and need strength. Since different people have different capabilities and needs it is important to be aware of individual differences that can moderate the linkages shown in Exhibit 4–14. If a person does not have a need for growth, job enrichment in any or all of the job core dimensions will probably have little impact.

Work behavior and individual job incumbent feelings appear to be more positive where there is a fit between the job and the person. Exhibit 4–15 depicts the results of a match and mismatch between individuals and the job.[20] The managerial implication of Exhibit 4–15 is that not all jobs should be designed to be high on the core job dimensions, and that the personal traits and characteristics of the persons' holding the job must be considered. *Not all jobs can be made interesting.*

The job analysis, job description, and job specification can be extremely valuable in determining whether or not a job can be enriched on any of the five core job dimensions.

---

[19]J. Richard Hackman and R. G. Oldham, "Motivation through the Design of Work: Test of a Theory," *Organizational Behavior and Human Performance,* August 1976, pp. 250–79, and J. Richard Hackman, G. Oldham, R. Janson, and K. Purdy, "A New Strategy for Job Enrichment," *California Management Review,* Summer 1975, pp. 57–71.

[20]John P. Wanous, "Who Wants Job Enrichment?" *S.A.M. Advanced Management Journal,* Summer 1976, pp. 15–22.

Exhibit 4–14 _____

The job characteristics model of work motivation

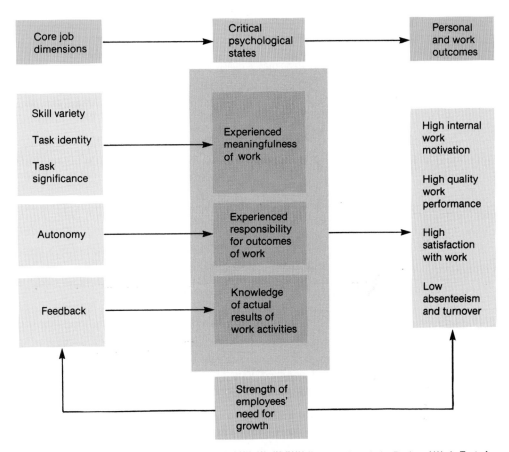

Source: Adapted from J. Richard Hackman and R. G. Oldham, "Motivation through the Design of Work: Test of a Theory," *Organizational Behavior and Human Performance*, August 1976, p. 256.

Thus, before job enrichment is even attempted two actions seem to be needed. First, the job has to be thoroughly understood. Job analysis can provide this needed information. Second, invididual preferences about job enrichment need to be considered. Do they want job enrichment? Can they tolerate an enriched job?

Prudential Life Insurances' Job Enrichment Program • The chief executive officer of Prudential decided that all jobs at Prudential should be made as interesting as possible. Each unit was charged with redesiging its own jobs with special attention to be paid to enrichment. The workers redesigned their jobs. The results were impressive:

- 57 percent of the units reported improvements in employee attitudes; only 4 percent indicated a deterioration.

Exhibit 4–15 _____

Degree of individual of job match

Degree of job enrichment	Intensity of desire for job enrichment	
	High	*Low*
Enriched	"Match" 1. Performance quality is high. 2. Satisfaction is high. 3. Absenteeism and turnover are low.	"Mismatch" 1. Employee is overwhelmed and possibly confused. 2. Performance is poor. 3. Absenteeism and turnover are high.
Simple	"Mismatch" 1. Employees feel underutilized. 2. Job satisfaction is low. 3. Absenteeism and turnover are high.	"Match" 1. Employees can be motivated by pay incentives in the absence of intrinsic motivation. 2. Performance is high.

- 31 percent of the units reported a decrease in turnover; only 5 percent reported an increase.
- 93 percent of the units indicate that the abilities of workers were being more fully utilized.
- Errors decreased in 50 percent of the units.[21]

General Food's Topeka Plant Job Enrichment Program • General Foods decided in 1968 to construct a new plant to manufacture pet foods. Management worked at designing a plant that contained enriched jobs—maximum variety, autonomy, and feedback.[22] The early resutls in the new plant were outstanding:

- Quality control improved.
- Turnover was down.
- Job attitudes were better than at other plants.
- Cost savings amounted to about $2 million per year.

These successes, however, began to fade about five or six years after the plant was built. One former employee noted

> Creating a system is different from maintaining it. There were pressures almost from the inception, and not because the system didn't work. The basic reason was power. We flexed in the face of corporate policy. People like stable states. This system has to be changing or it will die.

In fact, 70 workers ran the entire Topeka operation. The need for middle managers in the plant was eliminated. The result of the new plant arrangement was a power struggle of managers versus workers. Lyman Ketchum (the manager who had thought up the redesign experiment) was fired.

The Prudential experiment was a success, while the Topeka plant experiment with

_____

[21]James O'Toole, *Making America Work* (New York: Continuum, 1981), pp. 67–68.

[22]Richard E. Walton, "Teaching an Old Dog New Tricks," *Wharton Magazine*, Winter 1978, pp. 38–48.

job enrichment resulted in mixed findings—some successes and some failures. These two cases illustrate that job enrichment, or any redesign strategy, are not always successful. Some of the common problems with job enrichment reported in the literature include:

1. Technological constraints—the job simply can't be enriched because of machine constraints.
2. Costs. The costs of starting and sustaining job enrichment for tools, training, consultants is often high.
3. Failure to recognize job incumbent preferences—not everyone wants an enriched job.
4. Mickey Mouse changes—minor, insignificant changes in core dimensions are called job enrichment; they are so minor that they have no impact.
5. Managerial and union resistance—managers are sometimes threatened by increased subordinate autonomy. The union also may feel threatened because they see their power base shrinking.[23]

Job design is a process that influences the behavior and attitude of a job incumbent. The job is so important that it needs to be clearly understood, as well as modified in many situations. Jobs are not something that exist in a vacuum. They are dynamic and changing. Consequently, job analysis is an important technique that can capture the changing nature of jobs so that the best job design decisions can be made and implemented. P/HRM managers are involved in both job analysis decisions and decisions that reflect on job design. Exhibit 4–16 provides recommendations for use of job analysis and job design in terms of the model organizations.

Summary

This chapter has emphasized the major role that job analysis plays in P/HRM activities and programs. Each part of the diagnostic P/HRM model is in some way affected by job analysis. The job is the major building block of an organization. Therefore, it is essential that each characteristic of the jobs presence in an organization is clearly understood.

The chapter emphasized:

1. The six sequential steps in job analysis, starting with examining the total oranization and fit of jobs and concluding with the preparation of a job specification (see Exhibit 4–1).
2. The uses of job analysis information seems endless. Recruitment, selection, training, compensation, and job design actions all benefit immensely from job analysis information.
3. Job analysis is not for amateurs to conduct. Trained job analysts are worth their salaries and should be used.
4. Before conducting a job analysis, organization and process charts should be consulted to acquire an overview of the organization.
5. Four general job analysis techniques used separately or in some combination are observation, interviews, questionnaires, and job incumbent diary/logs.

---

[23]M. Fein, ''Job Enrichment: A Revolution,'' *Sloan Management Review,* Winter 1974, pp. 69–88; and E. A. Locke, D. Sirota, A. D. Wolfson, ''An Experimental Case Study of the Successes and Failures of Job Enrichment in a Government Agency,'' *Journal of Applied Psychology,* December 1976, pp. 701–11.

Exhibit 4–16

Recommendations for job analysis and job design for model organizations

Type of organization	Has a permanent job analysis unit	Use of JAIF-type instrument	Formal job analysis program	Observation method used	Interview method used	Questionnaire method used	Diary/log method used
1. Large size, low complexity, high stability		X	X		X	X	
2. Medium size, low complexity, high stability		X	X		X	X	
3. Small size, low complexity, high stability		X	X		X	X	X
4. Medium size, moderate complexity, moderate stability	X	X	X	X	X	X	
5. Large size, high complexity, low stability	X	X	X	X	X	X	
6. Medium size, high complexity, low stability	X	X	X	X	X	X	
7. Small size, high complexity, low stability		X	X	X	X	X	X

Case

Tim Huggins

What do you think now about Tim Huggins' job analysis process? He really acted like an amateur. Handing out questionnaires requires some careful preparation. The distribution of questionnaires without an explanation is bound to set off some negative feelings. Tim should have planned what he wanted to do. He was a new boss and this alone is threatening to many people. A new person has to establish some rapport before changing things. In the case of Sprowl Manufacturing, Tim's haste and poor preparation has now reached the boiling point. He needs to backtrack and slow down. Perhaps some memos, discussions with informal leaders, and working with job analysts can improve the atmosphere at Sprowl. What would you advise him to do about job analysis at this point?

6. Functional job analysis (FJA) is used to describe the nature of jobs, prepare job descriptions, and provide details on employee job specifications. The job is described in terms of data, people, and things.

7. The *Dictionary of Occupational Titles* is a listing of over 20,000 jobs on the basis of occupational code, title, industry.

8. The Position Analysis Questionnaire (PAQ) is a 194-item structured instrument used to quantitatively assess jobs on the basis of decision making, communication/social responsibilities, performing skilled activities, being physically active, operating vehicles and/or equipment, and processing information.

9. The Management Position Questionnaire (MPDQ) is a checklist of 208 items that assesses the concerns and responsibilities of managers.

10. Job design involves structuring job elements, duties, and tasks in a way to achieve optimal performance and satisfaction.

11. Job design was a concern of F. W. Taylor, the famous industrial engineer and father of what is called scientific management.

12. Job enrichment involves designing jobs so that job incumbent needs for growth, recognition, and responsibility are satisfied.

Questions for Review and Discussion

1. What role could job analysis play in the recruitment and selection of employees?

2. Are job descriptions the same as job specifications?

3. What is the difference between a job and an occupation?
4. What are the six major steps in the job analysis process?
5. Why would a manager be interested in using a combination of general job analysis techniques?
6. What is the problem with the claim that, "All jobs should be enriched?"
7. What is the job characteristics model?
8. It is claimed that "Job analysis is the cornerstone to all P/HRM activities." Do you agree? Explain.
9. Why is the PAQ considered a quantitative job analysis technique?
10. Should managerial jobs be subjected to job analysis? Why?

Glossary

Autonomy. The degree to which the job provides substantial freedom, independence, and discretion to the individual in scheduling the work and in determining the procedures to be used in carrying it out.

Feedback. The degree to which carrying out the work activities required by the job results in the individual's obtaining direct and clear information about the effectiveness of his or her performance.

Functional Job Analysis (FJA). A job analysis method that attempts to identify what a worker does in performing a job in terms of data, people, and things.

Job. A group of positions that are similar in their duties, such as a computer programmer or compensation specialist.

A Job Analysis. The process of defining a job in terms of tasks or behaviors and specifying the education, training, and responsibilities needed to perform the job successfully.

Job Analysis Information Format. A questionnaire that provides the basic core information about a job, job duties, and job requirements.

Job Characteristics Model. A model of job design that is based on the view that three psychological states toward a job affect a person's motivation and satisfaction level. These states are experienced meaningfulness, experienced responsibility, and knowledge of results. A job's skill variety, identity, and task significance contribute to meaningfulness; autonomy is related to responsiblity; and feedback is related to knowledge of results.

Job Description. The job analysis provides information about the job that results in a description of what the job entails.

Job Enrichment. A method of designing a job so that employees can satisfy needs while performing the job. The job characteristics model is used in establishing a job enrichment strategy.

Job Family. A group of two or more jobs that have similar job duties.

Job Specification. The job analysis also results in the specification of what kind of traits and experience are needed to perform the job.

Management Position Description Questionnaire (MPDQ). A checklist of 208 items related to concerns and responsibilities of managers.

Position. Consists of responsibilities and duties performed by an individual. There are as many positions as there are employees.

Position Analysis Questionnaire (PAQ). A structured questionnarie of 194 items used to quantitatively assess jobs. It assesses information input, mental processes, work output, relationships, job contacts, and various other characteristics.

Process Chart. A chart that displays how jobs are linked or related to each other.

Skill Variety. The degree to which the job requires a variety of different activities in carrying out the work, which involves the use of a number of an individual's skills and talents.

Task. A coordinated and aggregated series of work elements used to produce an output (e.g., units of production or service to a client).

Task Identity. The degree to which the job requires completion of a "whole" and identifiable piece of work—that is, doing a job from beginning to end with a visible outcome.

Task Significance. The degree to which the job has a substantial impact on the lives or work of other people—whether in the immediate organization or in the external environment.

Chapter Five

Planning

Case

Ted Sloane and Anne Wilson

"What do you mean we're going to lose the government contract?" asked the company president, Ted Sloane.

"We're going to lose it," said the personnel/human resource management vice president, Anne Wilson. "We don't have trained personnel to meet the contract specifications. We have to furnish records to show that we have an adequate number of employees with the right technical qualifications who meet the government's equal employment opportu-

nity goals. I don't have those kinds of records available at a moment's notice. You know I asked you to let me set up a computerized personnel planning information system, and we never got around to it."

Ted was like a ball lost in high weeds. He didn't know what Anne had in mind. Everything he ever heard about computer systems suggested that they were expensive and complex. He wanted to learn more about computerized planning systems.

Experiences like Ted's, described above, are common and suggest that many managers fail to plan for human resource needs. They never know what their needs are because they neglect personnel and employment planning (called human resource planning by some).

> Personnel and employment planning is the process which helps to provide adequate human resources to achieve future organizational objectives. It includes forecasting future needs for employees of various types; comparing these needs with the present work force, and determining the numbers and types of employees to be recruited or phased out of the organization's employment group.

People have always asked: "How do I get promoted? When will I be promoted? Will I have to relocate to be promoted? What is my future going to be?[1] Personnel and employment planning is a process that provides answers to these questions. Employees should know about the opportunities, plans, and development programs that exist for them.

---

[1]See Charles F. Russ, Jr., "Manpower Planning Systems: Part I," *Personnel Journal*, January 1982, pp. 40–45, and Charles F. Russ, Jr., "Manpower Planning Systems: Part II," *Personnel Journal*, February 1982, pp. 119–124.

Introduction to Personnel and Employment Planning

Exhibit 5–1 models the personnel and employment planning process. As the model indicates, top management examines the environment, analyzes the strategic advantages of the organization, and sets objectives for the coming period. Then the manager makes strategic and operating decisions to achieve the objectives of the organization. The P/HRM capabilities of the organization are among the factors analyzed in the strategic management process. An example of a strategic decision is General Electric's decision to sell its computer business. This meant that General Electric's supply of employees was cut when the business was sold to another company.

Once the strategy is set, the P/HRM unit does its part to assure its success and to achieve the organization's objectives. It does this by comparing the present supply of human resources with projected demand for them. This comparison leads to action decisions: add employees, cut employees, or reallocate employees internally.

Reasons for Personnel and Employment Planning

All organizations perform personnel planning, formally or informally. The formal employment techniques are described in this chapter because information methods are typically unsatisfactory for organizations requiring skilled human resources in a fast-changing

Exhibit 5–1 _____

The personnel and employment planning process

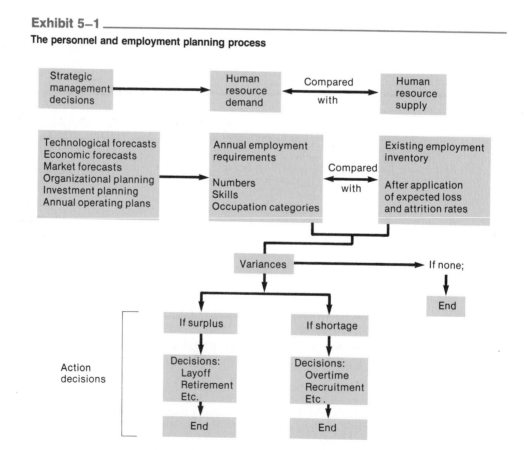

labor market. It is important to point out that most organizations do more talking about formal employment planning than actual performance.[2] Presently, only a minority of organizations actually engage in formal employment planning. Therefore, personnel and employment planning as a P/HRM activity is in Stage II of development, or early development (see Exhibit 1–2).

The major reasons for formal employment planning are to achieve:

- More effective and efficient use of human resources.
- More satisfied and better developed employees.
- More effective equal employment opportunity planning.

More Effective and Efficient Use of People at Work • Employment planning should precede all other P/HRM activities. For example, how could you schedule recruiting if you did not know how many people you needed? How could you select effectively if you did not know the kinds of persons needed for job openings? Careful analysis of all P/HRM activities shows that their effectiveness and efficiency, which result in increased productivity, depend on employment planning.

More Satisfied and Better Developed Employees • Employees who work for organizations that use good employment planning systems have a better chance to participate in planning their own careers and to share in training and development experiences. Thus they are likely to feel their talents are important to the employer, and they have a better chance to utilize those talents. This often leads to greater employee satisfaction and its consequences: lower absenteeism, lower turnover, fewer accidents, and higher quality of work.

More Effective EEO Planning • As pointed out frequently in this book, government has increased its demands for equal employment opportunities. Information systems that focus on personnel and employment planning help organizations formally plan employment distribution. Therefore, it is easier to complete the required government reports and respond satisfactorily to EEO demands using personnel and employment planning.[3]

In sum, effective employment planning assures that P/HRM activities and programs will be built on a foundation of good planning. This should cut down on the number of surprises that occur involving human resource availability, placement, and orientation. Not having the right person in the right place at a particular moment is a surprise and usually a problem. These kinds of surprises can be reduced through effective personnel and employment planning.

Who Performs the Planning?

Effectiveness in P/HRM activities requires the efforts and cooperation of P/HRM managers and operating managers. The activities described in this chapter are outlined in Exhibit 5–2, which shows the kind of planning activities that are performed by operating and by P/HRM managers.

---

[2]W. S. Wikstrom, "Manpower Planning: Evolving Systems," Report no. 521 (New York: Conference Board, 1971).

[3]A. Charnes, W. W. Cooper, K. A. Lewis, and R. J. Niehaus, "Equal Employment Opportunity Planning and Staffing Models," *Human Resource Planning,* Spring 1978, pp. 103–112.

Exhibit 5–2

Personnel and employment planning activities performed by P/HRM and operating managers

Personnel and employment planning activities	Operating manager (OM)	P/HRM manager
Strategic management decisions	Performed by OM with inputs from P/HRM	Provides information inputs for OM
Forecasting demands		Performed by P/HRM based on strategic management decisions
Job analysis	Provides information inputs for P/HRM	Performed by P/HRM with information inputs from OM
Analysis of supply of employees	Provides information inputs for P/HRM	Performed by P/HRM with information inputs from OM
Work scheduling decisions	Joint responsibility	Joint responsibility
Action decision: Analyzing the composition of the work force		Performed by P/HRM
Action decision: Shortage of employees	Provides information inputs for P/HRM	Performed by P/HRM with information inputs from OM
Action decision: Surplus of employees	Policy decisions by OM with inputs from P/HRM	Implementation decisions by P/HRM

A Diagnostic Approach to Personnel and Employment Planning

Exhibit 5–3 highlights the factors in the diagnostic model that are most important to planning. One of the most significant factors affecting planning is the goals of the controlling interests in the organization. If planning and effective utilization of human resources are not a significant goal for the organization, employment planning will not be performed formally, or it will be done in a slipshod manner. If the goals of top management include stable growth, employment planning will be less important than if the goals include rapid expansion, diversification, or other factors with a significant impact on future employment needs.

Government policies are another important factor in planning. Requirements for equal employment opportunity and promotion call for more personnel planning for women and other employees in minority groups and special categories. Other examples are the government's raising the age of mandatory retirement and the encouragement of hiring handicapped employees and veterans (see Chapter 3).

The conditions in the labor market also have a significant impact on the amount and type of employment planning done in an enterprise. For example, when there was 23 percent unemployment in the city of Grand Rapids, Michigan, in the fall of 1982, an employer had more hiring flexibility than when there was 7 percent unemployment in Houston, Texas.

To a lesser extent than the government, unions may restrict the ability to hire and promote employees, so they, too, are a factor in planning. In discussing the planning activity it is more realistic to take into consideration the important role played by the segments highlighted in Exhibit 5–3.

The types of people employed and the tasks they do also determine the kind of planning necessary. Needs for unskilled employees do not have to be planned two years ahead; but computer salespersons, for example, need years of training before coming on track. Planning for highly skilled employees usually require more care and forecasting.

Exhibit 5–3

Factors affecting personnel and employment planning and effectiveness

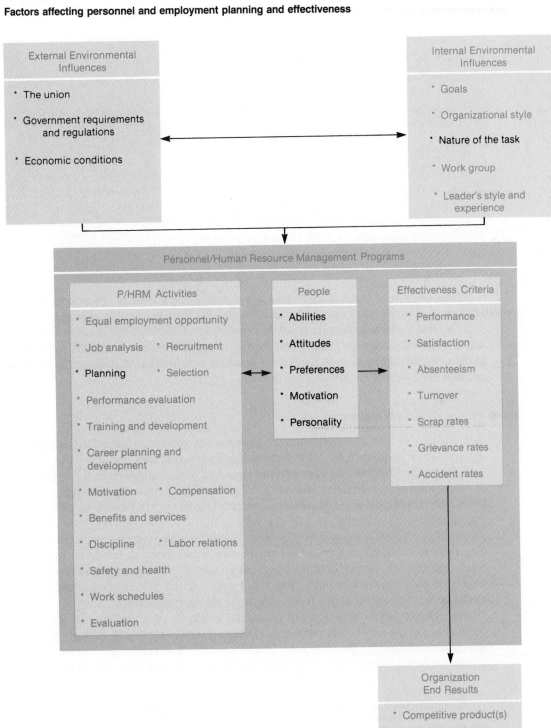

Forecasting Future Demand for Employees

> Scene: Board meeting at the Acme Publishing Company.
>
> *George Slone* (chairman and chief executive) Exhibit A is our planned budget and our objectives for next year. I'd appreciate your comments.
>
> *Martha Kemp* (outside director) George, I note that overall, you are projecting a modest growth trend for next year. You also have had a series of increased worker productivity projects going to cut employee costs. Just how many people will you employ next year to reach your sales and profit objectives?"
>
> *George:* That's a good question. Martha. I don't know exactly. John, what's the answer?
>
> *John Arturo* (vice president, personnel) That's hard to say. It depends on lots of factors.
>
> *Martha:* Frankly, John, that's not much of an answer. I can look at the figures in this exhibit and see how much money we need. The marketing people tell me how many units they are going to sell. Why can't you tell me how many people we'll need to get the job done—our people-cost figure?

John could have answered Martha's question if Acme's P/HRM department had developed an effective employee forecasting system—the first element of a planning system.

The employment requirements of an organization flow from the strategic decisions made by its top managers. Simply put, the top manager combines economic, technological, and market forecasts with investment planning to help P/HRM calculate the number of employees needed by skill and occupational categories.

Employment Forecasting Techniques

Essentially there are three organizational approaches to employment forecasting. The headquarters can forecast the total demand (top-down approach); the units can forecast their own demand (bottom-up approach); or there can be a combination of the other two.[4]

Four forecasting techniques will be described here: three top-down techniques—expert estimate, trend projection, and modeling—and the bottom-up unit-forecasting technique.

The Expert-Estimate Technique • The least sophisticated approach to employment planning is for an "expert" to forecast the employment needs based on her or his own experience and intuition. The P/HRM manager may do this by thinking about past employment levels and questioning future needs, which is a quite informal system. The expert-estimate technique can be more effective if the experts use the Delphi technique.

The Delphi technique is a set of procedures originally developed by the Rand Corporation in the late 1940s.[5] Its purpose is to obtain the most reliable consensus of opinion of a group of experts. Basically, the Delphi consists of intensive questioning of each expert, through a series of questionnaires, to obtain the desired data. The procedures are

---

[4]D. J. Bartholomew, ed., *Manpower Planning* (Harmandsworth, Eng.: Penguin Books, 1976). Also see Kendrith M. Rowland and Scott L. Summers, "Human Resource Planning: A Second Look," *Personnel Administrator,* December 1981, pp. 73–80.

[5]N. Dalkey, *The Delphi Method: An Experimental Study of Group Opinion* (Santa Monica, Calif. RAND, 1969.

designed to avoid direct meetings between the experts in order to maximize independent thinking.

A person who serves as intermediary in the questioning sends out the questionnaries to the experts and asks them to give, for example, their best estimates of employment needs for the coming year. The intermediary prepares a summary of the results, calculating the average response and the most extreme answers. Then the experts are asked to estimate the number again. Usually the questionnaires and responses tend to narrow down over these rounds. The average number is then used as the forecast.

A forecast by a single expert is the most frequently used approach to forecasting employment. It works well in small- and middle-sized enterprises which are in stable environments. The Delphi technique improves these estimates in larger and more volatile organizations.

← info obsolete quickly if fads.

The Trend Projection Technique • The second technique is to develop a forecast based on a past relationship between a factor related to employment and employment itself. For example, in many businesses, sales levels are related to employment needs. The planner can develop a table or graph showing past relationships between sales and employment. Exhibit 5–4 gives an example of a trend projection forecast for a hypothetical company, Rugby Sporting Goods Company. Note that as Rugby's sales increased, so did the firm's employment needs. But the increases were not linear. Suppose that in late 1979, Rugby instituted a productivity plan which led to 3 percent increased productivity per year. As Rugby forecasted employee needs, it adjusted them for expected productivity gains for 1983 and 1984.

Trend projection is a frequently used technique, though not as widely used as expert-estimate or unit demand. It is also an inexpensive way to forecast employment needs.

Modeling and Multiple-Predictive Techniques • The third top-down approach to prediction of demand uses the most sophisticated forecasting and modeling techniques. Trend projections are based on relating a single factor (such as sales) to employment. The more advanced approaches related many factors to employment, such as sales, gross national product, and discretionary income. Or they mathematically model the organization and use simulations, utilizing such methods as Markov models and analytical formulations.

Exhibit 5–4 _____

Sample trend protection employment forecast for Rugby Sporting Goods Company

Year	Sales	Employee census	Employee forecast adjusted for annual productivity rate increase of 3 percent
Actual data			
1979	$100,000,000	5,000	5,000
1980	120,000,000	6,000	5,825
1981	140,000,000	7,000	6,598
1982	160,000,000	8,000	7,321
	Sales forecast	Employee forecast	
Forecast			
1983	$180,000,000	9,000	7,996
1984	200,000,000	10,000	8,626

These are the most costly approaches to employment forecasting because of the cost of computer time and salaries of highly paid experts to design the models.

The use of the Markov chain analysis involves developing a matrix. This matrix would show the probability of an employee moving from one position to another or leaving the organization. A full treatment of P/HRM applications of Markov analysis is found in management science or operations management literature.[6]

In a public accounting firm, Markov analysis was used to calculate the length of time a person would spend at a particular job if he or she entered the firm at various levels. It was determined by use of statistical analysis and probabilities that if a person entered a firm as a junior (title), he or she would spend on the average 2.4 years as a junior, 1.4 years as a senior, 1.3 years as a manager, and about 1.3 years as a partner. This type of tenure expectation data was then used as a source of information to make recruitment and selection plans. Exhibit 5–5 summarizes the results of the Markov chain analysis calculations.

The Unit Demand Forecasting Technique • The unit (e.g., a unit may be an entire department, a project team, or some other group of employees) forecast is a bottom-up approach to forecasting demand. Headquarters sums these unit forecasts and the result becomes the employment forecast. The unit manager analyzes the person-by-person, job-by-job needs in the present as well as the future.

By analyzing present and future requirements on the job, and the skills of the incum-

---

Bill Foster (vice president, personnel) John, Bill Foster here. We're trying to get our forecast for employment needs together for next year so that we can get it into the budget. Will you get your net needs for next budget year to me by the end of the week? Use Form EP-1—it has a place for present employees in each of your units, less retirements, plus new employees needed for new business. Thanks!

John Jones (manager, division 1) Bill, I'll get right on it.

Exhibit 5–5 _____

Markov chain analysis results for planning decision

Number of Years Spent at This Level:

Junior	Senior	Manager	Partner		
2.4	1.4	1.3	1.3	Junior	
0	2.3	2.1	2.1	Senior	
0	0	5.4	5.4	Manager	Level when
0	0	0	22.9	Partner	entering firm

Note: A person who entered the firm as, say, a junior, would spend 2.4 years as a junior, 1.4 as a senior, 1.3 as a manager, and 1.3 as a partner. This information, in turn, can help a firm plan its human resource needs, by showing how many juniors, etc. must be hired if the firm knows it will need, say, 10 partners five years from today.

---

[6]Richard I. Levin and Charles A. Kirkpatrick, *Quantitative Approaches to Management* (New York: McGraw-Hill, 1980).

bents, this method focuses on quality of workers. Often it is initiated by a letter or a phone call.

Usually the manager will start with a list of the jobs in the unit by name. This list will also record the number of jobholders for each job. The manager evaluates both the numbers and skills of the present personnel. Consideration is given to the effects of expected losses through retirement, promotion, or other reasons. Whether the losses will require replacement and what the projected growth needs will be are questions the manager must answer and project into his or her calculations in determining net employment needs.

A manager's evaluation that is based on the present number of employees has two assumptions built into it: (1) that the best use has been made of the available personnel, and (2) that demand for the product or service of the unit will be the same for next year as this. With regard to the first assumption, the manager can examine the job design and workload of each employee. The manager may also attempt to judge the productivity of the employees in the unit by comparing the cost per product or service produced with those of similar units in the organization and others. Past productivity rates can be compared with present ones, after adjusting for changes in the job; or subjective evaluations can be made of the productivity of certain employees compared to others. In addition, it may be necessary to base employment needs on work force analysis, with adjustments for current data on absenteeism and turnover.

The unit analyzes its product or service demand by projecting trends. Using methods similar to the trend technique for the organization, the unit determines if it may need more employees because of a change in product or service demand. Finally, the unit manager prepares an estimate of total employment needs and plans for how the unit can fulfill these needs.

In larger organizations a P/HRM executive at headquarters who is responsible for the employment demand forecast will improve the estimates by checking with P/HRM and operating managers in the field. If the units forecast their own needs, the P/HRM executive sums their estimates, then this becomes the forecast. What happens if both the bottom-up and top-down approaches are used, and the forecasts conflict? In all probability, the manager reconciles the two totals by averaging them or examining more closely the major variances between the two. The Delphi technique could be used to do this. One or several forecast techniques can be used to produce a single employment forecast.

In the employment-demand forecasting aspect of employment planning, the bottom-up or unit-forecasting method calls for each unit to determine the number of people needed to accomplish the unit's objectives. The basic building blocks of this forecast is the number of jobs to be filled. The number of jobs in a unit can be reduced by more efficient job design, as discussed in Chapter 4. Recall that closely related to job design are job information procedures. Information about jobs is derived from job analysis, job description, and job specifications.

Analysis of the Supply of Present Employees *2 major probs – shortage of emp, overage of emp (RIF)*

After a manager has projected the employment needs of the organization, the next step in planning is to determine the availability of those presently at work in it—the supply of employees. On the basis of strategic management decisions, the P/HRM manager compares the demand for people needed to achieve the enterprise's objectives with the present supply of people to determine the need to hire, lay off, promote, or train. These are the *action decisions*.[7] The major tool of analysis used to compute employment supply is the *skills inventory*. In some enterprises, a separate skills inventory, called a management inventory, is developed just for the managerial employees.

This is one example of the uses of a skills inventory within an organization. There are many others. If the firm has a computerized skills inventory, Marjorie can give Howard an answer quickly. If there is no such inventory, she will have to call or write a lot of people and ask about many prospects.

Good skills inventories enable organizations to determine quickly and expediently what kinds of people with specific skills are presently available, whenever they decide to expand to accept new contracts or change their strategies. It is also useful in planning for training, management development, promotion, transfer, and related personnel activities.

A skills inventory in its simplest form is a list of the names, certain characteristics, and skills of the people working for the organization. It provides a way to acquire these data and makes them available where needed in an efficient manner.

For a small organization, it is relatively easy to know how many employees there are, what they do, and what they can do. A mom-and-pop grocery store may employ only the owners and have two part-time helpers to "plan" for. When they see that one part-time employee is going to graduate in June, they know they need to replace him. Sources of supply could include their own children, converting their other part-time helper into a full-time assistant, or the school's employment office.

It is quite a different situation with a school system employing hundreds at numerous locations, or such mammoth organizations as Procter & Gamble and IBM. These kinds of organizations must know how many full-time and peripheral employees they have working for them, and where. They must know what skills prospective employees would need to replace people who have quit, retired, or have been fired, or to relocate employees for new functions or more work.

The methods for handling such a challenge range from simple records on three-by-five inch index cards to sophisticated statistical and mathematical techniques such as sim-

---

Marjorie Lancer is vice president of personnel in a medium-sized firm. One of the division vice presidents, Howard Cantobello, calls her on the phone and says, after some small talk, "Marge, we've decided to enter the Latin American market and we need a person who has 10 years' experience, and a degree in industrial engineering and who can speak Spanish. Before I go outside, why not check to see if we have a person like that who might be interested in a job in our division. We can make it worthwhile financially, and the sky's the limit on promotions." Marjorie agrees to see what she can do.

---

[7]George T. Milkovich and Thomas A. Mahoney, "Human Resource Planning Models: A Perspective, *Human Resource Planning,* Spring 1978, pp. 19–30.

ulation and Markov chain analysis.[8] But the basic tool for assessing the supply of people and talents available within the organization is the skills inventory. Skills inventory tools can range from simple pieces of paper, forms, and three-by-five inch index cards to sophisticated computer information systems. The degree of sophistication necessary is related to the size, complexity, and volatility of the organization.

In smaller manual systems of skills inventories, the data are entered on cards, the more advanced cards having notches or loops which can be ''pulled'' by the use of long metal bars (Cardex). Thus, if an organization wants to get a list of employees speaking French fluently, it pulls all the cards notched at a particular place or with loop 15, for example, on the card. If there are multiple criteria, this subset is then checked for the next characteristic. This can also be done with summary overlays: all those with certain characteristics are punched onto cards; several of these summary cards are laid atop one another, and only those still visible on the last overlay fit the criteria for selection.

At the other extreme are very complex and sophisticated systems. Organizations such as IBM, RCA, and the U.S. Civil Service Commission and others have computerized inventories that allow them to plan employees' careers and define their business and other facts using these systems.

In the organization that maintains records and qualifications of thousands of employees a manual system is not efficient or even feasible. Thus, to deal with the need to plan for human resource needs, companies such as IBM have computerized their employment planning systems. The IBM system is called IRIS (IBM recruiting information system). Employees complete a booklet periodically called a data-pak. They answer questions about age, experience, education, skills, and qualifications. When there is a need to fill a vacancy, a manager describes the position and what he or she is looking for in terms of individual qualifications. The manager's requirements are entered into the computer. The IRIS system is used to match available candidates for the position described by the manager. The manager would then receive a computer listing of possible candidates.[9]

Another device that is less sophisticated then an IRIS-type system is the *replacement chart*. The replacement chart is used primarily with technical, professional, and managerial employees. It is a display of summary data about individuals currently in the organization. They are concise maps that can be readily reviewed to pinpoint potential problem areas in terms of exployment planning.

Exhibit 5–6 presents a replacement chart that can be easily reviewed by Wiley Department Store managers. This chart provides a lot of information about individuals in the organization in terms of age, performance, and tenure. This type of information can be combined with more extensive background data on each of the individuals shown on the chart to make planning decisions.

More on Skills Inventory Systems

Suppose that a manager decides that because of costs a skills inventory system will be used. The challenge facing the manager is what data the system should contain. An organization can only retrieve what is designed into the system.

---

[8]H. G. Heneman, III., and M. G. Sandver, ''Markov Analysis in human resource Administration,'' *Academy of Management Review,* October 1977, pp. 535–42.

[9]Gary Dessler, *Personnel Management* (Reston, Va.: Reston Publihing, 1981), p. 102.

Exhibit 5–6

Replacement chart: Wiley Department Stores

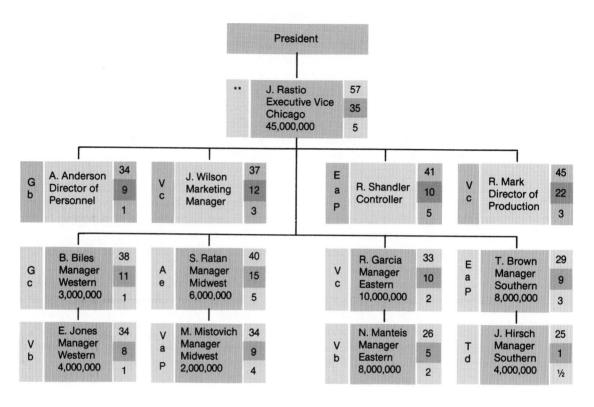

The list of data coded into skills inventories is almost endless, and it must be tailored to the needs of each organization. Some of the more common items include: name, employee number, present location, date of birth, date of employment, job classification or code, prior experience, history of work experience in the organization, specific skills and knowledge, education, field of education (formal education and courses taken since leaving school), knowledge of a foreign language, health, professional qualifications, publications, licenses, patents, hobbies, a supervisory evaluation of the employee's capabilities, and salary range. Items often omitted, but becoming increasingly important, are the employee's own stated career goals and objectives, including geographical preferences and intended retirement date.

Skills inventory data serve to identify employees for specific assignments which will

5. Performance and Potential Codes	1. Name 2. Title 3. Store Name and Classification 4. Volume	6. Age 7. Length of Service 8. Time in Job

1. Name—first name/middle initial/last name.
2. Title—Example: Mgr.,
3. Store Name and Classification.
4. Total sales volume in region.
5. Performance and Potential Codes (see below).
6. Age in years.
7. Length of service—number of years of unbroken service with company.
8. Time in job—number of years in current position.

	PERFORMANCE CODE	POTENTIAL CODE
E—Excellent	—Represents the top 10% of all executives in all categories.	a. Promotable now. One of two subdesignations must be made: P—"up"—will indicate readiness for promotion to a higher level. L—"lateral"—will indicate readiness for lateral promotion or transfer.
V—Very good	—Represents upper 25% in performance and generally indicates a high level of achievement of objectives.	
G—Good	—Represents the level of performance expected from most of our experienced executives and indicates upper-middlelevels of performance.	b. Promotable within two years or less. c. Potentially promotable—time uncertain. d. Potential good, but at present level only. e. Potential and future is questionable.
A—Adequate	—Represents the minimum level of performance that is acceptable under usual circumstances.	
U—Unsatisfactory	—Represents an unsatisfactory level of performance and indicates that failure to improve will result in termination or change of position.	
T—Too new to rate.		

fulfill not only organizational objectives but individual ones as well. Exhibit 5–7 is an example of the summarization of data from the forms used on a skills inventory, either computerized or manual. These summary cards provide the data that are used in assessing and analyzing the supply of people working for the organization.

Maintaining the Skills Inventory

While designing the system is the most difficult part of developing a skills inventory, planning for the gathering, maintaining, handling, and updating of data is also important. The two principal methods for gathering data are the interview and the questionnaire. Each method has unique costs and benefits. The questionnaire is faster and less expensive

Exhibit 5–7

Skills inventory summary card

NAME	DIV.	DEPT.	CLOCK	GROUP	SERIAL NO.	

QUALIFICATIONS INVENTORY SUMMARY CARD

I. A. EXPERIENCE CODES — YRS.
1.
2.
3.
4.
5.
6.

II. FOREIGN LANGUAGE CODES
1.
2.
3.
4.
5.

III. A. EDUCATION

	DEGREE CODES	MAJOR CODES	YEAR OF DEGREE	COLLEGE CODES
1.				
2.				
3.				
4.				

III. B. YEARS OF COLLEGE

CIRCLE EQUIVALENT TO FULL YEARS OF COLLEGE COMPLETED

0, 1, 2, 3, 4, 5, 6, 7, 7+

I. B. UNCODED EXPERIENCE — YRS.

Source: *W. Barnes, Identifying Manpower Potential* (New York: AMACOM, a division of American Management Associations, 1963).

when many employees are involved, but inaccuracies often prevail. People often do not spend enough time on a questionnaire. There are those who contend, therefore, that the trained interviewer can complete the reports more quickly and accurately, a procedure which in the long run more than offsets the costs of the interviewer.

A procedure for keeping the files updated also must be planned. The procedure depends on the frequency of change and the uses of the data. For some organizations, an annual update is adequate. In others, where changes are made often and use is frequent, shorter update periods may be necessary. Some organizations make provisions for monthly updating of changeable data and annual checks for less changeable data. One method is to include updating forms in payroll envelopes.

Finally a decision whether to store the data manually or on the computer must be made. This decision is based on costs of the computer and frequency of use of the data. The computer also provides the possibility of using comparative analyses of employment over a period of time.

Skills inventories are useful only if management uses the data in making significant decisions. Top management's support is necessary here. Before a manager uses the skills inventory for help in selection decisions, he or she must be trained to avoid system abuse. Examples of these are:

- Making requests simply on the basis that "it would be nice to know."
- Making requests for searches which are not backed up by bona fide requisitions that have been budgeted.
- Specifying too many characteristics for a desired employee so that no one fits all the characteristics.

As an example of the third type of abuse, consider the following request of a skills inventory system:

Wanted—A person with the following qualifications: B.S. in business, experience in finance and marketing, with at least two years with the company and making less than $20,000 per year.

Assume that the organization has 1,000 employees. The chance of finding a person with all these characteristics is the product of the percent of probability in each category. Thus if 20 percent of the 1,000 have a B.A. in business; 10 percent have experience in finance; 10 percent have experience in marketing; 70 percent have two years or more seniority; and 20 percent make more than $20,000, the chance of finding such a person is $0.20 \times 0.10 \times 0.70 \times 0.20$, or 0.0003, or less than one chance in a thousand. Those who set requirements must recognize that being overly specific reduces the chance of finding any suitable employee.

Action Decisions in Personnel and Employment Planning

There are several managerial decisions to be made once demand for people has been forecast and compared to supply. Exhibit 5–8 presents a more detailed outline of the action decisions. Another action decision which is not shown in the figure is increasingly important today: analyzing the work force to comply with government equal employment opportunity programs. We will discuss this problem first.

Exhibit 5–8

Employment planning action decisions

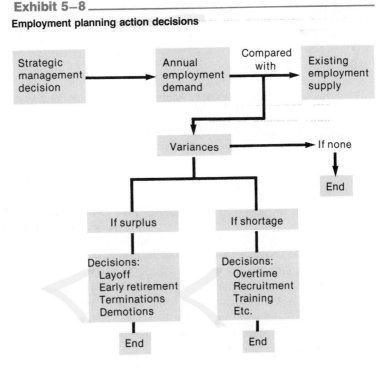

Analyzing the Composition of the Work Force

The extent to which the work force of an organization approximates the composition of the total work force for the area is an essential consideration in EEO programs. As stated in Chapter 3, government agencies enforce the EEO laws. The makeup of the present labor force in the United States and some discrepancies between the ideal of equal employment opportunity and the reality of these opportunities for certain groups was described in Chapter 2.

The organization must keep records of the distribution of employees by categories, levels (top management, professional, operative, and so on), and pay groups. If the statistics show that the organization's employment patterns are substantially different from the overall population in its geographic areas and by employment category, the employer is vulnerable to EEO legal action. This brings the threat of back-pay liability, mandatory hiring goals for women and minorities, and the like. Many socially responsible employers have voluntarily tried to improve the employment opportunities of these groups.

Antidiscriminatory programs enforced by government or promoted by popular opinion make it essential for the employer to examine the distribution of employees in protected categories (race, sex, and so on) at all levels to see if the organization has *in fact* discriminated against any group in its hiring and promotion practices. The organization cannot discriminate against any group solely on the basis of their personal characteristics. The purpose of this analysis is to assure that all potential employees of equal ability have an equal chance at hiring and promotion and other rewards. The specific programs used for analysis of these items will be discussed throughout the book.

Action Decisions with No Variance in Supply and Demand

It is possible for the organization, after matching the demand for employees with the supply at hand, to find that previous planning has been so excellent that the demand is matched exactly with the supply. In this case employment planning has served its purpose well in helping the organization to meet its objectives.

An exact match is rare. More frequently the total supply is correct, but there are variances in subgroups. These data become inputs to facilitate decisions about training, promotion, demotion, and similar decisions. Thus Exhibit 5–8 shows "end" if there are no variances, but the process may not end. It may require additional P/HRM decisions.

Action Decisions with a Shortage of Employees

affects efficiency
Do cost benefit analysis. If they can produce
profit, pay them whatever is required.

When employment specialists comparing demand to supply find the supply of workers is less than the demand, several possibilities are open to the organization. If the shortage is small and employees are willing to work overtime, it can be filled with present employees. If the shortage is of higher skilled employees, training and promotions of present employees, together with recruitment of lower skilled employees, are a possibility. This decision can also include recalling previously laid-off employees. Outside the organization, additional employees can be hired, either part time or full time, or some of the work can be contracted out to other organizations.

P/HRM Managers Close-Up

Paul S. Bernius
Hilti, Inc.

Biography

Paul S. Bernius has been director, manpower planning and development since joining Hilti, Inc., in 1979. Previously he held several positions with Sea-Land Service, Inc., a subsidiary of R. J. Reynolds Industries, including director, personnel administra-

tion and employee relations; manager, training and development; and manager, personnel services (European Division). From 1967 to 1972 he did extensive personnel administration and employee relations work with Standard Oil Company of California.

Bernius received a B.A. degree in sociology and psychology from St. Francis College in 1965. He later received a M.A. degree in Human Resource Development from the New School for Social Research in 1975.

Job description

As director, manpower planning and development, Paul S. Bernius is responsible for the acquisition and development of human resources necessary for Hilti, Inc., to achieve its business objectives. This work is accomplished through a staff of 16 professionals and includes activities such as labor force planning, recruiting, management development, succession planning, organization development, as well as the development of a broad range of programs aimed at increasing employee productivity.

Action Decisions in Surplus Conditions *affects efficiency & profit. Dysfunctional conflict betw competing employees.*

When comparison of employee demand and supply indicates a surplus, the alternative solutions include attrition, early retirements, demotions, layoffs, and terminations. Surplus employee decisions are some of the most difficult decisions managers must make, because the employees who are considered surplus are seldom responsible for the conditions leading to the surplus. A shortage of a raw material such as fuel, or a poorly designed or marketed product can cause an enterprise to have a surplus of employees.

As a first approach to deal with a surplus most organizations avoid layoffs by such means as attrition, early retirement, work creation, and work sharing. Many organizations can reduce their work force simply by not replacing those who retire or quit (attrition). Sometimes this approach is accelerated by encouraging employees close to retirement to leave early, but this can amount to layoffs of older employees if the organization is not careful. Another approach is for the organization to give surplus employees jobs such as painting the plant or extra maintenance chores to keep them on the payroll. Firms such as Kimberly Clark, Toyo Kogyo, Dow Chemical, Lockheed, American Shipbuilding, Aerojet General, and Raytheon have used this approach successfully.

Another variation of this approach is work sharing which will be discussed in detail in Chapter 20. Instead of attempting to decide whom to layoff, the organization asks all employees to work less than normal hours and thus share the work. Many unions favor this approach. During recessions, many firms give the employees a say in how to deal with surplus conditions, and some groups of employees decide for work sharing.

If there is a surplus of employees at higher levels in the organization hierarchy, demotion may be used to reduce the work force. After World War II, as the army reduced its size it had too many higher level officers to staff the number of positions left. As a result, many officers were demoted to their "permanent" rank, not the one they held in 1945. The numerous ways demotion can be handled include: lowered job status with the same salary or lowered salary; the same status with lower compensation; being bypassed in seniority for promotion; changing to a less desirable job; the same formal status, but with decreased span of control; being excluded from a general salary increase; insertion of positions above the person in the hierarchy; moving to a staff position; elimination of the position and reassignment; and transfer out of direct line for promotion. Demotions are very difficult for employees to accept, and valued employees may leave because of them.

Organizations such as Firestone Tire & Rubber, General Motors, and Wheeling-Pittsburgh Steel have asked workers to accept lower wages or fringe benefits. Uniroyal Inc.'s 16,600 U.S. employees pledged to give up over $20 million in wages for two years. Pay cuts hurt, but the alternative—layoff—can be even more painful.[10]

In managing a surplus through layoffs, employers take the surplus employees off the payroll "temporarily" to reduce the surplus. Some employers may feel more willing to accept this method because unemployment compensation plans are now available (see Chapter 13). If the layoff is likely to be semipermanent or permanent, it is in effect a termination and results usually in the payment of severance pay as well as unemployment compensation.

When the organization is getting close to the point where layoffs are necessary, employees know business is down, and the workplace buzzes with rumors. Managers should make layoff decisions as early as possible to give employees ample notice. This is especially important when there will be mass layoffs, as in the auto and steel industries in the mid-1970s and early 1980s.

Employees can become bitter at layoff time. For example, Ford Motor Company experienced sabotage in the midst of the layoffs in the mid-70s. Fear affects productivity and employee satisfaction, and most employers will try to avoid layoffs if at all possible.

How does a manager decide whom to lay off? Two criteria have been used: merit and seniority. In the past the most senior employee was laid off last. A second approach now is to lay off those with lower merit ratings. Merit means that those who do the job the best are kept; those who perform poorly are laid off. If merit ratings are not precise, unions may fight their exclusive use as a reason for laying off particular employees.

Using seniority as the only criterion may mean that recently hired minorities and women are laid off first. This pits minority rights against seniority rights, and the courts have been hard pressed to resolve the conflict. In a case with important implications for seniority systems, the U.S. Supreme Court decided that minority applicants who are discriminatorily rejected by an employer and later hired must be given seniority credit from

---

[10]Ralph E. Winter, "More Employees Accept Cuts in Pay to Help Their Companies Survive," *The Wall Street Journal*, October 22, 1980, p. 15.

the date of that rejection. Such seniority credits represent a breach in the tradition of seniority rights, but they do not apply to most minorities and women hired under EEO plans, for by and large they never were discriminately rejected. In short, federal EEO policies have not endangered seniority very much. While seniority has lost some judicial skirmishes to EEO, it remains the principal criterion of employment rights for hourly employees.

The final approach used to reduce employment surpluses is termination. Most employers use it as a last resort. Anyone who has watched Willy Loman in *Death of a Salesman* or the star of Neil Simon's *Prisoner of Second Avenue* knows why. Termination is usually very painful to both the employer and the employee. EEO requirements apply to terminations as well as layoffs. When terminations take place, many employers engage in outplacement: a serious attempt by the organization to help terminated employees find suitable jobs.

Summary

This chapter has pointed out the significant factors in the diagnostic model that affect personnel and employment planning. It began by emphasizing that this P/HRM activity is an integral aspect of strategic planning by top management. This P/HRM function assures the organization success in maintaining its P/HRM capacities by comparing the present supply of human resources with the projected demand for them. In summary:

1. The major reasons for formal employment planning are to achieve:

   a. More effective and efficient use of human resources.
   b. More satisfied and better developed employees.
   c. More effective equal employment opportunity planning.

2. The personnel and employment planning process is a joint responsibility of P/HRM and operating managers, with each performing specific functions in the process.
3. Four forecasting techniques used to determine work force needs described in the chapter are: expert-estimate, trend projection, modeling, and unit-forecasting techniques.
4. To provide realistic job information and to streamline efficient job design, three important processes are job analysis, job descriptions, and job specifications.
5. The next step in the planning process is to determine the availability of those presently employed by the organization who can fill projected vacancies. The skills inventory can serve this purpose.
6. Action decisions in a shortage of employees situation depend on the magnitude of the shortage: overtime, retraining of lower skilled employees, hiring additional employees, subcontracting some of the work.
7. Action decisions in surplus conditions include attrition, early retirement, demotions, layoffs, and terminations.
8. Organizations need to analyze the supply/demand match of employees in advance so as to take necessary steps to reschedule, recruit, or layoff employees. They will analyze work force composition to determine that it meets legal constraints.

Personnel and employment planning can be an integral part of the P/HRM program. It is most directly related to recruitment, selection, training, and promotion. By matching employment supply and demand, the organization can know how many persons of what

Case

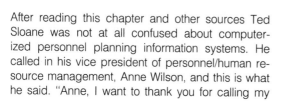

Ted Sloane and Anne Wilson

After reading this chapter and other sources Ted Sloane was not at all confused about computerized personnel planning information systems. He called in his vice president of personnel/human resource management, Anne Wilson, and this is what he said. "Anne, I want to thank you for calling my attention to the need for a computerized personnel planning information system. Without good forward planning we are going to be in trouble with the law. Let's move ahead and set up a computerized system. By the way are you familiar with the IBM "IRIS" system? It's a dandy."

Exhibit 5–9

Recommendations on personnel and employment planning for model organizations

Type of organization	Analysis of supply (skills inventory)		Method of demand analysis				Level where planning is analyzed		
	Manual	Compu-terized	Expert	Trend	Model/multiple	Unit	HQ	Unit	Both
1. Large size, low complexity, high stability		X			X	X	X		
2. Medium size, low complexity, high stability	X				X	X	X		
3. Small size, low complexity, high stability	X			X			X		
4. Medium size, moderate complexity, moderate stability	X			X		X		X	
5. Large size, high complexity, low stability		X		X		X			X
6. Medium size, high complexity, low stability	X			X		X		X	
7. Small size, high complexity, low stability	X		X					X	

type it needs to fill positions from within (by promotion or training) and how many it must acquire from outside (by recruitment and selection). (See Exhibit 5–9.)

Chapters 6 and 7 are devoted to recruitment and selection, filling employment needs from outside the organization when personnel and employment planning decisions show this need.

Questions for Review and Discussion

1. What is personnel and employment planning? How does it relate to other personnel activities?
2. What techniques are used for forecasting future employment needs?
3. Describe how you would choose a forecasting technique for several kinds of organizations, such as a small manufacturer of ashtrays, a large steel company, or a moderate-sized general hospital.
4. How could a replacement chart and a computerized system as ''IRIS'' be used to make better employment planning decisions?
5. How is analysis of employment supply related to demand analysis?
6. What is a skills inventory? Discuss how to design an effective skills inventory.
7. Why should an organization analyze the composition of its work force? How?
8. What action, decisions can be made when there is a worker shortage? Which is best?
9. What action decisions can be made when there is a worker surplus? Which is best?
10. How can a replacement chart be used to make better personnel and employment planning decisions?

Glossary

Handicapped Person. Any person who has a physical or mental impairment that may limit his-her work or job activities.

Personnel and Employment Planning. The process which helps to provide adequate human resources to achieve future organizational objectives. It includes forecasting future needs for employees of various types; accompanying these needs with the present work force, and determining the numbers of types of employees to be recruited or phased out of the organization's employment group.

Replacement Chart. A display or chart usually of technical, professional, and managerial employees. It includes name, title, age, length of service, and other relevant information on present employees.

Skills Inventory. A list of the names, certain characteristics, and skills of the people working for the organization. It provides a way to acquire these data and makes them available where needed in an efficient manner.

Chapter Six

Recruitment

Learning Objectives

After studying this chapter you should be able to:
- Discuss how to develop an effective recruiting program for an organization.

- Describe the recruiting process: who does it, how they do it, and where they seek recruits.

- Define what is meant by a realistic job preview.

- Identify typical flaws which college students find in recruiters.

- List sources of candidates for blue-collar, gray-collar, white-collar, and managerial, technical, and professional positions.

Chapter Outline

Case

Clark

Lewis

Ed

Clark Kirby is just entering the office of the vice president of personnel/human resource management, Lewis Yates. Clark has worked for Gunther Manufacturing for 10 years. After a short management training program, Clark spent almost two years as operating supervisor in a plant. After that, a position opened up in personnel. Clark had majored in personnel at California State University at Los Angeles and wanted to try it. He liked personnel and felt he was good at it. He had moved up in the department headquarters in Chicago during the next seven years.

Gunther is a growing firm. For a middle-sized operation, it has one of the fastest growth records in the industry. Now, Gunther is opening up a new plant in the quickly expanding Houston market. The plant's location is in one of Houston's suburbs, 15 miles from downtown.

Lewis has selected Clark to be the Houston plant personnel/human resource manager. This was what Clark had been waiting for: a chance to be on his own and to show what he can do for Lewis, who has been very supportive of his career, and for Gunther. He was very excited as he entered Lewis' office.

Lewis greeted him with, "Well, Clark, I hope you realize how much we are counting on you in Houston. Shortly you'll be meeting your new plant manager, Ed Humphrey. You'll be working for him, but responsible to me to see that Gunther's P/HRM policies are carried out.

"The plant will be staffed initially with the following employees. These are in effect your recruiting quotas:

Managers	38
Professional/technical	10
Clerical	44
Skilled employees	104
Semiskilled employees	400

Also note that you will receive a budget for maximum initial pay for this group shortly.

"You and Ed should work out the details. You are eligible to recruit some employees from the home office and other plants. But excessive raiding is not allowed. Remember too that Gunther has an equal employment opportunity problem. Wherever possible, try to hire qualified minorities and women to help us meet our goal.

"Your own P/HRM office consists of yourself, one P/HRM specialist to help you run the employment office, and one clerical employee. Good Luck!"

Clark quickly arranged for a meeting with Ed, his new boss. Ed is about 50 years old. He is a high school graduate who started with Gunther as a blue-collar employee when he was 18 years old. After 10 years in various blue-collar positions, Ed became a foreman. Eight years later he was selected as an assistant to the plant manager. After several years in this position, he was made one of the three assistant plant managers at one of Gunther's plants in Chicago. He held that position until being given the position of plant manager at the new Houston plant.

After introductions, Clark and Ed talked.

Clark Here are the figures for employees which Lewis gave me. He also said we could recruit some people from Gunther, but not to raid beyond company policy. Also, Lewis said we needed to do an exceptional job recruiting minorities and women because we have an EEO problem. In Houston, that means finding Hispanics, blacks, and women.

Ed Let's get something straight right off. You work for me now, not Lewis. Here's a list of 20 managers I want to take with me. It's your job to convince them to come to Houston with me. In cases where my help might persuade some to come along, call on me. But I'm very harassed now trying to get machinery ordered, the plant laid out, financing arranged, and so on. Call on me only when you must, you *understand*?

Oh, one more thing. That EEO * # /OX, you can forget that. The Houston plant is going to be the most efficient in the company, or else! And if that means hiring the best workers and they all turn out to be white, that's tough, you get me? Keep me posted on what's happening. Good to have you on board.

After some thought, Clark decided to use job posting as a method of attracting professional/technical and managerial employees at the Los Angeles office to the new plant in Houston. He also made the personal contacts Ed asked for in recruiting managerial employees, and the skills inventory was used to come up with more applicants. Clark contacted these also. He did not use job posting or the skills inventory for clerical, skilled, or semiskilled employees. He knew that for Gunther, as with most organizations, these categories of employees rarely wish to move to another location. Most companies don't want to pay transfer costs for these categories of employment, either.

Clark went to Houston and set up the employment office at the new location. He ran an ad in Houston's afternoon paper and placed a job listing with a private employment agency for the P/HRM specialist and clerk-typist for his office. Then he hired these two employees and set up the office to receive walk-ins. He provided application blanks and policy guidelines on when selection would proceed.

Clark listed the available positions with the U.S. Employment Service. He also contacted private agencies. He selected the private agencies after calling a number of P/HRM managers in the Houston area in similar businesses and who were also ASPA members. The P/HRM specialist notified the high schools, vocational-technical schools, and colleges of the positions. The schools selected included all the vocational-technical schools, the junior colleges, and the colleges in the Houston area. Also, all high school guidance counseling departments were notified. Now Clark wonders what other media he ought to use to publicize the positions.

Before an organization can make a job offer it must have people who want the job. This chapter describes effective ways to recruit the people needed to offset shortages in human resources which become apparent as a result of the personnel and employment planning process.

> Recruiting is that set of activities an organization uses to attract job candidates who have the abilities and attitudes needed to help the organization achieve its objectives.

> Job search is the set of activities a person undertakes to seek and find a position which will provide him or her with sustenance and other rewards.

Recruiting is related directly to a number of P/HRM activities, as shown in Exhibit 6–1.

Personnel and employment planning determines the number of employees needed, and all subsequent P/HRM activities (such as selection, orientation, development, compensation) cannot be effective unless good employees have been recruited. The Prentice-Hall/ASPA survey of 1,400 personnel executives found that they rated recruiting/selection as their most important function in a nonunionized firm.[1] Recruiting can be costly. For

---

[1] "The Personnel Executive's Job," *Personnel Management: Policies and Practices* (Englewood Cliffs, N.J.: Prentice-Hall, Inc., 1977).

Exhibit 6–1

Recruiting and other personnel activities

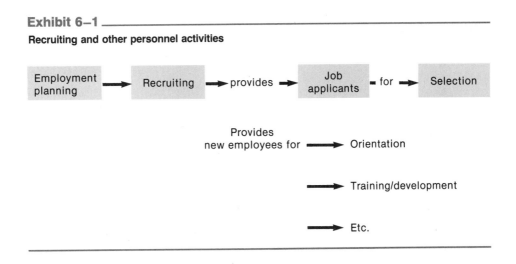

example, it has been estimated that recruiting cost the following percentages of the first-year salary of various specialists and managers: senior engineer, 68 percent; accountant, 61 percent; secretary, 51 percent; supervisor, 40 percent; middle manager, 33 percent; and top manager, 25 percent.[2] Thus for a $60,000-a-year executive, recruiting can cost $15,000; recruiting engineers can cost $11,900. Yet recruiting is not a well-developed personnel function; it is at Stage II or possibly Stage III (see Exhibit 1–1 in Chapter 1).

A Diagnostic Approach to Recruitment

Exhibit 6–2 examines how the recruiting process is affected by various factors in the environment. The recruiting process begins with an attempt to find employees with the abilities and attitudes desired by the organization and to match them with the tasks to be performed. Whether potential employees will respond to the recruiting effort depends on the attitudes they have developed toward those tasks and the organization, on the basis of their past social and working experiences. Their perception of the task will also be affected by the work climate in the organization.

How difficult the recruiting job is depends on a number of factors: external influences such as government and union restrictions and the labor market, plus the employer's requirements and candidates' preferences. External factors are discussed in this section, and the important interaction of the organization as a recruiter and the employee as a recruit is examined in the next section.

Since Clark Kirby has just moved to Houston he will have to learn about the external influences in the new location. Each area of the country has its own unique culture, problems, and situations that a P/HRM manager must study and understand. Clark will be doing a lot of studying of his new location.

---

[2]Robert Sibson, "The High Cost of Hiring," *Nation's Business*, February 1975, pp. 85–88.

Exhibit 6–2

Factors affecting recruitment of employees

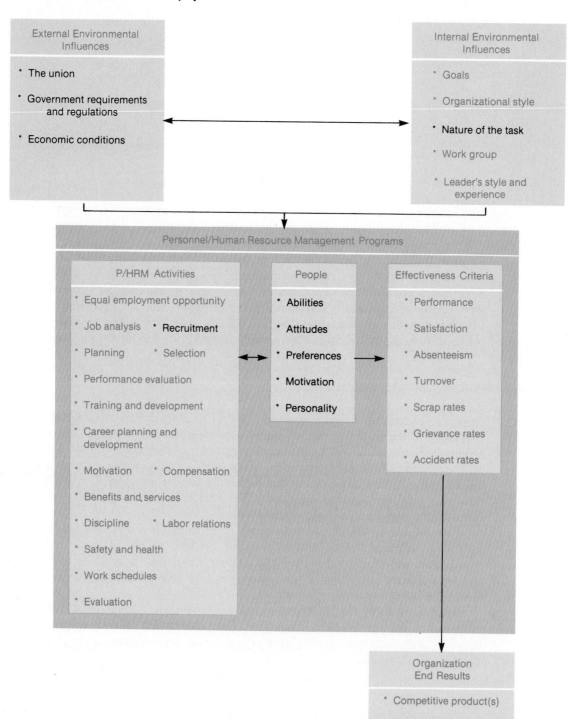

External Influences

Government and Union Restrictions • Government regulations prohibiting discrimination in hiring and employment have a direct impact on recruiting practices. As described in detail in Chapter 3 government agencies can and do review the following information about recruiting to see if an enterprise has violated the law:

- The list of recruitment sources (such as employment agencies, civic organizations, schools) for each job category.
- Recruiting advertising.
- Estimates of the firm's employment needs for the coming year.
- Statistics on the number of applicants processed by category (sex, race, and so on) and by job category or level.

The government may require an organization to use EEO programs to recruit qualified employees who are not well represented in the present work force. For example, a firm with no female managers may be required to recruit at women's colleges offering degrees likely to lead to management positions with the organization.

Exhibit 6–3 provides a guide to what recruiters can and cannot legally do or ask in recruiting interviews. Other personal characteristics recruiters need to be wary of, because they may discriminate or do not relate directly to performance, are birthplace; use of second names or aliases; religious affiliation; citizenship; membership in clubs, socities, and lodges; and social security numbers. In some states, it is illegal to ask about the type of military discharge and past police records. Many public organizations must be careful to follow state or local statutes on recruiting.

Obviously, these government restrictions affect who can be recruited, how, and where. In addition, some union contracts restrict recruiting to union hiring halls (as will be discussed in Chapter 7). This restriction does not apply for many employers, but where it does the recruiting function is turned over to the union, at least for those employees who are unionized.

Labor Market Conditions • The second external environmental factor affecting recruiting is labor market conditions (these were described in some detail in Chapter 2). The labor market affects recruiting in this way: If there is a surplus of labor at recruiting time, even informal attempts at recruiting will probably attract more than enough applicants. But when full employment is nearly reached in an area, skillful and prolonged recruiting may be necessary to attract any applicants that fulfill the expectations of the organization.

The employer can find out about the current employment picture in several ways. The federal Department of Labor issues employment reports, and state divisions of employment security and labor usually can provide information on local employment conditions. There are also sources of information about specific types of employees. Craft unions and professional associations keep track of employment conditions as they affect their members. Current college recruiting efforts are analyzed by the Conference Board, A. C. Nielsen, and the Endicott Report, which appears in *The Journal of College Placement*. Various personnel journals and *The Wall Street Journal* also regularly report on employment conditions.

Other sources provide summary data such as indexes of employment. One of the most interesting indexes is that of the Conference Board, which keeps track of help-

Exhibit 6–3

Dos and don'ts in recruiting interviews

Subject	Can do or ask	Cannot do or ask
Sex	Notice appearance.	Make comments or notes unless sex is a bona fide occupational qualification
Race	General distinguishing characteristics such as scars, etc. to be used for identification purposes.	Color of applicant's skin, eyes, hair, etc. or other direct or indirect questions indicating race or color.
Handicap	Are you able to carry out necessary job assignments and perform them well and in a safe manner?	What is the nature and/or severity of any handicaps you have?
Marital status	Ask status after hiring, for insurance purposes.	Are you married? Single? Divorced? Engaged? Are you living with anyone? Do you see your ex-spouse?
Children	Ask numbers and ages of children after hiring, for insurance purposes.	Do you have children at home? How old? Who cares for them? Do you plan more children?
Physical data	Explain manual labor, lifting, other requirements of the job. Show how it is performed. Require physical exam.	How tall are you? How heavy?
References	By whom were you referred for a position here?	Requiring the submission of a religious reference.
Criminal record	If security clearance is necessary, can be done prior to employment.	Have you ever been arrested, convicted, or spent time in jail?
Military status	Are you a veteran? Why not? Any job-related experience?	What type of discharge do you have? What branch did you serve in?
Age	Age after hiring. Are you over 18?	How old are you? Estimate age.
Housing	If you have no phone, how can we reach you?	Do you own your home? Do you rent? Do you live in an apartment or a house?

Source: Clifford M. Doen, Jr., "The Pre-Employment Inquiry Guide," *Personal Journal*, October 1980, p. 825–29. Reprinted with permission of *Personnel Journal*, Costa Mesa, Calif., all rights reserved; and *Business Week*, May 26, 1975, p. 77. Also see Stephen Sahlein, *The Affirmative Action Handbook* (New York: Executive Enterprises Publishing).

---

wanted advertising in 52 major newspapers across the nation, using 1967 as a base year of 100. Local conditions are more important than national conditions, unless the employer is recruiting nationwide.

Interactions of the Recruit and the Organization

After considering how external factors such as government, unions, and labor market conditions restrict the options of an organization to recruit (an applicant to be recruited), the next step in understanding the recruiting process is to consider the interaction of the applicants and the organization in recruiting.

In Exhibit 6–2 (the diagnostic model for recruitment), the nature of the organization and the goals of the managers are highlighted, as is the nature of the task. The techniques used and sources of recruits vary with the job. As far as the applicants are concerned, their abilities, attitudes, and past work experience affect how they go about seeking a job.

The recruiting process consists of the matching of the employer's desired qualifications with the applicant's qualifications. The employer offers a job with associated rewards; the organization is looking for certain characteristics in a potential employee. The recruit has abilities and attitudes to offer and is looking for a kind of job that meets his or her minimum expectations. A match is made when sufficient overlap exists between these two sets of expectations. The recruiting process usually requires some modifications and compromises on both sides.

The Organization's View of Recruiting

Three aspects affect recruiting from the organization's viewpoint: the recruiting requirements set, organization policies and procedures, and the organizational image.

Requirements for Recruits • Organizations specify the requirements they consider ideal in applicants for positions. The employer easily can have unrealistic expectations of potential employees: They might expect applicants who stand first in their class, are president of all extracurricular activities, have worked their way through school, have Johnny Carson's ability to charm, are good looking, have 10 years' experience (at age 21), and are willing to work long hours for almost no money. Or, to meet federal requirements, they might specify a black woman, but one who is in the upper 10 percent of her graduating class and has an undergraduate degree in engineering and an M.B.A.

As contrasted with this unrealistic approach, the effective organization examines the specifications that are absolutely necessary for the job. Then it uses these as its beginning expectations for recruits (see the section on job analysis, job description, and job specifications in Chapter 4).

Organization Policies and Practices • In some organizations P/HRM policies and practices affect recruiting and who is recruited. One of the most important of these is promotion from within. For all practical purposes, this policy means that many organizations only recruit from outside the organization at the initial hiring level. They feel this is fair to present loyal employees and assures them a secure future and a fair chance at promotion, and most employees favor this approach. Some employers also feel this practice helps protect trade secrets. The techniques used for internal recruiting will be discussed below.

Is promotion from within always a good policy? Not always. An organization may grow so stable that it is set in its ways. The business does not compete effectively, or the government bureau will not adjust to legislative requirements. In such cases, promotion from within may be detrimental, and new employees from outside might be helpful.

Other policies can also affect recruiting. Certain organizations have always hired more than their fair share of the handicapped, or veterans, or ex-convicts, for example, and they may look to these sources first. Others may be involved in nepotism to favor relatives. All these policies affect who is recruited.

Organizational Image • The image of the employer generally held by the public also affects recruitment. There are differences in attracting engineers, systems analysts, tool and die makers, marketing researchers, cost accountants, and employment specialists, for such diverse organizations and situations as:

NASA at the height of the space program, when men were walking on the moon.
Chrysler hiring engineers during the lull period in the company's history.

A small soap company, trying to hire salespersons, which must compete with Procter & Gamble for recruits.

IBM trying to recruit research scientists for its lab.

As you can imagine, the good or bad, well-known or unknown images of these organizations will affect how they are viewed by the public and job recruits. The organization's image is complex, but it is probably based on what the organization does and whether or not it is perceived as providing a good place to work. The larger the organization, the more likely it is to have a well-developed image. A firm that produces a product or service the potential employee knows about or uses is also more likely to have an image for the applicant. The probability is that a potential employee will have a clearer image of a chewing gum company than a manufacturer of subassemblies for a cyclotron.

The organization's image is also affected by its industry. These images change. In the past, petroleum had a positive image. The ecology movement has changed this universally good image. Petroleum organizations now actively advertise their positive contributions to society.

How does this image affect recruiting? Job applicants seldom can have interviews with all the organizations that have job openings of interest to them. Because there are time and energy limits to the job search, they do some preliminary screening. One of these screens is the image the applicants have of the organization, which can attract or repel them. They don't accept interviews with bad image organizations unless they have to.

In sum, the ideal job specifications preferred by an organization may have to be adjusted to meet the realities of the labor market, government or union restrictions, the limitations of its policies and practices, and its image. If an inadequate number of quality people apply, the organization may have to either adjust the job to fit the best applicant or increase its recruiting efforts.

The Potential Employee's View of Recruiting

Exhibit 6–2 highlighted several factors relevant to how a recruit looks for a job. The applicant has abilities, attitudes, and preferences based on past work experiences and influences by parents, teachers, and others. These factors affect recruits two ways: how they set their job preferences, and how they go about seeking a job. Understanding these is vital to effective recruiting by organizations.

Preferences of Recruits for Organizations and Jobs • Just as organizations have ideal specifications for recruits, so do recruits have a set of preferences for a job. A student leaving college may want a job in San Diego because of its quality of life, paying $25,000 a year, and with little or no responsibility or supervision. This recruit is unlikely to get *all* his expectations fulfilled. The recruit also faces the limits of the labor market (good or bad from the recruit's point of view, which is usually the opposite of the organization's), government and union restrictions, and the limits of organizational policies and practices. The recruit must anticipate compromises just as the organization does.

From the individual's point of view, organization choice is a two-step process. First, the individual makes an occupational choice—probably in high school or just after. Then she or he makes a choice of the organization to work for within the occupation chosen.

What factors affect the organization-choice decision? A number of researchers have found that more educated persons know the labor market better, have higher expectations

"Now, I hope you don't have the idea that working for I.T.T. is all intrigue and adventure."

Drawing by C. Barsotti; © 1973 The New Yorker Magazine, Inc.

of work, and find organizations that pay more and provide more stable employment. Although much of the research suggests that this decision is fairly rational, the more careful studies indicate that the decision is also influenced by unconscious processes, chance, and luck.

Some studies have indicated that the organizational choice tends to be correlated with single factors. One study found blue-collar workers went after the highest paying jobs;[3] another found workers trying to match multiple needs with multiple-job characteristics, such as high pay and preferred job type,[4] and a third found the approach varied by personality differences.[5]

Job Search and Finding a Job: The Recruit

Exhibit 6–4 outlines the pattern followed by effective job searchers. Examine Step 1: Realize that the first job choice is part of a career plan. Is this job the first in a chain of jobs with this company? Or is this just a job to get experience before starting your own business?

Step 2 is fulfilled by reading newspapers and professional publications in the area where the recruit wants to live, and describes desirable jobs. College placement offices have job information, as do professional associations, employment agencies, and search firms. Personal contacts also are a good source of information.

The data from Step 2 allow you to complete Step 3 with regard to industry. With regard to company type and job function, you need to analyze the answers to certain kinds of questions about potential employers.

[3]Dale Yoder, *Job Seeking Behavior of Workers* (New York: Organization for Economic Cooperation Development, 1965).

[4]Joseph Champagne, "Job Recruitment of the Unskilled," *Personnel Journal*, April 1969, pp. 259–68.

[5]John Morse, "Person-Job Consequence and Individual Adjustment and Development," *Human Relations*, December 1970, pp. 841–61.

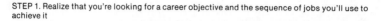

Exhibit 6–4 _____

Career decision strategy

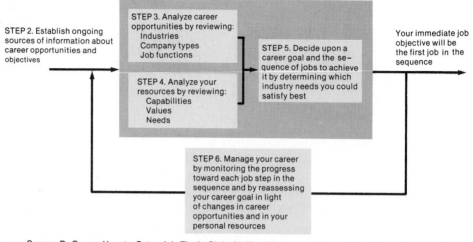

STEP 1. Realize that you're looking for a career objective and the sequence of jobs you'll use to achieve it

STEP 2. Establish ongoing sources of information about career opportunities and objectives

STEP 3. Analyze career opportunities by reviewing:
Industries
Company types
Job functions

STEP 4. Analyze your resources by reviewing:
Capabilities
Values
Needs

STEP 5. Decide upon a career goal and the sequence of jobs to achieve it by determining which industry needs you could satisfy best

Your immediate job objective will be the first job in the sequence

STEP 6. Manage your career by monitoring the progress toward each job step in the sequence and by reassessing your career goal in light of changes in career opportunities and in your personal resources

Source: B. Greco, *How to Get a Job That's Right for You* (Homewood, Ill.: Dow Jones-Irwin, 1975. © 1975 by Dow Jones-Irwin, Inc.).

At this point, you may have determined, for example, that what you really want is a job near home, in a small firm in the toy industry, that you can buy out some day. Answers to these questions will help you narrow the list of potential employers to a reasonable size.

As far as Step 4 is concerned, there are several questions you need to answer about your values and needs. Questions of this type are almost unlimited. What you must do first is rank them in importance so you know the trade-offs between them. You *will not* find a job with *all* the characteristics you choose.

Then you need to analyze what you have to offer that comprises your comparative advantages. These can include education (for example, grades, kinds of courses, skills developed), interpersonal skills, personality traits, and personal contacts.

After completing Steps 3 and 4, you are ready to look for a job. Use all the sources

Questions about Employers:

1. Do I have a size preference: small, medium, or large, or no size?
2. Do I have a sector preference (private, not for profit, public sector)?
3. What kinds of industries interest me? This is usually based on interests in company products or services. Do I prefer mechanical objects or counseling people? This is a crucial question.
4. Have I checked to make sure that the sector or product or service has a good future and will lead to growth in opportunity?

Questions about Me:

1. How hard do I like to work?
2. Do I like to be my own boss, or would I rather work for someone else?
3. Do I like to work alone, with a few others, or with large groups?
4. Do I like work at an even pace or in bursts of energy?
5. Does location matter? Do I want to work near home? In warmer climates? In ski country? Am I willing to be mobile?
6. How much money do I want? Am I willing to work for less money but in a more interesting job?
7. Do I like to work in one place or many? Indoors or outdoors?
8. How much variety do I want in work?

available to you: employment agencies, personal contacts, professional associations, and so on. If you use mail to send résumés, the letters should be personalized, and telephone follow-up is necessary. Personal contacts should be used wherever possible.

One study of over 200 personnel managers who normally screen applicants for positions found that it is essential for cover letters accompanying résumés to be personally typed, no longer than one page, and truthful.[6] They should include these items, in order of importance:

> Position you are seeking.
>
> Specific job objectives
>
> Your career objectives
>
> Reason you are seeking employment.
>
> An indication that you know something about the organization.

The same study found that preferred résumés were personally typed, no more than two pages in length, and on high quality paper, and so on. The most important items the managers surveyed in this study were looking for on a résumé were, in order: current address; past work experience; college major; job objectives and goals; date of availability for the job; career objectives; permanent address; tenure on previous jobs; colleges and universities attended; specific physical limitations; and job location requirements. Other items they preferred were, in order: overall health status; salary requirements; travel limitations; minor in college; grades in college major; military experience; years in which degrees were awarded; overall grade point average; membership in organizations; and awards and scholarships.

Successful job seekers prepare for job interviews. Some suggestions for this are given in Chapter 7. As with other skills, practice makes perfect. Practice interviewing before a videotape with a friend role playing the interviewer. You can learn from each other.

Once you have had job interviews, be sure to follow up those that interest you by sending a letter or calling the interviewer. This requires you to write down and remember the interviewer's name and some details of the job being offered.

---

[6]Hubert Feild and William Holley, "Résumé Preparation: An Empirical Study of Personnel Managers' Perceptions," *Vocational Guidance Journal,* March 1976, pp. 229–37.

Typical Questions Asked in Job Interviews:

1. What qualifications do you have that make you feel you will be a success in your field?
2. How much do you know about our company? Its product or service?
3. How did you pay for your college expenses?
4. Why did you choose this particular field of work?
5. What type of position are you most interested in?
6. Why do you want to work for our company?
7. What jobs have you held previously? How did you find them? Why did you leave? What have you learned from these positions that will help you in the job with our company?
8. Have you set a goal for yourself about the salary you expect by age 30? Why? 35? Why?
9. What is most important to you—making money or performing a service for people?
10. Do you have a geographic preference? For example, what size city do you prefer? Are you willing to relocate?
11. What do you see as your major weakness?

Who Does the Recruiting?

Clark Kirby's situation at Gunther illustrates that he is responsible for recruiting employees. This is an extremely important responsibility that will in the long run determine whether Gunther will be successful in the Houston area. The roles of operating and P/HRM managers in recruiting are shown in Exhibit 6–5.

Personnel and employment planning gives operating managers the data needed to set recruiting quotas. In larger organizations, sometimes this process is formalized by authorizations. That is, a budget is prepared showing the maximum number of people to be recruited and the maximum salary that can be paid. Lewis gave these items to Clark at Gunther Corporation.

Who does the recruiting? In larger organizations, the P/HRM department does it. The branch of the department with this responsibility is called the employment office or department. It is staffed by recruiters, interviewers, and clerical employees. This group also does the preliminary selection, as will be described in Chapter 7. Employment offices are specialized units which provide a place to which applicants can apply. They conduct the recruiting, both at the work site and away from it. A typical employment office is shown.

When applicants appear in person at the work site, the employment office serves a similar purpose. This initial meeting might be called the reception phase of employment. The applicant is greeted, supplied with an application blank, and perhaps given some information on present hiring conditions and the organization as a place to work. If the applicant is treated indifferently or rudely at this phase, he or she can form a lasting poor impression of the workplace.[7] The reception phase is a great deal like the initial contact a

---

[7]D. P. Rogers and M. Z. Sincoff, ''Favorable Impression Characteristics of the Recruitment Interviewer,'' *Personnel Psychology,* Summer 1978, pp. 495–504.

Exhibit 6–5

The roles of operating and P/HRM managers in recruitment

Recruiting function	Operating manager (OM)	Personnel/human resource manager (P/HRM)
Set recruiting goals	Set by OM with advice of P/HRM	Advises OM on state of labor market
Decide on sources of recruits and recruiting policies	Policy decision, outside versus inside, set by OM with advice of P/HRM	Advises OM on status of possible inside recruits
Decide on methods of recruiting	OM advises P/HRM on methods of recruiting	P/HRM decides on recruiting methods with advice of OM
College recruiting	OM occasionally recruits of colleges	P/HRM normally recruits at colleges
Cost/benefit studies of recruiting	OM evaluates results of cost/ benefit studies and decides accuracy	P/HRM performs cost/benefit studies

salesperson makes with a prospective customer. What kind of impression did the perspective employee in the cartoon get?

All applicants are potential employees, as well as clients for the organizations services or products. Therefore, it is vital that those who greet and process applicants (in person or by phone) be well trained in communication techniques and interpersonal skills. They should enjoy meeting the public and helping people in stressful conditions, for job seeking can be a difficult experience for many applicants.

"We'll be happy to put you on file, Mr. Bannister, but we don't have anything for an underling at the moment."

Drawing by Lorenz; © 1973 The New Yorker Magazine, Inc.

In smaller organizations, multipurpose P/HRM people do the recruiting, along with their other duties, or operating managers may take time to recruit and interview applicants. Sometimes the organization puts together a recruiting committee of operating and P/HRM managers.

The role of recruiter is very important. The recruiter is usually the first person from the organization that an applicant meets. Applicants' impressions about the organization are based to a large degree on their encounter with the recruiter. Effective recruiter behavior is described later in this chapter as an aspect of college training.

Sources of Recruits

Once the organization has decided it needs additional employees, it is faced with two recruiting decisions: where to search (sources), and how to notify applicants of the positions (methods). Two sources of applicants could be used: internal (present employees), and external (those not presently affiliated with the enterprise). Exhibit 6–6 lists many of the sources of recruits.

Job Posting and Bidding

If the employee shortage is for higher level employees, and if the organization approves of promoting from within, it will use the skills inventories to search for candidates (see Chapter 4). But P/HRM managers may not be aware of all employees who want to be considered for promotion, so they use an approach called job posting and bidding. In the job-posting system, the organization notifies its present employees of openings, using

Exhibit 6–6 _____

Sources for recruiting various types of employees

Sources	Blue collar	Gray collar	White collar	Managerial, technical, professional
Internal				
Job posting and bidding	X		X	X
Friends of present employees	X	X	X	
Skills inventories	X	X	X	X
External				
Walk-ins, including previous employees	X	X	X	
Agencies				
Temporary help			X	
Private employment agencies			X	
Public employment agencies*	X	X	X	
Executive search firms				X
Educational institutions				
High school	X	X	X	
Vocational/technical	X	X	X	X
College and universities				X
Other				
Unions	X			
Professional associations				X
Military services	X			X
Former employees	X	X	X	X

*Normally called U.S. Employment Service.

bulletin boards, company publications, and so on. About 25 percent of white-collar firms in one survey conducted by Dahl and Pinto used the system, as did most large Minnesota firms.[8] Most firms found the system useful; for example, the Bank of Virginia filled 18 percent of its openings as a result of job posting.

Dahl and Pinto provide a useful set of guidelines for effective job-posting systems.

- Post all permanent promotion and transfer opportunities.
- Post the jobs for about one week prior to recruiting outside the enterprise.
- Clarify eligibility rules. For example, minimum service in the present position might be specified as six months. Seniority may be the decision rule used to choose between several equally qualified applicants.
- List job specifications. Application forms should be available.
- Inform all applicants what happens in the choice.

Inside Moonlighting and Employees' Friends

If the labor shortage is short term or a great amount of additional work is not necessary, the organization can use inside moonlighting. It could offer to pay bonuses of various types to people not on a time payroll. Overtime procedures are already developed for those on time payrolls.

Before going outside to recruit, many organizations ask present employees to encourage friends or relatives to apply. In his study of the job-search behavior of 1,500 men, Ornstein found that 23 percent of white and 29 percent of black men found their jobs through friends, and 31 percent of both whites and blacks found their first jobs through help of the family.[9] These are *first* jobs; there presently are no data on what percentage of applicants for later jobs use these sources. These data indicate how powerful this source of recruits could be for organizations, should they use it wisely. Some equal employment opportunity programs prohibit using friends as a major recruiting source, however.

Employee referrals have to be carefully used by organizations. In a case involving *EEOC* v. *Detroit Edison (1975)*,[10] the U.S. Court of Appeals, Sixth Circuit found a history of racial discrimination that was related to recruitment. The court stated:

> The practice of relying on referrals by a predominantly white work force rather than seeking new employees in the marketplace for jobs was found to be discriminating.

This case suggests some caution about employee referrals. Unless the work force is racially and culturally heterogeneous to begin with, the referrals or friends tend to be the same in background, race, and attitude.

External Sources

Exhibit 6–6 also indicates a number of external sources of recruits and which sources supply applicants for various types of jobs. When an organization has exhausted internal sources, these sources are used. Studies indicating when each external source is used are not extensive.

---

[8]Dave Dahl and Patrick Pinto, "Job Posting: An Industry Survey," *Personnel Journal,* January 1977, pp. 40–42.

[9]Michael Ornstein, *Entry into the American Labor Force* (New York: Academic Press, 1976).

[10]*EEOC* v. *Detroit Edison Company.* U.S. Court of Appeals, Sixth Circuit (Cincinnati), 515 F. 2d. 301 (1975).

P/HRM Managers Close-Up

William M. Read
Atlantic Richfield Company

Biography

William M. Read is senior vice president of Atlantic Richfield Company in charge of employee relations.

Mr. Read, a native of Philadelphia, Pennsylvania, is a graduate of Washington and Lee University, Lexington, Virginia. He attended the University of Pennsylvania Graduate School.

He joined the Atlantic Refining Company in 1943 as a personnel clerk at the Philadelphia Refinery. He has served as a training assistant, manager of training, manager of personnel development and safety, and manager of personnel administration before

being elected a vice president in 1972 and a senior vice president in 1978.

Views of William M. Read—Atlantic Richfield

At Atlantic Richfield our employee relations professionals see their mission as one of helping managers achieve excellence in the management of their human resources. In carrying out this mission, the professional has four roles: (1) a service role, (2) a consulting role, (3) an advocacy role, and (4) a catalytic role.

The decade ahead offers a number of interesting human resource challenges:

1. National demographics indicate that there will be a shortage of persons with critical skills resulting from the zero population growth in the 50s and 60s. We in the Employee Relations profession must work with our management to intensify the training and development of minorities and females to fill this void and intensify efforts to retain older workers; that is, those who might be expected to retire.
2. We also face a middle-management crunch caused by the same demographics. Persons 35 to 45 who might anticipate rapid promotional movement will, in many companies in the second half of the decade, become blocked and frustrated by comparatively young managers filling the top-management jobs. This will require some creative re-thinking of how to retain the interest and enthusiasm of this important segment of the employee population.

The most fruitful of the outside sources is walk-ins. Ornstein found that one third of his sample got their first jobs that way.[11] Private employment agencies place some white-collar employees and serve as a source of recruits for many employers. Counselors in schools and teachers can also help, usually for managerial, professional, technical, and white-collar employees. The state employment security offices, partially using federal funds, have tried to serve more applicants and organization needs, but these agencies still provide primarily blue-collar, gray-collar, and only a few white-collar applicants. They try to tie into school counseling services, too. Still most studies, are very critical of the

---

[11]Michael Ornstein, *Entry into the American Labor Force* (New York: Academic Press, 1976).

costs and benefits of the public agencies. They do not help employees or applicants as much as they should. Thus, even though there appear to be many sources from which employees can be recruited, employers use only a few to recruit each type of employee.

Methods of Recruiting

A number of methods can be used to recruit external applicants; advertising, personal recruiting, computerized matching services, special-event recruiting, and summer internships are discussed here. There is also a separate section on college recruitment of potential managers and professionals.

To decide which method to use, the organization should know which are most likely to attract potential employees. Relatively few studies of the job-seeking procedures used by applicants have been made, but Exhibit 6–7 suggests the most likely media for various categories of employees.

Media Advertisements

Organizations advertise to acquire recruits. Various media are used, the most common of which are the daily newspaper help-wanted ads. Organizations also advertise for people in trade and professional publications. Other media used are billboards, subway and bus cards, radio, telephone, and television. Some job seekers do a reverse twist; they advertise for a situation wanted and reward anyone who tips them off about a job.

An example of an innovative recruiting ad is one used to staff Halls Crown Shopping Center, in Kansas City, this full-page ad in the Sunday *Kansas City Star* is reproduced below. Note how the ad disassociates the center from seeking clerks and attempts to recruit persons whose interests are likely to affect performance.

Another innovative way to attract prospective employees with particular skills is the use of recorded want ads. Want ad recordings were used by 40 companies recruiting engineers and scientists at a New York City convention. At a special recruiting center, job hunters were able to pick up a telephone and hear a three-minute taped recruiting message which included job description and company contract details.

Exhibit 6–7 _____

Methods of recruiting for various types of employees

Method	Blue collar	Gray collar	White collar	Managerial, professional, technical
Media advertisements				
Newspaper want ads	X	X	X	X
Professional journals and other media	X	X	X	X
Recruiters				X
Computer matching services				X
Special-event recruiting				X
Summer internships				X
Coop programs	Select highly skilled	Select highly skilled	Select highly skilled	

THIS IS A WANT AD

What we want is a show of hands from you out there who would be interested in pursuing your personal pastimes . . . . and getting paid for it.

For instance: are you a sports nut, a music buff, an antique collector, a candledipper, a Canoe Clubber, a shutterbug, a rock hound or a stargazer? If so, a very satisfying career awaits you on our Leisure-Lifestyle Level.

Or, do you have a personal passion for fabrics, jewels, furs, fine art, furniture, designer fashions? We think you could find happiness working on our Gracious-Lifestyle Level.

Or, are you a here-and-now type who loves the passing parade of things that are fun and topical, whether that means horoscopes or exciting new fashions? Then you'd never tire of your job on our New-Lifestyle Level.

Mind you, we're not looking for sales clerks. (If we were, we'd advertise in the Classified Section.) What we're seeking is people with a deep personal interest in all the exciting lifestyle concepts we'll be introducing at Halls Crown Center. The way we have it figured, nobody is better qualified to sell telescopes all day than the guy or gal who spends evenings stargazing. And nobody will be happier with the job.

Even if dealing with customers isn't your thing, come see us if you're interested in quality merchandising and all that goes with it. We need attendants, markers, receivers, packers, wrappers, handlers, finishers, fitters. In short, you can find an especially rewarding career at Halls Crown Center, whether or nor you're interested in selling.

Make sense to you? Then come tell us your dream . . . . and we'll show you ours.

Apply Now to Our Interviewing Office
Open 8:30 to 5:30, Monday through Friday

Help-wanted ads must be carefully prepared. Media must be chosen, coded for media study, and impact analyzed afterwards. If the organization's name is not used and a box number is substituted, the impact may not be as great, but if the name is used too many applicants may appear, and screening procedures for too many people can be costly. This is a difficult decision to make in preparing recruitment advertisements.

In addition, the ad must not violate EEO requirements by indicating preferences for a particular racial, religious, national origin, or sex group. The advertisement shown in Exhibit 6–8 is the type that will create trouble for a firm. Look at the questions that could be raised by this ad.

Use of Recruiters

Some organizations use recruiters or scouts who search the schools (as baseball scouts search the ball diamonds) for new talent. Recruiters can be ineffective as screeners of good applicants if they use stereotypes in screening or are more influenced by recent interviews than earlier ones. This will be made clearer in the discussion of college recruiters in this chapter and the problems of interviewing in Chapter 7.

Exhibit 6–8 _____

A questionable want ad

You can get into trouble very easily when you're hiring people these days. Look at this ad, and try to learn from its mistakes.

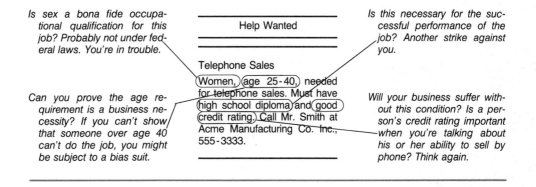

Is sex a bona fide occupational qualification for this job? Probably not under federal laws. You're in trouble.

Can you prove the age requirement is a business necessity? If you can't show that someone over age 40 can't do the job, you might be subject to a bias suit.

Help Wanted

Telephone Sales

Women, age 25-40, needed for telephone sales. Must have high school diploma and good credit rating. Call Mr. Smith at Acme Manufacturing Co. Inc., 555-3333.

Is this necessary for the successful performance of the job? Another strike against you.

Will your business suffer without this condition? Is a person's credit rating important when you're talking about his or her ability to sell by phone? Think again.

Computer Matching Services

Systems similar to the computer dating services that flourished a few years ago have been developed to match people desiring jobs and organizations needing people. These amount to extraorganizational skills inventories, and they are a natural use of the computer. The U.S. Employment Service's Job Bank is attempting to fill the need for a nationwide job-matching network to reduce unemployment. In addition to this government service, there are private-sector systems. Little is known about these sytems in practice, but they seem to have potential use for specifically qualified jobs.

Special-Event Recruiting

When the supply of employees available is not large or when the organization is new or not well known, some organizations have successfully used special events to attract potential employees. They may stage open houses, schedule headquarters visits, provide literature, and advertise these events in appropriate media. To attract professionals, organizations may have hospitality suites at professional meetings. Executives also make speeches at association meetings or schools to get the organization's image across. Ford Motor Company conducted symposia on college campuses and sponsored cultural events to attract attention to its qualifications as a good employer.

One of the most interesting approaches is to promote job fairs and native daughter and son days. A group of firms sponsors a meeting or exhibition at which each has a booth to publicize jobs available. Some experts claim recruiting costs have been cut 80 percent using these methods. They may be scheduled on holidays to reach college students home at that time or to give the presently employed a chance to look around. This technique is especially useful for smaller, less well-known employers. It appeals to job seekers who wish to locate in a particular area and those wanting to minimize travel and interview time.

Summer Internships

Another approach to recruiting and getting specialized work done that has been tried by many organizations is to hire students during the summer as interns. This approach has been used by businesses (Sherwin-Williams Company, Chase Manhattan Bank, Standard Oil Company of Ohio, Kaiser Aluminum, First National City Bank), government agencies (City of New York), and hospitals. Students in accredited graduate hospital programs, for example, serve a summer period called a preceptorship.

There are a number of purposes for these programs. They allow organizations to get specific projects done, expose them to talented potential employees who may become their "recruiters" at school, and provide trial-run employment to determine if they want to hire particular people full time. *The Wall Street Journal* has reported that some firms are using this technique to help recruit women and blacks.

From the student's point of view, the summer internship means a job with pay, some experience in the world of work, a possible future job, and a chance to use one's talents in a realistic environment. In a way, it is a short form of some co-op college work and study programs.

The organization usually provides supervision and a choice of projects to be done. Some of the projects the City of New York's college interns worked on during one summer were snow emergency planning, complaint handling, attitude survey of lower level employees, and information dissemination.

There are costs to these programs, of course. Sometimes the interns take up a lot of supervisory time, and the work done is not always the best. But the major problem some organizations have encountered concerns the expectations of students. Some students expect everything to be perfect at work. When it is not, they get negative impressions about the organization they have worked for, assuming that it is more messed up than others in the field. Such disillusioned students become *reverse recruiters*. This effect has caused some organizations to drop the programs. Others have done so when they found they were not able to recruit many interns.

College Recruiting

Many of you reading this section will be interested in learning how to improve your chances at getting a job. This section looks at college recruiting from the point of view of the enterprise.

The college recruiting process is similar in some ways to other recruiting. However, in college recruiting the organization sends an employee, usually called a recruiter, to a campus to interview candidates and describe the organization to them. Coinciding with the visit, brochures and other literature about the organization are often distributed. This literature is customarily expensively designed and produced. An organization may also run ads to attract students or conduct seminars at which company executives talk about various facets of the organization.

In the typical procedure, those seeking employment register at the college placement service. This placement service is a labor market exchange providing opportunities for students and employers to meet and discuss potential hiring. During the recruiting season (from about mid-October to mid-March), candidates are advised through student newspapers, mailings, bulletin boards, and so forth of scheduled visits. At the placement service, they reserve preliminary interviews with employers they want to see and are given brochures and other literature about the firms. After the preliminary interviews and before leaving the campus, each recruiter invites the chosen candidates to make a site visit at a later date. Those lower on the list are told they are being considered and are called upon if students chosen first decide not to accept employment with the firm.

Students who are invited to the site are given more job information and meet appropriate potential supervisors and other executives. They are entertained and may be given a series of psychological tests as well. The organization bears all expenses. If the organization desires to hire an individual, he or she is given an offer prior to leaving the site or shortly thereafter by mail or phone. Some bargaining may take place on salary and benefits, depending on the current labor market. The candidate then decides whether to accept or reject the offer.

With which companies do the students sign up to interview? They choose those whose work sounds interesting and whose recruiting program is well done and which have a good image. Generally speaking, the more interviews a student has, the greater variety of job offers he or she will get, and often the offers are better as well.

Various persons influence the applicant in job choice: peers, family, wife/husband or companion, and professors. The main influence appears to be the recruiter. You can learn a lot about the job situation by knowing what goes on on the recruiter's side of the desk. Mary Kale, a recruiter for Bethlehem Steel, has a recruiting day like the one described in the Close-Up on page 174.

So if, when you are interviewed, you suspect the recruiter is tired, usually you'll be right. Recruiters do not want prospects to have a stressful experience; rather they see a mutually satisfactory interview as a first step in your organizational choice. The college recruiting process is modeled in Exhibit 6–9. As you can see, effective recruiting efforts of both personnel and operating executives.

The Effective College Recruiter

In college recruiting, generally three elements are involved: the organization, the applicant, and the intervening variable—the recruiter. The recruiter is the filter and the matcher, the one who is actually seen by the applicants and is studied as a representative of the company. The recruiter is not just an employee but is viewed as an example of the kind of person the organization employs and wants in the future.

Students prefer recruiters who have work experience in their specialties and have some personal knowledge of the university they are visiting. Students also have preferences for specific behavior during the recruiting interview. Characteristics in the recruiter they want most are: friendliness, knowledge, personal interest in the applicant, and truthfulness. Second, some applicants prefer enthusiastic and convincing communicators.

Major flaws students have found in typical recruiters are:

Lack of Interest in the Applicant • They infer this if the recruiter's presentation is mechanical—bureaucratic—programmed. One student reported, "The company might just as well have sent a tape recorder."

Lack of Enthusiasm • If the recruiter seems bored, students infer that he or she represents a dull and uninteresting company.

P/HRM Manager Close-Up

Mary E. Kale
Bethlehem Steel
Corporation

Mary Kale is 28 and has been with Bethlehem for seven years. She was a metallurgist for two years and has been a recruiter for five. In 1976, she recruited 26 of the 106 persons Bethlehem hired and has a high acceptance rate among her recruits. She is one of the 3,500 full-time recruiters in the United States today.

Two recent weeks are typical of her work life. One week she interviewed for five days at Cornell; she had to drive three hours through a snow squall to get there. The next week, she flew and drove on Sunday to Grove City to interview there Monday. She drove to Youngstown, Ohio, and interviewed there Tuesday, then drove back to Pittsburgh. Wednesday and Thursday she interviewed at Carnegie Mellon and other Pittsburgh schools. Friday was spent in a hotel interviewing.

What's her day like? She eats an early breakfast and begins interviewing at 9 A.M. She interviews candidates for 30 minutes each, takes a 30-minute walk instead of lunch, and resumes interviews until 5:30 P.M. In brief open periods she tries to line up other candidates, but typically she interviews 54 people a week. After a quick supper, she spends the evening in her hotel room writing reports on the day's recruits, calling recruit prospects for later interviews, and reading the résumés of the next day's prospects.

In each interview, she begins by putting the recruit at ease, then asks the recruit about himself or herself. Next she discusses the job requirements and what the company has to offer, and asks for

questions. She sees herself as much as a job counselor as recruiter. She wants to help recruits find a direction for their lives, and also to acquire the best employees for Bethlehem.

Biography

Mary E. Kale, senior college relations representative for Bethlehem Steel Company, earned a B.S. in chemistry at Chatham College, Pittsburgh. Before her present position with Bethlehem Steel, Mary was a management trainee, metallurgical engineer, assistant college relations representative, and college relations representative. She travels extensively throughout the United States, meeting with industrial and government leaders as well as college placement officers and students. Mary has done videotaped news releases in connection with Bethlehem's communication effort and has served on specially appointed task forces and committees.

Job description

At Bethlehem Steel Corporation, a recruiter's job consists primarily of visiting college and university campuses to interview graduating seniors for employment with the corporation. During the interview, the recruiter's objective is to learn as much as possible about the candidate's academic qualifications, motivation, experience, and goals, in order to evaluate her or his overall suitability for the jobs available. This requires an in-depth knowledge of the corporation and the types of jobs to be filled. Once the recruiter evaluates the student, she or he must complete a written record of the interview, obtain a completed application form, and refer the file to the appropriate corporate department for further consideration and interview if desired.

In addition to interviewing, representatives visit key faculty and administration personnel on every campus at which the corporation conducts recruiting. Administrative tasks involved in college relations work include handling all correspondence with placement and faculty people concerning the campus visit, the completion of specification sheets describing the types of positions available and the degree required, and coordination of special events on campus, such as career fairs.

Exhibit 6–9

The college recruiting process

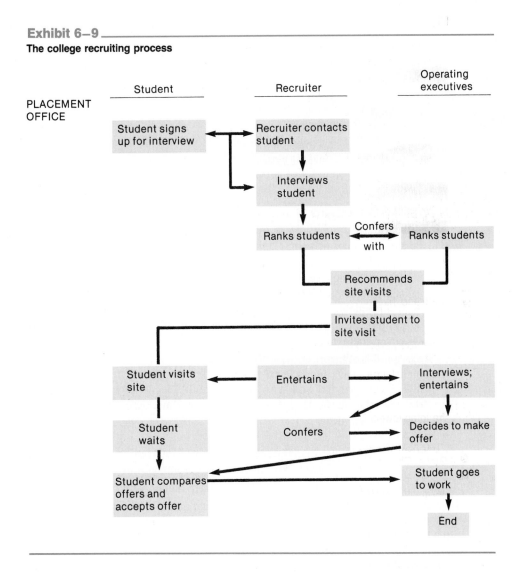

Stress or Too-Personal Interviews • Students resent too many personal questions about their social class, their parents, and so forth. They want to be evaluated for their own accomplishments. They also unanimously reject stress or sarcastic interviewing styles.

Time Allocation by Recruiters • The final criticism of recruiters has to do with how much time they talk and how much they let applicants talk or ask questions. From the point of view of the applicant, much of the recruiter's time is wasted with a long canned history of the company, number of employees, branches, products, assets, pension plans, and so forth. Many of the questions the recruiter asks applicants are answered on the application blank, anyway.

These findings reemphasize the need for an organization engaged in college recruiting to train effective recruiters and to have a well-planned visitation schedule. Too many enterprises do not plan the recruiting interview as well as they do their product sales presentations. The recruiter normally has 30 minutes per interview; this time should be used well. The applicant should receive printed material describing the less interesting aspects of information (such as organization history and details of organization operations). The interview period should be divided about equally between the recruiter and the applicant. Students want to hear about the job itself, the work climate, and the kind of person the organization is trying to hire for the job. Then they would like to be able to discuss how they might fit in and to ask a few questions. Too often, the recruiter talks for 25 minutes and almost as an afterthought asks if there are any questions.

Realistic Job Preview • It is also important for recruiters to provide realistic expectations of the job. When they do so, there is significantly lower turnover of new employees, and the same number of people apply. Researchers have found that most recruiters give general, glowing descriptions of the company rather than a balanced or truthful presentation.

Research suggests that recruitment can be made more effective through the use of realistic job previews (RJPs).[12] A realistic job preview means that a person is given pertinent information about the job without distortion or exaggeration. In traditionally providing job previews the job is presented as attractive, interesting, and stimulating. Some jobs are all of these things. However, most jobs have some unattractive features. The RJP presents the full picture, warts and all.

Exhibit 6–10 presents the typical consequences of traditional versus job previews. Studies conducted at Southern New England Telephone, Prudential Insurance Co., Texas Instruments, and the U.S. Military Academy have used and reported on the RJP.[13] The results indicate that:

> Newly hired employees who received RJP have a higher rate of job survival than those hired using traditional previews.
>
> Employees hired after RJPs indicate higher satisfaction.
>
> An RJP can "set" the job expectations of new employees at realistic levels.
>
> RJPs do not reduce the flow of highly capable applicants.

These findings suggest that RJPs can be used as an inoculation against disappointment with the realities of a job. This could be an important technique for reducing costly turnover and absenteeism.

Companies that wish to influence applicants should also review their recruiting literature to make sure it appeals to the most successful students. This literature, plus advertisements and articles in trade publications, are major factors in the organization-choice decision.

---

[12]John P. Wanous, "A Job Preview Makes Recruiting More Effective," *Harvard Business Review,* 1975, pp. 121–25.

[13]John P. Wanous, *Organizational Entry* (Reading, Mass.: Addison-Wesley, 1980), pp. 51–61. Also see J. Weitz, "Job Expectancy and Survival," *Journal of Applied Psychology,* August 1956, pp. 245–47; R. M. Macedonia, *"Expectations—Press and Survival.* "(unpublished doctoral dissertation, New York University, 1969).

Exhibit 6–10 _____

Typical consequences of job preview procedures

Traditional preview	_Realistic preview_
Set initial job expectations too high	Set job expectations realistically
↓	↓
Job is typically viewed as attractive, stimulating, and challenging	Job may or may not be attractive, depending on individual's needs
↓	↓
High rate of job offer acceptance	Some accept, some reject job offer
↓	↓
Work experience disconfirms expectations	Work experience confirms expectations
↓	↓
Dissatisfaction and realization that job not matched to needs	Satisfaction; needs matched to job
↓	↓
Low job survival, dissatisfaction, frequent thoughts of quitting	High job survival, satisfaction, infrequent thoughts of quitting

Source: adapted from John P. Wanous, "Tell It Like It Is at Realistic Job Preview," _Personnel,_ July–August 1975, p. 54.

Cost/Benefit Analysis of Recruiting

Many aspects of recruitment, such as the effectiveness of recruiters, can be evaluated. Organizations assign goals to recruiting by types of employees. For example, a goal for a recruiter might be to hire 350 unskilled and semiskilled employees, or 100 technicians, or 100 machinists, or 100 managerial employees per year. Then the organization can decide who are the best recruiters. They may be those who meet or exceed quotas and those whose recruits stay with the organization and are evaluated well by their superiors.

Sources of recruits can also be evaluated. In college recruiting, the organization can divide the number of job acceptances by the number of campus interviews to compute the cost per hire at each college. Then it drops from the list campuses that are not productive.

The methods of recruiting can be evaluated by various means. Exhibit 6–11 compares

Exhibit 6–11 _____

Yields of recruiting methods by various calculations

Source of recruit	_Yield_	_Total yield (percent)_	_Ratio of acceptance to receipt of resumé_	_Ratio of acceptance to offer_
Write-ins	2,127	34.77%	6.40	58.37
Advertising	1,979	32.35	1.16	39.98
Agencies	856	14.00	1.99	32.07
Direct college placement	465	7.60	1.50	13.21
Internal company	447	7.30	10.07	65.22
Walk-ins	134	2.19	5.97	57.14
Employee referrals	109	1.78	8.26	81.82

the results of a number of these methods. The organization can calculate the cost of each method (such as advertising) and divide it by the benefits it yields (acceptances of offers). After the interviews the organization can also examine how much accurate job information was provided during the recruitment process.

Summary

This chapter has demonstrated the process whereby organizations recruit additional employees, suggested the importance of recruiting, and shown who recruits, where, and how. To summarize, the following points are repeated:

1. Recruiting is the set of activities an organization uses to attract job candidates who have the abilities and attitudes needed to help the organization achieve its objectives.
2. External factors which affect the recruiting process include influences such as government and union restrictions and the state of the labor market.
3. Three aspects affect recruiting from the organization's viewpoint: the recruiting requirements set, organization policies and procedures, and the organizational image.
4. Applicants' abilities, attitudes, and preferences, based on past work experiences and influences by parents, teachers, and others, affect them in two ways: how they set job preferences, and how they go about seeking a job.
5. In larger organizations the P/HRM department does the recruiting; in smaller organizations, multipurpose P/HRM people or operating managers recruit and interview applicants.
6. Two sources of recruits could be used to fill needs for additional employees: present employees (internal) or those not presently affiliated with the enterprise (external).
   a. Internal sources can be tapped through the use of job posting and bidding; moonlighting by present employees; and seeking recommendations from present employees regarding friends who might fill these vacancies.
   b. External sources include walk-ins, referrals from schools, and state employment offices.
7. Advertising, personal recruiting, computerized matching services, special-event recruiting, and summer internships are methods which can be used to recruit external applicants.
8. The criteria which characterize a successful college recruiter are:
   a. Shows a genuine interest in the applicant.
   b. Is enthusiastic.
   c. Is neither too personal nor too stressful in approach.
   d. Allots enough time for applicant's comments and questions.
9. A better job of recruiting and matching employees to job will mean lower employee turnover and greater employee satisfaction and organizational effectiveness.
10. In larger organizations, recruiting functions are more extensively planned and elevated.

Likely approaches used by the seven-model organizations specified in Exhibit 1–8 (Chapter 1) are summarized in Exhibit 6–12. It should be noted that several of the model organizations employ different categories of employees. For example, a small, violatile

Exhibit 6–12

Recommendation on recruiting practices for model organizations

Type of organization	Employment conditions affect recruiting		Importance of image		Methods of recruiting							
	Greatly	Little	Crucial	Not too important	Employment agencies	Newspaper ads	Radio commercials	Present employees	Computer matching	Special events	College recruiting	Summer internships
1. Large size, low complexity, high stability	X			X	X	X	X		X		X	X
2. Medium size, low complexity, high stability		X		X	X	X		X	X		X	
3. Small size, low complexity, high stability	X		X		X	X	X	X		X		
4. Medium size, moderate complexity, moderate stability		X	X	X	X	X	X	X	X	X	X	
5. Large size, high complexity, low stability		X			X	X		X	X	X	X	X
6. Medium size, high complexity, low stability		X	X		X	X	X	X		X	X	
7. Small size, high complexity, low stability	X		X		X	X	X	X		X		X

Case

Clark Kirby got prices of ads from all the Houston papers, including suburban papers and ethnic papers. He also discussed the impact and readership of the papers with the personnel/human resource managers he'd befriended. On this basis, he chose the major Houston afternoon paper, the leading black newspaper, the leading Hispanic paper, and a suburban paper in an area near the plant.

He also investigated the leading radio stations and selected the one that had the highest rating of the top three and the lowest commercial cost. He chose commuter times to run the radio ads. The advertising approach was innovative.

The pay and working conditions offered at the Houston plant were competitive. After Clark's recruiting campaign, he had the following numbers of applicants:

Managerial positions.	68
Professional/technical.	10
Clerical	78
Skilled employees.	110
Semiskilled employees.	720

Clark notified Ed of the results. The next job is to select the best of the applicants for hiring. Clark knows that is no easy job. Effective selection/hiring is the subject of Chapter 7.

hospital and a small, volatile toy company employ different kinds of employees, and the sources of recruits used would vary in such organizations. Only a few of the aspects of recruitment have been summarized in this table.

Questions for Review and Discussion

1. What is recruiting? Job search?
2. Of what value would a realistic job preview be in attempting to reduce turnover?
3. Give some dos and don'ts in recruiting interviews as far as legality is concerned.
4. Describe a model of the recruiting/attraction process. How do organization requirements, organizational policies, and organizational pay affect the process?
5. How do career planning and job preferences relate to effective job finding? Outline an approach to specify the job characteristics you want prior to job search.
6. Describe how you plan to get your job when you leave college.
7. Who is responsible for recruiting?
8. What sources of recruits do organizations use for blue-collar, gray-collar, white-collar, and managerial recruits?
9. Compare and contrast the effectiveness of the methods of recruiting such as advertising, special events, internships, and others.
10. How do organizations recruit college students for jobs? What are effective and ineffective recruiters like?

Glossary

Job Posting.   A listing of job openings that includes job specifications, appearing on a bulletin board or in company publications.

Job Search.   The set of activities a person (job candidate) initiates to seek and find a position which will be comfortable and rewarding.

Realistic Job Preview.   Provides a job candidate with accurate and clear information about the attractive and unattractive features of a job. Being realistic so that expectations are accurate is the objective of a job preview.

Recruitment.   The set of activities an organization uses to attract job candidates who have the abilities and attitudes needed to help the organization achieve its objectives.

Chapter Seven

Selection

Learning Objectives

After completing this chapter, you should be able to:
- Define the steps in the selection process.

- List what selection criteria are available and how they can by used to make selection more effective.

- Describe how to use selection tools such as interviews and biodata more effectively.

- Compare the different types of validity—content, construct, and criterion related.

- Illustrate the methods used to observe and evaluate the performance of assessees in an assessment center.

Chapter Outline

I. A Diagnostic Approach to the Selection Process
   A. Environmental Circumstances Influencing Selection
   B. The Immediate Environment and Selection

II. Who Makes Selection Decisions?

III. Selection Criteria
   A. Formal Education
   B. Experience
   C. Physical Characteristics
   D. Personal Characteristics and Personality Type

IV. Reliability and Validity of Selection Criteria
   A. Reliability
   B. Validity

V. The Selection Process
   A. Step 1: Preliminary Screening Interview
   B. Step 2: Completion of Application Blank/Biodata Form
   C. Step 3: Employment Interview
   D. Step 4: Employment Tests
   E. Step 5: Reference checks and Recommentations
   F. Step 6: Physical Examinations

VI. Selection of Managers
   A. Assessment Centers

VII. The Selection Decision

VIII. Cost/Benefit Analysis of the Selection Decision

IX. Summary

Case
(continued from Chapter 6)

Clark

Clark Kirby is satisfied. He and his assistants have recruited 986 applicants for the 596 positions Gunther will have at its Houston plant. But before he gets too satisfied, he realizes that there is a big job ahead of him. Which 596 of the 986 should be hired? And who should do the hiring?

The P/HRM specialist has done some preliminary screening. Most of the applicants have completed an application blank. But where does he go from here?

Clark has called Ed Humprey, the plant manager, and asked if he wished to be involved in the hiring. Ed said that he only had time to choose his top management team. The rest is up to Clark. Clark reminded Ed that the company didn't want them to hire too many present employees; raiding this would be another Gunther plant. Ed said he knew that and would abide by company policy.

As Clark begins to plan how to make 596 decisions.

> Selection is the process by which an organization chooses from a list of applicants the person or persons who best meet the selection criteria for the position available, considering current environmental conditions.

This definition emphasizes the effectiveness aspect of selection, but selection decisions must also be efficient. The second purpose of selection is to improve the proportion of successful employees chosen from the applicant list at the least cost. Selection costs can be high. In 1981, it was estimated that it cost an organization such as Tenneco $25,000 to select a top-level executive, $6,000 to select a middle manager, $4,000 for a supervisor, $6,000 for an engineer, $9,000 for an accountant, and $3,000 for a secretary.[1]

The basic objective of selection is to obtain the employees most likely to meet the organization's standards of performance. The employees' satisfaction and complete development of their abilities are included in this objective.

A Diagnostic Approach to the Selection Process

As Clark Kirby sets out to hire 596 employees, he faces a selection process influenced by many factors. These factors are highlighted in the diagnostic model in Exhibit 7–1. We'll begin by examining the factors in the external and internal environment.

---

[1]Based on conversations with directors of P/HRM functions in large organizations in urban areas.

Exhibit 7–1 _____

Factors affecting selecting of human resources and effectiveness

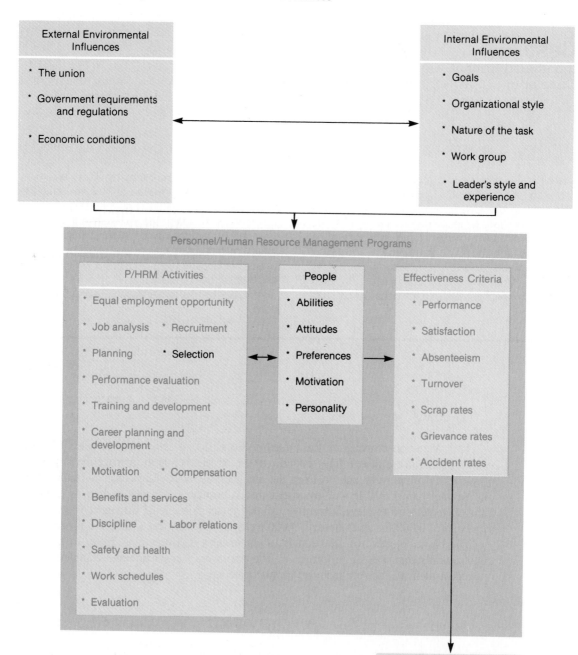

External Environmental
Influences

* The union

* Government requirements
  and regulations

* Economic conditions

Internal Environmental
Influences

* Goals

* Organizational style

* Nature of the task

* Work group

* Leader's style and
  experience

Personnel/Human Resource Management Programs

P/HRM Activities

* Equal employment opportunity

* Job analysis   * Recruitment

* Planning   * Selection

* Performance evaluation

* Training and development

* Career planning and
  development

* Motivation   * Compensation

* Benefits and services

* Discipline   * Labor relations

* Safety and health

* Work schedules

* Evaluation

People

* Abilities

* Attitudes

* Preferences

* Motivation

* Personality

Effectiveness Criteria

* Performance

* Satisfaction

* Absenteeism

* Turnover

* Scrap rates

* Grievance rates

* Accident rates

Organization
End Results

* Competitive product(s)

* Competitive service(s)

Environmental Circumstances Influencing Selection

The Internal Environment • The nature of the organization doing the selecting affects the process it uses. The private and third sectors use similar methods, but the public sector is different. Traditionally, in the public-sector selection has been made on the basis of either political patronage or merit. The patronage system gives jobs to those who have worked to elect public officials. This was the only method used in the public sector until the civil service reforms of the late 1800s. Patronage is still practiced today. In the private and third sectors friendship with managers or employees can become a factor in the choice, but this is not the same thing as patronage. Pure "merit" selection (choice based on the employee's excellence in abilities and experience) is an idea which systematic personnel selection tries to achieve but seldom does.

Other aspects of the organization which affect selection are the organization's size, complexity, and technological volatility. Systematic, reliable, and valid P/HRM selection techniques are sometimes costly to develop and use. When this is so, only large organizations can afford to use them. To justify the development of these techniques, there must be a sufficient number of jobs to fill and a pool of candidates to fill them. If the organization is complex and has a large number of jobs with only a few occupants, sophisticated selection techniques are not cost effective. The extent to which size dictates the number of employees each work group also affects the usefulness of the techniques. In sum, the size, complexity, technological volatility, and nature of the organization will determine which selection techniques are cost effective for the organization.

Nature of the Labor Market • The second circumstance affecting the selection process is the labor market within which the organization functions. If there are many applicants, the selection decision can be complicated. If there is only one applicant, it is relatively easy. The labor market for the organization is affected by the labor market in the country as a whole, the region, or the city in which the organization is located. It is further affected by the working conditions the organization offers, the job itself, and the organization's image. (These were discussed earlier in the book and will be covered in Chapters 13–15). For example, hospital dieticians trying to hire dishwashers or food preparation helpers do not have much of a selection decision to worry about. The job can be unpleasant, and it is performed at unpopular hours (the breakfast crew might have to arrive at 5:30 A.M.). The workday can be long, the pay is not good, and frequently there are no possibilities for promotion. For such jobs, an applicant who can walk in the door and is found to be free of a communicable disease will usually be hired. Rarely are there enough applicants. A civil service specialist who must choose from hundreds of applicants for foreign service postings to European embassies has a much more difficult selection decision to make.

Those who work in personnel/human resource management analyze this labor market factor by use of the selection ratio:

$$\text{Selection ratio} = \frac{\text{Number of applicants selected}}{\text{Number of applicants available for selection}}$$

Consider Clark Kirby's problem at Gunther. The selection ratios are: managers 38/68, or about 1:2; professional/technical, 10/10, or 1:1; clerical, 44/78, or about 1:2; skilled, 104/110, or about 1:1; semiskilled, 400/720, or almost 1:2. When the selection ratio is 1:1, the selection process is short and unsophisticated. It also means there are few applicants from which to select. With a selection ratio of 1:2, the process can be quite detailed, as described below. The larger ratio also means the organization can be quite selective in its choice. It is more likely that employees who fit the organization's criteria for success will be hired when the ratio is 1:2 than when it is 1:1.

Union Requirements • If the organization is wholly or partly unionized, union membership prior to or shortly after hiring is a factor in the selection decision. Sometimes the union contract requires that seniority (experience at the job with the company) be the only criterion—or at least a major one—in selection. If the union has a hiring hall, the union makes the selection decision for the organization. In many ways, openly and subtly, a union can affect an organization's selection process.

Government's Requirements • The fourth circumstance affecting selection is government. In the United States, governments have passed laws designed to guarantee equal employment opportunity and human rights. Some of the requirements were described in detail in Chapter 3 on selection decisions.

The Immediate Environment and Selection

You will note that in Exhibit 7–1 the people factor is emphasized. The basic objective, selection—to obtain high-performing employees—may be modified by the operating managers or controlling interests. It is management's responsibility to set selection objectives, such as:

- Employees who will stay with the company many years.
- Employees who have low accident rates.
- Employees who have high-quality standards.
- Employees who get along with their co-workers.
- Employees who get along with the customers.

These characteristics can influence the kind of employees selected. They do not, however, always correlate exactly with highest quantitative preformance.

Selection seeks to identify the abilities and attitudes of the applicant so that these can be matched up with job requirements. In Chapter 2, we discussed how human beings differ on every possible characteristic: physical, mental, and psychological. All of these characteristics are important considerations in making a selection decision.

Selection also seeks to identify the nature of the task. From job analysis (described in Chapter 4), job specifications which are up to date and related to behavior are developed. The job specifications are used to define the characteristics (criteria) needed for a person to perform a certain task effectively. The essence of selection is to match the right applicant, who has the right abilities and attitudes, with the right job and its specifications.

One more factor, which is not shown in Exhibit 7–1, influences the selection decision. This concerns how much time is available to make the selection decision. If there is adequate time the organization may be able to use all the selection tools it normally uses. If there is an emergency, the selection decision may be shortened by dropping one or several of the steps in the selection process.

The selection activity is in Stage IV of development or maturity (see Exhibit 1–6, Chapter 1). It is well developed, and many studies have analyzed the use of the various selection methods.

Who Makes Selection Decisions?

In smaller organizations with no P/HRM unit, the operating manager makes selection decisions. In medium-sized and larger organizations, both operating and P/HRM managers are involved in selection decisions, as Exhibit 7–2 indicates.

In larger organizations, the P/HRM manager in charge of selection is called the employment manager. An example is Audrey Johnson, employee relations manager of the Gillette Company (see page 188).

Some organizations also give employees a voice in the selection choice. Applicants are interviewed by employees who are then asked to express their preferences. For example, this procedure is used in university departments where the faculty expresses its preferences on applicants, and at the Lincoln Electric Company in Cleveland, in which the work group recruits and selects replacements or additions.

Generally, more effective selection decisions are made when many people are involved in the decision and when adequate information is furnished to those selecting the candidates. The operating manager and the work group should have more to say about the selection decision than the P/HRM specialist.

Selection Criteria

If a selection program is to be successful, the employee characteristics believed necessary for effective performance on the job should be stated explicitly in the job specification. The criteria usually can be summarized in several categories: education, experience, physical characteristics, and personal characteristics. Basically, the selection criteria should list the characteristics of present employees who have performed well in the position to be

Exhibit 7–2

The role of operating and personnel managers in selection

Selection function	Operating manager (OM)	Personnel/human resource manager (P/HRM)
Choice of selection criteria.	Selected by OM	Recommends and implements for selection criteria based on job specifications
Validation of criteria		Performed by P/HRM
Screening interview		Normally performed by personnel
Supervision of application/biodata form		Normally by P/HRM
Employment interview	OM and P/HRM	OM and P/HRM
Testing		Performed by personnel
Background/reference chart.		Normally performed by personnel
Physical exam.		Normally performed by personnel
Selection/decision	OM decides after considering P/HRM recommendation	Recommendation by P/HRM to OM

P/HRM Manager Close-Up

Audrey Johnson
The Gillette Company

Developed and instituted a comprehensive affirmative action plan which successfully stood a federal audit.

Streamlined and systematized employment practices and procedures to ensure their legality and efficiency.

Instituted compensation program with guidelines and controls to ensure uniform and equitable treatment for all employees.

Managed significant benefits changes, including installing a new dental insurance program and offering an HMO (Health Maintenance Organization) option.

Assessed training and development needs for all exempt employees.

Biography

Audrey Johnson, a graduate of the University of Minnesota with an M.B.A. in industrial relations, holds the title of employee relations manager for the Gillette Company, St. Paul, Minnesota. She holds a B.A. from St. Olaf College and is a graduate of the Harvard-Radcliffe Program in Business Administration. Johnson has had broad personnel experience. Before joining Gillette she worked as a personnel representative at the University of Minnesota. Some of her achievements in her current position include:

Job description

The position of employee relations manager for all personnel administrative functions in the manufacturing center of the Gillette Company, one of the nation's largest personal care manufacturers, involves responsibility for employment, affirmative action, compensation, work force, development and training, benefits, and employee services, along with a complete budget responsibility of $300,000. The employee relations manager also supervises a full-time staff of seven subordinates.

---

filled.[2] As in personnel and employment planning, however, if the list of characteristics desired is too long, it may be impossible to select anyone. And with no list of criteria, the wrong prospects are likely to be selected. Sometimes, because of limits on what the organization can offer or management's objectives, one gets criteria like those in the cartoon.

Formal Education

An employer selecting among applicants for a job wants to find the person who has the right abilities and attitudes to be successful. These cognitive, motor, physical, and interpersonal attributes are present because of genetic predisposition and because they were

---

[2] Scott T. Rickard, "Effective Staff Selection," *Personnel Journal*, June 1981, pp. 475–78.

"What we're really looking for is a not-too-bright young man with no ambition and who is content to stay on the bottom and not louse things up."

Reprinted by permission The Wall Street Journal.

learned in the home, at school, on the job, and so on. Most employers attempt to screen for abilities by specifying educational accomplishments.

Employers tend to specify as a criterion a specific amount (in years) of formal education and types of education. For the job of accountant, the employer may list as an educational criterion a bachelor's degree in accounting. The employer may prefer that the degree is from certain institutions, and that the gradepoint average is higher than some minimum, and that certain honors have been achieved. To be legal, such criteria must relate to past performance of successful accountants at the firm.

Formal education can indicate ability or skills present, and level of accomplishment may indicate the degree of work motivation and intelligence of the applicant. In general, other things being equal, employers tend to prefer more to less education and higher to lower grades. But these characteristics must be correlated with job success if the criterion is to be an effective predictor.

Thus the educational criteria must be validated against job performance. The employer must examine the amount and type of education that correlates with job effectiveness at the organization and use it as the selection criterion. This is more effective than relying on preferences, and is the legal, ethical way to set an educational criterion.

Experience

Another useful criterion for selection is experience. In general, employers prefer relatively more experience to less, relevant to irrelevant experience, and significant to insignificant experience. An employer known to be demanding of its employees would probably choose an applicant who has been successful in the same or a similar job. Employers equate experience with ability as well as with attitude, reasoning that a prospect who has performed the job before and is applying for a similar job likes the work, and will do it well. Since loyalty to the job and the organization are significant, most employers prefer to hire from within, as discussed in Chapter 6.

One way to measure experience within the organization is to provide each employee with a seniority rating, which indicates the length of time an employee has been employed. In the military, the date of rank is an equivalent seniority measure. Seniority is measured in various ways: as total time worked for the firm or time worked for the firm on a particular job or in a certain unit. Because some organizations in the past did not allow certain groups to hold certain jobs, the courts and the EEOC are assigning retroactive and compensatory seniority to some employees.[3]

Physical Characteristics

In the past, many employers consciously or unconsciously used physical characteristics (including how an applicant looked) as a selection criterion. Many times this discriminated against ethnic groups and females. The practice is now illegal unless it can be shown that a physical characteristic is directly related to work effectiveness. Studies show that employers were more likely to hire and pay more to taller men, airlines chose flight attendants on the basis of beauty (or their definition of it), and receptionists were often chosen on the same basis.

There are some tasks which require certain physical characteristics, usually stamina and strength, which can be tested. Candidates cannot legally be screened out by arbitrary height, weight, and similary requirements. The organization should determine the physical characteristics of present successful employees and use an attribute as a criterion *only* when all or most of them have it.

Personal Characteristics and Personality Type

The final criterion category is a catchall called personal characteristics and personality types. One personal characteristic is marital status. Some employers have preferred "stable" married employees, assuming this would lead to lower turnover and higher performance. Other firms prefer divorced or single persons because they are more willing to be transferred, to work weekends, and so on. Discrimination in selection based on marital status is illegal in some places, and unless an organization has data to support the relation of this criterion to performance, it makes little sense.

A second personal characteristic is age. It is illegal to discriminate against persons over 40 in the United States. It is not illegal to discriminate against young people, although protecting this group also has been proposed. Any age criterion should be examined by seeing how it relates to present successful employees.

Employers may prefer certain "personality" types for jobs. For example, to use Carl Jung's classification, they may prefer extroverts to introverts.[4] This can be an important

---

[3]Alfred J. Walker, "Management Selection Systems That Meet the Challenges of the 80s," *Personnel Journal*, October 1981, pp. 775–780.

[4]H. Read, M. Fordham, G. Adler, eds., C. G. Jung, *Collected Works* (Princeton, N.J.: Princeton University Press, 1953).

characteristic for employees who deal with the public, such as receptionists, salespersons, and caseworkers, but it may not be useful for other jobs, such as actuaries, lab technicians, or keypunch operators. The personality type specified should be based on past experience or be weighted lower than other, more directly relevant criteria.

Reliability and Validity of Selection Criteria

Before the organization can specify the characteristics to be sought in selection, the success criteria must be defined. Job analysis can indicate that the employee who meets minimum standards for a particular position processes 10 claims per hour, for example. This employee also receives an error rating of less than 5 percent and is absent less than six days per year.[5]

The next step is to determine ways of predicting which of the applicants can reach these levels of expectation. Sometimes direct success indicators (such as 10 claims per hour) are available. Other times proxies such as levels of intelligence, the presence of specified abilities, or certain amounts and types of experience are used.

Reliability

The main purpose of selection is to make decisions about individuals. One attempt to predict which candidates will be successful is to give applicants tests or simulations (more will be said about these later). If these selection tools are to be useful they must be dependable or *reliable*. Thus, if Dan scores a 70 on an employment test on Monday, a 40 on a similar version of the test on Wednesday, and a 95 on Friday, it would not be possible to determine which score is the best measure of Dan's ability. The test is too unreliable to use (assuming that Dan was not sick or tired on test days). The *reliability* of any selection technique refers to its freedom from systematic errors of measurement or its consistency under different conditions.

Unless interviewers judge the potential of a job applicant to be the same one day as they did yesterday or a few days ago, their judgments are unreliable. Likewise, Dan's test scores are unreliable. In practice, one way to assess reliabilities is to correlate the scores of applicants given the same or similar tests or interviews on two different occasions. This correlation indicates the *stability* of scores over time. Reliability can also be determined by correlating scores from two alternate forms of a selection device (e.g., test or interview). If the scores are the same or similar the test is said to yield reliable scores.[6]

Interrater reliability is another estimate of reliability. This is calculated by having scores independently assessed by two or more raters (e.g., performance evaluation, personality test). When nonobjective measures are used (e.g., performance evaluation) interrater reliability is important.

Validity

In addition to having reliable selection decision information it is important legally and organizationally to have valid information. *Validity* refers to the extent to which a score or measure is an accurate predictor of success. It should be noted that validity refers to

---

[5]L. R. Aiken, *Psychological Educational Testing* (Boston: Allyn & Bacon, 1971).
[6]Robert M. Guion, *Personnel Testing* (New York: McGraw-Hill, 1965), pp. 29–31.

the inferences made from the use of a procedure, not to the procedure (e.g., test) itself. Siegel contrasts reliability and validity in this way: he points out that the yardstick is a reliable measure of space; no matter how many times you measure a person's height, the result will be the same.[7] But a yardstick has no validity as a measure of muscular coordination. The message is: a selection technique can be reliable without being valid. That is, if it is not valid it is not measuring what it is suppose to measure.

It should be noted that reliability is *internally referenced:* it measures how well scores correlate with themselves, regardless of what they measure. On the other hand, validity is *externally referenced:* it measures how well scores relate to some other measure of behavior, such as job performance.

There are various types of validity that the P/HRM specialist must be familiar with: (1) content, (2) construct, and (3) criterion related. Knowledge about these forms of validity are needed to comply with EEO regulations involving P/HRM activities such as selection, performance evaluation, and job analysis.

Content Validity • The degree to which a test, interview, or performance evaluation measures the skill, knowledge, or ability to perform the job is called content validity. For example, employment tests used in the plumbing, bricklaying, and electrical construction trades are considered content valid when test content and job content correspond closely. Test and job content are directly observable, meaning that content validity is an appropriate type of validity.

Content validity is not appropriate for more abstract job behaviors, such as leadership potential, leadership style, or work ethic. When selection procedures involve the use of tests to measure leadership characteristics and/or personality, construct validity rather than content validity is appropriate.

Construct Validity • Suppose that a P/HRM specialist claims to have devised a paper-and-pencil test to measure creativity, a variable that is assumed to be important in screening candidates for managerial vacancies. It is necessary to find a relationship between the variable called creativity inferred from behavior and a set of test measures.

Suppose that candidates are hired without using the creativity test because it needs to be *validated.* Validation involves gathering necessary data and then evaluating the measure.[8] The individuals hired would be observed on the job over a period of time and then rated in terms of job behaviors indicative of creativity. The raters or observers would be unaware of the test scores. If the individuals with the highest creativity test scores are also rated the most creative, the people with the lowest creativity test scores are rated the least creative, the test is said to have construct validity. Thus, *construct validity* is defined as a demonstrated relationship between underlying traits inferred from behavior and a set of test measures related to those traits.

Criterion-Related Validity • The extent to which a selection technique is predictive of or correlated with important elements of job behavior is called criterion-related validity. Per-

---

[7]L. Siegel, *Industrial Psychology* (Homewood, Ill.: Richard D. Irwin, 1969). For a thorough discussion of validity, see *Principles for the Validation and Use of Personnel Selection Procedures* (Berkeley, Calif.: Division of Industrial Organizational Psychology, American Psychological Assoc., 1980).

[8]Validation is discussed in E. J. McCormick and J. Tiffin, *Industrial Psychology* (Englewood Cliffs, N.J.: Prentice-Hall, 1974), pp. 101–110.

formance on a test or in some simulated exercise is checked against actual on the job performance. The job performance is called the criterion. A criterion can be units of output, a supervisor's rating, an end of training program test, sales results, or whatever outcome is appropriate.

Two types of criterion-related validity popularly used are concurrent and predictive. Concurrent validity involves collecting criterion measures at the same time as test scores from present employees. Predictive validity involves collecting measures on candidates and then obtaining criterion data after they have been on the job for some time. The test scores are correlated with the criterion data to obtain a measure of predictive validity.

The Selection Process

All organizations make selection decisions, and most make them at least in part informally. The smaller the organization, the more likely it is to take an informal approach to selection decisions. Formal or systematic selection decisions were developed first during World Wars I and II, when employee shortages brought tremendous placement problems and the military had to select and place large numbers of men in many different jobs very quickly and efficiently.

In the past, selection was often thought to be an easy decision. The boss interviewed applicants, sized them up, and let his or her gut reaction guide the choice. Decisions were based on the subjective ''likes'' or ''dislikes'' of the boss. Selection tools were designed to aid this gut reaction. For most selection decisions, that is all the tools were intended to do; they were designed to increase the proportion of successful employees selected. Today, selection is viewed as being more than simply relying on intuitive feelings.

The selection decision is usually perceived as a series of steps through which applicants pass. At each step, a few more applicants are screened out by the organization, or more applicants accept other job offers and drop from the applicant list. Exhibit 7–3 illustrates a typical series of steps for the selection process.

This series is not universally used; for example, government employers test at Step 3 instead of Step 4, as do some private- and third-sector employers. Few organizations use all steps, for they can be time consuming and expensive, and several steps, such as 4, 5, and 6, may be performed concurrently or at about the same time. Generally speaking, the more important the job, the more each step is likely to be used formally. Most organizations use the screening interview, application blank, and interview. Tests are used by a relatively small (and declining) number of employers. Background and reference checks and physical exams are used for some jobs and not others.

Step 1: Preliminary Screening Interview

Different organizations can handle Step 1 in various ways, ineffectively or effectively. For some types of jobs, applicants are likely to walk into the employment office or job location. In these cases, a P/HRM specialist or line manager usually spends a few moments with applicants in what is called the preliminary screening. The organization develops some rough guidelines to be applied in order to reduce the time and expense of actual selection. These guidelines could specify, for example, minimum education or the

Exhibit 7–3 _____

Typical selection decision when all possible steps are used (private and third sectors)

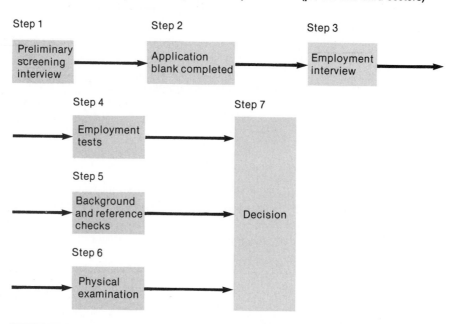

number of words typed per minute. Only those who meet these criteria are deemed potential employees and are interviewed.

If general appearance and personal characteristics are deemed important, preliminary screening is often done through a brief personal interview in which the personnel/human resource specialist or manager determines key information and forms a general impression of the applicant. On this basis, the successful applicant then moves to the next step in selection, perhaps with the knowledge that the lack of an essential characteristic has lessened the chances of being seriously considered for the job. In smaller organizations, if the applicant appears to be a likely candidate for the position the preliminary screening can proceed as an employment interview (Step 3).

The employer must be sure that the criteria used in this first step do not violate government antidiscrimination requirements. The EEOC has a publication, _Affirmative Action and Equal Employment: A Guidebook for Employers,_ which provides help on this issue (vol. 1, pp. 40–44).

Step 1 is part of the reception portion of recruiting (see Chapter 6). The organization has the opportunity to make a good or bad impression on the applicant in this step. James Metal Works made one kind of impression, Gunther Manufacturing another.

Step 2: Completion of Application Blank/Biodata Form

Applicants who come to an employment office are asked to complete an application blank after a screening interview. Recruiters often follow a similar procedure. In Gunther's employment office, all applicants who appear qualified, such as Jamie, would do so.

Jamie Meadows has just graduated from Martin Luther King High School. She is trying to decide which company to work for. She first goes to the P/HRM office at James Metal Works. John Walker, a P/HRM specialist, looks up after about 10 minutes. He stays seated.

John Yes?

Jamie I've just graduated from high school and am wondering if. . . .

John (interrupting) Can't you see the sign? Walker goes back to his paper work.

Over in the corner, Jamie notices a small sign that says: "We are not hiring now." Jamie leaves James Metal Works without another word.

Next she goes to Gunther's new employment office, where she is met by Terry Trovers. After her first experience, she approaches Terry somewhat reluctantly.

Jamie Hello, I'm Jamie Meadows. I just graduated from Martin Luther King High School, and I'm looking for a job.

Terry Nice to meet you Jamie. Let's sit down over here and talk about you and the jobs we have open right now.

One of the oldest instruments in P/HRM selection is the application blank.[9] Surveys show that all but the smallest organizations have applicants complete an application form or other biodata instrument (such as a biographical data form, biographical information blanks, an individual background survey, or an interview guide). Biodata forms are useful in selection, career planning and counseling, and performance evaluation. They are most likely to meet the EEOC's criticisms of other selection techniques.

Of course, application blanks and biodata forms could be illegal if they include items not relevant to job content. Items on the application blank should be kept to a minimum and should ask primarily for data which the enterprise's biodata studies indicate best predict effective performance. Exhibit 7–4 is an example of an application blank for the Thrifty Corporation.

Essentially, those advocating the biodata approach argue that past behavior patterns are the best predictor of future behavior patterns. Thus data should be gathered on a person's demographic, experiential, and attitudinal characteristics in a form that lends itself to psychometric evaluation and intrepretation. In constructing the biodata form, a variety of approaches is possible. According to experts the form should be brief; the items should be stated in neutral or pleasant terms; the items should offer all possible answers or categories plus an "escape clause"; and numbered items should add to a scale.[10] It is argued that sequenced items are preferable to nonsequenced items, and choose-one option items are better than multiple-choice items.

An important biodata substitute or supplement for the application blank is the *biographical information blank* (BIB). The BIB usually has more items than an application blank and includes different kinds of items, relating to such things as attitudes, health, and early life experiences. It uses the multiple-choice answer system. Instead of asking just about education, it might ask:

---

[9] Wayne F. Cascio, "Accuracy of Verifiable Biographical Information Blank Responses," *Journal of Applied Psychology,* December 1975, pp. 767–70.

[10] W. Owens, "Background Data," in *Handbook of Industrial and Organizational Psychology,* ed. M. Dunnette (Chicago: Rand McNally, 1976), pp. 609–44.

Exhibit 7–4

Application blank, Thrifty Corporation

Thrifty   **EMPLOYMENT APPLICATION**

                                  THRIFTY CORPORATION   STORE NO._____

(Use INK - PLEASE PRINT! Answer all questions accurately.)   DATE_____
NOTE: This application form is used for all Company jobs. Thus, any question deemed not job related may be omitted.

NAME	LAST	FIRST	MIDDLE	POSITION APPLIED FOR	FULL TIME___ PART TIME___
ADDRESS	NUMBER	STREET	HOW LONG?	SOC SEC NO	
CITY	ZIP CODE	STATE		PHONE NO.	

PERSONAL DATA

HOW WERE YOU REFERRED TO APPLY FOR WORK WITH THIS COMPANY?

   COMPANY IMAGE_____ NEWSPAPER_____ AGENCY_____ FRIENDS/RELATIVES_____ OTHER_____

DO YOU HAVE ADEQUATE TRANSPORTATION TO GET TO AND FROM WORK?_____

ARE YOU LEGALLY PERMITTED TO REMAIN PERMANENTLY IN THE U.S.? YES_____NO_____IF NO, VISA NO_____

WOULD YOU BE WILLING TO RELOCATE? YES_____NO_____ IF YES, DO YOU: OWN HOME?_____ RENT?_____LIVE WITH OTHERS?_____

DO YOU HAVE FAMILY, BUSINESS, HEALTH OR OTHER OBLIGATIONS THAT WOULD PREVENT YOU FROM:

   WORKING OVERTIME?_____TRAVELING?_____IF YES, EXPLAIN_____

LIST ANY OTHER NAMES USED OR UNDER WHICH YOU HAVE WORKED_____

LIST THE NAMES OF ANY FRIENDS/RELATIVES EMPLOYED BY THE COMPANY_____

EDUCATIONAL RECORD	NAME OF SCHOOL	LOCATION	DID YOU GRADUATE? YES NO	YEARS ATTENDED	DEGREE AND MAJOR	GRADE AVERAGE OR RANK IN CLASS
HIGH SCHOOL/ TRADE SCHOOL				✕		
JR COLLEGE						
COLLEGE UNIVERSITY						

ACTIVITIES IN WHICH YOU PARTICIPATED WHILE ATTENDING SCHOOL_____

ARE YOU CURRENTLY ATTENDING SCHOOL?_____ IF YES, LIST HOURS:_____

PRIOR THRIFTY EXPERIENCE (if any) FROM_____ TO_____ LOCATION_____LEFT BECAUSE_____

IF UNDER DIFFERENT NAME WHAT WAS THE NAME?_____

PREVIOUS EMPLOYMENT EXPERIENCE *In space below account for all time, including unpaid or volunteer work service, for the past 10 years, whether working or otherwise. Give complete names & addresses. If self-employed, give firm name and one business reference. Show month and year of employment.*

D A T E	FROM	PRESENT OR LAST EMPLOYER (FIRM NAME)			TITLE AND DUTIES		STARTING SALARY	ENDING SALARY
	TO	NO. & STREET	CITY	STATE	NAME OF SUPERVISOR	REASON FOR LEAVING		
D A T E	FROM	EMPLOYER (FIRM NAME)			TITLE AND DUTIES		STARTING SALARY	ENDING SALARY
	TO	NO. & STREET	CITY	STATE	NAME OF SUPERVISOR	REASON FOR LEAVING		
D A T E	FROM	EMPLOYER (FIRM NAME)			TITLE AND DUTIES		STARTING SALARY	ENDING SALARY
	TO	NO. & STREET	CITY	STATE	NAME OF SUPERVISOR	REASON FOR LEAVING		
D A T E	FROM	EMPLOYER (FIRM NAME)			TITLE AND DUTIES		STARTING SALARY	ENDING SALARY
	TO	NO. & STREET	CITY	STATE	NAME OF SUPERVISOR	REASON FOR LEAVING		

FORM NO. P-4 (352) FRONT (REV. 9/80)

SPECIAL SKILLS or JOB KNOWLEDGE

SHORTHAND WPM_____ TYPING WPM_____ CALCULATOR_____ 10 KEY ADDER_____

CASH REGISTER TYPES AND OTHER MACHINES YOU OPERATE_____

MERCHANDISE SPECIALTIES, IF APPLICABLE_____

OTHER, INCLUDING LANGUAGES YOU READ, SPEAK OR WRITE_____

PROFESSIONAL LICENSES YOU HOLD LIST TYPE AND LICENSE NUMBER_____

STORE WORK REQUIREMENTS
WORKING IN THE STORES AND COFFEE SHOPS REQUIRES VARIABLE SCHEDULES, INCLUDING
HOLIDAY, NIGHT, SATURDAY AND SUNDAY WORK   CAN YOU WORK THOSE HOURS?.............................YES_____ NO_____

IS SELLING PACKAGED LIQUOR OR TOBACCO ACCEPTABLE TO YOU?.......................................YES_____ NO_____

OTHER EMPLOYMENT
ARE YOU ASSOCIATED IN ANY WAY WITH ANY OTHER COMPANY WHERE YOU WILL CONTINUE WHILE EMPLOYED BY THIS COMPANY?

YES_____ NO_____ IF YES, EXPLAIN_____

HEALTH and PHYSICAL CONDITION
DO YOU HAVE ANY PHYSICAL CONDITION WHICH MAY RESTRICT YOUR PERFORMANCE OF THE FOLLOWING DUTIES
IN THE JOB FOR WHICH YOU ARE APPLYING? (PHYSICAL DUTIES INCLUDE STANDING 8 HOURS, WALKING, STOOPING, BENDING,
LIFTING, CLIMBING, REACHING, MODERATELY FAST WORKING SPEED).......................................YES_____ NO_____

IF YES, EXPLAIN_____

IF REQUIRED, ARE YOU WILLING TO LIFT OBJECTS WEIGHING UP TO 50 LBS? YES____ NO____. 100 LBS. YES____ NO____

BACKGROUND
HAVE YOU EVER BEEN   ARE YOU CURRENTLY ON BAIL OR
CONVICTED OF A FELONY?   YES_____ NO_____ RELEASED ON YOUR OWN RECOGNIZANCE?.... YES_____ NO_____

IF YES, EXPLAIN_____

HAVE YOU EVER BEEN DISCHARGED FOR ANY REASON? YES_____ NO_____

IF YES, GIVE BELOW DETAILS OF EACH INCIDENT_____

List HOME ADDRESSES in the United States for the past TEN years			
FROM	TO	ADDRESS	CITY AND STATE

PERSONAL REFERENCES
LIST THE NAMES AND ADDRESSES OF THREE (3) PEOPLE (NOT RELATIVES OR EMPLOYERS) WHO HAVE KNOWN YOU FOR FIVE (5) YEARS.

NAME	ADDRESS	OCCUPATION	PHONE
NAME	ADDRESS	OCCUPATION	PHONE
NAME	ADDRESS	OCCUPATION	PHONE

IN CASE OF EMERGENCY, PLEASE NOTIFY:

NAME_____ ADDRESS_____ PHONE_____

The statements made by me in this Employment Application form are true to the best of my memory and without error. The references listed
in this Employment Application form are authorized to provide this Company with information about my previous employment and education.
I understand that any false statement made in this Employment Application form may result in refusal of or dismissal from employment.

AFTER READING THE ABOVE STATEMENT, PLEASE SIGN BELOW.

Signature_____ Date_____

INTERVIEWER'S USE ONLY	DH	DNH
COMMENTS		

Interviewed by:_____

DOH_____

How old were you when you graduated from the 6th grade?

1. Younger than 10
2. 10–12
3. 13–14
4. 15–16

It also asks opinion questions such as:

How do you feel about being transferred from this city by this company?

1. Would thoroughly enjoy a transfer.
2. Would like to experience a transfer.
3. Would accept a transfer.
4. Would reject a transfer.

To use the BIB as a selection tool, the P/HRM specialist correlates each item on the form with the selection criteria for job success. Those criteria that predict the best for a position are used to help select applicants for that position.

Another variety of biodata form is the *weighted application blank,* an application form designed to be scored as a systematic selection device. The purpose of a weighted application blank is to relate the characteristics of applicants to success on the job. It has been estimated that to develop a weighted blank for a job takes about 100 hours. So it makes sense to develop such blanks only for positions with many jobholders.[11]

The typical approach is to divide present jobholders into two or three categories (in half, high or low; or in thirds, high, middle, or low), based on some success criterion such as performance as measured by production records or supervisor's evaluation, or high versus low turnover. Then the characteristics of high and low performers are examined. On many characteristics for a particular organization and job, there may be no difference by age or education level, but there may be differences on where applicants live and years of experience, for example. A weight is assigned to the degree of differences: for no difference, 0; for some difference, ±1; for a big difference, ±2. Then these weights are totaled for all applicants, and the one with the highest positive score is hired, assuming that the score meets the minimum which past and currently successful employees have attained.

These predictive characteristics vary by job and occupation. For example, sometimes the age of the applicant is a good predictor; other times it is not. They may also change over time. Weights need to be recomputed every several years or so, and the weighted application blank must be validated for each job and organization.

Most researchers have found that biodata approaches are reliable. They also find that biodata approaches have very high validity. Studies indicate, however, that although most organizations use application blanks, fewer than a third of the *larger* organizations have utilized weighted application blanks or other biodata approaches. Given the problems with tests, references, and other selection techniques, the percentage of organizations using biodata approaches is likely to increase.

---

[11]Larry Pace and Lyle Schoenfeldt, ''Legal Concerns in the Use of Weighted Applications,'' *Personnel Psychology,* (Summer 1977, pp. 159–66.

Step 3: Employment Interview

Employment interviews are part of almost all selection procedures. Studies indicate that over 90 percent of selection decisions involve interviews.[12] And a number of them, indicate that the interview is the *most important aspect* of the selection decision.

Types of Interviews • There are three general types of employment interview:

- Structured.
- Semistructured.
- Unstructured.

While all employment interviews are alike in certain respects, each type is also unique in some way. All three include interaction between two or more parties, an applicant and one or more representatives of the potential employer, for a predetermined purpose. This purpose is consideration of an applicant for employment. Information is exchanged, usually through questions and answers. The main differences in employment interviews lie in the interviewer's approach to the process, and the type used depends both on the kind of information desired and the nature of the situation.

In the *structured employment interview,* the interviewer prepares a list of questions in advance and does not deviate from it. In many organizations a standard form is used on which the interviewer notes the applicant's responses to the predetermined questions. Many of the questions asked in a structured interview are forced choice in nature, and the interviewer need only indicate the applicant's response with a check mark on the form.

If the approach is highly structured, the interviewer may also follow a prearranged sequence of questions. In such an interview the interviewer is often little more than a recorder of the interviewee's responses, and little training is required to conduct it. The structured approach is very restrictive, however. The information elicited is narrow and there is little opportunity to adapt to the individual applicant. This approach is equally constraining to the applicant, who is unable to qualify or elaborate on answers to the questions. The Bureau of National Affairs survey found that 19 percent of the companies used a written interview-form, while 26 percent employed a standard format for employment interviews.[13] Exhibit 7–5 is an example of a form used for a structured employment interview.

In the *semistructured interview* only the major questions to be asked are prepared in advance, though the interviewer may also prepare some probing questions in areas of inquiry. While this approach calls for greater interviewer preparation, it also allows for more flexibility than the structured approach. The interviewer is free to probe into those areas that seem to merit further investigation. With less structure, however, it is more difficult to replicate these interviews. This approach combines enough structure to facilitate the exchange of factual information with adequate freedom to develop insights.

The *unstructured interview* involves little preparation. The interviewer prepares a list of possible topics to be covered and sometimes does not even do that. The overriding advantage of the unstructured type is the freedom it allows the interviewer to adapt to the

---

[12]Eugene Mayfield, "The Selection Interview—A Re-evaluation of Published Research," *Personnel Psychology,* Autumn 1964, pp. 239–69; and Neal Schmitt, "Social and Situational Determinants of Interview Decisions: Implications for the Employment Interview," *Personnel Psychology,* Spring 1976, pp. 79–101.

[13]Bureau of National Affairs *Personnel Policies Forum,* Survey 114, September 1976.

Exhibit 7–5 _____

Patterned interview form—Executive position

Date _____ 19 ___

SUMMARY

Rating [1] [2] [3] [4]   Comments: _____ .
In making final rating, be sure to consider not only what the applicant can do but also his/her stability, industry,

perseverance, loyalty, ability to get along with others, self-reliance, leadership, maturity, motivation, and domestic situation and health.

Interviewer: _____   Job considered for: _____

Name _____   Date of birth _____ ; Phone No. _____
The age discrimination in the employment act and relevant FEP Acts prohibit discrimination with respect to individuals who are at least 40 but less than 65 years of age.

Present address _____ City _____ State _____ How long there? _____

Were you in the Armed Forces of the U.S.? Yes, branch _____ Dates _____ 19 ___ to _____ 19 _____
(Not to be asked in New Jersey)
_____ 19 ___ to _____ 19 _____

If not, why not? _____

Where you hospitalized in the service? _____

Are you drawing compensation?   Yes ___   No ___

Are you employed now?   Yes □   No □.   (If yes) How soon available? _____
What are relationships with present employer?

Why are you applying for this position? _____
Is his/her underlying reason a desire for prestige, security, or earnings?

WORK EXPERIENCE. Cover all positions. This information is very important. Interviewer should record last position first. Every month
since leaving school should be accounted for. Experience in Armed Forces should be covered as a job (in New Jersey exclude military questions).

LAST OR PRESENT POSITION

Company _____ City _____ From _____ 19 ___ to _____ 19 _____

How was job obtained? _____ Whom did you know there? _____
Has applicant shown self-reliance in getting jobs?

Nature of work at start _____ Starting salary _____
Will applicant's previous experience be helpful on this job?

In what way did the job change? _____
Has applicant made good work progress?

Nature of work at leaving _____ Salary at leaving _____
How much responsibility has applicant had?   Any indication of ambition?

Superior _____ Title _____ What is he/she like? _____
Did applicant get along with superior?

How closely does (or did) he/she supervise you? _____ What authority do (or did) you have? _____

Number of people you supervised _____ What did they do? _____
Is applicant a leader?

Responsibility for policy formulation _____
Has applicant had management responsibility?

To what extent could you use initiative and judgment? _____
Did applicant actively seek responsibility?

Source: Copyright, 1977, The Dartnell Corporation, Chicago, Illinois 60640. Developed by the McMurry Company.

situation and to the changing stream of applicants. Spontaneity characterizes this approach, but under the control of an untrained interviewer digressions, discontinuity, and
eventual frustration for both parties may result.

While the unstructured approach leads itself to the counseling of individuals with
problems, it is not limited to guidance. Students frequently encounter P/HRM recruiters
whose sole contribution, other than the opening and closing pleasantries, is "Tell me

about yourself." When used by a highly skilled interviewer, the unstructured interview can lead to significant insights which might enable the interviewer to make fine distinctions among applicants. As used by most employment interviewers, however, that is not the case, and it is seldom appropriate for an employment interviewer to relinquish control to such an extent.

Some interviewers try to induce stress into the employment interview process. Generally speaking, this is very dysfunctional to the employment interview process.

A number of studies have examined whether employment interviews are reliable sources of data.[14] Generally speaking, the more structured the interview and the more training the interviewer has, the more reliable the interview.

Interviewing is a skill that can be learned. The following sections describe the purposes and phases of effective interviews.

Purposes of Selection Interviews • Many employment interviewers perceive their only task as being to screen and select those individuals best suited for employment. While this is unquestionably the *main* function of the employment interview, it is not the only one. A second purpose is public relations: to impress the interviewees with the value of the interviewer's employer.

In addition to the selection and public relations roles, the employment interviewer also must function as an educator. It is the interviewer's responsibility to "educate" the applicants concerning details of the job in question which are not immediately apparent. The interviewer must be able to answer the applicant's questions with honesty and candor. To be effective, the interviewer must remain aware of all three of these functions while conducting the employment interview.

Step 4: Employment Tests

A technique some organizations use to aid their selection decisions is the employment test. Such a test is a mechanism (either a paper-and-pencil test or a simulation exercise)

FRANK AND ERNEST

© 1976 by Nea, Inc. Reprinted by permission of NEA.

---

[14]David Tucker and Patricia Rowe, "Relationship between Expectancy, Causal Attributions, and Final Hiring Decisions in the Employment Interview," *Journal of Applied Psychology,* February 1979, pp. 27–31; and Frank Landy, "The Validity of the Interview in Police Officer Selection," *Journal of Applied Psychology,* April 1976, pp. 193–98.

Summary of suggestions for effective interviewing:

1. Work at listening to what and how the applicant communicates to you. Unlike hearing, listening is an active process and requires concentration. Many interviewers plan their next question when they should be listening to the applicant's present response.

2. Be aware of the applicant's nonverbal cues as well as the verbal message. In attempting to get as complete a picture of the applicant as possible, you must not ignore what some consider the most meaningful type of communication, body language.

3. Remain aware of the job requirements throughout the interview. No one is immune to the halo effect, which gives undue weight to one characteristic. You must constantly keep the requirements of the job in mind. Sometimes an applicant possesses some personal mannerism or trait that so attracts or repels the interviewer that the decision is made mostly on the strength of that characteristic, which may be completely irrelevant to the requirements of the job in question.

4. Maintain a balance between open and overly structured questions. Too many of the former, and the interview becomes a meandering conversation; while too many of the latter turn the interview into an interrogation.

5. Wait until you have all of the necessary information before making a decision. Some interviewees start more slowly than others, and what may appear to be disinterest may later prove to have been an initial reserve which dissipates after a few minutes. *Don't evaluate on the basis of a first impression.*

6. Do not ask questions that violate equal employment opportunity laws and regulations (see list in Chapter 3). Focus the interview on the variables identified as crucial criteria for selection.

which attempts to measure certain characteristics of individuals, such as manual dexterity. Psychologists or P/HRM specialists develop these tests with a procedure that is similar to that described for the weighted application blank. First those most knowledgeable about the job are asked to rank (in order of importance) the abilities and attitudes essential for effective performance in a job. Thus for a secretarial position, the rank might be (A) ability to type, (B) ability to take shorthand, and (C) positive work attitudes. The psychologist prepares items or simulations which it is thought will measure these required characteristics. These are tried out to see if they can in fact separate the qualified from less qualified (on A and B) and easygoing from less easygoing (on C). On such items, psychologists prefer those that about half the applicants will answer with "right" answers and half with the opposite.

The terms or simulations that distinguish the best from the worst are combined into tests. A measure of effectiveness (a criterion) is developed, such as typing 75 words per minute with only 1 percent errors. All new applicants are given the test. After about two years, those items that prove to have been the best predictors of high performance are kept in the test used for selection, and those found not to be predictive are dropped. This is the validation process.

It is not easy or cheap to validate a test. In a study of 2,500 ASPA members, it was found that, on average, a validation study costs $5,000 per job, and some studies cost as much as $20,000.[15] This same study found the use of tests is declining, and they are used most frequently for clerical jobs. About half of the surveyed employers use tests in selection. Middle-sized firms are most likely to use them, followed by larger firms. The smaller firms are least likely to use them. Some industries (transportation and communications, offices, insurance) are more likely to use tests than manufacturers, hospitals, and retailers.

Of the 2,500 personnel managers consulted in this survey, 37.9 percent considered tests "about the same in importance," and 36.5 percent considered them less important than other selection techniques such as the interview and biodata. Less than 20 percent said they disqualified applicants on the basis of test scores alone.

Organizations today carefully weigh the value of tests relative to other selection techniques and in view of the law. One newspaper article indicated that "The use of testing is declining sharply in American business for reasons that have very little to do with its accuracy. Many employers feel that the guidelines applied to testing are so rigorous, expensive, and time consuming that they have decided to chuck it all and go back to the seat-of-the-pants approach to hiring and promotion."[16] These thoughts indicate that testing requires careful concern about validity, costs, and benefits.

Because of criticisms of the courts and P/HRM practitioners that tests discriminate against minority employees, separate validity studies may be required for minorities. Because this is expensive, many employers have abandoned the use of tests for minority employees. This criticism applies more to paper-and-pencil tests than performance tests.

Few organizations have the personnel, time, or money to develop their own tests. Instead, they often purchase and use tests developed elsewhere. The test organization provides a key (or notation) which lists the enterprises that have used the test in the past and the typical performance of good and bad employees. This is not enough, however; the test must be validated in each organization and for minority and nonminority employee groups before it can be useful.

There are various kinds of tests. The following will be discussed here: work sample performance tests, simulations of performance, paper-and-pencil tests, personality and temperament inventories, and others.

Job Sample Performance Tests • A job sample performance test is an experience that involves actually doing a sample of the work the job involves in a controlled situation.[17] Examples of performance tests include:

A. A programming test for computer operators.
B. Employees running a miniature punchpress.
C. A standard driving course as performance test for forklift operators.
D. The auditions used by symphony orchestras for hiring purposes. For example, when symphony orchestras select new musicians, the selection panel listens to them play the same piece of music with the same instrument. The applicants are hidden behind a screen at the time.

---

[15]"The Personnel Executive's Job," *Personnel Management: Policies and Practices* (Englewood Cliffs, N.J.: Prentice-Hall, 1976).

[16]*The Wall Street Journal,* September 5, 1975, p. 1.

[17]James J. Asher and James A. Sciarrino, "Realistic Work Sample Tests: A Review," *Personnel Psychology,* Winter 1974, pp. 519–33.

E. A tool dexterity test for machine operators.

F. Standardized typing tests. The applicants are asked to type some work. The speed and accuracy are then computed.

Variations of these performances tests exist in many organizations. The applicants are asked to run the machines they would run if they got the job, and quality and quantity of output are recorded.

Job sample tests tend to have the highest validities and reliabilities of all tests because they systematically measure behavior directly related to the job. This is not surprising. Imagine that you are an artist who is applying for graduate work in art. You typically must take the Graduate Record Exam, a paper-and-pencil test designed to measure verbal and mathematical "ability." You also must present 12 paintings, drawings, and watercolors (a portfolio) to the art department. Which of these selection devices appears likely to be the most reliable and valid measure of your painting ability? Or recall that when you took your driving test, you took two: a paper-and-pencil test, and, when you drove the car, a performance test. Which better tested your driving ability: the paper-and-pencil test, or that tension-filled drive, including the thrilling attempt at parallel parking? A similar principle applies to job selection. Which would be a better predictor of the forklift operator's job performance: the standardized test, in which the applicant drives the truck down and around piles of goods, or a paper-and-pencil test of driving knowledge, intelligence, or whatever?

Reliability and validity figures for all the standardized tests discussed here are available from the test developers. Many are reviewed in regular summaries such as the *Annual Review of Psychology*.

Performance Simulations • A performance simulation is a non-paper-and-pencil experience designed to determine abilities related to job performance. For example, suppose job analysis indicates that successful job occupants of a specific job require highly developed mechanical or clerical abilities. A number of simulations are available to measure these abilities. The simulation is not direct performance of part of the job, but it comes close to that through simulation. You may have learned to drive by performing first on simulation machines; it was not the same as on-the-street driving, but it was closer than reading about it or observing other drivers.

There are many of these simulation tests. Here are some:

Revised Minnesota Paper Form Board Test. Exhibit 7–6 is an excerpt from the MPFB, which is a test of space visualization. It is used for various jobs. For example, to be a draftsperson requires the ability to see things in their relation to space. The applicant must select the item (A–E) which best represents what a group of shapes will look like when assembled.

Psychomotor ability simulations. There are a number of tests which measure such psychomotor abilities as choice reaction time, speed of limb movement, and finger dexterity. One of these is the O'Connor Finger and Tweezer Dexterity Test (see Exhibit 7–7). The person being tested picks up pins with the tweezer and row by row inserts them in the holes across the board, or inserts the pins with the hand normally used. These tests are used for positions with high manual requirements for success, such as assemblers of radio or TV components and watches.

Clerical abilities. Exhibit 7–8 is the first page of the Minnesota Clerical Test. It is a typical test for clerical abilities. This simulation requires the applicants to check numbers and names, skills frequently used in clerical tasks.

Exhibit 7–6 _____

**Excerpt from Revised Minnesota
Paper Form Board Test**

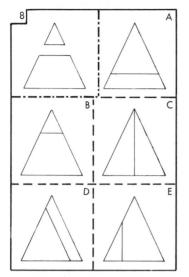

Exhibit 7–7 _____

**O'Connor Finger and Tweezer
Dexterity Test equipment**

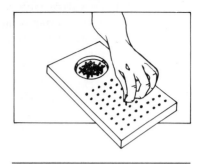

Exhibit 7–8 _____

MINNESOTA CLERICAL TEST
(formerly the Minnesota Vocational Test for Clerical Workers)
by Dorothy M. Andrew, Donald G. Patterson, and Howard P. Longstaff

Name _____   Date _____

TEST 1—Number Comparison	TEST 2—Name Comparison
Number Right _____	Number Right _____
Number Wrong _____	Number Wrong _____
Score = R − W _____	Score = R − W _____
Percentile Rating _____	Percentile Rating _____
Norms Used _____	Norms Used _____

INSTRUCTIONS

On the inside pages there are two tests. One of the tests consists of pairs of names and the other of pairs of numbers. If the two names or the two numbers of a pair are exactly the same make a check mark ($\sqrt{}$) on the line between them: if they are different, make no mark on that line. When the examiner says "Stop!" draw a line under the last pair at which you have looked.

SAMPLES done correctly of pairs of NUMBERS
79542____79524
1234567 $\sqrt{}$ 1234567

SAMPLES done correctly of pairs of NAMES
John C. Linder____John C. Lender
Investors Syndicate $\sqrt{}$ Investors Syndicate

This is a test for speed and accuracy. Work as fast as you can without making mistakes. Do not turn this page until you are told to begin.

Paper-and-Pencil Tests • In the third group of tests are paper-and-pencil tests designed to measure general intelligence and aptitudes.[18] Many employers assume that mental abilities are an important component of performance for many jobs. Intelligence and mental ability tests attempt to sample intellectual mental development or skills.

Some examples of paper-and-pencil tests are:

Otis Quick Scoring Mental Ability Test. This test samples several intellectual functions, including vocabulary, arithmetic skills, reasoning, and perception, totaling them to one score. It includes items such as the following:

(a) Which one of the five things below is soft?
   (1) glass (2) stone (3) cotton (4) iron (5) ice
(b) A robin is a kind of:
   (6) plant (7) bird (8) worm (9) fish (10) flower
(c) Which one of the five numbers below is larger than 55?
   (11) 53 (12) 48 (13) 29 (14) 57 (15) 16

Reproduced by permission. Copyright 1936, 1954 by Harcourt Brace Jovanovich, Inc., New York, N.Y. All rights reserved.

Wechsler Adult Intelligence Scale. The Wechsler is a comprehensive paper-and-pencil test of 14 sections grouped into two scores. The verbal score includes general information, arithmetic, similarities, vocabulary, and other items. The performance score includes picture completion, picture arrangement, object assembly, and similar items.

Wonderlic Personnel Test. The Wonderlic is a shortened form of the Otis test using a variety of perceptual, verbal and arithmetical items which provide a total score. Other well-known tests include the Differential Aptitude Test, the SRA Primary Mental Abilities Test, and multiple aptitude tests.

The above three tests are administered to individuals and are paper-and-pencil tests similar to those taken in school. There are also tests of mental ability designed to be administered to groups, including the following example:

California Test of Mental Maturity (adult level). This test is administered to groups and scored by machine. Scores are developed from a series of short tests on spatial relationships, verbal concepts, logic and reasoning, numerical reasoning, memory, and others. These scores are converted to IQ equivalents, and profiles are developed for analyzing performance.

The reliability and validity of paper-and-pencil tests have been studied extensively. In general, they are not as reliable as performance tests or other selection devices such as biodata forms or structured interviews.

Personality Inventories and Temperament Tests • The least reliable of the employment tests are those instruments that attempt to measure a person's personality or temperament. The most frequently used inventory is the Minnesota Multiphasic Personality Inventory. Other paper-and-pencil inventories are the California Psychological Inventory, the Minnesota Counseling Inventory, the Manifest Anxiety Scale, and the Edwards Personal Preference Schedule.

A different approach, not as direct as the self-reporting inventory, utilizes projective techniques to present vague stimuli, the reactions to which provide data on which psy-

---

[18]Anne Anastasi, *Psychological Testing* (New York: MacMillan, 1982).

Why does a fireman wear red suspenders?

A. ☐ *The red goes well with the blue uniform.*
B. ☐ *They can be used to repair a leaky hose.*
C. ☐ *To hold up his pants.*

Drawing by D. Fradon; © 1974 The New Yorker Magazine, Inc.

chologists base their assessment and interpretation of a personality. The stimuli are purposely vague in order to reach the unconscious aspects of the personality. Many techniques are used. The most common are the Rorschach Inkblot Test and the Thematic Apperception Test.

The Rorschach Inkblot test was first described in 1921. The test involves 10 cards, on each of which is printed a bilateral symmetrical inkblot similar to that illustrated in Exhibit 7–9.[19] The person responding is asked to tell what he or she sees in the inkblot. The examiner keeps a verbatim record of the responses, the time taken to make the responses, emotional expressions, and other incidental behavior. Then a trained interpreter analyzes the data set and reaches conclusions about the personality patterns of the person being examined.

Most of the tests like the Roschach were developed for use by psychiatrists and psychologists in counseling and mental health work, rather than in selection. Because of employee resistance, ethical problems in some questions, and lower reliability and validities, use of the inventories and temperament tests is likely to continue to decline in the future.

---

[19]H. Rorschach, *Psychodiagnostics: A Diagnostic Test Based on Perception* (Berne, Switz. Huber, 1942).

Exhibit 7–9 _____

An inkblot of the type employed in the Rorschach technique

The Polygraph • Another method currently used by some employers to test employees is the polygraph, sometimes erroneously called a lie detector. This is an instrument that records changes in breathing, blood pressure, pulse, and skin response associated with sweating of palms, and plots these reactions on paper. The person being questioned with a polygraph attached is asked a series of questions. Some are neutral, to achieve a normal response, others stressful, to indicate a response made under pressure. Thus the applicant may be asked: "Is your name Smith?" Then, "Have you ever stolen from an employer?"

Although originally developed for police work, the great majority of polygraph tests today are used to check data during selection. Approximately one fifth of American businesses use the polygraph today.[20] It is understandable why organizations need to determine certain facts about potential employees. On-the-job crime has increased tremendously, and it is estimated that dishonest employees cost employers about $5 billion per year. A good reference check may cost $100; a polygraph test only $25. Some employers offer applicants a choice: Take a polygraph test now, making it possible to make an immediate selection decision, or await the results of a reference check and run the risk of losing the job. Local, state, and federal agencies have begun to use the polygraph, especially for security, police, fire, and health positions.

There are many objections to the use of the polygraph in personnel selection. One is that this device is an invasion of the applicants' privacy and thus a violation of the Fourth Amendment to the Constitution. Second, it is believed that its use could lead to self-incrimination, a violation of the Fifth Amendment. A third objection is that it insults the dignity of the applicant.

As severe as these objections are, *the most serious question is whether the polygraph is reliable and can get the truth.* The fact is that the polygraph records *physiological* changes in response to stress, not lying or even the conditions necessarily accompanying lying. Many cases have come to light in which persons who lie easily have beaten the

---

[20]John A. Belt and Peter B. Hoden, "Polygraph Usage among Major U.S. Corporations," *Personnel Journal,* February 1978, pp. 80–86.

polygraph, and it has been shown that the polygraph brands as liars people who respond emotionally to questions. There is evidence that polygraphs are neither reliable nor valid. This is the conclusion reached following studies by a congressional committee and the Pentagon which made a thorough analysis of all the available data. Compounding this deficiency, one expert has estimated that 80 percent of 1,500 polygraph practitioners are not sufficiently trained to interpret the results of the tests, even if they were reliable and valid.[21]

Such criticisms have led to the banning of the polygraph for employee selection in many jurisdictions. Arbitrators have held against forcing employees to take such tests, and polygraph evidence is not admissible in court unless both sides agree. As a result of congressional hearings, the federal government has severely reduced the use of polygraphs. In spite of these criticisms however, it appears that the use of the polygraph in job selection will continue.

Employment Testing and the Law • Perhaps the first event signaling the involvement of the courts in employment testing was the *Myart* v. *Motorola* (1964) case.[22] In 1963, Leon Myart, a black, was refused a job as a "television phaser and analyzer" at one of Motorola's plants because his score on a five-minute intelligence test was not high enough although he had previous job-related experience. Myart filed a complaint charging that he had been racially discriminated against in his denial of the job. At the hearing, an examiner for the Illinois Commission ruled that: (1) Myart should be offered a job; (2) the test should no longer be used; and (3) every new test developed in its place should "take" into account the environmental factors which contribute to cultural deprivation. Although this ruling was eventually overturned for lack of evidence by the Illinois State Supreme Court, it set the precedent to hear employment testing complaints in the courts.

Testing will undoubtedly remain a part of many organizational selection programs. However, it is advisable for an organization to carefully choose selection tests, to examine the reliability and validity of the tests used, and to validate the tests used since it is likely that they will be challenged by some individuals. Furthermore, P/HRM specialists involved in testing should be familiar with the enforcement activities of the EEOC, OFCCP, and the Uniform Guidelines on Employee Selection Procedures.

Step 5: Reference Checks and Recommendations

If you have ever applied for a job, at some point you were asked to provide a list of references of past supervisors and others. In general, you picked people who could evaluate you effectively and fairly for your new employer—people who know and express your good and bad points equally.

For years, as part of the selection process, applicants have been required to submit references or recommendation letters.[23] These indicate past behavior and how well the applicant did at her or his last job. Studies indicate that this has been a common practice for white-collar jobs.

---

[21]John E. Reid and Fred E. Inbau, *Truth and Deception: The Polygraph Technique* (Baltimore: Williams & Wilkins, 1966).

[22]*Myart* v. *Motorola*, 110 Congressional Record 5662–64 (1964).

[23]Carole Sewell, "Pre-Employment Investigations: The Key to Security in Hiring," *Personnel Journal*, May 1981, pp. 376–79.

For a letter of recommendation to be useful, it must meet certain conditions:

The writer must know the applicant's performance level and be competent to assess it.
The writer must communicate the evaluation effectively to the potential employer.
The writer must be truthful.

If the applicant chooses the references, the first two conditions may not be met. With regard to the third, many people are reluctant to put in writing what they really think of the applicant, since he or she may see it. As a result, the person writing the reference either glosses over shortcomings or overemphasizes the applicant's good points. Because of these and other shortcomings, studies of the validity of written references have not been comforting to those using them in selection.

Kessler and Gibbs propose a method for potentially improving the validity of letters of reference as a selection too.[24] In their approach, letters of reference are required only for jobs which have had job analysis performed to develop job specifications (see Chapter 4). A panel of judges (three to six persons) familiar with the job ranks the specifications for relative importance. Then a reference letter is drafted asking the respondent to rate the

[24]Clemm C. Kessler, III., and Georgia J. Gibbs, "Getting the Most from Application Blanks and References," *Personnel*, January–February 1975, pp. 53–62.

applicant on the job specifications, which are listed randomly. A sample reference letter for the position of employment interviewer is given as Exhibit 7–10. The references must be familiar with the applicant's past employment. The rankings of the panel and the references are correlated, and the greater the correlation, the more likely is the applicant to be hired.

Congress has passed the Privacy Act of 1974 and the Buckley Amendment.[25] These allow applicants to view letters of reference in their files. The laws apply to public-sector employees and students. But private- and third-sector employers are afraid that the laws will soon apply to them, so many of them will now give out only minimal data: dates of employment, job title, and so on. If this becomes a common practice, reference letters may not be very useful.

When there is need to verify biodata, a more acceptable alternative for a letter might be a phone call to the applicant's previous supervisors. The organization can contact certain persons in order to cross-check opinions or to probe further on doubtful points. Most studies indicate that few employers feel written references alone are a reliable source of data. A majority of organizations combine telephone checks, written letters of reference, and data obtained from the employment interview. Items checked most frequently are previous employment and educational background (in that order).

Although little data for reliability exists, it appears to be very useful to find out how the applicant performed on previous jobs. This can be the most relevant information for predicting future work behavior. Reference checks would seem in order for the most crucial jobs at any time. Costs of these checks vary from a few cents for a few quick telephone calls to several hundred dollars for a thorough field investigation. It is not known whether privacy legislation is affecting telephone reference checks in the way it has written letters of reference.

Step 6: Physical Examinations

Some organizations require that those most likely to be selected for a position complete a medical questionnaire or take a physical examination. The reasons for such a requirement include the following:

- In case of later workers' compensation claims, physical condition at the time of hiring should be known.
- It is important to prevent the hiring of those with serious communicable diseases. This is especially so in hospitals, but it applies in other organizations as well.
- It may be necessary to determine whether the applicant is physically capable of performing the job in question.

These purposes can be served by the completion of a medical questionnaire, a physical examination, or a work physiology analysis. Chase has discussed the latter technique, which is neither a physical examination nor a psychomotor test.[26] Commonly used for selection of manual workers who will be doing hard labor, it attempts to determine, by physiological indexes (heart rate and oxygen consumption), the true fatigue engendered

---

[25]J. D. Rice, "Privacy Legislation: Its Effect on Pre-Employment Reference Checking," *Personnel Administrator,* February 1978, pp. 46–51.

[26]Richard Chase, "Working Physiology," *Personnel Administrator,* November 1969, pp. 47–53.

Exhibit 7–10 _____

Sample reference letter for applicant for employment interviewer positions

Dear _____

Mr. _____ is applying for a position with our company and has supplied your name as a reference. We would appreciate it if you would take a few moments to give us your opinions about him.

Listed below is a series of items that may describe skills, abilities, knowledge, or personal characteristics of the applicant to a greater or lesser degree. Will you please look at this list and rank them from most to least like the applicant by placing the appropriate letter in the space below. If you do not have an opinion about a specific item, skip it and rank what you can, beginning with Space 1.

A. Has the ability to develop scheduled and nonscheduled interview formats for various jobs.
B. Can conduct an interview using the nondirective approach
C. Has a neat appearance (clothes clean, in good condition)
D. Makes checks to see if people understand his meaning when he speaks to them.
E. Makes checks to see if he understands people when they speak to him.

1. _____ (Most characteristic of the applicant)
2. _____
3. _____
4. _____
5. _____ (Least characteristic of the applicant)

Now, on the rating scale below, please indicate with a check in the appropriate space the degree to which the applicant possesses the last ranked skill, ability, knowledge or personal characteristic. If he is very high in the characteristic, give a rating of 5; if he is very low, give him a rating of 1. Place your check in between the two extremes if you consider that a more appropriate rating.

Very low ⌊___|___|___|___|___⌋ Very high
           1   2   3   4   5

Comments about the applicant:

by the work. This is analyzed through simulated job performance. First, the analyst measures applicants and obtains baseline information on these indexes while they are seated. Then data are gathered while they are working. The data are analyzed and the workers are ranked; those with the lowest heart rate and oxygen consumption should be hired (all other factors being equal).

Physical examinations have *not* been shown to be very reliable as a predictor of future medical problems. This is at least partially so because of the state of the art of medicine. Different physicians emphasize different factors in the exam, based on their training and specialties. There is some evidence that correlating the presence of certain past medical problems (as learned from the completion of a medical questionnaire) can be as reliable as a physical exam performed by a physician and is probably less costly.

Selection of Managers

The selection process and the tools used vary with the type of employee being hired. The preceding section focused on blue-, gray-, and white-collar employees, but the general process is similar for the managerial employee.

Before a manager is hired, the job is studied. Then the criteria are selected, based on the characteristics of effective managers in the organization at present and likely future needs. *Each* organization must do this, since the managerial task differs by level, function, industry, and in other ways. Studies of successful managers across these groups have concluded that many (not all) successful executives have intelligence, drive, good judgment, and managerial skills. Most of the studies avoid the real-world problems like the following. Candidate A scores high on intelligence and motivation, low on verbal skills, and moderate on hard work. Candidate B scores moderate on intelligence, high on motivation, moderate on verbal skills, and high on hard work. Both have good success records. Which one would you choose? The trade-offs must be assessed for particular jobs and particular organizations.

One recruiter stated:

> I've read the studies about high intelligence, test scores, and so on in managerial selection. But I've found I've got to look at the job. For example, our most successful *sales managers* are those who grew up on a farm where they learned to work hard on their own. They went to the nearest state college (all they could afford) and majored in business. They got good to better than average grades. They might have done better gradewise if they hadn't had to work their way through school. Our best *accounting managers*, however, did not have that background.

The message is that these studies can indicate the likely predictors of success *in general*, but executive success must be analyzed in each organization. Each of the factors mentioned must be correlated with success measured several ways, to see which works for the organization. However, the focus of selection must be on *behavior*, not just on scores on tests or general impressions.

Once the criteria of managerial success are known, the selection tools to be used are chosen. In general, tests are not frequently used in managerial selection. Reference checks have been a major source of data on managerial applicants, but the legal problems with this tool also apply for executives. Biodata analysis is a major tool used for managerial selection. It is stated that, "Very often, a carefully developed typical behavior inventory based on biographical information has proved to be the single best predictor of future job behavior . . . biographic information has proved particularly useful for assessing managerial effectiveness."[27]

The most frequently used selection tool for managers is the interview. More often than not, it is used in conjunction with the other methods. But if only one method is used by an organization, it is likely to be the personal interview.

Studies indicate that more successful managers are hired using judgments derived in employment interviews than decisions based on test scores. This is no doubt so because these judgments can be based on factorially complex behavior, and typical executive performance is behaviorally complex. The interview is likely to continue to be the most used selection method because organizations want to hire managers they feel they can trust and feel comfortable with.

Assessment Centers → can be used for internal + external recruits

An assessment center is not a building or a place. It is a selection technique that involves a series of evaluative tests, exercises, and feedback sessions. Corporate-operated assessment centers have proliferated from just over 100 in 1973 to over 2,000 in 1981.[28] The popularity of the assessment center can be attributed to its capacity for increasing an organization's ability to select employees who will perform successfully in management positions. The assessment center was first used by the German military in World War II. The Office of Strategic Services (OSS) in the United States began to use it in the mid-1940s. American Telephone and Telegraph Company (AT&T) in the 1950s introduced assessment centers to the business world.

The core of an assessment center is the use of simulations, tests, interviews, and observations to obtain information about candidates (assesees). Exhibit 7–11 presents briefly a typical 2½ day assessment center schedule. Finkle states that "assessment center . . . refers to a group-oriented, standardized series of activities that provides a basis for judgments or predictions of human behaviors believed or known to be relevant to work performed in an organization setting.[29]

Most assessment centers are similar in a number of areas.

1. Groups of 12 assesses are evaluated. Individual and group activities are observed and evaluated.
2. Multiple methods of assessment are used—interviewing, objective testing, projective testing, games, role plays, and other methods.
3. Assessors doing the evaluation are usually a panel of line managers from the organization. They can, however, be consultants or outsiders trained to conduct assessments.

---

[27]John P. Campbell, Marvin Dunnette, Edward E. Lawler, III., and Karl E. Weick, Jr., *Managerial Behavior, Performance, and Effectiveness* (New York: McGraw-Hill, 1970), p. 146.

[28]Leland C. Nichols and Joseph Hudson, "Dual-Role Assessment Center: Selection and Development," *Personnel Journal*, May 1981.

[29]R. B. Finkle, "Managerial Assessment Centers," in *Handbook of Industrial and Organizational Psychology*, ed. M. Dunnette (Chicago: Rand McNally, 1976), pp. 861–88.

Exhibit 7–11 _____

Assessment center schedule (2½ days)

Day 1

A. Orientation of approximately 12 ratees.

B. Break-up into Groups of six or four to play management simulated game. (*Raters* observe: planning ability, problem-solving skill, interaction skills, communication ability.)

C. Psychological testing— Measure verbal and numerical skills.

D. Interview with Raters. (*Raters* discuss goals, motivation, and career plans.)

E. Small group discussion of case incidents. (*Raters* observe confidence, persuasiveness, decision-making flexibility.)

Day 2

A. Individual decision-making exercise—Ratees are asked to make a decision about some problem that must be solved. (*Raters* observe fact finding skill, understanding of problem-solving procedures, and risk-taking propensity.)

B. In-basket exercise. (*Raters* observe decision making under stress, organizing ability, memory, and ability to delegate.)

C. Role-play of performance evaluation interview. (*Raters* observe empathy, ability to react, counseling skills, and how information is used.)

D. Group problem solving. (*Raters* observe leadership ability and ability to work in a group.)

Day 3

A. Individual case analysis and presentation. (*Raters* observe problem-solving ability, method of preparation, ability to handle questions, and communication skills.)

B. Evaluation of other ratees. (Peer evaluations.)

_____

4. Assessment centers are relevant to the job and have higher appeal because of this relevance.

As a result of participating in the group and as individuals' completing exercises, interviews, and tests, the assessors have a large volume of data on each assessee. The assessees are evaluated on a number of dimensions such as organization and planning ability, decision-making decisiveness, flexibility, resistance to stress, poise, and personal styles.

The assessor judgments are consolidated and developed into a final report. Each assessee's performance in the center can be described if the organization wants this type of report. Portions of the individual reports are fed back to each assessee, usually by one or more members of the assessment team.

The assessment center exercises, tests, and interviews; the final reports permit the organization to make a number of decisions such as:

1. The qualifications of assessees for particular positions.
2. The promotability of assessees.
3. How assessees function in a group.
4. The type of training and development needed to improve behaviors of assessees.
5. How good assessors are in observing, evaluating, and reporting on the performance of others (assessees).

The results of research on assessment centers have been encouraging. The initial work at AT&T indicated that assessment centers can predict future success with some accuracy.

Assessor ratings were kept secret for eight years after one assessment center was conducted. In a sample of 55 candidates who achieved the middle-management level, the center correctly predicted 8 percent of them. Of 73 people who did not move beyond the first level of management, 95 percent were correctly predicted by the assessors.[30] Other research also indicates that the assessment center can be, if implemented correctly, an unbiased selection technique.[31]

In spite of some supportive research findings assessment centers are not without some disadvantages. Dunnette and Borman caution about the fact that "the rapid growth of assessment centers may be accompanied by sloppy or improper application of assessment procedures."[32] Everyone jumping on the bandwagon often leads to exaggerated claims and improper use. Another disadvantage is costs. Assessors' time, assessees' time, materials, exercises, and other center expenses cost money. Costs can be as high as $4,000 to $5,000 per assessee.

Why hasn't more work been devoted to costing out assessment center activities? In concise terms it is not an easy task. In fact, it requires quantifying many intangible characteristics. The work to quantify may certainly be worth the effort. A survey of 64 organizations reported on the cost and benefits from their assessment centers. Total yearly costs including staff personnel, facilities, and initial setup consultant fees averaged about $88,000, while yearly assessment center savings were estimated to be $364,000.[33]

The Selection Decision

These are three types of approaches to the selection decision.

Some studies have been done to contrast and evaluate the various selection techniques. Jauch proposes an interesting combination of the systematic and clinical approaches to the selection decision which is inexpensive and realistic enough for the aver-

> **Approaches to selection decisions:**
>
> *Random choice or chance approaches.* Examples of this approach include choosing the third applicant interviewed or putting names in a hat and drawing one out.
>
> *Emotional-clinical approach.* The manager unconsciously picks the applicant who was most likeable in the interviews.
>
> *Systematic quasi-rational approach.* A systemic approach using various selection techniques, while recognizing that unconscious emotional choices are likely to enter into the decision. This chapter focuses on the systematic quasi-rational approach.

[30]Douglas W. Bray and Donald L. Grant, "The Assessment Center in the Measurement of Potential for Business Management," *Psychological Monographs,* No. 625, vol. 80 (1966), p. 25.

[31]Larry Alexander, "An Exploratory Study of the Utilization of Assessment Center Results," *Academy of Management Journal,* March 1979, pp. 152–57, and Wayne Cascio and Val Silby, "Utility of the Assessment Center as a Selection Device," *Journal of Applied Psychology,* April 1971, pp. 107–18.

[32]M. D. Dunnette and W. Borman, "Personnel Selection and Classification Systems," in *Annual Review of Psychology,* ed. M. Rosenzweig and L. Porter (1979), pp. 477–526.

[33]Stephen L. Cohen, "Validity and Assessment Center Technology: One and the Same?" *Human Resource Management,* Winter 1980, pp. 2–11.

Exhibit 7–12

Selection decision matrix for paired-comparison technique

Criteria \ Candidates	A—Mr. Black	B—Mr. White	C—Ms. Neutral	D—Mrs. Other
I. Education	College grad.	High school grad.	High school grad.	2 years college
II. Test scores	130	110	115	120
III. Experience	None	5 years	8 years	2 years
IV. Job knowledge	Above average	Excellent	Excellent	Average
V. Past performance	Excellent	Average	Above average	Above average
VI. Desire	Above average	Average	High	Above average
VII. Stability	Low	Average	High	Below average
VIII. Inverviewer 1	1	3.5	2	3.5
IV. Interviewer 2	2	3	1	4
X. Interviewer 3	2	4	3	1

"Systemizing the Selection Decision," by Lawrence Jauch. Reprinted with permission *Personnel Journal* copyright © November 1976.

age manager to use.[34] He calls it the paired-comparison method, in which a matrix of the candidates and the criteria is developed, as shown in Exhibit 7–12. Each interviewer compares each candidate to the others on each criterion (I–VII) and ranks them relative to each other (VIII–X). These ranks then are summed or weighted according to the decision maker's evaluation of the opinion of each interviewer.

A method similar to Jauch's might be used to try to reconcile differences of opinion on selection between personnel specialists and operating managers. If that does not work it appears reasonable that the operating manager who will supervise the applicant should prevail, since this is the manager who must deal with an unsuitable or ineffective employee.

Cost/Benefit Analysis for the Selection Decision

One way to evaluate which selection techniques should be used is to consider the probabilities that particular methods will select successful candidates and the costs of these methods. The seven steps in the selection procedure and their probable costs are:

Method	Cost
1. Preliminary screening interview	Negligible
2. Application blank/biodata	Negligible
3. Employment interview	Time used × cost per hour
4. Employment tests	$5–$1,000
5. Background and reference checks	$100
6. Physical examination	$50
7. Decision	

Each of these steps can be regarded as a hurdle which will select out the least qualified candidates. Steps 1, 2, and 3 probably will be used in most cases. The questionable

[34]Lawrence Jauch, "Systematizing the Selection Decision," *Personnel Journal*, November 1976, pp. 564–66.

ones are 4, 5, and 6 for many persons, and Step 6 may not be appropriate. As for Step 5, the checks need not be used for many jobs which do not involve much responsibility. Each selection technique can be evaluated in terms of costs and benefits.

Costs of training and selecting personnel may have trade-off features which can be calculated. One final comment about the selection decision. The greater the number of sources of data into the decision, the more probable it is that it will be a good decision. Tests alone will not suffice. Interviews supplemented by background checks and some test results are better. Costs and time constraints however, are obviously crucial.

Summary

This chapter was designed to help you understand what is involved in making effective selection decisions. The basic objective of selection is to obtain the employees who are most likely to meet the organization's standards of performance and who will be satisfied and developed on the job. To do this, the following statements summarize this chapter's conclusions.

1. Selection is influenced by environmental characteristics: whether the organization is public or private, labor market conditions and the selection ratio, union requirements, and legal restrictions on selection.
2. Reasonable criteria for the choice must be set prior to selection.
3. The selection process can include up to six steps:
    a. Preliminary screening interview.
    b. Completion of application blank/biodata form.
    c. Employment interview.
    d. Employment tests.
    e. Reference checks and recommendation letters.
    f. Physical examinations.

4. For more important positions (measured by higher pay and responsibility), the selection decision is more likely to be formalized and to use more selection techniques.
5. The effective organization prefers to select persons already in the organization over outside candidates.
6. More effective selection decisions are made if both P/HRM managers and the future supervisors of potential employees are involved in the selection decision.
7. Using a greater number of accepted methods to gather data for selection decisions increases the number of successful candidates selected.
8. Larger organizations are more likely to use sophisticated selection techniques.
9. For more measurable jobs, tests can be used in the selection decision more effectively.
10. For lower jobs in the hierarchy, tests can be used more effectively in the selection decisions.
11. Even if the most able applicant is chosen, there is no guarantee of successful performance on the job.

If you were Clark Kirby, how would you select the 596 people? You should know that at present, Gunther is not unionized. Remember Lewis wants Clark to seriously consider EEO criteria in selection, and Ed doesn't want him to. And there are the two persons Clark wants to please with his decisions.

Clark doesn't have enough time to make all the selection decisions himself. A P/HRM specialist can help. But this won't be enough either if he is to follow all six steps of selection. Yet Gunther will not authorize additional help to select the people. If you were Clark, how would you proceed? (Plan your strategy before reading Clark's solution.)

Exhibit 7–13 summarizes the recommendations for use of the various selection methods in the model organizations (see Exhibit 1–8). While selection appears to be a universally used personnel activity, the techniques adopted are likely to be based on the types of personnel selected rather than the type of organization doing the selection.

Exhibit 7–13

Recommendations on selection methods for model organizations

Type of organization	Screening interview	Application blank, biodata	Employment interview	Performance and ability tests*	Telephoned background reference check†	Physical exam
1. Large size, low complexity, high stability	X	X	X	X	X	Hospital
2. Medium size, low complexity, high stability	X	X	X	X	X	
3. Small size, low complexity, high stability	X	X				
4. Medium size, moderate complexity, moderate stability	X	X	X	X	X	
5. Large size, high complexity, low stability	X	X	X	X	X	Hospital
6. Medium size, high complexity, low stability	X	X	X			
7. Small size, high complexity, low stability	X	X	X			Hospital

*Usually for blue- and white-collar positions.
†Usually for white-collar and managerial positions.

Case

This is what Clark Kirby did. He didn't have the resources or time to hire all 596. Besides, he believed that operating managers should participate in decisions. So his strategy was to hire the managers first. Then he had the managers help screen and hire the clerical and semiskilled employees.

As far as selection objectives were concerned, Clark accepted the home office's objectives. These were to hire those employees who were most likely to be effective and satisfied. He accepted the job specifications for the most similar positions he could find in the Chicago plant. These specifications listed minimum requirements in education and experience for managers and professional/technical employees. For clerical employees, the emphasis was on minimum experience, plus performance simulation test scores. For skilled employees, the job specifications included minimum experience and test scores on performance simulation tests. This was also true for semiskilled employees.

Clark decided that because of time pressures and the nature of the job differences, he would use the following selection process.

Managers: screening interview, application blank, interview, reference check.

Professional/technical: screening interview, application blank, interview, reference check.

Clerical: screening interview, application blank, interview, tests.

Skilled: screening interview, application blank, tests and interviews for marginal applicants.

Semiskilled: screening interview, application blank, tests and interviews for marginal applicants.

Clark and Ed hired the managers. Clark himself hired the professionals. While these groups were being hired, the personnel specialist administered the tests to the clerical employees and supervised the reference checking process on the managers and professionals. The P/HRM specialist hired the clerical employees. But the managers and professionals were involved in hiring the clerical personnel to be under their direct supervision.

Then Clark and the P/HRM specialist administered the tests to skilled and semiskilled employees. Clark hired the clearly well-qualified semiskilled employees, except in marginal cases. Candidates received a review and were interviewed by the managers to whom they would report. A similar process was used to hire the semiskilled employees. Since there were few choices among professional/technical and skilled employees, it was more efficient not to involve the new managers too.

Several problems developed. Clark and Ed had no trouble agreeing on 20 managerial candidates. But in 18 additional cases, Clark felt he had found better candidates. Ed wanted more Chicago people he knew. Lewis, reflecting the position of Chicago managers, objected. Clark found many more qualified minority and female managerial candidates than Ed wanted to accept. They compromised. Ed gave up half his choices to Clark, and Clark did likewise.

There were also problems in the skilled professional categories. These people generally wanted more pay than the budget called for. And the last 20 percent hired were somewhat below minimum specifications. Clark appealed for more budget, given these conditions. The home office gave him half of what he needed. He had to generate the other half by paying less for the bottom 20 percent of the semiskilled and clerical employees. Clark alerted Ed to the probable competence problem. He promised Ed that he'd begin developing a list of qualified applicants in these categories in case they were needed.

In sum, Clark hired the people needed within the adjusted budget, on time, and generally with the required specifications. He was able to make a contribution to equal employment opportunity objectives by hiring somewhat more minorities and women than the total population, less than he could have and less then Lewis wanted, but more than Ed wanted. All were qualified. No reverse discrimination took place.

Compare your solution with Clark's. In what ways was his better? Yours better?

Questions for Review and Discussion

1. What is personnel selection? Who makes these decisions? What factors influence personnel selection? How?
2. Why would an assessment center tend to be a costly selection technique?
3. What is a selection ratio? How does it apply to P/HRM selection?
4. What is the difference between content and construct validity?
5. Describe a typical selection process for a manual laborer; top executive; typist.
6. How are biodata forms used in selection? How effective are they? Are they reliable and valid? How frequently are they used?
7. What is an employment interview? How often is it used? What are three types of interview styles? Which are the most reliable?
8. What is a test? A performance test? A simulation? A paper-and-pencil test? Tests are increasing in use in the United States. Comment.
9. When would you use reference checks? For which jobs? How would you do the checks?
10. How does the process of selecting a manager differ from selecting a typist? How is it similar?

Glossary

Assessment Center. A selection technique that uses simulations, tests, interviews, and observations to obtain information about candidates.

Content Validity. The degree to which a test, interview, or performance evaluation measures skill, knowledge, or ability to perform.

Construct Validity. A demonstrated relationship between underlying traits inferred from behavior and a set of test measures related to those traits.

Criterion-Related Validity. The extent to which a selection technique is predictive of or correlated with important elements of job behavior.

Reliability. Refers to a selection technique's freedom from systematic errors of measurement or its consistency under different conditions.

Selection. The process by which an organization chooses from a list of applicants the person or persons who best meet the selection criteria for the position available, considering current environmental conditions.

Structured Interview. Interview that follows a prepared pattern of questions that were structured before the interview was conducted.

Weighted Application Blank. An application form designed to be scored and used in making selection decisions.

Part Two

Application Cases and Exercises

APPLICATION CASE II–1

AT&T: Human Resource Planning Issues*

American Telephone and Telegraph (AT&T) Company is actively involved in human resource planning decisions. W. S. Cashel is the vice chairman and chief financial officer of the company. Formerly, he was president of the Bell Telephone Company in Pennsylvania. Mr. Cashel believes that the manager's first concern with human resource planning is simply whether it is helping employees to do what they are committed to do. At AT&T this type of planning has become a rather complex job.

Today at AT&T many factors complicate the human resource planning job. EEO/affirmative action is a prime example. In the past, line managers, for instance, only had to think about whether or not they had the right number of installers. Now, they must think about whether they have the right number of both sexes, ethnic categories, and typically, eight or so establishments or labor market areas.

Another problem at AT&T involves managerial succession. To cite a few examples Mr. Cashel noted:

- One of our typical Operating Telephone Companies (OTC) will have to replace 55 of its 67 department heads by 1990.
- On a System base there will be about 50 percent turnover in the next few years.

A related concern is having enough strong candidates with experience and training in the right technical disciplines. AT&T estimates about 4,000 vacancies at the third level of management in the next few years.

Recently, an AT&T company, Western Electric, had to lay off 42,000 employees and close several manufacturing plants. This is another problem that is connected with human resource planning.

Cashel also believes that human resource planning needs to consider the notion of earnings. He states that

- Total compensation per employee has risen from $7,580 in the mid-1960s to about $28,330 in the early 1980s.
- 74 percent of AT&T operating expense dollars now go for people costs— about $14 billion a year.

Obviously these kind of cost figures raise the issue of capital versus human resources. This issue must be weighed in any human resource planning decision making.

Questions for Thought

1. What can AT&T do to efficiently handle managerial succession problems?
2. Is the area of employee layoffs a concern of human resource planning? Explain.
3. What is meant by the issue of capital versus human resources at AT&T?

---

*Adapted from W. S. Cashel, Jr., "Human Resource Planning in the Bell System," *Human Resource Planning* (1978), pp. 59–66.

APPLICATION CASE II–2

A New Recruitment Strategy at Hooker Chemical Corporation*

Few companies have seen their images suffer more than Hooker Chemical, a unit of Occidental Petroleum, following the surge of criticism of its Love Canal chemical dump in Niagara Falls, N.Y. How is a company with this kind of bad reputation in the public eye going to recruit enough talented people to keep itself going?

Prospective employees often look at the reputation of an organization when they are faced with a decision about whether to become a part of the firm. A company's image affects its ability to attract top talent. Hooker has had to take an active role in recruiting so that the flow of talent continues. The Hooker Chemical dumping of chemicals in Love Canal and polluting the water and environment, besides being the subject of major television documentaries on NBC, CBS, and ABC, has triggered Senate investigations, and has been reported in every major magazine and newspaper in the country. There has been a virtual flood of bad publicity, legal suits, and accusations, all resulting in a negative image.

Hooker has countered the negative stories and claims by publicizing its positive accomplishments, such as an $80 million garbage-burning power plant under construction at its Niagara complex. They have also held a two-day seminar for about 20 P/HRM consultants, flown to Niagara Falls from around the country. Hooker showed them slides of area housing, told its side of the Love Canal story and invited the consultants onto the links with Hooker managers for a few persuasive rounds of golf. The event was capped by a sundown cruise on the Niagara River.

The Hooker plan was expensive, time consuming, and purposefully designed to create a better image and name. Whether these tactics are successful is what management is worried about. This recruitment strategy could also be questioned from an ethical perspective. Is this really an ethical strategy of recruitment? Hooker seems to believe that it is ethical, cost efficient, and the best way to go about creating a larger pool of talent.

As a result of their image as a flagrant polluter, Hooker management has concluded that their new recruitment strategy is the proper course of action. The word was spread quickly about Hooker's bad image. They now want to have the word spread just as quickly that Hooker is a good company to work for and is also a good corporate citizen.

Questions for Thought

1. Do you believe that Hooker's recruitment strategy has ethical shortcomings?
2. How could Hooker determine if their recruitment strategy was worth the expense?
3. What other organizations that you are familiar with have recruitment image problems?

---

*Adapted from Erik Larson, "For Companies with an Image Problem, Hiring Top Talent Can Take Ingenuity," *The Wall Street Journal,* October 17, 1980, p. 48.

APPLICATION CASE II–3

Bechtel Power Corporation's Use of Objective Welding Tests*

Charles Ligons, a black, was a welder at the Iowa Electric Light and Power, Duane Arnold Energy Center Construction site at Palo, Iowa. He worked at the site for Bechtel Power Corporation. Bechtel required that its welders be qualified in accordance with standards of the American Society of Mechanical Engineers Code. That code prescribes objective criteria for testing welders on various types of welding work and for placing them in two categories: (1) A-LH, under which a welder qualifies to perform general welding jobs, and (2) AT-LH, involving more difficult welding procedures.

Prior to his arrival to the Palo site, Ligons passed a test which qualified him under AT-LH to perform heliarc welding. During his first week of employment, however, Ligons was required to report to the test shop for training and testing as a result of observations made by a welding engineer of a weld which Ligons had improperly prepared. Following a one-week training period, Ligons passed a simple plate welding test, but failed the same heliarc welding test which he had passed before coming to Palo. Ligons spent several weeks on at least three separate occasions training for upgrading testing to improve his competence in heliarc welding.

On February 9, approximately 18 months after coming to the Palo site, Ligons was laid off with 58 other welders, all of whom were white. Ligons was informed that he was eligible for rehire when more welders were needed. The layoff was a result of a general reduction of the Palo work force.

Ligons was rehired in September. He required further training and testing for recertification. After about one month of training, he passed only the test qualifying him for the least difficult type of welding. About four months after being rehired he was again laid off with five other welders.

Ligons believed that race was a motivating factor in the decision to lay him off. Bechtel claimed, however, that its testing procedures for upgrading a welder's qualifications had a relationship to the jobs for which they were used. They stated that the welding tests were based on objective welding standards set by the American Society of Mechanical Engineers. Bechtel was contractually bound to ensure that its welders were qualified and, that all welding performed on the job complied with the American Society of Mechanical Engineers Code.

Questions for Thought

1. Do you believe that welding tests are necessary for the type of job which Charles Ligon's worked on?
2. Was the first layoff of Ligons legitimate?
3. Did the company make an attempt to help Ligons maintain and upgrade his welding competence?

---

*Based on *Ligons* v. *Bechtel Power Corporation*, 23EPD 9 16, 233.

EXERCISE II

Practicing the Selection Interview

Objective. The exercise is designed to have students participate in structured and unstructured interviews involving selection decisions.

Set Up the Exercise

1. The class or group is to be divided into equal numbers of 6, 8, 10, 12, or 14 people. The best number to work with is 10.
2. Suppose that 10 people are in the group (make adjustments based on size of group). Two individuals will play the role of the job applicant Nick Thomas. The autobiography of Nick should be read.
3. Two other group members are to play the role of interviewers using the unstructured format. They should rereview the unstructured interview material in Chapter 7, the job description for the position, and Nick's job application.
4. Two other group members should conduct interviews with a structured format. Consult Chapter 7 on the structured format. Also read the job description for the position, and Nick's job application.
5. The remaining four members are to act as a panel of observers that will evaluate the structured versus unstructured format. Read all materials—Chapter 7 on interviews, job description, autobiography, and application.
6. First, the unstructured interview should be conducted (take no more than six or seven minutes).
7. Second, conduct the structured interview (take no more than six or seven minutes).
8. Observers should rate the interviewers using these criteria:
   a. Which format yielded the most valuable information?
   b. Which format was easiest to conduct?
   c. Which format was able to probe the applicant's attitudes and feelings?

A Learning Note

This exercise will illustrate that interviewing is a rather intricate task. One must be fully prepared to conduct any interview.

The Situation

Dante Foods is a chain of food stores operating in 20 locations in the Chicago area. The night manager of the Palmer Park store suddenly resigned, leaving a vacancy. The Palmer Park store has 40 full- and part-time employees. A brief job description of the night manager position was developed. Dante has a number of applicants and wants to fill the position as soon as possible. Nick Thomas seems a likely candidate for the vacancy.

Brief Job Description of Dante Night Manager

1. Reports directly to store manager.
2. Makes decisions concerning store tasks when on duty; usually from 6:00 P.M. to 12:00 A.M.
3. Supervises all night shift employees—full- and part-time.
4. Handles all emergencies and problems when on duty (e.g., customers, deliveries, special food orders).
5. Closes books at end of shift and prepares morning orders for stockouts—canned goods, produce, and bakery products.

Job Application—Dante Foods

Name: ____Nick Thomas____

Address: ____1711 Western Avenue, Chicago, Ill. 60615____

How Long at Present Address: ____3 years____

Date of Birth: ____March 18, 1960____

Marital Status: ____Single____

Number of Children: _____

U.S. Citizen: ____Yes____

Do you have any physical defects? ____No____ If yes, describe _____

Have you had any major illness in the past two years? ____No____

If yes, describe _____

Please List Former Employers

Year	Name and address	Position	Reason for leaving
From 1976 to 1978 (Summers)	Gassmans 3514 E. 92nd Street Chicago, Illinois	Clerk	College
From 1978 to Present	Safeway 10136 Commercial Chicago, Illinois	Checker, Assistant produce manager, and Produce manager	—

```
From
to
_____

From
to

_____

Hobbies: _____Fishing, Listening to Music, Exercise_____

Civic Organizations: _____
Professional Organizations: _____
```

Education	Date of Graduation	Major	Rank in Class and Grade Point Average
High School			
Bower	1978		65/275
College			3.1/4.0
University of Illinois/Circle		Business	65 credits completed

```
When could you begin to work for Dante?
                    Next Week 7/20
```

Nick Thomas Autobiography

I have lived in Chicago for the past 12 years. I was born in Washington, D.C., and lived for 11 years in Arlington, Virginia. I enjoy school and really like to work with people.

My work experience ranges from delivering papers as a youngster to my present position of produce manager. I plan to become an executive in the food business working for a chain or even starting my own business.

My strongest trait is a dogged determination to do the job well. In anything I do I work hard and always give my best effort. My weakest trait is that I sometimes become impatient with those people who do not do their best.

I enjoy fishing, listening to music, and staying in shape. Every year for the past three I have spent at least two weeks fishing on Lake Baribou in Wisconsin. I actively work out with Nautilus equipment and weights at least four times a week.

I would like to finish my degree at the Circle within the next four or five years. I have to keep working to put myself through school. This is the only way that I can receive a college education.

Part Three

U.S. Department of Labor

Part Three is concerned with performance evaluation and training and development. Chapter 8 focuses on the necessary managerial job of evaluating the work of employees. It clearly shows that performance evaluation is a difficult task for any rater (manager or supervisor). Chapter 9 discusses the orientation and training of employees. It focuses on improving the abilities and skills of employees. Chapter 10 discusses the development of human resources, with attention directed primarily toward organizational development (OD) in this chapter. Chapter 11 looks at career planning and development, an area of growing importance in organizations.

Performance Evaluation and Training and Development

U.S. Department of Labor

H. Armstrong Roberts

Chapter Eight

Performance Evaluation

Learning Objectives

After studying this chapter, you should be able to:
- Define what is meant by the term *performance evaluation.*

- Discuss various types of rating errors that managers make in performance evaluation programs.

- Compare the advantages of various performance evaluation techniques.

- Explain the role of a manager and his or her subordinate in a management by objectives program.

- Describe the importance of the evaluation feedback interview.

Chapter Outline

I. A Diagnostic Approach to Performance Evaluation

II. To Evaluate or Not to Evaluate
  A. In Favor of Evaluation
  B. Performance Evaluation and the Law
  C. Opposition to Evaluation

III. Potential Performance Evaluation Problems
  A. System design and operating problems
  B. Rater Problems
  C. Employee problems with performance evaluation

IV. Formal Evaluation
  A. Set policies on when, how often, and who evaluates
  B. Gather data on employees

V. Selected Evaluation Techniques
  A. Individual evaluation methods
  B. Multiple-person evaluation methods
  C. Other methods
  D. Which technique to use

VI. The Feedback Interview

VII. Make Decisions and File the Evaluation

VIII. Summary

Case

Felipe

Felipe Hernandez went to work in the maintenance department of Partridge Enterprise, a middle-sized firm, about a year ago. He enjoys being in maintenance, since he has always liked to work with his hands. His supervisor, Ed Smart, is a good maintenance man who helps Felipe when he doesn't understand a problem. But Felipe has often wished he knew what Ed thinks of him on the job. Ed never tells Felipe how he is doing. It seems that Ed chews him out about once a month. Felipe wonders: Doesn't he think I am trying to do a good job? Doesn't he think I am a good maintenance man?

Knowing the answers to these questions is important to Felipe, because someday he'd like to move up. He hears that Joe is going to retire next year. Joe's job is better and pays more. Felipe wonders if he has a chance to get the job. He also has heard that business is not good right now at some branches. People have been laid off. If the crunch hits the New York branch where Felipe works, he might get laid off. He knows seniority is a factor in layoffs. But so is performance. He wishes he knew how he was doing so that he could improve himself, move up, and avoid getting laid off.

This chapter focuses on *performance evaluation*—the P/HRM activity designed to satisfy Felipe's needs for performance feedback.

Performance evaluation is the P/HRM activity that is used to determine the extent to which an employee is performing the job effectively.

Other terms for performance evaluation include *performance review, personnel rating, merit rating, performance appraisal, employee appraisal,* or *employee evaluation.*

In many organizations, two evaluation systems exist side by side: the formal and the informal. Supervisors often think about how well employees are doing; this is the informal system. It is influenced by political and interpersonal processes so that employees who are liked better than others have an edge. On the other hand a

Formal performance evaluation is a system set up by the organization to *regularly* and *systematically* evaluate employee performance.

This chapter focuses only on formal performance evaluation systems.

A Diagnostic Approach to Performance Evaluation

Exhibit 8–1 highlights the relevant factors from the diagnostic model which have significance for performance evaluation. One factor is the task. A white-collar or supervisory task is more likely to be formally evaluated than some blue-collar tasks. In addition, the performance evaluation technique used will differ with the task being evaluated.

Another factor affecting performance evaluation is the government. Since the passage of antidiscrimination legislation, the government has investigated to determine if organizations discriminate against protected categories of employees in promotion, pay raises, and other rewards. Performance evaluation is the personnel method for allocating these rewards. By inducing organizations to keep better records to support their decisions, government action has indirectly encouraged better performance evaluation systems.

Another factor influencing performance evaluation is the attitudes and preferences of employees. For many people, especially those whose values fit the work ethic (such as Felipe) evaluations can be very important. But if this process is badly handled, turnover increases, morale declines, and productivity can drop. For employees with instrumental attitudes toward work, performance evaluation is just another process at work. Since work is not too important to them, neither are evaluations. They want a job to earn money, and that is it.

An important factor that can affect performance evaluation is the leader's (supervisor's) style. Supervisors can use the formal system in a number of ways: fairly or unfairly, in a supportive manner or punitively, positively or negatively. If the supervisor is punitive and negative with an employee who responds to positive reinforcement, performance evaluation can lead to the opposite of the results expected by the enterprise.

Finally, if there is a union present in the organization, performance evaluations might be affected. Different unions take different positions in support of or in opposition to formal performance evaluations. Most oppose the use of nonmeasurable, nonproduction-related factors in performance evaluation. They have good reason to doubt the usefulness of unclear factors such as "initiative" or "potential."

These are the major factors affecting the performance evaluation process. Now we will briefly examine the case for and against the use of formal performance evaluation.

To Evaluate or Not to Evaluate

Why hasn't Felipe ever been evaluated by his supervisor? In order to answer that question, picture the scene described on page 236.

In Favor of Evaluation

This meeting illustrates many of the arguments, pro and con, on formal performance evaluation. Let's sum them up. Those who favor formal performance evaluation contend that it serves several purposes:

> *Developmental purposes.*   It helps determine which employees need more
>   training. It helps evaluate the results of training programs. It helps the
>   subordinate-supervisor counseling relationship, and it encourages
>   supervisors to observe subordinate behavior to help employees.

Exhibit 8–1

Factors affecting performance evaluation

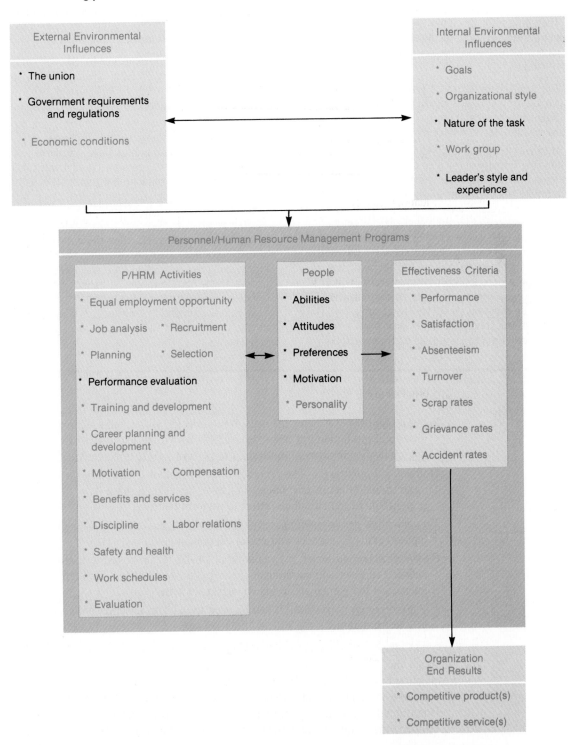

External Environmental Influences

* The union

* Government requirements and regulations

* Economic conditions

Internal Environmental Influences

* Goals

* Organizational style

* Nature of the task

* Work group

* Leader's style and experience

Personnel/Human Resource Management Programs

P/HRM Activities

* Equal employment opportunity

* Job analysis   * Recruitment

* Planning   * Selection

* Performance evaluation

* Training and development

* Career planning and development

* Motivation   * Compensation

* Benefits and services

* Discipline   * Labor relations

* Safety and health

* Work schedules

* Evaluation

People

* Abilities

* Attitudes

* Preferences

* Motivation

* Personality

Effectiveness Criteria

* Performance

* Satisfaction

* Absenteeism

* Turnover

* Scrap rates

* Grievance rates

* Accident rates

Organization End Results

* Competitive product(s)

* Competitive service(s)

Case

The setting: Office of the executive vice president of Partridge Enterprises. Present are the executive vice president and the vice presidents of the corporation.

Tom Smith (executive vice president) As you know, we're here to make a recommendation to John (the president) on what if anything to do about Mary's suggestion. Mary, why don't you review the issue?

Mary Hartford (vice president, personnel) You all received a copy of my memo to J. B. As you know, when I came here three years ago I felt one of our top priorities in personnel would be to get an evaluation system really running on line here. I want this because performance evaluation is an outstanding motivation technique. After much thought and planning, the results are in my memo. I recommend we institute an MBO-type evaluation system for vice presidents through section heads and a graphic rating scale for below that. The MBO would be done quarterly, the rating scale semiannually, and we'd tie rewards such as raises and promotions to the results of the evaluation.

The details are in these memos. We're too big and geographically dispersed now to continue using our informal system.

Tom Sounds good to me.

Dave Artem (vice president marketing) Me too.

Will Roxer (vice president, finance) Looks fine, Mary.

Fred Fairfax (vice president, manufacturing) Well, it doesn't to me. We had one of these papermill forms systems here 10 years ago, and it was a waste of time. It just meant more paper work for us down on the firing line. You staff people sit up here dreaming up more for us to do. We're overburdened now. Besides, I called a few buddies in big firms who have P.E. They say it involves a lot of training of evaluators and it makes half the employees mad when they don't get 100 percent scores on the "grade report." It gets down to a lot of politics when it's all said and done.

If you recommend this, I'll send J. B. a counterproposal and I'll call him to see I get my way, too.

Reward purposes. It helps the organization decide who should receive pay raises and promotions. It helps determine who will be laid off. It reinforces the employees' motivation to perform, more effectively.

Motivational purposes. The presence of an evaluation program has a motivational effect: it encourages initiative, develops a sense of responsibility, and stimulates effort to perform better.

Personnel and employment planning purposes. It serves as a valuable input to skills inventories and personnel planning.

Communications purposes. Evaluation is a basis for an ongoing discussion between superior and subordinate about job-related matters. Through interaction the parties get to know each other better.

P/HRM research purposes. It can be used to validate selection tools such as a test program.

These and other purposes served by a formal performance evaluation system indicate how important this P/HRM activity is to the organization. They also show how performance evaluation is job related and linked to other P/HRM activities—planning, selection, training, and development, research evaluation, and equal employment opportunity. Of all of the relationships between performance evaluation and other P/HRM activities the one between evaluation and equal employment opportunity has become extremely crucial.

Performance Evaluation and the Law

As mentioned in Chapter 3 the Equal Employment Opportunity Commission (EEOC), is responsible for administering and enforcing the Civil Rights Act of 1964. The EEOC issued the Uniform Guidelines on Employment Selection Procedures in 1978. These guidelines definitely have an impact on performance evaluation because evaluations are viewed as a selection procedure.[1] The guidelines state that a procedure such as a performance evaluation must not adversely impact any group protected by the Civil Rights Act.

Most performance evaluation procedures rely on paper-and-pencil methods to identify specific work behavior. Once ratings are made they are used as input in making promotion, pay, transfer, and other human resource decisions. In making these decisions there is the potential for bias and poor judgments in many parts of the evaluation process.[2] For example, managers who are serving as raters could use criteria that are not important in performing a job or place too little weight on significant job performance criteria.

A number of court rulings have identified the responsibilities of management in developing and using a performance evaluation system.

> *Griggs* v. *Duke Power Company (1971).*   Recall from Chapter 3 the central issue in this case was that an educational restriction on an employment decision is useless unless it can be proved that there exists a bona fide occupations qualificiation (BFOQ) between the test and actual job performance.

> *Brito* v. *Zia Company (1973).*   The Zia Company was found in violation of the law when a disproportionate number of protected group members were laid off on the basis of low performance evaluation scores. The Court ruled that the company had not shown that its performance evaluation instrument was valid in the sense that it was related to important elements of work behavior in the jobs where the employees were being evaluated.

> *Albermarle Paper Company* v. *Moody (1975).*   The Court ruled that in the process of validating their tests, the company had not conducted a job analysis to identify the critical requirements of jobs.

Since employers have been winning only about 5 percent of the race, sex, and age discrimination cases understanding the law seems to be a major concern. Previous Court rulings such as the three just cited provide managers with guidelines on the issues of criteria, validity, and reliability. These three concepts are extremely important if a case reaches the federal courts. Although an audit is necessary to ensure that an organization's performance evaluation system is able to withstand review, Several other steps that could be initiated by P/HRM specialists would be:[3]

1. Training evaluators (raters).
2. Clearly communicating the objectives of the performance evaluation to ratees and raters.

---

[1] Richard Henderson, *Performance Appraisal* (Reston, Va.: Reston Publishing, 1980), p. 217.

[2] See footnotes in Chapter 3 and Wayne F. Cascio and H. John Bernardin, "Implications of Performance Appraisal Litigation for Personnel Decisions," *Personnel Psychology,* Summer 1981, pp. 211–26.

[3] Diane E. Thompson and Debra Moskowitz, "A Legal Look at Performance Appraisal," *The Wharton Magazine,* Winter 1981–82, pp. 66–70.

3. Being sure that job relatedness of the performance evaluation can be demonstrated through job analysis.
4. Make the evaluation as objective as possible.
5. Building in privacy so that access to the evaluation is closely protected.

Opposition to Evaluation

Those who oppose the use of formal performance evaluation systems argue that:

They increase paperwork and bureaucracy without benefiting employees much. Operating managers do not use them in reward decisions. (Systems problems.)

Managers and employees dislike the evaluation process and are not effective. (Rater problems.)

Employees who are not evaluated in the top-performance category experience a reverse motivation effect: They slow down. (Employee problems.)

These problems will be discussed in the next section of the chapter. The examination of many performance appraisal systems now in use suggests that these three arguments have some merit in numerous settings.

Potential Performance Evaluation Problems

Any system can malfunction or fail. Performance evaluation is no exception. Performance evaluation can break down because of the kind of problems just mentioned.

System Design and Operating Problems

Performance evaluation systems break down because they are poorly designed. The design can be blamed if the criteria for evaluation are poor, the technique used is cumbersome, or the system is more form than substance. If the criteria used focus solely on activities rather than output results, or on personality traits rather than performance, the evaluation may not be well received. Some evaluation techniques take a long time to do or require extensive written analysis, both of which many managers resist. If this is the problem, another technique can be chosen. Finally, some systems are not on line and running. Some supervisors use the system, but others just haphazardly fill out the paperwork. Top management's support for performance evaluation can remedy this problem of ritualism.

Too often, a typical manager is like Ed. He knows there is a formal performance evaluation system, but he disregards it. Performance evaluation systems have to be so good that they can't be disregarded.

Rater Problems

Even if the system is well designed, problems can arise if the raters (usually supervisors) are not cooperative and well trained. Supervisors may not be comfortable with the process of evaluation, or what Douglas McGregor called "playing God."[4] This is often because

---

[4]Douglas McGregor, "An Uneasy Look at Performance Appraisal," *Harvard Business Review*, May 1957, pp. 90–94.

Case

Bob

Ed

Let's get back to Felipe and his supervisor, Ed Smart. Now that the vice presidents have had their meeting about performance evaluation, the tentative decision to start up Mary's plan has been passed on to the department heads.

Bob Woods (department head) I'm just reviewing your suggested pay and promotions for your unit, Ed. You know I try to delegate as much as I can. But I know some of the people you have set here for big raises and promotions, and I notice some surprising omissions. Since I'm responsible for the whole department, I'd like to review this with you. Understand, I'm not trying to undercut you, Ed.

Ed Smart (supervisor) Oh, I understand, Bob. No problem! Where do you want to start?

Bob Let me just highspot. I note that Mo Gibbs, who's always been in our high reward group, isn't here, nor is Felipe Hernandez, a good worker. And you do have Joe Berlioz in your high reward group. In the past, he never appeared there. How did you make these recommendations?

Ed I looked my people over and used my best judgment. That's what you pay me for, isn't it?

Bob Sure, Ed, but what facts did you use—did you look at the quarterly output printout, their personnel files, or what? How about performance evaluations—Partridge is thinking about a formal system to evaluate employees and help decide who should be promoted and get raises.

Ed I believe I know my people best. I don't need to go through a lot of paperwork and files to come up with my recommendations.

---

they have not been adequately trained or have not participated in the design of the program. Inadequate training of raters can lead to a series of problems in completing performance evaluations including:

- Standards of Evaluation.
- Halo Effect.
- Leniency or Harshness.
- Central Tendency.
- Recency of Events.
- Personal Bias.

Standards of Evaluation • Problems with evaluation standards arise because of perceptual differences in the meaning of the words used to evaluate employees. Thus *good, adequate, satisfactory,* and *excellent* may mean different things to different evaluators. Some teachers are "easy As," while others almost never give an A. *They* differ in their interpretation of *excellent*. If only one rater is used, the evaluation can be distorted. This difficulty arises mostly in graphic rating scales but may also appear with essays, critical incidents, and checklists.

For example, Exhibit 8–2 presents a rating scale with unclear standards for four difficult-to-rate performance dimensions. What does "good" performance for quality of work mean? How does it differ from a "fair" rating. How would you interpret the quality or quantity of performance? This rating scale is ambiguous as it now stands. Perhaps by defining the meaning of each dimension and by training raters to apply the five ratings consistently could reduce the potential rating problem.

The Halo Effect • Halo error in ratings is one of the major problems in most performance evaluation systems. It occurs when a rater assigns ratings on the basis of an overall impression (positive or negative) of the person being rated (ratee). Suppose that a retail store floor manager (rater) sees and overhears an argument between a clerk and a customer. If the rater assumed that because of this argument the clerk was not good at servicing customers, processing complaints, and ordering inventory he or she would be making a halo error. The one negative aspect of the clerk's behavior caused the rater to see the ratee in a negative light on other dimensions.

Eliminating halo rating errors are difficult. One procedure to reduce this type of error is to have the rater evaluate all subordinates on one dimension before proceeding to another dimension. The theory of this practice is that thinking in terms of one dimension at a time forces the rater to think in specific instead of overall terms when evaluating subordinates.

Leniency or Harshness Error • Performance evaluations require the rater to objectively reach a conclusion about criteria of performance. Being objective is difficult for everyone. Raters have their own rose-colored glasses with which they "objectively" view subordinates. What some raters see is everything good—these are lenient raters. Other raters see everything bad—these are harsh raters.

Exhibit 8–3 shows the distributions of lenient and harsh raters on a dimension called

Exhibit 8–2 _____

A graphic rating scale for laboratory scientists

Performance dimension	Scale: Place an X for rating of _____				
	Outstanding	Good	Fair	Below accepted	Poor
Quality of technical reports					
Quantity of technical reports					
Creativeness					
Social interaction ability					

Exhibit 8–3 _____

Distributions of lenient and harsh raters

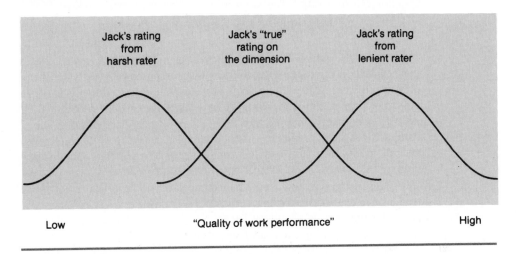

Jack's rating
from
harsh rater

Jack's "true"
rating on
the dimension

Jack's rating
from
lenient rater

Low   "Quality of work performance"   High

quality of work performance.[5] Suppose that Jack is a person working for this particular rater. His ratings would be low if rated by the harsh rater, and high if rated by the lenient rater.

Raters can assess their own harsh and lenient rating tendencies by examining ratings. This self-assessment is sometimes startling. Another method used to reduce harsh and lenient rating tendencies is to ask raters to distribute ratings—forcing a normal distribution (e.g., 10 percent of the subordinates will be rated excellent, 20 percent rated good, 40 percent rated fair, 20 percent rated below fair, and 10 percent rated poor).

Central Tendency Error • Many raters avoid using high or low ratings. They resort to a philosophy that everyone is about average and rate subordinates around a 4 on a 1 to 7 scale or a 3 on a 1 to 5 scale. This type of "average" rating is almost useless. It fails to discriminate between subordinates. Thus, it offers little information for making P/HRM decisions regarding compensation, promotion, training needs, or what should be fed back to ratees. Raters must be made aware of the importance of discriminating across ratees and the use of evaluations. This sometimes stimulates raters to use less central (or average) ratings.

Recency of Events Error • One difficulty with many of the evaluation systems is the time frame of the behavior being evaluated. Raters forget more about past behavior than current behavior. Thus many persons are evaluated more on the results of the past several weeks than on six month's average behavior. This is called a recency of events rating error.

Some employees are well aware of this difficulty. If they know the dates of the

_____

[5]Adapted from Wayne Cascio, _Applied Psychology in Personnel Management_ (Reston, Va.: Reston Publishing, 1978), p. 321.

evaluation, they make it their business to be visible and noticed in many positive ways for several weeks in advance. Many evaluation systems suffer from this difficulty. It can be mitigated by using a technique such as critical incident or management by objectives (MBO) or by irregularly scheduled evaluations.

Personal Bias Error • Various studies have indicated that rater's biases can influence their evaluation of employees.[6] If raters like certain employees better than others, this can influence the ratings they give. This problem is related to the effects of prejudices against groups of people. Pressures from governmental agencies and managerial values of fairness should lead to equal opportunity and fair performance evaluation. The result should be increased rewards, promotions, and significant careers for all employees, of both sexes and all races, religions, and nationalities. Some evaluation techniques (such as forced choice, field review, performance tests, and MBO) tend to reduce this problem.

Bias has been pointed out in a number of studies. One study found a systematic tendency to evaluate subordinates over 60 years of age lower on "performance capacity" and "potential for development" than younger subordinates.[7] In other research high-performing females were often rated significantly higher than high-performing males.[8]

Some of the evaluation difficulties and errors made in rating can perhaps be reduced through the use of better performance evaluation instruments (forms or scales used). By clearly defining the dimensions being rated and the scale value or descriptors (e.g., what is meant by the term *excellent, good, fair*) raters could become more confident about their ratings. Unfortunately, research to date indicates that improved instruments have little positive influence on reducing leniency and halo errors.[9] However, more research is needed before concluding that a clear, unambiguous, and meaningful rating scale is not more effective than an unclear, ambiguous, and meaningless rating scale.

Another approach used in reducing rater problems involves training. This training can be of many types: how to rate effectively, present rater tendencies and ways to become more accurate, how to feed back evaluation information, and how to get subordinates more involved in evaluation. Several research studies indicate that even brief training programs can reduce some of the rating errors so prevalent in performance evaluation programs.[10]

Employee Problems with Performance Evaluation

For the evaluation system to work well, the employees must understand it, must feel it is fair, and must be work oriented enough to care about the results. One way to foster this understanding is for the employees to participate in system design and be trained to some

---

[6]Walter C. Borman, "Format and Training Effect on Rating Accuracy and Rater Errors," *Journal of Applied Psychology,* August 1979, pp. 410–21.

[7]B. Rosen and T. H. Jerdee, "The Nature of Job Related Age Stereotypes," *Journal of Applied Psychology,* April 1976, pp. 180–83.

[8]William J. Bigoness, "Effect of Applicant's Sex, Race, and Performance on Employer's Performance Ratings: Some Additional Findings," *Journal of Applied Psychology,* February 1976, pp. 80–84.

[9]Donald P. Schwab, Herbert G. Heneman, III., and Thomas A. DeCotiis, "Behaviorally Anchored Rating Scales: A Review of the Literature," *Personnel Psychology,* Winter 1975, pp. 549–62.

[10]John M. Ivancevich, "Longitudinal Study of the Effect of Rater Training on Psychometric Errors in Rating," *Journal of Applied Psychology,* October 1979, pp. 502–08.

extent in performance evaluation. Another is the use of a self-evaluation system. With regard to fairness, performance evaluation is in some ways like grading systems in schools. If you have received grades that you thought were unfair and inequitable, that were incorrectly computed or based on the "wrong things" (always agreeing with the instructor), you know what your reactions were! Students will say "I got an A" for a course in which they worked hard and were fairly rewarded. They will say "*He* (or she) gave me a D" if they feel it was unfair. Their reactions sometimes are to give up or to get angry. Similar responses can come from employees as well. If performance evaluation raters are incompetent or unfair, the employees may resist, sabotage, or ignore them.

Performance evaluation may also be less effective than desired if the employee is not work oriented and sees work only as a means to an end sought off the job. It might be seen only as paperwork, unless the evaluation is so negative that the employee fears termination.

Some critics believe that employees who are rated poorly will not improve their performance but will give up. This is compounded if the technique used is viewed as a zero-sum game—that is, some win and some lose as a result of it. With a system such as forced distribution, 90 percent of the people must be told they are not highly regarded, whether they are or not. One study found that 77 percent of General Electric's personnel ranked themselves rather highly.[11] In a forced choice system only 10 percent would be rated highly, so 67 to 77 percent of them would find such an evaluation a deflating experience. Some of the performance evaluation tools (forced distribution, ranking, paired comparisons) do not include an explanation of why the person was ranked as he or she was. It might be argued that everyone cannot be tops, so the best are rewarded, and the worst will leave. Sometimes quite the contrary happens! Of those who were evaluated poorly at GE, 60 percent lost heart but stayed because they figured they had nowhere else to go.

But this analysis is too simple. In one summary of the research in how a person's expectations in the evaluation affected his or her reactions to evaluation and behavior afterward, it was found that reaction to positive and negative feedback varied depending on a series of variables: (1) the importance of the task and the motivation to perform it; (2) how highly the employee rates the rater; (3) the extent to which the employee has a positive self-image; and (4) the expectancies the employee had prior to the evaluation— for example, did the employee expect a good evaluation or a bad one?

The critics' analysis is based on one theory of the reactions to feedback (self-enhancement/esteem theory), but most research does not support this position. Rather, all four conditions listed above affect the likely results of evaluation.

Performance evaluation and promotion are personnel activities which are between Stage II and Stage III in development, as defined in Chapter 1 (Exhibit 1–8). There have been studies of evaluation, as in Stage II, but there is some conflict in the data from the studies, as is true of Stage III functions.

In sum, there are problems with performance evaluation: with the system, the rater, and the employee. However, following are some suggestions which can make performance evaluation a useful P/HRM activity.

---

[11]Paul H. Thompson and Gene W. Dalton, "Performance Appraisal: Managers Beware," *Harvard Business Review,* January–February 1970, pp. 149–57.

Formal Evaluation

John Partridge, president of Partridge Enterprises, reviewed the proposal from Mary Hartford and Fred Fairfax's complaints. He invited both in for a conference. He was pleased to see the general support for the proposal. But Fred is a key executive, and his support is needed, too.

Fred voiced his opposition, elaborating on the criticism he had given at the vice presidents' meeting. Then John asked Mary to review the reasons for formal performance evaluation. He approved of the formal approach, and he asked Mary to review briefly how formal performance evaluation would work. She then reviewed the six steps, the alternate approaches Partridge could use, and the one she was recommending.

For formal performance evaluation to be effective, six steps must be taken as follows:

1. Establish performance standards for each position and the criteria for evaluation.
2. Establish performance evaluation policies on when to rate, how often to rate, and who should rate.
3. Have raters gather data on employee performance.
4. Have raters (and employees in some systems) evaluate employees' performance.
5. Discuss the evaluation with the employee.
6. Make decisions and file the evaluation.

Step 1 was performed when job analysis and work measurement took place (see Chapter 4). But the key issue is: What is and should be evaluated?

The factors on which an employee is evaluated are called the criteria of the evaluation. Examples include quality of work, quantity of work, and how well the employee gets along with others at work. One of the major problems is that some systems make *person evaluations* rather than *performance evaluations*.

The criteria used are critical in effective performance evaluation systems. They must be established to keep EEO agencies satisfied, too. After a thorough review of the literature, Smith listed four characteristics of effective criteria:[12]

> *Relevant.* Reliable and valid measures of the characteristics being evaluated, and as closely related to job output as possible.
>
> *Unbiased.* Based on the characteristic, not the person.
>
> *Significant.* Directly related to enterprise goals.
>
> *Practical.* Measurable and efficient for the enterprise in question.

Do you think the criterion used in the cartoon, on page 245 fits these characteristics?

The evidence is very clear that single performance measures are ineffective because success is multifaceted. Most studies indicate that multiple criteria are necessary to measure performance completely. The multiple criteria are added together statistically or com-

---

[12]Patricia Smith, "Behaviors, Results, and Organizational Effectiveness," in *Handbook of Industrial and Organizational Psychology,* ed. M. D. Dunnette (Skokie: Rand McNally, 1976), pp. 745–75.

"Your work is fine, Perkins. It's your aftershave I can't stand."
Drawing by Frascino; © 1973 The New Yorker Magazine, Inc.

bined into a single multifaceted measure. The criteria choice is not an easy process. One must be careful to evaluate both activities (for example, number of calls a salesperson makes) and results (for example, dollars of sales). A variation is to evaluate both results and how they were accomplished.

Probably a combination of results and activities is desirable for criteria. How do you weigh the importance of multiple criteria? For example, if the salesperson is being evaluated on both number of calls and sales dollars and is high on one and low on the other, what is the person's overall rating? Management must weigh these criteria.

Keeley studies the evaluation of research scientists, whose job duties were not clear.[13] When the tasks are not clear and performance standards are hard to specify, he found the organization responds by asking third persons (such as employee peers and other supervisors) for their opinions of the employee's performance.

The criteria selected depend on the purpose of the evaluation. If the purpose is to improve performance on the job, they should be performance related. If social skills or personality are vital on this or future jobs, these should be stressed.

A BNA study found that for white-collar workers, performance factors such as the following were used by these percentages of organizations surveyed: quality of work (93 percent), quantity of work (90 percent), job knowledge (85 percent), and attendance (79

---

[13]Michael Keeley, "Subjective Performance Evaluation and Person-Role Conflict under Conditions of Uncertainty," *Academy of Management Journal,* June 1977, pp. 301–14.

percent).[14] Personality factors used were initiative (87 percent), cooperation (87 percent), dependability (86 percent), and need for supervision (67 percent). The data for blue-collar workers were parallel: performance factors included quality of work (used by 91 percent), quantity of work (91 percent), attendance (86 percent), and job knowledge (85 percent). Personality factors surveyed were dependability (86 percent), initiative (83 percent), cooperation (83 percent), and need for supervision (77 percent).

This study found that hard-to-measure personality traits are widely used. The key issue however, is weighing the factors. The personality factors may be evaluated but not weighed equally with performance.

Whether the evaluation should be based on actual or potential performance depends on the major purpose of the evaluation for the P/HRM function. In this respect there are three principal purposes of performance evaluation:

- Improvement of performance.
- Promotion consideration.
- Salary and wage adjustments.

If the main purposes are improved performance or wage adjustment, the evaluation should be based on actual performance. If the main purpose is possible promotion, a different evaluation is needed, one that will assess potential performance on a new job. This situation is similar to the selection decision, in which past performance on one job must be projected to possible performance on a different one: it is easier to do if the employee has had experience that is relevant to the new job. But here the emphasis is different, and assessment of future potential on a different job is more difficult than actual assessment of past performance. Exhibit 8–4 presents a promotability form used at Armstrong.

Set Policies on When, How Often, and Who Evaluates

When Should Evaluation Be Done? • There are two basic decision to be made regarding the timing of performance appraisal: one is when to do it, and the other is how often. In many organizations performance evaluations are scheduled for arbitrary dates such as the date the person was hired (anniversary date). Or every employee may be evaluated on or near a single calendar date (e.g., May 25). Although the single-day approach is conveenient administratively, it probably is not a good idea. It requires raters to spend a lot of time conducting evaluation interviews and completing forms at one time, which may lead them to want to "get it over with" quickly. This probably encourages halo effect ratings, for example. In addition, it may not be related to the normal task cycle of the employee, which can make it difficult for the manager to evaluate performance effectively.

It makes more sense to schedule the evaluation at the completion of a task cycle. For example, tax accountants see the year as April 16 to April 15. Professors consider that the year starts at the beginning of the fall term and terminates after the spring term. For others without a clear task cycle based on dates, one way to set the date is by use of the MBO technique, whereby the manager and employee agree upon a task cycle, terminating

---

[14]Bureau of National Affairs. "Employee Performance: Evaluation and Control," *Personnel Policies Forum,* Survey 108. (Washington, D.C., February 1975).

Exhibit 8—4 _____

Armstrong

CONFIDENTIAL BUSINESS INFORMATION

PERSONNEL PROMOTABILITY

Name _____ Employee No. _____

Following the Personnel Performance and Development Review with the individual, complete as appropriate:

A. PROMOTABILITY WITHIN UNIT. It appears that this individual has the potential to advance beyond the present position in this organizational unit, as follows:

	Ready Now	Ready By (Date)
(Title)		
(Title)		

B. PROMOTABILITY INTO OTHER UNITS. This individual should be considered for opportunities outside this organizational unit. It is suggested that these recommendations be reviewed with appropriate unit (s) management, where practical.

_____

_____

_____

C. INDIVIDUAL IS NOT PROMOTABLE. It appears this individual is not promotable beyond the present position. (Mark (X) for appropriate reasons.)

☐ Own desire, unwilling to change work locations, or similar personal reasons.

☐ Capabilities are now fully utilized.

☐ Other factors. (Specify) _____

_____

_____

_____

Evaluated by _____

Date evaluated _____

Reviewed by (Rater's Supervisor): _____

Please enclose the white copy of this form with Form 43289 and return to Director, Employee Relations, Lancaster. Retain buff copy.

in evaluation at a specific time. Another approach is to schedule an evaluation when there is a significant change (positive or negative) in an employee's performance.

How Often Should Evaluation Be Done? • The second question concerns how often evaluation should be done. A BNA study found that 74 percent of white-collar and 58 percent of blue-collar employees were evaluated annually, and 25 percent of white-collar and 30 percent of blue-collar employees were evaluated semiannually. About 10 percent were evaluated more often than semiannually.[15]

Psychologists have found that feedback on performance should be given frequently, and the closer the feedback to the action, the more effective it is. For example, it is more effective for a professor to correct an error on a computer program the first time the error appears and show the student how to change it than to wait and flunk the student at the end of the term.

Why, then, do so few firms evaluate frequently? Generally speaking, it is because managers and employees have lots of other things to do. One way to reconcile the ideal with the reality in this respect is for the manager to give frequent feedback to employees informally, and then formally summarize performance at evaluation time. This, of course, is based on the assumption that employees value evaluation and feedback.

As Exhibit 8–5 shows, performance evaluation is another P/HRM activity which involves both line managers and P/HRM specialists. For performance evaluation to be more than a yearly paperwork exercise, top management must encourage its use and use it to make reward decisions.

Who Should Evaluate the Employee? • Exhibit 8–4 indicates that the operating manager (the supervisor) does so. This is true in the vast majority of cases. Other possibilities include:

Exhibit 8–5 _____

Involvement of personnel and operating managers in performance evaluation

Performance evaluation function	Operating manager (OM)	Personnal Manager P/HRM
Establish performance standards....................	Approves the standards	Calculated by P/HRM and engineers
Set policy on when performance evaluation takes place	Approves the policy	Recommends the policy
Set policy on who evaluates	Approves the policy	Recommends the policy
Set policy on criteria of evaluation.....................	Approves the policy	Recommends the policy
Choose the evaluation system	Approves the system	Recommends the system
Train the raters		Done by P/HRM
Review employee performance......	Done by OM	
Discuss the evaluation with the employee	Done by OM	
File the performance evaluation		Done by P/HRM

_____
[15]Ibid.

Rating by a committee of several superiors. The supervisors chosen are those most likely to come in contact with the employee. This approach has the advantages of offsetting bias on the part of one superior alone and adding additional information to the evaluation, especially if it follows a group meeting format.

Rating by the employee's peers (co-workers). In the peer evaluation system the co-workers must know the level of performance of the employee being evaluated. For this system to work, it is preferable for the evaluating peers to trust one another and not be competitive for raises and promotions. This approach may be useful when the tasks of the work unit require frequent working contact among peers.

Rating by the employee's subordinates. Exxon has used this system, and it is used in some universities (students evaluate faculty). It is used more for the developmental aspects of performance evaluation than some of the other methods are.

Rating by someone outside the immediate work situation. This is known as the field review technique. In this method a specialized appraiser from outside the job setting, such as a personnel specialist, rates the employee. This is often costly, so it is generally used only for exceptionally important jobs. It might be used for the entire work force if accusations of prejudice must be countered. A crucial consideration is that the outside evaluator is not likely to have as much data as evaluators in any of the other four approaches and the data developed are from an atypical situation.

Self-evaluation. In this case the employee evaluates herself or himself, with the techniques used by other evaluators or different ones. This approach seems to be used more often for the developmental (as opposed to evaluative) aspects of performance evaluation. It is also used to evaluate an employee who works in physical isolation.

Finally, a combination of these approaches can be used. The supervisor's evaluation can be supplemented by a self-evaluation; when evaluation is done jointly, this can be an MBO exercise. The supervisor's results could be supplemented by subordinates' or peers' evaluations.

An example of the use of a combination program is the one at Glendale Federal Savings and Loan Association, Glendale, California.[16] The program has three critical elements:

1. Independent manager and employee completion of an evaluation instrument (see Exhibit 8–6 for employee's section which is similar to manager's section).
2. Two-way (rater-ratee) communication of job performance, career goals, and additional job responsibilities.
3. High-level managerial review of the completed appraisal.

This multiple-approach program involving a number of managerial levels has been well received to date. Managers complete their evaluations on time and key training and development data are extracted from the forms.

Unlike the Glendale Federal program, evaluation by superiors only is the most frequently used method, as noted above. Self-evaluation is used in about 5 percent of evaluations. Peer evaluation is sometimes used by the military and universities but is rarely used elsewhere.

It is probable that evaluation by superiors will continue to be the principal approach used. If the primary purpose of the evaluation is developmental, then the organization

---

[16]William J. Birch, "Performance Appraisal: One Company's Experience," *Personnel Journal,* June 1981, pp. 456–60.

Exhibit 8–6 _____

Glendale Federal Savings and Loan Association

SECTION I: EMPLOYEE'S COMMENTS

(To be completed by Employee)

MAJOR ACCOMPLISHMENTS: Briefly describe the major accomplishments you achieved in your position during the past appraisal period.

SUPPORT NEEDED: What type of assistance, guidance or support do you need from your supervisor or Glendale Federal Savings to improve your job related performance in the future?

MAJOR AREA(S) OF RESPONSIBILITY: Indicate 1 or 2 major areas of responsibility in your job that you would like to focus on during the next appraisal period.

DEVELOPMENTAL ACTIVITIES, Describe any developmental activities you are presently engaged in or have completed this appraisal period—i.e., courses, workshops, work assignments.

PERFORMANCE FACTORS: In each category below indicate ONE area you would describe as one of your major strengths by checking the appropriate circle. If strength is not evident, leave category blank. NOTE: Select only those factors which are appropriate for this job.

COMMUNICATING
- ○ Writes clearly & concisely
- ○ Speaks clearly & concisely
- ○ Works well with peers
- ○ Works well with subordinates
- ○ Works well with superiors
- ○ Courteous & helpful to customers
- ○ Presents ideas persuasively
- ○ _____

JOB SKILLS/KNOWLEDGE
- ○ Completes work assignments
- ○ Knows major aspects of job
- ○ Needs little supervision
- ○ Makes few errors
- ○ Meets schedules
- ○ Keeps up to date on current developments in field
- ○ _____

PLANNING
- ○ Sets realistic goals
- ○ Analyzes needs accurately
- ○ Gets results
- ○ Develops a variety of solutions
- ○ Effectively identifies & solves problems
- ○ _____

ORGANIZING
- ○ Keeps files & resources up to date
- ○ Delegates tasks appropriately
- ○ Checks effectiveness of actions
- ○ Establishes work priorities
- ○ Uses time efficiently
- ○ _____

SUPERVISING
- ○ Accurately judges subordinates' performance
- ○ Trains & prepares subordinates
- ○ Demonstrates effective leadership
- ○ Motivates subordinates
- ○ _____

CONTROLLING
- ○ Adheres to policies & procedures
- ○ Maintains acceptable quality standards
- ○ Keeps within expense limits
- ○ _____

OTHER
- ○ Knows where to find information
- ○ Develops creative ideas
- ○ Works well under pressure
- ○ Adjusts to changes
- ○ Makes good decisions
- ○ _____

Indicate specific area(s) from the lists above you would like to improve upon. NOTE: Indicate only areas that are job related.

1. _____   2. _____   3. _____

CAREER INTEREST: If appropriate, indicate other areas of career interest or long-range career goals.

EMPLOYEE'S SIGNATURE _____ DATE _____

When you have completed SECTION I give this form to your supervisor.

Source: "Performance Appraisal: One Company's Experience," By William J. Birch, copyright June 1981, p. 457.

P/HRM Manager Close-Up

Louis J. Bibri
Armstrong World Industries, Inc.

Biography

Louis J. Bibri is a vice president and director of employee relations for Armstrong World Industries, Inc., Lancaster, Pa. He joined the company is 1946 following his graduation from Grove City College and World War II service in the Navy.

He became assistant controller of the Lancaster Floor Plant, the company's largest manufacturing facility, in 1951.

In 1956 he was given the responsibility for administration of the Floor Plant's personnel and industrial relations program. Five years later, in 1961, he became manager of print production and inspection services at the Floor Plant, a post he held until 1963, when he was promoted to general manager of industrial relations for the entire company.

Mr. Bibri was named director of employee relations in 1968 and was elected a vice president of the company in January 1972.

Job description

As vice president and director of employee relations for Armstrong World Industries, Inc., Mr. Bibri has worldwide responsibility for Armstrong's industrial relations, training and development, employee communications, employee benefit programs, recruiting, equal employment opportunity and affirmative action programs, safety and health, and human resources planning and development. He reports to Armstrong's president and chief executive officer.

---

might consider supplementing it with subordinate evaluations or self-evaluation. If the purpose of the process is reward, then the organization might consider adding peer evaluation to superior's ratings. The field review approach would be used only in special cases. The key to successful performance evaluation appears to be well-trained, carefully selected raters who are knowledgeable about the performance of those being evaluated.

Gather Data on Employees

With regard to gathering data on employees, the raters gather information by observation, analysis of data and records, and discussion with the employees. The data they gather are influenced by the criteria used to evaluate, the primary purpose of the evaluation, and the technique used to do the evaluation.

Selected Evaluation Techniques

A number of techniques for evaluation will be described here. There are several ways to classify these tools. The three categories used here are: individual evaluation methods, multiple-person evaluation methods, and other methods.

Individual Evaluation Methods

There are a number of ways to evaluate the person individually. In these systems, employees are evaluated one at a time without *directly* comparing them to other employees.

Graphic Rating Scale • The most widely used performance evaluation technique is a graphic rating scale. It is also one of the oldest techniques in use. In this technique, the rater is presented with a graph such as that shown in Exhibit 8–7 and asked to rate employees on each of the characteristics listed. The number of characteristics rated varies from a few to several dozen.

The ratings can be in a series of boxes as in the exhibit, or they can be on a continuous scale (0–9, or so). In the latter case, the rater places a check above descriptive words ranging from *none* to *maximum*. Typically, these ratings are then assigned points. For example, in Exhibit 8–7, *outstanding* may be assigned a score of 4 and *unsatisfactory* a score of 0. Total scores are then computed. In some plans, greater weights may be assigned to more important traits. Raters are often asked to explain each rating with a sentence or two.

Two modifications of the scale have been designed to make it more effective. One is the Mixed Standard Scale.[17] Instead of just rating a trait such as *initiative*, the rater is given three statements to describe the trait, such as:

> She is a real self-starter. She always takes the initiative and her superior never has to stimulate her. (Best description.)
>
> While generally he shows initiative, occasionally his superior has to prod him to get his work done.
>
> He has a tendency to sit around and wait for directions. (Poorest description.)

After each description the rater places a check mark (the employee fits the description), a plus sign (the employee is better than the statement), or a minus sign (the employee is poorer than the statement). This results in a seven-point scale, which the authors contend is better than the graphic rating scale.

The second modification is to add operational and benchmark statements to describe different levels of performance. For example, if the employee is evaluated on job knowledge, the form gives a specific example: "What has the employee done to actually demonstrate depth, currency or breadth of job knowledge in the performance of duties? Consider both quality and quantity of work." The performance description statement to guide the rater on this gives these examples of persons deserving that rating (see Exhibit 8–8).

Forced Choice • The forced-choice method of evaluation was developed because other methods used at the time led to too many high ratings. In forced choice the rater must choose from a set of descriptive statements about the employee. Typical sets of these statements are given in Exhibit 8–9. The two-, three-, or four-statement items are grouped in a way that the rater cannot easily judge which statements apply to the most effective employee.

---

[17]Fritz Blanz and Edwin Ghiselli, "The Mixed Standard Scale: A New Rating System," *Personnel Psychology*, Summer 1972, pp. 185–99.

Exhibit 8–7 _____

Typical graphic rating scale

	Out-standing	Good	Satis-factory	Fair	Unsatis-factory
Name _____ Dept. _____ Date _____					
Quantity of work Volume of acceptable work under normal conditions	☐	☐	☐	☐	☐
Comments:					
Quality of work Thoroughness, neatness and accuracy of work	☐	☐	☐	☐	☐
Comments:					
Knowledge of job Clear understanding of the facts or factors pertinent to the job	☐	☐	☐	☐	☐
Comments:					
Personal qualities Personality, appearance, sociability, leadership, integrity	☐	☐	☐	☐	☐
Comments:					
Cooperation Ability and willingness to work with associates, supervisors, and subordinates toward common goals	☐	☐	☐	☐	☐
Comments:					
Dependability Conscientious, thorough, accurate, reliable with respect to attendance, lunch periods, reliefs, etc.	☐	☐	☐	☐	☐
Comments:					
Initiative Earnestness in seeking increased responsibilities. Self-starting, unafraid to proceed alone?	☐	☐	☐	☐	☐
Comments:					

Exhibit 8–8 _____

Standards of performance: Excerpts from graphic rating scale

Far below standard rating:

1. Has serious gaps in technical-professional knowledge
   Knows only most rudimentary phases of job
   Lack of knowledge affects productivity
   Requires abnormal amount of checking

2. Reluctant to make decisions on his own
   Decisions are usually not reliable
   Declines to accept responsibility for decisions

3. Fails to plan ahead
   Disorganized and usually unprepared
   Objectives are not met on time

4. Wastes or misuses resources
   No system established for accounting of material
   Causes delay for others by mismanagement

Typically, P/HRM specialists prepare the items for the form, and supervisors or others rate the items for applicability. That is, they determine which statements describe effective and ineffective behavior. The supervisor then evaluates the employee. The P/HRM department adds up the number of statements in each category (for example, effective behavior), and they are summed into an effectiveness index. Forced choice can be used by superiors, peers, subordinates, or a combination of these in evaluating employees.

Essay Evaluation • In the essay technique of evaluation, the rater is asked to describe the strong and weak aspects of the employee's behavior. In some organizations, the essay technique is the only one used; in others, the essay is combined with another form, such as a graphic rating scale. In this case, the essay summarizes the scale, elaborates on some of the ratings, or discusses added dimensions not on the scale. In both of these approaches the essay can be open ended, but in most cases there are guidelines on the topics to be covered, the purpose of the essay, and so on. The essay method can be used by raters who are superiors, peers, or subordinates of the employee to be evaluated.

Management by Objectives • In most of the traditional performance evaluation systems the rater makes judgments of past performance behavior. Any person making judgments is in a difficult and somewhat antagonistic role. McGregor believed that instead of creating

Exhibit 8–9 _____

Forced-choice items used by Exxon, Inc.

Most		1	Least
A	Does not anticipate difficulties.		A
B	Grasps explanations quickly.		B
C	Rarely wastes time.		C
D	Easy to talk to.		D
Most		2	Least
A	Leader in group activities.		A
B	Wastes time on unimportant things.		B
C	Cool and calm at all times.		C
D	Hard worker.		D

Source: Richard S. Barrett, *Performance Rating.* © 1966 by Richard S. Barrett.

antagonisms because of judgments, the superior should work with subordinates to set goals. This would enable subordinates to exercise self-control and management over their job performance behaviors. From the early beliefs of McGregor, Drucker, and Odiorne has emerged the management by objectives (MBO) approach.[18]

MBO is more than just an evaluation program and process. It is viewed as a philosophy of managerial practice, a method by which managers and subordinates plan, organize, control, communicate, and debate. By setting objectives through participation or by assignment from a superior the subordinate is provided with a course to follow and a target to "shoot for" while performing the job. Usually an MBO program follows a systematic process such as the following:

1. Superior-subordinate meetings to define key tasks of subordinate and to set a limited number of objectives (goals).
2. Setting objectives that are realistic, challenging, clear and comprehensive.
3. Setting up criteria for measuring and evaluating the accomplishment of the objectives.
4. Intermediate progress review dates are set.
5. Modifications in objectives are made when necessary at the review time.
6. A final evaluation by the superior is made and a meeting is held with the subordinate. This is more of a counseling, encouragement session.
7. Objectives for the next cycle are set keeping in mind the previous cycle and future expectations.

MBO-type programs have been used in organizations throughout the world.[19] Approximately 40 percent (200) of *Fortune's 500* largest industrial firms report use of MBO programs.[20] Various types of objectives have been set in these programs. A sample of some objectives taken from actual MBO evaluation forms are presented in Exhibit 8–10.

Exhibit 8–10

Examples of MBO evaluation form objectives

Occupation in organization	Type organization	Objective statement
Sales representative	Medium: Petrochemical firm	To contact six new clients in West AVA region and to sell at least 2 of these new clients within the next semiannual cycle.
Product manager	Large: Food processing plant	To increase market share of creamy peanut butter by at least 3.5 percent before next objective meeting (nine months from today) without increasing costs by more than 2 percent.
Skilled machinst	Small: Job shop	To reduce flange rejects by 8 percent by August 15.
Accountant	Small: CPA firm	To attend 2 auditing seminars to improve and up date audit knowledge by the end of summer (September 15).
Plant manager	Medium: Assembly line plant	Decrease absenteeism of operating employees from 18.9 percent to under 10 percent by January 1.
Engineer	Large: Construction company	To complete power plant tower project within 30 days of government specified target date of November 10.

[18]Douglas M. McGregor, *The Human Side of Enterprise* (New York: McGraw-Hill, 1960); Peter F. Drucker, *The Practice of Management* (New York: Harper & Row, 1954); and George S. Odiorne, *Management by Objectives* (New York: Pitman Publishing Corp., 1965).

[19]Gary P. Latham and Gary A. Yukl, "A Review of Research on the Application of Goal Setting in Organizations," *Academy of Management Journal*, December 1975, pp. 824–43 and Gary P. Latham and Edwin A. Locke, "Goal Setting—A Motivational Technique That Works," *Organizational Dynamics*, Autumn 1979, pp. 68–80.

[20]J. Singular, "Has MBO Failed?" *MBA*, October 1975, pp. 47–50.

Most of these objectives are stated in the language of the job or occupation. Some of them are routine, others are innovative, and some are personal such as the accountants.

Research indicates that a well-stated objective is clear, specific, challenging, and timely.[21] These criteria are easier to attain if the objectives are stated in quantitative terms and also specify a target date. A challenging objective leads to higher levels of performance if the objective is accepted by the subordinate. Thus, many firms have used participative goal setting to encourage subordinate acceptance of superior-subordinate established objectives.

An important feature of any MBO program is that discussions about performance evaluation center on results. The results hopefully can be seen, considered, and associated with certain work behaviors. The superior and subordinate dissect the objectives achieved and not achieved and this analysis serves to help develop subordinates. Theoretically development occurs because superiors have not unilateraly made judgments. The results were consulted, weighted, and reevaluated.

The enthusiastic support of MBO is easy to understand. First, MBO appeals to people because it doesn't require a superior to sit as a judge. Second, MBO seems simple to implement. Nothing can be further from the truth. In fact, MBO requires patience, objective writing skill, interview skills, and overall trust between superiors and subordinates. These attributes are complex and difficult to maintain in MBO programs. Third, the literature cites example after example of MBO success stories. Unfortunately, many of these success stories are based on anecdotal statements of consultants who are in the business of selling MBO to clients.

A number of pitfalls and problems with MBO have been identified. Some of these include:

- Too much paperwork.
- Too many objectives are set and confusion occurs. (It appears to be more efficient to work with four, five, or six objectives.)
- MBO is forced into jobs that are extremely difficult as far as establishing objectives are concerned.
- Failure to tie in MBO results with rewards. Why are we doing this is an often asked question.
- Too much emphasis on the short term.
- Failure to train superiors in the MBO process and the mechanics involved.
- Never modifying originally set objectives.
- Using MBO as a control device only.

These and other problems need to be considered if the MBO is to have any chance for success. MBO in some situations is very effective; in other cases it is costly and quite disruptive. Just like the other evaluation techniques available, managers need to examine the purposes, costs and benefits, and their preferences before selecting or discarding an MBO program.

Critical Incident Technique • In this technique, P/HRM specialists and operating managers prepare lists of statements of very effective and ineffective behavior for an employee. These are the *critical incidents*. The specialists combine these statements into

---

[21]George Labovitz and Lloyd S. Baird, "MBO as an Approach to Performance Appraisal," in *The Performance Appraisal Sourcebook,* ed. Lloyd S. Baird, Richard W. Beatty, and Craig Eric Schneier (Amherst, Mass.: Human Resource Development Press, 1982), pp. 51–56.

categories, which vary with the job. For example, Kircher and Dunnette described 13 categories they used for evaluating salespersons at the 3M Company.[22] Two of the categories are calling on all accounts and initiating new sales approaches. Another set of categories for evaluating managers generally includes, for example, control of quality, control of people, and organizing activities.

Once the categories are developed and statements of effective and ineffective behavior are provided, the rater prepares a log for each employee. During the evaluation period, the evaluator records examples of critical (outstandingly good or bad) behaviors in each of the categories, and the log is used to evaluate the employee at the end of the period. An example of a *good* critical incident of a sales clerk is the following:

> May 1—Dan Listened patiently to the customer's complaint, answered the woman's questions, and then took back the merchandise giving the customer full credit for the returned product. He was polite, prompt, and interested in her problem.

On the other hand a *bad* critical incident might read as follows:

> August 12—Dan stayed eight minutes over on his break during the busiest part of the day. He failed to answer three store manager's calls on the intercom to please report to cash register 4 immediately.

It is also *very useful* for the evaluation interview, since the rater can be specific in making positive and negative comments, and it avoids recency bias. The critical incident technique is more likely to be used by superiors than in peer or subordinate evaluations.

Checklists and Weighted Checklists • Another type of individual evaluation method is the checklist. In its simplest form, the checklist is a set of objectives or descriptive statements. If the rater believes that the employee possesses a trait listed, the rater checks the item; if not, the rater leaves it blank. A rating score from the checklist equals the number of checks.

A more recent variation is the weighted checklist. Supervisors or P/HRM specialists familiar with the jobs to be evaluated, prepare a large list of descriptive statements about effective and ineffective behavior on jobs, similar to the critical incident process. Judges who have observed behavior on the job sort the statements into piles describing behavior that is scaled from excellent to poor. When there is reasonable agreement on an item (for example, when the standard deviation is small), it is included in the weighted checklist. The weight is the average score of the raters prior to use of the checklist.

The supervisors or other raters receive the checklist without the scores and check the items that apply, as with an unweighted checklist. The employee's evaluation is the sum of the scores (weights) on the items checked. Checklists and weighted checklists can be used by evaluators who are superiors, peers, or subordinates, or by a combination.

Behaviorally Anchored Rating Scales • Smith and Kendall developed what is referred to as the behaviorally anchored rating scale (BARS) or the behavioral expectation scale (BES).[23] The BARS approach relies on the use of critical incidents to serve as anchor

[22]W. E. Kircher and M. D. Dunnette, "Using Critical Incidents to Measure Job Proficiency Factors," *Personnel*, September/October 1957, pp. 54–59.

[23]P. C. Smith and L. M. Kendall, "Retranslation of Expectations: An Approach to the Construction of Unambiguous Anchors for Rating Scales," *Journal of Applied Psychology*, April 1963, pp. 149–55.

statements on a scale. A BARS rating form usually contains 6 to 10 specifically defined performance dimensions, each with 5 or 6 critical incident anchors. Exhibit 8–11 presents one performance dimension for engineering competence. The rater would read the anchors and place an X at the appropriate position of the scale for the ratee.

A BARS scale usually contains the following features:

1. Six to 10 performance dimensions are identified and defined by raters and ratees (a group is selected to construct the form).
2. The dimensions are anchored with positive and negative critical incidents.
3. Each ratee is then rated on the dimensions.
4. Ratings are fed back using the terms displayed on the form.

Exhibit 8–11

Sample BARS dimension

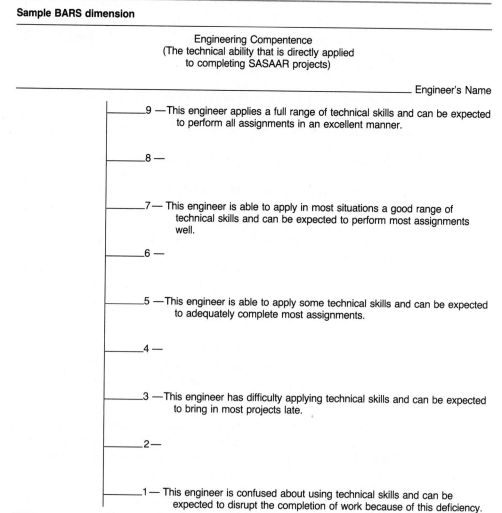

Engineering Compentence
(The technical ability that is directly applied
to completing SASAAR projects)

_____ Engineer's Name

9 —This engineer applies a full range of technical skills and can be expected to perform all assignments in an excellent manner.

8 —

7 — This engineer is able to apply in most situations a good range of technical skills and can be expected to perform most assignments well.

6 —

5 —This engineer is able to apply some technical skills and can be expected to adequately complete most assignments.

4 —

3 —This engineer has difficulty applying technical skills and can be expected to bring in most projects late.

2—

1 — This engineer is confused about using technical skills and can be expected to disrupt the completion of work because of this deficiency.

The exact construction of a BARS scale is too complex for presentation here.[24] However, it should be noted that usually two to four days are needed to develop a BARS. The results of the developmental work is a job-related, jargon free, superior-subordinate developed scale.

In terms of rating errors and problems, research fails to show the superiority of BARS over other techniques. Raters using BARS still make halo, harsh, and lenient rating errors.[25] However, there appears to be some important spin-offs from using a BARS program. It appears that subordinates involved with a BARS program are more committed, less tense, and more satisfied than counterparts using other programs.[26] Another possible benefit is that managers have feedback in the form of critical incident statements that are meaningful to subordinates. Thus, although the BARS system is costly, time consuming, and complex, it may make performance evaluation easier to accept for subordinates. After all they are usually involved in the development of the rating instrument.

In the decision of evaluation approaches and techniques, we have implied that each person is evaluated independent of others, unless the employee is one of the few being evaluated with a multiperson evaluation technique. However, this may not be strictly true: the evaluation of one employee can be affected by the evaluations of the others in the work group.

Laboratory research has indicated that when a work group included one employee with poor work attitudes who refused to obey orders, the supervisor evaluated other employees higher. In one study, 59 supervisors of 473 clerical employees were asked to evaluate their employees.[27] The researchers examined how the supervisors evaluated and rewarded the employees with promotions and pay raises. It was found that the presence of employees who were poor in ability and work attitudes (and the proprotion of the work group they comprised) affected how the supervisors evaluated *all* the employees. Specifically, when there is one or a small percentage of noncompliant employees, the supervisor gave a *much lower* evaluation of the noncomplaint employees and a slightly higher evaluation to the complaint employees. As the percentage of noncompliant employees increased, the supervisors raised the evaluations of the compliant employees *much higher*.

Case study research also indicates that some supervisors may perceive pressure not to evaluate all employees at the top of the range. They modify the ratings so that all employees do not seem "excellent." Therefore, at least some of the time evaluators are likely to be influenced in their evaluations of one employee by their evaluations of others in the work group, even when individual evaluation techniques are used.

---

[24]Gary P. Latham and Kenneth N. Wexley, *Increasing Productivity through Performance Appraisal* (Reading, Mass.: Addison-Wesley Publishing, 1981), pp. 51–64; and R. S. Atkin and E. J. Conlon, "Behaviorally Anchored Rating Scales: Some Theoretical Issues," *Academy of Management Review*, January 1978, pp. 119–28. Also see Frank J. Landy and James L. Fair, "Performance Rating," *Psychological Bulletin*, February 1980, pp. 72–107.

[25]Walter C. Borman and M. D. Dunnette, "Behavior-Based v. Trait-Oriented Performance Ratings: An Empirical Study," *Journal of Applied Psychology*, October 1975, pp. 561–65; and Paul O, Kingstrom and Alan R. Bass, "A Critical Analysis of Studies Comparing Behaviorally Anchored Rating Scales (BARS) and Other Rating Formats," *Personnel Psychology*. Summer 1981, pp. 263–89.

[26]John M. Ivancevich, "A Longitudinal Study of Behavioral Expectations Scales: Attitudes and Performance," *Journal of Applied Psychology*, April 1980, pp. 139–46.

[27]Ronald Grey, and David Kipnis, "Untangling the Performance Appraisal Dilemma: The Influence of Perceived Organizational Context on Evaluative Processes," *Journal of Applied Psychology*, June 1976, pp. 329–35.

Multiple-Person Evaluation Methods

The techniques described above are used to evaluate employees one at a time. Three techniques that have been used to evaluate an employee in comparison with other employees being evaluated are discussed in this section.

Ranking • In using the ranking method, the evaluator is asked to rate employees from highest to lowest on some overall criterion. This is very difficult to do if the group of employees being compared numbers over 20. It is also easier to rank the best and worst employees than it is to evaluate the average ones. Simple ranking can be improved by alternative ranking. In this approach, the evaluators pick the top and bottom employee first, then select the next highest and next lowest, and move toward the middle.

Paired Comparison • This approach makes the ranking method easier and more reliable. First, the names of the person to be evaluated are placed on separate sheets (or cards) in a predetermined order, so that each person is compared to all others to be evaluated. The evaluator then checks the person he/she feels is the better of the two on a criterion for each comparison. Typically the criterion is overall ability to do the present job. The number of times a person is preferred is tallied, and this results in an index of the number of preferences compared to the number being evaluated.

These scores can be converted into standard scores by comparing the scores to the standard deviation and the average of all scores. This method can be used by superiors, peers, subordinates, or some combination of these groups.

Forced Distribution • The forced-distribution system is similar to grading on a curve. The rater is asked to rate employees in some fixed distribution of categories, such as 10 percent in low, 20 percent in low average, 40 percent in average, 20 percent in high average, and 10 percent in high. One way to do this is to type each employee's name on a card and ask the evaluators to sort the cards into five piles corresponding to the ratings. This should be done twice for the two key criteria of job performance and promotability.

Exhibit 8–12 shows the results of forced-distribution evaluation of 20 employees. One reason forced distribution was developed was to try to alleviate such problems as inflated ratings and central tendency in the graphic rating scale.

A newer variation of forced distribution is the point allocation technique (PAT). In PAT, each rater is given a number of points per employee in the group to be evaluated, and the total points for all employees evaluated cannot exceed the number of points per

Exhibit 8–12

Forced-distribution evaluation of employees in a marketing research unit

High 10%	*Next 20%*	*Middle 40%*	*Next 20%*	*Low 10%*
Leslie Moore	Cinde Lanyon	Max Coggins	Art Willis	Wayne Allison
Tina Little	Sharon Feltman	Tina Holmes	Debbie Salter	Sherry Gruber
	Eddie Dorsey	Julis Jimenex	Tom Booth	
	Johnny Dyer	Lis Amendale	Lance Smith	
		Vince Gaillard		
		Missy Harrington		
		Bill King		
		Shelly Sweat		

employee times the number of employees evaluated. The points are allocated on a criterion basis. The forced distribution and PAT are most likely to be used by superiors but could be used by peers or subordinates.

Other Methods

Performance Tests • One approach to evaluation is to design a job performance test or simulation. Depending on how well the employees do on this test, they are promoted or their salaries are adjusted. One such test is used for operating personnel in the air force. The assessment center discussed in Chapter 7 utilizes another.

Field Review Technique • Unlike many of the approaches discussed above, the field review uses an "objective" outsider as evaluator. The person to be evaluated and the supervisor are questioned orally by an investigator, who usually is from the P/HRM department. The P/HRM evaluator probes and questions the supervisor about the employee. This results in an overall rating, such as outstanding, satisfactory, or unsatisfactory.

Which Technique to Use

Perhaps you now feel saturated with the large number of evaluation techniques. You should know that not all of them are used very often. It is generally recognized that the graphic rating scale is the most widely used technique. Studies indicate that the essay method is also widely used, usually as part of a graphic rating scale form. And checklists are widely used. Studies show that other methods, such as forced choice, critical incident, BARS, performance tests, field review, and MBO, *combined* equal only about 5 percent. Ranking and paired comparison are used by 10 to 13 percent of the employers. MBO is most likely to be used more for managerial, professional, and technical employees, not production and office personnel.[28]

Which technique should be used in a specific instance? The literature on the shortcomings and strengths, reliabilities, and validities of each of these techniques is vast. In essence, there are studies showing that each of the techniques is sometimes good, sometimes poor. The major problems are not with the techniques themselves but *how they are used* and *by whom*. Untrained raters or those that have little talent or motivation to evaluate well can destroy or hamper *any* evaluation technique. The rater is more critical than the technique in developing effective evaluation systems.

Evaluation techniques can be judged on a series of criteria such as costs and purposes. As noted in the discussion of the approaches to evaluation above, at least two major purposes are served by evaluation: Counseling and personal development and evaluation for rewards, such as an aid in promotion and decision. Some evaluation techniques serve one purpose better than others. Some systems cost more to develop and operate than others. Exhibit 8–13 scales the techniques on these criteria to help in the choice.

If the primary purpose of the evaluation is development, for example, the knowledgeable organization will use BARS, essay, critical incident, MBO, and field review tools. If the primary purpose of the evaluation is rewards, the organization might use graphic rating scales, field review, performance tests, forced distribution, MBO, critical incidents,

---

[28]Bureau of National Affairs, "Employee Performance: Evaluation and Control."

Exhibit 8–13

Selected criteria for choice of performance evaluation techniques

Evaluative base	Graphic rating scale	Forced choice	MBO	Essay	Critical incidents	Weighted checklist	BARS	Ranking	Paired comparison	Forced distribution	Performance test	Field review
Developmental cost	Moderate	High	Moderate	Low	Moderate	Moderate	High	Low	Low	Low	High	Moderate
Usage costs	Low	Low	High	High supervisory costs	High	Low	Low	Low	Low	Low	High	High
Ease of use by evaluators	Easy	Moderately difficult	Moderate	Difficult	Difficult	Easy	Easy	Easy	Easy	Easy	Moderately difficult	Easy
Ease of understanding by those evaluated	Easy	Difficult	Moderate	Easy	Easy	Easy	Moderate	Easy	Easy	Easy	Easy	Easy
Useful in promotion decisions	Yes	Yes	Yes	Not easily	Yes	Moderate	Yes	Yes	Yes	Yes	Yes	Yes
Useful in compensation and reward decisions	Yes	Moderate	Yes	Not easily	Yes	Moderate	Yes	Not easily	Not easily	Yes	Yes	Yes
Useful in counseling and development of employees	Moderate	Moderate	Yes	Yes	Yes	Moderate	Yes	No	No	No	Moderate	Yes

What kind of performance evaluation program did Partridge adopt? Mary Hartford described the first part of her proposal to John Partridge after reviewing the criteria, timing, and techniques. She explained that each person would be given specific objectives related to his or her job which were to be achieved. These were the standards for the system and were based on job analysis and work measurement.

For blue-collar and white-collar personnel, they were clear, multiple-purpose standards. They were based primarily on past standards, with some emphasis on future improvement.

The managerial group was to begin to participate in the management by objectives system. They would negotiate with the employees to improve performance. The MBO reviews would be quarterly.

Graphic rating scales would be used semiannually for nonmanagerial employees. The supervisors would choose times for review which matched the work cycle or when major changes in an employee's output were apparent. Personnel would keep track to see that two evaluations took place each year.

The P/HRM unit would put on training programs for evaluators and employees to demonstrate how to evaluate effectively and explain the purpose of the system. The evaluators were to be the employees' supervisors.

John thought the suggestions over and approved them. He took the time to explain his reasons to Fred and asked for his support. John also told Mary that when the new system was introduced, he would communicate his full support forcefully to all employees.

or BARS. If the primary purpose of the evaluation is developmental and costs are not a concern currently, then field review, MBO, or critical incident methods should be chosen. And if the primary purpose is development and costs are a consideration, the BARS or essay methods might be chosen.

The Feedback Interview

After the rater has completed the evaluation, the evaluation should be discussed with the employee. Some organizations use split evaluations to accomplish the dual purposes of evaluations. In evaluation for developmental purposes, the ratings are communicated and appropriate counseling takes place. And in evaluation to determine pay, promotion, and other rewards, the ratings sometimes are not given to the employee. In the usual evaluation, however, the employee acknowledges the evaluation in some way, often by signing a receipt form.

In 97 percent of the organizations with formal performance evaluation systems, the employee receives feedback, normally in the form of an evaluation interview.[29] The rater and ratee get together for an interview which allows the evaluator to communicate the employee's ratings and to comment on them.

---

[29]Bureau of National Affairs, "Employee Performance: Evaluation and Control," also see Randall Brett and Alan J. Fredian, "Performance Appraisal: The System Is Not the Solution," *Personnel Administrator,* December 1981, pp. 61–68.

Norman Maier describes three generally used approaches to these interview situations: tell and sell, tell and listen, and problem solving.[30] These are shown in Exhibit 8–14. Research on when each should be used indicates that the tell-and-sell approach is best for new and inexperienced employees, and that the problem-solving approach, which encourages employee participation, is useful for more experienced employees, especially those with work ethic attitudes.

The suggestions for conducting an effective evaluation interview are designed to reduce the arbitrariness and improve the clarity of the superior-subordinate interaction. Regardless of how or when the performance evaluation occurs there should be a formal evaluation interview. The closer the suggestions are followed the more effective the interview. It is the superior's responsibility to be a clear communicator, a good listener, to set a respectful tone, and to cover not only past performances but also future expectations and objectives.

Suggestions for effective evaluation interviews:

1. Superiors and subordinates should prepare for the meeting and be ready to discuss the employee's past performance against the objectives for the period.
2. The superior should put the employee at ease and stress that the interview is not a disciplinary session but a time to review past work, in order to improve the employee's future performance, satisfaction, and personal development.
3. The superior should budget the time so that the employee has approximately half the time to discuss the evaluation and his or her future behavior.
4. The superior should structure the interview as follows:
First, open with *specific positive remarks*. For example, if the employee's quantity of work is good, the superior might say: "John, your work output is excellent. You processed 10 percent more claims than was budgeted."
Second, sandwich performance shortcomings between two positive result discussions. Be specific, and orient the discussion to *performance* comments, *not personal* criticisms. Stress that the purpose of bringing the specific issues up is to alleviate the problems in the *future*, not to criticize the past. Probably no more than one or two important negative points should be brought up at one evaluation. It is difficult for many people to work toward improving more than two points. The handling of negative comments is critical. They should be phrased specifically and be related to *performance*, and it should be apparent to the employee that their purpose is not to criticize but to improve future performance. Many people become very defensive when criticized. Of course, the interviews should be private, between the employee and the evaluator.
Third, conclude with *positive* comments and overall evaluation results.
5. The superior should budget the time for these three aspects of the interview to match the rating. For example, if the employee is an 85 on a scale of 100, 85 percent of the time should be spent on positive comments to *reinforce* this behavior.
6. The final aspect of the interview should focus on *future* objectives and how the superior can help the employee achieve enterprise and personal goals. Properly done, the interviews contribute importantly to the purposes of performance evaluation.

---

[30]Norman Maier, *The Appraisal Interview: Three Basic Approaches* (La Jolla, Calif.: University Associates, 1976).

Exhibit 8–14

Three types of evaluation interviews

Method	Tell and sell	Tell and listen	Problem solving
Role of interviewer	Judge	Judge	Helper
Objective	To communicate evaluation To persuade employee to improve	To communicate evaluation To release defensive feelings	To stimulate growth and development in employee
Assumptions	Employee desires to correct weaknesses if he knows them Any person can improve who so chooses A superior is qualified to evaluate a subordinate	People will change if defensive feelings are removed	Growth can occur without correcting faults Discussing job problems leads to improved performance
Reactions	Defensive behavior suppressed Attempts to cover hostility	Defensive behavior expressed Employee feels accepted	Problem-solving behavior
Skills	Salesmanship Patience	Listening and reflecting feelings Summarizing	Listening and reflecting feelings Reflecting ideas Using exploratory questions Summarizing
Attitude	People profit from criticism and appreciate help	One can respect the feelings of others if one understands them	Discussion develops new ideas and mutual interests
Motivation	Use of positive or negative incentives or both (Extrinsic in that motivation is added to the job itself)	Resistance to change reduced Positive incentive (Extrinsic and some intrinsic motivation)	Increased freedom Increased responsibility (Intrinsic motivation in that interest is inherent in the task)
Gains	Success most probable when employee respects interviewer	Develops favorable attitude to superior which increases probability of success	Almost assured of improvement in some respect
Risks	Loss of loyalty Inhibition of independent judgment Face-saving problems created	Need for change may not be developed	Employee may lack ideas Change may be other than what superior had in mind
Values	Perpetuates existing practices and values	Permits interviewer to change his/her views in the light of employee's responses Some upward communication	Both learn, since experience and views are pooled Change is facilitated

Source: Reproduced from Norman R. F. Maier, *The Appraisal Interview; Three Basic Approaches* (La Jolla, Calif.: University Associates, 1976). Used with permission.

Make Decisions and File the Evaluation

Once the employees and their supervisor have discussed the evaluation, the superior reviews the evaluation. BNA found that 80 percent of office employees and 76 percent of production employees surveyed had their evaluations reviewed in this manner. Next the P/HRM department reviews the evaluation and places it on file.[31]

If the employee is unhappy with the evaluation, BNA found that 68 percent of the production employees and 56 percent of the office employees surveyed could appeal it through the union (if they are unionized) or to the rater's superior. This is less common in nonbusiness organizations than businesses. For more data on this, see Chapter 21.

These reviews are designed to prevent situations such as Felipe Hernandez's confusion and Ed Smart's failure to give him positive feedback. If the evaluation has been properly done, the employee knows where he or she stands and has received positive feedback on accomplishments and help on shortcomings. This is the developmental aspect of performance evaluation. The reward aspect can include pay raises (see Chapters 13 and 14).

Summary

Formal performance evaluation of employees is the P/HRM process by which the organization determines how effectively the employee is performing the job. It takes place primarily for white-collar, professional/technical, and managerial employees. It rarely is done for part-time employees, and only about half of all blue-collar employees experience it. Although the data are not entirely clear, it appears that, properly done, performance evaluation can be useful for most organizations and most employees. To summarize about performance evaluation, the following statements outline the major points:

1. Factors in the diagnostic model that have significance for performance evaluation are:

   a. The task performed.
   b. The government.
   c. The attitudes and preferences of the employee.
   d. The leader's or supervisor's style.
   e. The union (if present).

2. The purposes which formal performance evaluation can serve include:
   a. Developmental purposes.
   b. Reward purposes.
   c. Personnel planning purposes.
   d. Validation purposes.

3. Performance evaluation systems have problems because of:
   a. Systems design and operating difficulties.
   b. Problems with the rater:
      1. Standards of evaluation.

---

[31]Bureau of National Affairs, "Employee Performance: Evaluation and Control."

      2. The halo effect.

      3. Leniency or harshness.

      4. Recency of events.

      5. Personal biases.

   c. Employee problems with performance evaluation:

      1. Employees don't understand the system or its purpose.

      2. Employees are not work oriented.

      3. Evaluation may be below the employee's expectations.

4. For formal performance evaluation to be effective, six steps must be taken:

   a. Establish performance standards for each position.

   b. Establish performance evaluation policies on when and how often to evaluate, who should evaluate, the criteria for evaluation, and the evaluation tools to be used.

   c. Have raters gather data on employee performance.

   d. Discuss the evaluation with the employee.

   e. Make decisions and file the evaluation.

5. Performance appraisal interviews that involve feeding back evaluation information are dreaded because of the arbitrariness of many evaluation programs. Selecting the best program for the employees and supervisors to use is an important P/HRM decision.

6. Properly performed, performance evaluation can contribute to organizational objectives and employee development and satisfaction.

Exhibit 8–15 provides recommendations on the usage of evaluation tools in terms of the ability of the model organizations to use them. It should be obvious from this exhibit that some tools are more universally applicable (essay, critical incident, graphic rating scale, MBO, ranking, forced distribution). Others have fewer applications (performance test, field, review, forced choice), and still others are in the middle (assessment centers, BARS, weighted checklist).

The next two chapters discuss how the organizations can improve abilities and attitudes of employees through training and development activities.

Questions for Review and Discussion

   1. What is performance evaluation?

   2. "Performance evaluations cause as many problems as they are designed to solve." Comment. If you agree performance evaluation should take place, explain why.

   3. Describe the major problems which can arise for the system, the rater, and the employee in performance evaluation.

   4. How often should formal performance evaluations take place? Informal ones? How often do they take place?

   5. Who usually evaluates employees in organizations? Who should do so? Under what circumstances? What criteria should be used to evaluate employees? Which ones are used?

   6. Compare and contrast performance evaluation techniques. If you were to choose one to be used to evaluate you, which one would it be? Why?

Exhibit 8–15

Recommendations on evaluation techniques for model organizations

Type of organization	Graphic rating scale	Forced choice	MBO	Essay	Critical incident	Weighted checklist,	BARS	Ranking	Paired comparison	Forced distribution	Performance test	Field review
1. Large size, low complexity, high stability	X	X	X		X	X	X	X	X	X	X	X
2. Medium size, low complexity, high stability	X		X	X	X	X	X	X	X	X		
3. Small size, low complexity, high stability	X		X	X	X			X	X	X		
4. Medium size, moderate complexity, moderate stability	X		X	X	X	X		X	X	X		
5. Large size, high complexity, low complexity	X		X	X	X			X	X	X		X
6. Medium size, high complexity, low stability	X		X	X	X			X	X	X		
7. Small size, high complexity, low stability	X		X	X	X			X	X	X		

Case

Ed Smart was not too happy about having to take time out from his supervisory duties to go to this training session about the new evaluation system. But, he'd had some problems with his boss, Bob Woods, over pay and promotions. So even though it sounded like more paperwork and time, he decided to see what they had to say.

The training session began with some short lectures. But most of the session was involved in practice on how to complete the rating forms for several kinds of employees. The supervisors were encouraged to review their employees' files and to jot down notes about employees' good and bad performances. They also practiced the evaluation interviews on each other. Given the ratings, they completed interviews on a very good, an average, and a poor employee.

Other policies were also covered. They learned about the new MBO system and how it was going to work. Still, Ed was a bit skeptical.

About two months later, Ed decided he'd better start the evaluations, since Bob had asked him how they were going. Ed decided to do Felipe

Hernandez first. He still was a little worried about how it would go. Felipe had been trained in what to expect. Hope they hadn't built him up too high, Ed thought. In reviewing the files, his notes, and his observations, Ed realized he'd kind of overlooked how well Felipe had come along. Frankly, Ed hadn't been that fond of Puerto Ricans before Felipe had come along, but Felipe had done an excellent job, and so Ed had rated him highly.

Ed called Felipe in for the interview. Ed referred to his notes and started and ended the interview on a positive note. He talked just a little about the shortcomings he'd noticed and offered to help Felipe improve. At the beginning of the interview, Felipe had been nervous. But he beamed at the end.

Ed finished the interview by saying he was recommending Felipe for a good raise at the earliest chance. Over the next few days, Felipe seemed to be especially happy. Maybe it was Ed's imagination, but he seemed to be working a bit harder, too, although he was already a good worker.

That performance evaluation stuff works after all, Ed concluded.

7. What happens after the employee is evaluated? What should happen?
8. Describe how to conduct an effective evaluation interview with a new, inexperienced employee. With an experienced employee.
9. How could you determine if you were a lenient or harsh rater?
10. What did McGregor mean when he said that managers when they are involved in making judgments are placed in an antagonistic role?

Glossary

Behaviorally Anchored Rating Scale (BARS). A rating scale that uses critical incidents as anchor statements placed along a scale. Typically 6 to 10 performance dimensions, each with 5 to 6 critical incident anchors are rated per employee.

Central Tendency Error. Giving ratees an average rating on each criteria. That is, on a 1 to 7 scale circling all 4s, or on a 1 to 5 scale selecting all 3s.

Critical Incident Rating. Selecting very effective and ineffective examples of job behavior and rating whether an employee displays the type of behaviors specified in the critical incidents.

Halo Error. A rating error that occurs when a rater assigns ratings on the basis of an overall impression (positive or negative) of the person being rated.

Harshness Rating Error. Rating everyone low on the criteria being evaluated.

Leniency Rating Error. Rating everyone on every criteria high or excellent.

Performance Evaluation. The P/HRM activity that is used to determine the extent to which an employee is performing the job effectively.

Personal Bias Rating Error. The bias that a rater has about individual characteristics, attitudes, backgrounds, and so on, influence a rating more than performance.

Recency of Event Rating Error. Using the most recent events to evaluate a ratee's performance instead of using a longer more complete time frame.

Chapter Nine

Orientation and Training

Learning Objectives

After studying this chapter, you should be able to:
- Define what is meant by orientation, training, and development.

- Discuss the purposes of orientation, training, and development.

- Describe the characteristics of an orientation program.

- Explain the role that learning principles play in training and development.

- Compare on- and off-the job training methods and approaches.

- Illustrate the three phases in a training model used to define training more clearly.

Chapter Outline

Case

Art

Gigi   *Sam*

Art Johnson was so glad when he got the job at the Coca-Cola bottling works. Art really needed the job; he had been out of work for six weeks, and his wife, Betty was busy with their two-month-old daughter. Art wanted to do a good job; he wanted to keep the job and get ahead with the company. He certainly hoped they would explain how to do the job and what he was expected to get done in a good day's work.

* * *

Gigi Martinez reported to her first day's job at the department store. She didn't know where to go, so she went to the P/HRM office. She told the receptionist she had been hired as a new sales associate. The receptionist told Gigi to sit down and they'd get to her in a while. She sat there an hour. Finally, the P/HRM interviewer noticed her and said, "Gigi, what are you doing here? You're supposed to be in Men's Clothing."

Mumbling that no one told her, she rushed out and eventually found Men's Clothing. She approached several sales associates and finally found the department manager. He began: "So you're the new one. A bad start—late your first day. Well, get to work. If you need any help ask for it."

* * *

Sam Lavalle reported to P/HRM as the notice of employment said to do. After about six of the new employees were there, orientation began. Miss Wentworth welcomed them to the company and then the "paper blitz" took place. In the next 30 minutes, she gave them a lot of paper—work rules, benefits booklets, pay forms to fill out, and so on. His head was swimming. Then Sam got a slip telling him to report to his new supervisor, Andrew Villanueva, in Room 810. Andrew took him around the facility for three minutes and then pointed out Sam's new workbench and wished him good luck.

Art's attitude is an example of the attitude that many new employees have—ready to go to work and wanting so much to succeed. His case describes the orientation challenge. Gigi's case is an example of what happens to too many new employees: no help at all. Sam's case is an example of what most employees encounter: a formal orientation program that is adequate, but not all it could be.

Orientation is the P/HRM activity which introduces new employees to the organization and to the employee's new tasks, superiors, and work groups.

Walking into a new experience or job is often a lonely event. The newcomer doesn't usually know what to say or who to say it to, or even where he or she is supposed to be. It takes time to learn the ropes and a good orientation program can help make this time

be a positive experience. The first few days on the job are crucial in helping the employee get started in the right direction with a positive attitude and feeling.[1]

Orientation has not been studied a great deal.[2] Little scientific research has been done on whether the programs are adequate. Some experts view orientation as a kind of training. In terms of the stages of development of P/HRM functions discussed earlier and shown in Exhibit 1–8 (Chapter 1), it is a Stage II function.

A Diagnostic Approach to Orientation

Exhibit 9–1 highlights the environmental factors in the diagnostic model that are most important to effective orientation programs (indicated by an 0): the nature of the employee, and the nature of the task, the work group, and the leadership. The nature of the employee and the task are critical factors; for example, managers are given more detailed orientation programs than other employees. The orientation program focuses on introducing the new employee to the task, the work group, and the supervisor-leader. During orientation the work policies of the organization, the job conditions, and the people the employee will work with to get the job done are discussed.

The style an organization uses to orient new employees is affected by the organization and its climate. The diagnostic manager adapts the orientation program to the individual and gives it a different emphasis for a person with 20 years' experience in the industry than for a new employee who is just out of high school and from a disadvantaged background.

Part-time employees are likely to receive much shorter and less elaborate orientations. It is probable that orientation will be done by the P/HRM specialist, who will get them on the payroll, explain pay and hours, and turn them over to a supervisor. The supervisor is likely to explain her or his expectations for work, introduce new employees around, show them the job, and encourage them to ask for help.

The Purposes of Orientation

Effectively done, orientation serves a number of purposes. In general, the orientation process is similar to what sociologists call socialization. The principal purposes of orientation are:

To Reduce the Start-up Costs for a New Employee • The new employee does not know the job, how the organization works, or whom to see to get the job done. This means that for a while, the new employee is less efficient than the experienced employee, and additional costs are involved in getting the new employee started. These start-up costs

---

[1]Michael C. Gallegher, "The Economics of Training Food Service Employees," *The Cornell H.R.A. Quarterly,* May 1977, pp. 54–56.

[2]ASPA-BNA Survey No. 32: Employee Orientation Programs Bulletin to Management, No. 1436 (Washington, D.C.: Bureau of National Affairs, Inc., August 1977).

Exhibit 9–1

Factors affecting orientation (O), training, and development (T&D)

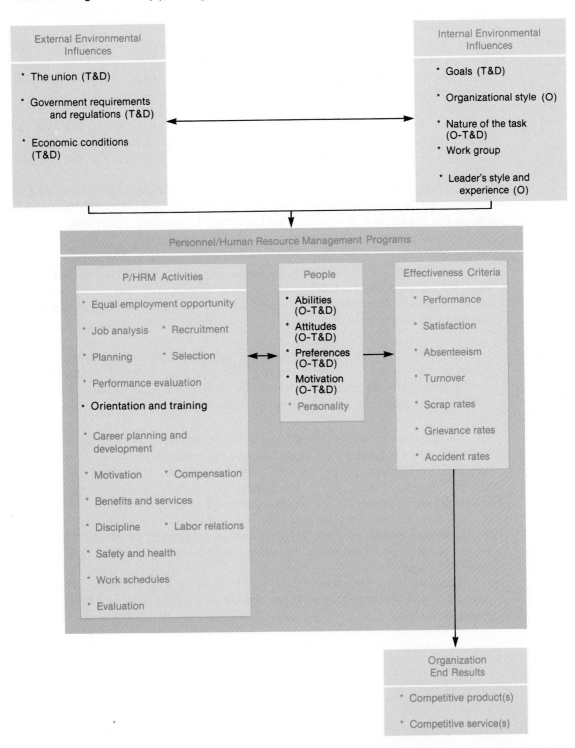

have been estimated for various positions as follows: top manager, $2,000; middle manager, $1,000; supervisor, $1,000; senior engineer, $900; accountant, $750; and secretary, $400.[3] Effective orientation reduces these start-up costs and enables the new employee to reach standards sooner.

To Reduce the Amount of Anxiety and Hazing a New Employee Experiences • Anxiety in this case means fear of failure on the job. This is a normal fear of the unknown focused on the ability to do the job. This anxiety can be made worse by hazing of the new employee.

Hazing takes place when experienced employees "kid" the new employee. For example, experienced employees may ask the new worker, "How many toys are you producing per hour?" When she answers, she is told, "You'll never last. The last one who did that few was no longer here after two days."

Such hazing serves several purposes. It lets the recruit know he or she has a lot to learn and thus is dependent on the others for his or her job, and it is "fun" for the old-timers. But it can cause great anxiety for the recruit. Effective orientation alerts the new person to hazing and reduces anxiety.

To Reduce Employee Turnover • If employees perceive themselves to be ineffective, unwanted, or unneeded and have similar negative feelings, they may seek to deal with them by quitting. Turnover is high during the break-in period, and effective orientation can reduce this costly practice.

To Save Time for Supervisor and Co-Workers • Improperly oriented employees must still get the job done, and to do so they need help. The most likely people to provide this help are the co-workers and supervisors, who will have to spend time breaking in new employees. Good orientation programs save everyone time.

To Develop Realistic Job Expectations, Positive Attitudes toward the Employer, and Job Satisfaction • In what sociologists call the older professions (law, medicine) or total institutions (the church, prison, the army), the job expectations are clear because they have been developed over long years of training and education. Society has built up a set of attitudes and behaviors that are considered proper for these jobs. For most of the world of work, however, this does not hold true. New employees must learn realistically what the organization expects of them, and their own expectations of the job must be neither too low nor too high.[4] Each worker must incorporate the job and its work values into his or her self-image.

Orientation helps this process. One way to illustrate how orientation serves these purposes is with the story of how Texas Instruments developed its new orientation program (see the box).

---

[3]Robert Sibson, "The High Cost of Hiring," *Nation's Business,* February 1975, pp. 85–86.

[4]Walter D. St. John, "The Complete Employee Orientation Program," *Personnel Journal,* May 1980, pp. 373–78.

Texas Instruments knew that anxieties existing in the early period of work reduced competence and led to dissatisfaction and turnover. The anxiety resulted from awareness on the part of the female assemblers that they must reach the competence level they observed in the experienced employees around them. Many times they did not understand their supervisors' instructions but were afraid to ask further questions and appear stupid. Sometimes this anxiety was compounded by hazing.

Anxiety turned out to be a very important factor in the study at Texas Instruments, which investigated whether an orientation program designed to reduce anxiety would increase competence, heighten satisfaction, and lower turnover. The control group of new recruits were given the traditional orientation program: a typical two-hour briefing on the first day by the personnel department. This included the topics normally covered in orientation and the usual description of the minimum level of performance desired. Then they were introduced to the supervisor, who gave them a short job introduction, and they were off.

The experimental group was given the two-hour orientation the control group received and then six hours of social orientation. Four factors were stressed in the social orientation:

1. They were told that their opportunity to succeed was good. Those being oriented were given facts showing that over 99 percent of the employees achieved company standards. They were shown learning curves of how long it took to achieve various levels of competence. Five or six times during the day it was stressed that all in the group would be successful.

2. They were told to disregard "hall talk." New employees were tipped off about typical hazing. It was suggested that they take it in good humor but ignore it.

3. They were told to take the initiative in communication. It was explained that supervisors were busy and not likely to ask the new worker if she "needed help." Supervisors would be glad to help, but the worker must ask for it, and she would not appear stupid if she did so.

4. They were told to get to know their supervisor. The supervisor was described in important details—what she liked as hobbies, whether she was strict or not, quiet or boisterous, and so forth.

This social orientation had dramatic results. The experimental group had 50 percent less tardiness and absenteeism, and waste was reduced by 80 percent, product costs were cut 15 to 30 percent, training time was cut 50 percent, and training costs cut about 66 percent.

Who Orients New Employees?

Exhibit 9–2 describes how operating and P/HRM managers run the orientation program in middle-sized and large organizations. In smaller organizations, the operating manager does all the orienting. In some unionized organizations, union officials are involved. P/HRM also helps train the operating manager for more effective orientation behavior.

A new and progressive idea about who should orient employees is being used at Hewlett Packard (H-P) in San Diego, California. At this H–P plant and also one in Waltham, Massachusetts, retired employees perform the orientation training. The response

Exhibit 9–2

Relationship of operating and P/HRM managers in orientation

Orientation function	Operating manager (OM)	P/HRM manager (P/HRM)
Design the orientation program		P/HRM is consultant with OM
Introduce the new employee to the organization and its history, personnel policies, working conditions, and rules. Complete paperwork		P/HRM performs this
Explain the task and job expectations to employee	OM performs this	
Introduce employee to work group and new surroundings. Encourage employees to help new employee	OM performs this	

according to Joe Costi, employee relations manager at the San Diego facility, has been fantastic. "Many newcomers comment this must be a good place to work, if retirees come back. . . ."[5]

How Orientation Programs Work

Orientation programs vary from quite informal, primarily verbal efforts to formal schedules which supplement verbal presentations with written handouts. Formal orientations often include a tour of the facilities or slides, charts, and pictures of them. Usually, they are used when a large number of employees must be oriented.

The formal program usually covers such items as:

- History and general policies of the enterprise.
- Descriptions of the enterprise's services or products.
- Organization of the enterprise.
- Safety measures and regulations.
- Personnel policies and practices.
- Compensation, benefits, and employee services provided.
- Daily routine and regulations.

The material can be presented in a variety of forms. For example, in an experiment at Union Electric Company in St. Louis it was found that programmed learning approaches were efficient and effective.[6] The written material may be in the form of handouts and booklets or combined into a single employee handbook. The literature and handouts should be examined to see that the reading level is right for the employees in question. Frequently they are too technical or are written at too high a reading level for the employee. A study of the orientations of disadvantaged employees found that initial

---

[5]"Companies Calling Retirees Back to the Workplace," *Management Review*, February 1982, p. 29.

[6]Marian McClintock et al., "Orienting the Employee with Programmed Instruction," *Training and Development Journal*, May 1967, pp. 18–22.

presentations should be in oral form, followed by written materials, to avoid a feeling of communication overload.[7] The oral, then written, communication pattern should be followed by both P/HRM specialists and supervisors.

To make sure that the orientation program is complete and works well, larger organizations prepare checklists of what should be covered. Some are completed by supervisors (see Exhibit 9–3). To make sure the supervisor covers all the important points, some organizations also prepare an orientation checklist to be filled out by employees.

Orienting Management Trainees

Management trainees are in a special orientation category. Most of these recruits must adjust from college life to work life. Many organizations have prepared rather elaborate orientation programs for potential managers which are called management training programs. There is little doubt that initial experiences with an organization are important predictors of future managerial performance. Research studies make that clear.

Formal Management Training Programs

After recruits have been selected to become managers, there are two distinct approaches to their orientation and placement. The first is to orient them briefly and let them go to work. This is the approach most organizations take with nonmanagerial employees. The second is to orient and train them in a management training program and then assign them to specific positions. Studies indicate that the most effective management training programs:

Are short (of four to five months' duration, if possible).

Use on-the-job training and minimize classroom teaching.

Guidelines for conducting an employee orientation:

1. Orientation should begin with the most relevant and immediate kinds of information and then proceed to more general policies of the organization.

2. The most significant part of orientation is the human side, giving new employees knowledge of what supervisors and co-workers are like, telling them how long it should take to reach standards of effective work, and encouraging them to seek help and advice when needed.

3. New employees should be "sponsored" or directed by an experienced worker or supervisor in the immediate environment who can respond to questions and keep in close touch during the early induction period.

4. New employees should be gradually introduced to the people with whom they will work, rather than given a superficial introduction to all of them on the first day. The object should be to help them get to know their co-workers and supervisors.

5. New employees should be allowed sufficient time to get their feet on the ground before demands on them are increased.

---

[7]Michael M. Petty, "Relative Effectiveness of Four Combinations of Oral and Written Presentations of Job-Related Information To Disadvantaged Employees," *Journal of Applied Psychology*, February 1973, pp. 105–6.

Exhibit 9–3

Supervisor's orientation checklist

	Discussion completed (please check *each* individual item)
Employee's Name:	
I. Word of welcome	
II. Explain overall departmental organization and its relationship to other activities of the company	
III. Explain employee's individual contribution to the objectives of the department and his starting assignment in broad terms	
IV. Discuss job content with employee and give him a copy of job description (if available)	
V. Explain departmental training program(s) and salary increase practices and procedures	
VI. Discuss where the employee lives and transportation facilities	
VII. Explain working conditions: a. Hours of work, time sheets b. Use of employee entrance and elevators c. Lunch hours d. Coffee breaks, rest periods e. Personal telephone calls and mail f. Overtime policy and requirements g. Paydays and procedure for being paid h. Lockers i. Other_____	
VIII. Requirements for continuance of employment—explain company standards as to: a. Performance of duties b. Attendance and punctuality c. Handling confidential information d. Behavior e. General appearance f. Wearing of uniforms	
IX. Introduce new staff member to manager(s) and other supervisors. Special attention should be paid to the person to whom the new employee will be assigned.	
X. Release employee to immediate supervisor who will: a. Introduce new staff member to fellow workers b. Familiarize the employee with his work place c. Begin on-the-job training	

If not applicable, insert N/A in space provided.

_____   _____
Employee's Signature   Supervisor's Signature

_____   _____
Date   Division

Form examined for filing: _____   _____
                                              Date   Personnel Department

Source: Joan Holland and Theodore Curtis, "Orientation of New Employees," in Joseph Famularo, ed., *Handbook of Modern Personnel Administration* (New York: McGraw-Hill, 1972), chap. 23.

Encourage high job and training expectations in trainees.

Provide trainees with frequent feedback on their progress or lack of it.

Generally, these qualities are desired by both companies and trainees. Both prefer a minimum of formal classroom work and a maximum of actual work so the company gets productivity sooner and the individual receives rewards sooner. Most of the trainees want to test themselves against the challenge of the real world to see if they can do the job. Training programs that do not allow this and emphasize lectures or allow only observation of how departments work will satisfy neither of these objectives.

Perhaps most crucial to an effective management training program is an effective supervisor for the trainee. Too often the trainees are roadblock executives who see themselves as failures because they have not been promoted beyond a certain point. They are likely to haze recruits and give them tough experiences, always supposedly for their own good. Instead, recruits need a good supervisor who understands their problems and wants to get them off to a good start. An example of an effective manager who was an excellent trainer of new employees is given in the accompanying box.

Happy is the trainee whose supervisor is a Ray Scheid (see box below) instead of a frustrated person who takes out his or her aggressions by hazing the trainees.

Assignment, Placement, and Orientation Follow-Up

The final phase of the orientation program is the assignment of the new employee to the job. At this point, the supervisor is supposed to take over and continue the orientation program. But as the Texas Instruments study demonstrated, supervisors are busy people, and even though they might be well intentioned, they can overlook some of the facts needed by the new employee to do a good job.

One way to assure adequate orientation is to design a feedback system to control the program, or use the management by objectives technique. A form could be used to communicate this feedback from the trainee. The new employee could be instructed to: "Complete this checklist as well as you can. Then take it to your supervisor, who will go over

---

When I was in the food business, I observed one of the best "trainers" in the business. Ray Scheid was also one of the most effective purchasing agents in the food business, the head grocery buyer at the Cincinnati branch of the Kroger Company. Because he was very good at his job, earlier in his career he had been offered many promotions. As is often the case with such promotions, each would have involved a geographic transfer. He liked Cincinnati, and for this and other reasons he preferred to stay in his position there. Scheid liked his job and found it rewarding, but one of his most important rewards was training new managers for Kroger. He often told me of the men he had trained—some of whom later became his bosses. He was as proud of them as if they were his sons. His joy was to teach them all he knew so they could be promoted elsewhere and advance in their careers. He showed no jealousy or desire to be in their shoes. He had had his chances and had chosen a different life. His career was satisfying to him and he lived theirs vicariously. He had all that was needed: technical expertise, a sincere desire to help people learn, and reward when they had learned all he had to teach.

it with you and give you any additional information you may need.'' The job information form is signed by employee and supervisor. An appointment set up with the orientation group in the first month on the job provides a follow-up opportunity to determine how well the employee is adjusting and permits evaluation of the orientation program. The form is designed not to test knowledge but to help improve the process of orientation.

Summary: Orientation

Orientation programs are an important part of the employment process. The diagnostic manager will recognize that the amount and emphasis of orientation varies with the complexity of the task, the experience of the employee, and the climate in the work group. The manager will adjust the orientation program accordingly, following these basic principles:

1. The principal purposes of orientation include:
   a. To reduce start-up costs for a new employee.
   b. To reduce fear and anxiety of the new employee and hazing from other employees.
   c. To reduce turnover.
   d. To save time for supervisors and co-workers.
   e. To develop realistic job expectations, positive attitudes toward the employer, and job satisfaction.
2. In small enterprises the operating manager does all the orienting; in middle-sized or larger enterprises the operating and P/HRM managers share this task.

Art Johnson was lucky. Even though the Coca Cola Bottling Works was small, it had a well-developed, though informal, orientation program. The personnel manager got Art to complete the required employment forms. Then he chatted with Art about work rules and similar matters. He described Art's new supervisor, Ida Averill, and talked about what the work group was like.

Ida introduced Art around the work group. Then she spent 20 minutes talking about what a good work group it was and what each employee was like. Finally, she talked to Art about what job performance was expected. Then she put Art with Ted Carson. Ted was to be Art's "work buddy" and help train him. Six months later, Art was one of the highest performing employees at the plant, and he loved his job.

* * * *

Gigi Martinez was not so lucky. Her first experience at the department store was typical. Her "orientation" consisted of being assigned to a work center and being told, "Well, get to work. If you need help ask for it." But when she did ask for help, people were too busy. Two weeks later when her boss criticized her in front of others for poor performance, she quit.

* * * *

Sam Lavalle got a better start than Gigi. And he made friends with the man at the next workbench, Lionell Narda. When he needed help, Lionell helped. He also filled Sam in on how to get along with his co-workers and with Andrew, the supervisor, who was a bit distant. Six months later, Sam was still at the workbench and performing about average. He seemed to like his work pretty well.

Case

Harold

Gwen

Harold Matthews was unhappy. He'd just had an unpleasant visit with his boss, William Custer. Harold is vice president of operations of Young Enterprises, a firm employing about 1,600 persons in the Los Angeles area. The firm manufactures parts for a large aircraft firm nearby.

Since Young Enterprises serves primarily one customer, costs are a major factor in their negotiations. Bill Custer told Harold that the new contract was not as good as the last one. Costs needed to be cut. Since labor costs are a high percentage of the total, Harold must begin to work on these. At the same time, Purchasing was working on reducing materials costs and Finance was trying to find ways to reduce the cost of capital.

Harold has decided to consult two groups of persons about the cost cutting: P/HRM and his supervisors. First he calls a meeting of the department heads and key supervisors and prepares his figures. The facts are:

- Their labor costs are rising faster than their competitors' are, and faster than the cost of living.
- These costs are higher any way you measure them: number of employees per unit of output, cost per unit of output, and so on. What's more, the trend is worsening.

At the meeting, Harold explained the facts. Then he asked the supervisors for suggestions. He gave them strong "encouragement" to supervise each employee closely and to make sure that the firm gets a fair day's work for a fair day's pay. Harold took notes of the comments his supervisors made. Some of the better ones were:

Sally Feldman (supervisor): One of my problems is that the people P/HRM sends me are not up to the output standards of the people I've lost through quits and retirement.

Art Jones (department head): Let's face it, when you look at the records, our recent output isn't up to what we expected when we installed the new machines.

Sam Jacobs (supervisor): The problem is our current crop of employees. They ain't what they used to be!

Harold wondered if they were just passing the buck—or if there was some truth to the complaints. He invited Gwen Meridith, the personnel vice president, in for help.

Harold Gwen, production costs are up and labor efficiency is down. The supervisors are blaming it on the employees. We put new machinery in to get production up. It's up, but not to what it should be, given our investment. What do you think is going on?

Gwen I suspect that part of what they say has some truth to it. Lately the job market is tight. Last week, I had 20 jobs to fill and only 20 applicants. About half really were somewhat marginal. And let's face it, we put the new machinery in with little preparation of the employees.

Harold What can we do? We have a serious cost problem.

Gwen The job market is still tight. I don't see any improvement in the quality of labor in the near future. Sounds like we ought to gear up that training program I've been talking about.

Harold You prepare something for Bill. Then you and I will go to see him about it.

3. A formal orientation program covers:

    a. History, general policies, description of the organization's products or services, and organization of the enterprise.

    b. Safety measures and regulations.

    c. P/HRM policies and practices.

    d. Compensation, benefits, and employee services provided.

    e. Daily routine and regulations.

4. The shorter the management training and orientation program is, and the closer it is to actual work experience, the more effective it will be.

5. More effective orientation programs include a minimum of technical information and emphasize the social dimensions of the new job (supervisor's expectations, encouragement, climate of work group, etc.)

Recommendations for use of orientation programs by model organizations are given in Exhibit 9–4.

Introduction to Training and Development

Harold and Gwen have just described one of the several reasons why training and development takes place in organizations. Training and development is, in short, an attempt to improve current or future employee performance. The following specific factors are important to know:

> *Training* is the systematic process of altering the behavior of employees in a direction to increase organizational goals.

Exhibit 9–4 _____

Recommendations on orientation programs for model organizations

Type of organization	Informal orientation programs	Formal orientation programs	Informal placement follow-up	Formal placement follow-up
1. Large size, low complexity, high stability		X		X
2. Medium size, low complexity, high stability		X		X
3. Small size, low complexity high stability	X		X	
4. Medium size, moderate complexity, moderate stability	X		X	
5. Large size, high complexity, low stability		X		X
6. Medium size, high complexity, low stability		X		X
7. Small size, high complexity, low stability	X		X	

Management development is the process by which managers gain the experience, skills, and attitudes to become or remain successful leaders in their organizations.

A *formal training program* is an effort by the employer to provide opportunities for the employee to acquire job-related skills, attitudes, and knowledge.

Learning is the act by which the individual acquires skills, knowledge, and abilities which result in a relatively permanent change in his or her behavior.

Another way to define training and development is to model it. A model is given in Exhibit 9–5.[8] Each phase of the training and development process will be discussed. This section of the chapter will focus on training programs to improve managerial and employees' abilities. For example, training programs can be geared toward improving typing

Exhibit 9–5

Training model

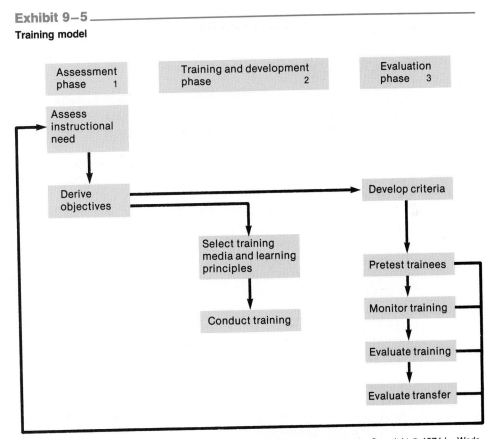

Source: From *Training Program Development and Evaluation* by I. L. Goldstein. Copyright © 1974 by Wadsworth Publishing Company, Inc. Reprinted by permission of the publisher, Brooks/Cole Publishing Company, Monterey, California.

---

[8]Irwin I. Goldstein, *Training: Program Development and Evaluation* (Monterey, Calif.: Brooks/Cole Publishing, 1974). Also see "Guides for Designing Training Programs," *Training and Development Journal,* April 1981, pp. 6–7.

skills, salesmanship abilities, lathe operation techniques, and so on. Chapter 10 will deal with methods of developing attitudinal change and interpersonal skills in both managers and nonmanagers.

Since training is a form of education, some of the findings regarding learning theory logically might be applicable to training. These principles can be important in the design of both formal and informal training programs. The following is a brief summary of the way learning principles can be applied to job training.[9]

The Trainee Must Be Motivated to Learn • This motivation involves two factors: awareness of the need to learn, based on the individual's own inadequacy in this regard, and a clear understanding of what needs to be learned. The learner must secure satisfaction from the learning. He/she must see the usefulness of the material in terms of his or her own needs.

The Learning Must Be Reinforced • Behavioral psychologists have demonstrated that learners learn best with fairly immediate reinforcement of appropriate behavior. The learner must be rewarded for new behavior in ways that satisfy needs, such as pay, recognition, promotion. Standards of performance should be set for the learner. Benchmarks for learning will provide goals and give a feeling of accomplishment when reached. These standards provide a measure for meaningful feedback.

The Training Must Provide for Practice of the Material • Learning requires time to assimilate what has been learned, to accept it, to internalize it, and to build confidence in what has been learned. This requires practice and repetition of the material.

The Material Presented Must Be Meaningful • Appropriate materials for sequential learning (cases, problems, discussion outlines, reading lists) must be provided. The trainer acts as an aid in an efficient learning process.

The learning methods used should be as varied as possible. It is boredom that destroys learning, not fatigue. Any method—whether old-fashioned lecture or programmed learning or the jazziest computer game—will begin to bore some learners if overused.

The Material Presented Must Be Communicated Effectively • Communication must be done in a unified way, and over enough time to allow it to be absorbed.

The Material Taught Must Transfer to the Job Situation • The trainer does her or his best to make the training as close to the reality of the job as possible. Thus, when the trainee returns to the job, the training can be applied immediately.

As each aspect of training program design and implementation is discussed, you will see how these learning theory principles are applied. Training and management development are closely related to many P/HRM activities. For example, performance evaluation provides the data needed for training. Employment planning decisions may also dictate the need for added training.

Employee training is moderately well developed—a Stage III or possibly Stage IV function in P/HRM. But management development is a Stage II P/HRM function. Most people do it, but scientific evaluation of its results is slim.

---

[9]E. R. Hilgard and G. H. Bower, *Theories of Learning* (New York: Appleton-Century-Crofts, 1966).

A Diagnostic Approach to Training and Development

Refer back to Exhibit 9–1 which highlights those aspects of the diagnostic model that are especially important to employee training and development (T&D notation is used). The most important determinants of training are the task to be done and the employees' abilities and attitudes. If the current employees have work ethic attitudes and the skills needed to do the jobs, training may not be too important for the organization. More often, because of conditions in the labor market, the organization is losing some employees to other enterprises who provide better rewards.

It is also unlikely that the task demands are stable. More frequently, because of volatile technology and market conditions, the jobs are changing, and this requires more training so employees can meet current effectiveness standards. For example, when computers are introduced or new production or operating techniques are instituted, employees must be retrained.

The U.S. government also is becoming a vital influence on training. This has been happening in two ways. One is the pressure for equal employment opportunities and human rights. If in an organization minorities and women work only at the lowest paid, least skilled positions, pressure will be applied to upgrade the skills of those who have the potential for upward mobility. This increases the demand for training or retraining.

The second way government influences training is that it provides many training programs. These programs frequently have public policy purposes, such as reduction of unemployment, upgrading the incomes of minority groups, or increasing the competitiveness of underdeveloped regions of the country.

In the United States, the federal government, through the Comprehensive Employment and Training Act (1974) and other work force legislation, has allocated large sums of the training of potential workers for jobs.[10] The government reimburses training organizations (schools, business, unions) or trains the workers itself. This program, however, was cut back severely by the Reagan budget cuts in 1982.

The Canadian government also operates several work force training programs. In fact, Canada spent over $2 billion, three to four times the per capita spending of the United States in this area between 1967 and 1975.[11]

Some unions are also involved in employee training, especially in industries such as construction in which the union is larger than the employer. In these cases, the union often does most or all of the training. A large proportion of this type of training occurs in apprenticeship programs.

Finally, the goals of management affect training and development. For example, organization development programs are likely to be chosen by managers who feel that full development of employees is an appropriate enterprise goal.

The implications are that employee training is a major undertaking for employers. Almost all large organizations and most medium-sized ones run their own training programs. They employ 50,000 full-time trainers and spend approximately $100 billion per year on their programs.[12] As P/HRM personnel know, training can be a costly endeavor.

---

[10]William Mirengoff and Lester Rindler, "The Comprehensive Employment and Training Act. Impact on People, Places, and Programs (Washington, D.C.: National Academy of Sciences, 1976).

[11]Larry Truesdall, "Determinants of the Demand for Manpower Training," *Relations Industrielles*, Fall 1975, pp. 424–34.

[12]Thomas Gilbert, "The High Cost of Knowledge," *Personnel*, March–April 1976, pp. 11–23.

Exhibit 9–6 _____

Average costs of training a salesperson*

Type of firm	1980
Industrial products (e.g., an engineering salesperson)	$20,093
Consumer products (e.g., a person selling food products to a grocery store)	13,625
Services[†]	12,772

*Includes salary, instructional materials, transportation, and living expenses incurred for training, instructional staff, outside seminars, and management time when it is part of training budget.

[†]Includes insurance, financial, utilities, transportation, and sales personnel.

Reprinted with permission from *Sales & Marketing Management* magazine. Copyright 1981.

Exhibit 9–6 illustrates how an industrial firm could easily spend $50,000–$100,000 or more training just five or six salespeople. Whether an organization has management or professional development programs depends a great deal on its size. Smaller enterprises rarely run their own formal development program; the programs are informal at best. Larger organizations have elaborate formal programs combining on-the-job with off-the-job development. Others, such as General Motors, the U.S. Military, Exxon, and AT&T, have established large complex training and development centers for their managers. The Federal Executive Institute at Charlottesville, Virginia, is set up to develop federal government executives, as is the Executive Seminar Center in Berkeley, California, and the U.S. Post Office Center in Norman, Oklahoma. There has been tremendous growth in this area in the past 30 years, and the trend is expected to continue.

Purposes of Training and Development

There are many reasons why organizations engage in training and development programs. The most frequently mentioned reasons are:

- To improve the quantity of output.
- To improve the quality of output.
- To lower the costs of waste and equipment maintenance.
- To lower the number and costs of accidents.
- To lower turnover and absenteeism and increase employees' job satisfaction, since training can improve the employees' self-esteem.
- To prevent employee obsolescence.

In effect, training and development help the organization become more efficient and effective and the employee to develop and become more satisfied. Given here are the viewpoints of two executives on the purpose of training.

Remember Harold Matthew's problem at Young Enterprises? The employees are not producing the quality and quantity of output expected, and it appears that training may help reduce costs to make the firm more competitive. Well-trained employees also tend to be more satisfied with their positions and better able to perform their jobs more effectively.

Edgar Speer, chairman and chief executive officer of United States Steel, says:

We support training and development activities to get results. . . . We're interested in specific things that provide greater rewards to the employee, increased return to the stockholder, and enable reinvestment needs of the business. In other words, [we're interested in] those things which affect the "bottom line." Although you cannot always evaluate training as readily as some other functions, as people improve their performance it is reflected in on-the-job results as well as all aspects of their lives.

William Murray, chairman of the board and chief executive officer of Harris Bank of Chicago, says:

I readily relate to the fundamentals of good technical training. . . . The training function plays an integral role in the bank by helping upgrade employee performance and the from hire to retire approach provides continuity in the developing process of bank personnel. While we can't measure the absolute results of training programs, our record as an organization indicates we're doing something right.

Who is Involved in Training and Development?

For training and development to be effective, top management must support it, as Mr. Speer and Mr. Murray do. They provide the budget and personal support.

As with other P/HRM activities both operating and P/HRM managers are involved in training. Exhibit 9–7 indicates how. Occasionally more than these two groups are involved. For example, at General Telephone of Florida, the training, labor relations, and public affairs departments combined forces to prepare video training programs to train managers to handle grievances and arbitration. Community theater actors performed the roles to show participants how to perform while on the job.

In larger organizations, the P/HRM manager most involved in the work described in

Exhibit 9–7 _____

The role of operating and P/HRM managers in training and development

Training and development function	Operating manager (OM)	P/HRM manager (P/HRM)
Determining training needs and objectives	Approved by OM	Done by P/HRM
Develop training criteria	Approved by OM	Done by P/HRM
Choosing trainer	Jointly chosen: nominated by OM	Jointly chosen: approved by P/HRM
Developing training materials	Approved by OM	Done by P/HRM
Planning and implementing the program		Done by P/HRM
Doing the training	Occasionally done by OM	Normally done by P/HRM
Evaluating the training	OM reviews the results	Done by P/HRM

P/HRM Manager Close-Up

John Barrows
Packaging Corporation of America

Biography

John F. Barrows is director—training and development for Packaging Corporation of America. He joined the company as a recruiting and compensation specialist in 1967 and subsequently held positions as personnel manager and area personnel and industrial relations manager before assuming his present position.

Barrows received a B.S. degree in Business Administration from Northeastern University and subsequently received an M.B.A. degree from the Harvard Graduate School of Business. He joined Sears, Roebuck & Company as a personnel specialist before moving to Packaging Corporation of America.

Job description

The director—training and development is to contribute to the profitability and growth of the company by providing to management timely and relevant information; and accepted advice, service and training in the area of management development, job skills, and personal motivation that contribute to effective employee performance.

Specific responsibilities include: the administration of management development and training programs, the development of new programs as needs are identified, and the research of new ideas and concepts for improving human performance.

Views about the personnel function at Packaging Corporation of America

The function in Packaging Corporation of America is titled personnel and industrial relations to reflect the wide scope of its contributions and responsibilities.

Personnel and industrial relations, hereafter referred to as P&IR, is critical to the organization as recognized by its senior vice president reporting directly to the chairman of the board and chief executive officer.

Our executives have long realized that the continued success and growth of the company is dependent on the sustained and collective good performance of all its employees. In order to maintain this success and growth, our operating and key staff managers must have available highly professional and varied P&IR services to meet their individual human resource needs.

The value of P&IR can only grow given the constant and increasing complexities of change that influence human values, needs, expectations, and behavior. It will take creative and committed P&IR professionals to find the approaches where both the needs of the individual and the company can be realized.

Chapters 9 and 10 is called the training director, or training and development manager. A typical training director is John F. Barrows. His work history and the job description for his position, director—training and development for Packaging Corporation of America and a few of his thoughts are given here.

Case

Bob

Young Enterprises did not have a separate training department. So Gwen, with the assistance of Bob McGarrah, the director of training and development, began to think about a training program to help Harold Matthews reach his goal. The program might not have been needed if the job market weren't so tight. But since applicants are so scarce, the training program was very important at this point.

Gwen Bob, what we need to determine is what training programs we should have right now. What do you suggest we do?

Bob The typical approach is to use organizational analysis, operational analysis, and person analysis. Besides, we need to do some sort of feasibility or cost/benefit analysis to see if the training is worth the effort. This will give us a set of training objectives for a program or set of programs. Then we design the program content and methods around these. After the program is run, we evaluate it.

Gwen At this point, let's set the objectives and design the program. Then we'll go back to Harold to see if he has any additional suggestions.

Managing the Training Program

Determining Training Needs and Objectives

The first step in managing training is to determine training needs and set objectives for these needs. In effect, the trainers are preparing a training forecast (this is the assessment phase in Exhibit 9–5).

There are four ways to determine the training needs:[13]

1. By observing the employees to be trained.
2. By listening to the employees to be trained.
3. By asking their supervisors about the employees' training needs.
4. By examining the problems the employees have.

In essence, any gaps between expected and actual results suggest training needs. Active solicitation of suggestions from employees, supervisors, managers, and training committees can also provide training needs ideas.

From the analysis of training needs, the training manager proposes specific training programs to meet specific measurable objectives. These objectives include knowledge,

---

[13]Donald Kirkpatrick. "Determining Training Needs," *Training and Development Journal,* February 1977, pp. 22–25.

skill, job performance, and output objectives. For example, an objective for clerical training might be "to operate the IBM Selectric typewriter at 60 words per minute with less than two errors per page."

The cost and feasibility assessment is an attempt to determine (before formal evaluation) whether the training costs can be offset by the benefits or whether another approach, such as selection improvements, is more effective.

Determining training needs helps the organization achieve several of the learning principles mentioned in the beginning of the chapter:

- If the employee to be trained is involved in assessing training needs, he or she will become more aware of the training needs.
- If specific objectives are set, standards of performance for feedback are designed.
- If the standards are set properly, it is likely that the training program will help transfer results to the job situation.

Although it is obviously desirable to analyze training needs, studies indicate that less than half of larger organizations (and, one assumes, smaller percentages of medium-sized and smaller organizations) formally assess training needs and set formal training objectives.[14]

Choosing Trainers and Trainees

Great care must be exercised in hiring or developing effective instructors or trainers. To some extent, the success of the training program depends upon proper selection of the person who performs the training task.[15] Personal characteristics (the ability to speak well, to write convincingly, to organize the work of others, to be inventive, and to inspire others to greater achievements) are important factors in the selection of trainers.

Although much formal training is performed by professional trainers, often operating supervisors may be the best trainers technically, especially if the training manager helps them prepare the material. Using operating managers as trainers overcomes the frequent criticism that "Training is O.K. in the classroom, but it won't work on the shop floor or back on the job." The presence of *trained* trainers is a major factor in whether the training program is successful. It will help if these principles of learning are followed:

- Provide for practice of the material.
- Require practice and repetition of the material.
- Communicate the material effectively.

Another planning factor is the selection of trainees who will participate in the programs. In some cases this is obvious; the program may have been designed to train particular new employees in certain skills. In some cases, the training program is designed to help with EEO goals; in others it is to help employees find better jobs elsewhere when layoffs are necessary or to retrain older employees. Techniques similar to selection procedures may be used to select trainees, especially when those who attend the program may be promoted or receive higher wages or salaries as a result. If formal selection

---

[14]Bureau of National Affairs, "Training Employees," Personnel Policies Forum, Survey No. 88 (Washington, D.C.: U.S. Government Printing Office, 1969).

[15]Lyle Sussman, Edwin Talley III., and Virginia Pattison, "Training Non-Trainers for Training," *Training and Development Journal,* May 1981, pp. 132–36.

techniques are not used, quotas, supervisor nominations, self-nominations, and seniority rules may develop unofficially or officially as selection mechanisms for the programs.

This discussion of trainee selection is normative, however; it implies that organizations rationally select those employees who need the training and train them. Roderick and Yaney studied selection of and participation in training programs by 1,247 young males who worked for businesses over a four-year period.[16] Only 1 out of 7 received any formal training during the period. The companies tended to select for further training those men with the best educational backgrounds and from the highest socioeconomic group. This "creaming" meant that those who needed the training the most did not get it, and the gap between the trained and untrained widened. Also because of these selection procedures, blacks received much less training than white males. The companies seemed to select trainees based on the most probable "success ratio" for the training, not on those needing the training the most.

Training and Development Phase

After needs and objectives have been determined and trainees and trainers have been selected, the program is run. This is the second phase shown in Exhibit 9–5. This phase includes selection of content and methods to be used and the actual conducting of the training.

Selection of Training Content

From the analysis of the training needs, the training director derives the content of the training. In the case of Young Enterprises, the company installed new machinery without training the employees in its use. Introduction of new equipment, as in this case, often causes employees' skills to become obsolete, without developing the new skills to cope effectively with the redesigned job.

Since there are well over 20,000 jobs listed in the *Dictionary of Occupational Titles*, the number of skills to be developed can be quite large. For example, communication, leadership, and budgeting skills, are frequent subjects of training programs. But all kinds of skills can be taught. The ones *to be* taught are derived from the training needs analyses. They can vary from typing skills improvement, to learning a new computer language, to effective use of a new machine.

Training Approaches for Employees

Both training for the unskilled and retraining for the obsolete employee follow one of four approaches which combine elements of the *where* and *what* of training. The four principal types of training are apprenticeship, vestibule, on-the-job training, and off-the-job training.

Apprentice Training • Apprentice training is a combination of on-the-job and off-the-job training. It requires the cooperation of the employer, trainers at the workplace and in schools (such as vocational schools), government agencies, and the skilled-trade unions.

Governments regulate apprentice training. In the United States, the major law is the Apprenticeship Act of 1937. Typically the government also subsidizes these programs.

---

[16]Roger Roderick and Joseph Yaney, "Developing Younger Workers: A Look at Who Gets Trained," *Journal of Management*, Spring 1976, pp. 19–26.

The U.S. Department of Labor funds apprenticeship programs in the building trades, mining, auto repair, oil, and other fields. The department also issues standards and regulations governing these programs. About 30,000 persons are trained yearly by this method.

The apprentice commits herself or himself to a period of training and learning that involves both formal classroom learning and practical on-the-job experience. These periods can vary from two years or so (barber, ironworker, foundryman, baker, meat cutter, engraver) through four or five years (electrician, photoengraver, tool and die maker, plumber, job pressman), up to 10 years (steelplate engraver). During this period, the pay is less than that for the master workers.

Research evaluating construction workers trained by the apprenticeship method versus on-the-job training indicates that apprentices are better trained, get promoted sooner, and experience less unemployment later.[17] Thus apprentice training can be effective.

Vestibule Training • In vestibule training, the trainee learns the job in an environment that simulates the real working environment as closely as possible. An example would be the simulated cockpit of a Boeing 767 used to train airline pilots in operating that specific airplane.[18] United Airlines had in use in 1982, 16 jet simulators. A machine operator trainee might run a machine under the supervision of a trainer until he learns how to use it properly. Only then is he sent to the shop floor. This procedure can be quite expensive if the number of trainees supervised is not large, but it can be effective under certain circumstances. Some employees trained in the vestibule method have adjustment problems when they begin full-time work, since the vestibule area is safer and less hectic.

On-the-Job Training • Probably the most widely used method of training (formal and informal) is on-the-job training. The employee is placed into the real work situation and shown the job and the tricks of the trade by an experienced employee or the supervisor. Although this program is apparently simple and relatively less costly, if it is not handled properly the costs can be high in damaged machinery, unsatisfied customers, misfiled forms, and poorly taught workers. To prevent these problems, trainers must be carefully selected and trained. The trainee should be placed with a trainer who is similar in background and personality. The trainer should be motivated by training and rewarded for doing it well. The trainer should use effective training techniques in instructing the trainee.

One approach to systematic on-the-job training is the job instruction training (JIT) system developed during World War II.[19] In this system, the trainers first train the supervisors, who in turn train the employees. Exhibit 9–8 describes the steps of JIT training as given in the War Manpower Commission's bulletin, "Training within Industry Series in 1945." These are the instructions given to supervisors on how to train new or present employees.

Another frequently used on-the-job training technique is job rotation. In this approach, the trainee is taught several positions in succession over a period of time so the trainee can be used in several positions.

---

[17]William Franklin, "A Comparison of Formally and Informally Trained Journeymen in Construction," *Industrial and Labor Relations Review,* July 1973, pp. 1086–94.

[18]Shelby Hodge, "Flights of Fancy Qualify Pilots on the Ground," *Houston Chronicle,* August 9, 1981, p. 3AA.

[19]Fred Wickert, "The Famous JIT Card: A Basic Way to Improve It," *Training and Development Journal,* February 1974, pp. 6–9.

Exhibit 9–8 _____

Job instruction training (JIT) methods

First, Here's what you *must do* to *get ready* to teach a job:
1. Decide what the learner must be taught in order to do the job efficiently, safely, economically, and intelligently.
2. Have the right tools, equipment, supplies, and material ready.
3. Have the workplace properly arranged, just as the worker will be expected to keep it.

Then, you should *instruct* the learner by the following *four basic steps:*

Step I—*Preparation* (of the learner)
1. Put the learner at *ease.*
2. Find out what he or she already knows about the job.
3. Get the learners interested and desirous of learning the job.

Step II—*Presentation* (of the operations and knowledge)
1. *Tell, show, illustrate* and *question* in order to put over the new knowledge and operations.
2. Instruct slowly, clearly, completely, and patiently, one point at a time.
3. Check, question, and repeat.
4. Make sure the learner really knows.

Step III—*Performance tryout*
1. Test learner by having him or her perform the job.
2. Ask questions beginning with *why, how, when* or *where.*
3. Observe performance, correct errors, and repeat instructions if necessary.
4. Continue until you *know learner knows.*

Step IV—*Follow-up*
1. Put the employee "on his own."
2. Check frequently to be sure learner follows instructions.
3. Taper off extra supervision and close follow-up until person is qualified to work with normal supervision.

Remember—if the learner hasn't learned, the teacher hasn't taught.

On-the-Job Experiences in Management Development • There are four approaches to on-the-job management development. These programs are not mutually exclusive; often they are run simultaneously. On-the-job management development is the preferred type from many points of view, especially because of its relevance and immediate transferability to the job.

Coaching and counseling. One of the best and most frequently used methods of developing new managers is for effective managers to reach them.[20] The coach-superior sets a good example of what a manager is (does). He or she also answers questions and explains why things are done the way they are. It is the coach-superior's obligation to see

---

Approaches to on-the-job management development:

Coaching and counseling in the present position.
Transition to new job experiences while staying at the old job.
Self-improvement programs.
Job rotation and transfer career plans.

---

[20]Walter Mahler and William Wrightnour, *Executive Continuity* (Homewood, Ill.: Richard D. Irwin, 1973), chaps. 6, 7.

to it that the manager-trainee makes the proper contacts so that the job can be learned easily and performed in a more adequate way. In some ways, the coach-superior-manager-trainee relationship resembles the buddy system in employee training.

One technique the superior may use is to have decision-making meetings with the trainee. During these meetings procedures are agreed upon. If the trainee is to learn, the superior must give him or her enough authority to make decisions and perhaps even make mistakes. This approach not only provides opportunities to learn, it requires effective delegation, which develops a feeling of mutual confidence. Appropriately chosen committee assignments can be used as a form of coaching and counseling.

Although most organizations use coaching and counseling as either a formal or an informal management development technique, it is not without its problems. Coaching and counseling fail when inadequate time is set aside for them, when the subordinate is allowed to make no mistakes, if rivalry develops, or the dependency needs of the subordinate are not recognized or accepted by the superior.

In sum, many experts contend that coaching and counseling, when coupled with planned job rotation through jobs and functions, is an effective technique. It can fit the manager's background and utilizes the principle of learning by doing, which has been proven effective. Finally, the method involves the supervisors, which is essential to successful management development.

Transitory, anticipatory experiences. Another approach to management development is to provide transitory experiences. Once it has been determined that a person will be promoted to a specific job, provision is made for a short period before the promotion in which he learns the new job, performing some of his new duties while still performing most of his old ones. This intermediate position is labeled differently in various organizations as assistant-to, understudy, multiple management, or management apprenticeship.

The main characteristic of this type of program is that it gives partial prior experience to a person likely to hold a position in the future.[21] In some approaches, the trainee performs a part of the actual job; thus, an assistant-to does some parts of the job for the incumbent. In multiple management, several decision-making bodies make decisions about the same problem and compare them—a junior board or group's decisions are compared to those of senior management groups. Another variation is to provide trainees with a series of assignments that are part of the new job in order to train them and broaden their experiences.

To the extent that transitory experiences simulate the future job and are challenging, and the trainees' supervisors are effective managers themselves, they seem to provide an eminently reasonable approach to management development. Little systematic study has been made of the effectiveness of this approach, however, and it appears to be used less often than coaching or counseling.

Self-improvement programs. The third approach to on-the-job experience is a self-improvement program pursued while on the job. The manager may take a correspondence course or study individually at home to improve job skills, attend local professional association meetings in the evenings or at lunchtime, and take part in annual or quarterly professional meetings.

---

[21]Roger O'Meara, "Off the Job Assignments for Key Employees," in *Manpower Planning and Programming,* ed. Elmer Burack and James Walker (Boston: Allyn & Bacon, 1972), pp. 339–46.

Transfers and rotation. In the fourth on-the-job approach, trainees are rotated through a series of jobs to broaden their managerial experience. Organizations often have developed programmed career plans which include a mix of functional and geographic transfers.

Advocates of rotation and transfer contend that this approach broadens the manager's background, accelerates the promotion of highly competent individuals, introduces more new ideas into the organization, and increases the effectiveness of the organization. But some research evidence questions this.[22] Individual differences affect whether or not the results will be positive, and generalists may not be the most effective managers in many specialized positions.

Geographic transfers are desirable when fundamentally different job situations exist at various places. They allow new ideas to be tried instead of meeting each situation with the comment, "We always do it that way here." As in many other types of development, trained supervisors can make this technique more effective.

In general, because of the perceived relevance of on-the-job experience, it should be provided in management development programs. Because of individual differences in development and rewards by organizations, however, off-the-job development programs should supplement them where expertise is not readily available inside the organization. Exclusively on-the-job programs lead to a narrow perspective and the inhibition of new ideas coming into the organization.

Off-the-Job Training • Other than apprenticeship, vestibule training, and on-the-job training, all other training is off-the-job training, whether it is done in organization classrooms, vocational schools, or elsewhere. Organizations with the biggest training programs often use off-the-job training. The majority of the 50,000 trainers in the United States and the $100 billion spent on training is in off-the-job training. A survey of training directors in *Fortune 500* companies examined their views of which off-the-job training technique were the most effective for specific objectives. The training directors indicated that if knowledge acquisition were the objective it would be best to use programmed instruction. On the other hand, if the training was intended to improve the problem-solving skills of participants then it would be better to use the case method of training (i.e., having participants analyze job-related cases). Exhibit 9–9 summarizes the major results of the study. The most frequently used methods for on-the-job training are the conference/discussion, programmed instruction, computer-assisted, and simulation approaches.[23]

Conference/discussion approach. The most frequently used training method is for a trainer to give a lecture and involve the trainee in a discussion of the material to be learned. The effective classroom presentation supplements the verbal part with audiovisual aids such as blackboards, slides, mockups. Frequently these lectures are videotaped or audio taped. The method allows the trainer's message to be given in many locations and to be repeated as often as needed for the benefit of the trainees. Videotape recording also allows for self-confrontation, which is especially useful in such programs as sales training and interpersonal relations.[24] The trainee's presentation can be taped and played back for analysis.

---

[22]Robert Pitts, "Unshackle Your 'Comers'," *Harvard Business Review,* May 1977, pp. 127–36.

[23]Goldstein, *Training.*

[24]Willard Thomas, "Shoot the Works with Videobased Training," *Training and Development Journal,* December 1980, pp. 83–87.

Exhibit 9–9 _____

Training directors' ratings of effectiveness of alternative training methods for specific training objectives

Training method	Knowledge acquisition mean rank	Changing attitudes mean rank	Problem solving skills mean rank	Interpersonal skills mean rank	Participant acceptance mean rank	Knowledge retention mean rank
Case study	2	4	1	4	2	2
Conference (discussion) method	3	3	4	3	1	5
Lecture (with questions)	9	8	9	8	8	8
Business games	6	5	2	5	3	6
Movie films	4	6	7	6	5	7
Programmed instruction	1	7	6	7	7	1
Role playing	7	2	3	2	4	4
Sensitivity training (T-group)	8	1	5	1	6	3
Television lecture	5	9	8	9	9	9

Note: 1 = highest rank.

Source: Adapted from Stephen J. Carroll, Frank T. Paine, and John M. Ivancevich, "The Relative Effectiveness of Training Methods— Expert Opinion and Research," *Personnel Psychology,* 33 (1972) pp. 495–509.

Programmed instruction and computer-assisted instruction. A popular method used in organizational training is programmed instruction.[25] Material can be presented on teaching machines or in text form, and behaviorist learning principles are followed closely. Programmed instruction is a useful method for self-instruction when the development cost of the materials has been paid by another organization and the materials are available. It might also be a useful method if there are enough trainees to amortize the development cost, if the trainees are likely to be motivated enough to move ahead with this approach, and if the material presented is suitable to the method. Programmed instruction has been described as follows:

> Programmed instruction is a technique for instructing without the presence or intervention of a human instructor. It is a learner-centered method of instruction, which presents subject-matter to the trainee in small steps or increments, requiring frequent responses from him and immediately informing him of the correctness of his responses. The trainee's responses may be written, oral, or manipulative. A response may be constructed, as in the completion type; it may be selected from among several alternatives, as in the multiple-choice type; or it may assume one or more of a variety of other styles.[26]

Features of programmed instruction are:

> Instruction is provided without the presence or intervention of a human instructor. The learner learns at his own rate (conventional group instruction, films, television,

_____

[25]A. N. Nash, Jan P. Muczyk, and F. L. Vettori, "The Role and Practical Effectiveness of Programmed Instruction," *Personnel Psychology,* Autumn 1971, pp. 397–418.

[26]Leonard Silvern, "Training: Man-Man and Man-Machine Communications," in *Systems Psychology,* ed. Kenyon De Greene (New York: McGraw-Hill, 1970), pp. 383–405.

and other media and methods that do not allow learner control do not satisfy this criterion).

Instruction is presented in small incremental steps requiring frequent responses by the learner; step size is a function of the subject matter and the characteristics of the learner population.

There is a participative overt interaction, or two-way communication, between the learner and the instructional program.

The learner receives immediate feedback informing him of his progress.

Reinforcement is used to strengthen learning.

The sequence of lessons is carefully controlled and consistent.

The instructional program shapes and controls behavior.[27]

Programmed instruction may have wide application in organizational training programs, especially for programs whose characteristics fit those discussed above. It can also be developed in computer-assisted forms.

No matter which training and development approach is used, it must be evaluated. This is the third phase of the model shown in Exhibit 9–5. Evaluation of training and development will be discussed in Chapter 10.

Summary: Training *See pg 282 also*

Training is a significant part of an organization's investment in human resources. Supervisors train new employees and retrain older ones. More experienced employees help train less experienced employees. P/HRM training specialists provide technical training and coordinate the overall training effort of the organization. To summarize the training process, the following points are listed:

1. Training is a form of education to which the following learning principles can be applied:

   a. The trainee must be motivated to learn.
   b. The learning must be reinforced.
   c. The training must provide for practice of the material.
   d. The material presented must be meaningful.
   e. The material taught must transfer to the job situation.

2. Purposes of training and development include:
   a. To improve the quantity of output.
   b. To improve the quality of output.
   c. To lower the costs of waste and equipment maintenance.
   d. To lower the number and costs of accidents.
   e. To lower turnover and absenteeism and increase employee job satisfaction.
   f. To prevent employee obsolescence.

3. When employee turnover is great, it is more important for the organization to provide formal technical training for employees.

---

[27]Ibid.

Exhibit 9–10

Recommendations on management training and development programs for model organizations

Type of organization	Formal program	Informal program	On-the-job programs	Off-the-job programs
1. Large size, low complexity, high stability	X		X	X
2. Medium size, low complexity, high stability		X	X	
3. Small size, low complexity, high stability		X	X	
4. Medium size, moderate complexity, moderate stability		X	X	X
5. Large size, high complexity, low stability	X		X	X
6. Medium size, high complexity, low stability		X	X	
7. Small size, high complexity, low stability		X	X	

4. Effective organizations design their training programs only after assessing the organization's and individual's training needs and setting training objectives.
5. Effective training programs select trainees on the basis of the trainees' needs as well as organizational objectives.
6. Effective training programs carefully select and develop trainers for the programs.
7. Effective organizations evaluate training programs against the program objectives (effectiveness measure) and cost/benefit ratios (efficiency measures).
8. Effective management development programs emphasize on-the-job development programs and supplement them with off-the-job experiences and programs.
9. Training approaches for employees are:
   a. Apprenticeship.
   b. Vestibule.
   c. On-the-job training (coaching and counseling; transitory experiences; self-improvement programs; transfers and rotation).
   d. Off-the-job training (conference/discussion; programmed instruction; computer assisted; simulation approaches).

The recommendations on management training and development programs for model organizations are presented in Exhibit 9–10.

Questions for Review and Discussion

1. What are the main purposes of orientation programs? What aspects of orientation seem to be the most neglected?
2. Describe the study of Texas Instruments' orientation program. What does it indicate to you about how to operate an orientation program?

After Bob and Gwen performed the training needs analysis, he isolated the skills training necessary. The supervisors and employees told him the key need was improved training in the use of the new equipment. He also identified other work-related skills which appeared to decrease employee efficiency.

Then Bob prepared a proposed training program. The training needs analysis had identified the employees who needed the training the most. For trainers, he decided to propose that the manufacturer of the new equipment should provide a trainer. This person would train Bob and several supervisors who appeared to have the greatest potential to run employee training programs. He also proposed that the manufacturer provide a mockup of the machines to use in the training (if available). Lacking that, slides would be used. Then the firm would use several machines for training alone— a semivestibule approach. The cost would be minimal. The manufacturer would provide the training free.

Harold approved the plan, and the training sessions were conducted. Two months after the training was completed, however, there was little change in results. Gwen realized that they had not done as good a job in cost feasibility study as they should have. No formal evaluation of the training had been planned or done.

Gwen and Bob went back to the supervisors to interview them on what had happened. Some of the comments were:

Sandy Feldman (supervisor) I told you people the problem was who you hired. Training bimbos like I got won't help.

Sam Jacobs (supervisor) I thought that training would help. It did a little, for a while. But my problem has become discipline. They know how to do the job—they just don't seem to want to do it.

Harry Samson (supervisor) Maybe the problem was *how* the training was done—I don't know. I see little real results so far.

Bob and Gwen decided to do a formal evaluation of training on the next program. As for what to do now, performance evaluation time was coming up. Maybe the use of rewards for better employees would help. Maybe more and better training would have results. And maybe the labor market had opened up and some terminations and rehirings would be the answer. They'd just have to keep working on it until they could really help Harold and the company. (There will be more about this case in Chapter 10.)

3. Describe a typical orientation program. Which parts of it would you describe as important, very important, or less important? To the employee? To the employer?
4. What is training? Management training and development?
5. Can everyone learn or be trained?
6. What principles of learning affect training? How?
7. Why do organizations perform training? Management development?
8. Who is involved in the planning and operating of formal training in organizations?
9. How do training managers determine training needs and objectives? Why do they do so (or should they)?
10. Describe the major training methods. Which are best?

Glossary

Apprentice Training. A combination of on-the-job and off-the-job training. The apprentice, while learning the job, is paid less than the master worker. Some of the jobs in which one serves as an apprentice include electrician, barber, tool and die maker, and plumber.

Learning. The act by which a person acquires skills, knowledge, and abilities which result in a relatively permanent change in his or her behavior.

Management Development. The process by which managers gain the experience, skills, and attitudes to become or remain successful leaders in their organizations.

Orientation. The P/HRM activity which introduces new employees to the organization and the employee's new tasks, superiors, and work groups.

Training. The systematic process of altering the behavior of employees in a direction to increase organizational goals.

Vestibule Training. A trainee learns a job in an environment that closely resembles the actual work environment. For example, pilots at United Airlines train (vestibule) in a jet simluation cockpit.

Chapter Ten

Development of Human Resources

Learning Objectives

After studying this chapter, you should be able to:
- Define the meaning of organization development (OD).

- Discuss the differences in an OD program that is targeted for individuals, groups, and the total organization.

- Explain the importance of evaluating training and development programs.

- Illustrate how the diagnosis portion of OD is conducted.

- Compare the characteristics of sensitivity training, transactional analysis, and team building.

- Describe the six phases of a Grid OD program.

Chapter Outline

I. Introduction to Development

II. Approaches for Developing Managers
  A. Predecessors to Current Development Programs
  B. The Case Method
  C. Role Playing
  D. The In-Basket Technique
  E. Management Games
  F. Which Methods and Approaches Should Be Used?
  G. Behavior Modeling

III. The Nature of Management Development

IV. Development: An Overview
  A. The Importance of Diagnosis: OD's Base

V. OD: Individual and Interpersonal Techniques
  A. Sensitivity Training
  B. Transactional Analysis

VI. OD: A Group Technique
  A. Team Building

VII. OD: An Organizationwide Technique
  A. Grid OD

VIII. Evaluation of Training and Development

IX. Summary

Case (continued from Chapter 9)

Later the same year, Gwen Meridith, Young Enterprises's P/HRM vice president was faced with another problem. She received the results of Young's third annual attitude survey from the firm's consultant. (An attitude survey is an instrument to measure employee's feelings about their employer.)

Bob McGarrah, the director of training and development was called in to discuss them.

Gwen Bob, look at the results of the items on training and development. Even though we have not had the desired results on our new training program, Item 17 indicates that the blue- and white-collar employees are very satisfied with our technical training program. So are the managers. Now look at the questions on development. There seems to be serious dissatisfaction there on the part of the employees and managers. With regard to the employee dissatisfaction, this may be related to Item 27. There is a fair amount of dissatisfaction with their supervisors' management styles. Maybe

that is why our training program has not given us the desired results! What do you think?

Bob Well, Gwen, we haven't done much on nontechnical training here at Young. We have not tried to run off-the-job development programs. We don't do career development. Nor have we ever considered organizational development programs. How do you feel about them?

Gwen As you know, Bob, my background is labor relations. I have kept up in other areas such as EEO, OSHA, and compensation. But I'm asking for your help on this. I'm not too familiar with these programs. Why don't you get together a report to tell me what's happening in development these days.

Bob prepared a summary of the current trends and happenings in development for managers and employees. The next section covers many of the points Gwen wanted to know about development programs.

Introduction to Development

This chapter completes the two-chapter unit on training and development of managers and employees. Chapter 9 focused primarily on the training of managers and employees to improve their abilities. In addition, training and development can also focus on interpersonal skills, attitudes, and the total organization system. It can be argued that effective interpersonal skills are also abilities, but typically these programs have as their goals the changing of attitudes as well as the development of skills.

Organizations use attitude-change and interpersonal skills training programs for many reasons. One is to improve the effectiveness of employees, especially managers, in their day-to-day work or in specific programs. The latter might be designed to improve meetings and conferences or to help employees adjust their attitudes toward overseas assignments. A second and very important purpose is to help the organization's managers and employees understand themselves better and learn how to cope with modern living. Some programs designed to affect attitudes are oriented toward the attitudes, interpersonal skills, and climate of whole organizational units. These programs are called *organization development* (OD).

A number of other programs could be described. The ones that will be emphasized here are:[1]

---

[1]For more complete treatment of organization development, see Edgar Huse, *Organization Development and Change* (St. Paul: West Publishing, 1980); and Michael Beer, *Organization Change and Development* (Santa Monica, Calif: Goodyear Publishing, 1980).

- Behavioral modeling.
- Sensititivy training.
- Transactional analysis.
- Team building.
- The Managerial Grid.

In these programs various training techniques are used such as the case method, role playing, and in-baskets. These and other training techniques will be discussed in this chapter. Although this chapter indicates that all employees participate in development programs, most organizations focus primarily on the development of managerial and professional employees.

Approaches for Developing Managers

As mentioned in Chapter 9, the variables diagnosed for and the purposes of training and development programs are similar. The people involved in development programs are similar to those who supervise training, therefore, these sections of Chapter 9 will not be repeated here. It should be pointed out, however, that there is a somewhat greater tendency for firms to hire outside consultants and trainers to oversee development programs than is done for training programs.

Predecessors to Current Development Programs

The earliest programs designed to affect employee and managerial attitudes, called human relations programs, were oriented toward individual development. Human relations programs were an outgrowth of the human relations movement, which fostered consideration of the individual in the operation of industry in the 1930s to the 1950s. The rationale of the movement from the organization's point of view, was that an employee-centered, liberal supervisory style would lead to more satisfied employees. This in turn would reduce absenteeism, employee turnover, and strikes. Sometimes the style also increased performance. But, as was discussed in Chapter 2, effective performance has multiple causes, and supervisory attitudes and behavior are only one factor influencing it.

The effectiveness of these general human relations programs was measured by direct improvement in objectively measured results, such as a reduction in turnover. They were also called effective if they changed the attitudes of the managers in the direction desired or if the managers participating said the programs were worthwhile. In reviewing the evidence on the effectiveness of human relations programs; it has been determined that 80 percent of the programs evaluated had significant positive results, as measured by attitudes and opinions about these programs.[2]

Such positive results have encouraged organizations to continue to conduct interpersonal skills and attitude-change programs. A number of the training techniques are used in interpersonal skills and attitude-change programs. Those most frequently used are the case, role playing, in-basket, and management games techniques.[3]

---

[2]John P. Campbell, Marvin D. Dunnette, Edward E. Lawler, III, and Karl E. Weick, Jr., *Managerial Behavior, Performance, and Effectiveness*. (New York: McGraw-Hill, 1970).

[3]John P. Campbell, "Personnel Training and Development" in *Annual Review of Psychology*, (Palo Alto: Annual Reviews, 1971); and B. M. Bass and J. A. Vaughan, *Training in Industry* (Belmont, Calif.: Wadsworth, 1966).

The Case Method

One widely used technique is the case method. A case is a written description of a real decision-making situation in the organization or that occurred in another organization. Trainees are asked to study the case to determine the problems, analyze them for their significance, propose solutions, choose the best solution, and implement it. More learning takes place if there is interaction between the trainers and trainees as well as among trainees themselves.

The case method lends itself more to some kinds of material (business policy) than to well-structured material. It is easier to listen to a lecture and be given a formula than to tease the formula out of a case, for example. With proper trainers and good cases, the case method is a very effective device for improving and clarifying rational decision making.

Variations on the Case Method • One variation of the case method is the incident method. In the incident method, just the bare outlines of the situation are given initially, and the students are assigned a role in which to view the incident. Additional data are available if the students ask the right questions. Each student "solves" the case, and groups based on similarity of solutions are formed. Each group then formulates a strong statement of position, and the groups debate or role play their solutions. The instructor may describe what actually happened in the case and the consequences, and then everyone' compares their solutions with the results. The final step is for participants to try to apply this knowledge to their own job situations.

Role Playing

Role playing is a cross between the case method and an attitude development program. Each person being developed is assigned a role in a training situation (such as a case) and asked to play the role and to react to other players' role playing. The player is asked to pretend being a focal person in the situation and to react to the stimuli as that person would. The players are provided with background information on the situation and the players. There is usually a brief script provided to the participant. Sometimes the role plays are videotaped and reanalyzed as part of the development situation. Often role playing is done in trainee groups of a dozen or so persons. The success of this method depends on the ability of the players to play the assigned roles believably.

A comparison of the general forms of role playing and the case method suggest the following differences between the two:[4]

Case study	*Role playing*
1. Presents a problem for analysis and discussion.	1. Places the problem in a real-life situation.
2. Uses problems that have already occurred in the company or elsewhere.	2. Uses problems that are now current or are happening on the job.
3. Deals with problems involving others.	3. Deals with problems in which participants themselves are involved.
4. Deals with emotional and attitudinal aspects in an intellectual frame of reference.	4. Deals with emotional and attitudinal aspects in an experiential frame of reference.
5. Emphasis is on using facts and making assumptions.	5. Emphasis is on feelings.
6. Trains in the exercise of judgment.	6. Trains in emotional control.
7. Furnishes practice in analysis of problems.	7. Provides practice in interpersonal skills.

---

[4]A. R. Solem, "Human Relations Training: Comparison of Case Study and Role Playing," *Personnel Administrator*, (September/October 1960), pp. 29–37.

The In-Basket Technique

Another method used to develop managerial decision-making abilities is the in-basket technique. The participant is given a set of material (typically memos or descriptions of things to do) which includes typical items from a specific manager's mail and a telephone list. Important and pressing matters such as out-of-stock positions, customer complaints, or the demand for a report from a superior are mixed in with routine business matters such as a request to speak at a dinner or a decision on the date of the company picnic four weeks hence. The trainee is analyzed and critiqued on the number of decisions made in the time period allotted, the quality of decisions, and the priorities chosen for making them.

Management Games

Essentially, management games describe the operating characteristics of a company, industry, or enterprise. These descriptions take the form of equations which are manipulated after decisions have been made.

In a typical game procedure, teams of players are asked to make a series of operating (or top-management) decisions. In one business game, for example, the players are asked to decide on such matters as the price of the product, purchase of materials, production scheduling, funds borrowing, marketing, and R&D expenditures. When each player on the team has made a decision, the interactions of these decisions are computed (manually or by computer) in accordance with the model. For example, if price is linearly related to volume, a decrease in price of x percent will affect the volume, subject to general price levels. Players on the team first reconcile their individual decisions with those of the other team members prior to making a final decision. Then each team's decision is compared with those of the other teams. The result of that team's profit, market share, and so forth is compared and a winner or best team performance is determined.

Games are used to train managers in all sectors. Advantages of games include the integration of several interacting decisions, the ability to experiment with decisions, the provision of feedback experiences on decisions, and the requirement that decisions be made with inadequate data, which usually simulates reality. The main criticisms of most games concern their limitation of novelty or reactivity in decision making, the cost of development and administration, the unreality of some of the models, and the disturbing tendency of many participants to look for the key to win the game instead of concentrating on making good decisions. Many participants seem to feel the games are rigged, and a few factors or even a single factor may be the key to winning.

Which Methods and Approaches Should be Used?

This choice is made on the basis of the number of trainees for each program, the relative costs per trainee for each method, the availability of training materials in various forms (including the trainers' capabilities), and the employees' relative efficiency in learning. In general, it is true that the more active the trainee, the greater the motivation to learn. The probability of success is higher in that instance. If there are only a few trainers, individualized programmed instruction may be considered. If none of the trainers is capable of giving certain instructions, outside trainers may be contacted, or movies or videotapes might be used. Finally, the method used should reflect the degree of active participation desired for the program, as illustrated in Exhibit 10–1.

Inevitably, the question as to the effectiveness of each form of training must be answered. There are studies to support the effectiveness of all methods; if a method is appropriate for the particular program in question, it should be used.

Studies have been found the following training methods are used by larger companies with advanced P/HRM practices: 53 percent used the lecture method; 29 percent, the conference method; and 20 percent, programmed instruction.[5] One survey found that almost all organizations used lectures and conferences. Other techniques such as simulation, role playing, and programmed instruction were used by about 15 percent of the companies.[6]

Behavior modeling

A relatively new approach to training in interpersonal skills is behavior modeling, which is also called interaction management or imitating models.[7] In behavior modeling, as

Exhibit 10–1 _____

Roles of participants affected by different approaches

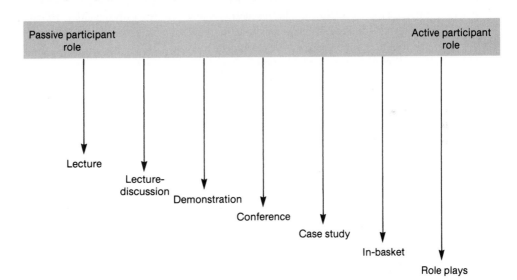

Source: From *Handbook of Creative Learning Exercises*, by Herbert M. Engel. Copyright © 1973 by Gulf Publishing Company, Houston, Texas. Used with permission. All rights reserved.

---

[5]NICB, *Office Personnel Practices* no. 197; *Personnel Practices in Factory and Office* (New York: The Conference Board, 1965).

[6]S. B. Utgaard and R. V. Davis, "The Most Frequently Used Training Techniques," *Training and Development Journal,* April 1970, pp. 40–43.

[7]See Allen Kraut, "Developing Managerial Skills Via Modeling Techniques: Some Positive Research Findings—A Symposium" (other articles in this series cover modeling), *Personnel Psychology,* Autumn 1976, pp. 325–61; and Gary Latham and Lise Saari, "Application of Social Learning Theory to Training Supervisors through Behavior Modeling," *Journal of Applied Psychology,* June 1979, pp. 239–46.

developed by Goldstein and Sorcher, the development model is as shown in Exhibit 10–2.[8] The key to behavior modeling is learning through observation or imagination. Thus, modeling is a "vicarious process" which emphasizes observation.

One behavior modeling approach begins by identifying 19 interpersonal problems that employees, especially managers face. Typical problems are gaining acceptance as a new supervisor, handling discrimination complaints, delegating responsibility, improving attendance, effective discipline, overcoming resistance to change, setting performance goals, motivating average performance, handling emotional situations, reducing tardiness, and taking corrective action.[9]

There are four steps in the process:

1. Modeling of effective behavior—often by use of films.
2. Role playing.
3. Social reinforcement—trainees and trainers praise effective role plays.
4. Transfer of training to the job.

A typical behavior modeling training module is shown in Exhibit 10–3. Modeling applies the principles of learning described in Chapter 9 to the development situation. Exhibit 10–4 shows how.

Behavior modeling has been introduced into a number of organizations including AT&T, General Electric, IBM, RCA, Boise Cascade, Kaiser Corporation, Olin, and B. F. Goodrich. So far, the research evidence is generally positive. In a series of studies, the groups trained in behavior modeling have outperformed those who received no training or traditional management development training.[10]

Another interesting program using behavior modeling was reported in a study conducted in the manufacturing operation of a major forest products company.[11] A training program was divided into seven weekly workshop sessions, each lasting about six hours. The sessions focused on a particular problem-solving situation such as dealing with a performance problem or motivating a subordinate.

Exhibit 10–2 _____

Model of behavior modeling training program

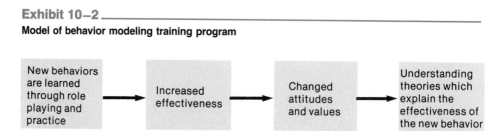

Source: From *Training: Program Development and Evaluation* by I. L. Goldstein. Copyright © 1974 by Wadsworth Publishing Company, Inc. Reprinted by permission of the publisher, Brooks/Cole Publishing Company, Monterey, California.

---

[8]A. P. Goldstein and M. Sorcher, *Changing Supervisory Behavior* (Elmsford, N.Y.: Pergamon Press, 1974).

[9]P. D. Johnson and M. Sorcher, "Behavior Modeling Training: Why, How, and What Results," *Journal of European Training,* No. 2, 1976, pp. 62–72.

[10]Charles C. Manz and Henry P. Sims, Jr., "Vicarious Learning: The Influence of Modeling on Organizational Behavior," *Academy of Management Review,* January 1981, pp. 105–14; and B. L. Rosenbaum, "New Uses of Behavior Modeling," *Personnel Administrator,* July 1978, pp. 27–28.

[11]Jerry I. Porras and Brad Anderson, "Improving Managerial Effectiveness through Modeling-Based Training," *Organizational Dynamics,* Spring 1981, pp. 60–77.

Exhibit 10–3

Behavior modeling

Administrator announces the interaction skill being considered and the supervisors read an overview of the interaction skill	5 minutes
Administrator describes critical steps in handling the interaction	5 minutes
Administrator shows a film or video tape of a supervisor effectively handling the interaction with an employee..	10 minutes
Administrator and supervisors discuss how the supervisor depicted handled the critical steps	5 minutes
Three supervisors take turns in skill practice exercises by handling similar situations with employees. Background information is provided the "supervisor" and "employee" in each skill practice exercise. The handling of the situations is observed by the other supervisors and the administrator using specially prepared Observer Guides. The use of positive reinforcement by the observers helps to build confidence and skill in skill-practicing supervisors	60 minutes
Supervisors write their own interaction situations based on job-related problems, using forms provided in workbooks	10 minutes
Supervisors take turns in skill practice sessions by becoming the "employee" in the participant-written situations, while other supervisors use the interaction skills to handle these situations. These skills practice exercises are also observed and discussed	60 minutes
Supervisors read a summary of the skill module. Using specially designed forms, they plan on-the-job applications of the interaction skills. The administrator hands out a Critical Steps card for supervisors to utilize on the job...	10 minutes

Source: William Byham and James Robinson, "Interaction Management: Supervisory Training That Changes Performance," *The Personnel Administrator,* February 1976.

The specific training approaches used were:

1. A conceptual lecture.
2. A videotape demonstration of the skills being taught.
3. A rehearsal period for practicing the behaviors.
4. A feedback and reinforcement period for refining the behaviors.

Exhibit 10–4

Learning theory principles applied to behavior modeling (conditions for effective learning)

Learning principles	*Behavior modeling method*
Principles whereby learner:	
Is motivated to improve	
Understands desired skills	Modeling
Actively participates ⎱	
Gets needed practice ⎰	Role playing
Gets feedback on performance ⎱	
Is reinforced for appropriate skills ⎰	Social reinforcement
Experiences well-organized training ⎱	
Simple to complex ⎬	Transfer of training
Easy to hard ⎰	
Undergoes training performance akin to job	

Source: Allen Kraut, "Developing Managerial Skills via Modeling Techniques," *Personnel Psychology* 29 (1976), pp. 325–28.

5. Participants entered into contracts and committed themselves to the newly acquired skills on the job.

6. A follow-up discussion on how things were going on the job.

These six phases were built into each workshop session. Each session covered critical incidents selected from a survey of all first-line supervisors in the company. The supervisors had been asked to identify the most difficult problems they faced in managing their subordinates.

The second phase of each session involved a modeled demonstration. The supervisors in the training program observed a videotape that depicted a company supervisor successfully employing skills to solve the problem. The videotaped model performed each step in solving the problem. As participants watched, they were asked to identify the steps being taken and make comments of it in their notebooks for future reference. After observing the models the participants rehearsed the skill in the classroom.

Improved supervisory behavior in dealing with 10 difficult problems led to improved performance on the job. Average daily production of trained supervisors versus controls increased. Furthermore, grievance rates decreased and absenteeism steadily declined. This behavior modeling program, then, has the kind of positive impact organizations desire.

Modeling offers a number of promising possibilities in organizations. One especially important need in organizations is to train and develop effective leaders. Modeling appears to be a useful technique for leadership training especially if used in conjunction with videotape methods.[12] The leadership training participants could view their style, behaviors, strengths, and weaknesses and learn from this personal, first-hand view. Seeing oneself in action is a vivid reminder that we can all benefit from training and practice.

The other approach to making this decision is to evaluate a method or approach after it is used. These evaluations are kept and become an input to future decisions. Evaluation, the last phase of training and development is discussed later in this chapter.

The Nature of Management Development

In Chapter 9 we primarily discussed training employees in the skills they need to effectively perform their job. The present chapter is more concerned with the development of human resources. That is, the focus is on developing employees for future tasks, responsibilities, and assignments. The P/HRM department is involved in both the training and development of employees. Conducting training and development requires diagnosis, and involves scheduling training and development sessions, selecting participants, obtaining instructors, and evaluating the training and development efforts all part of the P/HRM specialist's job.

The line manager also is involved in development planning and implementation activities. He or she is often involved in the actual development and training sessions with the specialist. The line manager also selects participants and makes suggestions about areas in which development is needed.

---

[12]Henry P. Sims, Jr. and Charles C. Manz, "Modeling Influences on Employee Behavior," *Personnel Journal,* January 1982, pp. 58–65.

Each of the techniques just mentioned—the case method, role playing, the in-basket technique, and management games—are classroom practices used in both skills training and development programs. In addition to these popular methods behavior modeling has become widely used.

Organization Development: An Overview

Organizations and their environments are dynamic and constantly changing. New technologies are developed, competitors enter and leave markets, inflation increases, and productivity fluctuates. These are the kind of changes that managers in general and specifically P/HRM managers face. Organizational development (OD) is an approach to change that involves the continuing development of human resources. It is a newly emerging area of study directed toward using behavioral science knowledge to deal with problems of change. There is still no definition of organization development that is universally accepted. Perhaps the most quoted definition of OD is that it is:

> . . . an effort *(a)* planned, *(b)*, organizationwide, *(c)* managed from the top, to *(d)* increase organization effectiveness, and health through *(e)* planned intervention in the organization's "processes" using behavioral science knowledge.[13]

According to this definition, OD is planned, since it requires systematic diagnosis, development of a program, and the mobilization of resources (e.g., trainers, participants, teaching aids). It involves either the entire system or an entire unit. It must have top-management commitment if it is to be a success. The definition also suggests that OD is not a specific technique such as behavior modeling, transactional analysis, or sensitivity training. These techniques and others often are part of an OD effort, but they are used only after their relevance and utility is demonstrated by a careful diagnosis.

The Importance of Diagnosis: OD's Base

An important characteristic of any OD intervention is that is should follow diagnosis.[14] A manager's perception of a problem is not a sufficient reason to implement a technique such as behavior modeling. Only after data are collected in a scientific way through interviews, observation, questionnaire, and/or checks of records should a planned OD intervention be considered and selected. Exhibit 10–5 presents the diagnosis phase of OD in a schematic diagram.

The collection of diagnostic data is considered to be a part of the action research orientation of OD.[15] Action research involves seven main steps:

1. Problem identification.
2. Consultation among experts in change and OD. This could involve hired consultants, P/HRM specialists, and senior executives.

---

[13]This definition was originally developed by R. Beckhard, *Organization Development: Strategies and Models* (Reading, Mass.: Addison-Wesley Publishing, 1969, p. 16.

[14]David Nadler, *Feedback and Organization Development: Using Data-Based Methods* (Reading, Mass.: Addison-Wesley Publishing 1977, pp. 34–40.

[15]Peter A. Clark, *Action Research and Organizational Change,* (New York: Harper & Row, 1972).

Exhibit 10–5

Diagnosis steps in OD programs

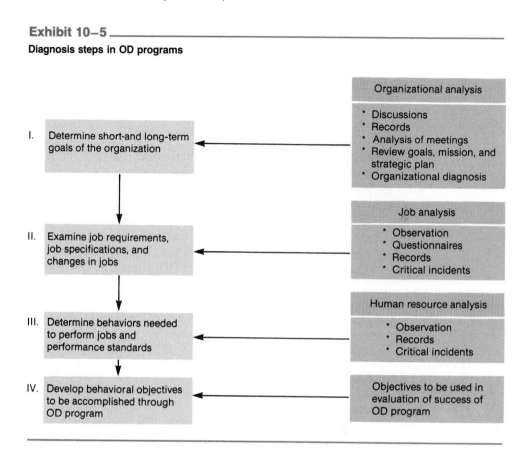

3. Data collection and diagnosis.
4. Feedback of findings to key people.
5. Group discussion of the diagnostic data and findings.
6. Action. The adoption of techniques such as sensitivity training, transactional analysis, and team building.
7. Evaluation of the action steps taken in Step 6.

The P/HRM department of specialists may be involved in any or all of these seven action research steps. For purposes in this book the action step is extremely important for developing human resources; it involves determining which planned interventions or techniques are available for use as part of OD programs.

OD: Individual and Interpersonal Techniques

One way to classify OD techniques is on the basis of the target area they are intended to affect. There are four target areas: individual, interpersonal, group, and organizational. Sensitivity training or T group training is designed to improve the awareness of individuals. Transactional analysis is suppose to help people understand the principles of trans-

P/HRM Manager Close-Up

J. William Streidl
Tenneco Inc.

Biography

J. William Streidl is director of management education and development for Tenneco Inc. in Houston, Texas. After receiving his B.S. degree from the School of Natural Resources at the University of Michigan, Streidl worked for a short time as an industrial engineer for the Hamilton Manufacturing Company. He served as an army officer in Korea and returned to the University of Michigan where he received his M.B.A. degree majoring in personnel and industrial management.

Streidl joined the Filer City, Michigan Paper Mill of Packaging Corporation of America (a Tenneco company) as an employment supervisor in 1955. He moved through various personnel, labor relations, training, and organization, planning and development assignments until becoming director of manpower planning and development for Packaging Corporation in 1967. He was promoted and transferred to the corporate staff of Tenneco Inc. in 1975.

Job description

J. W. Streidl, as director of management education and development for Tenneco Inc. He directs the activities of the professional staff which carries out formal management education and development programs for all Tenneco companies on an international basis. In addition, he assures the effective use of university level executive development programs and assures that enrollments in such programs are related to corporate executive resource plans.

Views about personnel development— J. William Streidl

The human assets of any organization can appreciate rather than depreciate over a period of time if the organization provides the environment and resources for such appreciation to occur.

This "personal growth environment" depends upon:

- The individual employee who must be personally concerned with self-development.
- The employee's immediate supervisor who must assure that the job environment sustains and reinforces the employee's self-development efforts.
- The resources provided by the organization as a whole. These resources in larger organizations are typically assigned to the education and development staff.

Tenneco's management education and development staff provides formal programs which are designed to accelerate the acquisition of participant's management concepts and skills so they can perform more effectively on their current or future jobs. Our management course participants come from almost all of the United States and many countries of the free world. They represent many different industries, organizational levels, and national cultures because of the diversity of Tenneco's companies and their operations. It is a challenge to provide meaningful and helpful programs which provides the opportunity for continual personal development for those who participate.

Tenneco's management firmly believes that we will be successful as long as we provide such opportunities for human resource development on a continuing basis.

actions with others so that more meaningful interpersonal interactions occur. Team building which focuses on the group and the grid which addresses the organization as a target will be covered in the next sections.

Sensitivity Training

The first sensitivity training course was held in 1946 in New Britain, Connecticut. Since this beginning it has been used by psychotherapists, counselors, trainers, and P/HRM specialists.[16] Overall sensitivity training focuses on:

- Making participants aware of and sensitive to the emotional reactions and expressions in themselves and others.
- Increasing the ability of participants to perceive, and to learn from, the consequences of their actions through increased attention to their own and other's feelings.

The Group • The sensitivity group process varies from trainer to trainer. However, a typical meeting involves a group of 10 to 12 people, meeting away from the job.[17] The emphasis is on: "How do you feel right now?" "What do you feel about others in the group?" "What will it take to make you feel better?" There is little structure imposed by the trainer on the group. Each group member is encouraged to say what he or she is thinking and how they see others in the group.

Because of its nature, the sensitivity training group is a controversial OD technique. Some believe that it is unethical, impractical, and dangerous.[18] However, some research suggests that sensitivity training can change participant behavior. Participants can increase their sensitivity when working with other people. Furthermore, a few studies indicate that sensitivity training can improve organizational performance. It has, however, been shown that sensitivity training can increase the anxiety levels of some participants.[19]

A survey of personnel directors of large firms found that about twice as many respondents indicated a negative response toward the use of sensitivity training as those who said they would recommend it.[20] These directors may be listening more closely to the critics than to some of the supportive research results. Two things are certain about sensitivity training; only qualified trainers should be used, and only employees who volunteer to participate should attend this type of training program.

Transactional Analysis

Transactional analysis, or TA, is not really accepted by most OD experts as a full-fledged technique to use in developing human resources. Instead, TA is considered as a useful tool or technique to help people better understand themselves.

---

[16]Leland Bradford, Jack R. Gibbs, and Kenneth Benne, eds., *T-Group Theory and Laboratory Method* (New York: John Wiley, & Sons, 1964).

[17]K. Back, *Beyond Words: The Story of Sensitivity Training and the Encounter Movement* (New York: Russell Sage Foundation, 1972).

[18]George Odiorne, "The Trouble with Sensitivity Training," *Training Directors Journal,* October 1963, pp 19–37.

[19]Robert J. House, "T-Group Training: Good or Bad?" *Business Horizons,* December 1969, pp. 69–77.

[20]William J. Kearney and Desmond D. Martin, "Sensitivity Training: An Established Management Development Tool?" *Academy of Management Journal,* December 1974, pp. 755–60.

Eric Berne is usually credited with starting the interest in TA with his book, *Games People Play.*[21] TA remains popular today and is not just a fad, perhaps because it is based on the psychoanalytic theories of Freud.[22] Three important ego states are used in TA: child, adult, and parent.

Child State • This is the state where a person acts as an impulsive child. Immature behavior is displayed. An example would be an employee who, when reprimanded by a boss even after doing a good job, throws a temper tantrum and shouts, cusses, and screams about the unfairness of the system.

Adult State • In this state the person acts like a mature adult. The adult state person is fair, objective, and careful in what he or she does. An example would be a manager who in reviewing the production record of a subordinate states, ''Well output is down a little, but we can look at it together and see what went wrong—was it equipment, not enough help, or poor quality parts?''

Parent State • In this state people act like domineering and nagging parents. They are critical and all knowing in their interactions often talking down to others. A manager who states, ''You shouldn't horse around because we are paying you to put in a fair day's work, not to play.''

Generally people exhibit all three ego states, but one often dominates the other two. The emphasis in TA development training seminars or courses is on encouraging participants to engage in *adult state behaviors*. It is this state that leads to effective interpersonal relations. A TA training program emphasizes the analysis of the transactions between people. It is these interactions of ego states that can significantly influence behavior.

Exhibit 10–6 shows effective interaction between a P/HRM manager and a subordinate. The two ego states involved are adult to adult. The two parties are communicating at the same ego state.

Exhibit 10–6

Effective interaction

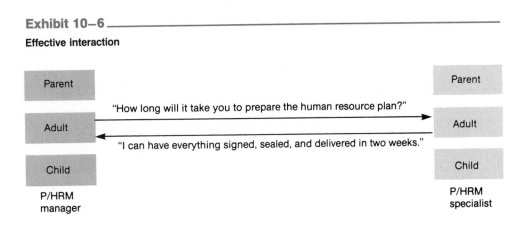

---

[21]Eric Berne, *Games People Play* (New York: Ballantine Books, 1964).

[22]Sigmund Freud, ''Psychopathology of Everyday Life,'' *The Standard Edition of the Complete Psychology Works of Sigmund Freud,* ed. J. Strackey (London: Hogarth Press, 1960).

Exhibit 10–7

Impaired interaction

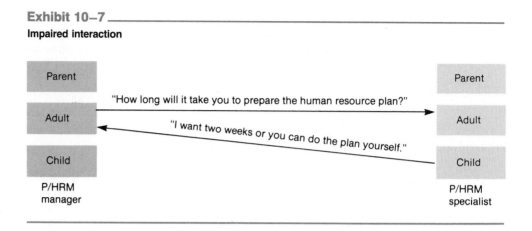

A different kind of interaction is displayed in Exhibit 10–7. The P/HRM manager speaks as an adult, but the specialist replies as a child. This weakens the communication between the two.

In Exhibit 10–8 there is a breakdown in interaction. The adult P/HRM manager speaks to the adult in the specialist. However, the child in the specialist replies to the parent in the P/HRM manager.

Two other concepts in TA are strokes and games. *Strokes* mean that people need cuddling, affection, recognition, and praise. Strokes can be viewed as reinforcers. A "Good morning," a "Hello," or a "How are you doing?" from a boss may be a positive stroke which helps interactions.[23]

TA is also concerned with games people play. A game is a superficial set of transactions. The outcome of games is that one person wins and another loses. Some of the frequently played games are presented in Exhibit 10–9.

When used as an OD technique, TA training is designed to develop more adult states in people so that effective interactions occur. To date few studies have been reported on

Exhibit 10–8

A breakdown in interaction

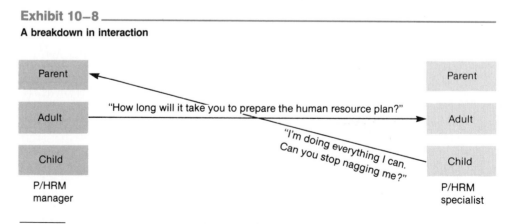

---

[23]Dorothy Jongerward and Philip Seyen, *Choosing Success* (New York: John Wiley & Sons, 1978).

Exhibit 10–9 _____
Games people play in organizations

Name of game	*Brief description of game*
1. Now I've Got You, You S.O.B. (N.I.G.Y.Y.S.O.B.)	One employee gets back at another by luring her into what appears to be a natural work relationship. Actually the situation is rigged so that the other will fail. When the inevitable mistake is made, the game player pounces on the associate and publicly embarrasses her.
2. Poor Me	The person depicts himself to the boss as helpless. Criticisms for inadequate performance are avoided because the boss truly feels sorry for the individual, who may actually begin to feel sorry for himself.
3. Blemish	The boss appears to be objectively evaluating an employee's total performance. In reality, the boss is looking for some minor error. When the error is found, the employee is berated for the poor performance, the inference being that the whole project/task/report is inadequate.
4. Hero	The boss consistently sets up situations where employees fail. At some point, the boss steps in to save the day miraculously.
5. King of the Hill	The boss sets up situations where employees end up in direct competiton with her. At the end, she steps in and demonstrates her competence and superiority while publicly embarrassing her employees.
6. Cops and Robbers	An employee continuously walks a fine line between acceptable and unacceptable behavior. The boss wastes unnecessary time desperately trying to catch the employee, while the employee stays one step ahead and laughs to himself through the day.
7. Prosecutor	The employee carefully carries around a copy of the union contract or organization regulations and investigates management practices. This employee dares the boss to act in an arbitrary manner. Once he does, the employee files a grievance and attempts to embarrass the boss.
8. If It Weren't for You . . .	The employee discusses her problems openly but carefully works the conversation around so that she can rationalize her failure by blaming the boss for everything that goes wrong.
9. Yes, but . . .	In this game the boss responds with "Yes, but . . ." to every good answer or idea that the subordinate may have. By doing this the boss can maintain a superior position and keep subordinates in their place. It represents a form of pseudoparticipation; that is, the boss asks for participation but answers every suggestion with "Yes, but . . ."

Source: Adapted from Fred Luthans and Mark J. Martinko, *The Practice of Supervision and Management*. Copyright © 1979 McGraw-Hill, pp. 386 –87, which in turn is adapted from the literature on transactional analysis. Used with the permission of McGraw-Hill Book Company.

_____

the scientific analysis of TA interventions.[24] Instead, testimony of TA consultants dominates the literature supporting this approach. Until more rigorous research is conducted on the effectiveness of TA as an OD tool, P/HRM managers and specialists must cautiously consider its relative value for their situation or problem.

OD: A Group Technique

There are numerous OD techniques that focus on improving the effectiveness of groups (the target), such as process consultation, survey feedback, and team building. In order to understand more fully these types of techniques, team building is presented.

_____

[24]Donald D. Bowen and Rayhu Nath, "Transactional Analysis in OD: Applications within the NTL Model," *Academy of Management Review*, January 1978, pp. 86–87.

Team Building

Any organization depends on the cooperation of a number of people if it is to be successful. Consequently, teams of people have to work on a temporary or permanent basis in harmony.[25] Task forces, committees, project teams, or interdepartmental groups are the kind of teams that are frequently brought together.

In one organization, team building followed this pattern:[26]

1. *A team skills workshop*. Production teams in the firm went through a 2 ½ day workshop working on various experiential exercises.
2. *Data collected*. Attitude and job data were collected from all teams (individual members).
3. *Data confrontation*. Consultants presented data to teams. It was discussed and problem areas sorted out. Priorities were also established by each team.
4. *Action planning*. Teams developed their own tentative plans to solve problems.
5. *Team building*. The teams finalized plans to solve all the problems identified in Step 4 and to consider barriers to overcome.
6. *Intergroup team building*. The groups that were interdependent met for two days to establish a collaborate plan.

The advantages of team building is that participation is encouraged and sustained. There also can be improved communication and problem solving within and between teams. Team building has proven to be successful especially when the technique is tailored to fit the needs and problems of the groups involved.

OD: An Organizationwide Technique

By "organizationwide," OD experts mean the total system is involved or that a clearly identifiable unit, department, or plant is the target. The independence of the identifiable system or subsystem is extremely important when using an organizationwide technique.

Grid OD

One of the most publicized programs in OD was first introduced and researched by Blake and Mouton and is called the Managerial Grid®[27] It consists of six phases directed toward enhancing organizational performance. The completion of the six-phase Grid program would cover a period of three to five years.

The Grid OD program is built upon a framework for understanding leadership styles of managers, as presented in Exhibit 10–10. The Grid depicts five different patterns of leadership, although 81 cells represent the two leadership concerns, production and people. Each person completes a questionnaire resulting in a determination of their leadership

---

[25]W. G. Dyer, *Team Building: Issues and Alternatives* (Reading, Mass.: Addison-Wesley Publishing, 1977).

[26]Warren R. Nielsen and John R. Kimberly, "The Impact of Organizational Development on the Quality of Organizational Output," *Academy of Management Proceedings*, 1973, pp. 528–29.

[27]Robert R. Blake and Jane S. Mouton, *The Managerial Grid* (Houston: Gulf Publishing, 1964); and Robert R. Blake and Jane S. Mouton, *The New Management Grid* (Houston: Gulf Publishing, 1978).

style. Blake and Mouton propose that the best way to lead is to be a 9, 9—which typifies high concern for both production and people.

The specific objectives of a Grid OD program are to:

- Study the organization as an interacting system and apply techniques of analysis in diagnosing problems.
- Understand the rationale of systematic change.
- Gain insight into the strategies of Grid OD for increasing performance.
- Examine the documents and forms used in different phases and simulate their application to the participant's own situation.
- Evaluate the styles of leadership and techniques of participation most likely to produce high-quality results.
- Assess the effort and expense required and risks involved relative to the potential of increased profit and human effectiveness.[28]

Exhibit 10–10

The Managerial Grid®

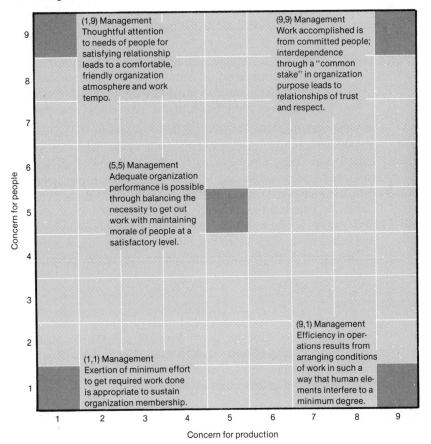

Source: Robert R. Blake and Jane S. Mouton, *The Managerial Grid* (Houston: Gulf Publishing, 1964), p. 10.

---

[28]Brochure from Scientific Methods, Inc., Austin, Texas.

These objectives are accomplished according to Blake and Mouton, by following the six-phase program.[29]

Phase I: *Study of the Grid.* Concepts about the various leadership styles are taught. The participants' styles are evaluated and reviewed. 50 hours of problem-solving tasks and exercises are completed.

Phase II: *Team Development.* Participants spend time analyzing their leadership styles and group skills. The key objective in the first two phases is to build trust and respect within the teams.

Phase III: *Intergroup Development.* Emphasis is on intergroup relationships. Joint problem solving is used in simulated situations.

Phase IV: *Developing an Organization Model.* The emphasis is on the importance of strategic planning and to bring together top-and lower management groups. Linking the top and lower levels by establishing a framework is one result of this phase.

Phase V: *Implementing the Model.* Groups are given tasks to implement the Phase IV developed model. Structural, process, and personnel plans are established to use the model.

Phase VI: *Evaluation.* The evaluation of the overall Grid is part of this phase. Modifications are made and a critique of the program is also part of this final phase. A standardized 100-item questionnaire is part of the evaluation in order to examine such areas as individual behavior, teamwork, intergroup relations, problem solving, and corporate strategy.

The Grid has been adopted totally or in part by thousands of organizations. Almost 20,000 persons have participated in public Grids, while an additional 200,000 have attended in-company Grid sessions.[30] A large amount of the support for Grid OD comes from its founders, Blake and Mouton.[31] However, a comprehensive review of OD does give some support to Blake and Mouton's claims.[32] It has been found to have a positive impact on intergroup relationship and teamwork as well as on performance and satisfaction. But, as is true with most training and development techniques, Grid OD needs to be researched more. This means that P/HRM managers considering the use of Grid OD must cautiously weigh the potential costs and benefits of this extremely popular technique.

Evaluation of Training and Development

In Chapter 9, the problem Gwen Meridith and Harold Matthews faced was deciding whether the training offered was effective. They had not designed a formal evaluation of the training program. This is also an issue in the current development program Gwen is proposing. This section focuses on that issue.

---

[29]A summary is provided in Robert R. Blake and Jane S. Mouton, "An Overview of the Grid," *Training and Development Journal,* May 1975, pp. 29–37.

[30]"Using the Managerial Grid to Ensure MBO," *Organizational Dynamics,* Spring 1974, p. 55.

[31]Fred Luthans, *Organizational Behavior* (New York: McGraw-Hill, 1981), p. 618.

[32]Jerry Porras and P. O. Berg, "The Impact of Organizational Development," *Academy of Management Review,* April 1978, pp. 259–60.

Recall that evaluation of training is the final phase of the training and development program. Cost/benefit analysis generally is more feasible for training and development than for many other P/HRM functions. Costs are relatively easy to compute: they equal direct costs of training (trainer cost, materials costs, and lost productivity, if it is done on company time) and indirect costs (a fair share of administrative overhead of the P/HRM department).

Essentially, the evaluation should be made by comparing the results (the benefits) with the objectives of the training and development program which were set in the assessment phase. It is easier to evaluate the results of some training programs (e.g., typing) than others (e.g., decision making and leadership). The criteria used to evaluate training and development depend on the objectives of the program and who sets the criteria: management, the trainers, or the trainees. For example, one study found that trainees who were asked to develop their own evaluative criteria chose standards which varied from knowledge of the subject to the amount of socializing allowed during training sessions.[33]

There are three types of criteria for evaluating training: internal, external, and participant reaction. *Internal criteria* are directly associated with the content of the program—for example, did the employee learn the facts or guidelines covered in the training program. *External criteria* are related more to the ultimate purpose of training—for example, improving the effectiveness of the employee. Possible external criteria include job performance rating, increases in sales volume, or decreases in turnover. *Participant reaction,* or how the subjects feel about the benefits of a specific training or development experience, is commonly used as an internal criterion.

Most experts argue that it is more effective to use multiple criteria to evaluate training.[34] Others contend that a single criterion, such as the extent of transfer of training to on-the-job performance or other aspects of performance, is a satisfactory evaluation approach.

One design for a multiple-criterion evaluation system was developed by Kirkpatrick.[35] He suggests measuring the following:

Participant Reaction. Whether subjects like or dislike the program.

Learning. Extent to which the subjects have assimilated the training program.

Behavior. An external measure of changes or lack of changes in job behavior.

Results. Effect of the program on organizational dimensions such as employee turnover or productivity.

At present, most firms assess reaction, but very few measure behavioral results.

A number of evaluation instruments and methods can be used to measure results of training and development (see the box). Data that can be used for evaluation include information on the trainee in the program; the trainee's immediate superiors and superiors above immediate supervisors; the trainee's subordinates (where applicable); nonpartici-

---

[33]Jack Retting and Matt Amano, "A Survey of ASPA Experience with Management by Objectives, Sensitivity Training, and Transactional Analysis," *Personnel Journal,* January 1976, pp. 26–29.

[34]Karen Brethower and Gary Rummler, "Evaluating Training," *Training and Development Journal,* May 1979, pp. 12–15.

[35]Donald L. Kirkpatrick, ed., *Evaluating Training Programs* (Madison, Wis.: American Society for Training and Development, 1975).

Evaluation Methods for Training and Develoment Programs:

Company Records. Either existing records or those devised for the evaluation of training or development, used to measure production turnover, grievances, absenteeism, and so on.

Observational Techniques. Interviewing, field observation, and other methods to evaluate skills, ability, communication, and productivity.

Critical Incidents. Using crucial incidents that occur on the job.

Ratings. Judgments of ability, performance, or ratings of satisfaction with various factors.

Questionnaires. A variety of types to measure decision making, problem solving, attitudes, values, personality, perceptions, and so on.

Tests. Written examinations or performance tests to measure changes in ability or knowledge.

pants from the work setting, including the subject's peers; company records; and nonparticipants from outside the work setting who might be affected by the program (e.g., clients).

One useful device to address the evaluation issue is to work with a systematic evaluation matrix. A matrix, because of its organization can help those involved with training and development programs to systematically review relevant issues or questions. Exhibit 10–11 presents such a matrix that could be used as a guideline for evaluating any of the programs and techniques covered in Chapters 9 and 10.

The relevant issues, skill improvement, training and development materials, costs, and long-term effects, are crucial questions that can be answered by use of evaluation. It is important to understand that the issues and questions provide only the direction which evaluation can take. The actual design and data collection of the evaluation phase of training and development requires following the scientific method as used by behavioral scientists. Simply asking participants if they liked the program after attending a sensitivity group or a behavioral modeling session is not very scientific. What would you expect to be the answer? Certainly, most of us like new experiences, new ideas. However, this does not mean that a program is good or beneficial for improving performance or increasing interpersonal skills on the job.

Someone in authority (usually someone above the P/HRM specialist involved in the training or development such as a director of human resources or vice president of operations) must hold the trainers and developers of people accountable. The efficient use of people, dollars, and facilities must be clearly shown. This can only be done if the evaluation phase is completed and sound research designs are used. Evaluation is certainly not easy, but it is a necessary and often glossed over part of training and development.[36]

In sum, formal training has been shown to be more effective than informal training or no training. But the results tend to be assumed rather than evaluated for most training and development programs.

---

[36]For an interesting view of one of the pioneers of OD, see "A Dialogue with Warren Bennis," *Training and Development Journal*, April 1981, pp. 19–26.

Exhibit 10–11

An evaluation matrix: Issues to consider

The relevant issues to cover and evaluate	Examples of what to measure	What to examine for answers?	How to collect data to answer issue questions?
1. Are the participants learning, changing attitudes, and/or improving skills?	Participants' attitudes and/or skills before and after (even during training or development sessions)	Comments Method of participation Co-workers Superiors	Interview Questionnaires Records Observation
2. Are the training or development materials used on the job?	Participants on-the-job performance, behavior, and style	Subordinate performance, attitudes, and style	Records Interview Questionnaires Critical incidents Observation
3. What are the costs of training and development programs and techniques?	The fixed and variable costs of conducting the training or development	Cost of trainers Participant time Travel expenses Consultant fees Training aids Rent Utilities	Budget records
4. How long does the training or development have an effect on participants?	Participants on-the-job performance, behavior, and style over an extended period of time.	Subordinate performance, attitudes, and style	Records Interview Questionnaires Critical incidents Observation (collected a number of times)

Summary

This chapter has introduced the important areas of the development of human resources and the evaluation of training and development programs. In summary, the following points were made:

1. Managment development is the process by which managers gain the experience, skills, and attitudes to become or remain successful leaders in their organizations.
2. Management and professional development is designed to reduce obsolescence and to increase employee satisfaction and productivity.
3. Methods which can be used to modify employee and managerial attitudes and interpersonal skills include behavior modeling, sensitivity training, transactional analysis, and team building.
4. An organizationwide OD program of great popularlity is the Managerial Grid which was first introduced by Blake and Mouton.
5. Organization development programs such as the Grid overlap the other methods. It seeks to change attitudes, values, organization structure, and managerial practices to improve performance.
6. The final phase of any training and development program is evaluation. It is unfortunately often bypassed by organizations.

Exhibit 10–12 provides some recommendations for the use of various OD programs and techniques for the model organization.

Exhibit 10–12 _____

Recommendations for use of OD in model organizations

	Types of OD				
Type of organization	Behavior modeling	Sensitivity training	Transactional analysis	Team building	Grid OD
1. Large size, low complexity, high stability		X	X		
2. Medium size, low complexity, high stability		X	X		
3. Small size, low complexity, high stability			X		
4. Medium size, moderate complexity, moderate stability	X	X	X	X	X
5. Large size, high complexity, low stability	X	X	X	X	X
6. Medium size, high complexity, low stability	X	X	X	X	X
7. Small size, high complexity, low stability	X		X	X	

Case

After absorbing the material Bob has brought her, Gwen approaches Lester Young, Young Enterprise's president on an informal basis.

Gwen You know, Les, our last attitude survey indicated major dissatisfaction with our development program at Young. We've been doing some research in our shop about development programs. I'm sure I couldn't work it into this year's budget. But we're only six weeks away from the new budget time. I feel it is very important at this time. As you know, we were not completely satisfied with the training program on the new machinery. In addition, one or two or our supervisors have come in to complain about the lack of any organization development program for them. How would you like us to proceed?

Lester I have heard some talk about OD at a recent American Manufacturers Association meeting. I hear its quite costly. We may have some problems in this area, but we're in no position to make a major investment in development at the present time in view of our earnings situation. Why not work up a modest program for presentation to the budget and goals meeting six weeks from now—no more than 5 percent of your current budget as an increment.

Gwen Will do, Les.

Gwen and Bob put together a proposal which they viewed as Phase 1. They proposed a supervisory development program with some help from the P/HRM department for one half of 1 percent of current budget.

After investigating the potential costs of an OD consultant, they felt they should begin to move in the development area. They proposed some beginning funds for planning an OD program, the first phase of which would involve initial diagnosis and small sample data collection. They proposed to set up an experiment using a behavior-modeling program in one unit for supervisory style, with a control group. Evaluation procedures were to be formal. They specified desired outputs: better readings from the attitude survey, some improvements in turnover and absenteeism, and some results in the productivity problem.

Lester and the budget and goals committee accepted the proposal. Phase 1 began, and it was successful. Little by little, the company accepted a development program. The results were encouraging to all—Lester, Gwen, Bob, Harold, and Sally.

Questions for Review and Discussion

1. Describe the characteristics of a few OD programs designed to improve interpersonal skills and affect attitudes. Describe the ones you'd like to participate in.
2. What is organization development?
3. Under what conditions is organizational development effective?
4. Why do you think that many organizations fail to evaluate their training and development programs?
5. Why do you think that TA is such a popular technique?
6. What type of organization would implement a full-fledged Grid OD program?
7. What skills would be needed to conduct a good evaluation program?
8. Why would some people be frightened by the prospect of being required by their organization to attend a sensitivity training program?
9. Why would an organization enter into attitude-change and interpersonal skills training programs?

10. The predecessor of current development programs was called human relations programs. What was the major emphasis of these programs, and how effective were they?

Glossary

Behavior modeling. Participants learn by observing a role model behavior. The fundamental characteristic modeling is that learning takes place by observation or imagination of another individual's experience.

Case method. A training technique in which a description (a case) of a real situation is analyzed by participants. The interaction of the participants and trainer is valuable in improving the degree of learning that occurs.

Grid OD. A program that involves six phases that is designed to improve organizational performance. The phases include determining the participants' leadership styles, team building, intergroup development, and evaluation.

Role Playing. The acting out of a role by participants. Participants play act a role which others in the training session observe. Participants play an active part in role plays.

Sensitivity Training. A training technique that was first used in 1946. In it small groups of participants focus on emotions and how they feel about themselves and the group. Usually little structure is imposed by the trainer. The group members are encouraged to say or do what they feel.

Team Building. A development method that attempts to improve the cooperation between teams.

Transaction Analysis. A training technique that is designed to help the people participating better understand their own ego states and those of others; to understand the principles behind transactions; and to interact with others in a more comfortable way.

Chapter Eleven

Career Planning and Development

Learning Objectives

After studying this chapter, you should be able to:

- Define what is meant by the term *career*.

- Describe some of the problems faced by recent hirees, midcareer managers, and preretirement employees.

- Explain why organizations need to be concerned about dual careers.

- Discuss how career pathing can be used within an organization.

- State how career planning is done in organizations.

Chapter Outline

Case

Jim Lucio and Norbert Wislinski

Jim Lucio was a 50-year-old executive with Neal Engineering Construction Company in Katy, Texas, a suburb of Houston. Despite his age, his professional engineering training, and his good position, he was having an identity problem. The recent conversation between Jim and Norbert Wislinski, his boss, indicates a midcareer concern.

Norb Jim, you're really moving on the south Texas project. Costs are under control and you've been able to control Tony (the chief engineer).

Jim To be honest, Norb, I'm sick of the project, Tony, and everything about the job. I can't sleep, eat, or relax.

Norb I'm sorry to hear that. Do you need some time off?

Jim No. I need to rethink my whole career. I've just lost my intensity. It hasn't been sudden. Been growing over the last year.

Norb You know I'll do anything I can to help you. You're what made this company a success.

Jim Thanks. But I have to really do some soul-searching. I've always wanted to own my own business, be my own boss. I just haven't been brave enough to take the plunge.

Norb Jim, you know I'm selfish. I need you here at Neal, but if you make the break I'll help you any way I can.

Jim Thanks again, Norb. I have to think more about this. It is a whole career change. Serious business for a 50-year-old engineer.

Organizational change and growth require managers to pay attention to developing people and placing them in key positions. Organizational growth through expansion, mergers, and acquisitions creates new management positions and changes the responsibilities of exising positions. Capable people must be available to fill the new and bigger jobs. Moreover, the contemporary concern for developing the full potential of all employees through job opportunities which provide responsibility, advancement, and challenging work reinforces such efforts. Even organizations facing a stable or a contracting future recognize that a key to performance is the development of human resources.

As organizations change, so do their employees. For example, a recently hired P/HRM manager has different needs and aspirations than does the midcareer or the preretirement P/HRM manager. All of us move through a fairly uniform pattern of phases during our careers. The different phases produce different opportunities and stresses which affect job performance. Effective managers comprehend these implications and facilitate the efforts of employees who wish to confront and deal with their career and life needs.

Finally, it should be noted that managers should be concerned with their own career development. By their nature, managers are likely to be concerned with their career goals and with the paths that are most likely to lead to those goals. Yet managers often lack the ability and the information that are needed to develop their career plans in systematic and explicit ways. But we see more and more evidence of growing interest in providing individuals with information that will help them to identify their goals and to understand what they should do to reach them.

Jim Lucio has changed and now he is trying to cope with his thoughts and feelings. This is a difficult time in Jim's life. He seems to have it all, but something is missing. He is not satisfied. Norb is an understanding manager who also seems to realize that Jim Lucio is at a midcareer point in life and wants to make a change.

In this chapter we will review a number of programs which organizations and managers can use to plan and develop careers. Some of these programs have been used in management for many years to identify and select promising managerial talent. For example, assessment centers and performance appraisal programs have long been used to develop managers, though the traditional emphasis of these programs have been placed on the satisfaction of organizational needs. More recently, the programs have been revised to include the consideration of employee needs as well.

A Diagnostic Approach to Career Planning and Development

Exhibit 11–1 highlights the diagnostic factors most important to career planning and development as a P/HRM activity. People have always had careers, but only recently has serious P/HRM attention been directed to the way careers develop and the type of planning that is needed to achieve career satisfaction. The key to the diagnostic factors influencing careers is not in the person, external environmental influences, or the internal influences themselves, but rather the ways in which these major factors interact.

Certainly careers do not just happen in isolation from environmental and personal factors. Every person's career goes through a series of stages. Each of these stages may or may not be influenced by attitudes, motivation, the nature of the task, economic conditions, and so forth. Those in P/HRM must be sensitive to the "career cycle" and the role that different influences such as those shown in Exhibit 11–1 can play at different points.

An adequate matching of individual needs, abilities, preferences, and motivation and organizational opportunities will not just happen. Individuals, organizations, and experts in areas such as P/HRM all must take responsibility for things they can control. For example, organizations and P/HRM must know what the needs of employees are. On the other hand, employees must have a clear picture of the opportunities available now and anticipated in the future. Organizations should not guess or assume some set of career needs. Likewise employees should not have to guess how career development occurs in the "the organization." A sharing of information, and understanding of the "career stage," and concern about the kind of forces highlighted in Exhibit 11–1 must be established as part of an ongoing career planning and development effort. Anything less will probably result in the inefficient use of human resources.

The Concept of Career

The concept of career has many meanings. The popular meaning is probably reflected in the idea of moving upward in one's chosen line of work—making more money; having more responsibility; and acquiring more status, prestige, and power. Although typically

Exhibit 11–1

Factors affecting career planning and development

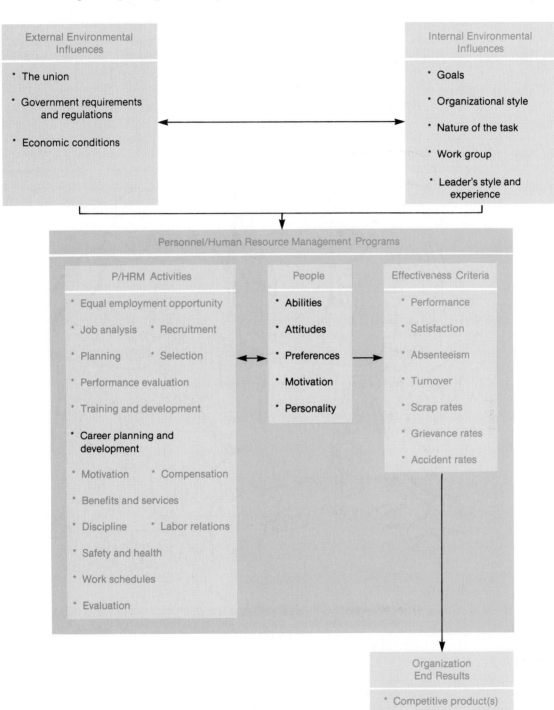

"I find this work truly fulfilling in many ways—there's the exercise, the sense of accomplishment, and, most important, the opportunity to make lots of noise."

Reprinted by permission The Wall Street Journal

restricted to lines of work which involve gainful employment, the concept of career can apply to other life pursuits. For example, we can think of homemakers, mothers, and volunteer workers as having careers. For they too advance in the sense that their talents and abilities to take on larger responsibilities grow with time and experience. It goes without saying that the mother of married children plays a far different role than she did when the children were preschoolers.

Here our discussion will center on the careers of those in occupations and professions. The definition of career that we will use follows closely the one recently devised by an important contributor to this field. Accordingly:

> The career is the individually perceived sequence of attitudes and behaviors associated with work-related experiences and activities over the span of the person's work life.[1]

This definition emphasizes that the term *career* does not imply success or failure except in the judgment of the individual, that a career consists of both attitudes and behaviors, and that it is an ongoing sequence of work-related activities. Yet even though the concept of career is clearly work-related, it must be understood that a person's non-work life and roles play a significant part in it. For example, the attitudes of a 50-year-old midcareer manager about a job advancement involving greater responsibilities can be quite different from those of a manager nearing retirement. A bachelor's reaction to a promotion involving relocation is likely to be different from that of a father of school-age children.

Now that you have started to think about the notion of careers, it would be useful for you to consider your own career aspirations. The exercise which follows will enable you to think about a career and its meaning. Although you can do the exercise without inputs from others, it would be helpful to share and compare the results. The exercise is presented in a step-by-step format, and it can be completed on a separate sheet of paper.

1. Draw a horizontal line which depicts the past, present, and future of your *career*. On that line, mark an *X* to show where you are now.
2. To the left of the *X,* that part of the line which represents your *past,* identify the events in your life which gave you genuine feelings of fulfillment and satisfaction.
3. Examine these historical milestones, and determine the specific factors which seem to have caused those feelings. Does a pattern emerge? Did the events occur when you were alone or when you were with other people? Did you accomplish some objective alone or with other people? Write down as much as you can about the events and your reactions to them.
4. To the right of the *X,* that part of the line represents your *future,* identify the career-related events from which you expect to realize genuine fulfillment and satisfaction. You should describe these events as explicitly as possible. If you are only able to write such statements as ''Get my first job'' or ''get my first raise,'' you probably have ill-defined career expectations.
5. After you have identified these future career-related events, rank them from high to low in terms of how much fulfillment and satisfaction you expect to derive from them.

---

[1] Douglas T. Hall, *Careers in Organizations* (Santa Monica, Calif.: Goodyear Publishers, 1976), p. 4.

6. Now go back to step 3 and rank the historical events from high to low in terms of the actual fulfillment and satisfaction you derived from them. Compare your two sets of ranked events. Are they consistent? Are you expecting the future to be the same as or different from the past? If you expect the future to be considerably different from the past, are you being realistic about the fulfillment and satisfaction that you think the future events will provide?

7. Discuss your results with your classmates and your instructor. How do you compare with your classmates in terms of your self-understanding and your understanding of the role of a career in providing personal fulfillment and satisfaction?

Career Stages

The idea that individuals go through distinct but interrelated stages in their careers is widely recognized. The simplest version would include four stages: (1) the prework stage (attending school), (2) the initial work stage (moving from job to job), (3) the stable work stage (maintaining one job), and (4) the retirement stage (leaving active employment). Most working people prepare for their occupation by undergoing some form of organized education in high school, trade school, vocational school, or college. They then take a first job, but the chances are that they will move to other jobs in the same organization or in other organizations. Eventually they settle into a position in which they remain until retirement. The duration of each stage varies among individuals, but most working people go through all of these stages.

Studies of career stages have found that needs and expectations change as the individual moves through the stages.[2] Managers in American Telephone and Telegraph (AT&T) expressed considerable concern for safety needs during the initial years on their jobs. This phase, termed the *establishment* phase, ordinarily lasted during the first five years of employment. Following the establishment phase is the *advancement* phase, which lasts approximately from age 30 to age 45. During this period the AT&T managers expressed considerably less concern for the satisfaction of safety needs and more concern for achievement, esteem, and autonomy. Promotions and advancement to jobs with responsibility and opportunity to exercise independent judgment and characteristics of this phase.

The *maintenance* phase follows the advancement phase. This period is marked by efforts to stablize the gains of the past. Although no new gains are made, the maintenance phase can be a period of creativity since the individual has satisfied many of the phychological and financial needs associated with earlier phases. Although each individual and each career will be different, it is reasonable to assume that esteem and self-actualization would be the most important needs in the maintenance phase. But as we will see, many people experience what is termed the *midcareer* crisis during the maintenance phase. Such people are not achieving satisfaction from their work, and consequently they may experience physiological and psychological discomfort.

The maintenance phase is followed by the *retirement* phase. The individual has, in effect, completed one career, and he or she may move on to another one. During this phase the individual may have opportunities to experience self-actualization through activ-

---

[2]Douglas T. Hall and Khalil Nougaim, "An Examination of Maslow's Need Hierarchy in An Organizational Setting," *Organizational Performance and Human Behavior,* 1968, pp. 12–35.

ities that it was impossible to pursue while working. Painting, gardening, volunteer service, and quiet reflection are some of the many positive avenues that are available to retirees. But the individual's financial and health status may make it necessary to spend the retirement years in satisfying safety and physiological needs. The relationship between career stages and needs is summarized in Exhibit 11–2.

The fact that individuals pass through different stages during their careers is evident. It is also understandable that individual needs and motives are different from one stage to the next. But managing the careers of others requires a more complete description of what happens to individuals during these stages. One group of individuals whose careers are of special significance to the performance of modern organizations are the *professionals*. Knowledge workers—such as professional accountants, scientists, and engineers—are one of the fastest growing segment of the work force. This segment constitutes 32 percent of the work force at present (blue-collar workers make up 33 percent).[3] These professionals spend their careers in large, complex organizations after having spent several years in obtaining advanced training and degrees. The organizations which employ them expect them to provide the innovativeness and creativity that are necessary for organizational survival in dynamic and competitive environments. Obviously, the performance levels of professional employees must be of the upmost concern for the organizations' leaders.

The effective management of professionals begins with understanding the crucial characteristics of the four stages of professional careers. Professional employees could avoid some disappointments and anxieties if they also understood more about their own career stages.

Stage I • Young professionals enter an organization with technical knowledge, but without an understanding of the organization's demands and expectations. Consequently, they must work fairly closely with more experienced persons. The relationship that develops between the young professionals and their supervisors is an *apprenticeship*. The central activities in which apprentices are expected to show competence include *learning* and *following directions*. To move successfully and effectively through Stage I, one must be able to accept the *psychological state of dependence*. And some professionals cannot cope with being placed in a situation similar to that which they experienced while in school. They found that they are still being directed by an authority figure, just as they were in

Exhibit 11–2

Career stages and important needs

Important needs	Safety, security, physiological	Safety, security	Achievement esteem, autonomy	Esteem, self-actualization	Self-actualization
Age	0 ⟷ 25	⟷ 30	⟷ 45	⟷ 65	⟷
Career stage	Prework	Establishment	Advancement	Maintenance	Retirement

[3]Gene W. Dalton, Paul H. Thompson, and Raymond L. Price, "The Four Stages of Professional Careers—A New Look at Performance by Professionals," *Organizational Dynamics*, Summer 1977, pp. 19–42.

school. Yet they had anticipated that their first job would provide considerably more freedom. Those who do not cope successfully can compromise their careers if they engage in sloppy and slipshod work behavior.

Stage II • Once through the dependent relationship characteristic of Stage I, the professional employee moves into Stage II, which calls for working independently. But passage to this stage depends on having demonstrated competence in some specific technical area. The technical expert may be in a content area, such as taxation, product testing, or quality assurance, or it may be in a skill area, such as computer applications. The professional's primary activity in Stage II is to be an *independent contributor* of ideas in the chosen area. The professional is expected to rely much less on direction from others. The *psychological state of independence* may pose some problems because it is in such stark contrast to the state of dependence required in Stage I. Stage II is extremely important for the professional's future career growth. Those who fail at this stage do so either because they do not have the requisite technical skill to perform independently or because they do not have the necessary self-confidence to do so.

In the case at the beginning of this chapter, there is an indication that Jim Lucio is at Stage II in his career development. As the case stated, Jim really values his independence. He wants to be his own boss, run his own business. Independence is a high priority for him, as it is for most professionals at Stage II.

Stage III • Professionals who enter Stage III are expected to become the mentors of those in Stage I. They also tend to broaden their interests and to deal more and more with people outside the organization. Thus, the central activities of professionals at this stage are *training* and *interactions* with others. Stage III professionals assume *responsibility for the work of others,* and this characteristic of the stage can cause considerable psychological stress. In previous stages the professional was responsible only for his or her own work. But now it is the work of others which is of primary concern. Individuals who cannot cope with this new requirement may decide to shift back to Stage II. Individuals who derive satisfaction from seeing other people move on to bigger and better jobs may be content to remain in Stage III until retirement.

Stage IV • Some professional employees remain in Stage III; for these professionals Stage III is the career maintenance phase. Other professionals progress to yet another stage. This stage is not experienced by all professionals, because its fundamental characteristic is that it involves *shaping the direction of the organization itself.* Although we usually think of such activity as being undertaken by only one individual in an organization—its chief executive—in fact it may be undertaken by many others. For example, key personnel in product development, process manufacturing, or technological research may be Stage IV types. As a consequence of their performance in Stage III of their careers, Stage IV professionals direct their attention to long-range strategic planning. In doing so, they play the roles of manager, entrepreneur, and idea generator. Their primary job relationships are to *identify* and *sponsor* the careers of their successors and to interact with key people outside the organization. The most significant shift for a person in Stage IV is to accept the decisions of subordinates, without second-guessing them. Stage IV professionals must learn to influence; that is, to practice leadership through such indirect means as idea planting, personnel selection, and organizational design. These shifts can be difficult for an individual who has relied on direct supervision in the past.

The concept of career stages is fundamental for understanding and managing career development. It is necessary to comprehend *life stages* as well. Individuals go through career stages as they go through life stages, but the interaction between career stages and life stages is not easy to understand.

Life Stages

Our understanding of the stages of life for children and youth is relatively well developed as compared to our understanding of adult life stages. Psychology has provided much insight into the problems of early childhood, but far less insight into the problems of adulthood. More and more, however, we are finding that adulthood is defined by rather distinct phases. The demands, problems, and opportunities presented in these phases must be taken into account by managers who are concerned with developing the careers of their subordinates.

One view of the life stages emphasizes developmental aspects. That is, each life stage is marked by the need to work through a particular developmental task before the individual can move successfully into the next stage.[4] In this regard, moving through the stages of life is analogous to Maslow's need hierarchy. The stages and their developmental tasks are as follows.

Adolescence • For most people this stage occurs from age 15 to age 25. Prior to this stage is *childhood,* but since our primary concern is the life stages as related to the career stages, childhood is relatively unimportant for our purposes. Essential for normal progression through adolescence is the achieving of *ego identity*. Adolescents are much concerned with settling on a particular career or occupational choice. They can become confused by the apparent gaps between what they think they can do and what they think they must do to succeed in a career. The latter years of the adolescent stage usually coincide with initial employment; and if ego identity has not been achieved, one can expect difficulties during this first employment opportunity.

Young Adulthood • The years between 25 and 35 ordinarily involve the development of *intimacy and involvement with others*. During this life stage, individuals learn to become involved not only with other persons but also with groups and organizations. The extent to which individuals pass through this phase successfully depends on how successful they were in establishing their ego identities as adolescents. In terms of career stages, young adulthood corresponds with the *establishment* of a career and the initial stages of *advancement*. Conflicts may develop between life stage demands and career stage demand if, for example, the demands of the career stage include behaviors that are inconsistent with the development of relationships with others.

Adulthood • The 30 years between 35 and 65 are devoted to *generativity,* a term that implies concern for actions and achievements which will benefit *future generations*. Individuals experiencing this life stage emphasize the productive and creative use of their talents and abilities. In the context of work experience, adulthood involves building or-

---

[4]Erik H. Erikson, *Childhood and Society,* 2d ed. (New York: W. W. Norton, 1963), as presented in Hall, *Careers in Organizations,* pp. 48–52.

Exhibit 11–3 _____

The relationships between career stages and life stages

Career stages	Prework		Establishment	Advancement		Maintenance		Retirement

Age 0 ←——→ 15 ←——→ 25 ←——→ 30 ←— 35 ←——→ 45 ←————→ 65 ←——

Life stages	Childhood	Adolescence	Young adulthood		Adulthood		Maturity

ganizations, devising new and lasting products, coaching younger people, and teaching others. This life stage coincides with the later years of the advancement career stage and the full duration of the maintenance stage. Successful development of the adulthood stage depends on having achieved ego identity and commitment to others, the developmental tasks of the preceding two stages.

Maturity • The last life stage is maturity, and people pass through this stage successfully if they achieve *ego integrity;* that is, if they do not despair of their lives and of the choices they have made. In a sense, this stage represents the culmination of a productive and creative life served in the interests of others to the satisfaction of self. This life stage coincides with the retirement career stage.

The relationships between life stages and career stages are shown in Exhibit 11–3. Successful careers are evidently a result, in part, of achieving certain career stages at certain ages. For example, a study of scientists in two research and development companies attempted to determine the relationship between performance and career stage for those over 40. The results are shown in Exhibit 11–4. In these two companies it is apparent that individuals whose career stages were not in step with their life stages were relatively low performers. Notice that 100 percent of the employees over 40 who were classified as at Stage I of their careers were considered to be below-average performers. For whatever reasons, these employees were unable to establish themselves as independent contributors of ideas and thus to move on to Stage II. Perhaps this was because they had been unable to achieve ego identity during the early stages of their lives. Managers must recognize the interaction between career stages and life stages in designing effective career development programs.

Exhibit 11–4 _____

Relationship between age, career stage, and performance (40 years or older)

	Stage I	Stage II	Stage III	Stage IV
Above-average performance	0%	18%	79%	100%
Below-average performance	100%	82%	21%	0%

Source: Based on Gene W. Dalton, Paul H. Thompson, and Raymond L. Price, "The Four Stages of Professional Careers—A New Look at Performance by Professionals," *Organizational Dynamics,* Summer 1977, p. 36.

Career Development: A Commitment

When an organization understands the importance of career development, it typically offers numerous opportunities to employees. These opportunities can involve simply a tuition reimbursement program or a detailed counseling service for developing individual career path plans. An example of the type of career development programs available in various organizations and industries is presented in Exhibit 11–5.

Exhibit 11–5

Career development programs

Career counseling:
  Career counseling during the employment interview
  Career counseling during the performance appraisal session
  Psychological assessment and career alternative planning
  Career counseling as part of the day-to-day supervisor/subordinate relationship
  Special career counseling for high-potential employees
  Counseling for downward transfers

Career pathing:
  Planned job progression for new employees
  Career pathing to help managers acquire the necessary experience for future jobs
  Committee performs an annual review of management personnel's strengths and weaknesses and then
    develops a five-year career plan for each
  Plan job moves for high-potential employees to place them in a particular target job
  Rotate first-level supervisors through various departments to prepare them for upper management
    positions
Human resources:
  Computerized inventory of backgrounds and skills to help identify replacements
  Succession planning or replacement charts at all levels of management

Career information systems:
  Job posting for all nonofficer positions; individual can bid to be considered
  Job posting for hourly employees and career counseling for salaried employees

Management or supervisory development:
  Special program for those moving from hourly employment to management
  Responsibility of the department head to develop managers
  Management development committee to look after the career development of management groups
  In-house advanced management program

Training:
  In-house supervisory training
  Technical skills training for lower levels
  Outside management seminars
  Formalized job rotation programs
  Intern programs
  Responsibility of manager for on-the-job training
  Tuition reimbursement program

Special groups:
  Outplacement programs
  Minority indoctrination training program
  Career management seminar for women
  Preretirement counseling
  Career counseling and job rotation for women and minorities
  Refresher courses for midcareer managers
  Presupervisory training program for women and minorities

The programs presented in Exhibit 11–5 are most valuable when they are: (1) regularly offered; (2) open for all employees; (3) modified when evaluation indicates that change is necessary. The overall objective of these programs is to match employee needs and goals with current or future career opportunities in the organization. Thus, a well-designed career development effort will assist employees in determining their own career needs, develop and publicize available career opportunities in the organization, and match employee needs and goals with the organization. This commitment to career development can delay the obsolescence of human resources that is so costly to an organization.

At Owens-Illinois, Inc., a formal career opportunity program is used. It is the firm's policy to promote persons from within the company whenever possible. The career opportunity program provides several services to employees:

1. It makes available a broad range of information about jobs that are open and the qualifications needed to fill them.
2. It provides a system through which qualified employees may apply for these positions.
3. It helps employees establish career goals.
4. It encourages a meaningful dialogue between employees and supervisors about the employees' career goals.

Exhibit 11–6 presents one of the career opportunity responses forms that is completed by employees and managerial personnel. The selecting supervisor who makes the hiring decision explains why he or she made the decision that was reached. No matter who is selected for the job, the form is returned to the employee who submitted it for consideration.

Three points in the careers of individuals are particularly crucial for career development. The *recent hiree* begins his or her career with a particular job and position. Experiences on this first job can have considerable positive and negative effects on future performance. The *midcareer* person is subject to pressures and possibilities different from those of the recent hiree, but he or she is also at a critical point. The *preretirement* person is uncertain and anxious about the future. The following sections describe some career development problems of recent hirees, midcareer managers, and preretirement employees.

Career Development for Recent Hirees

Recently hired employees face many anxious moments. They have selected their positions on the basis of expectations regarding the demands that the organization will make of them and what they will receive in exchange for meeting those demands. Young managers, particularly those with college training, expect opportunities to utilize their training in ways which lead to recognition and advancement. In too many instances, recently hired managers are soon disappointed with their initial career decisions. Although the specific causes of early-career disappointments vary from person to person, some general causes have been identified.

Causes of Early Career Difficulties

Studies of the early-career problems of young managers typically find that those who experience frustration are victims of "reality shock." These young managers perceive a mismatch between what they thought the organization was and what it actually is. Several factors contribute to reality shock, and it is important for young managers and their managers to be aware of them.

The Initial Job Challenge • The first jobs of young managers often demand far less of them than they are capable of delivering. Consequently, young managers believe that they are unable to demonstrate their full capabilities and that in a sense they are being stifled. This particular cause is especially damaging if the recruiter has been overly enthusiastic in "selling" the organization to the managers when they were recruited.

Some young managers are able to *create* challenging jobs even when their assignments are fairly routine. They do this by thinking of ways to do their jobs differently and better. They may also be able to persuade their managers to give them more leeway and more to do. Unfortunately, many young managers are unable to create challenge. Their previous experiences in school were typically experiences in which challenge had been given to them by their teachers. The challenge had been created for them, not by them.

Initial Job Satisfaction • Recently hired managers with college training often believe that they can perform at levels beyond those of their initial assignments. After all, they have been exposed to the latest managerial theories and techniques, and in their minds at least, they are ready to run the company. Disappointment and dissatisfaction are the sure outcomes, however, when they discover that their self-evaluations are not shared by others in the organization. The consequence of unrealistic aspirations and routine initial assignments is low-job satisfaction in particular, low satisifaction of growth and self-actualization needs in general.

Initial Job Performance Evaluation • Feedback on performance is an important managerial responsibility. Yet many managers are inadequately trained to meet this responsibility. They simply do not know how to evaluate the performance of their subordinates. This management deficiency is especially damaging to new managers. They have not been in the organization long enough to be socialized by their peers and other employees. They are not yet sure of what they are expected to believe, what values to hold, or what behaviors are expected of them. They naturally look to their own managers to guide them through this early phase. But when their managers fail to evaluate their performance accurately, they remain ignorant and confused as to whether or not they are achieving what the organization expects of them.

Certainly, not all young managers experience problems associated with their initial assignments. But those who do and who leave the organization as a consequence of their frustrations represent a waste of talent and money. One estimate placed the cost of replacing a manager (including recruiting costs, training expenses, and subpar performance during the early phases) at $50,000 in the first year alone.[5] Thus, it is apparent that the cost of losing capable young managers outweighs the cost of efforts and programs designed to counteract initial job problems.

---

[5]"What Does It Cost to Train New People?" *Training/HRD*, March 1981, p. 16.

Exhibit 11–6

Career opportunity response form—Owens-Illinois

Form 5287-R6

Owens-Illinois Career Opportunity Program Response Form

O·I

Section 1

Name		Soc. Sec. No.		Home Phone	O-I Ext.	O-I Mail Location
Present Job Title		Div.	Department			☐ Hourly ☐ Salary
Present Supervisor			Supervisor's Signature *			
Is your supervisor aware that you have responded to this Career Opportunity Program? ☐ Yes ☐ No					Number of months on current position	

Job You Are Responding to

Job Title		Div.	Department		Rate Group/Points	Location
Divisional Personnel Coordinator		Posting Dates	HRS Requisition No.		Date Form Completed	

To Apply

1. Compare your experience, education, and skills against the selection criteria stated on the posting.

2. Complete Sections 1 and 2 of this form and the Career Summary Form and forward to
   Career Opportunity Program – 2, OIB, Human Resource Systems.

3. Please do not keep any pages of this form. A copy of this form will be returned to you by the Divisional Personnel Coordinator.

* Supervisor Approval

4. Your supervisor must approve your responding to a job under the following policies:

   - Non-exempt and hourly –
     if you have been on the job less than 12 months.

   - Exempt through 129 points –
     if you have been on the job less than 18 months.

   - Greater than 130 points –
     if you have been on the job less than 24 months.

   - All personnel responding –
     before you may receive an interview.

Human Resource Use Only

Date Received

(**White** and **Canary** copies – Return to Employee, **Pink** copy – Retained by Division)

Form 5287-R6

Owens-Illinois Career Opportunity Program Response Form

O·I

Section 1

Name		Soc. Sec. No.		Home Phone	O-I Ext.	O-I Mail Location

Present Job Title	Div.	Department	☐ Hourly ☐ Salary

Present Supervisor	Supervisor's Signature

Is your supervisor aware that you have responded to this Career Opportunity Program? ☐ Yes ☐ No	Number of months on current position

Job You Are Responding to

Job Title	Div.	Department	Rate Group/Points	Location
Divisional Personnel Coordinator	Posting Dates	HRS Requisition No.	Date Form Completed	

Section 2

Candidate
State how your qualifications meet posted criteria

Section 3

Divisional Personnel Coordinator
1. Review all responses.   2. Turn down, interview or forward files to Selecting Supervisor.
3. If turned down, state reason why candidate is **not** being considered further and return Response Form and Career Summary Form to candidate.

Section 4

Selecting Supervisor
1. Review all responses.
2. If no further consideration is given, indicate reason why and return Response Form and Career Summary Form to Division Personnel Coordinator.
3. If you wish to interview, schedule interviews through your Division Personnel Coordinator.
4. If candidate is not offered position after the interview, state reason and return Response and Career Summary Forms to Div. Personnel Coordinator.

Date	Signed

Section 5

Divisional Personnel Coordinator
1. Complete Referral Summary Form indicating status of candidates and return form to HR Systems.
2. Return Response and Career Summary Forms to candidate.

Date	Signed

(White and **Canary** copies – Return to Employee, **Pink** copy – Retained by Division)

Programs and Practices to Counteract Early-Career Problems

Managers who wish to improve the retention and development of young management talent have several alternatives.

Realistic Job Previews • One way to counteract the unrealistic expectations of new recruits is to provide realistic information during the recruiting process. Remember from Chapter 6 that this practice is based on the idea that a recruit should know both the bad and the good things to expect from a job and the organization. Through *realistic job previews* (RJPs) recruits are given opportunities to learn not only the benefits that they may expect, but also the drawbacks. Studies have shown that the recruitment rate is the same for those who receive RJPs as for those who do not. More important, those who receive RJPs are more likely to remain on the job and to be satisfied with it than are those who have been selected in the usual manner. The practice of "telling it like it is" is used by a number of organizations, including the Prudential Insurance Company, Texas Instruments, and the U.S. Military Academy.

A Challenging Initial Assignment • Managers of newly hired people should be encouraged to slot them into the most demanding of the available jobs. Successful implementation of this policy requires managers to take some risks, because managers are accountable for the performance of their subordinates. If the assignments are too far beyond the ability of the subordinates, both the managers and the subordinates share the cost of failure. Thus, most managers prefer to bring their subordinates along slowly by giving them progressively more difficult and challenging jobs, but only *after the subordinates have demonstrated their ability*. Newly hired managers have *potential for performance*, but have not *demonstrated performance*. Thus, it is risky to assign an individual to a task for which there is a high probability of failure. But studies have indicated that managers who experienced initial job challenge were more effective in their later years.[6]

An Enriched Initial Assignment • Job enrichment is an established practice for motivating employees with strong growth and achievement needs. If the nature of the job to be assigned is not intrinsically challenging, the newly hired manager's manager can enrich the assignment. The usual ways to enrich a job include giving the new manager more authority and responsibility, permitting the new manager to interact directly with customers and clients, and enabling the new manager to implement his or her own ideas (rather than merely recommending them to the boss).

Demanding Bosses • A practice which seems to have considerable promise for increasing the retention rate of young managers is to assign them initially to demanding supervisors. In this context, "demanding" should not be interpreted as "autocratic." Rather, the type of boss most likely to get new hires off in the right direction is one who has high but achievable expectations for their performance. Such a boss instills in the young managers the understanding that high performance is expected and rewarded and, equally important, that the boss is always ready to assist them through coaching and counseling. Apparently, 9, 9 leaders would be effective for this purpose, but if these are unavailable, task-oriented leaders would be more effective than person-oriented leaders.

---

[6]Hall, *Careers in Organizations,* p. 67.

The programs and practices that are intended to retain and develop young managers—particularly recent hires with college training—can be used separately or in combination. A manager seeks to establish policies which would retain those recent hires who have the highest potential to perform effectively. The likelihood of that result is improved if the policies include realistic job previews coupled with challenging initial assignments supervised by supportive, performance-oriented managers. Although such practices are not perfect, they are helpful not only in retaining young managers but also in avoiding the problems which may arise during the middle phase of a manager's career.

Career Development for Midcareer Managers

Managers in the midstages of their careers are ordinarily "key people" in their organizations. They have established a place for themselves in society as well as at work. They occupy important positions in the community, often engage in civic affairs, and are looked upon as model achievers in our achievement-oriented culture. Yet popular and scholarly articles and books appear yearly which discuss the "midcareer crisis" and the "middleaged dropout." Executives disappear from their jobs and are later found driving taxis, drinking heavily, or, at worst, on skid row. Such lost talent is expensive to replace, and more and more organizations are initiating practices to deal with the problems of the midcareer manager.

The Midcareer Plateau

Managers face the midcareer plateau during the adult stage of life and the maintenance phase of careers. At this point the likelihood of additional upward promotion may be quite low. Two reasons account for the plateau. First, there are simply fewer jobs at the top of the organization, and even though the manager has the ability to perform at that level, no opening exists. Second, openings may exist, but the manager may lack either the *ability* or the *desire* to fill them.[7]

Managers who find themselves stifled in their present jobs tend to cope with the problems in fairly consistent ways. They suffer from depression, poor health, and fear and hostility toward their subordinates. Eventually they "retire" on the job or leave the organization physically and permanently. Any one of these ways of coping results in lowered job performance and, of course, lowered organiztional performance.[8]

The midcareer, middle-aged crisis has been depicted in novels, movies, dramas, and psychological studies. Although each individual's story is different and unique, the scenario has many common features. Each story and research indicates that the midcareer crisis is real and has psychological and often physical effects that can become dangerous if not properly handled. Jim Lucio, for example, has insomnia, loss of appetite, and is on the edge because of his midcareer crisis.

Of course, not all managers respond to their situations in the same ways. Some, perhaps most, cope constructively. But to the extent that effective managers experience

[7]Thomas P. Ference, James A. F. Stoner, and E. Kirby Warren, "Managing the Career Plateau," *Academy of Management Review,* October 1977, p. 604.

[8]Duane Schultz, "Managing the Middle-Aged Manager," *Personnel,* November–December 1974, pp. 8–17.

disruptive psychological, physical, and professional traumas, organizational performance will suffer. The cost of impaired managerial effectiveness indicates that organizations should implement programs to counteract midcareer plateau problems.

Programs and Practices to Counteract Midcareer Problems

Counteracting the problems that managers face at midcareer involves providing *counseling* and *alternatives*.

Midcareer Counseling • Organizations such as IBM, DuPont, Alcoa, and Western Electric employ full-time staff psychiatrists to assist employees in dealing with career, health, and family problems.[9] In the context of such counseling, midcareer managers are provided with professional help in dealing with the depression and stress they may experience. Since midcareer managers are usually well educated and articulate, they often only need someone to talk to, someone skilled in the art of listening. The process of verbalizing their problems to an objective listener is often enough to enable midcareer managers to recognize their problems and to cope with them constructively.

Midcareer Alternatives • Effective resolution of the problems of midcareer crises requires the existence of acceptable alternatives. The organization cannot be expected to go beyond counseling on personal and family problems. But when the crisis is precipitated primarily by career-related factors, the organization can be an important source of alternatives. In many instances, the organization simply needs to accept career moves that are usually viewed as unacceptable. Three career moves which have potential for counteracting the problems of midcareer managers are lateral transfers, downward transfers, and fallback positions.[10]

Lateral transfers involve moves at the same organizational level from one department to another. A manager who has plateaued in production could be transferred to a similiar level in sales, engineering, or some other area. The move would require the manager to learn quickly the technical demands of the new position, and there would be a period of reduced performance as this learning occurred. But once qualified, the manager would bring the perspectives of both areas to bear on decisions.

Downward transfers are associated in our society with failure; an effective manager simply does not consider a move downward to be a respectable alternative. Yet downward transfers are in many instances not only respectable alternatives, but entirely acceptable alternatives, particularly when one or more of the following conditions exist:

> The manager values the quality of life afforded by a specific geographic area and may desire a downward transfer if this is required in order to stay in or move to that area.

> The manager views the downward transfer as a way to establish a base for future promotions.

---

[9]Manfred F. R. Kets de Vries, "The Midcareer Conundrum," *Organizational Dynamics,* Autumn 1978, p. 58.

[10]Douglas T. Hall and Francine S. Hall, "What's New in Career Management," *Organizational Dynamics,* Summer 1976, pp. 21–27.

The manager is faced with the alternatives of dismissal or a downward move.

The manager desires to pursue autonomy and self-actualization in non-job-related activities—such as religious, civic, or political activities—and for that reason may welcome the reduced responsibility (and demands) of a lower level position.

The use of *fallback positions* is a relatively new way to reduce the risk of lateral and downward transfers. The practice involves identifying in advance a position to which the transferred manager can return if the new position does not work out. By identifying the fallback position in advance, the organization informs everyone who is affected that some risk is involved but that the organization is willing to accept some of the responsibility for it and that returning to the fallback job will not be viewed as "failure." Companies such as Heublein, Procter & Gamble, Continental Can, and Lehman Brothers have used fallback positions to remove some of the risk of lateral and upward moves. The practice appears to have considerable promise for protecting the careers of highly specialized technicians and professionals who make their first move into general management positions.

The suggestion that organizations initiate practices and programs to assist managers through midcareer crises does not excuse managers from taking responsibility for themselves. Individuals who deal honestly and constructively with their lives and careers will early on take steps to minimize the risk of becoming obsolete or redundant. At the outset of their management careers, they can begin to formulate their *career plans and paths*. Often they will be assisted in this process by the organization which employs them.

Career Development for Preretirement

The extension of mandatory retirement to age 70 was signed into U.S. law in April 1978. It has given rise to the reference of the "graying of America." The impact of this legislation on career planning and development can be significant. Will people still want to retire at an earlier age than 70? What is the organization's responsibility in preparing employees for retirement? Will dissatisfied workers and those with good pension plans retire early? Is the inflationary spiral dampening the urge to retire early?

Most organizations are ill-prepared to deal with the effects of the legislation, have few programs that cope with the preretirement employee, and are unable to answer the questions raised above. Management needs to consider in much more depth the following issues:

- When do employees plan to retire?
- Who is attracted to early retirement?
- What do employees plan to do during retirement? Can the organization help them prepare for these activities?
- Do retirees plan a second career? Can the organization assist in this preparation?
- Which retirees can still be consulted by the organization to help new employees?

Programs and Practices to Minimize Retirement Adjustment Problems

These and other similar questions can be addressed through counseling and education programs for preretirees. Retirement is feared by some and anticipated by others. Counseling and education programs can make the transition from being employed to retirement much smoother.

In most cases the retired person must learn to accept a reduced role, to manage a less structured life, and to make new accommodations to family and community. Educational workshops and seminars, and counseling sessions are invaluable for the preretirement person to make the transition from work to retirement. These activities can be initiated by P/HRM departments.

IBM is one organization that has attempted to aid in this transition. They offer tuition rebates for courses on any topic within three years of retirement. The subject matter can cover any area. Many IBM preretirees have decided to prepare for second careers (learning new skills, professions, and small business management).[11]

Those P/HRM departments that are truly dedicated to the development of human resources will become more involved with the preretiree's problems, fears, and uncertainties in the 1980s. Perhaps a new measure of concern for human resources will be the degree of organizational commitment to those who have devoted their careers in the form of preretirement preparation.

Career Planning and Pathing

The practice of career planning involves matching an individual's career aspirations with the opportunities available in an organization. *Career pathing* is the sequencing of the specific jobs that are associated with those opportunities. The two processes are intertwined. Planning a career involves the identification of the means for achieving desired ends, and in the context of career plans, career paths are the means for achieving aspirations. Although career planning is still a relatively new practice, many organizations are turning to it as a way to *proact* rather than *react* to the problems associated with early and midcareer career crises.

The career planning and career pathing process is depicted in Exhibit 11–7. Its successful employment places equal responsibility on the individual and the organization. The individual must identify his or her aspirations and abilities and, through counseling, recognize what training and development are required for a particular career path. The organization must identify its needs and opportunities and through work force planning, provide the necessary career information and training to its employees. Such companies as Weyerhaeuser, Nabisco, Gulf Oil, Exxon, and Eaton use career development programs to identify a broad pool of talent that is available for promotion and transfer opportunities. Companies often restrict career counseling to managerial and professional staff, but IBM, GE, TRW, and Gulf Oil provide career counseling for both blue-collar and managerial personnel.

---

[11]Jeffrey Sonnonfeld, "Dealing with the Aging Work Force," *Harvard Business Review,* November/December 1978, pp. 81–92.

Exhibit 11–7
A career planning process

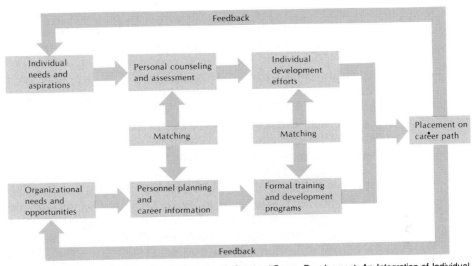

Source: Based on John C. Alpin and Darlene K. Gerster, "Career Development: An Integration of Individual and Organizational Needs," *Personnel*, March–April 1978, p. 25.

Career Planning: How It's Done

Individual and organizational needs and opportunities can be matched in a variety of ways. According to a recent American Management Association (AMA) survey, the most widely used approaches are (1) informal counseling by the personnel staff and (2) career counseling by supervisors. These approaches are often quite informal. Somewhat more formal and less widely used practices involve workshops, seminars, and self-assessment centers.

Informal Counseling • The P/HRM staffs of organizations often include counseling services for employees who wish to assess their abilities and interests. The counseling process can also move into personal concerns, and this is proper, since, as we have already seen, life concerns are important factors in determining career aspirations. In this context, career counseling is viewed by the organization as a service to its employees, but not as a primary service.

Career counseling by supervisors is usually included in perfomance evaluations. The question of where the employee is going in the organization arises quite naturally in this setting. In fact, the inclusion of career information in performance appraisal preates the current interest in career planning. A characteristic of effective performance evaluation is to let the employee know not only how well he or she has done, but also what the future holds. Thus, supervisors must be able to counsel the employee in terms of organizational needs and opportunities not only within the specific department, but throughout the organization. Since supervisors usually have limited information about the total organization, it is often necessary to adopt more formal and systematic counseling approaches.

Formal Counseling • Workshops, assessment centers, and career development centers are being used increasingly in organizations. Typically, such formal practices are designed to serve specific employee groups. Management trainees and "high-potential" or "fast-track" management candidates have received most of the attention to date. However, women employees and minority employees have been given increased attention. Career development programs for women and minority employees are viewed as indications of an organization's commitment to affirmative action.

One example of a formal organizational career planning system is Syntex Corporation's Career Development Center. The center was the result of the realization that the managers in Syntex were unable to counsel their subordinates because they (the managers) were too caught up in their own jobs. The center's staff first identifies the individual's strengths and weaknesses in eight skill areas which Syntex believes to be related to effective management. These eight areas are: (1) problem analysis; (2) communication; (3) goal setting; (4) decision making and conflict handling; (5) selecting, training, and motivating employees; (6) controlling employees; (7) interpersonal competence; and (8) the use of time. On the basis of scores in the eight areas, each manager sets career and personal goals. The center's staff assists the manager to set realistic goals which reflect his or her strengths and weaknesses in the eight areas.

The highlight of each manager's career planning effort is attendance at a weeklong seminar. Usually attended by 24 managers at a time, the seminar places each participant into simulated management situations which require applications of the eight skill areas. Subsequently, each candidate reviews his or her own career plan, a plan which includes career goals, timetables, and required personal development. The purpose of the seminar is to encourage realistic self-appraisal. Following the seminar, participants meet with their immediate supervisors to set up their career development plans.

Organizations can use a variety of practices to facilitate their employees' career plans. One of the oldest and most widely used practices is some form of *tuition aid program*. Employees can take advantage of educational and training opportunities available at nearby schools, and the organization pays some or all of the tuition. J. I. Case, a Tenneco company with corporate offices in Racine, Wisconsin, is but one of many organizations that provide in-house courses and seminars as well as tuition reimbursement for courses related to the individual's job.

Another practice is *job posting;* that is, the organization publicizes job openings as they occur. The employees are thus made aware of the opportunities. Effective job posting requires more than simply placing a notice on the company bulletin board. At a minimum, job posting should meet the following conditions:

1. It should include promotions and transfers as well as permanent vacancies.
2. The available jobs should be posted at least three to six weeks prior to external recruiting.
3. The eligibility rules should be explicit and straightforward.
4. The standards for selection and the bidding instructions should be stated clearly.
5. Vacationing employees should be given the opportunity to apply ahead of time.

6. Employees who apply but are rejected should be notified of the reason in writing, and a record of the reason should be placed in their personnel files.[12]

Whatever approach is used, the crucial measure of its success will be the extent to which *individual and organizational* needs are satisfied.

Career Pathing

The result of career planning is the placement of an individual into a job which is the first of a sequential series of jobs. From the perspective of the organization, career paths are important inputs into work force planning. An organization's future work force depends on the projected passage of individuals through the ranks. From the prospective of the individual a career path is the sequence of jobs which he or she desires to undertake in order to achieve personal and career goals. Although it is virtually impossible to completely integrate the organizational and individual needs in the design of career paths, systematic career planning has the potential for closing the gap between the needs of the individual and the needs of the organization.

Traditional career paths have emphasized upward mobility in a single occupation or functional area. When recruiting personnel, the organization's representative will speak of engineers', accountants', or salespersons' career paths. In these contexts, the recruiter will describe the different jobs that typical individuals will hold as they work progressively upward in an organization. Each job, or "rung," is reached when the individual has accumulated the necessary experience and ability and has demonstrated that he or she is "ready" for promotion. Implicit in such career paths is the attitude that failure has occurred whenever an individual does not move on up after a certain amount of time has elapsed. Such attitudes make it difficult to use lateral and downward transfers as alternatives for managers, who no longer wish to pay the price of upward promotion.

An alternative to traditional career pathing is to base career paths on real-world experiences and individualized preferences. Paths of this kind would have several characteristics:

1. They would include lateral and downward possibilities as well as upward possibilities, and they would not be tied to "normal" rates of progress.
2. They would be tentative, and they would be responsive to changes in organizational needs.
3. They would be flexible enough to take into account the qualities of individuals.
4. Each job along the paths would be specified in terms of *acquirable* skills, knowledge, and other specific attributes, not merely in terms of educational credentials, age, or work experience.[13]

Realistic career paths, rather than traditional ones, are necessary for effective employee counseling. In the absence of such information the employee can only guess at what is available.

---

[12]David R. Dahl and Patrick R. Pinto, "Job Posting: An Industry Survey," *Personnel Journal,* January 1977, pp. 40–42.

[13]James W. Walker, "Let's Get Realistic about Career Paths," *Human Resource Management,* Fall 1976, pp. 2–7.

Exhibit 11–8 _____

Career path, general management in a telephone company.

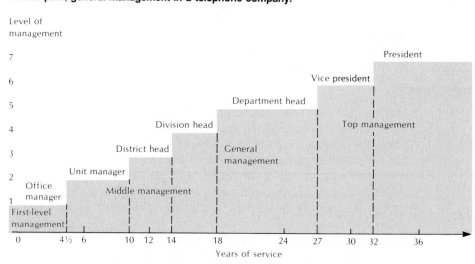

An example of a career path for general management in a telephone company is depicted in Exhibit 11–8. According to the path, the average duration of a manager's assignment in first-level management is 4 years—2½ years as a staff assistant in the home office and 1½ years as the manager of a district office in a small city. By the 14th year the average manager should have reached the fourth level of management. The assignment at this level might be that of division manager of Commercial Sales and Operations Division. Obviously not all managers reach the fifth level, much less the seventh, president. As one nears the top of the organization, the number of openings declines and the number of candidates increases.

Career Development Problems and Issues

Organizations which undertake career development programs are certain to encounter some difficult issues along the way.[14] The following problems are based on the actual experiences of some organizations.

Integrating Career Development and Work Force Planning

The relationship between career development and work force planning is obvious. Career development provides a *supply* of talents and abilities; work force planning projects the *demand* for talents and abilities. It would seem that organizations which undertake one of these activities would undertake the other. Surely it makes little sense to develop people and then have no place to put them; or to project needs for people, but have no program to supply them. In fact, some organizations do have one or the other but not both.

---

[14]This section is based on Hall and Hall, "What's New in Career Management," pp. 27–30.

P/HRM Managers Close-Up

Adrianne H. Geiger
Owens-Illinois, Inc.

Biography

Adrianne H. Geiger is manager, human resource systems (HRS), for Owens-Illinois, Inc., Toledo, Ohio. She was graduated from Ohio State University with a B.A. in premedicine. While rearing a family of four and working part-time as a professional musician, she returned for graduate work. She holds an M.B.A. and a Ph.D. in organization development from the University of Southern California's School of Public Administration.

Dr. Geiger held faculty positions at several universities and was a private consultant in organizational effectiveness in California before going into industry in 1979. She joined Owens-Illinois as an organization development specialist working in the manufacturing plants for several divisions of the company. She was also involved in the writing and training of programs for middle management and supervisory skills training.

Job description

As manager, HRS, Adrianne Geiger is responsible for management progression and succession planning systems, including forecasting, work force planning and career pathing. Additional responsibilities include improvement of career opportunity programs such as job posting and search activities and the performance appraisal systems. She also administers a wide variety of management development programs for high-level managers.

Views about the changing role of personnel in the 1980s—Adrianne H. Geiger

The technical skills required to be a personnel professional have changed drastically over the past decade. The standard industrial relations specialist who traditionally negotiated the labor contracts and, therefore, rose to become head of the personnel department, has been replaced by the human resource specialist. A good grounding in psychology, human motivation, group dynamics, and organization development are essential to the personnel professional of the 1980s.

The next technical requirement will be mastery of computerized personnel information systems which enhance the ability of personnel professionals to better manage a company's people resources. The demographics of the 1980s and people's changing work values contribute to make employee demands ever present. They wish to know (1) how they're doing against standards of the job, (2) what their next career step will be, and (3) what are their chances of getting there. Employees want to be a part of the decision making—on the job, about the job, and for choices around the next job. All of this is difficult to do in large, complex organizations unless the computer keeps track of job performance, growth potential and career interests for you, the personnel professional. Human resource planning will be a necessity for all well-managed companies into the next century. It will affect bottom-line profits and productivity. The personnel professional will find the challenge an exciting one, but also one that mandates constant learning and updating of skills.

Even companies which make use of both career development programs and work force planning have difficulty in integrating the efforts of the two. One reason is that each is done by different specialties. Career development is often done by psychologists, and work force planning is the job of economists and systems analysts. Practitioners of these two disciplines have difficulty in communicating with each other. Their training and backgrounds create potential barriers to effective communication.

A second reason for failure to integrate the efforts of career development and work force planning is related to the *organization structure*. Career development is usually the function of *personnel departments*. Work force planning is the function of *planning staffs*. The two activities are carried out in two organizationally distinct units. The manager who is responsible for both units may be the chief executive officer or a group executive.

Managing Dual Careers

As more and more women enter the working world and pursue careers, managers will increasingly confront the problems of *dual careers*. The problem arises because the careers of husbands and wives may lead them in different directions. An obvious problem can arise when the organization offers the husband or wife a transfer (involving a promotion), but is rejected because the required relocation is incompatible with the spouse's career plans. One study reports that one in three executives cannot or will not relocate because this would interfere with the career of the spouse.[15] Thus, organizations *and* individuals lose flexibility as a consequence of dual careers.

The incidence of dual careers will probably rise as more women enter the labor force. At present, more than 46 million employed men and women are two-career couples. There is no reason to believe that the number will decrease with time; in fact, the reasonable assumption to make is that both the number and the proportion of dual-career couples will increase.[16] The problems associated with this phenomenon are relatively new, but those who have studied these problems offer the following advice:

1. An organization should conduct an employee survey which gathers statistics and information regarding the incidence of dual careers in its *present* and *projected* work force. The survey should determine *(a)* how many employees are at present part of a two-career situation, *(b)* how many people interviewed for positions are part of a dual-career situation, *(c)* where and at what level in the organization the dual-career employees are, *(d)* what conflicts these employees now have, and *(e)* whether dual-career employees perceive company policy and practices to be helpful to their careers and careers of their spouses.

2. Recruiters should devise methods which present realistic previews of what the company offers dual-career couples. Orientation sessions conducted by P/HRM departments should include information which helps such couples identify potential problems.

---

[15]Francine S. Hall and Douglas T. Hall, "Dual Careers—How Do Couples and Companies Cope with the Problem?" *Organizational Dynamics,* Spring 1978, p. 58.

[16]Randolph Flynn and Judith V. Litzsinger, "Careers without Conflict," *Personnel Administrator,* July 1981, pp. 82–83.

3. Career development and transfer policies must be revised. Since the usual policies are based on the traditional one-career family, they are inapplicable to dual-career situations. The key is to provide more flexibility.
4. The company should consider providing career couples with special assistance in career management. Couples are typically ill prepared to cope with the problems posed by two careers. Young, recently hired couples are especially naive in this regard.
5. The organization can establish cooperative arrangements with other organizations. When one organization desires to relocate one dual-career partner, cooperative organizations can be sources of employment for the other partner.
6. The most important immediate step is to establish flexible working hours. Allowing couples the privilege of arranging their work schedules so that these will be compatible with family demands is an effective way to meet some of the problems of managing dual-career couples.[17]

It would be a mistake to believe that dual-career problems exist only for managerial and professional personnel. More and more nonmanagerial personnel are also members of two-career families. Managers will confront problems in scheduling overtime for these people, and in transferring them to different shifts. Like the needs of managerial and professional people, the needs of blue-collar individuals must be considered.

One company which has responded to the needs of its dual-career employees is the Morgan Adhesives Company in Stow, Ohio. Tom and Vickie Barker are employed by the company. Vickie finally won her bid to run a machine which applies an adhesive coating to films, foils, foams, and papers. She is responsible for monitoring and controlling the machine's output and for directing the work of two helpers. One of her helpers is her husband, Tom. After Vickie had won her bid, Tom put in a bid to be her helper so that they could be on the same shift. The company has no difficulty with the arrangement. As Bill Wyers, Morgan Adhesives' personnel manager said, "Our only policy is performance, and the Barkers are delivering."[18]

The issues of managing dual careers both from the couple's and the organization's viewpoint are only beginning to emerge. P/HRM managers of the 1980s will find these issues to be among their most significant career development challenges.

Middle-Aged Women Looking for a Career

After 20 years of raising children, being a good wife, and doing her bit for the community, Ruth Sugerman, 43 years old, of Lawrenceville, N.J., wanted a job. But those 20 years had left a big gap in her résumé. To help fill the void she became an intern. The intern program is run by Creative Alternative for Women.[19]

The program Ruth joined offers women a chance to develop confidence in their abilities to succeed in business. The program involves courses, workshops, and seminars designed to help the women identify their work interests.

---

[17]Ibid. pp. 72–76.

[18]"At Home on the Coating Line," Management Review, September 1978, p. 46.

[19]Erik Larson, "Firms Providing Business Internships Lure Middle-Aged Women Looking for Work," *The Wall Street Journal,* September 2, 1981, p. 21.

After completing the classroom work the internships follow. They are salaried and usually last three to six months. The jobs include market research, public relations, data processing, and banking.

Ruth Sugerman interned with Educational Testing Service, Inc., as a researcher. Now she is a full-time senior research assistant on the same project. The career reentry program restored Ruth's confidence and permitted her to retool while being paid. This, however, is a point of contention. Some P/HRM experts believe that interns shouldn't be paid since they are hired as unknown quantities. What do you think? Should interns, men or women, be paid?

Dealing with EEO Problems

The initial thrust of affirmative action programs is to recruit and place women and minority employees into managerial and professional positions. Many organizations have been successful in that effort, but their success has created additional problems. For example, the career development needs of women and minority employees require nontraditional methods. A potentially explosive additional problem is coping with the reactions of white male employees.

Apparently the key to meeting the career development needs of women and minority employees is to integrate recruitment, placement, and development efforts. For example,

NOTICE
THIS IS AN
EQUAL
OPPORTUNITY
KITCHEN

Reprinted by permission The Wall Street Journal

Virginia National Bankshares, the holding company of Virginia National Bank (VNB), has 155 offices throughout Virginia. Despite the fact that 72 percent of its employees are women, only 25 percent of them are in management positions. To correct the imbalance, VNB started a program which is designed to move more women into management. VNB appointed an advisory board consisting of eight women from various specialities within the bank. The advisory board interviewed all present female managers to determine what women considered to be their problems. The board then surveyed 109 nonmanagerial women to find out how many actually aspired to be managers.

The advisory board discovered a large number of women who stated that they were willing to undergo whatever training was necessary to move into management. The board also identified three crucial problem areas which had to be resolved before these women could realize their aspirations: (1) misconceptions about women and outdated attitudes toward women, (2) lack of lending experience among women, and (3) lack of management skills among women. The bank's management accepted the advisory board's recommendation that a rotational program be implemented. Women would be placed in all major credit areas throughout the bank. They would be trained in three lending skills: accounting, economics/finance, and financial statement analysis. They would spend one month in each credit area: branch management, credit review, marketing, branch lending, commercial loans, mortgage loans, and national accounts. In addition to the rotational program, the bank sponsors seminars prepared by the National Association of Bank Women and conducts life planning seminars to help women function effectively in their careers and in other areas of their lives.[20]

The VNB program is representative of career development that is designed to meet the specific needs of employees in a specific situation. Traditional, "canned" programs are directed toward mainstream employees and are too general in focus and content to meet the needs of women and minority employees. Although the VNB program's target group was women, its principles could be equally applicable to minority employees.

In the midst of EEO and affirmative action concerns, the employees most likely to feel threatened are white males of average competence. The threat is most keenly felt when the economy slows down and what few promotions are available go to women and minority employees. White males are not much comforted to be told that such practices are temporary and are intended to correct past injustices. The white male of average competence is the one who often loses the promotion, and he is the one who is most threatened. Above-average white males will usually progress; below-average performers will always lag behind. So what can managers do to help the average performers?

No company practice can guarantee that average-performing white male employees will go along with affirmative action programs. But some practices offer promise. First, the company should provide open and complete information about promotions. Instead of being secretive about promotions (in the hope that if white males aren't told that they are being passed over for promotion, they won't notice it), the organization should provide information which permits white males to see precisely where they stand. If given such information, they will be less likely to overestimate their relative disadvantage and will be able to assess their position in the organization more accurately.

A second practice that seems promising is to make sure that white males receive as much career development assistance as other groups. White males may also need infor-

---

[20]"Making Room at the Top," *Management Review*, April 1978, p. 45.

mation about occupational opportunities *outside the company*. Since their upward mobility may be temporarily stifled by the company's affirmative action efforts, the average white males should be given the opportunity to seek career mobility elsewhere. But the management of any company that is sincerely pursuing affirmative action through career development must not expect all employees to go along with and support the effort. Vested interests are at stake when one group progresses at the expense of another.

Summary

This chapter has been designed to introduce you to the area of career planning and development. In summary, the following points are made:

1. A career is an ongoing sequence of work-related activities. It is not something that occurs in isolation, but is work related.
2. Individuals go through four career stages—prework, initial work stage, the stable stage, and the retirement stage.
3. In thinking about career stages it is relevant to also consider life stages— adolescence, young adulthood, adulthood, and maturity.
4. Three points in careers are of particularly crucial importance for career development—when a person is just hired, at midcareer, and at preretirement.
5. Programs to combat problems of the new hiree include realistic job previews, challenging initial assignments, and demanding bosses.
6. Problems to combat midcareer problems include counseling midcareer alternatives (e.g., transfers).
7. Programs to combat preretirement problems include counseling, workshops, and seminars on what to expect, alternative careers, and coping with change.
8. Career pathing can inform people about the sequence of job opportunities in the organization.
9. Career planning involves matching a person's aspirations with opportunities. Some commonly used practices involve counseling, seminars, and even self-assessment centers.
10. A growing issue of importance is the dual-career couple. Organizations need to become more active in finding ways to minimize problems of dual-career couples.

After thinking about his goals, present position, and the future he saw at Neal, Jim Lucio made the decision to leave the company. It wasn't easy and he had some fears, but Jim really felt that a second career was best for him. He didn't make a hasty decision; he knew all about the idea of a midcareer crisis. Jim decided to go after the thing he always wanted, his own business. He now is a partner in a data-based management system company in Hamilton, Ohio. He felt good, slept well, and jumped into his second career with enthusiam. Norb and everyone at Neal wished him well. His co-workers even had a party for Jim to show him that they really cared and wanted him to be happy in his new career as a business owner in the computer field.

Unlike other chapters, Chapter 11 will not include a chart with recommendations on career planning and development for model organizations. The concern of organizations and specifically P/HRM departments is still relatively new to make these predictions. More progressive organizations of all sizes in different industries are recognizing the need to develop formal career planning and development programs.

Questions for Review and Discussion

1. Do individuals have a responsibility to manage their own career?
2. Why do recently retired persons need to be prepared for the differences between work and retirement?
3. What should be included in a workshop for preretirement employees?
4. What is the meaning of the terms *career success* to an individual?
5. Are some people satisfied with what is identified as a midcareer plateau?
6. What can organizations do to cope with dual-career issues?
7. What is a realistic career path?
8. What role can a demanding boss play for a new hiree?
9. How are life and career stages related?
10. Where are you with regard to your own career?

Glossary

Career. Individually perceived sequences of attitudes and behaviors associated with work-related experiences and activities over the span of an individual's work life.

Career Path. A sequence of positions through which an organization moves an employee.

Career Stages. The notion that individuals go through distinct stages in their careers. The typical stages include prework, initial work, stable work, and retirement.

Dual Careers. A situation in which a husband and wife have careers.

Midcareer Plateau. A point reached during the adult stage of life where a person feels stifled and not progressing as he or she had planned or would like.

Part Three

Application Cases and Exercises

APPLICATION CASE III–1

Performance Evaluation of Store Managers at Firestone Tire & Rubber

The Firestone Tire & Rubber Co. is the second largest tire company in the United States with about 18 percent of the market. Firestone manufactures and sells tires and related products for cars, trucks, buses, tractors, and airplanes. The tires are sold to automakers and consumers through 2,100 Firestone stores and many independent dealers, including Montgomery Ward. The stores are the vital link with the ultimate consumer.

A vital person in the link with consumers is the store manager. It is the store managers who are the key human resource in determining whether sales and profits will be sufficient. Listed below is a description of the store managers' duties and a portion of the performance evaluation form used to appraise store managers. Each store manager is evaluated annually by his/her immediate supervisor.

Descriptions of Store Manager Responsibilities

Summary of Duties

Has responsibility for securing maximum sales volume and maximum net profits. Supervises all phases of store operation—selling, merchandise display, service, pricing, inventories, credits and collections, operation, and maintenance. Responsible for the control of all store assets and prevention of merchandise shortages.

Interviews, selects, trains, and supervises all employees, following their progress and development. Conducts employee meetings and follows closely for satisfactory productivity.

Sets sales quotas for employees and follows for accomplishment. Works with salespeople and personally calls on commercial and dealer accounts.

Interprets and explains store operating policies and procedures to subordinates and follows for adherence. Investigates complaints and makes adjustments. Maintains store cleanliness.

A. *Personnel administration*—30 percent
   1. Directly supervises pivotal employees and through them the other employees, directing activities, schedulling duties and hours of work, following for productivity and sales results. Instructs or directs the instruction of new and present employees in work procedure, results expected, sales quota program, product and price information, etc., and follows for adherence to instructions. (Daily)
   2. Interviews applicants, obtains formal applications, determines qualifications (using employment questionnaires) and makes selection of best persons for open jobs or files applications for future consideration. (Weekly)
   3. Determines number of employees needed for profitable store operations, considering individual sales productivity, salary expense, anticipated personnel requirements, etc. (Monthly)
   4. Prepares plans for and conducts employee meetings, instructing concerning new products and policies, developing sales enthusiam, explaining incentive programs, holding sales demonstrations, etc. (Semimonthly)
   5. Trains and directs the training of new employees, following established training programs for effective utilization, conducting on-the-job training, and supervising training activities for own employees and those being trained for other assignments. (Weekly)

B. *Selling and sales promotion*—30 percent
1. Breaks down stores sales into individual daily amounts for each employee, follows progress of employees in meeting quotas, determines and takes action necessary to help them reach the objective. (Daily)
2. Works with salesperson in setting up sales objectives and reviewing accomplishments, using call and sales record sheets, and following to secure maximum sales effort effective use of time. Makes calls with salespeople to determine effectivess of contacts, reasons for lack of progress, etc., giving help in closing sales, and securing additional business. (Daily)
3. Contacts personally and by telephone, inactive accounts and prospective customers, promoting and soliciting the sale of merchandise and services, and following to close the sales. Reviews prospect cards, assigns them to employees,and follows to secure sales from each. (Daily)
4. Contacts selected commercial and dealer accounts for special sales promotion and solicitation, determining sales possibilities and requirements, selling merchandise and services, etc. (Daily)
5. Prepares advertising copy, following merchandising program suggestions, and arranges for insertion of advertisements in local newspaper. Make certain employees are alerted and store has merchandise to back up advertising. (Weekly)
6. Maintains a firm retail, commercial and wholesale pricing program according to established policies.

I.

Setting standards and recording results

Instructions: This worksheet is to be used during the year for the purpose of providing supporting information for the annual employee assessment. First list the six most important job duties of the employee in decreasing order of importance. Establish standards for each major job duty. Record the employee's performance against the standards established (1, 2, 3, or 4). Refer to the employee's work results in the performance feedback or post-assessment interview.

Major Job Duties (Taken From Job Description)	Standard Of Performance (Measure Or Criterion Of Success)	Less Than 50%	50% to 75%	76% to 89%	90% Or More
1.					
2.					
3.					
4.					
5.					
6.					

Employee's Performance (Percentage Of Time Standard Is Met)

II. _____

Work review comments

Instructions: Review the employee's performance against the standards established. Analyze the employee's performance
in terms of quality (how good), quantity (how much), and work methods (how the employee went about getting
work results). What job duties are being handled particularly well by the employee? What job standards
are not being met? Complete this section before conducting the interview with the employee.

```
PERFORMANCE STRENGTHS ABOVE JOB STANDARDS: _____
_____
_____
_____
PERFORMANCE AREAS BELOW JOB STANDARDS: _____
_____
_____
_____
```

III. INTERVIEW RESULTS AND DEVELOPMENT PLAN

Instructions: The work counseling interview is an important part of any work results program. Section III should be
completed after holding the interview. Comment on the employee's reaction to performance feedback and
the plan you and the employee have developed for improving work results. Be specific in your description
of the results of the interview and the developmental steps you and the employee have agreed upon.

```
EMPLOYEE REACTION TO PERFORMANCE FEEDBACK: _____
_____
_____
PLAN FOR IMPROVING WORK RESULTS: _____
_____
_____
_____
```

```
                                        Employee's Signature
```

```
RATER TO PROCEED TO SECTION IV
```

C. _Inventory sales and expense control_—15 percent
   1. Reviews stock turnover records for overstock conditions, determines steps necessary to correct and takes the appropriate action. Establishes stock levels and orders accordingly based on sales results as recorded in the stock ledgers for new tires and retreads. (Also major appliances.)
   2. Prepares sales and expense budget covering projected sales and expenses for the period. (Monthly)
   3. Reviews expense control sheet, comparing actual expenses with budget figures, determines and takes action necessary to keep within the approved budget. (Daily)
   4. Is responsible for the completeness and accuracy of all inventories, accounting inventories, markup, markdown inventories, etc.
D. _Checking_—10 percent
   1. Checks stock, automotive equipment, service floor, etc., continually observing store activities, and determining that equipment is maintained in good operating condition. Makes inspection trips through all parts of the store, checking observance of safety and fire precautions, protection of company assets, etc. Checks credit information secured for commercial and dealer accounts, and works with office and credit manager in setting up credit limits. (Weekly)
   2. Manager is responsible and investigates all cash shortages, open tickets and missing tickets.

    3. Investigates customer compliants, making adjustments or taking appropriate action for customer satisfaction. (Daily)

E. *Miscellaneous functions*—15 percent

    1. Reads and signs Store Operating Policy and Office Procedure Letters, analyzes and puts into operation new policies and procedures as received. (Weekly)

    2. Prepares letter to district manager covering progress of the store, sales plans, results secured, market and special conditions, etc. (Monthly)

    3. Inspects tires and other merchandise in for adjustment, determines appropriate settlement, prepares claim forms, and issues credit, replaces, etc. (Makes all policy adjustments.) (Daily)

    4. Attends district sales and civic organization meetings, and takes part in civic affairs, community drives, etc. (Weekly)

Questions for Thought

1. Do you consider the description of the Firestone store managers' responsibilities as important information that the raters of managers need to be knowledgeable about?
2. Does the portion of the performance evaluation form used at Firestone require any subjective judgments or considerations on the part of the rater?
3. Suppose that a Firestone manager received an outstanding performance evaluation. Does this mean that he or she is promotable? Why?

APPLICATION CASE III–2

Training Factory Workers at Honeywell*

Like many industrial plants, Honeywell Residential group uses primarily two methods to teach a new employee a task:

1. A knowledgeable work director and trainer, called a group leader.
2. An engineering-generated written methods description, called an assembly procedure.

Honeywell decided to provide the group leader with training tools to facilitate the training of new production workers. These tools were developed for tasks in which verbal and/or written instructions were insufficient. The tools were then combined into "training packages." (A package included everything needed to complete the training, brought

---

*Adapted from Carol L. Fey, "Factory Skills Training at Honeywell," *Training and Development Journal,* February 1981, pp. 92–95.

together into one unit.) If learning a job required the worker to read a wiring diagram, select and insert parts, solder, and then visually inspect, the training package provided instruction, practice, and feedback.

A variety of media were used in the training packages. Some of them are as follows:

- *Slide Shows.* *Used for orientation-type presentation. The scripts with the slides are general. For example, one slide show, "The Factory Quality Slide Show," emphasizes the importance of the worker in quality control.*
- *Self-Instruction Manuals.* Manuals are read at the work station which present instructions and examples. Included are self-tests to check on worker learning. The manuals are very attractive, colorful, and laminated.
- *Picture Book.* Very few words are used—only enough to label photographs that depict, the correct way of doing a job.
- *Classroom Instruction.* Very little of this kind of training is used at Honeywell. Group leaders use this form of training much more than the workers.
- *Hybrid Programs.* A hybrid program uses multiple instructional media. Influencing the trainee with as many sensory stimuli as possible is the objective of hybrid programs.

Questions for Thought

1. Is the use of picture books or slides too simplistic for training Honeywell production-line workers? Why?
2. What does Honeywell management mean when they state that hybrid programs are an attempt to influence the senses of trainees?.
3. Why do you feel that Honeywell has decided to minimize the use of classroom instruction for training factory workers in their plants?

APPLICATION CASE III–3

General Food's Method of Needs Assessment*

The history of training and development at General Foods Corporation is a long one and continues to be supported throughout the company. General Foods relies on its training and development effort to achieve optimum performance levels. Some of General Food's (GF) philosophy is captured in statements made by executives of the firm:

---

*Adapted from J. I. Lazer, A. W. Olkewicz, and J. W. Bevans, "Training in Plants: A Realistic Approach," *Training and Development Journal,* October 1980, pp. 91–96.

- GF believes people want and should be given the opportunity for individual growth and development and should be encouraged to increase their knowledge and improve their skills.
- Training and development is the responsibility of each employee and his/her manager.
- The results of training and development must be evaluated.

At the hub of the training and development process is the determination of needs. All of the aspects of training and development revolve around the "needs." Thus, the first important step of training and development is the identification of needs. Exhibit III–1 presents the needs model used at GF's plants. Note that the needs assessment is a cooperative effort of employees, supervisors, management, and P/HRM staff. The purpose of this first crucial training and development step is to collect qualitative and quantitative data.

The needs assessment at GF is conducted at the organizational and individual levels— separately or concurrently. This is considered an important requirement for acquiring a total picture of needs. GF places significant emphasis on the role of the line manager in assessing needs. Since managers are concerned about performance, they must be responsible for closing the gap between actual and expected performance.

It is, however, the responsibility of the P/HRM department to act as consultants once the line managers assess their needs. Thus, a dual responsibility for training and development at GF rests in line managers and the P/HRM department.

Exhibit III–1

Training and Development needs identification determine plant objectives and activities necessary for an efficient operation to accomplish those objectives.

Based on		*As discovered by*		*To determine*
1. Analysis of organizational problems and conditions and 2. Analysis of employees' performance, problems, and potential	1. Asking—	Employees Supervisors Top management Staff offices	Questionnaire Interview Surveys	1. What is the problem or situation that makes us want to do something? 2. What causes this problem or situation? 3. Exactly what do we really want? 4. What do we have now? 5. What do we need? 6. Which of these needs have greatest priority? 7. What can we do about them? 8. How shall we go about doing it?
	2. Observing—	Employees Their work Work flow Relationships		
	3. Studying—	Records and reports Public reaction to service Jobs (job analysis) Organization structure Program plans Organization policies		

A cooperative effort of employees, supervisors, management, and P/HRM staff

Questions for Thought

1. Would the needs model shown in Exhibit III–1 be of any value to the General Foods line manager?
2. Why does General Foods collect qualitative and quantitative data in the needs assessment step?
3. Since there is a dual responsibility between line managers and the P/HRM department at General Foods, do you think that they will cooperate with each other? Explain.

EXERCISE III–A

Making Responses

Objective. The exercise is designed to have students apply the three ego states of transactional analysis—Child, adult, parent

Set up the Exercise

1. Divide the class into groups of four or five.
2. Individually complete the transactional analysis response form.
3. Discuss in the group the individual responses. Consult Chapter 10 to review the child, adult, parent states.

Transactional Analysis Response Form

Make a child, adult, and parent response to each of the following statements:

A. Is P/HRM an important function in organizations?

Child:

Adult:

Parent:

B. Eating nutritional food is good for your health.

Child:

Adult:

Parent:

C. Are you a good driver?

Child:

Adult:

Parent:

D. Do you litter the highways?
   Child:

   Adult:

   Parent:

E. Jim (Anne) is a good student in this course (program).
   Child:

   Adult:

   Parent:

F. You always force your views on other people.
   Child:

   Adult:

   Parent:

4. Which of these states is the dominant one for you?

A Learning Note

This exercise will illustrate clearly the differences in the three ego states. It will also illustrate that the adult state is much more relevant and effective when answering any kind of question or issue.

EXERCISE III–B

Career: A Self-Assessment

Objective. This exercise is designed to encourage students to think about themselves in terms of a career. It also requires students to engage in the development of a personal career plan of action.

Set up the Exercise

1. Individually complete the self-assessment career exercise. Take your time, give each section serious thought, and after careful thought make any necessary changes that are needed.

2. The instructor will set up groups of four or five to discuss any aspect of the self-assessment that individuals want to talk about. Each individual should at least discuss *one* part or issue of his/her career assessment.
3. After the discussion each individual is to complete the action plan form.

Career Self-Assessment Form

A. *What is the ideal* career?
   Describe briefly what appears to you to be the ideal career. This is not necessarily the career you want or are in, but what you feel is ideal.
B. What skills do I have?
   List the three most obvious skills that you possess.
   1.

   2.

   3

C. List the job experience that you have had.
D. Rate each of the outcomes you want from a job.

	Extremely important						Not really important
1. Job security	7	6	5	4	3	2	1
2. Pay	7	6	5	4	3	2	1
3. Advancement opportunity	7	6	5	4	3	2	1
4. Social interaction	7	6	5	4	3	2	1
5. Challenge	7	6	5	4	3	2	1
6. Travel	7	6	5	4	3	2	1
7. Respect of colleagues	7	6	5	4	3	2	1
8. Feedback	7	6	5	4	3	2	1
9. Variety	7	6	5	4	3	2	1
10. Autonomy	7	6	5	4	3	2	1
11. Power	7	6	5	4	3	2	1
12. Recognition	7	6	5	4	3	2	1

E. Describe how often you think about your ideal career. What kind of things do you usually think about?

Career Action Plan

Now that you have thought about a career and have discussed it in a group, it is time to consider preparing your own career action plan. State the kind of actions that you really plan to do. Also seriously consider the potential obstacles in your path. Only work on *two* specific career planning goals.

A Learning Note

The difficulty of career progress evaluation will be highlighted. It will also help students compare an ideal career with their own career plans, experience, and preferred outcomes.

Action for Goal	*When will I do it*	*Obstacles*	*How obstacles can be overcome*
Action for Goal I Description:			
Action for Goal II Description:			

Now describe how you will determine whether your two action plans were successful. That is, how will you evavluate the progress being made?

Evaluation description

Action Plan I

Action Plan II

Part Four

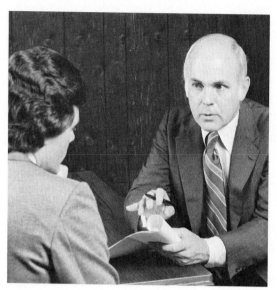

H. Armstrong Roberts

Part Four discusses an extremely important part of a firm's overall P/HRM program: motivation, rewards, and discipline.

Chapter 12 introduces the major concern of all managers of subordinates—motivation. It discusses four popular theories of motivation: (1) Maslow's need hierarchy; (2) Herzberg's two-factor theory; (3) expectancy theory; and (4) equity theory. How these theories influence and form the basis of motivational programs are viewed in terms of behavior modification and quality circles.

Chapter 13 introduces the subject of compensation and pay. It discusses the potential impact of pay on employees and discusses pay level, pay structure, and individual pay determination. Chapter 14 completes this discussion by focusing on incentives and pay programs, managerial compensation, and several significant policy issues regarding compenstion.

Chapter 15 covers benefits, services, and pensions. The potential impact of benefits and services is considered, and the major benefits that employers provide for employees are discussed.

Chapter 16 discusses the issue of discipline. It presents some of the methods used to deal with and modify employee problem behaviors.

Motivation, Rewards, and Discipline

U.S. Department of Labor

U.S. Department of Labor

Chapter Twelve

Motivation

Learning Objectives

After studying this chapter, you should be able to:
- Define the meaning of motivation.

- State why individuals react differently to being frustrated or blocked in satisfying their needs.

- Describe why behavior modification and quality circles are not always successful.

- Explain the differences between expectancy theory and behavior modification.

- Discuss the types of rewards used in behavior modification and quality circle programs.

Chapter Outline

Case

Tanya Collins and Don Marchant

Tanya Collins was discussing a problem she was having with her subordinate, Mark Kelsey. Listening to her was a colleague, Don Marchant, who really wasn't saying too much. He was simply listening and watching Tanya really become involved in her story.

Tanya I just can't understand Mark. He has everything that is needed to do the job. Ability, experience, and the right training. He just doesn't seem to put everything together. He isn't even performing at the level of a brand new trainee. Can you imagine that? I'm going to have to try

something to get him on the right track. If he wasn't such a promising employee and a nice person I'd fire him today. Six months of poor performance and no hope for improvement really has me puzzled. Maybe it's me. What do you think, Don?

Don Tanya, Mark doesn't seem to be motivated.

Tanya Don, now you sound like a psychiatrist. I think it might be me or the company.

Don Think about motivation. It is something inside the person. Don't just blame yourself, the pay plan, or the company in general.

Introduction

Don suggested to Tanya that Mark might be losing interest in his job because he wasn't motivated. Every manager can have an influence on subordinates' levels of motivation. Likewise the P/HRM department can affect motivation indirectly by contributing to a better organizational climate. P/HRM, through involvement in the structure and type of rewards administered, the establishment of efficient performance evaluation and development programs, and the creation of cooperative relations with employees are part of an organization's motivational climate.

A caring, concerned P/HRM department can create a climate of supportiveness that employees can identify and feel. Such a climate can directly affect employees' perceptions, attitudes, and behaviors. If the effect is positive, some possible results are improved rates of absenteeism, turnover, and accident frequency. Tanya failed to really look at the notion of Mark's internal or personal level of motivation. Let us now examine some of the important facts about motivation that managers in any department within an organization need to understand.

Motivation is concerned with the ''why'' of human behavior, with what it is that makes people do things. Why doesn't Mark Kelsey perform at his level of competence, or why does Dianne work so much harder than Jim? These questions can be partially answered with an understanding of human motivation. Whenever we ask managers what their biggest problem is, the answer in the vast majority of cases comes back—motivating subordinates. How can I motivate my people? This is a challenging question that will not go away. Therefore, this chapter will provide a discussion about programs that managers can use to create conditions which will motivate subordinates to exert the necessary effort to achieve performance.

Before we examine the elements of motivation, it is vital that we clearly understand exactly what the term means. *Motivation* has been defined as "all those inner striving conditions described as wishes, desires, drives, etc. . . . It is an inner state that activates or moves."[1]

More specifically, the term *motivation* has often been called an *intervening variable*. Intervening variables are internal psychological processes which are not directly observable and which account for behavior. Thus, motivation cannot be seen, heard, or felt, but can only be inferred from behavior. In other words, we can judge how a person like Mark is motivated only by observing his behavior; Tanya cannot measure motivation directly because it is unobservable.

A Diagnostic Approach to Motivation

Exhibit 12–1 highlights the factors in the diagnostic model that are extremely important to understanding motivation among employees. The individual factors are very significant. A person's abilities, attitudes, preferences, and internal motivational level all play a role. For example, if Mark Kelsey has a bad attitude or views the organization in negative terms he may be motivated to resist attempts to improve performance. Though Mark's attitudes or views can't be seen by Tanya (or any manager), his behavior *can* be seen, and conclusions reached about his attitude and motivation.

Internal environmental factors also play a major role in motivation. The task itself may stimulate an employee. On the other hand, it may bore or understimulate an employee. A work group can also stimulate behavior and work effort. If a group is positively motivated to accomplish goals, its members are influenced to work harder and longer. A leader can also play major role in motivation. Some individuals are motivated by aggressive, "take-charge" leaders, while others prefer the type of leader who shares power with subordinates. In any event, leader style and action can stimulate or dampen an employee's motivation.

Motivation and Behavior

A commonly accepted principle is that all behavior is motivated and that people have reasons for doing the things they do or for behaving in the manner that they do. This means that all human behavior is designed around the desire for *need satisfaction*.

---

[1]Bernard Berelson and Gary A. Steiner, *Human Behavior: An Inventory of Scientific Findings* (New York: Harcourt Brace Jovanovich, 1964), p. 239.

Exhibit 12–1

Factors affecting motivation

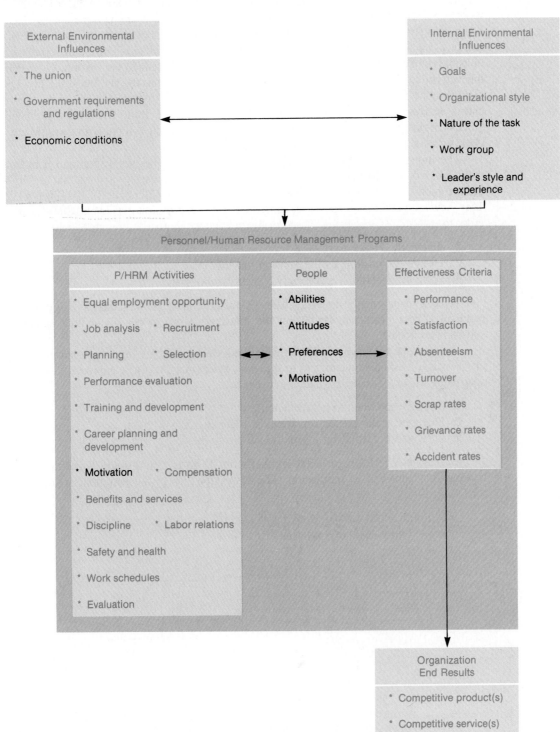

The Process of Motivation

As shown in Exhibit 12–2, an unsatisfied need is the starting point in the process of motivation. That need is deficiency within the individual, and it provides the spark which begins the chain of events leading to behavior. An unsatisfied need causes tension (physical or psychological) within the individual, leading the individual to engage in some kind of behavior (seek a means) to satisfy the need and thereby reduce the tension. Note that this activity is directed toward a goal; arrival at the goal satisfies the need, and the process of motivation is complete. For example, a thirsty person *needs* water, is *driven* by thirst, and is *motivated* by a desire for water in order to satisfy the need. Thus, the continuous process begins with an unsatisfied need and ends with need satisfaction, with goal-directed behavior as a part of the process.

The importance of understanding the relationships between motivation and behavior was underscored by McGregor.[2] He proposed that managers usually assume that employees are motivated by one of two ways. The traditional way, is referred to as Theory X. This view suggests that managers assume that they must coerce, control, and threaten in order to motivate subordinates. These mangerial actions are needed because employees:

1. Inherently dislike work.
2. Dislike responsibilities for decision making.
3. Have little ambition and want job security above all.

Thus, a manager who accepts Theory X would engage in authoritarian and directive practices. These practices result from the manager's assumptions about how and why subordinates behave.

The opposite of Theory X McGregor called Theory Y. McGregor believed that Theory Y was a reasonable alternative to the more traditional Theory X approach. The manager using Theory Y assumed that employees are:

1. Not lazy and want to do challenging work.
2. Interested under proper conditions in accepting responsibility.
3. Interested in displaying ingenuity and creativity.

An analysis of McGregor's Theory X-Theory Y distinction displays a traditional and a behavioral approach to motivation. The distinction lies in the assumptions managers

Exhibit 12–2 _____

The process of motivation

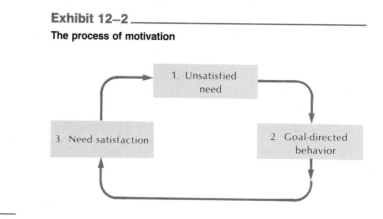

---

[2]Douglas McGregor, *The Human Side of Enterprise* (New York: McGraw-Hill, 1960).

"Good show, Wilkins. A busy office is a happy office."

Cartoon by Dean Vietor in Management Review, February, 1982

make about the needs of subordinates. If workers are assumed to have Theory X needs, management will create tighter controls and use coercion to motivate better performance. On the other hand, if Theory Y assumptions are made about subordinates, managers would probably seek to create an environment under which a full range of needs can be satisfied. In most cases managers, generally practice using a bit of Theory X and some Theory Y. Knowing how one approaches motivation, the degree of Theory X versus Theory Y, is important in the managerial world. The manager's behavior and approach has a significant impact on the behvavior displayed by employees.

Individual Needs and Motivation

As we have already mentioned, unsatisfied needs are the starting point in the process of motivation. These needs may be classified in different ways. Many of the early writers on management regarded monetary incentives as prime means for motivating the individual. These writers were influenced by the classical economists of the 18th and 19th centuries, who emphasized the rational pursuit of economic objectives and believed that economic behavior was characterized by rational economic calculations. Today, many psychologists hold that while money is obviously an important motivator, people seek to satisfy other than purely economic needs. In fact, Freud was the first psychologist to state that much of a person's behavior may not even be rational, and that behavior may be influenced by needs of which the individual is not aware.

Although most psychologists agree that human beings are motivated by the desire to satisfy many needs, there is a wide difference of opinion as to what those needs and their relative importance are. Most psychologists, however, take the pluralistic view, emphasizing many different types of needs whose satisfaction is a key determinant of behavior.

The Need Hierarchy

Maslow's need hierarchy theory has enjoyed widespread acceptance particularly in the writings of behavioralists. This theory of motivation stresses two fundamental premises:

1. Each person is a wanting animal whose needs depend on what he or she already has. Only needs not yet satisfied can influence behavior. A satisfied need is not a motivator.
2. Needs are arranged in a hierarchy of importance. Once one need is satisfied, another emerges and demands satisfaction.

Maslow believed that five levels of needs exist. These levels are (1) physiological, (2) safety, (3) social, (4) esteem, and (5) self-actualizaiton.[3] He placed them in a framework referred to as the *hierarchy of needs*. This framework is presented in Exhibit 12–3.

Maslow stated that if all of a person's needs are unsatisfied at a particular time, the most basic needs will be more pressing than the others. Needs at a lower level must be satisfied before higher level needs come into play, and only when they are sufficiently satisfied do the next needs in line become significant. Let us briefly examine each need level.

[3] Abraham H. Maslow, *Motivation and Personality* (New York: Harper & Row, 1954), pp. 93–98.

Exhibit 12–3

The hierarchy of needs

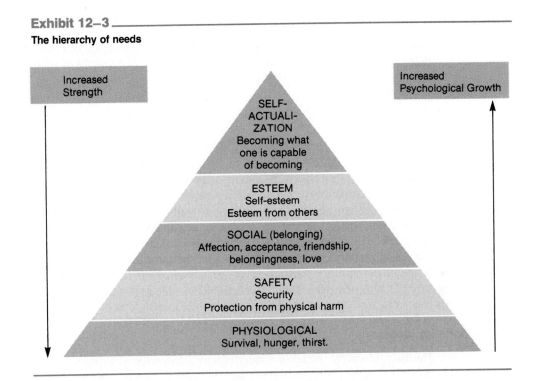

Physiological Needs

This category consists of the basic needs of the human body, such as food, water and sex. Physiological needs will dominate when all needs are unsatisfied. In such a case, no other needs will serve as a basis for motivation. As Maslow states, "A person who is lacking food, safety, love, and esteem would probably hunger for food more strongly than for anything else.[4]

Safety Needs

These needs include protection from physical harm, ill health, economic disaster, and the unexpected. From a managerial standpoint, safety needs manifest themselves in attempts to ensure job security and to move toward greater financial support.

Social Needs

These needs are related to the social nature of people and to their need for companionship. This level in the hierarchy is the point of departure from the physical or quasi-physical needs of the two previous levels. Nonsatisfaction of this level of needs may affect the mental health of the individual.

---

[4]Ibid., p. 82.

Esteem Needs

These needs comprise both the need for the awareness of one's importance to others (self-esteem) and the need for the actual esteem of others. The esteem of others must also be regarded as warranted and deserved. The satisfaction of esteem needs leads to self-confidence and prestige.

Self-Actualization Needs

Maslow defines these needs as the "desire to become more and more what one is, to become everything one is capable to become more and more what one is, to become everything one is capable of becoming."[5] This means that the individual will fully realize the potentialities of his or her talents and capabilities.

Obviously, as a person's role varies, so will the external aspects of self-actualization. Whether the person is a college professor, a corporate manager, a parent, or an athlete, being effective in that particular role is the need. Maslow assumes that the satisfaction of self-actualization needs is possible only after the satisfaction of all other needs. Moreover, he proposes that the satisfaction of self-actualization needs will tend to increase the strength of those needs. Thus, when people are able to achieve self-actualization they will tend to be motivated by increased opportunities to satisfy that level of needs.

Implications for Managers

The need hierarchy model is widely accepted and referred to by practicing managers. It is easy to comprehend, has a great deal of "commonsense" validity, and points out some of the factors that motivate people in organizations. Most organizations in the United States and Canada have successfully satisfied lower level needs. Through the wages or salary they receive, individuals are able to satisfy the physiological needs of themselves and their families. Through both salary and fringe benefit programs, organizations also aid in satisfying safety needs. Finally, organizations aid in satisfying social needs by allowing interaction and association with others on the job. In one way, all of this may create future problems for management. Since human behavior is primarily directed toward fulfilling unsatisfied needs, how successful a manager is in motivating subordinates in the future may be a function of the ability to satisfy their higher level needs.

Although Maslow's need hierarchy does not provide a complete understanding of human motivation or the means to motivate people, it does provide an excellent starting point for the student of management. We shall use it in this chapter as the foundation for an understanding of motivation in organizations.

Management's Use of the Need Hierarchy Model

Nonsatisfaction of Needs

Unsatisfied needs of subordinates must be determined by managers who are attempting to create a positive motivation setting. Individuals are often unsuccessful in their attempts to satisfy needs. In order to improve our understanding of motivation, it is necessary to explore what happens when needs are not satisfied.

---

[5]Ibid, p. 92.

As noted previously, unsatisfied needs produce tensions within the individual. Such needs motivate the individual to behavior which will reduce the tension. When the individual is unable to satisfy needs (and thereby reduce the tension), *frustration* is the result. The college male who plots conscientiously for half a semester to secure a date with a coed in his personnel/human resource management class only to have her refuse is probably quite frustrated. His goal of getting a date has been blocked.

The reactions to frustration vary from person to person. Some people react in a positive manner (constructive behavior), others in a negative manner (defensive behavior).

Constructive Behavior • The reader is undoubtedly familiar with the constructive adaptive behavior in which people engage when attempts to satisfy needs have been frustrated. An assembly-line worker who has been frustrated in attempts for recognition because of the nature of the job may seek recognition off the job by winning election to leadership posts in fraternal or civic organizations. In order to satisfy social and belonging needs, a worker may conform to the norms and values of a group which bowls on weekends. Finally, a college student named Mike may settle for a date with Susan or may attend a party without a date but with some friends. Each of these is an example of constructive adaptive behavior which individuals employ to reduce frustration and satisfy needs.

Defensive Behavior • Individuals who are blocked in attempts to satisfy their needs may exhibit defensive behavior instead of constructive behavior. All of us employ defensive behavior in one way or another because such behavior performs an important protective function in our attempts to cope with frustration. In most cases, defensive behavior does not handicap the individual to any great degree. Ordinarily, however, it is not adequate for the task of protecting the self. As a result, adults whose behavior is continually dominated by defensive behavior usually have great difficulty in adapting to responsibilities of work and of social relationships.

What happens when needs are not satisfied is difficult to understand but is worth considering. A few general patterns of defensive behavior have been identified, of which three of the more common are discussed below.

Withdrawal. One obvious way to avoid reality is to withdraw, or avoid situations which will prove frustrating. The withdrawal may be physical (leaving the scene), but more than likely it will be expressed as apathy. Workers whose jobs provide little in the way of need satisfaction may withdraw, and this is reflected by excessive absences, latenesses, or turnover.

Aggression. A very common reaction to frustration is aggression. In some cases, this may take the form of a direct attack on the source of the frustration. Unfortunately, all too often the aggression is directed toward another object or party. This is known as *displacement*. For example, a supervisor may displace aggression onto a subordinate production worker, who, in turn, may displace his aggression onto his wife.

Rationalization. This occurs when an individual presents a reason for behavior which is less ego-deflating or more socially acceptable than the true reason. An example of this defense mechanism is perceiving one's own poor performance as the result of obsolete equipment rather than personal deficiency.

Every person relies to some extent on defense mechanisms. In fact, these are useful in maintaining mental health. However, subordinates' overreliance on defensive behavior can be minimized if managerial decisions provide conditions which encourage constructive behavior. In addition, a manager who understands defensive behavior will have greater empathy with those who use it and will realize that such behavior may not be a true indication of the person's actual character.

What has been said thus far about motivation is summarized in Exhibit 12–4. The diagram indicates that an unsatisfied need results in tensions within the individual and motivates a search for ways to relieve the tensions. The diagram also indicates that if a person is successful in achieving a goal, the next unsatisfied need emerges. If, however, attempts are met with frustration, the person either engages in constructive behavior (note the plus sign to indicate its adaptive/positive nature) or resorts to defensive behavior (indicated with a minus sign because of its negative effects). In either case, the person returns to the next unsatisfied need which emerges.

The Two-Factor Theory

Frederick Herzberg advanced an approach to motivation based on a study of need satisfactions and on the reported motivational effects of those satisfactions on 200 engineers and accountants. His approach is often referred to as the *two-factor theory of motivation*.[6]

In their study, Herzberg and his associates asked the subjects to think of times when they felt especially good and especially bad about their jobs. Each subject was then asked to describe the conditions which led to those feelings. The subjects identified different work conditions for each of the feelings. For example, if managerial recognition for doing an excellent job led to good feelings about the job, the lack of managerial recognition was seldom indicated as a cause of bad feelings.

Maintenance and Motivation Factors

Based on this research, Herzberg reached the following two conclusions.

1. Although employees are dissatisfied by the absence of some job conditions, the presence of those conditions does not build strong motivation. Herzberg called the conditions *maintenance factors,* also called hygiene factors, since they are necessary to maintain a reasonable level of satisfaction. He also

Exhibit 12–4 _____

A motivational model

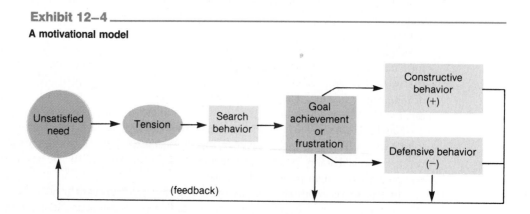

[6]See Frederick Herzberg, B. Mausner, and B. Snyderman, *The Motivation to Work* (New York: John Wiley & Sons, 1959).

noted that these factors have often been perceived by managers as factors which can motivate subordinates, but that they are, in fact, more potent as dissatisfiers when they are absent. He concluded that there were 10 maintenance factors, namely:

a. Company policy and administration.
b. Technical supervision.
c. Interpersonal relations with supervisor.
d. Interpersonal relations with peers.
e. Interpersonal relations with subordinates.
f. Salary.
g. Job security.
h. Personal life.
i. Work conditions.
j. Status.

2. Some job conditions build high levels of motivation and job satisfaction. However, the absence of these conditions does not prove highly dissatisfying. Herzberg described six of these *motivational factors,* or satisfiers:

a. Achievement.
b. Recognition.

"So no one actually sends you compliments. Isn't __this__ enough?"

    c. Advancement.
    d. The work itself.
    e. The possibility of personal growth.
    f. Responsibility.

In summary, the absence of maintenance factors causes much dissatisfaction, but these factors do not provide strong motivation when they are present. On the other hand, the presence of the factors in the second group leads to strong motivation and satisfaction, but their absence does not cause much dissatisfaction. In Exhibit 12–5 the Herzberg idea of a two-factor continuum is presented and contrasted to the traditional view.

The motivational factors are job-centered; that is, they relate directly to the job itself, the individual's job performance, the job responsibilities, and the growth and recognition obtained from the job. The maintenance factors are peripheral to the job itself and are more related to the external environment of work. Another important finding of Herzberg's study is that when employees are highly motivated, they have a high tolerance for dissatisfaction arising from the absence of maintenance factors.

The distinction between motivational and maintenance factors is similar to the distinction between what psychologists have described as *intrinsic* and *extrinsic* motivators. Intrinsic motivators are part of the job and occur when the employee performs the work. The opportunity to perform a job with intrinsic motivational potential is motivating because the work itself is rewarding. Extrinsic motivators are external rewards that have meaning or value after the work has been performed or away from the workplace. They provide little, if any, satisfaction when the work is being performed. Pay, of course, is a good example of what Herzberg classifies as a maintenance factor and what some psychologists call an extrinsic motivator.

Criticisms of Two-Factor Theory

One limitation of Herzberg's original study and conclusions is that the subjects consisted of engineers and accountants. The fact that these individuals were in such positions indicates that they had the motivation to seek advanced education and that they expected to

Exhibit 12–5 _____

Traditional versus Herzberg view of satisfaction

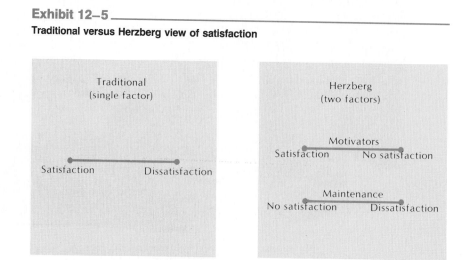

be rewarded for it. The same may not hold true for nonprofessional workers. In fact, some testing of Herzberg's model on blue-collar workers showed that some of Herzberg's maintenance factors (pay, job security) are regarded as motivational factors by blue-collar workers.[7]

Individuals evaluating Herzberg's ideas have also cited other problems.[8] It has been claimed that Herzberg's conclusions concerning the differences between dissatisfiers and motivators cannot be completely accepted, and that the differences in the stated sources of satisfaction and dissatisfaction in Herzberg's study may be the result of defensive processes within those responding. Critics point out that people are apt to attribute the causes of satisfaction to their own achievements, but are more likely to attribute their dissatisfaction to obstacles presented by company policies or superiors than to their own deficiencies.

Another group has criticized Herzberg's oversimplification of the true relationships between motivation and dissatisfaction as well as between the sources of job satisfaction and job dissatisfaction.[9] These authors reviewed several studies which showed that one factor can cause job satisfaction for one person and job dissatisfaction for another. They concluded that further research is needed to be able to predict in what situations worker satisfaction will produce greater performance.

Since conducting the original study, Herzberg has cited numerous and diverse replications which support his position.[10] These studies were conducted on professional women, hospital maintenance personnel, agricultural administrators, nurses, food handlers, manufacturing supervisors, engineers, scientists, military officers, managers ready for retirement, teachers, technicians, and assemblers; and some of the studies were conducted in other cultural settings—Finland, Hungary, Russia, and Yugoslavia.

This discussion indicates that Herzberg's theory has generated a great deal of controversy. Therefore, the readers should not view his theory as the answer for all motivation problems in organization, but as a starting point which they can use when attempting to develop their own approaches to motivation in the work situation.

Even after considering the legitimate criticisms, few would argue that Herzberg has not contributed substantially to our thinking on motivation at work. He has certainly extended Maslow's ideas and made them more applicable to the work situation. In addition, he has drawn attention to the critical importance of job-centered factors in work motivation which previously had been given little attention by behavioral scientists. This insight has resulted in an increased interest in *job enrichment,* an effort to restructure jobs so as to increase worker satisfaction. (See Chapter 4.)

There is much similarlity between Herzberg's and Maslow's models. A close examination of Herzberg's ideas indicates that what he is actually saying is that some employees may have achieved a level of social and economic progress in our society such that the higher level needs of Maslow (esteem and self-actualization) are the primary motivators. However, these employees must still satisfy their lower level needs in order to maintain

---

[7]Michael R. Malinovsky and John R. Barry, "Determinants of Work Attitudes," *Journal of Applied Psychology,* (December 1965), pp. 446–51. For a discussion of other alternative interpretations of the two-factor theory and the research support for the various interpretations, see N. King, "Clarification and Evaluation of the Two-Factor Theory of Job Satisfaction," *Psychological Bulletin,* July 1970, pp. 18–31; and D. A. Ondrack, "Defense Mechanisms and the Herzberg Theory: An Alternate Test," *Personnel Psychology,* March 1974, pp. 79–89.

[8]Victor H. Vroom, *Work and Motivation* (New York: John Wiley & Sons, 1964), pp. 128–29.

[9]R. J. House and L. A. Wigdor, "Herzberg's Dual-Factor Theory of Job Satisfaction and Motivation: A Review of the Evidence and a Criticism," *Personnel Psychology,* Winter 1967, pp. 369–89.

[10]Frederick Herzberg, *Work and the Nature of Man* (Cleveland: World Publishing, 1966).

their current state. Thus, we can see that money might still be a motivator for nonmanagement workers (particularly those at a minimum wage level) and for some managerial employees. The power of money as a motivator may be taking on new meaning in an economy with a high annual inflation rate. Herzberg's model adds to the need hierarchy model because it draws a distinction between the two groups of motivational and maintenance factors and because it points out that the motivational factors are often derived from the job itself. Exhibit 12–6 compares the two models.

Expectancy Theory

A theory of motivation has been developed by Vroom that expands on the work of Maslow and Herzberg.[11] The expectancy theory views motivation as a process governing choices. Thus, an individual who has a particular goal must perform some behavior in order to achieve the goal. The individual, therefore, weights the likelihood that various behaviors will achieve the desired goal, and if a certain behavior is expected to be more successful than others, that behavior will probably be selected.

An important contribution of the expectancy theory is that it explains how the *goals* of individuals influence their *effort* and that the behavior individuals select depends on their assessment of whether it will successfully lead to the goal. For example, the members of an organization may not all place the same value on such job factors as compensation, promotion, job security, and working conditions. Vroom believes that what is important is the perception and value that the individual places on certain goals. Suppose that one individual places a high value on salary increases and perceives high performance as instrumental in reaching that goal. Accordingly, this individual will strive toward superior performance in order to achieve the salary increases. However, another individual

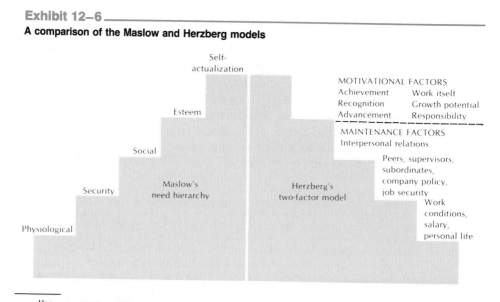

Exhibit 12–6 _____

A comparison of the Maslow and Herzberg models

[11]Vroom, *Work and Motivation.*

may value a promotion and perceive knowing the right person as related to achieving it. This individual, therefore, is not likely to emphasize superior performance to achieve the goal. The reader is now encouraged to think of this in terms of student motivation, where one student has the goal of an A grade and another the goal of a C grade in a particular course. How might their respective efforts and behaviors in the course vary?

The strength of a person's preference for one outcome in relation to another is called *valence.* The strength of a person's belief that an act will lead to a particular goal (e.g., an outcome) is called expectancy. If a student is perfectly certain that she has no chance to receive an A by working hard, then expectancy is *zero.* If, however, she is sure that hard work will lead to an A in the course, expectancy is 1.

In short, valence is a person's desire for an outcome and expectancy is the probability that a person's action will achieve the outcome. When valence is multiplied by expectancy the result is a person's state of motivation. Expectancy theory assumes that people make motivational decisions on how they perceive the valence, the relationship between rewards and performance, and expectancy of performing a task. The level of motivational effort will be high if people perceive *(a)* they can perform the task, *(b)* that their performance will be rewarded, and *(c)* the rewards satisfy their needs. Do you agree with this theory? What about with regard to your study and the results for the last examination you took? Think about your behavior in terms of expectancy theory.

The expectancy model is certainly more abstract than the need hierarchy and the two-factor models. However, the expectancy model adds insight into the study of motivation at work since it attempts to explain how *individual goals* influence *individual performance.* But note that the common thread running through each of these three theories is that behavior is goal directed.

Equity Theory

Another popular way to explain behavior is in terms of *equity.* While the hierarchy of needs emphasized unsatisfied needs, Herzberg's theory emphasized job conditions which are motivators, and expectancy theory focused on a person's choice or decision making, equity theory is concerned with the fairness of distributed rewards. The equity explanation of motivators rests in two assumptions.[12] First, it is assumed that individuals engage in a process of evaluating their social relationships. That is, people make contributions and expect something in return or outcomes. If Joe works hard (input) he expects the company to reward him (outcome). Second, it is assumed that people compare their input-outcome ratio with others to determine their relative position. That is, Joe examines his work-reward situation with a co-worker, Dan, and considers whether his situation is equitable or not.

The equity situation exists if the ratio of a person's perceived outcomes to inputs is equal to the ratio of the other's outcomes to inputs. Or when:

$$\frac{O_p}{I_p} = \frac{O_0}{I_0}$$

---

[12]J. S. Adams, ''Injustice in Social Exchange,'' *Advances in Experimental Social Psychology,* ed. L. Berkowitz (New York: Academic Press, 1965).

Inequity exists when these two ratios are unequal:

$$\frac{O_p}{I_p} > \frac{O_0}{I_0} \quad \text{or} \quad \frac{O_p}{I_p} < \frac{O_0}{I_0}$$

The conditions necessary to produce a state of inequity are based on the person's perceptions of inputs and outcomes. If a person has a distorted view of the compensation received by a co-worker, this distortion will be incorporated into his/her calculations of equity or inequity. The inequity can occur when the person is relatively underpaid or overpaid. Of course, individuals are more willing to accept overpayment than underpayment.

The Consequences of Inequity

There are some obvious consequences if inequity exists. First, perceived inequity creates tension within an individual. Second, the tension is proportionate to the magnitude of the inequity. Third, the tension will motivate an individual to reduce it. Finally, the strength of motivation to reduce the tension is proportionate to the perceived inequity.[13]

In reality people have a number of actions they can take to reduce inequity. A few of these actions are:

1. *To alter the inputs.* For example, underpaid people may reduce their job efforts or increase absenteeism, while overpaid people may work harder.
2. *To alter the outcomes.* For example, the union works to increase wages and fringe benefits without an increase in employee effort.
3. *Leave the situation.* For example, quitting or transferring permits the person to get away from the comparison person.
4. *Changing the comparison person.* For example, finding someone else to compare oneself to is a method of bringing the ratios into balance.

Through these and other actions, individuals attempt to cope with situations thay they believe are unfair. Their actions and motivations are largely aimed at returning to a state of equity and reduced tension.

The Manager's Role

The equity theory of motivation emphasizes the importance to managers of the comparisons people make. For example, increasing someone's pay or redesigning a job may not improve a person's performance if the changes do not change the input-outcome ratio. If employees still believe that inequities exist even after such changes, there will probably be no improvement in effort (motivation). Do you ever make comparisons? It's human nature to do so!

Furthermore, the importance of perception in employee motivation is clearly spelled out in the equity theory. If employees perceive that they are inequitably treated, they will respond sometimes in a manner that is contrary to company objectives. For example,

---

[13]Rick T. Mowday, "Equity Theory Predictions of Behavior in Organizations," *Motivation and Work Behavior,* ed. R. M. Steers and L. W. Porter (New York: McGraw-Hill, 1979).

P/HRM Manager Close-Up

Betty Bessler
Mary Kay Cosmetics, Inc.

Biography

Betty Bessler, whose title is director of personnel, joined Mary Kay Cosmetics, Inc., in 1975 as personnel manager in a former manufacturing subsidiary with the responsibility to establish a personnel function in that organization. Prior to joining Mary Kay she was personnel manager of Liquid Paper Corporation for five years, where she had established the corporate personnel function.

Ms. Bessler received a B.A. degree from the University of Dallas, and has done graduate work in business at the University of Dallas and Southern Methodist University.

Job description

In 1981 Ms. Bessler assumed responsibility for Mary Kay's total personnel function, which includes responsibility for employment, employee relations, compensation, benefits, and management and organizational development.

Views about personnel/human resource management at Mary Kay Cosmetics

The personnel department of Mary Kay continues the historical departmental responsibility to maximize the contribution of the human resources of the organization to meet corporate goals and objectives. The planning, controlling and effective utiliza-

tion, training and motivation of "people" assets has been and continues to be a major concern of the company. The role of the personnel department in this effort is to serve the organization as a catalyst, to be a resource to management in the recruitment and retention of a highly competent and motivated employee group.

The personnel department's focus is to implement and maintain systems to assure that the challenges of a high-growth organization with rapidly changing technologies can be met in the areas of employment services, employee relations, training and development programs, and recognition and reward systems.

Rapid changes in technology throughout the organization and rapid growth places an increased responsibility on the employment staff to recruit only those candidates who are above average in competence and technical expertise and who are self-motivated, flexible, and adaptable. Not only must the company employ talented people, but the resulting employee group must be utilized in such a way that commitment to the accomplishment of company goals is built. Communication and appropriate recognition and reward systems become key elements in this effort. The training and development of employees to ensure competency at all levels of the organization carries a high priority as well.

Another major challenge is to assure that the "people philosophy" which built the company is not lost as the company grows. The personnel department will play an important role in adapting the emphasis on individual recognition which built the company in the 1970s to a larger and more diverse employee population in the 1980s.

This means that members of the personnel staff must continue to grow and develop professionally, to become experts in strategic problem solving and planning, to know and understand our industry as well as the profession of personnel management. I've personally seen the personnel profession change and mature as personnel executives have increasingly become effective partners with management in achieving the goals and objectives of the organization. The personnel profession offers personal reward and satisfaction for the bright professionals now entering the field who are willing to accept the challenges before all of us who concentrate our efforts on the maximizing of human resources.

quitting or staying home from work are actions that people use to respond to inequities. Are your perceptions always accurate?

Also, the equity theory requires managers to do a better job at evaluating inputs or contributions. If people really do make comparisons then the organization needs some record of contributions upon which rewards are allocated. The allocation of rewards must be based on equity or contribution. One way to work toward equitably distributing rewards is to use a valid and reliable performance evaluation program (see Chapter 8).

Application of Motivation Theories

The four motivation theories discussed in this chapter are often criticized for being merely theoretical. This implies that they are interesting but of little practical value to managers. However, in reality many applications of significant value use parts or the entire explanation of motivation theories. Understanding the four theories presented provides managers with the tools and knowledge to examine various motivational problems like that facing Tanya Collins in the opening case. Tanya might ask: (1) Are Mark's needs being satisfied by the job? (2) What motivators can be built into the job? (3) What are Mark's preferred goals and can he accomplish them on the job? (4) Does Mark feel that he is receiving his fair share of the rewards?

Two specific and currently popular motivational programs are behavior modification and quality circles. They are being used in organizations throughout the industrialized world. In some cases they have been successful in terms of improving either or both performance and attitudes. However, in some situations they have been improperly implemented or placed in organizations where managers were not trained or knowledgeable in their application.

Behavior Modification

One method for improving employee productivity which has emerged in recent years is *behavior modification*. This method is based largely on the theory and research of B. F. Skinner[14] who emphasizes the effect of environmental influences on behavior,

Skinner distinguishes between *respondent behavior* and *operant behavior*. Respondent behavior occurs because of some prior stimulus. It is unlearned, instinctive behavior. One does not learn to sneeze or to cough. Operant behavior, on the other hand, must be learned.

The fundamental difference between respondent behavior and operant behavior can be further illustrated by the relationship between response and the environment. In respondent behavior the environment acts on the person and there is a response. The doctor taps a knee and the leg moves—respondent behavior. However, the patient must first call the doctor for an appointment—operant behavior.

In studying this distinction, Skinner introduced the concept of *operant conditioning*. In Skinner's theory operant behavior is learned on the basis of its consequences. *Thus, learned behavior operates on the environment to produce a change.* If the behavior causes the desired change, then Skinner states that this behavior is *reinforced* and will probably be repeated. For example, being permitted to drive across a toll bridge is contingent on

---

[14]B. F. Skinner, *Contingencies of Reinforcement* (New York: Appleton-Century-Crofts, 1969).

inserting the proper change in a coin meter. If the proper change is inserted, the green light will flash and the gate will go up. The *behavior* is inserting the coin, and the *consequence* is the gate going up. Thus, behavior can be conditioned by adjusting its consequences.

Over the years, scientific experimentation has produced the information needed to implement behavioral modification in organizations. Three specific strategies have emerged from this work—positive reinforcement, negative reinforcement, and punishment. The strategies can and are used singly or in various combinations to improve performance.

Positive reinforcement refers to an increase in the frequency of a response which is followed by a positive reinforcer. Such reinforcers are often called rewards. For example, employees repeatedly produce large quantities of parts (a frequent response) because they are paid on a piece-rate basis. Something is reinforcing the behavior to produce the large quantities. In this example, pay is the positive reinforcer (reward) that increases the frequency with which the workers produce large quantities.

Take a few minutes and think about the four motivation theories. Skinner showed little concern with a person's needs. He was more concerned about determining how rewards influence behavior. Expectancy theory is more relevant in explaining how behavior modification works than are any of the other three theories. Using expectancy theory would require that the manager determine which rewards his or her employees prefer.

Negative reinforcement refers to the increased frequency of a response which is brought about by removing a disliked event immediately after the response occurs. An example would be an employee whose supervisor continually nags about producing more units. By producing more, the worker causes the supervisor to stop nagging. The elimination of the nagging results in more production.

Punishment decreases the frequency of a response by introducing something disliked or removing something liked following that response. A worker may tell the supervisor that she has discovered a way to reduce machine downtime. The supervisor publicly reprimands her for wasting time working on stupid projects like this and tells her to get back to work. The actions of the supervisor are punishment oriented and will probably reduce the tendency of the worker to be creative.

Organizational applications of behavior modification • Emery Air Freight has used positive reinforcement as a behavior modification strategy. Under the directions of Edward J. Feeney, a vice president when behavior modification was introduced at Emery, the company reported a saving of $2 million over a three-year period. Feeney developed what he called a *Performance Audit* for identifying performance-related behaviors and strengthening them with positive reinforcement.[15]

An audit was conducted to find the job behaviors that were most closely linked to profit. The strategy was to tell the individuals who were responsible for profit-oriented behaviors how they were doing. This feedback was a part of learning for the employees. They found out on a regular basis how they were doing and what the company thought about their work.

The Emery program is kept simple in each unit. First, the audit identifies the key performance behaviors. Second, management establishes a realistic goal and gives the

---

[15]W. C. Hamner and E. P. Hamner, "Behavior Modification on the Bottom Line," *Organizational Dynamics,* Spring 1976, pp. 3–21.

employees frequent feedback on how they are performing. Third, improved performance is strengthened by positive reinforcement such as praise and recognition. The main thrust of the Emery program is to provide timely feedback and to use positive reinforcement that is contingent on performance improvement.

B. F. Goodrich Chemical Company uses a positive reinforcement program. One production section in a B. F. Goodrich plant in Ohio was not performing well. After identifying some problems, the production manager introduced a positive reinforcement program. The program provided cost, scheduling, and goal accomplishment information directly to the first-line supervisors once a week. Daily meetings were also held to discuss how each group in the section was doing. This program allowed the supervisor and the subordinates to look at the performance of the group on a regular basis. Illustrative charts were developed that showed achievements as compared to objectives in terms of sales, costs, and production.

The evaluation of this program by company representatives indicated that production increased over 300 percent in five years. Production costs went down. The company believed that these impressive results were largely the result of providing the supervisors and employees with feedback about their performance.

Criticisms of Behavior Modification • Despite impressive results from behavior modification, there have been many critics of this approach.[16] Some of the major criticisms of behavior modification are:

It is coercive.

It is bribery.

It is dependent on extrinsic reinforcers.

It requires continual reinforcement.

One means to avoid coercion is to have employees participate in the development of the reinforcement program. Participative behavior modification programs are certainly possible.

In some programs, tokens are used to reward employees for not being absent or for performing well. The critics charge that this is an illicit use of rewards, and also that it demeans the persons who receive them. They point out that mental institutions sometimes give tokens to patients who display socially acceptable behavior, and they argue that tokens ought not to be applied to employees.

Some critics object that reinforcement leads to a dependence on reinforcers. As a result, extrinsic reinforcers might always be required in order to secure acceptable performance. The issue here is whether enough extrinsic reinforcers can be found to continue the program. If the same reinforcers are used over and over again, they become boring and lose their effect.

The final criticism focuses on the necessity for continual reinforcement. To be successful, behavior modification requires that supervisors closely monitor the performance of their subordinates and reward desired behavior. However, in many organizations managers simply do not have sufficient time for such close supervision. This criticism, however, applies as well to any of the motivation theories that are put into practice by a

---

[16]Fred L. Fry, "Operant Conditioning in Organizational Setting: Of Mice or Men," *Personnel,* July–August 1974, pp. 17–24.

manager. For example, applying Herzberg's motivators requires continual attention and involvement of a manager.

Behavior modification, like the use of a good pay plan or of job enrichment, will work in some organizations but not in others. The evidence of success is not overwhelming, but it does appear promising. Of course, failures are usually not as widely publicized as successes. It appears that Skinner's ideas may be used by some managers to obtain some degree of performance improvement.

Quality Circles

During the past 10 years American and Canadian industries have been experiencing a quiet revolution. Faced with sluggish productivity, an increasingly competitive world market, and inflation, some managers have discovered and experimented with *Quality Circles* (QCs). Quality Circles are small groups of workers (7–12) who meet regularly (weekly in most cases) with their supervisor as the Circle leader to solve work-related problems (e.g., quality, quantity, cost).

From management's point of view, the Quality Circle is a motivational program that has significant potential. One expert stated that, "There is scarcely a study in the entire literature that fails to demonstrate that . . . productivity increases accure from a genuine increase in decision-making power . . . the participative worker is an involved worker, for his job is an extension of himself and by his decisions he is creating his work, modifying and regulating it."[17] Circles leave time for managers to manage. The motivation is assumed to be in the task itself.

QCs give the employee the opportunity for involvement, social need satisfaction, participation in work improvement, challenge, and opportunity for growth. They are, in essence, a vehicle for enabling employees to satisfy lower and upper level needs (as stated by Maslow) and job condition motivators (as described in Herzberg's theory). Participation in QCs provides the vital Herzberg-type motivators to even the lowest level employee. Members assume responsibility to identify and analyze problems in their work areas.

Although in most cases QCs meet for only about an hour a week, this meeting carries over into the rest of the week. Circle activities are carried to break and lunch times. Also, members continue to think about the points raised in the meetings. Frequently, Circle members meet on their own time to complete QC assignments such as charting or graphing. One QC often compares its progress to that of other QCs.

The employee in a Quality Circle is part of a team which seeks common goals. Matching the worker's needs to company goals can be accomplished in a QC. Organizational goals can be reached while personal needs keep the progess moving forward.

The QC: The Final Answer? • Like any managerial program with motivational overtones, QCs have some risks. Assuming that QCs are the answer to all motivational problems is, of course, misleading and untrue. The Japanese popularized the use of QCs. A concern is whether a Japanese model of motivation can work in the United States or Canada. Japan is not the same technologically as the United States or Canada. Furthermore, Japan has a homogeneous culture which treats organizational life as an extension of family life.

---

[17]Mignon Mazique, "The Quality Circle Transplant," *Issues and Observations,* May 1981, pp. 1–4.

This is not the case in plants, offices, and construction projects in Detroit, Chicago, Los Angeles, Toronto, and elsewhere in North America.

Culture is certainly a powerful force that must be considered. However, there is also the need to determine whether labor and management is willing to work together in QCs. Instead of initiating the Japanese style of QCs, it seems more realistic to develop an American style QC, a Canadian style QC, and so forth. The appropriate QC style must be developed by labor and management through a cooperative team effort. If such cooperation is not possible then QCs, no matter how they are designed, have little chance to be successful in motivating participants.

The American aerospace industry has used QCs successfully. It is an industry that is concerned with quality because one small error can have a devastating price in terms of human lives. There is also a history of labor-management cooperation in the aerospace industry. The results of QCs in the industry have been positive—higher productivity and morale. This particular industry is well suited for QCs.

On the other hand, the use of QCs in the auto industry has been much more difficult. For years the relationship between management and labor has been antagonistic and difficult to overcome through the use of QCs. The common good, common interest, and common goals will not be accomplished if labor and management are not inclined to cooperate and work together.

Another potential problem with QCs is managerial resistance. QCs encourage people at the bottom levels of the organization to voice opinions, make suggestions, and display their ideas about work. This theoretically reduces the administrative distance between worker and manager. The result is that some managers are threatened by what they perceive as a loss of power, status, prestige, and authority. They may consciously or subconsciously hinder the work and processes of the QC. A QC can die if managers do not become involved and supportive of its efforts.

Managerial resistance doesn't have to be the case. YKK is a Japanese zipper manufacturer with 22,000 employees working in 36 overseas plants. An interesting experiment is going on at the Montreal, Canada, YKK plant. The employees are divided into worker groups that resemble quality circles.[18] Each division manager organizes his staff into either a technical or production group. The technical staff meets once a month to discuss the maintenance of the plant's machinery. Almost all the other workers are organized into 14 groups of 10 people each. Once a week after work, they discuss production and quality issues.

The manager is a key communication point and is actively involved in the YKK arrangement. Communication from the top down and vice versa is expected and encouraged. The manager is able to be involved because he or she is the key to the worker groups. So far the YKK experiment has been a success—absenteeism is down, turnover is down, and managers like the major roles they are playing in the groups.

Still another potential area of difficulty is the role of the Circle leader. This role is usually occupied by the manager or supervisor. However, in the QC the leader is not in an authority position. He or she is instead a facilitator, a discussion leader who helps the group reach solutions. The leader who attempts to autocratically enforce his or her viewpoints quickly loses the respect, cooperation, and attention of the QC members. Many managers have a difficult time making the transition from a legitimate authority position in the formal hierarchy to the role of a facilitator in a QC.

---

[18]Robert Collison, ''The Japanese Fix,'' *Canadian Business,* November 1981, p. 42.

Case

Tanya

Tanya is now more familiar with the role that motivation plays in explaining Mark Kelsey's performance deficiencies. She is aware that Mark's problem could be motivational. She is presently sitting at her desk developing a plan to work with Mark and really explore his plight. Tanya feels that maybe she can create a better work environment for Mark and her other subordinates. She is going to have a long discussion with Mark about his goals and preferences. Tanya is proceeding with care since she wants Mark to be relaxed and comfortable about the discussion. She knows that it is impossible to tell Mark to be motivated. Motivation, after all, is something inside Mark and Tanya wants to use her knowledge about motivation to learn about his needs, preferences, feelings about the fairness of the reward system, and his goals.

The continued introduction and research of QCs in American and Canadian industry will undoubtedly continue in the 1980s. Whether or not QCs can work as well in North America as they have in Japan remains to be tested in the next few years. They are worthy of consideration from managers and organizations who are willing to allow employees to participate in job-related problem solving.[19]

Summary

Motivation is at the top of any manager's list of topics of extreme importance. A manager with the most skilled employees in the world is in trouble if these talented subordinates are not motivated. This chapter points out the following:

1. Motivation is concerned with the "why" of human behavior. It is an internal process which is not directly observable.
2. All behavior is motivated to achieve certain goals.
3. A number of theoretical explanations are available to help managers understand and deal with motivation. Maslow's need hierarchy suggests that unsatisfied needs stimulate a person.

[19]Elaine Rendall, "Quality Circles—A 'Third Wave' Intervention," *Training and Development Journal*, March 1981, pp. 28–31. Also see Edwin G. Yager, "The Quality Circle Explosion," *Training and Development Journal*, April 1981, pp. 98–99, 101–5 and Michael LeBoeuf, *Productivity Challenge: How to Make It Work for America and You*, New York: McGraw-Hill, 1982.

4. The nonsatisfaction of needs may result in constructive behavior which results in a person attempting to satisfy needs. However, individuals who are blocked in attempts to satisfy their needs may exhibit defensive behaviors such as withdrawal, aggression, or substitution.

5. Herzberg developed a two-factor theory of motivation. One factor results in creating no dissatsifaction but little motivation. The other factor serves as motivating behavior. The motivators include achievement, recognition, and responsibility.

6. The expectancy theory of motivation involves explaining the choices people make in achieving goals. Individuals are assumed to weigh the likelihood that various behaviors will achieve the desired goal and act accordingly.

7. The equity theory assumes that people evaluate their social relationships in terms of inputs versus outcomes. Their input-outcome situation is compared to input-outcomes of others. If the ratios are equal there is little tension to change.

8. The test of theories in managerial terms is whether they can be applied. Many applications of theory exist. Two popular motivational applications were selected for inclusion—behavior modification and Quality Circles. These applications use such factors as needs, goals, comparisons, and external motivators. That is, they borrow from theories of motivation.

Questions for Review and Discussion

1. Do you make the kind of comparisons discussed in the equity theory of motivation? Explain.

2. Are there any differences between expectancy theory and behavior modification?

3. The manager of clerical personnel was overheard saying, "I believe that money is the best of all possible motivators. You can say what you please about all that other nonsense, but when it comes right down to it, if you give a person a raise, you'll motivate him or her. That's all there is to it." In light of what we have discussed in this chapter, advise this manager.

4. Think of a situation from your personal experience in which two individuals reacted differently to frustration. Discuss each situation and the reactions of the two individuals. Can you give a possible explanation of why the two individuals reacted differently?

5. Some critics of behavior modification and Quality Circles state that most of the declared successes are based on short-term results. These critics contend that a proper evaluation over a longer period of time would show less positive results for these programs. Comment.

6. A student remarked after reading and discussing this chapter that "a person can't motivate another person. A person can only engage in self-motivation." What do you think?

7. In this chapter it was emphasized that managers must be familiar with the fundamental needs of people in order to motivate employees successfully. Select two individuals with whom you are well acquainted. Do they differ,

in your opinion, with respect to the strength of various needs? Discuss these differences, and indicate how they could affect behavior. If you were attempting to motivate those persons, would you use different approaches for each? Why?

8. Can a student be motivated by an instructor? How?

9. Assume that you have just read that the *goals* of individuals influence their *effort* and that the behavior which they select depends on their assessment of the probability that the behavior will successfully lead to the goal. What is your goal in this course? Is it influencing your effort? Do you suppose that another person in your class might have a different goal? Is his or her effort (behavior) different from yours? Could this information be of any value to your professor?.

10. Why should a manager be concerned about the consequences of inequity?

Glossary

Constructive Behavior. Positive behavior that a person uses to satisfy needs when they have been thwarted or frustrated.

Defensive Behavior. Negative behaviors, such as withdrawal aggression and rationalization, that a person resorts to when attempts to satisfy needs have been frustrated.

Expectancy. The strength of a person's belief that an act will lead to a particular goal.

Extrinsic Motivation. External rewards that have meaning or value after the work has been performed or away from the workplace—according to Herzberg pay is extrinsic.

Intrinsic Motivation. There are motivators that are part of the job and occur when the person performs the work—feeling good about doing a good job.

Motivation. All those inner striving conditions described as wishes, desires, drives, and so on. It is an inner state that activates or moves.

Need Hierarchy. A motivation theory proposed by Maslow. He believed that five levels of needs exist; that these needs are arranged in a hierarchy of importance, and that only needs not yet satisfied can influence behavior.

Operant Conditioning. According to B. F. Skinner, operant behavior is learned on the basis of its consequences. If reinforced, operant behavior will probably be repeated.

Quality Circles. Small groups of workers who meet regularly with their supervisor as the Circle leader, to solve work-related problems.

Valence. The strength of a person's preference for one outcome in relation to another.

Chapter Thirteen

Compensation: An Overview

Learning Objectives

After reading this chapter, you should be able to:

- Define what is meant by job evaluation.

- Describe four widely used methods of job evaluation.

- Discuss how pay surveys help management compare their pay systems to other organizations.

- Explain how external factors influence pay levels and policies.

- Illustrate a pay-class graph and pay trend line.

Chapter Outline

I. Introduction
   A. Objectives of Compensation
   B. Compensation Decision Makers
   C. Compensation Decisions

II. A Diagnostic Approach to Compensation

III. Compensation and Employee Satisfaction

IV. Compensation and Employee Performance

V. External Influences on Pay Levels
   A. Government Influences
   B. Union Influences on Compensation
   C. Economic Conditions and Compensation
   D. Nature of the Labor Market and Compensation

VI. Pay Surveys and Comparable Pay Levels
   A. Who Conducts Wage Surveys?
   B. How Pay Surveys Are Conducted and Used

VII. Organizational Influences on Pay Levels
   A. The Labor Budget
   B. Goals of Controlling Interests and Managerial Pay Strategies

VIII. The Pay-Level Decision

IX. Pay Structures
   A. Job Evaluation
   B. Pay Classes, Rate Ranges, and Classifications

X. Individual Pay Determination

XI. Summary

Case

Poppa Joe

Guido

Cardeson National Bank is a small firm which was founded in suburban Pittsburgh 14 years ago. For the first year and a half, it operated out of a prefabricated building on a small lot across from the shopping center. Then it built a nice building on the site. Later it added two branch offices in adjoining suburbs. CNB now employs about 150 persons.

The founder of the bank and still president is Joseph Paderewski, an entrepreneur who made his first career in construction and building. Poppa Joe, as everyone calls him, was 64 years old. He spent most of his energies building the bank. He did this by raising money from the original stockholders, developing a marketing plan to get enough depositors to use CNB, and finding good locations at which to build banks.

Poppa Joe did almost all the hiring. He also established the pay rates himself for each employee, based on experience, potential, and how much the employee needs to help support self and family. Recently, Guido Panelli, his executive vice president, started bringing Poppa Joe some problems he didn't have time for. Guido has mentioned something about salaries, but Poppa Joe hasn't given it much thought.

Poppa Joe has always had an open-door policy. Yesterday a teller, Arte Jamison, came in to see him.

Arte Jamison Poppa Joe, you hired me five years ago. I came in to tell you that I'm quitting. I had to tell Mr. Panelli about this problem a couple of times and nothing happened. So I'm gone. I'm going to work for Pittsburgh National Bank for more money.

Poppa Joe Arte, don't quit for money. What do you need? I'll take care of it.

Arte That's not the point. You keep hiring in people with less experience than me at more pay. There's no future here with a situation like that. I quit.

Poppa Joe Sure sorry to see you go, Arte.

Poppa Joe sat in his office. He'd always liked Arte. What was happening? He called in Guido.

Poppa Joe Guido, what's happening around here? Arte Jamison just quit. He's a good man.

Guido Boss, I've tried to bring the subject up lots of times, and you're always too busy. We've got a poor pay system around here.

Poppa Joe What do you mean? I've always been fair.

Guido You think you've been fair. But you're too busy to do all you've been doing. You hire people at one pay level and others doing the same job at another. Some get behind and never get a raise. It's a mess.

I've asked one of our vice presidents, Mary Renfro, to take a course at the University of Pittsburgh's night MBA program on P/HRM, and to look especially at compensation. She's done it. Now: Should I ask her to study the problem and talk to us about it?

Poppa Joe O.K., let her do a study. But I'm not convinced we've got such a big problem because a few people quit.

Guido Please boss, let's keep an open mind about this. Pay has an awfully important impact on employees.

Introduction

Compensation is part of a transaction between an employee and an employer which results in an employment contract. From the employee's point of view, pay is a necessity in life. Few people are so wealthy they do not accept financial remuneration for their work. The compensation received for work is one of the chief reasons people seek employment. Pay is the means by which they provide for their own and their family's needs. For people with instrumental attitudes toward work (as discussed in Chapter 2), compensation may be the only (or certainly a major) reason why they work. Others find compensation a contributing factor to their efforts. Pay can do more than provide for the physiological needs of employees, however. It can also serve their recognition needs.

Compensation is one of the most important P/HRM functions for the employer, too. Compensation often equals 50 percent of the cash flow of an organization, and a larger percentage in service enterprises. It may be the major method used to attract the employees needed to get the work done, as well as a means to try to motivate more effective performance. Compensation is also significant to the economy. For the past 30 years, salaries and wages have equaled about 60 percent of the gross national product of the United States and Canada.

Compensation or pay is only one way the employee is rewarded for work. Work also provides benefits (Chapter 15), such as promotions and status, intrinsic benefits of the job and other rewards. The relative importance which employees attach to pay as compared to the other rewards varies with their preferences.

Objectives of Compensation

The objective of a compensation system is to create a system of rewards which is equitable to the employer and employee alike, so that the employee is attracted to the work and *motivated* to do a good job for the employer. Patton suggests that in compensation policy there are seven criteria for effectiveness.[1] The compensation should be:

> *Adequate*. Minimum governmental, union, and managerial levels should be met.
>
> *Equitable*. Each person is paid fairly, in line with his or her effort, abilities, training, and so on.
>
> *Balanced*. Pay, benefits, and other rewards provide a reasonable total reward package.
>
> *Cost effective*. Pay is not excessive, considering what the organization can afford to pay.
>
> *Secure*. The extent to which the employee's security needs relative to pay and the needs which pay satisfies are met.
>
> *Incentive providing*. Pay motivates effective and productive work.
>
> *Acceptable to the employee*. The employee understands the pay system and feels it is a reasonable system for the enterprise and himself or herself.

How well do you think Cardeson National Bank's pay plan is achieivng these objectives?

---

[1] Thomas Patton, *Pay* (New York: Free Press, 1977).

> At present Cardeson National Bank has a rudimentary P/HRM manager, much less a compensation manager. Poppa Joe is making almost all decisions.

Compensation Decision Makers

A number of persons are involved in making compensation decisions. Top management makes the decisions which determine the total amount of the budget that goes to pay, the pay form to be used (time pay versus incentive pay), and pay policies, such as secrecy. They also set the pay strategy (discussed below). Usually the P/HRM department advises them of all these issues. As always, the operating managers at the supervisory and middle-management level also have an impact on P/HRM decisions, including pay. The relationships between P/HRM and operating managers in pay matters are given in Exhibit 13–1.

Exhibit 13–1 describes a typical modern compensation manager. This person normally is a department head in a P/HRM department.

Compensation is a Stage IV P/HRM function. It is mature in that all work organizations compensate employees, and there is a good deal of empirical data with which to analyze the relative effectiveness of various compensation methods.

Compensation Decisions

Perhaps you believe that pay can be detemined by a manager and employee sitting down and talking it over, or you think the government or unions determined pay. In fact, pay is influenced by a series of internal and external factors. A diagnostic approach can be used to help you understand these factors better.

Pay can be determined absolutely or relatively. Some have argued that a pay system

Exhibit 13–1 _____

The roles of operating and P/HRM managers in making pay decisions

Pay decision factor	Operating manager (OM)	P/HRM manager (P/HRM)
Compensation budgets	OM approves or adjusts P/HRM preliminary budget	P/HRM prepares preliminary budget
Pay-level decisions: Pay survey design and interpretation		P/HRM designs, implements, and makes decisions
Pay structure decisions: Job evaluation design and interpretation		P/HRM designs, implements, and makes decisions
Pay classes, rate ranges, and classification design and interpretation		P/HRM designs, implements, and makes decisions
Individual pay determination	Joint decision with P/HRM	Joint decision with OM
Pay policy decisions: method of payment	OM decides after advice of P/HRM	P/HRM advises OM
Pay secrecy	OM decides after advice of P/HRM	P/HRM advises OM
Pay security	OM decides after advice of P/HRM	P/HRM advises OM

P/HRM Manager Close-Up

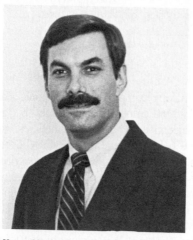

Henry Oliver
University Computing Company

Biography

Henry Oliver is manager of compensation and benefits for University Computing Company. Prior to his present assignment, he served the company as ad-

ministrator of compensation of benefits and as a staff recruiter. He has been with UCC since 1976. Before his association with UCC, he was regional director of personnel for the Massachusetts Indemnity and Life Insurance Company and a national accounts officer with the First City National Bank of Houston. He was born in Houston, Texas, and holds a B.A. degree in economics from the University of the South at Sewanee, Tennessee.

Job description

Henry Oliver is responsible for ensuring that UCCs employees are compensated at an equitable level relative to each other and to people who hold similar positions outside the company. He is also charged with the responsibility of maintaining benefits at levels which remain competitive and which provide real assistance to an employee at a time of death, disability, or retirement. Additionally, Oliver also recruits professionals for the company's corporate staff and provides personnel-related assistance for a remote subsidiary.

---

set by a single criterion for a whole nation or the world, an absolute control of pay, is the best procedure. However, in one of the few recorded attempts to use this approach, in Denmark, it was not a great success. Since absolute pay systems are not used, the pay for each individual is set *relative* to the pay of others.

Nash and Carroll point out that pay for a particular position is set relative to three groups.[2] These are:

- Employees working on similar jobs in other organizations (Group A).
- Employees working on different jobs within the organization (Group B).
- Employees working on the same job within the organization (Group C).

The decision to examine pay relative to Group A is called *the pay-level decision.* The objective of the pay-level decision is to keep the organization competitive in the labor market. The major tool used in this decision is the pay survey. The pay decision relative to Group B is called *the pay-structure decision.* This uses an approach called job evaluation. The decision involving pay relative to Group C is called *individual pay determination.*

---

[2]Allen Nash and Stephen J. Carroll, Jr., *The Management of Compensation* (Monterey, Calif.: Brooks/Cole Publishing, 1975).

Consider Joe Johnson, custodian at Cardeson National Bank. Joe's pay is affected first by the pay-level policy of the bank: whether CNB is a pacesetter or a going-wage employer. Next his pay is affected by how highly ranked *his* job is relative to other jobs, such as teller. Finally, his pay depends on how good a custodian he is, how long he has been with the enterprise, and other individual factors (individual pay determination).

A Diagnostic Approach to Compensation

Exhibit 13–2 highlights the diagnostic factors most important to compensation as a P/HRM activity. The nature of the task affects compensation primarily in the method of payment for the job, such as payment for time worked or incentive compensation, which depends on the task performed. These issues, and executive compensation, which differs in many ways from other types, are discussed in Chapter 14.

One of the most significant factors in compensation is the nature of the employee. How employee attitudes and preferences directly affect performance is discussed in the section. Employee attitudes and preferences also affect the pay structure.

There are other factors which affect compensation. The factors external to the organization—the government, unions, economic conditions, and labor market conditions—all have an effect in pay or wage surveys. Organizational factors are managerial goals and pay structures, labor budgets, and the size and age of the organization. Discussion of these factors in the sections below illustrates why employees and managers are paid the amounts they receive and which methods are used to pay people.

Compensation and Employee Satisfaction

Does a well-designed pay system motivate employees to greater performance, higher quality performance, or greater employee satisfaction? The answer to this question has varied from the yes of scientific management in the early 1900s to the no of human relations theorists in the 1930s. The controversy still rages. It is not possible to settle this age-old dispute here, but the various positions will be presented briefly .

All would agree that effective compensation administration is desirable in efforts to increase employee satisfaction. And satisfaction with pay is important because, as many researchers have found, if pay satisfaction is low, job satisfaction is low.[3] As a consequence, absenteeism and turnover will be higher and more costly.

A summary of research on pay satisfaction indicates a number of important points:[4]

> *Salary level.* The higher the pay, the higher the pay satisfaction within an occupational group at each job level. (For example, higher paid presidents are more satisfied than lower paid presidents.)

> *Community cost of living.* The lower the cost of living in a community, the higher the pay satisfaction.

---

[3]Graef S. Crystal, "Pay for Performance—Even If It's Just Luck," *The Wall Street Journal,* March 2, 1981, p. 16.

[4]J. D. Dunn and Frank Rachel, *Wage and Salary Administration* (New York: McGraw-Hill, 1971).

Exhibit 13–2

Factors affecting compensation and end results

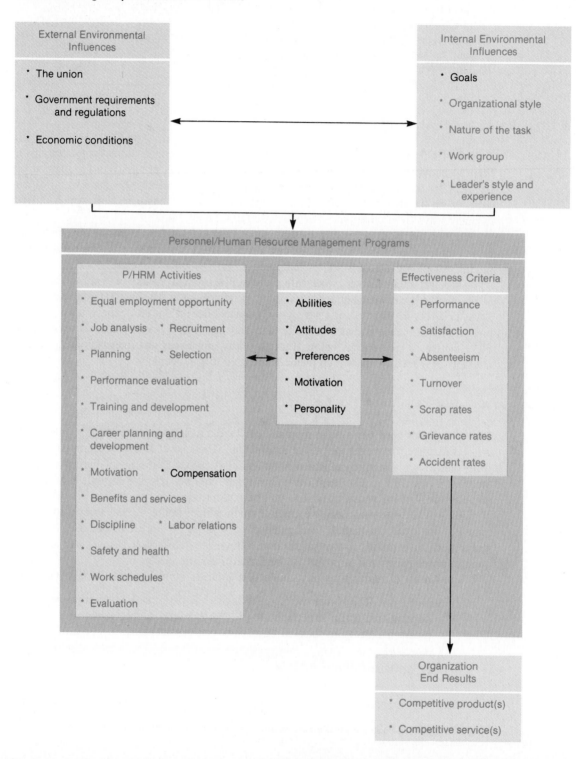

Education. The lower the educational level, the higher the pay satisfaction.

Future expectations. The more optimistic the employee is about future job conditions, the higher the pay satisfaction.

Other personal characteristics. The more intelligent, self-assured, and decisive a person is, the lower the pay satisfaction.

Pay basis. The more pay is perceived to be based on merit or performance, the greater the pay satisfaction.

In sum, most people believe it is desirable to have a pay system that leads to pay satisfaction. However, research indicates a relatively weak relationship between pay and satisfaction. One reason that the relationship is not stronger is that people have different ideas about what their pay should be. Another reason for the weak relationship is that how pay is determined is not clearly understood by employees. That is, nonjob factors such as being agreeable with the boss, having a pleasant personality, or making donations to the supervisor's favorite charity, may be factors in the pay decision. Whether they are or not is sometimes not known to the employees.

Compensation and Employee Performance

As we have seen, high performance requires much more than employee motivation. Employee ability, adequate equipment, good physical working conditions, effective leadership and management, employee health, and other conditions all help raise employee performance levels. But employee motivation to work harder and better can be an important factor. And most compensation experts believe that pay can increase the motivation of employees to perform more effectively on the job. A number of studies indicate that if pay is tied to performance, the employee produces a higher quality and quantity of work.[5]

Not everyone agrees with this, some researchers argue that if you tie pay to performance, you will destroy the intrinsic rewards a person gets from doing the job well.[6]

**"Oh, I've found inner peace.
Now I'm seeking financial peace."**

Reprinted by permission The Wall Street Journal.

---

[5]Edward J. Lawler, III., *Pay and Organizational Effectiveness* (New York: McGraw-Hill, 1971).

[6]Herbert Meyer, "The Pay for Performance Dilemma," *Organizational Dynamics,* Winter 1975, pp. 39–50; and Edward Deci, *Intrinsic Motivation* (New York: Plenum Publishing, 1975).

These are powerful motivators too. But the research behind these concerns is in its earliest stages. The importance of money to employees varies among individuals. And if the organization claims to have an incentive pay system and in fact pays for seniority, the motivation effects of pay will be lost.

In sum, at present there are theorists who suggest that pay is a useful mechanism to motivate and satisfy employees. Others disagree. Because of individual differences in employees and jobs, it seems more fruitful to redirect this research to examine (1) the range of behaviors which pay may affect positively or negatively; (2) the amount of change pay can influence; (3) the kind of employees that pay influences positively and negatively; and (4) the environmental conditions that are present when pay leads to positive and negative results.

An important issue concerning compensation and performance involves being to reliably and validly measure performance. In Chapter 8 we pointed out the difficulty of measuring performance. If pay rewards cannot be linked to measurable performance, management has a problem. That is, if performance measures are poorly developed, employees will have difficulty perceiving the connection between pay and performance. Thus, if compensation is to have any influence on motivation it is important to develop accurate measures of performance.

External Influences on Pay Levels

Among the factors which influence pay and compensation policies are those outside the organization: the government, unions, the economy, and the labor market.

Government Influences

The government directly affects compensation through wage controls and guidelines, which prohibit an increase in compensation for certain workers at certain times, and laws directed at the establishment of minimum wage rates, wage and hour regulations, and the prevention of discrimination directed at certain groups.

Wage Controls and Guidelines • Several times in the past quarter century or so, the United States has established wage freezes and guidelines. President Harry Truman imposed a wage and price freeze from January 1951 to 1953, and President Richard Nixon imposed freezes from 1971 to 1974, which came to be called Phases I–IV. Wage freezes are government orders which permit no wage increases. Wage controls limit the size of wage increases. Wage guidelines are similar to wage controls, but they are voluntary rather than legally required restrictions.

Economists and compensation specialists differ on the usefulness of wage and price freezes. The critics argue that the controls are an administrative nightmare, that they seriously disrupt the effective resource allocation market process and lead to frustration, strikes, and so on. Even the critics admit, however, that during times of perceived national emergencies and for relatively brief periods, the controls might help slow (but not indefinitely postpone) inflation. Those favoring them believe that controls reduce inflation. The important point is that employers must adjust their compensation policies to any governmental wage guidelines and controls. Considerable data gathering is necessary when such programs are in effect, and the employer must be prepared to justify any proposed wage increases. Even when the controls have been lifted, frequently there are wage and price advisory groups—government or quasi-government groups which some politicians use to try to "jawbone" executives into keeping price increases lower. These bodies at times might influence prices, which in turn could limit the profits needed to give wage increases. One proposed solution is TIP (tax-based income policy). In TIP, when employers give employees bigger raises then government standards, the employer receives a tax increase; when the raise is below standard, he receives a tax reduction.

Wage and Hour Regulations • The Fair Labor Standards Act of 1938 is the basic pay act in the United States. It has been amended many times, most recently in 1974. In 1982 over 55 million American workers were covered by the Fair Labor Standards Act. This law has a number of provisions, including the following:

Minimum wages. All employers covered by the law (all but some small firms and some specific exemptions) must pay an employee at least a minimum wage per hour. Exempt are small businesses whose gross sales did not exceed $325,000 in 1980, or $362,000 in 1981. In 1938, the minimum wage was 25 cents per hour. In 1982 the minimum was $3.35. A number of economists question the desirability of minimum wages, arguing that this law may price the marginal worker out of a job. All do not agree, however, many experts propose a lower minimum wage for trainees and teenagers to help reduce the unemployment problem.

Overtime pay. An employee covered by the law who works more than 40 hours per week must be paid one and one half times the base wage. If bonuses are also paid on a monthly or quarterly basis, the overtime pay equals one and one half the base pay and bonuses. Overtime pay tends to reduce the scheduling of longer hours of work.

Child labor prohibition. The law prohibits employing persons between 16 and 18 in hazardous jobs such as meatpacking and logging. Persons under 16 cannot be employed in jobs in interstate commerce except for nonhazardous work for a parent or guardian, and this requires a temporary permit.

There are certain categories of employees exempt from the act or various provisions. Employee exemption occurs because of responsibilities, duties, and salary provisions. In most cases executives, managers, and professionals are exempt from the act.[7]

Government agencies such as the Department of Labor's Wage and Hour Division enforce the wage and hour law. It has the right to examine employers' records and issue orders for back pay, get an injunction to prohibit future violations, and prosecute violators and send them to prison. For example, the department estimates that in 1976 U.S. employers underpaid employees by $89 million, in violation of minimum wage and overtime regulations. The department forced employers to pay $32 million to 293,000 employees for minimum wage violations, and 262,000 workers recovered $33 million from employers violating overtime regulations.

The Equal Pay Act (1963) amendment to the Fair Labor Standards Act is the first antidiscrimination law relating directly to females. The act applies to all employers and employees covered by the Fair Labor Standards Act, including executives, managers, and professionals. The Equal Pay Act requires equal pay for equal work for men and women and defines equal work as work requiring equal skills, effort, and responsibility under similar working conditions.[8]

---

[7]Description of exemption is found in U.S. Department of Labor, *Executive, Administration, Professional and Outside Salesmen Exemption* (Washington, D.C.: U.S. Government Printing Office, 1973).

[8]Based on Richard I. Henderson, *Compensation Management* (Reston, Va.: Reston Publishing, 1979), pp. 85–86.

Under the Equal Pay Act, an employer can establish different wage rates on the basis of (1) senority; (2) merit; (3) performance differences—quantity and quality; and (4) any factor other than sex. Shift work differentials are also permissible. All these exemptions must apply equally to men and women alike.

Comparable worth. Today, American women working full time earn only about 60 percent of what men earn. In an effort to close this earnings gap, there has been a growing movement in the last few years to have the widely accepted concept of equal pay for equal jobs expanded to include equal pay for comparable jobs. The issue of comparable worth has been ruled on by the Supreme Court. In a 5 to 4 decision on June 9, 1981, the Supreme Court ruled that a sex descrimination suit may be brought under the 1964 Civil Rights Act on a basis other than discrimination based on "equal or substantially equal work."[9] The suit involved Washington County, Oregon, prison matrons claiming sex discrimination because male prison guards, whose jobs were somewhat different, received substantially higher pay. The country had evaluated the man's jobs as having 5 percent more job content than the female jobs, and paid the males 35 percent more.

Until the *Gunther* vs. *Washington* prison matron's case, the courts were split on the issue of comparable worth.[10] However, the ruling although not mentioning the comparable worth concept, now permits women to bring suit on the grounds that they are paid lower then men holding jobs of comparable, or less then comparable, are paid disproportionately low based on job content evaluations.

In San Jose, California, in 1981, several hundred women employees of the city walked off their jobs of the comparable worth issue. One eye-opening example in this situation was that senior librarians, typically female, earned 27 percent less than senior chemists, typically male, although the two jobs were rated comparably.

The union and city reached a settlement on July 14, 1981, with the city agreeing to pay $1.45 million in raises for several hundred female employees to make their pay more equitable with men. A few other pay equity cases in the lower courts are these:[11]

1. Nurses working for the city of Denver, Colorado, starting at $1,000 per year less than painters, tree trimmers, and tire servicemen.
2. Jobs held primarily by females in a Westinghouse plant in Trenton, New Jersey, in general paying less than male jobs that were rated comparably by the company's job evaluation system.
3. Women handling health and beauty aids for a division of Super Value Stores, Inc., in western Pennsylvania, eastern Ohio, and northern West Virginia, being paid $3,500 less than men handling perishable food.

In each of these cases and almost every instance of a case reaching the court, the claim revolved around the job evaluation system (job evaluation will be discussed later in this chapter). The selection of the factors used in any job evaluation plan involves making subjective judgments. P/HRM specialists must be extremely careful about how job eval-

---

[9]Michael F. Carter, "Comparable Worth: An Idea Whose Time Has Come?" *Personnel Journal*, October 1981, pp. 792–794.

[10]James T. Brinks, "The Comparable Worth Issue: A Salary Administration Bombshell," *Personnel Administrator*, November 1981, pp. 37–40; and Richard J. Schonberger and Harry W. Hennessey, Jr., "Is Equal Pay for Comparable Work Fair?" *Personnel Journal*, December 1981, pp. 964–968.

[11]Carter, *"Comparable Worth,"* p. 793.

uation data is used. They must also work at developing job evaluation systems that are valid and reliable. Comparable worth is an issue that requires a number of P/HRM responses such as:

- A sound job evaluation system.
- Comparing pay across jobs on a regular basis. Are low-paying jobs being occupied by females and minorities? If so look at this closely.
- Documentation of the pay system.
- Clarifying and documenting the role that performance appraisal plays in pay.

Today comparable worth is still a controversial issue. However, the courts are now involved. Thus, P/HRM departments will be forced to defend their company's pay system.

Other Pay Legislation • The Civil Rights Act of 1964, and the Age Discrimination Act of 1967 are designed to assure that all persons of similar ability, seniority, and background receive the same pay for the same work. The Equal Employment Opportunity Commission enforces the Civil Rights Act, while the Wage and Hour Division enforces the Equal Pay Act and the Age Discrimination Act.

The Walsh-Healey Act of 1936 requires firms doing business with the federal government to pay wages at least equal to those prevailing in the area where the firm is located. It parallels the Fair Labor Standards Act on child labor and requires time-and-a-half pay for any work performed after eight hours a day. It also exempts some industries. The Davis-Bacon Act of 1931 requires the payment of minimum wages to workers engaged in federally sponsored public works—construction jobs. The McNamara-O'Hara Service Contract Act requires employers that have contracts with the federal government of $2,500 per year or more or that provide services to federal agencies as contractors or subcontractors to pay prevailing wages and fringe benefits to their employees.

In addition to federal laws, 39 states have minimum wage laws covering intrastate employees and those not covered by federal laws. Some of these minimiums are higher than the federal minimum. In such cases, the state minimums apply.

The government directly affects the amount of pay the employee takes home by requiring employers to deduct funds from employees' wages. For the federal government, this entails federal income taxes (withholding taxes) and social security taxes. The employer may also be required to deduct state and local income taxes.

The federal government also has other laws governing pay deductions. The Copeland Act (1934) and Anti-Kickback Law (1948) are designed to protect the employee from unlawful or unauthorized deductions. The Federal Wage Garnishment Act (1970) is designed to limit the amount deducted from a person's pay to reduce debts. It also prohibits the employer from firing an employee if the employee goes in debt only once and has his pay garnished. The employer may deduct as much from the paycheck as required by court orders for alimony or child supprt, debts due for taxes, or bankruptcy court requirements.

Other Government Influences • In addition to the laws and regulations discussed above, the government influences compensation in many other ways. For example, if the government is the employer, it may legislate pay levels by setting statutory rates. For example, for teachers, the pay scale may be set by law or by edict of the school board, and pay depends on revenues from the current tax base. If taxes decline relative to organizations' revenue streams, no matter how much the organization may wish to pay higher wages, it cannot.

The government affects compensation through its employment-level policy too. One of the goals of the government is full employment of all citizens seeking work. The government may even create jobs for certain categories of workers, which reduces the supply of workers available and affects pay rates.

Union Influences on Compensation

Another important external influence on employer's compensation program is labor unionization. Unions have an effect whether or not the organization's employees are unionized, if it is in an area where unionized enterprises exist. For unions have tended to be pacesetters in demands for pay, benefits, and working conditions. There is reasonable evidence that unions tend to increase pay levels, although this is more likely where an industry has been organized by strong unions. If the organization elects to stay in an area where unions are strong, its compensation policies will be affected.

During hard economic times, union and nonunion employees have taken cuts in pay to keep their companies afloat. Uniroyal, Inc's. 16,000 employees gave up $27 million in compensation in 1980 and 1981. This savings was essential for Uniroyal to survive. Public Service Electric and Gas CO. extended the workweek for 3,000 employees at its Neward, New Jersey, headquarters to 40 hours from 35 hours. This increase in time occurred without any pay increase. It means that the firm gets more work for the same payroll dollar.[12]

A series of legal cases has required employers to share compensation information with the unions if employees are unionized. For example, in *Shell Development* v. *Association of Industrial Scientists—Professional Employees,* Shell was required to provide the union with a written explanation of salary curves and the merit system, as well as copies of current salary curve guides, merit ratings, and so on. In *Time Incorporated* v. *Newspaper Guild, Time* was required to provide the union with a list of salaries of employees. In *General Electric* v. *International Union of Electrical Workers,* GE was required to provide the union with the pay survey information it had gathered to form compensation decisions. Thus employers would do well to communicate with and try to influence the union on compensation policy and levels.

Unions do try to bargain for higher pay and benefits, of course. The union is more likely to increase the compensation of its members when the organization is financially and competitively strong and the union is financially strong enough to support a strike; when the union has the support of other unions; and when general economic and labor market conditions are such that unemployment is low and the economy is strong.

Unions also bargain over working conditions and other policies that affect compensation. There is a tendency for unions to prefer fixed pay for each job category, or rate rangee that are administered to primarily reflect seniority rather than merit increases. This is true in the private and other sectors. Unions press for time pay rather than merit pay when the amount of performance expected is tied to technology (such as the assembly line).

---

[12]Ralph E. Winter, "More Employees Accept Cuts in Pay to Help Their Companies Survive," *The Wall Street Journal,* October 22, 1980, p. 23.

Economic Conditions and Compensation

Also affecting compensation as an external factor are the economic conditions of the industry, especially the degree of competitiveness, which affects the organization's ability to pay high wages: Certain industries are more profitable than others at any one time, which is often related to the degree of competitiveness in the industry. The more competitive the situation, the less able is the organization to pay higher wages. Ability to pay is also a consequence of the relative productivity of the organization or industry or sector. If a firm is very productive, it can pay higher wages. Productivity can be increased by advanced technology, more efficient operating methods, a harder working and more talented work force, or a combination of these factors.

One productivity index is used by many organizations as a criterion in the determination of a general level of wages is the Bureau of Labor Statistics' "Output per Man-Hour in Manufacturing." This productivity index is published in each issue of the *Monthly Labor Review*. For about 70 years, productivity increased at an average annual rate of approximately 3 percent. The percentage increase in average weekly earnings in the United States is very closely related to the percentage change in productivity, plus the percentage change in the consumer price index. Unfortunately in the past few years productivity in the United States has been less than 2 percent. In fact, as discussed in Chapter 1, worker productivity in 1982 lags behind that found in Japan, West Germany, France, Italy, and the Netherlands.

The degree of profitability and productivity is a significant factor in determining the ability of firms in the private and third sector to pay wages. In the public sector, the limitations of the budget determined the ability to pay. If tax rates are low or the tax base is low or declining, the public-sector employer may be unable to give pay increases even if they are deserved.

Nature of the Labor Market and Compensation

The final external factor affecting compensation to be discussed is the state of the labor market. Although many feel that human labor should not be regulated by forces such as supply and demand, this does in fact happen. In times of full employment, wages and salaries may have to be higher to attract and retain enough qualified employees; in depressions, the reverse is true. Pay may be higher if few skilled employees are available in the job market. This may be because unions or accrediting associations limit the numbers certified to do the job. In certain locations, due to higher birthrates or a recent loss of a major employer, more persons may be seeking work than others. These factors lead to what is called *differential pay levels*. At any one time in a particular locale, unskilled labor rates seek a single level, and minimally skilled clerical work rates seek another. Research evidence from the labor economics field provides adequate support for the impact of labor market conditions on compensation.

Besides differences in pay levels by occupations in a locale, there are also differentials between government and private employees and exempt and nonexempt employees, as well as international differences. For example, there are differences in pay levels between the United States and Canada.

Increases in productivity are typically passed on to employees in the form of higher pay. Studies indicate that, in general, employers do not exploit employees when market

Case

Mary

Guido Panelli went to Mary Renfro as he had promised Poppa Joe. He told her to go ahead and prepare a report which would point out the problems in P/HRM, especially in compensation, that CNB was facing. Mary remembered worrying about the situation at Cardeson National Bank after learning about the effect of pay on performance and satisfaction. At the bank some employees seemed to be paid for seniority, others for family need. People doing the same job at about the same performance levels received different paychecks, and they knew it. This seemed to be a bomb about to go off.

She knew the bank was following the legal requirements of compensation with regard to minimum wage and overtime. But equal-pay requirements were another situation. Often single people were paid less than married people, and married people with several children were paid more than those who were childless or had only one child. Single females were paid the least.

At present the bank was not unionized; few banks were. The labor market was good for the bank right now. There always were more applicants than needed. This has helped CNB with its problem of high turnover, for there are many eager replacements. But what would happen if the labor market should change or if the inequities in the pay rates are not corrected?

conditions do not favor the employees. Employers use compensation surveys and general studies of the labor market in the area to serve as inputs to their pay-level compensation decision. The pay survey is the major pay-level decision tool.

Pay Surveys and Comparable Pay Levels

You do it + give other co's a copy. Share info.

Pay surveys (also called wage surveys) are surveys of the compensation paid to employees by all employers in a geographic area, an industry, or an occupational group. They are the principal tool used in the pay-level decision, as noted above.

Want to be equitable in industry + still be reasonable

Who Conducts Wage Surveys?

Pay surveys are made by large employers, professional and consulting enterprises, trade associations, and the government. Some examples are described here.

Professional and Trade Association Surveys • *American Management Association.* AMA conducts surveys of professional and managerial compensation and provides about 12 reports on U.S. executives' salaries and 16 reports on foreign executives' salaries. The *Top Management Report* shows the salaries of 31,000 top executives in 75 top positions in 3,000 firms in 53 industries. The *Middle Management Report* covers 73 key exempt jobs between supervisor and top executives. The sample includes 640 firms with 15,000 middle-level executives. The *Administrative and Technical Report* covers jobs below the middle management level. The sample is 568 firms. The *Supervisory Management Report* provides national and regional data on salaries of 55 categories of foremen and staff supervisors in 700 companies.

Administrative Management Society. This group compiles records on the compensation of clerical and data processing employees. AMS surveys 7,132 firms with 621,000 clerical and data processing employees in 132 cities throughout the United States, Canada, and the West Indies. The data are gathered on 20 positions. A directory published every other year by cities and regions reports interquarterly ranges of salaries.

American Society for Personnel Administration. ASPA conducts salary surveys for personnel executives and others every other year.

Surveys by Other Organizations • Other organizations which do pay surveys include Pay Data Service (Chicago). Management Compensation Services, Bureay of National Affairs, and American Society of Corporate Securities. Many journals report on compensation, including: *Compensation Review, Business Week, Dun's, Forbes, Fortune, Hospital Administration, Nation's Business, and Monthly Labor Review.*

Government Surveys • U.S. government pay surveys include those by Federal Reserve banks, which survey private industry pay to set their employees' pay, and the Bureau of Labor Statistics (BLS). The BLS publishes three different surveys:

Area wage surveys. Annually, BLS surveys about 200 areas (usually the Standard Metropolitan Statistical Areas) on the pay and benefits for white-collar, skilled blue-collar, and indirect manufacturing labor jobs (in alternate years).

Industry wage surveys. The BLS surveys 50 manufacturing industries, 20 service industries and public employees. Blue- and white-collar employees are covered. The surveys are done on yearly, and three- and five-year cycles. Some industries are surveyed nationally (utilities, mining, manufacturing), and others by metropolitan area (finance, service, and trade).

Professional, administrative, technical, and clerical (PATC) surveys. BLS also annually surveys 80 occupational work-level positions on a nationwide basis. Occupaions covered by the PATC survey include accountancy, legal services, engineering, drafting, clerical, and chemistry. Although the BLS studies tend to follow the most sophisticated survey methods, they often do not relate to the area in which a firm is doing business.

How Pay Surveys Are Conducted and Used

How are these surveys done? One method is the personal interview, which develops the most accurate responses but is also expensive. Mailed questionnaires are probably the most frequently used method, and one of the cheapest. The jobs being surveyed by mail must be clearly defined, or the data may not be reliable. Telephone inquiries are used to follow up the mail questionnaires or to gather data. This procedure is quick, but it is also difficult to get a great deal of detailed data over the phone.

There are a number of critical issues determining the usefulness of the surveys: the jobs to be covered, the employers to be contacted, and the method to be used in gathering the data. Other employers cannot be expected to complete endless data requests for all the organization's jobs, so the jobs that are surveyed should be the 2 to 20 most crucial ones. If the point method of job evaluation is used (see below), the key jobs might be selected for surveying, since they cover all ranges. The jobs which most employees hold should also be on the list (clerk-typists, underwriters, and keypunch operators for an insurance company, for example).

The second issue concerns who will be surveyed. Most organizations tend to compare themselves with similar competitors in their industry. American Airlines may compare its pay rates to those of United Airlines, for example. It has been shown that employees may not compare their pay to that offered by competitors at all. Their basis of comparison might be friends' employers, or employers that they worked for previously. If the survey is to be useful, employees should be involved in choosing the organizations to be surveyed. The employers to be surveyed should include the most dominant ones in the area and a small sample of those suggested by employees.

Government agencies use pay surveys of comparable private-sector jobs to set their pay levels. The evidence suggests that private-sector organizations use their own pay surveys more than those provided by the government or other services, and they use the surveys primarily as general guidelines or as only one of several factors considered in pay-level decisions. In fact, there is some evidence that organizatons weigh job evaluation and individual pay determination more heavily than external pay comparisons. This makes sense because pay surveys are not taken often (perhaps yearly), and are sometimes hard to interpret meaningfully.

Much care and thought must go into how the pay survey is conducted, and many factors, such as the source of data, must be considered. An employer might not know if there is a pay differential between the job he offers and others, how much of the difference is due to differences in the job or other fringe benefits provided, the time of the survey, the pay level of the two areas, or other factors that affect the pay survey. Remember too that there are many surveys an employer can use and many organizations and locales it can survey. This can give the employer a great deal of maneuvering room to handle problems such as relative ability or inability to pay certain wages or to deal with cost-of-living problems, and similar pay bargaining issues.

Organizational Influences on Pay Levels

In addition to the external influences on compensation discussed above, several internal factors affect pay levels: the size and age of the organization, the labor budget, and the goals of its controlling interests.

We don't know a great deal about size and pay. Generally speaking, it appears that larger organizations tend to have higher pay levels. Little is known about age of the organizations and pay, but some theorists contend that newer enterprises tend to pay more than old ones.[13]

+ more profitables pay better

---

[13]Bruce R. Uly, ''Compensation Management: Its Past and Its Future,'' *Personnel,* May–June 1977, pp. 30–40.

The Labor Budget

The labor budget of an organization normally identifies the amount of money available for annual employee compensation. Every unit of the organization is influenced by the size of the budget.[14] A firm's budget normally does not state the exact amount of money to be allocated to each employee, but they do state how much is available to the unit. The discretion in allocating pay is then left to department heads and supervisors. These allocations form the basis of a manager's strategy.

The department heads and supervisors are in the best position to allocate the unit's labor budget dollars, assuming that they have the closest contract and best view of the employees. Theoretically, the contract and performance evaluation should permit a proper allocation of dollars. Thus, the department heads and supervisors take the budget amounts and, based on observation and evaluation, recommend who should get what amount of compensation. Exhibit 13–3 briefly describes some of the pay allocation decisions. Each of these decisions is significantly influenced and constrained by what amount it budgeted to a particular unit.

Goals of Controlling Interests and Managerial Pay Strategies

Another organizational influence deals with the goals of controlling interests and the specific pay strategy that managers select. The final authority in pay decisions as shown in Exhibit 13–4 is top-level or senior management. The views of managers and supervisors about pay differ as much as the employees' views. For example, some believe their employees should be compensated at high-pay levels because they deserve it. They also accept or reject the idea that high pay or merit pay leads to greater performance or employee satisfaction. These attitudes are reflected in the pay-level strategy chosen by the managers of the organization. This is a major strategic choice top managers must make. Essentially, three pay-level strategies high, low, or comparable—can be chosen by supervisors and managers (the term *manager* will henceforth be used to reflect these two levels of compensation decision makers).

Exhibit 13–3 _____

Allocation decisions based on labor budget

Position	Responsibility
Employees' immediate supervisor	Appraises performance; makes pay recommendation to supervisor.
Department head	Reviews each recommendation and initiates action based on budgeted amounts.
P/HRM: Compensation specialists	Review department head recommendations and considers equity, budget, objectives, and future plans. Consults with department heads on specialist's recommendations.
Senior or top-level management.	Makes final decision on pay recommendations. Decision is based on labor budget and departmental allocations plus recommendations passed through various levels (supervisor, head, specialist).

---

[14]Henderson, *Compensation Management*, p. 429.

Exhibit 13–4

Factors affecting the pay-level decision

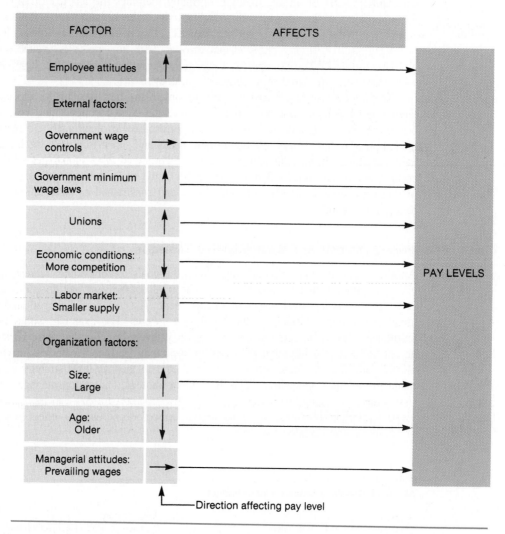

The High-Pay-Level Strategy • In this strategy, the managers choose to pay higher than average pay levels. The assumption behind this strategy is that you get what you pay for. These managers believe that paying higher wages and salaries will attract and hold the best employees, and this is the most effective long-range policy. This strategy is sometimes called the pacesetter. It may be influenced by pay criteria such as paying a living wage or paying on the basis of productivity.

The Low-Pay-Level Strategy • At the opposite extreme is the low-pay strategy. In this case, the manager may choose to pay at the minimum level needed to hire enough employees. This strategy may be used because this is all the organization can pay–the ability to pay is restricted by other internal or external factors such as a limited labor budget or a forecasted decline in sales and profits.

FRANK AND ERNEST

© 1975 by NEA, Inc. Reprinted by permission of NEA.

The Comparable-Pay-Level Strategy • The most frequently used strategy is to set the pay level at the going-wage level. The wage criteria are comparable wages, perhaps modified by cost of living or purchasing power adjustments. For example, the Federal Pay Comparability Act of 1970 limits federal government compensation to the comparable pay paid in the private sector at the time. This going wage is determined from pay surveys (discussed above). Thus the policy of a manager of this type is to pay the current market rate in the community or industry, ±5 percent or so.

These three strategies are usually set for the total organization, although the strategy might have to be modified for a few hard-to-fill jobs from time to time. The choice of strategy in part reflects the motivation and attitudes held by the manager. If the manager has a high need for recognition, the high-pay strategy might be chosen; otherwise, the low-pay strategy might be chosen. Another factor is the ethical and moral attitude of the manager. If the manager is ethically oriented, then a low-pay strategy is not likely to be chosen willingly.

The Pay-Level Decision

The pay-level decision is made by managers, who compare the pay of persons working inside the organization with those outside it. This decision is affected by multiple factors in interaction with one another, as shown in Exhibit 13–4. These factors affect pay levels laterally, upward, or downward. Most employees' unions and minimim wage laws push the level up. Wage controls steady the level or tend to hold it down. More competition and older organizations hold it down. Managerial attitudes toward prevailing wages would steady the level. Larger size of the organization would tend to increase pay level, as would a smaller supply of employees in the labor market.

This is an example of how some of the factors in the compensation activity affect the pay-level decision. When factors such as managerial attitudes, the labor market, and competition change, the pressures on pay level shift.[15]

---

[15]Robert J. Greene, "Thoughts on Compensation Management in the '80s and '90s," *Personnel Administrator*, May 1980, pp. 27-28.

But remember: The many external factors affecting the process, such as government and unions, are compounded by employees' job preferences which include pay and non-pay aspects. And many employees do not have a sophisticated or comprehensive knowledge of all these factors. So you can see that the organization has a great deal of maneuvering room in the pay-level decision.

Pay Structures

In addition to relating pay to pay levels paid for comparable jobs in other organizations, the enterprise must also determine pay structures for its employees having different jobs *within* the organization. Factors similar to those affecting pay levels affect these pay structures too.

Managers can cope with the attempt to provide equal pay for positions of approximately equal worth by arbitrary management decisions, collective bargaining, or job evaluation. If managers try to make these decisions without help from tools such as job evaluation, unsystematic decision making is likely to lead to perceived inequities. Bargaining alone can lead to decisions based solely on relative power. Therefore, most management experts suggest that managerial decisions should be influenced both by the results of collective bargaining and job evaluation.

Job Evaluation

Job evaluation is the formal process by which the relative worth of various jobs in the organization is determined for pay purposes. Essentially, it attempts to relate the amount of the employee's pay to the extent that her or his job contributes to organizational effectiveness.

It is not always easy to evaluate the worth of all jobs in an organization. It may be obvious that the effective physician will contribute more to the goals of patient care in the hospital than the nurse's aid. The point at issue is *how much* the differential is worth.[16]

Since computing exactly how much a particular job contributes to organizational effectiveness is difficult, proxies for effectiveness are used. These proxies include skills required to do the job, amount and significance of responsibility involved, effort required, and working conditions. Compensation must vary with the differing demands of various jobs if employees are to be satisfied and if the organization is to be able to attract the personnel it wants.

Job evaluation is widely used. At least two thirds of all jobs have been evaluated. The following are among the reasons often cited for using a job evaluation program:[17]

- To establish a systematic and formal structure of jobs based on their worth to the organization.
- To justify an existing pay structure or to develop one that provides for internal equity.

---

[16]Carter, "Comparable Worth."

[17]Henderson, *Compensation Management*, p. 210.

- To provide a basis for negotiating pay rates when bargaining collectively with a union.
- To identify to employees a hierarchy of pay progression.
- To comply with equal pay legislation.
- To develop a basis for a merit or pay-for-performance program.

Once an organization decides to use job evaluation, a series of decisions must be made to ensure its effectiveness. Part of the decision to use job evaluation, or the first step in using it effectively, is for management to involve employees (and, where appropriate, the union) in the system and its implementation. Most experts emphasize that job evaluation is a difficult task which is more likely to be successful if the employees whose jobs are being evaluated are involved in the process by being allowed to express their perceptions of the relative merits of their jobs compared to others. This participation affords an opportunity to explain the fairly complicated process of job evaluation to those most directly affected by it, and it will usually lead to better communication and improved employee understanding.

After the program is off to a cooperative start, usually a committee of about five members evaluates the jobs. Ideally, the committee includes employees, managers, and P/HRM specialists. All members should be familiar with the jobs to be evaluated.

Job evaluation is usually performed by analyzing job descriptions and occasionally job specifications. Early in the process, it is imperative that job evaluators check the availability and accuracy of the job descriptions and specifications (see Chapter 4). It is usually suggested that job descriptions be split into several series, such as managerial, professional/technical, clerical, and operative. It makes sense in writing job descriptions to use the words that are keyed to the job evaluation factors.

Another essential step in effective job evaluation is to select and weigh the criteria (factors) used to evaluate the job. Although there is not a lot of research in this area, it appears that the results are the same whether all factors or just a few factors are considered especially if the job evaluation is carefully designed and scaled. Typical of the most frequently used factors for job evaluation are education, experience, amount of responsibility, job knowledge, work hazards and working conditions. It is important that the factors used be accepted as valid for the job by those being evaluated.

Once the method of evaluating the job (to be discussed below) is chosen, the evaluators make the job evaluations. Basically, those familiar with the jobs tend to rate them higher, especially if they supervise the jobs. It seems useful for each committee member to evaluate each job individually. Then the evaluators should discuss each job on which the ratings differ significantly, factor by factor, until agreement is reached.

Job Evaluation Methods • The four most frequently used job evaluation methods are:

Job ranking.
Factor comparison.
Classification.
The point system.[18]

Job evaluation systems can be related as shown in Exhibit 13–5.

---

[18]See H. D. Janes, "Union Views on Job Evaluation: 1971 vs. 1978," *Personnel Journal*, February 1979, pp. 80–85; and David W. Belcher, *Compensation Administration* (Englewood Cliffs, N.J.: Prentice-Hall, 1974).

Exhibit 13–5 _____

Comparison job evaluation systems

Comparison basis	Nonquantitative comparison (job as whole)	Quantitative comparison (parts of factors of jobs)
Job versus job	Job ranking	Factor comparison
Job versus scale	Job griding or classification	Point system

Ranking of Jobs • The system, used primarily in smaller, simpler organizations, is job ranking. Instead of analyzing the full complexity of jobs by evaluating parts of jobs, the job-ranking method has the evaluator rank order *whole* jobs, from the simplest to the most challenging.

Sometimes this is done by providing the evaluator with the information on cards. The evaluator sorts the jobs into ranks, allowing for the possibility of ties. If the list of jobs is large, the paired-comparison method, whereby each job is compared to every other job being evaluated, can be used. The evaluator counts the number of times a particular job is ranked above another, and the one with the largest number of highest rankings is the highest ranked. There is no assurance that the ranking thus provided is composed of equal-interval ranks. The differential betweeen the highest job and next highest may not be exactly the same as that between the lowest and next lowest. If the system is used in an organization with many jobs to be rated, it is clumsy to use, and the reliability of the ratings is not good. Because of these problems, ranking is probably the least frequently used method of job evaluation.

Classification or Grading System • The *classification* or *grading system* groups a set of jobs together into a grade or classification. Then these sets of jobs are ranked in levels of difficulty or sophistication. For example, the least challenging jobs in the federal service are grouped into GS–1, the next most challenging into GS–2, and so on.

The classification approach is more sophisticated than ranking but less so than the point system or factor comparison. It can work reasonably well if the classifications are well defined. It is the second most frequently used system. It is used widely in the public sector, as well as in the private and third sectors.

The Point System • The greatest number of job evaluation plans use the point system. It is the most frequently used because it is more sophisticated than ranking and classification systems, but it is relatively easy to use.

Essentially, the point system requires evaluators to quantify the value of the elements of a job. On the basis of the job description or interviews with job occupants, points are assigned to the degree of various factors required to do the job. For example, skill required, physical and mental effort needed, degree of dangerous or unpleasant working conditions involved, and amount of responsibility involved in the job. When these are summed, the job has been evaluated.

Many point systems evaluate as many as 10 aspects or subaspects of each job. The aspects chosen should not overlap, should distinguish real differences between jobs, should be as objectively defined as possible, and should be understood and acceptable to both management and employees. Because all aspects are not of equal importance in all jobs, different weights reflecting the differential importance of these aspects to a job must be set. These weights are assigned by summing the judgments of several independent but knowledgeable evaluators. Thus a clerical job might result in the following weightings education required, 50 percent; experience required, 25 percent; complexity of job, 12 percent; responsibility for relationships with others, 8 percent; working conditions and physical requirements, 5 percent.

Once the weights are agreed upon, reference to a point manual is appropriate. Experience required by jobs varies, as does education. A point manual carefully defines degrees of points from first (lowest) to fifth, for example. Experience might be defined in this way:

First degree, up to and including three months . . . . 25 points
Second degree, more than three months but less than six . . . . 50 points
Third degree, more than six months to one year . . . . 75 points
Fourth degree, more than one year and up to three years . . . . 100 points
Fifth degree, more than three years . . . . 125 points

These definitions must be clearly defined and measurable to ensure consistency in ratings of requirements from the job description to the job evaluation. The preliminary point manuals must be pretested prior to widespread use.

As displayed in Exhibit 13–6, factor 1, education, has five degrees, as do factors 2 and 3. On the other hand factor 4 has three degrees, while factor 5 has four degrees. The maximum number of points is calculated by multiplying the points in the system by the assigned weights. For education, the maximum points would be 250 (50 percent weight multiplied by 500 maximum points).

Factor Comparison • The factor comparison method was originated by Eugene Benge. Like the point system, it permits the job evaluation process to be done on a factor-by-factor basis. It differs from the point method in that jobs are evaluated or compared against "benchmark" or key points. A factor comparison scale, instead of a point scale, is used. Five universal job factors used to compare jobs are:

- *Responsibilities*—The money, human resource, records, and supervisor responsibilities of the job.
- *Skill*—The facility in muscular coordination and training in the interpretation of sensory requirements.
- *Physical effort*—The sitting, standing, walking, lifting, moving, and so on.
- *Mental effort*—The intelligence, problem solving, reasoning, and imagination.

Exhibit 13–6

Evaluation points for insurance clerical job

Factor	Weight	Degree points (500 point system;				
		1st	2d	3d	4th	5th
1. Education	50	50	100	150	200	250
2. Experience	25	25	50	70	100	125
3. Complexity of job	12	12	24	36	48	60
4. Relationships with others	8	8	24	40		
5. Working conditions	5	10	15	20	25	

Exhibit 13–7

Ranking four benchmark jobs by factors

| | Factors | | | | |
Jobs	Responsibility	Skill	Physical effort	Mental effort	Working conditions
Tool and die maker	2*	1	2	2	3
Shipping clerk	4	2	1	4	4
Systems analyst	1	4	4	1	2
Secretary	3	3	3	3	1

*1 is high, 4 is low. For working conditions, the higher the rating the poorer the conditions.

- *Working conditions*—The environmental factors such as noise, ventilation, hours, heat, hazards, fumes, and cleanliness.

The evaluation committee follows six formal steps in examining jobs. First, the comparison factors are selected and defined. The five universal job factors will be used in working through an example. Factors, of course, could differ across executive, supervisory, and operating employee jobs. Second, the benchmark or key jobs are selected. These are common jobs, found in the firm's labor market. Often a committee is used to select from 10 to 20 benchmark jobs. Third, the evaluators rank the key jobs on each of the comparison factors. The ranking is based on job descriptions and job specifications. Four benchmark jobs for the Moser Manufacturing company of Tulsa, Oklahoma, are presented in Exhibit 13–7.

Fourth, job evaluators allocate a part of each key job's wage rate to each job factor as shown in Exhibit 13–8. The proportion of each wage assigned to the different critical factors depends on the importance of the factor. Each evaluator first makes an independent decision. Then the committee or group of evaluators would meet to arrive at an apportionment consensus about assigning money values to the factors.

Fifth, the two sets of ratings (the ranking and assigned money), would be compared to determine the evaluator's consistency. Exhibit 13–9 displays this consistency of rating comparisons at Moser.

Sixth, a job comparison chart displays the benchmark jobs and the money values for each factor is constructed. The chart is used to rate other jobs as compared to the benchmark jobs. These jobs would be placed in an appropriate position in the chart. Exhibit 13–10 illustrates the Moser job comparison chart.

Exhibit 13–8

Apportionment of wages to benchmark jobs

| | | Factors | | | | |
Jobs	Hourly wage	Responsibility	Skill	Physical effort	Mental effort	Working conditions
Tool and die maker	$8.40	2.00 (2)	2.50 (1)	1.60 (2)	1.50 (2)	.80 (3)
Shipping clerk	$5.80	.60 (4)	1.90 (2)	1.80 (1)	.60 (4)	.90 (4)
Systems analyst	$7.10	2.30 (1)	1.10 (4)	1.20 (4)	1.90 (1)	.60 (2)
Secretary	$5.00	1.00 (3)	1.50 (3)	1.30 (3)	1.00 (3)	.20 (1)

Exhibit 13–9

Rank versus money comparisons

	Factors									
Jobs	Responsibility		Skill		Physical effort		Mental effort		Working condition*	
	R[†]	$[‡]	R	$	R	$	R	$	R	$
Tool and die maker	2	2	1	1	2	2	2	2	3	3
Shipping clerk	4	4	2	2	1	1	4	4	4	4
Systems analyst	1	1	4	4	4	4	1	1	2	2
Secretary	3	3	3	3	3	3	3	3	1	1

*Note that working condition is reversed, poorer conditions receive more money.
[†]Rankings.
[‡]Money amounts.

The factor comparison method has some advantages and disadvantages. One advantage is that it is a step-by-step formal method of evaluation. Furthermore, it permits you to see how the differences in factor rankings translate into dollars and cents. Probably the most negative aspect of the factor comparison method is its complexity. Although the method is easy to explain to subordinates, it is difficult to show them how much a system is developed. There is also the issue of subjectivity. Despite the systematic nature of the

Exhibit 13–10

Moser job comparison chart

Money amounts	Responsibility	Skill	Physical effort	Mental effort	Working conditions
$2.50		Tool and die maker			
	Systems analyst				
2.00	Tool and die maker	Shipping clerk	Shipping clerk	Systems analyst	
			Tool and die maker		
1.50		Secretary		Tool and die maker	
			Secretary		
			Systems analyst		
1.00	Secretary	Systems analyst		Secretary	
					Shipping clerk
					Tool and die maker
0.50	Shipping clerk			Shipping clerk	Systems analyst
					Secretary
0					

factor comparison method it still relies on a committee's or a group of evaluator's subjective judgments. Of course this disadvantage is also found with each of the other job evaluation methods.

Pay Classes, Rate Ranges, and Classifications

After completion of the job evaluation, the pay-structure process is completed by establishing pay classes, rate ranges, and job classifications for ease of administration.[19] A pay class (also called a pay grade) is a convenient grouping of a variety of jobs that are similar on work difficulty and responsibility requirements. If an organization uses the factor comparison or point system of job evaluation, this is accomplished by use of pay-class graphs or point conversion tables. An example of a pay-class graph is given in Exhibit 13–11.

At intervals of say 50 points, a new pay class is marked off. The pay curve illustrated in Exhibit 13–11 is based on information obtained from wage and salary surveys and modified as necessary to reflect the organization's policy to pay at, above, or below prevailing rates. This exhibit shows a single-rate pay system rather than a rate-range system in that all jobs within a given labor class will receive the same rate of pay. In this example, pay classes are determined by the point value determined through a point system method of job evaluation.

Exhibit 13–12, another pay-class graph, demonstrates how wage and salary survey data are combined with job evaluation information to determine the pay structure for an organization. A compensation trend line is derived by first establishing the general pay pattern, plotting the surveyed rates of key jobs against the point value of these jobs. The trend line can then be determined by a variety of methods, ranging from a simple eyeball estimate of the pay trend to a formalized statistical formulation of a regression line based on the sum of the least squares method. The appropriate pay rate for any job can then be

Exhibit 13–11 _____

Pay classes and pay curve

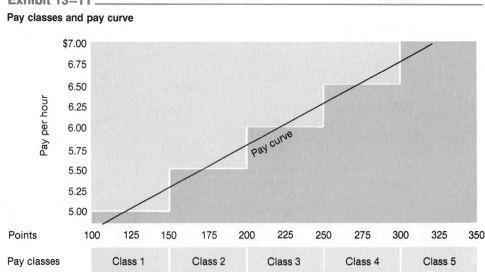

[19]Nash and Carroll, *Management of Compensation*.

Exhibit 13–12

Pay-class graph with range of pay

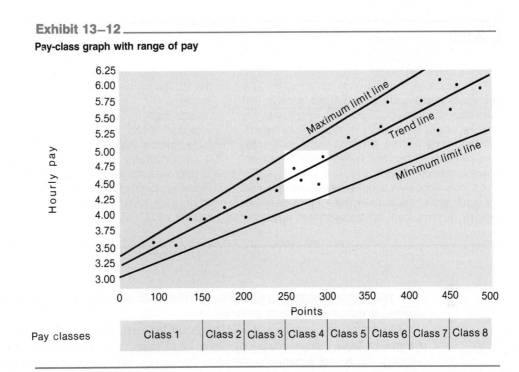

ascertained by calculating the point value of the job and observing the pay level for that value as shown by the trend line. By taking a set percentage (e.g., 15 percent) above and below the trend line, minimum and maximum limit lines can be established. These limit lines can be used to help set the minimum and maximum rates if a pay range is used instead of a single rate for each job. The limit lines can also be used in place of the trend line for those organizations that wish to establish pay levels above market—the pay leaders—or those that want to pay slightly under the prevailing rates.

Although it is possible for a pay class to have a single pay rate (as in Exhibit 13–11), the more likely condition is a range of pays. These ranges can have the same spread, or the spread can be increased as the pay rate increases.[20] An example of a pay structure with increasing rate ranges is given in Exhibit 13–12. The ranges are usually divided into a series of steps. Thus, within Class 4 (250–300 points), there might be four steps:

	Pay range
Step 1.	$4.20 – 4.40
Step 2.	4.40 – 4.60
Step 3.	4.60 – 4.85
Step 4.	4.85 – 5.10

These steps in effect are money raises within a pay range to help take care of the needs of individual pay determination (to be discussed shortly). Similar ranges would ordinarily be determined for all other classes to illustrate the pay structure for all jobs in the pay

[20]David J. Thomsen and Robert A. Smith, "What Are Average, and Above-Average Salaries?" *Compensation Review*, Second quarter 1974, pp. 18–26.

Case

Mary sat at her desk a few days later. She thought over the problems the bank was facing again. She had spent weeks learning about pay surveys, job evaluation, pay classifications, rate ranges—all the aspects of pay-level and pay-structure decisions. CNB had done nothing about any of these issues. How could they keep employees without much attention to pay practices?

As Mary wondered about these issues, she had the report she's prepared for her P/HRM class before her. It compared the turnover and absentee-ism rates at CNB to those of other banks like it in the Pittsburgh area. CNB was clearly in the worst shape.

She had interviewed supervisors and others who had talked with employees leaving CNB. A large number gave better pay as the reason for leaving. And even more often, fairness in treatment of pay was the reason given. She'd passed her report on to Guido. But would anything happen—other than receiving a grade in class for her report?

---

plan. Within-grade increases are typically based upon seniority, merit, or a combination of both, as described in the next section.

The entire pay structure should be evaluated periodically and adjusted to reflect changes in labor market conditions, level of inflation, and other factors affecting pay. Although the typical structure is shown as linear, generally a more fair structure is curvilinear, with rates increasing exponentially as pay increases.

Individual Pay Determination

The final group used to establish pay for an employee is the employees working on the *same* job in an organization. This comparison leads to setting the pay of each individual, within the pay ranges that have been established. This is called individual pay determination. It is done first when the employee is hired. Then it takes place each year (or more frequently in some cases) when the employee's pay is reconsidered, often tied to performance evaluation (Chapter 8). It also is closely tied to raises (see pay administration in Chapter 14). Essentially the issue is: Given that a job can pay varying amounts within a range, which pay rate should this individual receive?

A *crucial* aspect of setting pay is individual pay determination. The persons most employees know and can compare their own pay to are other employees doing similar jobs *within the* organization.

Compensation specialists say that individual pay determination should be based on differences in current performance. Thus, if welder 1 makes 10 percent more welds than welder 2, and if the quality of all the welds is similar, welder 1 ought to be paid higher in the rate range, according to most compensation specialists. Most white-collar employees, managers, and professional employees agree with compensation specialists in this regard.

But many other employees (perhaps a majority) believe that seniority, age, and therefore *past* performance and loyalty should have equal or greater weight in individual pay determination. And managers may claim they have merit or performance-based pay systems, but many studies indicate they are more accurately based on current performance plus seniority, or seniority alone. This can have the effect of reducing the motivations of higher performing, younger employees. It also has been shown that sex, race, personal appearance, and lifestyle influence individual pay, although many believe that this should not be.

Summary

Chapter 13 has begun the discussion of compensation and pay structures which will be concluded in Chapter 14. The objectives of compensation have been stated, and premises dealing with the multiple meanings of pay at work, pay level, external and internal factors influencing pay level, and pay structures and their determination, have been covered. Some comments that summarize the chapter's main points are:

1. Pay is the monetary reward paid by an organization for the work done by an employee.
2. To promote employee satisfaction, compensation should be adequate, equitable, balanced, cost effective, secure, incentive providing, and acceptable to the employee.
3. Compensation decisions are the joint responsibility of operating executives, supervisors, and P/HRM specialists.

4. Because of individual employee preferences and jobs, research on motivation and compensation should be directed to examine:
   a. The range of behaviors which pay may affect positively or negatively.
   b. The amount of change pay can influence.

Case

Guido called Mary into his office the next day to go over her findings. She decided to use her term report to illustrate possible solutions for CNB's dilemma.

Guido I've read your paper. I like the way it deals with the problems here at CNB. It was a good idea to calculate how much turnover costs the bank. This may have an impact on Poppa Joe. You've also prepared recommendations for changes in our pay program, as I asked you to do. Let me see if I understand your plan. Basically, you propose setting up a point system of job evaluation and establishing standardized pay classes and ranges which would allow for pay variations based on individual pay factors. You also recommend that we set up a pay policy according to going wages. In view of our profit picture, that seems reasonable.

I'll present this plan to Poppa Joe tomorrow, with my endorsement.

Mary I'll be interested to see if it has any impact.

The next day Guido gave the report to Poppa Joe to read and comment on.

Questions:
1. Do you think Poppa Joe will approve changing the pay system at CNB? Why or why not?
2. If Guido were president of the bank and he accepted the report, how long would it take to implement the new program?
3. What problems would you anticipate, especially with those employees who are "overpaid" according to the job evaluation program?

(This case will be continued in Chapter 14.)

    c. The kind of employee pay influences positively and negatively.

    d. The environmental conditions that are present when pay leads to positive and negative results.

5. External influences on pay levels include government influences, union influences, economic conditions, and the nature of the labor market.

6. The pay-level decision involves the pay of employees working on similar jobs in other organizations: high, medium, or low pay.

7. The pay-structure decision involves employees working on different jobs within the organization: Which job is worth the most, which the least, which is in between?

8. Individual pay determination involves employees working on the same job within the organization: How much experience, education, seniority, and so on is necessary for each pay range?

9. Pay surveys are the principal tool used in the pay-level decision.

10. Job evaluation is the formal process by which the relative worth of various jobs in the organization is determined for pay purposes.

11. After job evaluation is completed, rate ranges and pay classes are developed for each job category as the basis for individual pay determination decisions.

Questions for Review and Discussion

1. What is compensation? How does it fit into the total reward system of organization?

2. Distinguish pay-level decisions, pay-structure decisions, and individual pay determination decisions.

3. Does compensation affect employee satisfaction? Performance?

4. What are the external factors affecting pay-level decisions? How do they affect the decisions?

5. Discuss the major laws affecting compensation. How do they affect the organization's pay level?

6. What is a pay survey? What is the best way to run one?

7. What are the organization factors affecting pay level?

8. How does management's pay strategy affect pay level? Give an example of the most typical pay strategy. Which strategy would you pursue?

9. What is a pay structure?

10. What is job evaluation? What are the techniques for performing it?

11. Distinguish and describe the interrelationships among pay classes, rate changes, and pay classifications.

12. How are individual pay determination decisions made?

Glossary

Classification or Grading System. A job evaluation method that groups jobs together into a grade or classification.

Comparable Worth. An issue that has been raised by women and the courts in recent years. It means that the concept of equal pay for equal jobs should be expanded to the notion of equal pay for comparable jobs. If a job is comparable to other jobs as determined by job content analysis that pay should be comparable.

Factor Comparison Method.   A job evaluation method that uses a factor-by-factor comparison. A factor comparison scale, instead of a point scale is used. Five universal job factors used to compare jobs are: responsibilities, skills, physical effort, mental effort, and working conditions.

Job Evaluation.   The formal process by which the relative worth of various jobs in the organization is determined for pay purposes.

Minimum Wage.   The Fair Labor Standards Act of 1938 as amended states that all employees covered by the law must pay an employee at least a minimum wage. In 1982 the minimum was $3.35 per hour.

Pay Class.   A convenient grouping of a variety of jobs that are similar on work difficulty and responsibility requirements.

Pay Surveys.   Surveys of the compensation paid to employees by all employers in a geographic area, an industry, or an occupational group.

Point System.   The most widely used job evaluation method. It requires evaluators to quantify the value of the elements of a job. On the basis of the job description or interviews with job occupants, points are assigned to the degree of various factors required to do the job.

Ranking of Jobs.   A job evaluation method often used in smaller organizations which has the evaluator rank jobs from the simplest to the most challenging—for example, clerk to research scientist.

Chapter Fourteen

Compensation: Methods and Policies

Learning Objectives

After studying this chapter, you should be able to:
- Describe three types of incentive plans used by organizations.

- Discuss the mechanics and process of the Scanlon Plan.

- Define what is meant by the terms *perk, bonus,* and *cost-of-living adjustment.*

- Explain how the government is involved in the employee stock ownership trust (ESOT) plan

Chapter Outline

I. Methods of Payment
   A. Payment for Time Worked
   B. Individual Incentives
   C. Group Incentives
   D. Organization Incentive Plans

II. Executive Compensation
   A. Executive Salaries
   B. Bonuses
   C. Stock Options, Performance Shares, and Book-Value Devices
   D. Executive Perquisites
   E. Executive Compensation Policy

III. Compensation Administration Issues
   A. Pay Secrecy or Openness
   B. Security in Pay
   C. Pay Raises
   D. Pay Compression

IV. Summary

Case (continued from Chapter 13)

Poppa Joe Paderewski sat in his big office in the rear of the Cardeson National Bank. Guido Panelli, his executive vice president, came in to drop off Mary Renfro's report on compensation, and to discuss other problems CBN was having with people and pay.

"For one thing, Poppa Joe, our executive turnover has been increasing. Mary is wondering if the executive compensation package is contributing to the problem. The employees who have quit have indicated a lack of adequate compensation, but we all know this is the most acceptable reason to give an employer for leaving. In any case, it's a problem, and we have to face it."

"CBN pays the going rate for salaries," Poppa Joe declared. "And there's our bonus system—when profits allow it."

"But some of those leaving said their new employers would have performance-share programs," Guido said.

Poppa Joe wondered what that meant, and he thought, "Maybe I should hire a consultant to advise us on the executive compensation program."

Meanwhile, over at Branch 1, Tom Nichols, the manager of the branch, was having a meeting with the tellers' supervisors to discuss pay. He hadn't wanted to attend the meeting; he didn't like meetings, and he knew this one would be bad. The tellers were never satisfied with their pay. Back in school, Tom had learned that pay was one thing that was never easily settled; people were always griping about it.

The meeting went like this:

Chet Tom, we're here because the troops are unhappy.

Tom The troops are always unhappy.

Chet Sure, But this time it's serious. My people are tired of punching time clocks and getting paid by the hour. Everyone else here at the bank gets salaries—52 weeks a year. Why don't my tellers?

Tom Well, you know, it's always been done that way. Besides . . .

Chet Don't give me that "it's-always-been-done-that-way" stuff. You can do something about it. Talk to Poppa Joe. My people want the security of a regular paycheck and the dignity of no time clock. You know the union's been around. What are we going to do about it?

The other supervisors shook their heads, and Tom didn't know what to say.

Branch 2 was having its own problems. One day there was an incident involving two tellers and a supervisor. It all started when the following dialogue took place:

Martha Did you hear that Joanne makes $1.50 more an hour than me? I've been here longer than she has. What is this?

Sandra Why not go to June about it? She's the boss.

Martha (to June) How come Joanne makes $1.50 more than me? I've been here longer.

June How do you know that's true? We don't reveal salaries around here, and it's against company policy to discuss other people's pay.

Martha Never mind how I found out. And let's cut the company policy stuff. Why is Joanne paid more than I am?

It is now raise time again, and Poppa Joe is getting flack from all sides. He believes he can afford about 10 percent for raises. But who should get them?

After Guido left his office, Poppa Joe went over the situation in his mind. "Some deserve no raise, really," he thought. "Others deserve something; a few deserve a lot. But how should I divide the money? Should I really give no raise at all to some? With inflation what it is, that's like getting a pay cut, and they don't deserve *that*. And how much should the *average* employee get? The cost of living has gone up 7 percent. If I give them much more than that, there won't be enough to give big raises to the people who really deserve them, like Mary and Guido. And that says nothing about the people who deserve raises because, as Mary keeps saying, their base pay is too low, and what about the people who are being promoted? How am I going to allocate this raise money?"

After thinking it over, Poppa Joe decided to talk to Mary about the problems and her report. He asked her to come in and give him a brief summary of some of the major points about compensation she learned in the college course she had taken.

Poppa Joe Mary, I'm having problems with pay again, as you know. Will you give me a rundown on some of the highlights of that course you took? I don't have a lot of time, though. That's why I'd rather have you tell me than read your report.

Mary I know you don't have much time. Let's cover some basics that we haven't discussed already.

With that, Mary briefed Poppa Joe on pay methods, executive compensation, and some key compensation issues raised in the incidents she and Guido had told him about.

Let's pick up where we ended in Chapter 13 and complete the discussion of the seven criteria for effective compensation introduced there. A compensation system which meets all these criteria will accomplish the objective of providing a system of rewards which is equitable to employer and employee alike, so that the employee's satisfaction and production are both heightened. As we discussed, an effective compensation system should be:

Adequate. Chapter 13 gave the legal definition of adequacy as set forth in minimum wage and other legislation. The managerial definition of adequacy, or pay-level policies designed to pay the going wage, was also described.

Equitable. Chapter 13 discussed job evaluation as one technique to be used to attain equity. Chapter 14 will touch upon the related policy issue of whether all employees should be paid salaries.

Incentive providing. Chapter 13 discussed the theory behind the merit or incentive pay system. This chapter will discuss how incentive pay systems are designed and how raises are used as a form of incentive.

The other four criteria, which will be discussed primarily in this chapter, state that the compensation plan should be:

Secure. The extent to which the employee's pay seems secure to him or her.

Balanced. The extent to which pay is a reasonable part of the total reward package, which includes benefits, promotions, and so on. Chapter 15 discusses benefits.

Cost effective. The extent to which the pay system is cost effective for the organization.

Acceptable to the employee. Whether employees think the pay system makes sense. Three aspects of this will be discussed: whether pay should be secret; compensation communication to achieve acceptability; and employee participation in pay decision making.

Methods of Payment

Employees can be paid for the time they work, the output they produce, or a combination of these two factors.

Payment for Time Worked

The majority of employees are paid for time worked, in the form of wages or salaries. Paying for time worked and establishing compensation systems based on time were the compensation methods discussed in Chapter 13. Pay surveys are used to establish competitive pay for the industry, and job evaluation is the principal method for setting time-pay schedules. Then pay ranges, pay classifications, and similar tools are developed for individual pay determination, the final step in a time-based pay system.

Salaries for Everyone? • Typically, most employees are paid salaries. Exceptions are blue-collar and some clerical employees who are paid hourly wages. One issue in the time-pay system is whether everyone should be paid a salary. (Tom Nichols's dilemma in dealing with hourly paid employees is an example.) Would you rather be paid strictly by the hour and not know your income week to week, month to month, or be paid a salary so you could plan your life? In general, most blue-collar employees are given hourly pay, but there has been a movement to place all employees on salaries and give them the same benefits and working conditions others have. Firms such as IBM, Texas Instruments, Polaroid, and Avon have experimented with this plan.

The advantage claimed for this move is that blue-collar workers become more integrated into the organization, and this improves the climate of employee relations. No study claims that it improves productivity, and the reports of its effects on absenteeism are mixed.[1] Some studies claim absenteeism decreases. Other have found that it increases, but management controls and peer pressure later bring it down to acceptable levels.[2]

Some individuals purpose that if all employees are paid salaries, it is possible that the long-run security of positions will be diminished. With hourly workers, if business is down it is relatively easy for an organization to reduce the hours worked daily or weekly, save the labor costs, and adjust to the realities of the marketplace. On the other hand, if everyone is on salary, management tends to look toward full layoffs or reduction in the labor force by attrition or terminations. *Providing salaries for everyone changes labor costs from variable to fixed, and this can have serious employment security implications.*

The success of a total-salaries program requires stable, mature, responsible employees, a cooperative union, willing supervisors, and a work load that allows continuous employment. Caution is urged in adopting this approach until the full range of possible consequences is carefully evaluated.[3]

The methods for paying employees on the basis of output are usually referred to as incentive forms of compensation. Incentives can be paid individually, to the work group, or on an enterprisewide basis. Incentive compensation assumes it is possible and useful to tie performance directly to pay, an issue discussed in detail in Chapter 13.

Individual Incentives

Perhaps the oldest form of compensation is the individual incentive plan, in which the employee is paid for units produced. Today the individual incentive plan takes several

---

[1] Edward E. Lawler III., *Pay and Organizational Effectiveness: A Psychological View* (New York: McGraw-Hill, 1971).

[2] Ibid.

[3] W. J. Keaney, "Pay for Performance? Not Always," *MSU Business Topics,* Spring 1979, p. 6.

forms: piecework, production bonus, and commissions.[4] These methods seek to achieve the incentive goal of compensation.

Straight piecework usually works like this. An employee is guaranteed an hourly rate (probably the minimum wage) for performing an expected minimum output (the standard). For production over the standard, the employer pays so much per piece produced. This is probably the most frequently used incentive pay plan. The standard is set through work measurement studies, as modified by collective bargaining. The amount of the base rate and piece rates may emerge from data collected by pay surveys.

A variation of the straight piece rate is the differential piece rate. In this plan, the employer pays a smaller piece rate up to standard and then a higher piece rate above the standard. Research indicates that the differential piece rate is more effective than the straight piece rate, although it is *much less* frequently used.[5]

Production bonus systems pay an employee an hourly rate. Then a bonus is paid when the employee exceeds standard, typically 50 percent of labor savings. This system is not widely used.

Commissions are paid to sales employees. Straight commission is the equivalent of straight piecework and is typically a percentage of the price of the item. A variation of the production bonus system for sales is to pay the salesperson a small salary and commission or bonus when she or he exceeds standard (the budgeted sales goal).

"Our incentive plan is quite simple. Make one mistake and you're through!"

Reprinted by permission of George Dole.

---

[4]Richard I. Henderson, *Compensation Management* (Reston, Va.: Reston Publishing, 1979), pp. 355–83.

[5]Edwin Locke, et al., "Goods and Intentions as Mediators of the Effects of Monetary Incentive on Behavior," *Journal of Applied Psychology*, April 1968, pp. 104–21.

Individual incentives are used more frequently in some industries (clothing, steel, textiles) than others (lumber, beverage, bakery), and more in some jobs (sales, production) than others (maintenance, clerical).

Are individual incentives effective? The research results are mixed.[6] Most studies indicate they do increase output. Although production increases, other performance criteria may suffer. For example, in sales, straight commission can lead to less attention being paid to servicing accounts. There is also evidence that there are individual differences in the effect of incentives on performance.[7] Some employees are more inclined to perform better than others. This should not surprise you, since we know that people have varying motivations to work.

Incentive systems may be designed to affect outputs other than performance. For example, employers may use them to try to lower absenteeism and turnover. At least for some employees, incentive pay may lower satisfaction, however. Employees may be dissatisfied if they have to work harder or if they feel manipulated by the system.

For incentive plans to work, they must be well designed and administered. It appears that an individual incentive plan is likely to be more effective under certain circumstances.[8] These are when:

- The task is liked.
- The task is not boring.
- The supervisor reinforces and supports the system.
- The plan is acceptable to employees and managers and probably includes them in the plan's design.
- The standards are carefully designed.
- The incentive is financially sufficient to induce increased output.
- Quality of work is not especially important.
- Most delays in work are under the employees' control.

Group Incentives

Piecework, production bonuses, commissions, and other individual incentives can also be paid to groups of individuals. This might be done when it is difficult to measure individual output, when cooperation is needed to complete a task or project, and when management feels this is a more appropriate measure on which to base incentives. Group incentive plans also reduce administrative costs.

Group incentive plans are used less frequently than individual incentive plans. Less research has been done on group incentives, though some studies suggest that group incentives are less effective than other incentive plans but more effective than straight-time wages or salaries.[9] A problem is that the group may not work well together, or less motivated members might decide to coast along on the work of others.

Another problem incentive compensation schemes face is restriction of output. The

---

[6]Lawler, *Pay and Organizational Effectiveness.*

[7]Mitchell Fein, ''Let's Return to Now for Incentives,'' *Industrial Engineering,* January 1979, pp. 34–37

[8]Allen Nash and Stephen Carroll, *The Management of Compensation* (Monterey, Calif.: Brooks/Cole Publishing, 1975), chap. 7.

[9]Manuel London and Greg Oldam, ''A Comparison of Group and Individual Incentive Plans,'' *Academy of Management Journal,* March 1977, pp. 34–41.

Supreme Court ruled (*Schofield et al.* v. *National Labor Relations Board et al.*) that a union can discipline a member who exceeds the piecework norm. This legitimizes restriction of output and makes it more difficult to install group incentive plans.

Organization Incentive Plans

In an attempt to minimize the problems of interindividual and intergroup competition, some organizations have elected to use organization level incentive plans. Competition can result in withholding information or resources, political gamesmanship, not helping others, and even sabotaging the work of others. These behaviors can certainly be costly to an organization to use organization level incentive plans.

In an interesting use of an organization incentive plan, Robert Collings, president of Data Terminal Systems (DTS) used a vacation reward program.[10] DTS was experiencing some growing problems with too much interdepartmental conflict and jealousy. Collings gave employees an offer that was difficult to refuse: if the firm doubled sales and earnings he would treat everyone to a week's vacation in Disney World or London. Sales didn't quite make that goal, but earnings more than doubled. Collings closed the doors for one week and off the employees went (310 employees, 326 dealers, and about 300 husbands, wives, and friends [they paid their own way]). The vacation incentive cost DTS about $200,000.

The next year, Collings offered a trip to Rome. Again the goals were met and off the company went. Each employee received full pay, most expenses, $100 spending money, and cost rates for their families. The Rome travels and leisure cost DTS about $500,000. But DTS remained committed to organizationwide incentives because the entire employee team was able to pull together to accomplish a common or superordinate goal.

Four approaches to incentive plans are used at the organizational level: suggestion systems; company group incentive plans; profit sharing; and stock ownership plans.

Suggestion Systems • Most large- and medium-sized organizations have suggestion systems designed to encourage employee input for improvements in organization effectiveness. Typically, the employee submits the suggestion in writing, perhaps placing it in a suggestion box. If, after being screened by a committee, the idea is tried and proven useful, the employee receives a financial reward. If the savings due to the idea are hard to compute, the employee is given a standard reward, such as $25 or $100. If they are measurable, the employee receives a percentage of the first year's savings, typically 10 to 20 percent.

Effective administration of the suggestion program is essential to its success. General Electric has disbursed over $3 million to its employees in one year for more than 69,000 suggestions.[11] The reasons for rejecting a suggestion must be carefully explained to the submitter. If a group idea is successful it is useful to reward the whole group rather than

---

[10]S. Solomon, "How a Whole Company Earned Itself a Roman Holiday," *Fortune,* January 15, 1979, pp. 80–83.

[11]Henderson, *Compensation Management,* p. 379.

an individual. In general, suggestions systems seem to be useful incentive plans. But this is not always true. Some of the reasons for failure are:

1. Management lacks interest and fails to support the system.
2. There has been insufficient time to review and analyze the suggestions.
3. Those developing suggestions fear the impact of changes brought about by the suggestions on co-workers (e.g., improving technology, equipment, and work flow may result in layoffs or cutbacks in overtime pay).
4. Supervisors consider suggestions to be a personal threat.[12]

Company Group Incentive Plans • Several companies have developed elaborate group incentive and participation schemes which generally have been quite successful. The most successful group incentive plan at a single company is the Lincoln Electric Plan.[13] The benefits of the plan are impressive: stable prices for customers, good employee-management relations, and large financial rewards to employees. Individual workers have received huge bonuses year in and out, into the thousands of dollars, in addition to competitive wages. From 1933 to 1951, the bonuses per worker averaged $40,000! The employee's share in the bonus is based on a merit rating three times a year.

Lincoln Electric, with $120 million yearly in sales of welding and similar equipment, has multiple incentives for its workers tied to a participation scheme. An advisory board of several executives and about 30 employees reviews and makes suggestions for company

"Dear Sir: Here are two thousand suggestions for the betterment and efficiency of the corporation. One . . ."

Drawing by Herbert Goldberg; © 1974 The New Yorker Magazine, Inc.

---

[12]Ibid., pp. 379–80.
[13]James Lincoln, *Incentive Management* (Cleveland, O.: Lincoln Electric Co., 1969).

improvements. The suggestion system pays 50 percent of savings in the first year. The base rate of wages is a piece rate. The firm also has a stock-purchase plan in which about two thirds of the employees participate; they now own about one third of the total stock. The stock is privately traded and not sold on any exchange.

Lincoln Electric has been extraordinarily successful in mobilizing employee energies. Employees hire the replacements for vacancies in their work group. The company basically subcontracts the work to the work group, using its past performance and time studies as standards. When these standards are beaten, the employees share generously. This bonus is not used as a substitute for adequate wages and benefits, either. Needless to say, some individuals bid to go to work for Lincoln Electric.

Scanlon Plan companies. The Scanlon Plan is a combination group incentive, suggestion, and employee participation scheme that has been adopted by about 100 smaller and medium-sized manufacturing firms and at least one large firm, Midland Ross.[14] It is named after Joseph Scanlon, its designer. The Scanlon Plan avoids many of the problems of the other group incentive schemes. Here is how it works. Each department of the firm has a production committee composed of the foreman and employee representatives elected by the members or appointed by the union. The committee screens the suggestions for improvements made by employees and management. The number of suggestions that come from workers in these plans is about double the normal suggestion-plan rate, and about 80 percent of them are usable. If accepted, the cost of savings is paid to the work group, not just to the person suggesting it.

The plan also involves a wage formula. Gains from increased productivity are paid in bonus form to all employees: operative workers, supervisors, indirect workers such as typists, and salespersons. They receive bonuses in proportional shares. Management receives its share of productivity gains in increased profits.

Advocates of the Scanlon Plan contend that there are positive results for everyone. These include increased participation by employees, better acceptance of change on everyone's part, greater efficiency for the company, and improved union-management relations. Most of the research studies are positive.

The Scanlon Plan is a promising incentive system. However, for the plan to succeed, management must be willing to encourage and work with participating workers. All employers must provide their fair shares of suggestions and work. The union must develop a new degree of cooperation. It is likely to be more successful in small- and medium-sized organizations. It also has worked well in troubled companies, providing there are the necessary conditions of participation, communication, and identification.

Profit-Sharing Plans • Essentially, profit sharing is the payment of a regular share of company profits to employees as a supplement to their normal compensation. The plans must be approved by the Internal Revenue Service, which issued a "model plan" in late 1976 to fit the 1976 tax revision law in the United States.

The number of plans is growing in smaller firms and declining in larger ones. Profit-sharing plans divide a set percentage of net profit among employees. The percentage varies, but 25 percent is about normal. The funds can be divided equally based on the base salary or job grade, or in several other ways. The profit share can be paid often

---

[14]James W. Driscoll, "Working Creatively with a Union: Lessons from the Scanlon Plan," *Organizational Dynamics*, Summer 1979, pp. 61–80.

(such as quarterly) or less frequently (such as yearly), or deferred until retirement. The latter plan has tax advantages for the recipient.

Advocates of profit sharing contend that the plans successfully motivate greater performance by employees. Many firms also see profit sharing as a way to increase employee satisfaction and quality workmanship and to reduce absenteeism and turnover. Essentially, they contend that employees who have profit-sharing plans identify more closely with the company and its profit goals and thus they reduce waste and increase productivity.[15]

However, there are some potential problems with profit sharing.[16] First, an organization cannot share what it does not have. And in bad years, there are no profits to share. The employees may have cut costs and worked hard, but perhaps a recession slowed sales and thus profits, or management chose an expensive but ineffective marketing program. After several bad years the employee no longer links his extra efforts to increased financial rewards. Often, even in good years, it is difficult for the employee to see the significance of extra work to profit sharing a year away, or worse, at retirement 40 years later.

Profit sharing has had limited success because of the difficulty of tying individual rewards to effort and the problems raised when there are no profits to share. The plans probably are more successful in smaller firms because the employees can identify more closely with a smaller organization and can see the relation between their productivity and company profits more easily. Plans restricted to executives have been more successful, as will be discussed later in the chapter.

In the United States, the passage of the Employee Retirement Income Security Act of 1974 (ERISA; see Chapter 15) influenced more companies to set up profit-sharing plans. The payment of annual profit-sharing funds are not subject to ERISA's requirements, and some employers probably choose to use the profit-sharing mechanism to avoid the financial and paperwork problems associated with ERISA. However, the Tax Reform Act of 1976 created disadvantages for profit-sharing plans.

Stock Ownership Plans • Many companies encourage employee purchase of company stock (often at advantageous prices), to increase employees' incentives to work, satisfaction, and work quality, and to reduce absenteeism and turnover. Purchase plans often allow for payroll deductions or company financing of the stock. Sometimes the company will agree to buy the stock back at a guaranteed rate if it appears that the employee would take a significant loss. Companies use these plans for the same reasons as they do profit-sharing plans; when employees become partners in the business, they work harder.

Some of these plans (such as Procter & Gamble's) are very successful. In general, stock purchase plans have most of the disadvantages of profit sharing. It is hard for the truck driver to identify his working harder with an increase in the value of his stock. It is more difficult when the stock drops in price. Many stock ownership plans were terminated in the 1930s because of big drops in stock prices.

A major change in U.S. laws may have increased the usage of stock ownership plans. Recently, Congress authorized an establishment of an employee stock ownership plan (ESOP) through the mechanism of an employee stock ownership trust (ESOT). Firms have a number of incentives for setting up an ESOT. ERISA views an ESOT as an employee benefit plan. The Tax Reduction Act of 1975 allows firms with an ESOT to

---

[15]"Employee Wrath Hits Profit-Sharing Plans," *Business Week,* July 18, 1977, pp. 25, 28.

[16]Randy G. Swad, "Stock Ownership Plans: A New Employee Benefit," *Personnel Journal,* June 1981, pp. 453–55.

take an extra 1 percent investment tax credit in addition to the 10 percent investment tax credit. The Trade Reform Act gives a company with an ESOT preference in receiving government expansion funds for growth in areas where foreign competition has hurt.[17] And the De-Couper Industries ruling by the Securities Exchange Commission (SEC) appears to allow a firm to convert a standard profit-sharing fund into an ESOT.

The ESOT has been popularized by Louis Kelso.[18] Essentially the firm setting up an ESOT puts into the trust unissued stock or stock held by a dominant stockholder. The shares are sold to the trust, and the trust uses the stock as collateral and borrows the value of the stock from a bank. The trust then turns the cash over to the company and pays the trust back by making tax-deductible contributions to the ESOT (a maximum of 15 percent of eligible payroll of pretax income). This allows the company to borrow at half the normal cost (it pays back principal only, not the interest) and creates a market for the shares of smaller and middle-sized firms. The retiring employee (or the family of an accidentally killed employee) is given his or her share of the ESOT.

It is clear that for the corporation an ESOT improves liquidity and cash flow, can help the firm acquire life insurance for key stockholders, and can be useful in effecting divestitures and mergers. One expert maintains that the ESOT is best for an organization that is doing well financially, is in the full corporate income tax bracket, is a domestic corporation (not a subchapter S corporation or partnership), and is labor intensive; that is, has a minimum "covered" payroll of at least $500,000 annually.[19] Compensation specialists foresee the spread of ESOTs and ESOPs.

Not everyone has a positive opinion on ESOPs. Some critics feel it is a loophole in ERISA and can endanger employee pension funds. The problems with profit-sharing plans (stocks decline in value, and so will retirement funds) could be worse for ESOPs if all the funds are invested in the company stock. ESOPs also have the effect of diluting earnings per share and thus stockholder equity.[20]

Case

Mary and Poppa Joe's conversation on compensation continues:

Mary In summary, Poppa Joe, one of our problems is that we pay some people salaries, and pay others by the hour. That was the problem Chet brought to Tom Nichols at Branch 1. Of course, lots of banks do this, but we could change it.

We also have not tried incentive pay here.

Most banks don't offer it, but we might consider it. At least we probably ought to have a suggestion system. We might even consider a Scanlon Plan or profit sharing.

Poppa Joe I don't know. What about our executive compensation problem?

Mary I'm going to get to that next.

---

[17]Paul Burke, "Total Compensation Planning under the 1976 Tax Reform Act," *Personnel Journal*, March 1977, pp. 137–39, 150.

[18]Ibid.

[19]Wallace F. Forbes and Donald P. Partland, "Pros and Cons of Employee Stock Ownership Plan," *Business Horizons*, June 1976, pp. 5–12.

[20]Based on William G. Flanagan, "More Sweets to the Suite," *Forbes*, June 8, 1981, pp. 107–44.

Executive Compensation

Executives in the public and third sectors are normally compensated by salaries. In the private sector, business executives receive salaries too, but many of them also receive incentive compensation such as bonuses. In addition, executives in all sectors receive benefits and special treatment which are usually called perqusites (perks).

A fundamental question in executive compensation is why business executives should be paid incentives as well as salaries. A number of answers can be given. First, it is argued that these incentives improve performance, and that is good for stockholders and employees. A second reason is that incentive compensation is a way of retaining talented executives. Many have alternative employment opportunities with other corporations or as entrepreneurs. The third reason is that business executives are more likely to control their own compensation in the private sector than in the public sector, where legislative bodies determine it, or in the third sector, where boards, normally from outside the enterprise, have a great deal of control. For these and other reasons, the compensation of business executives tends to be lucrative and innovative enough to sidestep the everchanging tax laws.

Executive Salaries

Salaries of executives in the public sector are generally known to the public. Salaries of executives in the third sector have not been widely studied. In general, the highest salaries are paid in the private sector.[21] There are many studies of this form of compensation.

To give you some idea of the salaries and bonuses of some top executives in organizations you probably have done business with, let's look at some 1980 data. Remember these figures are just for the salary and bonus portions of compensation. Exhibit 14–1 provides a look at 10 executives in companies that are in the news.

Some studies have been done on the relationship of the size and kind of business to salary amount. With regard to size, in general, as the firm increases in size, the top executive's salary increases. Several studies have examined the relative salaries of exec-

Exhibit 14–1 _____

Ten chief executives: Salary and bonus for 1980

Name	Age	Company	Salary and bonus
Albert V. Casey	61	American Airlines	$ 372,000
David W. Mitchell	53	Avon Products	547,000
Thomas H. Wyman	51	CBS	1,361,000
Philip Caldwell	61	Ford	400,000
Reginald H. Jones	63	General Electric	1,000,000
William E. C. Dearden	58	Hershey Foods	300,000
Frank T. Cary	60	IBM	871,000
Bernard M. Fawler	58	K mart	450,000
Peter E. Haas	62	Levi Strauss	397,000
Fred L. Turner	48	McDonald's	375,000

Source: Forbes, June 8, 1981, "Who Gets the Most Pay," Copyright 1981, Forbes, Inc.

---

[21]Arch Patton, "Top Executive Pay," *Harvard Business Review*, September–October 1966, pp. 94–97. Also see Carol J. Loomis, "The Madness of Executive Compensation," *Fortune*, July 12, 1982, pp. 42–52.

utives in different industries. For example, one study found that in companies with sales larger than $10 billion, motor vehicle companies paid the highest, followed (in order) by conglomerates and firms in office machines and oil.[22] In the $5 billion category the order was motor vehicles, office machines, conglomerates, and oil. In the $2.5 billion sales category, the order was pharmaceuticals, packaged goods, forest products, chemicals, and food processors. In the $500 million sales category, the order was packaged goods, pharmaceuticals, chemicals, office machines, and forest products.

Various experts have tried to explain industry differences in executive compensation. Patton suggested that industries that pay higher salaries are dynamic, decentralized, and results oriented. Industries that pay poorly tend to be be static, centralized, seniority oriented, and monopolies with a great deal of regulation. In a later study he added that high-paying companies tend to have stock that is widely held.[23]

Most studies also find that the salaries below the CEO level fit a percentage pattern by industry grouping. For example, the second highest executive is usually paid about 71 percent of the CEO's salary in all except retail trade, where it is 84 percent. The third highest executive tends to be paid 55–60 percent of the CEO's salary.

If top managers believe that pay is a motivator to higher performance, it follows that they will pay themselves in a way that rewards performance. And if performance is defined as more profits, pay should be correlated with profits. Some studies indicate that this is done. Other studies show that top executive pay is correlated with sales, a proxy for size.[24]

More sophisticated studies point out that simple correlations such as these are not likely to explain very much. The factors which influence executive pay are ownership and market concentration. One study found that in closely held firms, executive pay was correlated with profitability. Other studies agree with this, and it makes sense.[25] In firms where the owners can put pressure, executives are likely to encourage higher profitability. In firms with no strong ownership interest, executives can set their salaries similar to those of executives in equal-size firms, regardless of profitability.

Bonuses

A bonus is a compensation payment that supplements salary and can be paid in the present or in the future. In the latter case, it is called a deferred bonus. Exhibit 14–2 shows the top 10 paid executives of publicly held companies in 1980. Their compensation consists of salaries, bonus, benefits (see Chapter 15), contingent pay or the amounts of deferred compensation received based on performance incentives, and stock gains or gains from shares or cash from exercising stock options.

While reviewing the figures of the "Top 10" you probably asked yourself, "Is any one person worth millions of dollars to a business?" Apparently many firms believe that the talents, experience, and decision-making skills of the kind of individuals presented in Exhibit 14–2 are worth the price.

---

[22]Arch Patton, *Men, Money, and Motivation* (New York: McGraw-Hill, 1961).

[23]Robert Sibson, "Executive Pay: The Long Term Is Where the Action Is," *Nation's Business,* November 1971, pp. 29–33.

[24]Marc Wallace, "Type of Control, Industrial Concentration and Executive Pay," *Proceedings,* National Academy of Management, 1976.

[25]John Dearden, "How to Make Incentive Plans Work," *Harvard Business Review,* July–August 1972, pp. 117–24.

Exhibit 14-2 _____

The top 10

Name	Company	Salary and bonus	Benefits	Contingent	Stock gains	Total
1. Thomas B. Pickens, Jr.	Mesa Petroleum	$ 415,972	$ 169,145	$ 45,165	$7,235,549	$7,865,831
2. George T. Scharffenberger . . .	City Investing	569,000	11,839	120,941	4,464,112	5,165,892
3. Robert A. Charpie.	Cabot	799,000	1,222,533	1,376,048	1,308,625	4,706,206
4. Walter J. Sanders III	Advanced Micro Devices	538,246	27,907	8,106	3,706,560	4,280,819
5. Milton F. Rosenthal	Engelhard Minerals	1,825,000	476,592	1,698,625	—	4,000,217
6. Clifton C. Garvin, Jr..	Exxon	1,043,431	60,551	227,564	2,016,437	3,347,983
7. Fred L. Hartley	Union Oil California	875,767	370,387	463,313	1,419,441	3,128,908
8. Ray C. Adam	NL Industries	662,225	21,845	247,483	2,161,500	3,093,053
9. David S. Lewis	General Dynamics	455,173	8,875	—	2,556,746	3,020,794
10. Robert Anderson.	Rockwell International	865,000	18,562	919,900	1,163,531	2,966,993

Source: Forbes, June 8, 1981, "Who Gets the Most Pay," Copyright 1981, Forbes, Inc.

A majority of large firms pay bonuses, in the belief that this leads to better profitability and other advantages for organizations. Bonuses involve large expenditures of funds. They vary from 80 percent of top executives' salaries to 20 percent of the salaries of lowest level participants. In spite of wide usage and high costs, there is little research support for their effectiveness. Unless more research does support the payment of bonuses, many may conclude they are an example of management's power to pay itself what it wants. This is an issue that can have an impact on the image the public holds about the ethics of chief executives running organizations.

Dearden suggests a systematic and logical approach to bonuses.[26] His plan has these features:

- The total bonus for top executives is based on percentage of net profits after a reasonable earnings per share for the stockholder.
- The standard bonus per executive is based on number of bonus points

© King Features Syndicate Inc., 1977. World rights reserved.

_____
[26]"Special Privileges," *The Wall Street Journal*, September 18, 1975, p. 1.

assigned to the job, based on the position's potential impact on company profitability.
- The actual bonus payments are spread over a three- to five-year period.
- A limit (cutoff level) is put on the total of the bonus to be paid in one year. The excess funds are reserved for leaner years.

Stock Options, Performance Shares, and Book-Value Devices

Another form of executive compensation used in the private sector is a set of devices tied to the firm's stock (see Exhibit 14–2). The oldest form is the *stock option,* which gives executives the right to purchase company stock at a fixed price for a certain period of time. The option's price usually is close to the market price of the stock at the time the option is issued. The executive gains if the price rises above the option price during the option period enough to cover the capital gains tax on the stock should it be purchased.

The popularity of stock options has risen and fallen with the tax laws (especially the 1976 and 1981 laws), the level of interest rates, the state of the stock market, and the feelings of stockholders about them. At present, because of tax law changes and these other factors, the use of stock options as incentive compensation is decreasing.

Is this a great loss? Probably not. There was little research to indicate that stock options led to better performance; what evidence there was tended to indicate that they did not. But one implication of the research is that as management's income from ownership-related sources (dividends and capital gain) increases, these instruments can serve to improve performance.

Innovative tax lawyers and tax accountants have worked up some new compensation forms to replace the stock option and still provide ownership and incentive compensation. Several variations are primarily incentive compensation oriented, others ownership oriented, and still others a mix of the two. The ownership-oriented devices are:

Market-Value Purchases • The company lends the executive funds at low interest rates to buy company stock at current market value. The executive repays the loan by direct payment or receives credits on the loan payments for staying with the company and/or achieving a certain performance level.

Book Value Purchases • The executive is offered a chance to buy the company stock at book value (or some similar nonmarket value measure) but can resell it to the company later, using the same formula price.

Exercise Bonuses • Payment to an executive when he or she exercises a stock option that is equal to or proportionate to the option gain is called an exercise bonus. This helps the executive keep the stock rather than sell it to pay the taxes on the gain.

One device appears to be primarily a form of compensation that is linked to stocks. This is *performance shares and performance units,* used by such companies as General Motors, Gulf, Texaco, Pepsico, and International Nickel. Performance shares grant stock units due the executive in the future (such as five years later) if performance targets are met. These units appreciate or depreciate as the stock does. Performance units are performance shares paid in cash instead of stock. The units are compensation unless they are to be used to buy stock. Both are viewed as compensation by the IRS.

Another device, *stock appreciation rights,* can be either compensation or ownership oriented. This device, attached to a stock option, allows the executive to accept appreciation in value in either stock or cash.

Most of these devices are fairly new and are still rarely used. All could have performance implications for the organization, but there is inadequate research at this stage to determine under what conditions they do so. The key to their success is the definition and identification of what constitutes performance.

Executive Perquisites

All over the world and in all sectors of the economy, executives receive special perquisites and extras called perks. These tend to be larger in Europe than in the United States. The European executive can receive free housing and other niceties in lieu of or in addition to higher salaries. The differences can be easily explained. Some perks are taxed as income in the United States, but are not taxed elsewhere. The mood of Congress and the Internal Revenue Service regarding executive perks mellowed when the Reagan administration came into power in 1981.

The American Management Association studied perks in 742 companies: 34 perks were examined, but only 7 were regularly available in more than half of the companies studied. These include better office decor, choice office location, a company car, reserved parking, a car for personal use, and first-class air tickets.[27]

A list of executive perks is presented in Exhibit 14–3. Some of these perks are also called benefits (as noted in the exhibit, these are discussed in Chapter 15). Research indicates that executives prefer the following perks the most: insurance (96 percent), company car (87 percent), club memberships (84 percent), financial counseling (77 percent), travel (66 percent), loans (57 percent), company airplane (56 percent).

Perks have not been widely studied. In terms of Maslow's hierarchy of needs, however, they are likely to fulfill the physiological and especially the recognition needs of the executive. Obviously, a big office provides for recognition needs. But a company car, club membership, financial counseling, and so on provide the executive with nontaxable income—something many of them prefer to taxable income.

Executive Compensation Policy

How does an organization choose the compensation package for its executives? Effective executive compensation must meet the needs of both the organization and the individual executive. With regard to the organization, the total compensation must be competitive with that of similar enterprises. Thus it makes no sense to look at total compensation of executives, or averages. The effective firm determines the compensation of executives in similar-sized organizations in the same industry group with the same degree of competitiveness. Executive compensation must also be directly tied to the organization's strategy and objectives, so executive rewards will promote achievement of the organization's goals.

One way organizations try to satisfy the needs and desires of their executives is to adjust compensation methods to changing tax laws. This often leads to the use of more deferred compensation methods. Another way is to study the preferences and attitudes of

---

[27]Robert Sbarra, "The New Language of Executive Compensation," *Personnel,* November–December 1975, pp. 10–18.

Exhibit 14–3 _____

Executive perquisites: A selected list

Insured or Internal Revenue Service Qualified Benefits
Voluntary supplement retirement benefits*
Voluntary supplementary life insurance and disability insurance*
Officers and directors liability insurance
Profit-sharing, thrift saving, stock purchase plans

Special Privileges:
Financial counseling services*
Company loans for stock option exercise, stock purchase, home purchase, education, personal investment,
   and so forth
Company cars
Paid memberships (initiation and dues) to country clubs, athletic clubs, luncheon clubs, dinner clubs,
   professional associations
Liberal expense accounts
Extra time off from work, sabbatical leaves
Company housing, hotel suites
Income deferral
Employment or termination contracts
Combined business and vacation trips
Second office in-home or near-home location
Executive medical examinations
Executive dining room privilege
Unique investment opportunities
Special office decorating allowance

Expense Assumptions:
Educational assistance (tuition, dependent scholarships or loans)
Discounts on company products, services, or use of company facilities
Uncovered family medical and dental expenses

*A benefit discussed in Chapter 15.
Source: Robert Sbarra, "The New Language of Executive Compensation," *Personnel,* November–December 1975, p. 12. Reprinted by permission of AMACOM, a division of American Management Associations. All rights reserved.

executives toward the various compensation approaches. However, since each executive is different and has differing needs for compensation, studies of pay preferences are only partly indicative of what an enterprise should do. In one study of the pay preferences of 300 executives in seven large companies, it was found that executives' compensation preferences vary widely.[28] One consistency was a preference for 75 percent of total compensation in cash and 25 percent in benefits and deferred items, which would mean a shift from the present 85/15 percent division to include more benefits.

A way to deal with these differences is to set up a cafeteria compensation system. The cafeteria approach permits executives to determine the range of their compensation between present pay, deferred compensation, and benefits and services. This approach is described in more detail in the next chapter, where the cafeteria approach to benefits is considered for all employees. It does not change the total compensation (that could lead to perceived inequities), but the mix of how the compensation is received. Although there are administrative hurdles to be overcome, this approach fits compensation theories and makes sense.

_____

[28] Wilbur Lewellen and Howard Lanser, "Executive Pay Preferences," *Harvard Business Review,* September–October 1973, pp. 115–22.

Case

Mary So you see, boss, we've really only scratched the surface on compensation at CNB. Our executive compensation system consists of salaries (and not high ones at that), and a few perks like free memberships. We haven't tried bonuses or stock options, performance shares, or anything else. Our executive turnover is probably related to our executive compensation system.

Poppa Joe Yeah, but high turnover also could be happening because we've hired a great group of executives. Now we're a likely target for others to pirate executives from.

Mary I doubt it, boss.

Poppa Joe O.K. What's left?

Mary What's left are some key compensation administration issues.

At present the cafeteria system is not feasible in the public sector because of the usual rigid pay classifications and the system of a single salary plus fixed benefits. But it is possible and is being used in the private and third sectors.

Compensation Administration Issues

Managers must make policy decisions on three issues in compensation administration for employees and executives. These issues involve the extent to which (1) compensation will be secret, (2) compensation will be secure, and (3) raises will vary with performance.

Pay Secrecy or Openness

The first compensation issue to be discussed is the extent to which the pay of employees is known by others in the enterprise. (This is the issue Martha raised in the beginning of the chapter.) How would you feel if your co-workers could find out what you make? Would you care? As in other issues, employees differ on this.

There are degrees of secretiveness and openness on pay information. In many insti-

© 1977 by NEA, Inc. Reprinted by permission of NEA.

tutions and organizations, pay ranges and even an individual's pay are open to the public and fellow employees. Examples are public-sector salaries (federal, state, and local governments), some universities, and unionized wage employees. This is called the open system.

The opposite is the secret system, in which pay is regarded as privileged information known only to the employee, her or his superior, and such staff employees as P/HRM and payroll. In the most secrecy-oriented organizations, employees are told they cannot discuss pay matters and specifically their own pay. Recently, the National Labor Relations Board ruled that this is not a legitimate policy.

In the private and third sectors, secrecy is clearly the predominant pattern. For example, a BNA study found that only 18 percent of personnel officials felt pay should be an open matter.[29] Only a minority of organizations provide general pay information, such as pay rates, and even less provide data on individual's pay.

Should this be changed? Research is mixed. Some findings favor the open system, others the secret system. Before an open system is tried, the individual's performance must be objectively measurable, and the measurable aspects of the jobs to be rewarded must be the significant ones. There should be little need for cooperation among jobs, and employees in the system should have a direct causal relationship on performance. The employees must also prefer the open system.

There is increasing recognition that some employees want a more open pay system. The opening up of a system and providing more information to employees certainly has its costs and benefits. However, if an organization wishes to reduce the manipulative aura surrounding pay, actual or perceived, it is going to have to share additional pay information with employees. As more firms post job openings to make employees aware of opportunities, information on pay becomes a critical decision point.

As a step in deciding how much secrecy or how much openness is needed, managers first must clearly determine through observation (listening, talking, discussions in groups) what their employees want to know about pay. Then managers must decide if providing pay information will harm or benefit the firm. Finally, the conditions cited above concerning the objective measuring of performance, degree of interdependence, and causal relationships on performance must be carefully weighed.

Security in Pay

Current compensation can be a motivator of performance. But the belief that there will be future security in compensation may also affect it. Various plans for providing this security have been developed: the guaranteed annual wage, supplementary unemployment benefits, severance pay, seniority rules, and the employment contract.

A few companies provide a guaranteed annual wage to employees who meet certain characteristics. For this type of plan to work, general employee-management relations must be good. And the demand for the product or service must be steady. The best known such plans are those of Procter & Gamble, Hormel Meats, and the Nunn-Bush Shoe Company. In one plan, the employer guarantees the employee a certain number of weeks of work at a certain wage after the worker has passed a probation period (say, two years). Morton Salt Company guarantees 80 percent of full-time work to all employees after one year of standard employment. Procter & Gamble has invoked its emergency clause only

---

[29]Bureau of National Affairs, *Personnel Policies Forum*, Survey No. 97 (Washington, D.C. 1972).

P/HRM Manager Close-Up

Howard Falberg
Associated Dry Goods Corporation

Biography

Howard Falberg is vice president of personnel for Associated Dry Goods Corporation. He is a graduate of Columbia College and has a M.B.A. from Columbia University's Graduate School of Business. After a tour of duty with the U.S. Army, he held personnel positions with U.S. Steel Corporation and Continental Can Company. His experience in the retailing field began in 1965 and he spent the next 10 years in both corporate and division positions with

Federated Department Stores. He then spent two years as personnel vice president of Famous Barr Division of May Company and joined Associated Dry Goods as corporate vice president of personnel in 1976.

Job description

His areas of responsibility include labor force planning and development, executive search, compensation, labor relations, benefits, organization development and affirmative action.

Views about P/HRM by Howard Falberg

Ours is a labor intensive business. Our investment is not in heavy equipment but rather in the individuals who perform both executive and nonexecutive tasks. To a large degree, our success depends upon our ability to attract, train, and develop optimal people at all levels. We live in a period of time which one could describe as "manpower poor." This scarcity of talented people makes it essential for those companies who wish to retain the best individuals to put great emphasis on the environment in which people work. My job is basically to see to it that we can attract and retain those people who are able to further their personal growth along with the growth of our company.

once since 1923—in 1933 for a brief period at three plants. In the Hormel and Spiegel plans and others, a minimum income is guaranteed.[30]

In the supplementary unemployment benefits approach, the employer adds to unemployment compensation payments to help the employee achieve income security if not job security (as in the GAW). The auto, steel, rubber, garment, and glass industries, among others, contribute to a fund from which laid-off employees are paid. During the 1973–74 recession, many of these funds in the auto industry went bankrupt. They provided less income security than was thought. Studies on plans where unemployment was less severe than in autos show the system has helped in employment security.

In many organizations, the employer provides some income bridge from employment to unemployment and back to employment. This is severance pay. Typically, it amounts to one week's pay for each year of service. About 25 percent of union contracts require such severance pay. This doesn't guarantee a job, but it helps the employee when a job is lost.

---

[30]Robert Zager, "Managing Guaranteed Employment," *Harvard Business Review,* May–June 1978, pp. 103–115.

In times of layoff the basic security for most employees is their seniority. If an organization is unionized, the contract normally specifies how seniority is to be computed. Seniority guarantees the jobs (and thus the compensation) to the employees with the longest continuous employment in the organization or work unit. Even in nonunionized situations, a strong seniority norm prevails which gives some security to senior employees.

Pay Raises

The issues involved in pay increases, or raises, are the main ones bothering Poppa Joe. The first issue is the timing of raises. If the organization accepts the position that pay affects performance favorably, raises should be closely tied to performance. Employees generally prefer raises to be as frequent and as large as possible (except possibly for executives with tax problems), but there may be individual differences in timing preferences. However, administrative costs for personnel and supervisory evaluation usually limit pay raises to annual events. Annual raises can be given to everyone at the same time or tied to annual performance reviews dating from the date of hire.

One problem with the current timing of raises is that raises tend to get "buried." A raise usually is given on an annual basis, so it is divided into 12 parts and mixed up with increases in taxes and insurance deductions. The take-home paycheck often looks the same after the raise. A new attempt to deal with this problem is the lump-sum raise. This allows the employee to elect to spread the raise over as many as 12 paychecks as desired or to take it at one time—in a lump sum. If the employee elects the lump-sum raise for the entire year at the start of the year, the employer deducts the interest that would otherwise accrue to the sum and pays it out. If the employee leaves before the full year is over, the proportion of the raise not earned is deducted from the last paycheck.

The second aspect of raises is the use of the cost of living as a criterion. Most pay experts believe that an organization must adjust its pay scale to reflect the amount of inflation in the economy to some degree, so employees will not perceive a growing inequity as compared to those who receive cost-of-living adjustments. A 1981 survey showed that only a few occupational groups actually gained in buying power because of taxes and inflation.[31] Exhibit 14–4 presents a few of the gainers and losers in the race against taxes and inflation.

There are several ways to adjust for cost-of-living increases. Pay can be adjusted yearly or at regular intervals, or by automatic cost-of-living adjustment (COLA). In

Exhibit 14–4

Who's staying ahead of taxes and inflation?

Occupations	Average weekly pay before taxes	Change in pay from 1980	Change in real pay after allowing for inflation and taxes
Oil-refining workers	$524.17	+115.36	+37.74
Aluminum workers	497.21	+ 72.06	+ 7.43
Social security recipients	74.65	+ 9.34	+ 2.42
Steelworkers	500.58	+ 54.67	− 6.53
Retail trade workers	154.96	+ 11.14	− 9.22
Schoolteachers	332.00	+ 24.96	−11.21
Local-bus drivers	277.87	+ 1.66	−27.03
Farm operators	174.90	+ 31.02	−45.85

[31]"Who's Ahead, Who's Behind in Real Pay?" *U.S. News & World Report,* May 18, 1981, p. 93.

COLA plans, when the Bureau of Labor Statistics's Cost-of-Living Index increases by a rounded percentage, the wages and salaries are automatically increased by that percentage. COLA adjustments are not made each time an increase takes place, to help reduce the costs of administration. Typically the employer informs employees of the adjustment, how it was calculated, and how it affects them as wages or salaries are adjusted. The number of employees covered by COLA plans has increased from 26 percent in 1965 to about 58 percent in 1980.[32]

The third issue is what criteria should be used to allocate raises, other than cost-of-living factors. This takes us back to the issue of pay for performance or for merit or seniority. The negative impact on employees who do not receive merit raises can be a problem in merit pay systems. Many employees feel a fair pay raise system includes merit pay for current and past performance (seniority, and so).

The final issue is: How large must a raise be for it to affect satisfaction and performance? Not much research has been done in this area. Several theories have been advanced to suggest that pay increases should be related to current pay, past pay increases, current consumption, or some combination of these if they are to influence the employee's satisfaction or performance. One study found large individual differences in regard to an effective pay increase policy.[33] The researchers studied two groups of employees: those who perceived the increase as primarily a form of recognition for their performance, and those who saw it as satisfying physiological needs through money. The best predictors of a satisfactory increase for those who saw the raise in terms of recognition were *anticipated changes in the cost of living and expected pay increases*. For those who valued the money increase itself, the best predictors were *expected changes in the cost of living, the last pay increase, and current pay satisfaction*. Either these groups were influenced by different factors, or all individuals were influenced by more than one factor. The researchers recommend against flat percentage increases in view of their findings, because current pay was not a significant factor in predicting meaningful pay increases.

This research shows how preceding studies oversimplified the specification of raises. More research is needed to provide better guidelines on the size of effective pay raises, given these individual differences. Perhaps a cafeteria approach to pay and benefits, including pay raises, might help with this problem. Obviously the organization's ability to pay and other factors are important, in addition to the employees' perceptions of "what a good raise is."

Pay Compression

The Fair Labor Standards Act (FLSA) sets a legal minimum wage that must be paid employees. However, union power and labor market conditions often push for higher minimum rates of pay. These pressures often result in setting higher levels of pay at the levels. This further results in what is called *pay compression*.

Pay compression exists when jobs requiring advanced levels of education and experience, more skills, and higher degrees of responsibility receive smaller increases in compensation opportunities. Those performing jobs requiring more knowledge, greater skills, and increased responsibilities find that rewards are inadequate for these added contributions.

[32]"Inflation's COLA Cure," *Time*, July 29, 1980, p. 57.

[33]Henderson, *Compensation Management*, p. 436.

Case

Poppa Joe

In summing up what she had told Poppa Joe about compensation, Mary Renfro said, "Poppa Joe, that's it. We've discussed a lot of Personnel/Human Resource Management problems." Then she summarized the situation at Cardeson National Bank for him, as follows:

- You are making all the pay decisions. You hire people and pay them what you think they are worth, based on their experience (as you see it), their potential (as you see it), and their needs (as you see them). This has caused us a lot of inequity problems. Remember Arte Jamison. He was really underpaid and we lost him. You don't use pay surveys. You don't use job evaluation. You don't have pay classifications—nothing. It's all in your head, and it varies with your feelings at the moment. You have ignored the equal pay laws.

- You give raises similarly and throw in some factor for seniority—how, we don't know.

- Our turnover and absenteeism are high. I think

that's largely because of pay problems. Turnover and absenteeism are complex factors, like profit. But you have been hearing a lot of complaints about pay lately, haven't you? Where there's smoke. . . . I've shown you the cost figures on turnover and absenteeism. It's a real cost. And that doesn't count morale problems directly—surly tellers, and so on.

- Executive turnover is high, too. It appears low pay and few incentives are one cause.

- There is pressure to put everyone on salary—as Tom Nichols knows.

- In spite of our pay secrecy policy, word about the differential pay situation is getting out. Remember Martha.

- We don't have a raise policy. We don't have a pay strategy.

- Should we continue time pay only, or go to an incentive plan like a suggestion system or profit sharing?

While Poppa Joe is pondering these points,

To illustrate pay compression suppose that the job of a mechanic in a food-processing plant of General Mills is difficult to fill. Furthermore, pay for mechanics has increased by 12 percent partly because of the shortage of qualified candidates. There is, however, an abundant supply of mechanic supervisors, so that their pay increases this year averaged about 6.5 percent. The pay differential between the operative mechanic and the mechanic supervisor has become smaller—it has been compressed. To overcome pay compression problems, some firms state that there must be at least a 15 percent differential between the pay received by the highest level nonmanagerial personnel and that of their immediate supervisors.[34]

---

[34]John M. Ivancevich, "Management and Compensation," in *Making Organizations Humane and Productive*, eds. H. Meltzer and Walter R. Nord (New York: John Wiley & Sons, 1981), p. 82.

Guido stops by the office to help Mary make her points.

Guido Boss, Mary has some specific suggestions for you. They're all in her report that I've given you. I've discussed them with some of the other VPs and they generally agree. . . .

Poppa Joe Oh, they do, do they? I'll bet it'll all cost a lot of money. How can you build a bank like I'm trying to do and give away all the profits? I've been fair with everybody. And what do I get—complaints!

Well, Mary, show me where your specific suggestions for our personnel needs are in your report and I'll read them. I'll let you know.

Mary's report contained the following recommendations:

1. That one of the vice presidents be delegated to handle day-to-day P/HRM matters. Poppa Joe would deal only with policy decisions.
2. That a job evaluation point system be set up to determine proper pay. No person would have his or her pay lowered. But some people being paid below the suggested pay level should be raised as soon as possible. Those overpaid should be held at the same level until they are in the right category.
3. That area wage surveys be consulted in making pay decisions.
4. That a pay structure be set up.
5. That a pay strategy of paying going wages be approved.
6. That a systematic raise policy be established as soon as possible, fixing timing, amount, and criteria for raises.
7. That the pay secrecy policy be continued.
8. That current use of hourly pay and salaries be continued.
9. That the possibility of incentive pay for executives and other employees be investigated.

Question

1. Which (if any) of these suggestions do you believe Poppa Joe accepted? Explain your answer.

Some firms are also paying supervisory personnel for overtime work. Supervisory personnel typically are exempt under the FLSA from overtime pay. However, overtime pay is one way to attract more qualified employees into the managerial field and provide fair compensation. It keeps some pay differential between supervisors and nonsupervisors.

Summary

Chapter 14 has continued the discussion of compensation by adding some very important concepts: methods of payment, executive compensation, and compensation administration issues. These statements will highlight the concepts introduced:

1. Methods of payment are:

   a. Payment for time worked
      (1) Hourly wage.
      (2) Salary.
   b. Incentive plans
      (1) Individual incentives.
      (2) Group incentives.
      (3) Organization incentives.

2. Most employees are paid salaries; exceptions ars blue-collar and some clerical employees.

3. Individual incentive plans are the most effective methods to tie pay to performance; group incentive plans are the next most effective; organizationwide plans the least effective.

4. Group and organization incentive plans provide more nonpay rewards (such as social acceptance, esteem) than individual incentive plans.

5. The least effective plans for tying pay to performance are across-the-board raises and seniority increases.

Case

Poppa Joe

Mary

A week later, Mary and Guido caught Poppa Joe in his office. He'd spent much of the time since their last meeting at the branch offices—very unusual behavior for him.

Guido Boss, are you free?

Poppa Joe I'm very busy. But come in for a moment.

Guido Mary and I have been wondering if you've had a chance to decide on those pay policy issues.

Poppa Joe Yes, I have. I believe we are a small bank. We don't need a lot of paperwork and bureaucracy. So I decided to chuck the whole report in the wastebasket.

Then I thought it over and decided I ought to compromise. So I accept suggestions 5, 7, and 8. I've already appointed John Bolts to investigate who is letting out the salary information around here. Now, I'm very busy. So please excuse me.

Six months later, Mary Renfro left the bank. Executive and employee turnover had continued to increase. Guido Panelli took early retirement at age 55, about six months after Mary left. The bank still has two branches and about the same number of employees. Profitability has declined some, but the bank is still profitable.

6. Executives are the most likely to think that pay should be tied to performance.
7. The more executive compensation is tied directly to performance for executives, the greater the impact on performance.
8. Managers make policy decisions on three issues in compensation involving the extent to which:
   a. Compensation information will be open or secret.
   b. Compensation will be secure.
   c. Raises will vary with performance.

Questions for Review and Discussion

1. What is the most typical payment method: time based or output based? Why?
2. Are individual incentive pay plans effective? Which of the individual incentive pay plans are used most frequently?
3. Are group incentive pay plans effective? Why or why not?
4. Compare and contrast the positive and negative aspects of suggestion plans, company group incentive plans, profit-sharing plans, the Scanlon Plan, and the stock ownership plan.
5. Business executive compensation is excessive today. No executive is worth a $1 million-a-year salary. Comment.
6. Are executive salaries effective in increasing performance? Are perks? Bonuses? Stock options and performance shares?
7. Should compensation be kept secret? Why or why not?
8. Should compensation be made more secure? Why or why not? How?
9. When should raises be given? Should raises be given for cost-of-living changes?
10. How big should raises be to have an influence on performance?

Glossary

Bonus. A compensation payment that supplements salary and can be paid in the present or in the future.

COLA Plans. The adjustment of pay by automatic cost-of-living adjustment (COLA). In COLA plans, when the Bureau of Labor Statistic's Cost of Living Index increases by a rounded percentage, the wages and salaries are automatically increased by that percentage.

Incentive Compensation. Paying employees on the basis of output.

Pay Compression. A pay situation in which jobs requiring advanced levels of education and experience, more skills, and higher degrees of responsibility receive smaller increases in compensation opportunities.

Profit-Sharing Plan. A compensation plan in which payment of a regular share of company profits to employees is made as a supplement to their normal compensation.

Scanlon Plan. A combination group incentive, suggestion, and employee participation plan developed by Joseph Scanlon. Gains from increased productivity are paid in bonus form to all employees.

Stock Option. Provides employees with the right to purchase company stock at a fixed price for a certain period of time.

Chapter Fifteen

Employee Benefits and Services

Learning Objectives

After studying this chapter, you should be able to:

- Define what is meant by the terms *benefits, services,* and *pensions.*

- Explain why organizations provide benefits and services to employees.

- Discuss the three-legged stool notion that most elderly people use to provide security. Namely, social security, savings, and private pensions.

- Identify the value of preretirement programs to employees.

- Illustrate the costs of benefits and services to employers in different industries.

Chapter Outline

Case

Carl Reems and Pete Lakich

Carl Reems was the president of Coy Manufacturing of Whiting, Indiana. It was Carl's intention to keep his work force as satisfied and productive as possible. A number of problems concerning the Coy employee benefits and services package have come to a head over the past few months. Carl listened to a presentation that Pete Lakich, Coy's director of personnel/human resources, made to the firm's executive committee. In the presentation, Pete used some figures that seemed wrong to Carl. Pete claimed that in manufacturing firms in the Whiting area (located just southeast of Chicago), the average fringe benefit and services costs per worker totaled $6,240. In fact Pete gave a specific item-by-item breakdown of these costs to the committee.

After the meeting Carl had this talk with Pete:

Carl Pete, where did you get those fringe benefit figures? They seem wrong.

Pete Carl, these are facts based on my program of monitoring costs and benefits of fringes.

Carl We must be paying the highest fringe benefits in the entire area!

Pete As a matter of fact, we are a little on the low end of the scale. Of all the similar firms in our area we are in the bottom one third in fringe benefit costs.

Carl Do you think this is one of the reasons we are not able to recruit and hold skilled employees?

Pete I'm not certain, but there is probably some connection. You know how employees exchange and compare wage, fringe, and service information.

Carl Let's look at the entire range of our fringe benefits and services and see what is needed to become more competitive. We could probably even improve production and morale by improving benefits and services.

Pete We do need to take a look, but we can't be so certain that more and better fringes and services can make productivity and morale jump up.

Carl Pete, you're just too conservative about the power of money. The carrot and the stick can always do the job, even in Whiting, Indiana.

Pete Boss, don't jump to conclusions.

Do you agree with Carl or Pete about the motivational power of benefits and services?

Introduction

Employee benefits and services are a part of the rewards (including pay and promotion) which reinforce loyal service to the employer. Major benefits and services programs include pay for time not worked, insurance, pensions, and services.

This definition is a bit vague because the terms *benefits and services* is applied to hundreds of programs, as we shall see. Some programs that are sometimes called benefits or services (for example, stock-purchase plans) have already been discussed. This chapter will indicate that Pete's opinions about the impact of benefits and services is a valid position in most situations.

Why Do Employers Offer benefits and Services?

The programs offered in work organizations today are the product of efforts in this area for the past 40 years. Before World War II, employers offered a few pensions and services because they had the employees' welfare at heart, or they wanted to keep out the union. But most benefit programs began in earnest during the war, when wages were strictly regulated.

The unions pushed for nonwage compensation increases, and they got them. Court cases in the late 40s confirmed the right of unions to bargain for benefits: *Inland Steel* v. *National Labor Relations Board* (1948) over pensions, and *W. W. Cross* v. *National Labor Relations Board* over insurance. The growth of these programs indicates the extent to which unions have used this right. In 1929, benefits cost the employer 3 percent of total wages and salaries; by 1949, the cost was up to 16 percent; and in the 70s, it was nearly 30 percent; by the mid-1980s costs of benefits are expected to total about 50 percent.[1]

Some employers provide these programs for labor market reasons; that is, to keep the organization competitive in recruiting and retaining employees in relation to other employers. Or they may provide them to keep a union out, or because the unions have won them.

Another reason often given for providing benefits and services is because they increase employee performance. Is this reason valid? In a study of benefits, it was found that none of these reasons explained the degree to which benefits and services were provided.[2] They found that only the *size* of the organization explained this factor. Thus, under Parkinson's law, as organizations grow in size, they offer more benefits. According to these researchers, the move to provide employee benefit and services is just another manifestation of the bureaucracy.

Who Is Involved in Benefit Decisions?

How the benefit and services decision is made is discussed later in the chapter. Exhibit 15–1 shows who is involved in benefit decisions within the organization. P/HRM executives often seek professional advice from specialists such as a member of the Society of Professional Benefit Administrators. These persons are independent consultants or are employed by benefit carriers like insurance companies. In very large organizations, the compensation department may have a specialist in benefits, usually called a manager of employee benefits, such as Ernest J. E. Griffes of Levi Strauss & Co.

Benefits are still primarily a Stage I function. Many authorities argue that all organizations should have benefits and services, but there is little concrete evidence that they affect employee productivity or satisfaction.

---

[1] K. A. Randall, "Rethinking Employee Benefits Assumptions" (New York: Conference Board, 1978), p. v.

[2] Robert Ashall and John Child, "Employee Services: People, Profits, or Parkinson?" *Personnel Management*, Fall, 1972, pp. 10–22.

Exhibit 15–1 _____

The role of operating and P/HRM managers in Benefits and services

Benefits and services function	Operating manager (OM)	P/HRM manger (P/HRM)
Benefits and services budget	Preliminary budget approved or adjusted by top management	Preliminary budget developed by P/HRM
Voluntary benefits and services	Programs approved by OM (top management)	Programs recommended by P/HRM
Communication of benefits and services	OM cooperates with P/HRM	Primary duty of P/HRM
Evaluation of benefits and services		Done by P/HRM
Administration of benefit and services programs		Done by P/HRM

P/HRM Manager Close-Up _____

Ernest J. E. Griffes
Levi Strauss & Company

Biography

Ernest J. E. Griffes is director of employee benefits with Levi Strauss & Co. in San Francisco. A graduate of Grand Valley State College, Allendale, Michigan, with a B.A. in economics, Griffes has previously held positions as a bank operations manager, an office manager-personnel officer, a consultant (employee benefit plans), and a personnel and financial officer. Over the past several years, he has achieved a highly respected national reputation through his frequently published articles, his participation in seminars and workshops, and his lectures on the subjects of pension planning and legislation. He serves as chairman of the American Society for Personnel Administration (ASPA) National Committee on Retirement Income Systems. Griffes prepared ASPA's position paper to the U.S. Congress on the subject, "Providing Adequate Retirement Income for the American People," in which he outlined ASPA's position on pension legislation.

Job description

The primary responsibility of this position is dynamic, results-oriented management of employee benefit plans to maximize the cost effectiveness of benefit expenditures for both company and employee. The incumbent develops and installs new or modified plans, administers existing plans, assures compliance with all laws, determines whether "to make or buy" group insurance, and also develops and implements corporate benefit policies, alerting management to trends.

A Diagnostic Approach to Benefits and Services

Exhibit 15–2 highlights the most important factors in the diagnostic model of the P/HRM function which affect the administration of employee benefits and services. Unions have had a great impact on benefits. In the 1940s and 1950s, a major thrust of their bargaining was for increased or innovative benefits. Union pressure for additional holidays is being followed by demands for such benefits as group auto insurance, dental care, and prepaid legal fees. Union leaders have varied the strategy and tactics they use to get "more." The long-range goal is getting employers to perceive benefits not as compensation but as part of their own social responsibility.

Government requirements have affected the benefits area significantly. Three major benefits are legally required: workers' compensation, unemployment compensation, and social security. Progressive income taxes and the policy of the Internal Revenue Service to allow deductions of benefits costs as expenses have encouraged their development. In 1971 the federal government mandated four long holiday weekends. Passage of the Welfare Fund Disclosure Act requires descriptions and reports of benefits plans. The National Labor Relations Board and the courts have stringent rules on eligibility for benefits and the employer's ability to change an established benefits plan. Finally, the government's tax policy influences benefits. At present, benefits are tax free, though some agencies (in Canada, for example) appear interested in taxing benefits as income.

Economic and labor market conditions influence benefit decisions because in tight labor markets, organizations seeking the best employees compete by offering better benefits and services packages, which are nontaxable income.

The goals of managers and controlling interests affect the benefits-services package offered. Managers or owners may aim at employee satisfaction or may oppose unions. Other goals also can influence whether a benefits program is set up and how generous it is.

Competition can induce an organization to add to or adjust its benefits-services plan. Certain companies are pacesetters in benefits. These pacesetters introduce the newer benefits first. One example is the American Telephone and Telegraph Company. Other leading employers follow the practice, and then organizations who follow the leading companies set the program up. The benefits managers of the pacesetters regularly discuss benefit trends and read surveys of what the competition is offering.

The final factor affecting benefits and services is the preferences and attitudes of employees toward them. For benefits to have an effect on employee satisfaction:

> Employees must know about their benefits.
>
> Employees must prefer the organizations benefits to those offered by other organizations.
>
> Employees must perceive the organization's benefits as satisfying more of their needs than competing employers' benefits would.

Presumably, if employees are satisfied with their benefits package, they will be absent less, be reluctant to quit, produce higher quality products, and have fewer accidents. For benefits to affect employee performance:

> Employees must see them as a strongly preferred end.
>
> Employees must perceive that by performing better they can increase their benefits.

Exhibit 15–2 _____

Factors affecting benefits, services, and pensions and end results

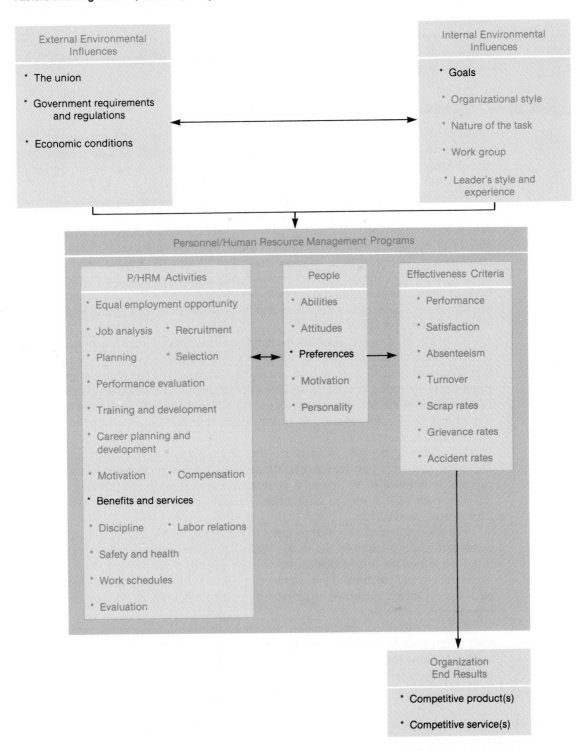

Mandated Benefit Programs

There are three benefit programs which the private- and third-sector employers have no choice but to offer to employees. An employer who wishes to change these programs or to stop offering them must get involved in the political process and change the laws. These three programs, as noted above, are unemployment insurance, social security, and workers' compensation (see Chapter 19).

Unemployment Insurance

In the 1930s, when unemployment was very high, the government was pressured to create programs to take care of people who were out of work through no fault of their own. Unemployment insurance (UI) was set up in the United States as part of the Social Security Act of 1935.

Unemployment insurance is designed to provide a subsistence payment to employees between jobs. The employer contributes to the UI fund (in Alabama, Alaska, and New Jersey, so do employees). The base payment is increased if there is more than an average number of employees from an enterprise drawing from the fund (this is called the experience rating). Unemployment insurance and allied systems for railroad, federal government, and military employees covers about 65 million employees. Major groups excluded from UI are self-employed workers, employees of small firms with less than four employees, domestics, farm employees, state and local government employees and nonprofit employers such as hospitals.

To be eligible for compensation, the employee must have worked a minimum number of weeks, be without a job, and be willing to accept a suitable position offered through a state Unemployment Compensation Commission. A Supreme Court decision granted unemployment insurance benefits to strikers after an eight-week strike period. The Court ruled that neither the Social Security Act nor the National Labor Relations Act specifically forbids making benefits payments to strikers. Each state decides on whether to permit or prohibit such payments.[3]

The employee receives compensation for a limited period. Typically the maximum is 26 weeks, although a few states extend the term beyond this in emergency situations. The payment is intended to be about 50 percent of a typical wage and varies from a few dollars to over $200 a week in some states. Unemployment compensation averages about $109 a week nationally.

The unemployment insurance program is jointly run by the federal and state governments and is administered by the states. Federal guidelines indicate that presently the tax is 3.4 percent on the first $6,000 earned by each employee. Each state has its own set of interpretations and payments. Payments by employers and to employees vary with benefits paid, the experience ratings of organizations, and the efficiency of different states in administering the program.

At present there are serious problems with UI funding, because of increased benefits, high unemployment, extended length of benefits, poor administration, and cheating by some claimants. Hard economic times seem to tempt more Americans to cheat on unemployment. Some individuals keep collecting unemployment checks after they find work.

---

[3]*New York Telephone Co. et al.* v. *New York State Department of Labor et al.*, U.S. Supreme Court, No. 77–961, March 21, 1979.

It is estimated that approximately \$3 billion a year may be wasted on unemployment insurance fraud.[4] In 1982 the government initiated a program to cut unemployment insurance fraud. They are now using computers and extensive interviews to block costly fraudulent claims.

What can the employer do about UI cost increases? Responsible employers want to pay their fair share but do not want to support abusers. They also do not want their experience ratings to increase costs. Much expert advice has been offered on how to cut costs to the program by stabilizing employment, keeping good records, challenging fraudulent claims, and issuing effective claim control procedures. Careful hiring and separation procedures, and claims verification and control can also cut costs. Effective managers try to control the costs of unemployment insurance just as much as inventory, advertising, or other costs.

Social Security

In 1935 the pension portion of the social security system as established under the Old-Age, Survivors and Disability Insurance (OASDI) program. (See Chapter 19 for disability and other provisions.) The goal of the pension portion was to provide *some* income to retired persons to *supplement* savings, private pensions, and part-time work. It was created at a time when the wealthy continued to live alone, the average person moved in with relatives, and the poor with no one to help them were put in a "poor house," or government-supported retirement home.

The basic concept was that the employee and employer were to pay taxes that would cover the retirement payments each employee would later receive in a self-funding insurance program. Initially, two goals were sought: adequate payments for all, and individual equity, which means that each employee was to receive what he or she and the employer had put into the fund. In the past 15 years, however, individual equity has lost out.

The program has a worthwhile objective. No one wants older people to live out their last years in crushing poverty and with little or no dignity. Anyone whose grandparents had to live with their children because they could not survive any other way knows how hard this can be on everyone involved.

Social security taxes are paid by *both* employers and employees. Both pay a percentage of the employee's pay to the government. The percentage, the maximum income the percentage is paid on, the maximum tax to be paid are respectively 6.70 percent, \$33,900, and \$2,271.30 in 1983, and 6.70 percent, \$36,000, and \$2,412 in 1984. The percentage will continue to rise, to 7.65 percent for employee and employer in 1990. The maximum tax will rise to \$3,046 in 1987 for an employee earning \$42,600. How much is paid by employee and employer is calculated on the average monthly wage (weighted toward the later years).

Those receiving social security pensions can work part time, up to a maximum amount which is increased each year to reflect inflation. The maximum a person aged 65 to 70 can earn before loss of social security benefits is \$6,000 in 1982 and thereafter. Just about all employees except civilian federal government employees are eligible for social security coverage. Self-employed persons can join the system. They will pay 10.75 percent in 1990, a tax of \$4,579 for a person earning \$42,600.

---

[4]Joann S. Lublin, "Government Starts Cracking down on Unemployment Insurance Fraud," *The Wall Street Journal,* February 9, 1982, p. 27.

Employees become eligible to receive full benefits at age 65, or for lower benefits at age 62. If an employee dies, a family with children under 18 receives survivor benefits, regardless of the employee's age. An employee who is totally disabled before age 65 becomes eligible to receive insurance benefits. Under Medicare provisions of the social security system, eligible individuals 65 and older receive payments for doctor and hospital bills, as well as other related benefits and services.

President Reagan in 1982 called attention to some of the problems with the social security system. Specifically he pointed out that the trust fund set up to pay the pensions was being rapidly depleted. This was happening for a number of reasons, including:

- Unrealistic inflation rate assumptions by the system's actuaries.
- Inaccurate assumptions of the birthrate.
- Unrealistic assumptions of the productivity increases by employees.
- Addition by Congress of beneficiaries who did not pay into the system fully.
- Withdrawal of many government employees from the system.

Another area of concern for the social security system is that many people continue to believe that social security is not just a supplement but should provide full support in retirement, at almost the same standard of living they had when they were working. Unfortunately, some voters reward congressmen and senators who vote their way on a single issue. Social security is such a value charged issue that voters listen very carefully about how a politician regards this benefit. The goal of providing full retirement support through social security benefits simply cannot be reached without a dramatic increase in taxes.

Probably the best way to save social security is to create a significant *communication* program to tell people the facts about retirement and social security. Everyone must understand these facts and comprehend their applicability to their own situations.

Benefit and Retirement Plans

In addition to the benefits required by the law, many employers also provide other kinds of benefits: compensation for time not worked, insurance protection, and retirement plans. There are many differences in employers' practices regarding these benefits.

FACTS ABOUT SOCIAL SECURITY

Social security is a *supplement.* You cannot live on it alone. And if population trends for the foreseeable future prevail, the country will be unwilling to tax wage earners enough so that social security could cover all expenses.

You must expect to save during your lifetime to supplement social security payments in retirement.

If possible, you should try to get a job with a private pension to supplement social security.

You probably will have to lower your standard of living when you retire in order to pay your expenses, even if you have savings, social security, and a private pension. You may have to work part time in retirement or even live with relatives to make ends meet.

Compensation for Time off

Can you imagine a life in which you went to work six days a week, 12 hours a day, 52 weeks a year for life? That's what life used to be like, although it has been shown that employees did not always work hard all that time. The concepts of a paid holiday or vacation with pay did not exist. Now most employers compensate for some time that they have not worked: break time, get-ready time, washup time, clothes change time, paid lunch and rest periods, coffee breaks, and so on. Employers also pay employees when they are not actually at work—holidays, vacations, sick leave, funeral leave, jury duty, and other personal leaves, such as to fulfill military obligations.

Studies of employees' preference indicate that work breaks are not strongly preferred; they are just expected.[5] Vacations are generally a highly preferred benefit. Preferences for holidays vary, and lower paid and women employees have stronger preferences for sick leave. Unions have negotiated hard for added time off to give their members more leisure and to create jobs.

Paid Holidays • Probably the most frequently offered of these time-off-with-pay items is paid holidays. At one time, every employee was paid only for actual holidays off with pay. The typical number of paid holidays has been increasing. Currently, nine or more paid holidays are provided to full-time employees. The most typical holidays are: New Year's Day, Good Friday, Memorial Day, July 4, Labor Day, Thanksgiving Day, Christmas, President's Day, Friday after Thanksgiving, December 24, and January 2. The new minivacation dates created by Congress through the federal Monday-holiday law allow for three-day weekends in February for President's Day, in May for Memorial Day, in October for Columbus Day, and in November for Veteran's Day.

Paid Vacations • Another example of voluntary compensation offered for time not worked is paid vacations. This is the most expensive benefit for American employers. Most organizations offer vacations with pay after a certain minimum period of service. The theory behind vacations is that they provide an opportunity for employees to rest and refresh themselves; when they return, hopefully, they will be more effective employees. Employees have pressed for more leisure to enjoy the fruit of their labors.

Government and military employers traditionally have given 30 days' vacation. The typical vacation is one week of paid vacation for an employee of less than a year's service, and two weeks for 1–10 years' service. Three-week vacations are offered annually to veterans of 10–20 years, and four weeks to the over 20-year tenured. Over one fourth of the companies studied by the Conference Board now offer five- and six-week vacations usually for 25-year employees.[6] The trend in paid vactions for unionized employees is upward. As you can see from the cartoon on page 470, vacations need to be well planned to allow the firm to continue to operate effectively.

Personal Time Off • Many employers pay employees for time off for funerals, medical/dental appointments, sickness in the family, religious observances, marriage, personal-choice holidays, and birthdays as holidays. If an organization uses flexitime scheduling

---

[5]Jerry Geisler and William Glueck, ''Employee Benefit Preferences and Employee Satisfaction,'' University of Georgia Paper, 1977.

[6]Mitchell Meyer and Harland Fox, ''Profile of Employee Benefits,'' *Basic Patterns Union Contracts* (Washington, D.C.; 1975).

"Let me see that vacation schedule again, Hawkins."

Jack Markou, from True Magazine.

(see Chapter 20), the need for time off is minimized. A BNA survey found that 9 out of 10 firms provide paid jury duty; 9 out of 10 provide paid leave for funerals of close relatives; and 7 out of 10 provide paid leave for military duty time. Typically, the pay is the difference between normal pay and military pay. A variety of policies apply to leaves for personal reasons, such as sickness in the family or marriage. A typical policy is to allow no more than five days per year personal time.[7]

[7]Bureau of National Affairs, *Paid Leave and Leave of Absence Policies,* Personnel Policies Forum, Survey 111 (Washington, D.C., November 1975).

Sick Leave

Illness has a significant effect on the productivity of an organization. In most situations, organizations allow and pay for one sick day per month or 12 per year. The movement in society toward improved health has certainly found its way into organizations. There is now a trend toward emphasizing wellness instead of sick pay among employees.

At Scherer Brothers, a lumber company in Minnesota, a wellness program has been implemented.[8] The firm has removed candy machines, cigarette machines, caffeinated coffee, and high-fat foods from the noontime meals served free to employees. In addition, recreation facilities are available for use by employees and their families, including a gym, exercise equipment, and a sauna. Coupled with this was well pay—two hours extra pay for employees who had been neither tardy nor absent during the previous month. The result is that absenteeism is now 0.3 percent compared to an industry rate of between 3 and 4 percent.

Other firms are using what are called sick-leave banks to cut down on sick leave. Employees deposit a set portion of their earned sick-leave days into a company pool. Should an employee use all of his or her compensated sick leave, an application for withdrawal from the sick-leave bank may be made. However, these requests are carefully screened by a committee.

The sick-leave bank has psychological benefits. Members become conservative in using banked days, using only what they need so that co-workers will have what they need in case of long-term illnesses or accidents.

Employer-Purchased Insurance

The many risks encountered throughout life—illness, accident, and early death, among others—can be offset by buying insurance. Many employers can buy insurance cheaper than their employees can, and insurance is frequently offered as a benefit. The employer may provide it free to the employee or pay part of it, and the employee "participates" by paying a share. Four major forms of insurance are involved: health, life, disability-accident, and maternity leave.

Health Insurance • One of the most costly kinds of insurance, health or medical insurance, is financed at least partially by employers as a benefit for employees. What studies have been done indicate that employees prefer it over most other benefits. Health insurance includes hospitalization (room and board and hospital service charges), surgical fees (actual surgical fees or maximum limits), and major medical fees (maximum benefits, typically $5,000–$10,000 beyond hospitalization and surgical payments). In the 1980s increased coverage has been provided in major medical and comprehensive health insurance plans. Surveys report that almost all organizations have hospitalization plans, almost all nonblue-collar workers are provided with surgical and major medical plans, and about three fourths of blue-collar employees have major medical insurance. The rising costs of hospital care, as shown in Exhibit 15–3, point out how important health insurance is to employees.

Typically, all employees get basic coverage. Beyond this, plans differ. Plans for

---

[8]Miriam Rothman, "Can Alternatives to Sick Pay Plays Reduce Absenteeism?" *Personnel Journal,* October 1981, pp. 788–90.

Exhibit 15–3 _____

Cost of hospital care

	1976	1981	1986 estimate
Semiprivate room rate (per day)	$ 55.00	$ 116.50	$ 233.00
Laboratory test (P).	2.78	5.89	11.20
X ray (P)	5.05	10.95	21.90
Nursing (P)	46.10	95.30	190.60
Bandages, supplies (P).	7.90	15.82	31.60
Medicines (P).	10.21	21.45	42.90
Food (P)	5.05	9.48	19.00
Ambulance	16.20	42.00	96.50
Emergency room.	15.50	39.52	83.00
Operating room	110.20	301.05	648.00
Recovery room.	22.90	50.67	114.00
Anesthesiologist.	40.16	91.66	206.00
Appendectomy.	250.00	580.00	1,335.00
Tonsils and adenoids	107.00	250.00	575.00
Hemorrhoidectomy	193.00	450.00	1,035.00
Heart bypass	2,500.00	8,000.00	21,000.00
Pacemaker.	1,200.00	2,500.00	4,000.00
Vasectomy	90.00	210.00	483.00
Cesarean birth	340.00	790.00	1,820.00
Hysterectomy	430.00	1,000.00	2,300.00

Source: Chicago Tribune Graphic. Reprinted by permission of Tribune Company Syndicate, Inc.

salaried employees typically are of the major medical variety and provide "last-dollar coverage." This means that the employee must pay the first $50 of the cost or a similar deductible. The benefits may be based on either a specified cash allowance for various procedures or a service benefit which pays the full amount of all reasonable charges.

Negotiated plans for time-pay workers generally have expanded coverage which provides specific benefits rather than comprehensive major medical coverage. This approach is preferred by union leaders because they feel individual benefits which can be clearly labeled will impress members. And these benefits can be obtained with no deductible payments by employees. Also, until recently, coverage of some desired services was not available under major medical plans. Some of the more rapidly expanding benefits of the negotiated plans are prescription drugs, vision care, mental health services, and dental care. For example, typical dental care ranges from $1,000 to $2,000 yearly. About one employer in eight provides this insurance now.[9]

Life Insurance • Group life insurance is one of the oldest and most widely available employee benefits. The employer purchases life insurance for each employee, to benefit the employee's family. Group life insurance plans provide coverage to all employees without physical examinations, with premiums based on the characteristics of the group as a whole.

Employee preference for group life insurance is not high. Surveys indicate that almost all employers offer group life insurance. In a typical program for a large company, the

_____

[9]Thomas Patton and Phillip Dutton, "Employee Dental Insurance Plans for Today and Tomorrow," _MSU Business Topics._ Autumn 1976, pp. 13–25.

amount of insurance provided by the plan increases as salary increases, the typical amount being twice the salary in life insurance. But about a third of the companies surveyed have different plans for blue-collar employees, who usually get a flat amount (usually $5,000). Initially the organization pays part of the premium, the employee the rest (contributory plan). The trend is moving toward noncontributory plans in which the company pays it all. But 34 percent of blue-collar, 38 percent of white-collar, and 40 percent of managerial plans are still contributory. In view of employee preferences, it probably should stay that way. Continued life insurance coverage after retirement, usually one third the coverage while working, is provided by 72 percent of large American companies.[10]

Long-Term Sickness and Accident Disability Insurance • What happens to employees who have accidents at work which leave them unable to work, temporarily or permanently? Workers' compensation pays a very small part of these costs, since it was designed primarily to take care of short-term disability problems (see Chapter 19). Employer-funded, long-term disability insurance is designed to cover these cases, with payments supplementing benefits from workers' compensation, social security, and other agencies.

Some disability payments are very large. Recently a roofer who fell off a roof received over $5 million. About 75 percent of larger firms have this kind of insurance. Usually blue-collar workers are covered by flat-amount coverage (usually $5,000– $10,000). For other employees coverage is tied to salary level. Usually there is noncontributory coverage for all employees. The goal is to provide employees with at least half pay until pension time, but the primary recipients have been nonblue-collar employees.

The majority of long-term sickness and accident disability insurance plans provide benefits for up to 26 weeks. But about 20 percent provide these benefits for a year. About 75 percent of organizations provide such sickness and accident coverage.[11]

Maternity Leave Benefits

The Pregnancy Discrimination Act is technically an amendment to Title VII of the Civil Rights Act. The Pregnancy Discrimination Act became law in 1978. It requires that pregnancy be treated just like any other temporary disability. Before the act, temporary disability benefits for pregnancies were paid in the form of either sick leave or disability insurance, if at all. It was common organizational practice to limit pregnancy benefits to about six weeks.

The current practice in organizations is very different. One survey reported that about 96 percent of over 300 firms permits the pregnant employee who is able to do the job to work as long as she wants.[12] This ability to work must of course be certified by her physician. Maternity leave is typically granted for up to six months. Extensions are granted if a physician certifies the employee's continued disability. Thus, a woman can go on leave in the seventh month of her pregnancy and return to work four months after her child is born and receive disability payments for the entire period.

An interesting program was initiated in 1979 by American Telephone and Telegraph

---

[10]Bureau of National Affairs, *Employee Health and Welfare Benefits,* Personnel Policies Forum, Survey 105 (Washington, D.C.; 1974).

[11]Ibid.

[12]M. Meyer, *Women and Employee Benefits* (New York: Conference Board, 1978).

Co. (AT&T). AT&T established a program under which new fathers can take up to six months of unpaid leave to help care for a newborn and still return to their jobs. Workers of either sex adopting infants are also eligible for the unpaid six-month leave. Pregnant employees at AT&T can take paid leave as long as they have been certified by a physician as unable to work. As long as the employee is certified as disabled, she can receive 52 weeks of half-pay maternity benefits (with six months of service) or 52 weeks of full pay (with 25 years of service). Certainly the program is innovative, but one must ask about the 52 weeks of full-pay provision. How many women with 25 or more years of service are having babies? Probably not very many even in a firm as large as AT&T.

Income in Retirement

Retired employees can receive income from a number of sources: (1) savings and investments, (2) individual retirement accounts, (3) government pensions, and (4) employer pension plans. The first two are discussed in this section and the government and employer pension plan are discussed in separate sections.

Retirement Income from Savings and Work

One source of income for retirees is postretirement work and savings. One study of 5,000 families found that 52 percent of persons expected to earn money by part-time employment after retirement.[13] The percentage who planned to work expected to earn about 20 percent of their current salaries in this way.

Another source of income is from savings. Studies find that persons save more (percentagewise and absolutely) the higher their income, and those with private pensions are more likely to save money for retirement than those without them.[14]

Until the mid-1970s, little change in savings took place after social security started. As people were forced to pay social security taxes, their private savings for retirement tended to decline. But social security does not allow much work after retirement, and thanks to medical science, people are living longer. So they have seen the need to save more during their working years and have begun to do so. More persons will have to work to supplement social security payments in view of inflation, but if social security benefits increase substantially, people will save less during their work years.

The government has encouraged people with and without private pensions to save for retirement. In 1981, the Economic Recovery Tax Act became a law. This law made important changes that affect individual retirement accounts (IRAs), Keogh plans, and other compensation plans.

IRAs and Voluntary Contributions

Under the 1981 law, all employees can make annual tax-excludable contributions to an individual retirement account (IRA) or voluntary contributions to pension, profit sharing, or compensation, whichever is smaller.

---

[13]George Katona, "Private Pensions and Individual Savings," Monograph 40 (Ann Arbor: Survey Research Center, University of Michigan, 1965).

[14]Alicia Munnell, *The Effect of Social Security on Personal Savings* (Cambridge, Mass.: Ballinger Publishing Co., 1974).

An employee can have both a qualified voluntary employee contribution (QVEC) plan and an IRA[15] A qualified voluntary employee contribution means that the employee pays, but the employer doesn't. The money is deposited with a qualified pension, profit-sharing or similar plan. An employee who contributes say $1,000 to a QVEC can deposit only $1,000 in an IRA.

The employer has a number of alternatives under the 1981 law. The employer can add a QVEC provision to one or more of its existing plans or adopt a new plan offering employees a QVEC opportunity. Also the employer can ignore QVECs altogether. Employees under the law will then probably turn to the many IRAs offered by banks, insurance companies, and other financial institutions if they wish to accumulate tax deductible contributions.[16] Or perhaps the employer may decide to sponsor an IRA by arranging for withholding of employee pay and the transmittal of contributions to the employee-designated IRA agency. What management chooses, and how it affects its choice, is likely to have long-term implications for a company's benefit program and for its P/HRM policies overall.[17]

Private Pensions

As we shall see shortly, the Employee Retirement Income Security Act of 1974 (ERISA) requires that all persons participating in pensions must be notified about them in writing and in language *they can understand.* The U.S. Department of Labor set out a six-page notification form in "laymen's language" which employers could use to notify retirees about their pensions. One firm sent this report, littered with pension terms such as *vested benefits* and *fiduciary,* to its retirees. "The reaction of retired employees who received the letters was near hysteria," according to Mr. Donnelly, personnel director at Vulcan, and the company's pension-plan administrator. "Nearly half of them called the company, desperate to learn whether the gobbledygook meant their pensions were going to be raised or cut".[18] Let's examine some of the so-called pension terms.

Nonfunded
Portability
Vesting
Uninsured
Pension payments
Funded
Noncontributory
Insured
Benefit formula
Fiduciary
Contributory

Vesting • This is the right to participate in a pension plan. Pension plans state how long a person must be employed before he or she has a right to a pension or a portion of it should he quit. When the employee has completed the minimum time after which he has a right to a pension, he is said to be vested in the pension.

Portability • This is the right to transfer pension credits accrued from one employer to another. It becomes possible when several employers pool their pensions through reciprocal agreements.

Contributory or Noncontributory • Some pension plans require employees to pay some of the costs of the pensions during employment (contributory). Other employers pay all the pension costs (noncontributory).

---

[15]Philip M. Alden, Jr., "New Tax Law's Voluntary Employee Contributions Forcing Management to Make Hard, Long-Term Choices," *Management Review,* December 1981, pp. 21–23.

[16]G. Christian Heil, "Fierce Competition for IRA Cash Breaks out in the Financial Industry," *The Wall Street Journal,* January 18, 1982, p. 23.

[17]Frederick W. Rumack and David H. Gravitz, "New Opportunities in Compensation and Benefits under the 1981 Tax Act," *Management Review,* November 1981, pp. 8–12.

[18]David Ignatius, "Paper Weight," *The Wall Street Journal,* July 16, 1976, p. 12.

Funded or Nonfunded • Some pension plans finance future payments by setting money aside in special funds. These are called funded pension plans. Nonfunded or pay-as-you-go plans make pension payments out of current funds.

Insured or Uninsured • Funded plans can be administered by insurance companies. Under the insured method, the payments made for each employee buy him an annuity for the retirement years. An uninsured or trustee plan is usually administered by a bank or trust company. In these cases, the administrators invest the pension funds in securities, real estate, and so on, from which pension payments are generated.

Pension Payments • Pensions can be paid in one of two ways: a flat or defined dollar payment, or an annuity. The defined benefit approach uses a benefit formula, as described below. In an annuity, the payments vary according to the value of the investment trust used to pay the pensions. If the value increases, the payment increases, and *the reverse* is also true. In the stock market decline of the early 1980s, some pensioners learned that valuable annuities vary downward as well as upward.

Fiduciary • Fiduciaries are persons responsible for pension trust funds, such as pension trustees, officers, or directors of the company, controlling shareholders, and attorneys.

Benefit Formula • A benefit formula is used to calculate the size of a pension payment. It expresses the relationship between wages and salaries earned while employed and the pension paid.

The first step in determining the formula is to indicate which earning figure should be used as a base in this computation. Some experts have noted a trend toward using the average of the final several years of employment as the base earnings figure. An earlier approach was to average career earnings, but this is not fair in an inflationary period.

Once average earnings are determined, by whichever formula approach is used, the actual pension benefit is determined by multiplying the average earnings times the number of years of service times the stipulated percentage, generally between 1 and 3 percent. Some firms offset this figure to some degree by social security benefits. This approach is generally designed to yield a monthly benefit, including social security; that is approximately 50 percent of the individual's projected salary during the final year of employment.

Criticisms of Private Pensions

Most elderly Americans believe that security in the later years rests on a three-legged stool consisting of social security, savings, and private pensions. An average retired couple has an income of about $14,700 per year, of which 33 percent comes from social security, 13 percent from private pensions, and 17.5 percent from savings, stocks, or other assets. At this time, that stool is very shaky. President Reagan on a number of occasions in 1981 considered cutbacks in social security retirement benefits. Personal savings are no longer considered a secure nest egg. Inflation has wiped out much of the purchasing power of money in the bank.[19]

---

[19] "Facing the Pension Dilemma," *Time*, October 19, 1981, pp. 76–77.

Since two of the stool legs are shaky, people are looking more closely at their private pensions programs. There are now about 500,000 private employer pensions plans that cover more than 75 percent of American's nonfarm workers over age 25. Exhibit 15–4 shows the percentage of people receiving income from specific sources and what each source contributes to a family's income.

There is loud criticism of the private pension system. The criticisms center on mismanagement, misrepresentation of funds, and failure to keep up with inflation. For example, some people who thought they were covered were not because of complicated rules, insufficient funding, irresponsible financial management, and employer bankruptcies. Some pension funds, including both employer-managed and union-managed funds,

Exhibit 15–4

Sources of income: Retirement

Families with head 65 years and older		Percent receiving income from specific sources	Source as percent of total income
$14,726 Mean income	Social Security	92.6	33.2
	Savings and other assets	75.5	17.5
	Wages	45.2	33.4
	Pensions (private and government-employer)	44.6	13.3
	Supplemental Security (aid to the aged, blind, and disabled)	7.6	0.9
	Public assistance (aid to families with dependent children)	2.4	0.3
	Other payments (unemployment and veterans' benefits)	10.4	1.5

Source: Committee for Economic Development (1979 figures).

were accused of mismanagement, and others required what the critics considered unusually long vesting periods. Over the years, therefore, pension regulation laws were regularly debated. ERISA was passed in 1974 to respond to some of the criticisms.

Status of Private Pensions

Like many other benefits, private pensions are relatively new; the private pension plans in existence prior to 1950 covered less than one sixth of the nonagricultural work force. In the 1950s many new plans were introduced and coverage doubled, so that by 1960 about 15 million workers were covered. Coverage during the 60s remained rather stable, and the percentage participating had also stabilized. Studies have found that the kinds of employees covered vary greatly. Certain industries (mining; manufacturing, especially nondurable goods; construction; transportation; communication; and public utilities) tend to provide pensions more than others (retailing and services). Larger firms are more likely than smaller firms to have pensions. The higher the employee's income, the more probable it is that a pension exists. Unionized employees are more apt to be covered than nonunion employees. And everyone working for employers with pension plans is not covered by them; the Treasury Department estimates that 35 to 45 percent of employees of companies with pension plans are not covered. Part-time employees, for example, are rarely included in pension plans.

Inflation Protection

More and more companies are beginning to design pension plan options that provide at least some inflation protection. H. J. Heinz Co. has introduced an indexing option. A worker may choose to take a lower initial retirement benefit and then pension checks will be increased each year by a fixed percentage based on the increase in the consumer price index. The pension benefit is tied (indexed) to the consumer price index.

Other organizations have voluntarily increased the pensions of their retirees because of inflation. For example, in 1980 Exxon boosted the annual benefits for 21,000 former employees. Similar steps were taken by RCA, the Continental Group, and New York's Chemical Bank.[20]

Government Regulation of Private Pensions

The law regulating private pensions is the Employee Retirement Income Security Act (ERISA) of 1974. As noted above, ERISA was designed to cover practically all employee benefit plans of private employers, including multiemployer plans. Basically, the legislation was developed to ensure that employees covered under pension plans would receive the benefits promised.

Existing regulations were tightened in ERISA, but the major impact of the law is in the minimum standards established, which all plans are required to meet. ERISA *does not*

---

[20]Ibid., p. 77.

require an employer to have a private pension plan. Indeed, many existing private pension plans were terminated rather than meet ERISA's requirements. The major provisions of the law are as follows.

Eligibility Requirements

Organizations were prohibited from establishing requirements of more than one year of service, or an age greater than 25, whichever is later. An employee hired before the age of 22 who continues unbroken service must at age 25 be given at least three years' service credit for vesting purposes. An exception is allowed employers who provide immediate 100 percent vesting in that they may require a three-year eligibility period.

Vesting Practices

The employer may choose from three vesting alternatives: (1) the 10-year service rule, whereby the employee receives 100 percent vesting after 10 years of service; (2) the graded 15-year service rule, whereby the employee receives 25 percent vesting after 5 years of service, graded up to 100 percent after 15 years; and (3) the rule of 45, which provides 50 percent vesting when age and service equal 45 (if the employee has at least five years of service), graded up to 100 percent vesting five years later.

The new vesting standards appear to provide a major advantage to employees. Previously, those who changed employment after 10 or 15 years of service did not receive benefits; now they will. Although small, the benefits received will increase the total income at retirement.

Portability Practices

From the employee's point of view, it is desirable for pensions to be transferable or portable. Employers, however, find portability an expensive provision. Under ERISA, portability becomes a voluntary option of the employee and his or her employer. If the employer agrees, a vested employee leaving a company is permitted to transfer (tax free) the assets attributable to his or her vested pension benefits or vested profit-sharing or savings plan funds to an individual retirement account (IRA). The benefit to employees is in the opportunity to defer the payment of taxes on the funds.

Fiduciary Responsibility

Because of the need to provide more effective safeguards for pension funds, the law has imposed new standards for fiduciaries and parties-in-interest such as trustees, officers or directors of the company, controlling shareholders, or attorneys. The "prudent man" rule is established as the standard for handling and investing pension plan funds.

A fiduciary is prohibited from engaging in certain activities. He may not: (1) deal with the fund for his own account; (2) receive personal consideration from any party dealing with the fund in connection with a transaction involving the fund; (3) make loans between the fund and a party-in-interest; and (4) invest more than 10 percent of the assets of the pension plan in securities of the employer. These prohibitions have caused a great deal of concern, and it is expected that Congress will amend the standards.

Other Provisions

ERISA provides for plan termination insurance to ensure vested pension benefits (similar to FDIC provisions at banks). The Pension Benefit Guaranty Corporation was set up to pay pensions to employees of firms whose pension plans become bankrupt.

Reporting and disclosure provisions of the law require the employer to provide employees with a comprehensive booklet describing major plan provisions, and to report detailed information concerning the operation and financing of the plan annually to the secretary of labor. The act also imposes limits on contributions and benefits and changes the tax rules related to lump-sum distributions to employees.

What about those who have no employer-sponsored pension plan or who are self-employed? Persons having an employer but without a pension plan can set aside 15 percent of their compensation or $1,500, whichever is less, and pay no taxes on this income until they are 70.5 years old. IRAs (individual retirement accounts) are managed by banks and other financial institutions. ERISA limits the investment of these funds to specific choices: savings accounts, certificates of deposit, retirement annuities, endowment or retirement income policies, mutual funds, trust accounts, individual retirement bonds, and others. The money cannot be withdrawn before age 59.5 without tax penalty. Firms without pension plans can set up IRAs for their employees. Self-employed persons can set up IRAs or Keogh plans. Legislation allows a self-employed person to set aside up to 15 percent (or $7,500) in tax-deferred trusts. There is more flexibility for investment of Keogh funds than IRA funds, and the withdrawal provisions are the same.

Public Pensions

Employees in the public sector also receive pensions. The Tax Foundation estimates the pensions are now almost universally available at the state and local levels. Federal employees are covered by civilian or military pensions plans, and about two thirds of state and local government employees are also covered by social security. Typically, public pensions are contributory. The bulk of the costs is paid by the government and investment income. The employee usually contributes about 7 percent of wages or salary.

One study comparing private with public pensions found that the benefit levels of the latter are approximately *twice* the level of those in private industry.[21] Even adjusting for the portion paid for by the employees themselves, public pensions are still one third larger than industry's. The plans are not coordinated with social security. Since public pension and social security payments have been rising dramatically, a number of public servants now retire at greater net income than they had when working. Needless to say, this is a strong inducement to retire and has helped lead to a crisis in public pensions. The crisis is this: As public pensions rose (often because politicians gave public employees greater pensions than wage increases and left the bill for their successors to pay), funding did not. All the studies show a consistent pattern: a rising spread between funds and payouts. Exhibit 15–5 illustrates how, as benefits rose, contributions did not.

There are only two ways to take care of this: raise taxes *dramatically,* or lower pension checks. A third answer, to place the public plans under ERISA, is not helpful. A

---

[21]Robert Tilove, *Public Employee Pension Funds,* Twentieth-Century Fund Report (New York: Columbia University Press, 1976).

Exhibit 15–5

Public pensions and funding

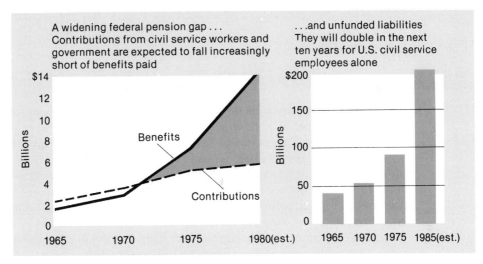

A widening federal pension gap ...
Contributions from civil service workers and
government are expected to fall increasingly
short of benefits paid

...and unfunded liabilities
They will double in the next
ten years for U.S. civil service
employees alone

Source: John Perham, "The Mess in Public Pensions." Reprinted with the special permission of *Dun's Review*, March 1976. Copyright, 1976, Dun & Bradstreet Publications Corporation.

better solution is to reform the public pensions so that benefit payouts are coordinated with social security and total no more than private industry's payout of about 55 percent of final salary. The length of service required to receive full pensions should be more like that in private industry, too. Taxes must rise or benefits must fall, or the total government budget could be going to pensions.

Preretirement and Retirement

Retirement has mixed meaning for people: some look forward to it, others dread it. Various policies affect the way people will live in retirement. These include compulsory *or* OR flexible retirement policies, early retirement policies, and employer preretirement programs.

Compulsory *or* Flexible Retirement

A major issue regarding retirement has been whether it should be compulsory or flexible. There are advantages to both of these policies. Flexible retirement policies take account of individual differences but can cause difficulty in administration, especially in regard to favoritism. Compulsory retirement assures a predictable turnover of older employees, opening up positions for younger ones, and equality of treatment for all employees. When new job openings come up, EEO requirements can be fulfilled more easily. However, those closest to retirement age favor flexible retirement policies, not compulsory ones.

Nevertheless, legislation that became effective January 1, 1979, stipulated that the private and third sectors cannot have mandatory retirement policies that specify less than 70 years of age. The only exception is that firms may retire top executives and policy-makers who at age 65 have employer-financed pension or retirement benefits of at least $27,000 per year (exclusive of social security). Prior to this new legislation, federal employees could be forced to retire at age 70. There now is no maximum age limit for federal employment.

Early Retirement

The opposite of the movement to keep older employees working is early retirement. Some employees prefer not to work up until normal retirement age. In recent years, more than 90 percent of pension plans studied have made provision for early retirement.

Typically, the minimum age for early retirement is 55; others call for a minimum age of 60. Most early retirement plans require a minimum number of years of work (typically 10 or 15 years) before the employee is eligible for early retirement. As far as benefits are concerned, all plans will pay the actuarial equivalent of the normal retirement benefits, but 30 percent of the plans pay more than that. One study found that in a typical year an average of 10 percent of those eligible retire early, but this is related to the benefits paid. Only 5 percent of those with nonliberalized payments retire early, whereas 30 percent of those eligible for early retirement with liberalized benefits do so.[22] The U.S. Census Bureau found that more men than women retire early.

Several studies have examined which employees take early retirement. They have found that black men have a lower propensity to retire early than white men.[23] One study also found that the employee is more likely to retire early the higher the pension benefits, the smaller the number of dependents, the higher the assets, and the poorer the health. Blue-collar workers are more likely to retire early than white-collar workers. Executives are especially averse to early retirement. Government workers retire early more frequently than private-sector employees. But in general, people are reluctant to retire early in times of inflation.

© 1978 by NEA., Inc. Reprinted by permission of NEA.

---

[22]Meyer and Fox, ''Profile of Employee Benefits.''
[23]''Hanging in There after 65,'' *Business Week*, January 17, 1977, p. 20–21.

Employers' Preretirement Programs

Today there are about 25 million retirees and 50 million people are over 50 years old. What have American employers done to smooth the way for these potential retirees? Until recently, very little.

In more recent years, many organizations have begun providing preretirement counseling. A recommended, comprehensive, preretirement program includes these topics:

> *First meeting: Developing a healthy attitude for a happy retirement.* This session emphasizes the positive steps society has taken to ease the financial burdens on senior citizens by reducing the costs of recreation, housing, and taxes. The potential retirees are encouraged to keep mentally and physically active, and programs designed to help, such as adult education, are discussed.

> *Second meeting: Leisure time converted to happiness.* Potential retirees are acquainted with the variety of leisure time activities, and they are encouraged to choose specific goals and to take steps to develop plans that will bring them to fruition.

> *Third meeting: Is working in retirement for me?* Retirees are given lectures on service projects and part-time job experiences that may provide variety in the retirement period.

> *Fourth meeting: Money matters.* This session discusses the sources of funds available to retirees: social security, pensions, and supplementary jobs. Personal budgeting is developed for each retiree to help him or her adjust to the new income level more smoothly.

> *Fifth meeting: Relocation in retirement.* The advantages and disadvantages of living in retirement communities, staying in present quarters (if possible), or moving in with children are discussed.

> *Sixth meeting: Other subjects.* Rights under Medicare are discussed. Retirement publications such as *Harvest Years* and *Modern Maturity* are analyzed. The preparation of wills is encouraged. Social and marital adjustment problems during retirement are covered.

At present, the great majority of firms do the counseling when employees are 64 or 65 years old. About a third counsel employees between the ages of 60 to 65. Very few do so prior to age 60. Preretirement counseling is an inexpensive benefit which can help the employee a great deal.

Employee Services

"Employee services" is something of a catchall category of voluntary benefits. It includes all other benefits or services provided by employers. These are such varied programs as cafeterias; saunas and gyms; free parking lots; commuter vans; infirmaries; ability to purchase company products at a discount; and death, personal, and financial counseling. Several of the more frequently provided services will be discussed here.

Education Programs • Many organizations provide for off-the-job general educational support for their employees. This varies from teaching basic skills such as reading to illiterate workers, to tuition-refund programs for managers, to scholarship and loan plans for employees' children.

Where employers provide for tuition refunds for courses, they usually place some restrictions on them. The courses must be relevant to the work being done, and a minimum grade level must be achieved. One study of some 620 U.S. and Canadian firms found some form of educational assistance at 96 percent of the companies.[24] A large majority required the course of study to be either directly or indirectly related to the employee's present job in order to qualify for reimbursement. Approximately half of the companies paid 100 percent of the tuition costs. A few firms based the degree of remuneration on the grade attained in the course. More than 75 percent of the firms made refunds only upon completion of the course.

Financial Services • Some organizations give their employees help and encouragement to save funds through employee savings plans, credit unions, and thrift plans. Essentially, savings plans encourage employee thrift by matching all or part of an employee's contribution, up to, say 5 percent of the wage or salary. Credit unions help employees avoid loan sharks and wage garnishments.

In the thrift plans, most funds are often invested for distribution at retirement. When companies have thrift plans, about 85 percent of employees participate. As with many other services, it is difficult to tie performance or even employee satisfaction to such plans. However, they may contribute to the perception of the organization as a good place to work and thus attract better employees.[25]

Social and Recreational Programs • Today more than 50,000 organizations provide recreation facilities for employees, on or off the job. Some experts foresee a growing trend to release employees from work time to participate in company-sponsored sports activities, which are intended to keep employees physically fit and tie them to employers. In one survey, three fourths of companies responding said they sponsored recreation programs, and half of them sponsored athletic teams.[26] The median expenditure is $6 per employee per year.

There are no available studies of the value, if any, of such benefits to the employer. These plans could be extensions of the paternalistic antiunion activities of some employers in the 1920s and later. Studies of the preferences of employees indicate that recreational services are *the least preferred* of all benefits and services offered by organizations.

Cost/Benefit Analysis of Benefits

Conrad Fiorello tells the story about a gunman who suddenly appeared at the paymaster's window at a large plant and demanded: ''Never mind the payroll, Bud. Just hand over the welfare and pensions funds, the group insurance premiums, and the withholding taxes.'' As indicated earlier, costs of benefits are going up twice as fast as pay.

---

[24]Meyer and Fox, ''Profile of Employee Benefits.''

[25]''Hanging in There,'' p. 21.

[26]Meyer and Fox, ''Profile of Employee Benefits.'' Also see Karen Debats, ''Industrial Recreation Programs: A New Look at an Old Benefit,'' *Personnel Journal*, August 1981, pp. 620–27.

When benefit costs increase the price of products and services, they are less competitive with other products, especially those from countries where the government pays for benefits. Higher benefits can reduce permanent employment, also, since it is cheaper to pay overtime or to hire part-time employees than to pay full-time wages and benefits. It may also reduce employee mobility, but most evidence thus far is that it does not affect turnover at all.

It is rational for employees to want additional benefits since they are tax-free income. For example, in 1980, the typical employee in the petroleum industry received over $10,000 in fringe benefits—tax free. The costs of such benefits, however, have been rising substantially, and many organizations cannot afford to offer benefits and high wages as well. Just what does it cost employers to provide these benefits for their employees?

Various groups, including the Department of Labor and the U.S. Chamber of Commerce, report on the costs of benefits. Exhibits 15–6 and 15–7 present some of the latest Chamber figures, by industry and per employee. These studies indicate that benefits (not including services) cost 14–60 percent of payroll, although they vary by size of employer and industry. The most typical figures are 20–30 percent. For example, retailers and textile firms offer low benefits. Petroleum and chemical and public utilities offer a high level of benefits. The most costly benefits are time off with pay (holidays, rest periods, vacations), insurance (especially health insurance), and pensions. In sum, benefits are very costly and getting more so.

In addition to the direct costs of benefits, there are added burdens, or indirect costs. One is the administration of these plans. They can become complicated, and paperwork proliferates. Because administrative costs at smaller organizations are especially high, some smaller organizations get together in joint benefit plans for their employees.

Exhibit 15–6

Weekly employee benefits, per employee, 1969 and 1980

	1969	1980	Percent change
Old-age, survivors, disability and health insurance taxes	$ 6.44	$ 18.35	+185
Private pensions (nongovernment)	5.88	17.08	+190
Insurance (life, accident, hospitalization, etc.)	5.00	18.27	+265
Paid vacations	6.17	15.54	+152
Paid rest periods, lunch periods, wash-up time, etc.	4.12	11.10	+169
Paid holidays	3.85	10.58	+175
Workers' compensation	1.29	5.02	+289
Paid sick leave	1.10	4.29	+290
Profit-sharing payments	1.25	4.13	+230
Unemployment compensation taxes	1.63	3.88	+138
Christmas or other special bonuses	0.67	1.12	+67
Contributions to employee thrift plans	0.23	1.00	+335
Salary continuation or long-term disability	N.A.	0.79	N.A.
Employee meals furnished free	0.29	0.56	+93
Discounts on goods and services purchased from company by employees	0.17	0.42	+147
Other employee benefits	1.25	2.06	+65
Total employee benefits	$ 39.46	$117.00	+197
Average weekly earnings	$141.44	$315.37	+123

N.A. = Data not available.
Source: *Nation's Business*, December 1981.

Exhibit 15–7 _____

Weekly employee benefits cost, by industry, 1980

	Per employee, per week
All industries	$117.00
Manufacturers	
Petroleum industries.	203.42
Chemicals and allied industries	144.10
Primary metal industries	143.73
Transportation equipment	142.29
Machinery (excluding electrical)	127.02
Rubber, leather, and plastic products	106.96
Electrical machinery, equipment, and supplies.	121.02
Food, beverages, and tobacco	111.69
Fabricated metal products (excluding machinery	
and transportation equipment)	119.46
Stone, clay, and glass products	110.94
Printing and publishing.	114.50
Instruments and miscellaneous products	108.50
Pulp, paper, lumber, and furniture	104.37
Textile products and apparel.	67.96
Nonmanufacturing industries	
Public utilities.	158.42
Miscellaneous nonmanufacturing industries (mining,	
transportation, research, hotels, etc.).	109.81
Banks, finance and trust companies	112.08
Insurance companies.	106.83
Wholesale and retail trade.	80.96
Hospitals	74.13
Department stores	70.31

Source: *Nation's Business,* December 1981.

Financing benefits can also be complicated. Some companies have found that they can save money by creating tax-exempt trusts for benefit funds as disability pay; examples include Westvaco, General Electric, TRW, and FMC Corporation.

An organization can compare its costs to those of other firms with the aid of data from an industry or professional group or published sources such as the Chamber of Commerce. Some other examples of such sources are the Conference Board, Bureau of Labor Statistics, *Nation's Business,* and *Business Week.*

Costs can be compared on four bases:

1. Total cost of benefits annually for all employees.
2. Cost per employee per year—basis 1 divided by number of employee hours worked.
3. Percentage of payroll—basis 1 divided by annual payroll.
4. Cost per employee per hour—basis 2 divided by employee hours worked.

Costs of benefits can be calculated fairly easily. The benefits side of the equation is another issue, however. There has been little significant empirical research on the effects of benefits on productivity.

Managing an Effective Benefit Program

When top managers make benefit and services decisions such as the cost decision discussed above, they must consider the following facts:

- At present, there is little evidence that benefits and services really motivate performance. Nor do they necessarily increase satisfaction.
- The costs are escalating dramatically.
- As regards mandated programs, managers have no choice but to offer them.
- With regard to voluntary programs, unions, competitors, and industry trends put pressures on the manager to provide or increase benefits.

To manage the benefit program effectively, certain steps are necessary. Four of these are discussed in this section.

Step 1: Set Objectives and Strategy for Benefits

There are three strategies for benefits:

1. *Pacesetter strategy.*   Be first with the newest benefits employees desire.
2. *Comparable benefit strategy.*   Match the benefit programs similar organizations offer.
3. *Minimum benefits strategy.*   Offer the mandatory benefits and those which are most desired and least costly to offer.

The decision about which strategy to use is made on the basis of management's goals, as discussed early in the chapter. The third strategy may be chosen because of inability to pay more benefits, or because management believes the employees want more pay and fewer benefits. Before these costly benefits and services are offered, management must set objectives that fit its benefit strategy.

Step 2: Involve Participants and Unions in Benefit Decisions

Whatever strategy is chosen, it makes sense to find out what those involved desire in benefits and services. Yet in most organizations, top managers *alone* judge which benefits the employees prefer. Without getting some employee-preference input, it is impossible to make these decisions intelligently. It is similar to a marketing manager trying to decide on consumer preferences with no market research input.

Therefore it is wise to permit (and encourage) employee participation in decision making on benefits and services. When employees share in benefit decisions, they show more interest in them. One way for employees to participate in the decisions is to poll them with attitude surveys. Another is to set up employee benefits advisory committees.

Steps in managing a benefit program:

1. Develop objectives and a benefit strategy.
2. Involve participants and unions in the benefit programs.
3. Communicate the benefits effectively.
4. Monitor the costs closely.

Will these devices work? Many believe so, but others think employees are not well enough informed to be of much help. Others oppose asking employees about benefits because this might raise their expectations so that they expect more. Instead, supervisors and union leaders might be asked about workers' preferences; most research shows they are good predictors of employee preferences.

A more direct way of allowing employee participation in benefit decisions and dealing with the problem of major preference differences is called the cafeteria approach to benefits. Each employee is told how much money the employer has set aside for benefits plans, after provision for mandated programs and minimal health insurance. Then the employee can choose to receive the funds in cash in lieu of benefits, or decide which benefits are wanted. This approach lets employees know how much the employer is spending on the programs. Because they pick the benefits they want for themselves, their performance and satisfaction are more likely to be affected favorably.

When the organization is unionized, it is vital that the union leadership be involved. Many times the leadership knows what employees want in benefits. Sometimes, the leadership tries to maximize benefits without having determined what employees want. It is useful to involve the union leadership in preference studies so that all parties are seeking benefits desired by the employees.

Step 3: Communicate Benefits Effectively

Another method for improving the effectiveness of benefits and service is to develop an effective communication program. How can benefits and services affect the satisfaction and performance of employees if they do not know about the benefits or understand them? Yet most studies of employees and executives indicate they are unaware of the benefits or significantly undervalue their cost and usefulness.

It has always been desirable to improve benefit communications for this reason. But now there is another reason. For pensions, ERISA requires employers to communicate with employees by sending them an annual report on the pension plan and basic information on their pensions in language they can understand.

Many communication media can be used: employee handbooks; company newspapers, magazines, or newsletters; booklets; bulletin boards; annual reports; payroll stuffers; and employee reports. Other communication methods include filmstrips, cassettes, open houses and meetings with supervisors and employees. A typical employee report is Exhibit 15–8 which spells out the value of the benefits to each employee. How much employees would need to save to provide this coverage themselves should be stressed. Another direct means of communication is to send employees copies of bills paid by the company for medical expenses on their behalf.

The problem is retention of the message and learning it in its entirety. Most organizations handle these problems by using multiple media and sending the message many times. For example, when the First National Bank of Chicago changed its benefits package, it told about the plan with a range of communications. These included, from first to last, the following:

> A letter from the president was sent to each employee's home to explain the purpose and general nature of the changes. This letter was tested out on 15 "typical" employees for readability prior to sending it.

Exhibit 15–8 _____

Summary page from a 1982 benefit-audit statement

YOUR TOTAL PAY PACKAGE

	Your yearly contributions	Estimated cost if you bought it all
Basic and major medical...........................	$ 204	$ 1,257
Salary continuation and		
disability insurance............................	none	2,464
Life and accident insurance	none	946
Pension plan......................................	none	3,458
Social security...................................	709	2,130
Total.....................................	$ 913	$10,255
Net value of benefits	$ 9,342	
Annual salary	$38,000	
Total pay package value	$46,396	

This report tells you what your company-provided benefits can mean to you and your family at retirement or in case of illness, disability, or death. There is no way of knowing how many dollars you will actually receive. The table above, however, shows your yearly contributions and the estimated cost in annual individual insurance and benefit policy premiums if you were to buy this protection and income yourself. The company pays the full cost of your basic and major medical insurance, salary continuation, long-term coverage, and your pension. You and the company together share the cost of social security and the medical insurance program.

_____

The company newsletter carried several articles per week for weeks after.

Employee handouts were distributed to explain the plan.

Meetings of 40 employees each were held.

Each employee was exposed to easy-to-read loose-leaf binders explaining the benefits.

Finally, employees received their individual annual benefits reports explaining what the benefits meant to them.

In sum, organizations are spending billions on benefits and very little on benefit communications. To make these billions pay off, they need to increase the quantity and improve the quality of their communications about the benefits they represent.

Step 4: Monitor the Costs Closely

In addition to considering costs in choice of benefits, it is vital that managers make sure the programs are administered correctly. Especially important is the review of insurance claims. Miller has shown how Rockwell International and Goodyear Tire and Rubber have lowered insurance costs by studying claims to make sure they are covered by the policy and reasonable.[27] Large savings resulted. More efficient administration procedures using computerized methods also can lead to greater savings and more satisfied employees.

Together, these four steps will make any benefit program more effective.

_____

[27]Allan Miller, "How Companies Can Train Employee Health Benefit Claims," *Harvard Business Review,* January–February 1978, p. 608.

Summary

Chapter 15 has described benefits and services as part of the rewards which reinforce loyal service to the employer. The chapter described mandated and voluntary employee benefits and some critical benefit decisions such as communication, administration, retirement benefits, and employee participation. Let's sum up the major points:

1. Mandated benefit programs in the private and third sectors include:

    a. Unemployment insurance.
    b. Social security.
    c. Worker's compensation (Chapter 19).

2. To be eligible for unemployment insurance, an employee must have worked a minimum number of weeks, be without a job, and be willing to accept a position offered through a state Unemployment Compensation Commission.

3. Three kinds of benefits many employers provide voluntarily are:

    a. Compensation for time not worked (break time, coffee breaks, clothes change time, holidays, sick leave, vacations, and so on).
    b. Insurance protection (health, disability-accident, and life).
    c. Employee services (various benefits which can include cafeterias, gyms, free parking lots, discounts, and so forth).

4. Retirement income is received from three principal sources:

    a. Savings and investments and part-time work.
    b. Private pension plans.
    c. Government program—Social security.

Carl Reems

Case

After talking to other presidents and reading some literature that Pete gave him, Carl understood better Pete's conservatism about benefits and services. Carl reviewed what researchers have found and became convinced that pouring money into benefits and services doesn't mean that absen-teeism will decrease, production will increase, and loyalty toward Coy will improve. "Employees have simply come to expect employers to provide competitive benefits and services," Carl thought, "I'm sure glad Pete brought this to my attention."

5. The Employee Retirement Income Security Act of 1974 is the law regulating private pensions.
6. To manage the benefit program effectively, follow these steps:
    a. Develop objectives and a benefit strategy.
    b. Involve participants and unions in the benefit programs.
    c. Communicate the benefits effectively.
    d. Monitor the costs closely.

7. To avoid administrative nightmares, employers should concentrate on fewer benefit plans, and those preferred by most employees.

The benefit plans recommended for the model organizations are given in Exhibit 15–9.

Remember for the benefits and services program to be effective, the operating manager and P/HRM manager must work together. The operating manager helps the P/HRM

Exhibit 15–9

Recommendations on benefit and service programs for model organizations

Type of organization	Benefits and services							
	Legally required benefits	Vacation plans	Paid holi-days	Group life insur-ance	Hospital-medical insur-ance	Accident-disability insurance	Employee pension program	Services
1. Large size, low complexity, high stability	X	*	*	*	X	X	X	*
2. Medium size, low complexity, high stability	X	*	*	*	X	X	X	*
3. Small size, low complexity, high stability	X	*	*	*	X	X	X	*
4. Medium size, moderate complexity, moderate stability	X	*	*	*	X	X	X	*
5. Large size, high complexity, low stability	X	*	*	*	X	X	X	*
6. Medium size, high complexity, low stability	X	*	*	*	X	X	X	*
7. Small size, high complexity, low stability	X	*	*	*	X	X		*

*Minimized.

manager know what the employees prefer in benefits and asks for help in explaining the benefits and getting administrative problems cleared up. The P/HRM manager helps the operating manager communicate the benefits to employees and administer the program.

Questions for Review and Discussion

1. What are employee benefits and services?
2. Why do employers have benefit and service programs?
3. Which benefits and services do employees prefer? Which do you prefer? Why are these preferences significant?
4. Describe government-mandated benefits and services. Should these programs exist? How can they be improved?
5. What is social security?
6. Are early retirement programs a good idea? Have they been successful?
7. What are the major provisions of ERISA regarding vesting and portability?
8. Which of the benefits and services are the most costly?
9. How can managers make better benefits decisions?
10. How can managers communicate about benefits better?

Glossary

Individual Retirement Account. A plan in which a person is able to save or invest for retirement up to $2,000 which is not subject to taxes.

Portability. The right of an employee to transfer pension credits accrued from one employer to another.

Unemployment Insurance. Established by the Social Security Act of 1935 to provide a subsistence payment to employees when they are between jobs. The employer and employee contribute to a fund which then pays when the employee is out of work.

Vesting. The right of employee to participate in a pension plan.

Chapter Sixteen

Discipline and the Difficult Employee

Learning Objectives

After studying this chapter, you should be able to:

- List four categories of employees that are designated "difficult."

- Describe steps that can be taken to prevent employee theft.

- Discuss the elements of a disciplinary system.

- Define what is meant by the term *dehiring*.

- Explain why discharge is more widely used in a nonunionized situation as opposed to a unionized situation.

Chapter Outline

I. A Diagnostic Approach to Discipline

II. Categories of Difficult Employees
   - A. Category 1: The Ineffective Employee
   - B. Category 2: Alcoholic and Addicted Employees
   - C. Category 3: Participants in Theft, Crime, and Illegal Acts
   - D. Category 4: The Rule Violators
   - E. Are Certain Types of Employees Likely to Be Difficult?

III. The Discipline Process

IV. Administration of Discipline
   - A. Hierarchical Discipline Systems
   - B. Other Discipline and Appeal Systems

V. The Disciplinary Interview: A Constructive Approach

VI. Summary

Case

Managers supervise a variety of types of employees as part of their work. Most employees perform effectively most of the time. But any management development session eventually comes around to a discussion of employees like Al, Susan, Joyce, or Tom. These four employees are employed by a small conglomerate in the Boston area, Judge Incorporated. Judge owns manufacturing and retailing units.

- Al is the salesman who had the largest sales increases of any of the sales force just after he was hired. Later, his sales dropped off. When his supervisor checked, Al was found to be making just enough sales calls to reach his quota.
- Susan is often a good worker. Then there are days when all the forms she types have serious errors on them. These are the days Susan is drinking.

- Joyce seems to do good work. She is courteous to the customers. She puts the stock up quickly and marks the prices accurately. But Joyce takes more than her paycheck home every week.
- Tom is a pretty good employee. But John, his supervisor, is driven up the wall by him. Tom just can't seem to follow the company rules. And when John tries to talk to him about it, Tom gives him a hard time and may even seem to threaten him if he tries to do anything about the problem.

At present, Judge Incorporated has no well-organized discipline system.

These examples illustrate a time-consuming and worrisome aspect of the P/HRM job: dealing fairly with the difficult employee. The seriousness of the problem is shown by the fact that the largest number of cases going to arbitration involves disciplinary matters. Unionized organizations have ways of dealing with these incidents, but most employees do not work in a unionized situation.

This chapter is concerned with the characteristics of difficult employees and some of the reasons for their problems. It also considers systems of discipline and appropriate means for rehabilitating difficult employees. Too often discipline has been oriented toward punishment for past misdeeds. This is required in Joyce's case, but more important for the others is behavioral change to improve employee productivity.

The emphasis of the chapter will be on *on-the-job behavior*. Organizations such as the military have tried to control the total behavior of the employee; the military often will court-martial and punish soldiers for civilian offenses such as speeding, whether or not civilian authorities prosecute. The work organization, however, should be concerned with off-the-job behavior only when it affects work behavior. Thus if Susan drinks before work so that she cannot do her job, this is of concern to her employer. If she has a few drinks after work and this in no way affects her job, it is none of her employer's business, even if the boss happens to be a teetotaler.

Generally, the operating supervisor is the person primarily involved in disciplining employees. P/HRM specialists may be involved as advisers if they are asked to do so by the operating manager. Sometimes the P/HRM manager serves as a second step in investigation and appeal of a disciplinary case. Or, when the union is involved, the P/HRM manager may advise the operating manager on contract interpretation for a specific case.

Discipline is a Stage III P/HRM activity as defined in Exhibit 1–6 (Chapter 1). Some studies have been performed on the topic, but there is a wide divergence in the disciplinary practices applied in various organizations.

A Diagnostic Approach to Discipline

Exhibit 16–1 highlights the factors affecting the discipline process in an organization. As we have seen, an employee's attitude toward work is a crucial factor in productivity or performance, and discipline may play an important part in this attitude. (The kind of discipline system used is normally related to the organization.) It will be more formal in larger organizations, especially those that are unionized. It is quite informal in smaller organizations.

How strict discipline is depends on the nature of the prevailing labor markets. In times of high unemployment, for example, it can be quite strict. It is also related to the supportiveness of the work group (if the work group "covers" for the employee and feels the issue is unimportant, management's ability to discipline will be limited), and to the nature of the leader or supervisor (a liberal leader's approach to discipline will be quite different from a conservative leader's). The government and the legal system may provide support for employer or employee.

The effective operating or P/HRM manager will try to diagnose each of these factors in the discipline situation. For example, the supervisor may try to diagnose the difficult employee's motivation, with a view to improving performance. This is not always easy to do. If the manager does not know the employee well, because there are many employees or for other reasons, it may be virtually impossible. Discipline is one of the most challenging areas in the P/HRM function. The diagnostic approach has many advantages over the "give him a fair trial before you hang him" approach in dealing with the difficult employee.

Categories of Difficult Employees

This chapter will focus on discipline and behavior modification of four kinds of employees whose behavior can be described as difficult.

Categories of difficult employees:

Category 1. Those whose quality or quantity work is unsatisfactory due to lack of abilities, training, or job motivation. (Al is an example.)

Category 2. Those whose personal problems off the job begin to affect job productivity. These problems can include alcoholism, drugs, or family relationships. (Susan is an example.)

Category 3. Those who violate laws while on the job by such behavior as stealing from the organization or its employees or physical abuse of employees or property. (Joyce is an example.)

Category 4 Those who consistently break company rules and do not respond to supervisory reactions. (Tom is an example.)

Exhibit 16–1 _____

Factors affecting the discipline of personnel

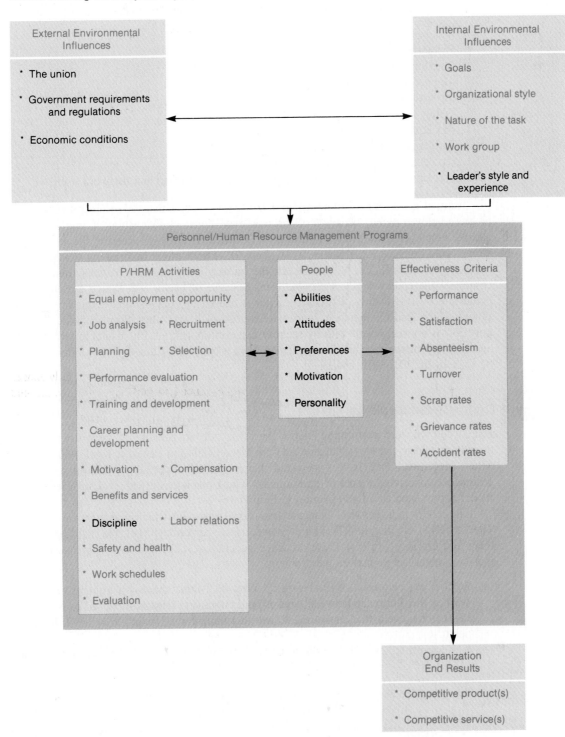

The difficulty of determining the causes of any human behavior pattern was noted in Chapter 2. It is especially difficult to assess the causes of undesired behavior, but Miner has devised a scheme for analyzing deficient behavior which provides a checklist of possible causes:[1]

I. Problems of intelligence and job knowledge.
II. Emotional problems.
III. Motivational problems.
IV. Physical problems.
V. Family Problems.
VI. Problems caused by the work group.
VII. Problems originating in company policies.
VIII. Problems stemming from society and its values.
IX. Problems from the work context (e.g., economic forces) and the work itself.

Many of these causes can influence deficient behavior, which can result from behavior of the employee alone, behavior of the employer alone, or interaction of the employee and the employer. Al's behavior (Category 1), which is directly related to the work situation, could be caused by Factors II, III, and VII. Susan might be drinking (Category 2) because of Factors II, IV, V, and others; the primary cause of her behavior is outside the control of the employer. Or she could drink because of Factor VII, which the employer could remedy. Frequently, difficult behavior is caused by personal and employment conditions which feed one another. Joyce's behavior—theft and other illegal activities (Category 3)—is normally dealt with by security departments and usually results in termination and possibly prosecution of the employee. Tom's behavior (Category 4) is often caused by Factors III, VII, VIII, and IX.

Category 1: The Ineffective Employee

one of easier to correct   Responsible to work rules;
just can't meet standard. When interview, assume trainable.
Sometimes make mistakes. Train, relocate, discharge

Employees who are performing ineffectively may do so because of factors which are directly related to the work situation and are theoretically the easiest to work with and to adjust Mager and Pipe have systemized this pattern of undesirable behavior and have designed a conceptual model of questions by which management can deal with it.[2] Their model is presented as a flow diagram in Exhibit 16–2.

The model indicates that there are four key issues with which managers must cope. The first (I on the diagram) is: The employee is not performing well; the manager thinks there is a training problem. There are three general questions and follow-up questions a manager might use to analyze the problem:

1. *What is the performance discrepancy?* Why do I think there is a training problem? What is the difference between what is being done and what is supposed to be done? What is the event that causes me to say that things aren't right? Why am I dissatisfied?
2. *Is it important?* Why is the discrepancy important? What would happen if I left the

---

[1]John Miner, *The Challenge of Managing* (Philadelphia: W. B. Saunders, 1975).
[2]Roger Mager and Peter Pipe, *Analyzing Performance Problems* (Palo Alto, Calif., Feron Publishers, 1970).

Exhibit 16–2

Analyzing undesirable employee behavior

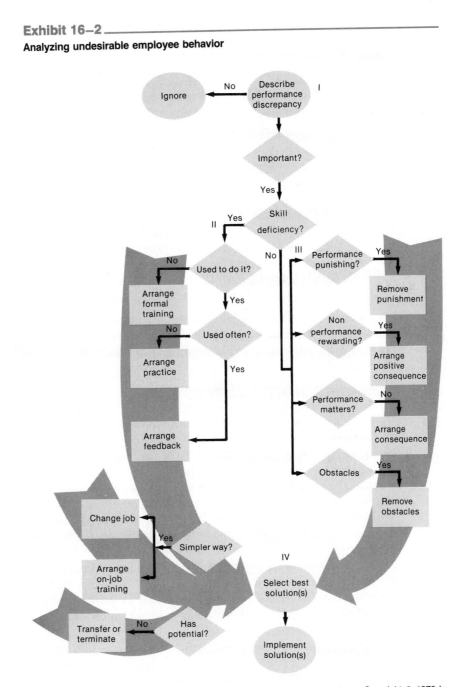

Source: Robert Mager and Peter Pipe, *Analyzing Performance Problems.* Copyright © 1970 by Fearon-Pitman Publishers, Inc., 6 Davis Drive, Belmont, California. Reprinted by permission.

discrepancy alone? Could doing something to resolve the discrepancy have any worthwhile result?

3. *Is it a skill deficiency?* Could he do it if he really had to? Could he do it if his life depended on it? Are his present skills adequate for the desired performance?

Question 3 leads to II on the diagram. Key issue I is solved: Yes, it is a skill deficiency. To check this further, general questions 4–7 can be used.

4. *Could he do it in the past?* Did he once know how to perform as desired? Has he forgotten how to do what I want him to do?

5. *Is the skill used often?* How often is the skill or performance used? Does he get regular feedback about how well he performs? Exactly how does he find out how well he is doing?

6. *Is there a simpler solution?* Can I change the job by providing some kind of job aid? Can I store the needed information some way (written instructions, checklists) other than in someone's head? Can I show rather than train? Would informal (i.e., on-the-job) training be sufficient.?

7. *Does he have what it takes?* Could he learn the job? Does he have the physical and mental potential to perform as desired? Is he overqualified for the job?

At this point it might appear that the conclusion to II was not correct, or the question may have been answered no in the first place. In this case the key issue would be: It is not a skill deficiency; he could do it if he wanted to. At III, general questions 8–11 apply:

8. *Is desired performance punishing?* What is the consequence of performing as desired? Is it punishing to perform as expected? Does he perceive desired performance as being geared to penalties? Would his world become a little dimmer (to him) if he performed as desired?

9. *Is nonperformance rewarding?* What is the result of doing it his way instead of my way? What does he get out of his present performance in the way of reward, prestige, status, jollies? Does he get more attention for misbehaving than for behaving? What event in the world supports (rewards) his present way of doing things? (Are you inadvertently rewarding irrelevant behavior while overlooking the crucial behaviors?) Is he "mentally inadequate," so that the less he does the less he has to worry about? Is he physically inadequate, so that he gets less tired if he does less?

10. *Does performing really matter?* Does performing as desired matter to the performer? Is there a favorable outcome for performing? Is there an undesirable outcome for not performing? Is there a source of satisfaction for performing? Is he able to take pride in his performance, as an individual or as a member of a group? Does he get satisfaction of his needs from the job?

11. *Are there obstacles to performing?* What prevents him from performing? Does he know what is expected of him? Does he know when to do what is expected of him? Are there conflicting demands on his time? Does he lack the authority? . . . the time? . . . the tools? Is he restricted by policies or by a "right way of doing it" or "way we've always done it" that ought to be changed? Can I reduce interference by improving lighting? . . . changing colors? . . . increasing comfort? . . . modifying the work position? . . . reducing visual or auditory distractions? Can I reduce "competition from the job"—phone calls, "brush fires," demands of less important but more immediate problems?

Finally, we arrive at IV, the key issue: Which solution is best? Mager and Pipe suggest these questions to analyze that problem:

> Are any solutions inappropriate or impossible to implement? Are any solutions plainly beyond our resources? What would it "cost" to go ahead with the solution? What would be the added "value" if it did? Is it worth doing? Which remedy is likely to give us the most result for the least effort? Which are we best equipped to try? Which remedy interests us most? (Or, on the other side of the coin, which remedy is most visible to those who must be pleased?)

This is a useful approach to dealing with a Category 1 employee.

Category 2: Alcoholic and Addicted Employees

(recognize, but don't try to deal w/!) approach it on basis of performance, not on ... hard to substantiate prob. If they admit it & ask for help, you can help, otherwise document! performance. If meet T (drugs) must wait for harm to show! (blued on arm) Can't force rehab or fire unless poor perform)

Abuse of alcoholic consumption which affects an employee's job performance is a serious problem with effects on organizations everywhere throughout the world. More and more, alcoholism is being viewed by the courts and by therapists as an illness, a *treatable* illness. More often than not it is treated as humorous, as in the Frank and Ernest cartoon. Those who know and love people who are alcoholics don't think it is funny at all!

Estimates of the number of alcoholics employed in America vary, but about 10 percent of the labor force are alcoholics and another 10 percent are borderline alcoholics.[3] The greatest incidence of alcoholism is in people aged 35–55 who have been employed at the same enterprise 14–20 years. The direct cost to industry alone is estimated at $8 billion a year in lost productivity and allied expenses. This estimate may be low because alcoholics often are sent home as "sick" rather than as drunk.

Of course, alcoholic consumption does not affect all employees the same at work, nor does it affect performance of tasks equally. Studies indicate that alcoholic intake tends to reduce some ability performance levels (for example, cognitive and perceptual-sensory skills) more than others (psychomotor skills).[4] For many persons, it takes about an hour

SORRY WE'RE LATE, SIR, BUT WE WERE UP UNTIL THREE THIS MORNING CELEBRATING BOSS APPRECIATION DAY.

FRANK & ERNEST

© 1978 by NEA, Inc. Reprinted by permission of NEA.

---

[3]National Industrial Conference Board, *Company Controls of Alcoholism,* Studies in Personnel Policy 167 (New York: Conference Board, 1969).

[4]Jerrold Levine, Gloria G. Kramer, and Ellen N. Levine, "Effects of Alcohol on Human Performance An Integration of Research Findings Based on an Abilities Classification," *Journal of Applied Psychology,* June 1975, pp. 285–93.

for the alcohol to affect performance negatively. About a third of America's largest employers have set up alcoholism control programs. Many medical plans now cover the costs of treatment for alcoholism if the employee will take it, and if they refuse, many companies fire them.

Generally the successful program for alcoholics includes a conference between supervisor and employee. These points are covered:

> The supervisor documents the effects at work of the employee's alcoholism to the employee.
>
> The supervisor offers to help.
>
> The supervisor *requires* the employee to participate in a rehabilitation program such as Alcoholics Anonymous (which has been evaluated as by far the best program).
>
> The supervisor notifies the employee that the consequences of not participating in rehabilitation is loss of the job.

Many unions are now participating in joint employer-union programs designed to deal with alcoholism.

In larger organizations, the medical or occupational health department helps alcoholics. In medium-sized and smaller organizations, P/HRM refers them to consultants and the treatment programs. P/HRM and operating managers need documentation to support their decision, in arbitration hearings if necessary.

The Addicted Employee • Employers also are finding more employees addicted to drugs such as cocaine and heroin and are becoming more aware of this problem area. Drug addiction manifests itself in ways similar to alcoholism. The problem may be less well known to employers because of laws against possession and use of drugs, which causes employees to hide their habit.

How many drug addicts there are in the employment situation is not known precisely. In 1971 the American Management Association studied 23 companies.[5] More than half of the companies surveyed said they had dealt with problems of employee drug abuse during the preceding year. The drugs involved were marijuana (29 percent), amphetamines (18 percent), heroin (17 percent), cocaine (2 percent), and other (10 percent).

Companies believe that absenteeism, turnover, accidents, and lower productivity are caused by drug addiction, and some thefts are caused by addicts trying to support their habit. What have they done about it? One survey of 108 companies on employees' use of drugs found that 81 percent tried to find out if the employee had used drugs prior to hiring, and 51 percent have company policies against drug use by employees.[6] Their responses to the problem include detection methods to determine the extent of the problem, more careful recruitment and selection, educational programs for supervisors, policy statements, and counseling programs which refer addicts to rehabilitation programs.

Companies follow similar control programs for drugs as they do for alcohol, although

---

[5]Susan Halspern, *Drug Abuse and Your Company* (New York: American Management Association, 1972).

[6]Carl D. Chambers and Richard Heckman, *Employee Drug Abuse* (Boston: Cahners Books, 1972). Also see William G. Wagner, "Assisting Employees with Personal Problems," *Personnel Administrator,* November 1982, pp. 59–64.

treatment methods vary more in the drug area. Drug usage is illegal, and public attitudes are much more negative on drugs than on alcohol. In industry, the company health department can try to rehabilitate drug users. Often, however, the ultimate decision is discharge and discipline, although this may lead to arbitration. A summary of arbitration rulings on the subject and a survey of members of the National Academy of Arbitrators by Levin and Denenberg found that because of the legal implications and the difficulty drug users would have in getting future jobs, arbitrators demand full and complete proof of drug usage.[7] This is sometimes difficult for employers to provide. Employers can help protect themselves by asking the employee to certify previous drug experiences. If it can be shown this record is falsified, arbitrators view this as grounds for discharge or discipline. If company policy is to discipline or discharge employees who use drugs, company rules and employment controls should be explicit about this prohibition. Evidence must also be given that these prohibitions have been communicated clearly to all employees.

Kimberly-Clark has an employee assistance program (EAP) for chemical dependency and other special health problems affecting work performance.[8] The EAP screened over 250 employees and family members in 1980. About half of these had chemical dependency problems. The company's rehabilitation program was able to reduce chemical dependency and improve the job performance of about 65 percent of the participants. Absenteeism and accident data for employees in the EAP showed a 43 percent reduction in absenteeism and a 70 percent reduction in accidents for a one-year period following treatment (using a pre- and posttreatment design).

Arbitrators have discharged drug-using employees if their habit ruins a firm's reputation or causes it to lose business. They are more likely to uphold discharges for drug usage after conviction than after arrest alone, and they discipline drug pushers more severely than drug users. In general, arbitrators tend to urge employers to give drug-using employees a second chance if they agree to rehabilitation programs.

Category 3: Participants in Theft, Crime, and Illegal Acts   *internal theft bigger $ than shoplifter.*

Employers often have to deal with employees who engage in various illegal acts. Employers may steal (remember Joyce), misuse company facilities or property, disclose trade secrets, embezzle, or kidnap executives for terrorist purposes. They may sabotage products, or use company telephones and credit cards for personal purposes, or pirate company materials or labor to repair their own homes. One source estimates that 75 percent of stolen goods is taken by employees and suppliers. Yet some arbitrators have recently ruled that employee property (such as their cars in the parking lot) cannot be searched without a warrant. The organization must also be concerned with thefts and similar crimes by visitors and guests. Organizations try to deal with employee theft and similar problems in a number of ways. One is to try to screen out likely thieves. For example, a weighted application blank has been developed to help with this.

Other organizations try to prevent thefts by training and preventive measures. Ten ways to prevent theft are given in the accompanying box.

Set up internal control procedures.

---

[7]Edward Levin and Tia Deneberg, ''How Arbitrators View Drug Abuse,'' *The Arbitration Journal*, March 1976, pp. 97–108.

[8]Robert E. Dedmon and Mary Katherine Kubiak, ''The Medical Director's Role in Industry,'' *Personnel Administrator*, September 1981, pp. 59–64.

Ways to prevent employee theft:

1. The employee should be made to feel that the job is worth keeping and it would not be easy to earn more elsewhere.
2. Normal good housekeeping practices—no piles of rubbish or rejects or boxes, no disused machines with tarpaulins on them, and no unlocked, empty drawers—will help assure that there are no places where stolen goods can be hidden. The first act of the thief is to divert merchandise from the normal traffic flow.
3. Paperwork must be carefully examined and checked at all stages so invoices cannot be stolen or altered.
4. Employees' cars should not be parked close to their places of work. There should be no usable cover between the plant doors and the cars.
5. Women employees must not be allowed to keep their handbags next to them at work. Lockers that lock must be provided for handbags. Merchandise has a way of disappearing into a handbag, and once the bag is closed a search warrant is needed to get it open again.
6. Whether the plant is open or closed at night, bright lights should blaze all around the perimeter so no one can enter or leave without being seen.
7. There should be adequate measures to control issuance of keys. There have been cases where a manager or supervisor would come back at night for a tryst with a girlfriend and would give her an armload of merchandise to take home with her. Key control is very important.
8. As far as possible, everyone entering or leaving should have an identification card.
9. Unneeded doors should be kept locked. If only two must be open to handle the normal flow of traffic, the rest should be bolted.
10. Everything of value that thieves could possibly remove, not just obvious items, must be safeguarded.

A method organizations can use to oversee these procedures is to set up a security department or program. Often this responsibility is assigned to the P/HRM department. Typically, the protection program is called industrial security and includes security education, employment screening, physical security, theft and fraud control, and fire prevention.

Most companies engage in at least minimal industrial security operations such as identification or "badge" systems, prior employment screening, special safeguards for or destruction of sensitive documents, and escort services for visitors.

Studies suggest that the larger the organization, the greater the likelihood that security measures will be used.[9] Most organizations also attempt at least some industrial security planning in selecting sites and designs for remodeling or construction of facilities. Security vulnerabilities are assessed and structural barriers such as fences, lighting, and the building itself are designed to reduce security hazards.

Operating and P/HRM managers may both be involved in disciplinary matters involving Category 3 employees. Often firings and legal action are considered. Visitors involved in illegal acts may also face the law.

---

[9]Jerry L. Wall, "Industrial Espionage in American Firms." (Ph.D. diss., University of Missouri, 1974).

Category 4: The Rule Violators *Most common . Must be consistent . Rules SB explicit.*

If needed, write in flexibility to

Difficult employees of the fourth category consistently violate company rules, such as those prohibiting sleeping on the job, having weapons at work, fighting at work, coming in late, or abusing the supervisor. An especially difficult issue is verbal and physical abuse of supervisors. It is useful (though not necessary) for the organization to have an established rule prohibiting verbal and physical abuse. Disputes charging abuse often go to arbitration. In general, arbitrators take the position that the decisions of supervisors deserve respect. Their rulings have been influenced by several facets of the cases:

> *The nature of the verbal abuse.*   If the shop talk is usually obscene, unless the employee personally applies the obscenities to the supervisor arbitrators are not likely to uphold disciplinary measures for use of obscene words.
>
> *The nature of the threat.*   Discipline will be upheld if an employee *personally* threatens a supervisor, not if the employee talks vaguely about threats.
>
> *The facts in physical abuse cases.*   If the employee directly attacks the supervisor personally or indirectly (e.g., abusive phone calls) *and if* the employee was not provoked, the disciplinary decision will be upheld by arbitrators.

One study found that in 54 percent of the cases studied, arbitrators have reduced disciplinary penalties given by supervisors.[10] They take into account mitigating circumstances like prior excellent work records and how fairly the management has treated the employee prior to and at the time of the incident. They also check to make sure that management has consistently disciplined other employees in similar cases and that the disciplinary decisions have been consistent. Arbitrators have treated altercations between supervisors and union stewards differently from those between supervisors and other employees. They view the supervisor and steward as equal and feel the steward need not be as ''respectful'' as other employees.

It is more difficult to establish rules about other infractions. Many organizations prohibit gambling on company grounds, to avoid lowering productivity and losing time from fights over gambling losses. Yet few work very hard to prohibit nickel-dime poker at lunch.

Organizations usually have rules prohibiting employees from making decisions when there is a conflict of interest (such as a purchasing agent who has an interest in a supplier) or when they are indebted to others. Many organizations prohibit their employees from accepting gifts over some nominal value or from being guests at lavish parties. Conflict-of-interest dealings are usually specifically prohibited.

More and more organizations should have rules prohibiting sexual harassment, but they are difficult to investigate or enforce. Women who have had to put up with sexual harassment to hold a job are turning to the EEOC and the courts to resolve this issue.

---

[10]Ken Jennings, ''Verbal and Physical Abuse toward Supervision,'' *Arbitration Journal,* December 1974, pp. 258–71.

This is a difficult problem for management. Not too long ago, management was criticized for rules prohibiting fraternization between employees as constituting an invasion of privacy.

The problem of the ex-convict as an employee is a long-standing one. Many can become excellent employees, others will not. P/HRM must be especially careful in the supervision and discipline of ex-convicts if they are to be developed as good employees.

Are Certain Types of Employees Likely to Be Difficult?

Various experts have tried to identify the personality characteristics of the difficult employee. This search is as elusive as trying to find the personality characteristics of good leaders.

One researcher studied 1,635 hourly workers in two plants of a manufacturing company in the eastern United States.[11] She was searching for the "marginal worker"—the one who consistently and frequently is difficult, as measured by more frequent absences, turnover, firings, discipline cases, grievances, and accidents. She *thoroughly* reviewed the literature prior to testing hypotheses and found that the marginal worker was most likely to be one of a *few* employees who caused the most problems. Characteristically, this type of employee was a production worker in a large production department, working on a late shift and receiving high overtime or incentive pay rather than the day rate.

The Discipline Process

Exhibit 16–3 is a model of the discipline process. The employer establishes goals and rules and communicates them to employees. Employee behavior is then assessed, and modification may be found desirable. This process is an attempt to prevent difficulties and is positive in nature. It is designed to help employees succeed.

The first element in the process is the establishment of *work and behavior rules*. Work goals and standards were discussed as part of performance evaluation (Chapter 8). Through whatever method is used (time and motion study, examination of past performance or performances by others, management by objectives), a set of minimally accept-

Exhibit 16–3

Elements in a disciplinary system

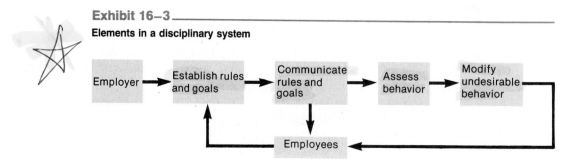

---

[11]Claire Anderson, "The Marginal Worker: A Search for Correlates." (Ph.D. diss. University of Massachusetts, 1976).

P/HRM Manager Close-Up

Denise Wilkerson
Dailey Oil Tools, Inc.

Biography

Denise Wilkerson graduated cum laude from the University of Houston. She holds a B.S. degree in business technology with a specialization in personnel management. Denise's professional experience includes working as an employment specialist and also being involved with recruiting, interviewing, orientation, counseling, salary administration, systems development and management and benefits program development.

Job description

Denise is currently assistant director of industrial relations with Dailey Oil Tools, Inc., in Houston, Texas. She is responsible for establishing new personnel policies and procedures, conducting salary and benefit surveys, providing orientation to new employees, handling EEO requirements and reports, evaluating job descriptions, and handling personnel problems such as administering discipline programs when required.

---

able work goals is established. Behavior rules cover many facets of on-the-job behavior. They can be categorized as concerning behavior that is directly or indirectly related to work productivity. Both types are often negatively described as prohibited behavior. Exhibit 16–4 lists some examples of employee behavior rules.

The second important element in the disciplinary process is the *communication* of the rules to all employees. Unless employees are aware of the rules, they can hardly be expected to follow them. Closely related is a willingness to accept the rules and their enforceability. If employees or their representatives participate in the formation of the rules, their cooperation is more likely to be assured. Employees must be convinced that the rule is *fair and related to job effectiveness*.

It is useful for management to seek employee advice on periodic revision of rules. The objective is to reduce the number of rules to the minimum and enforce those that are important. Customs and conditions change. Rules, like laws, need regular updating to achieve the respect and acceptance necessary for order in the workplace.

The third element of the disciplinary process is an *assessment mechanism*. In most organizations, performance evaluation is the mechanism for assessing work behavior deficiency. Rule-breaking behavior usually comes to the attention of management when it is observed or when difficulties arise and investigation reveals certain behavior as the cause.

Finally, the disciplinary process consists of a system of *administering punishment or attempting to motivate change*. This varies from supervisory administration of discipline to formal systems somewhat like courts or grievance procedures.

Exhibit 16–4 _____

Examples of employee behavior rules

I. Rules Directly Related to Productivity
   A. Time rules
      1. Starting and late times.
      2. Quitting times
      3. Maximum break and lunch times.
      4. Maximum absenteeism.
   B. Prohibited-behavior rules
      1. No sleeping on the job.
      2. No leaving workplace without permission.
      3. No drinking on the job.
      4. No drug taking on the job.
      5. Limited nonemployer activities during work hours.
   C. Insubordination rules
      1. Penalties for refusal to obey supervisors.
      2. Rules against slowdowns and sit-downs.
   D. Rules emphasizing laws
      1. Theft rules.
      2. Falsification rules.
   E. Safety rules
      1. No smoking rules.
      2. Safety regulations.
      3. Sanitation requirements.
      4. Rules prohibiting fighting.
      5. Rules prohibiting dangerous weapons.
II. Rules Indirectly Related to Productivity
   A. Prevention of moonlighting.
   B. Prohibition of gambling.
   C. Prohibition of selling or soliciting at work.
   D. Clothing and uniform regulations.
   E. Rules about fraternization with other employees at work or off the job.

Administration of Discipline

Another important issue in discipline is how it is accomplished so as to protect employees' rights. In unionized organizations, the employee has a formalized procedure which provides adequate protection: the grievance procedure discussed in Chapter 18. In nonunionized situations, the hierarchical system is the most prevalent. However, management today is no longer free in any type of situation, union or nonunion, to administer discipline without concern for potential legal challenges.

Hierarchical Discipline Systems

Discipline is administered to most nonunion employees by the supervisor, who also evaluates the employee. When the employee is found to be ineffective, the supervisor decides what needs to be done. In this hierarchical system, the conditions allow a supervisor who might be arbitrary, wrong, or ineffective himself to be police officer, judge, and jury over the employee.

A person accused of a crime such as speeding in many of our courts can have counsel, the judge is not the arresting officer, and the penalty may be a $50 fine. In the employment situation, where the employee has none of these safeguards, the penalty for an infraction of work rules may be his or her job and salary. Even if convicted of speeding, the employee can appeal to a higher court. What can the employee do if he/she is unfairly fired by the supervisor? There is, of course, the *open-door policy:* the employee could appeal to the supervisor's superior. But this is usually no help at all. The whole value system of the hierarchy is based on support of the supervisors to build a good management team. Of course, the informal open-door policy can lead to a quasi-legal form of justice such as that developed by IBM, in which the employee's case is recorded and systematically reviewed at several levels. A strictly hierarchical justice system is more prevalent in businesses than in other work organizations.

A feeling of helplessness and lack of due process for employees can become a *powerful* force leading to the unionization of enterprises. To work at all, hierarchical systems must be considered fair by employees. There must be adequate proof of any deviance. Employees will support discipline only if they feel that the disciplined employee was treated fairly and consistently compared to other past offenders. Mitigating circumstances must be considered if disciplinary procedures are taken. The minimal safeguard to prevent serious injustice in the hierarchical system is the mandated right to job transfer in disputes with less than overwhelming evidence against the employee.

If hierarchical systems are to be effective and fair, operating and P/HRM managers must administer discipline equitably. There have been a few studies of the extent to which this is so. One study on the subject found that even in companies with a well-developed discipline system, discipline was unevenly administered.[12] Other studies have found that prejudice against minorities or union members has led to unequal discipline. The data on differences in degree of discipline provide reasons for having systems of appeal besides the open-door policy to supplement or supplant the hierarchical approach.[13]

If discipline is called for, the manager can apply a series of sanctions to improve future performance or behavior. These vary from the brief parental chat to discharging the employee. A typical discipline system follows a progress pattern of steps. Each step in the progression becomes more severe for the disciplined employee.

The first step in a progressive pattern involves what is called counseling or a verbal discussion or warning. This is the most frequent method of disciplinary action. The supervisor determines if in fact a violation took place, explains to the employee why the violation significantly affects productivity, and suggests that it should not happen again. Sometimes the supervisor pushes counseling to the "chewing out" stage.

If a second or more serious violation takes place, the supervisor again counsels the employee, this time noting that the incident will be entered in the employee's personnel file. This is actually called the written warning step in a progressive pattern of discipline. If the violation was sufficiently serious, the employee may also be given an oral or written warning of the consequences of a future recurrence. An example of an employee warning report from Dailey Oil Tools, Inc. is presented in Exhibit 16–5. This report is placed in the employee's file.

If the incident concerns ineffective productivity, the employee may request transfer or be asked to transfer to another job. The employee may have been placed in the wrong job, there may be a personality conflict between the employee and the supervisor, or more training might help. In some rare cases, demotions or downward transfers are used.

---

[12]Edward L. Harrison, "Legal Restrictions on the Employer's Authority to Discipline," *Personnel Journal,* February 1982, pp. 136–41.

[13]Phillips Shaak and Milton S. Schwartz, "Uniformity of Policy Interpretation among Managers in American Industry," *Academy of Management Journal,* March 1973, pp. 77–83.

If counseling and warnings do not result in changed behavior, and if a transfer is not appropriate, the next progressive step is normally a *disciplinary layoff*. If damage resulted from the deviant behavior, the deductions may be made from employee's pay over a period of time to pay for the damage. Most disciplinary action will not require such a severe step. The layoff is usually of short duration, perhaps a few days up to a week.

The next most severe form of progressive discipline is what is referred to as *dehiring*, and most people call getting an employee to quit.[14] Getting the unsatisfactory employee to quit has many advantages over termination, for both employee and employer. Both save face. The employee finds another job and then quits, telling the peer group how much better off he or she is at the new location. The employer is happy because he or she has gotten rid of an ineffective employee without having to fire him or her. Dehiring is not a forthright approach to discipline. Many supervisors find it unethical. It should be used only if the supervisor prefers it to the next step: discharge.

The ultimate progressive discipline step is discharge or termination of employment. To many inexperienced managers, discharge is the solution to any problem with a difficult employee. Often discharge is not possible, because of seniority rules, union rules, too few replacements in the labor market, or a number of other reasons. Discharge has many costs, both direct and indirect. Directly, it leads to a loss of all the human resource

---

[14]Lawrence Steinmetz, *Managing the Marginal and Unsatisfactory Performer* (Reading, Mass.: Addison-Wesley Publishing, 1969).

Exhibit 16—5

Employee Warning Report

DAILEY OIL TOOLS, INC.
HOME OF THE
L. I. Drilling Jars
SPECIALTY SERVICE SINCE 1945

EMPLOYEE WARNING REPORT

Employee's Name _____ Date of Warning _____ Dept. _____ Shift _____
Clock or
Payroll No. _____

Type of Violation	□ Attendance □ Carelessness □ Disobedience □ Safety □ Tardiness □ Work Quality □ Other _____

W
A
R
N
I
N
G

Violation Date _____

Violation Time _____ a.m. / p.m.

Place Violation Occurred _____

Company Statement

Employee Statement

Check Proper Box

□ I concur with the Company's statement.

□ I disagree with the Company's statement for the following reasons:

I have entered my statement of the above matter.

Employee's Signature _____ Date _____

Warning Decision

Approved By _____
Name _____ Title _____ Date _____

List All Previous Warnings Below
When Warned And By Whom

Previous Warning:	**1st Warning**
Date _____	
Verbal _____	
Written _____	
Previous Warning:	**2nd Warning**
Date _____	
Verbal _____	
Written _____	
Previous Warning:	**3rd Warning**
Date _____	
Verbal _____	
Written _____	

I have read this "warning decision" and understand it.

Employee's Signature _____ Date _____

Signature of person who prepared warning _____ Title _____ Date _____

Supervisor's Signature _____ Date _____

Copy Distribution

□ Employee   □ Supervisor   □ Foreman
□ Industrial Relations   □   □ Union Rep.

DOT 704 (R 12/80)

"Basford, I want to put an end to this rumor that you're going to be fired. You're fired!"

Reprinted by permission The Wall Street Journal

investments already made, for recruiting, selection, evaluation, and training; many organizations also pay severance pay. Then these same investments must be made again for the replacement, and frequently there is a period during which the new employee is not as productive as the former employee was. The indirect costs are the effect on other employees of firing one of their numbers. If it is a blatant case of severe inability or deviant behavior, there is not too much problem with peer group resentment. But too often, the facts are not clear, and other employees may feel the employer acted arbitrarily. Some employees may seek employment elsewhere to prevent an arbitrary action happening to them. Others may reduce productivity in protest.

Thus discharge is the *last alternative* to be tried—when all else fails or in very serious cases, such as discovery of fraud or massive theft. One subtle reason restrains many supervisors from suggesting discharges. If the supervisor has had the employee a long time, management may begin to ask: "If the employee is so bad, why wasn't he downgraded sooner? Why didn't the supervisors get rid of the employee sooner? Why did he hire him in the first place? Do you think he's a good judge of employees? Is he supervisory timber?" Many discharges are reversed by arbitrators. For these reasons, actual discharges are rare and when they occur a record is made of the reasons. Exhibit 16–6 presents the documentation used at Dailey Oil Tools for terminated or discharged employees.

A few cases will illustrate how the law views discharge as part of a firm's discipline system. For the most part employees not covered by collective agreements (a contract) are in jeopardy and can be discharged even for the flimsiest reasons.[15] What do you think about these actual rulings?

- A salesperson who had worked for U.S. Steel Corporation for 14 years was discharged. The reason, he claimed, was that he questionned his superiors whether the steel tubes he was selling had been adequately tested and were

---

[15]Clyde W. Summers, "Protecting All Employees against Unjust Dismissal," *Harvard Business Review,* January–February 1980, pp. 132–39.

Exhibit 16–6
Termination Report

DAILEY OIL TOOLS, INC.
HOME OF THE
L. I. Drilling Jars
SPECIALTY SERVICE SINCE 1941
D.O.T.
HOUSTON, TEXAS

TERMINATION REPORT

PROFILE DATA (To Be Completed By Employee's Immediate Manager)

EMPLOYEE NAME	SOCIAL SECURITY NUMBER
ADDRESS	MANAGER/SUPERVISOR
POSITION	

☐ EXEMPT ☐ NON-EXEMPT ☐ FULL-TIME ☐ PART-TIME ☐ TEMPORARY

AGE	HIRE DATE	SALARY

LAST PERFORMANCE RATING

NOTICE GIVEN?   ☐ NO   ☐ YES, _____ DAYS   ☐ VERBAL   ☐ WRITTEN

REASONS FOR TERMINATION (Check Appropriate Reason(s) and Explain Fully).

VOLUNTARY

____ Personal Reasons
____ Medical Reasons
____ Domestic Reasons
____ Another Position
____ Dissatisfied (Wgs., Hrs., Wk.)
____ Transportation Difficulties
____ Marriage
____ Leaving Area
____ Attend School
____ Military
____ Deceased
____ Retirement
____ Other (Specify)

INVOLUNTARY

____ Unadaptable or Unsatisfactory
____ Unsatisfactory Attendance
____ Attitude Unsatisfactory
____ Excessive Tardiness
____ Violation of Company Rules
____ Refused to do assigned work
____ Extensive Absence due to illness
____ Lack of Work
____ Other (Specify)

IMPACT ON COMPANY

Do the Circumstances of this Termination Qualify the Employee for Unemployment Benefits Taxable to the Company?
☐ YES   ☐ NO   ☐ QUESTIONABLE

EVALUATION (Check One and Explain Below)
☐ SIGNIFICANT LOSS (Key Employee)   ☐ LOSS   ☐ NO IMPACT   ☐ ADVANTAGE

WOULD YOU RECOMMEND REHIRE?   ☐ NO   ☐ YES   ☐ SIMILAR JOB   ☐ DIFFERENT JOB

INTERNAL CORRECTIVE ACTION INDICATED?   ☐ NO   ☐ YES

COMMENTS:

EVALUATION BY:	DATE

DOT-728 (R 4/81)

safe. His superiors told him to follow orders. He did but also expressed his misgivings to a vice president of sales. The company reevaluated the tubes in question, withdrew them, and discharged the complaining salesperson. He sued, claiming that his discharge was without cause. The Pennsylvania Supreme Court dismissed his suit, declaring, "The law has taken for granted the power of either party to terminate an employment relationship for any or no reason."

- In California, a secretary who received a jury service questionnaire was told by her superior that she should indicate she was unavailable. She indicated that she was available and was discharged. The court acknowledged that the firm was "quite reprehensible, selfish, and shortsighted," but declared that, "Her employer could discharge her with or without cause. It makes no difference if the employer had a bad motive in so doing."

- A foreman with 25 years seniority at Westinghouse Electric Corporation was dismissed without notice of hearing for alleged unsatisfactory performance. He brought suit, claiming that the cause of his termination was the plant manager's false report to company officials that he was sympathetic with efforts to unionize the plant. The Louisiana Court of Appeals threw out his suit, declaring that he was, in the words of the common law, "an employee at will," and therefore, could be discharged at any time.

Most employers pay severance allowances to all discharged employees except to those in Category 3. They differ on whether severance pay should be offered to Category 1 employees and the most blatant cases of laziness and so forth in Category 4 employees.

Other Discipline and Appeal Systems

Although the progressive discipline and grievance system is *by far* the most used in industry, other employing organizations use different models more often. A few business organizations have also taken steps to design systems which may protect the employee from arbitrary supervisory action more effectively than the hierarchical model does. The alternatives to the hierarchical models are peer, quasi-judicial, and modified hierarchical approaches. In the peer system, a jury of peers evaluates and punishes. The quasi-judicial approach uses an independent arbitrator or ombudsman to resolve disputes. Modified hierarchical systems are regular appeals channels *inside* the organization, but including someone other than the supervisor's superior. One mechanism is to have all disputed dismissals or behavior modification plans submitted to specified management executive or executives far removed from the scene hear the facts and judge whether proper action was taken.

Nonhierarchical systems are used by such varied organizations as unions like the United Auto Workers, the Civil Service Commission in the U.S. government, and the American military. The private sector almost never uses nonhierarchical systems.

It must be noted that there is little or no empirical evidence that providing nonhierarchical systems necessarily provides fairer treatment of employees. But a study of the history of justice under various systems in the public domain would indicate justice is much more likely under systems that provide for independent assessment of evidence and judgments than one in which the superior is prosecutor, judge, and jury.

The Disciplinary Interview: A Constructive Approach

As previously mentioned, managers in some cases must tell an employee in clear terms that his or her behavior or job performance is below par. Suppose that this is accomplished through a discussion of poor performance, which is in essence a disciplinary interview.[16] There are several guidelines that can help the manager accomplish a constructive discussion with the ineffective performer.

1. *Root out the Causes.* The manager needs to determine if personal problems are playing a role in the poor performance (e.g., fatigue, alcohol, insomnia). This can be done by listening to the employee, to his or her co-workers, and by observation of the employee on the job.

2. *Analyze Other Reasons for Poor Performance.* If personal problems are not the main cause of poor performance, examine such factors as:
   a. Lack of skill and training to do the job.
   b. Low effort.
   c. No motivation by employee because good performance is not rewarded.
   d. Situation circumstances beyond the employee's control.

3. *Prepare for the Disciplinary Interview.* After analyzing possible causes and reasons for poor performance prepare for the interview. Check the employee's previous record and even talk to previous supervisors about the employee.

4. *Conduct the Interview with Care and Professionalism?*
   a. Keep it private—public criticism is too stark and often so negative.
   b. Criticize selectively—emphasize job-related performance causes. Tell the employee what you think and try to avoid being aggressive. Stay calm and be polite at all times.
   c. Let the employee speak—be a good listener; don't rush the meeting. Allow the employee to give his or her side of the story. A good rule is to show that you are listening by asking questions that indicate you are receiving the message being delivered.
   d. Take one point at a time—don't confuse points. Focus on one problem at a time.
   e. Attack the problem and not the person—in focusing on each point remember to attack the act and not the self-concept.

5. *Issuing the Discipline.* Don't make a joke of having to discipline the employee. There really is nothing funny about being disciplined for poor performance or inappropriate behavior. Prescribe the disciplinary steps to be taken in specific terms and with a specific timetable. Do not end the disciplinary interview until you are certain that the employee understands the discipline and what is expected. Also assure the employee his or her future performance will be judged without considering past ineffective performance problems.

6. *Don't Expect to Win a Popularity Contest.* A person who administers discipline in an equitable and firm manner will not win popularity contests. However, this person will be respected and a manager who is respected is invaluable to an organization. The disciplinary interview is a serious part of the management job that unfortunately must be conducted regularly.

---

[16]Guvene G. Alpander, ''Training First-Line Supervisors to Criticize Constructively,'' *Personnel Journal,* March 1980, pp. 218–21.

These few guidelines are designed to correct a problem or modify ineffective behaviors and are not supposed to embarrass or publically ridicule an employee. A constructive discipline interview can play an instrumental role in converting an ineffective performer into a productive member of the organization.

Summary

Some of the most difficult human and personnel problems involve handling the difficult or ineffective employee. Guidelines for assessing the causes and how to deal with this situation follow:

1. Most deviant or difficult employees' problems probably have multiple causes. Some of these are listed below:
   a. Problems of intelligence and job knowledge.
   b. Emotional problems.
   c. Motivational problems.
   d. Physical problems.

Case

Jeremy Schultz, the P/HRM vice president at Judge Incorporated, is reflecting on the results of his interviews with four supervisors this week. These supervisors are responsible for Al, Susan, Joyce, and Tom.

Because of these four and many similar employees, Jeremy decides to set up a formal disciplinary system. In conjunction with supervisors and a sample of employees, he sets up in written form the rules of working at Judge. The performance evaluation system is strengthened to make the goals clearer.

Jeremy runs some training sessions and communicates the new system to the employees. The new discipline system sets up a step-by-step process and a set of "costs":

1st violation or problem: Counseling by supervisor

2d violation or problem: Counseling by supervisor and recording in personnel file.

3d violation or problem: Disciplinary layoff.

4th violation or problem: Discharge.

For alcohol or drug problems, mandatory counseling at counseling centers is required, or discharge will result. Legal violations result in discharge and prosecution.

In all cases of disciplinary layoff, the employee will receive counseling from P/HRM. If there appear to be problems between supervisor and employee, Jeremy will serve as an ombudsman.

With regard to Al, Susan, Joyce, and Tom, Jeremy recommends the following actions:

Al Transfer to a new supervisor. There appeared to be a personality conflict between Al and his supervisor. (The transfer did not help. Eventually Al received a disciplinary layoff and was terminated, in spite of much counseling.)

Susan Ask her to join Alcoholics Anonymous. (She did, and got her drinking problem under control).

Joyce Watch for evidence that she is stealing. (When the evidence was clear, she was terminated and prosecuted. The judge gave her a suspended sentence.)

Tom Give him counseling about his behavior. (The supervisor reported later that Tom was a better employee.)

All in all, Jeremy felt the new disciplinary system was working rather well.

    e. Family problems.

    f. Problems caused by the work group.

    g. Problems originating in company policies.

    h. Problems stemming from society and its value.

    i. Problems from the work context (e.g., economic forces) and the work itself.

2. Categories of employees which cause discipline problems include:

    a. The ineffective employee.

    b. Alcoholic and addicted employees.

    c. Participants in theft, crime, and illegal acts.

    d. The rule violators.

3. The discipline process involves:

    a. Employer establishes rules and goals.

    b. These rules and goals are communicated to the employees.

    c. Employee behavior is assessed.

    d. Undesirable behavior is modified, punished, and so on.

    e. Depending on the behavior, its severity, and the number of offenses, continued violation might result in termination.

4. Employers should concentrate on trying to modify the effects and advise rehabilitation and counseling for such problems as alcoholism and drug addition.

5. For discipline systems to be effective, the disciplinary review must take place as soon after the action as possible. It must be applied consistently and impersonally.

    Exhibit 16–7, gives the recommendations for the use of different kinds of justice systems in the model organizations defined in Chapter 1.

Exhibit 16–7

Recommendations for model organizations on difficult employees and discipline

Type of organization	Hierarchical justice systems	Reinforce hierarchical justice systems with:		
		Peer committees	Ombudsmen	Outside committees
1. Large size, low complexity, high stability	X		X	X
2. Medium size, low complexity, high stability	X		X	
3. Small size, low complexity, high stability	X	X		
4. Medium size, moderate complexity, moderate stability	X		X	
5. Large size, high complexity, low stability	X		X	X
6. Medium size, high complexity, low stability				
7. Small size, high complexity, low stability	X	X		

It is important to remember that discipline is an area in which help is needed from many areas: supervisors, P/HRM, the work group, arbitrators, and top management. Each has a crucial role to play if the discipline system is to be effective.

Questions for Review and Discussion

1. What is discipline?
2. What are the four categories of difficult employees?
3. What are the major causes of difficult job behavior?
4. Describe the ineffective employee. How do Mager and Pipe suggest analyzing undesirable behavior?
5. How serious a problem is the alcoholic employee at work? How should the alcoholic employee be handled?
6. How serious a problem is the addicted employee? How should the addict be dealt with?
7. How serious is the employee who violates laws? How should this employee be dealt with?
8. Describe the discipline process.
9. Contrast various discipline philosophies. Which one do you accept?
10. Describe the disciplinary methods available and when you would use each.

Glossary

Progressive Pattern of Discipline. A discipline program that proceeds from less severe disciplinary actions (a discussion) to a very severe actions (being discharged). Each step in the progression becomes more severe.

Part Four

Motivation, Rewards, and Discipline

APPLICATION CASE IV–1
Honeywell Believes in Quality Circles

APPLICATION CASE IV–2
Nucor Uses Money as a Motivator

APPLICATION CASE IV–3
St. Benedict's Employee Assistance Program

EXERCISE IV–A
Paying People for Work

EXERCISE IV–B
Developing a Sales Positive Reinforcement Program

APPLICATION CASE IV–1

Honeywell Believes in Quality Circles*

The list reads like a corporate who's who—RCA, General Electric, Ford, Control Data, Memorex, Polaroid, Westinghouse, Bethlehem Steel, and Hughes Aircraft. These are users of Quality Circles (QCs). Each of these and thousands of other firms encourage QCs to meet on company time every week to identify, analyze, and resolve work-related problems.

Honeywell was one of the first American firms that imported the innovative Japanese concept of QCs. Honeywell has over 300 QCs spread through various installations. The firm estimates savings of several million dollars have resulted from the work of QCs.

Instead of only examining quality or quantity improvement Honeywell believes there is another benefit from QCs that has been largely neglected. Honeywell management believes that American workers aspire not only to an improved work life but also to jobs offering a personal sense of participation in the decisions that affect them. Is the worker of the 1980s any different than the worker of the 1950s? Yes, claims Honeywell; the worker today is better educated, more individualistic, less responsive to authority figures.

The QC is considered by some to be an ideal way to resolve the "we/they," labor-management conflict. With this belief that workers have changed, the environment is changing, and action steps are needed to correct productivity decreases, Honeywell has begun to use more and more QCs.

Perhaps Honeywell is correct in assuming that QCs not only step up productivity but also create an atmosphere for self-motivation. However, the cautious cynic must ask: if QCs are so good and is a superior motivational technique why haven't more organizations adopted them? Perhaps not everyone is as optimistic as Honeywell and other users of QCs.

Questions for Thought

1. What is wrong with the statement that Honeywell estimates that savings of several million dollars resulted from the use of QCs?
2. Do you agree with Honeywell's assumption that employees want a personal sense of participation in decision making?
3. Do you feel that one reason why more American firms haven't adopted QCs is that the approach originated in Japan? Explain.
4. Which motivation theory discussed in Chapter 12 fits best with the Honeywell assumptions about the worker of the 1980s?

---

*Adapted from Arnold Kanarick, "The Far Side of Quality Circles," *Management Review,* October 1981, pp. 16–17.

APPLICATION CASE IV–2

Nucor Uses Money as a Motivator*

Nucor Manufacturing Corporation has a management team that believes, unlike Herzberg, that money is the best motivator. Most Nucor employees are unskilled or semiskilled when they are hired. Furthermore, Nucor employees seem to place a high value on job security which management works hard to provide.

Nucor currently operates five steel joist fabrication plants. The entire organization has only five organizational levels from the president to the operating employee. There are no assistant managers, group managers, or directors. All of Nucor's facilities are in rural areas. These structural features and plant locations are rather unique in the steel joist fabrication industry.

The company currently has four incentive compensation programs. All of them are designed around groups, not individuals. The incentive systems are for production employees, department heads, secretaries, accounting clerks, accountants, engineers, and senior officers alike. The groups range in size from 25 to 30. Approximately 2,500 Nucor employees are under the main program or what is called production incentive system.

To a certain extent Nucor views each of the 25 to 30 production employee grups in business for themselves. What they earn is largely dependent directly upon their performance in terms of production. There are no bonuses paid when equipment is not operating.

The rules for absenteeism at Nucor are simple. There are four grace days per year. Additional days off are approved for military service or jury duty. Anyone who is not there for other days loses their bonus for the week. Additionally, if someone is more than a half hour late they lose their bonus for the day.

The production incentive program is only one part of the Nucor system. At the department head level the company has an incentive compensation program based on the division contribution of the particular division in which the department manager works on the company as a whole.

The third incentive plan applies to employees who are not in a production function or are not at the department manager level. This applies to accountants, secretaries, clerks, and so on. The bonus they receive is based on either the division's return on assets or the corporation's return on assets. Every month each division receives a report showing, on a year-to-year basis, their return on assets. This chart is posted in the employee cafeteria or break area together with the chart showing the bonus payout.

The fourth Nucor program is for senior officers. They receive no profit-sharing, no pension or retirement plans, or other similar executive perks. More than half of each of Nucor's officers' compensation is based directly on company earnings. If the firm is doing well, the executives do well. Their base salaries are set at 70 percent of what an individual in a comparable position with another company would receive.

Nucor does not have a retirement plan that is actuarially based; rather they have a profit-sharing plan with a deferred trust. Under the plan 10 percent of the firm's pretax

---

*Adapted from John Savage, "Incentive Programs at Nucor Corporation Boost Productivity," *Personnel Administrator,* August 1981, pp. 33–36, 49.

earnings is put into profit sharing annually. Of this amount, 20 percent is set aside to be paid to employees in March of the following year as cash profit sharing. The remainder is put into a trust.

Vesting in the profit sharing trust is much like that of a retirement plan. An employee is 20-percent vested after a year in profit sharing with an additional 10-percent vesting each year thereafter.

Another example of incentive at Nucor is the service awards program. Instead of handing out pen and pencil sets or the clips or gift certificates for seniority, Nucor issues company stock. After five years of service an employee receives five shares of Nucor stock. Another five years of service they receive another five shares and so on.

Questions for Thought

1. Consider the type of retirement plan at Nucor. What does the amount of retirement income for Nucor employees depend upon?
2. Do you feel that Nucor's program would have any success if most employees were from urban rather than rural backgrounds? Why?
3. What is your opinion of Nucor's senior officer incentive program? Would you like to work under such a program? Why?

APPLICATION CASE IV–3

St. Benedict's Employee Assistance Program*

In 1981 it was estimated that over 2,500 U.S. corporations in all types of industries have employee assistance programs (EAP). The argument for EAPs is that it is more desirable both economically and socially to rehabilitate previously proven and trained employees than it is to have to discharge them for alcoholism, drug dependency, emotional or other problems.

St. Benedict's is a 198-bed, nonprofit, acute general hospital. Services are typical of a medium-sized general hospital. The hospital has a staff of 700 employees and a medical staff of 224 physicians. The director of human resources was designated coordinator and referral source for employees' needing assistance.

The EAP has voluntary and mandatory aspects. The employee who has a personal problem and recognizes it can voluntarily seek help. The mandatory aspect calls for man-

---

*Adapted from H. Joe Featherston and Robert J. Bednaiek, "A Positive Demonstration of Concern for Employees," *Personnel Administrator,* September 1981, pp. 43–44, 47.

agers to look for deteriorating job performance as the basis for referring an employee to the employee assistance coordinator for diagnosis and referral to appropriate professionals. The referrals are made to family counselors, mental health specialists, private psychiatrists, and credit counseling services.

It was decided that St. Benedict's managers had to be trained in the use of the EAP. Retraining of supervisors on the specifics of the EAP occurs annually, with new supervisors receiving a one-on-one orientation by the director of human resources.

National estimates indicate that in most organizations about 10 percent of the employees need counseling of some kind. During the first two years of the program, St. Benedict's had 67 employees in for counseling which is slightly below 10 percent. Of the 67 counseled, it was determined through interviews, observation, and self-report surveys that 25 had their problems resolved (i.e., an alcoholic who successfully completed treatment and is back to work and maintains sobriety); 24 had shown considerable improvement; 6 showed no improvement and 3 of the six were terminated.

Other interesting statistics kept on the EAP were:

A. Clients referred: 55 women; 12 men.
B. Nature of referral: 27 involuntary, 40 voluntary.
C. Average tenure: 3.9 years.
D. Classification of clients: 30 professional, 15 technical and 20 nonprofessional, 1 volunteer, and 1 doctor's spouse.
E. Category of problem:
   1. Financial—21.
   2. Psychiatric or psychological—10.
   3. Absenteeism—5.
   4. Alcohol/drugs—8.
   5. Marital or family—12.
   6. Legal aid—5.
   7. Personal problems—5.
   8. Theft—1.

The hospital was considering how it could assess the cost/benefits of the EAP. One suggestion was to assess turnover, selection, training, and insurance opportunities versus costs of the program. It is assumed that most of the EAP's clients were problem-type employees and considered high-risk employees.

Questions for Thought

1. Do you feel that employee assistance programs should have a mandatory requirement like the one at St. Benedict's?
2. What do you think the training for managers in the use of the St. Benedict's EAP involved?
3. How could St. Benedict's management assess the costs/benefits of its EAP? Help them set up an assessment program.

EXERCISE IV–A

Paying People for Work

Objective. The exercise encourages students to think about job conditions and occupations in terms of the most appropriate, if any, method of payment.

Set up the Exercise

1. Listed below are several job conditions. Decide whether payment should be made on the basis of time worked (e.g., hour, week, month) or on the basis of number of units produced or output (e.g., generators, cars painted, vouchers filed).

Job condition	Time payment	Output payment
1. Quality is very important.	_____	_____
2. Quantity is difficult to measure.	_____	_____
3. Worker's perceive little relationship between effort-performance and rewards.	_____	_____
4. Equipment is unreliable; thus there are large chunks of downtime.	_____	_____
5. Management wants to create more competition between workers.	_____	_____
6. Incentive systems have been very successful.	_____	_____

Now examine the jobs listed below. Decide whether payment should be made on the basis of time or output.

Job	Time payment	Output payment
Police officer	_____	_____
Auto worker	_____	_____
Coal miner	_____	_____
College professor	_____	_____
Trucker	_____	_____
Neurosurgeon	_____	_____
Professional baseball player	_____	_____
Air traffic controller	_____	_____
Homemaker	_____	_____
Accountant	_____	_____
Judge (lawyer)	_____	_____
Carpenter	_____	_____
Nurse	_____	_____
Cashier at checkout	_____	_____

2. The instructor will form groups to discuss the individual ratings.
3. What did each group find? Was there a lot of similarities or differences in opinions? Have a group spokesperson discuss the findings.

A Learning Note

This exercise encourages you to think about how payment for work decisions are made difficult by the characteristics of the job. It also raises issues how individuals in various occupations are paid.

EXERCISE IV-B

Developing a Sales Positive Reinforcement Program

Objective. The exercise is designed to have students apply principles of motivation in designing a positive reinforcement program for sales personnel.

Set up the Exercise

1. Please read the facts individually.

   Mary Day Cosmetics is a small firm with 15 salespeople in the New York City area. The salespeople put on demonstrations to sell a full line of women's cosmetics in the homes of customers. Each demonstration will have between 10 to 15 neighborhood women in attendance. The Mary Day salesperson has a specific New York area territory. Usually the territories are the areas in which the salesperson lives. The salespeople receive commissions at the rate of 12 percent on gross sales. Bonuses are paid if sales exceed a previously set sales goal established jointly by the sales director and each salesperson. Pension and insurance benefits are paid by the company.

   Two years ago Mary Day had four salespeople. Currently the company has 15 sales persons, and plans to add 15 more in two years because of the growth in sales. Unfortunately, there has been some turnover (five women have left and been replaced) in the past nine months.

   The president of Mary Day, Sonja Kimslow, believes that applying behavior modification can improve performance, reduce turnover, and increase the morale of the sales force. She would like a skeleton plan that outlines what the company can do in terms of a positive reinforcement program to accomplish these objectives.
2. The class or group is to be divided into groups—six, seven, or eight persons are ideal.
3. Each group is to develop a positive reinforcement program for Sonja's review. Think about the following points in developing the plans:
   a. What reinforcers should be used? How were they determined to be what was needed?
   b. How and when should the reinforcers be used?
   c. How should the consequences be assessed?
   d. Should punishment be included in any plan to improve performance at Mary Day?
   e. What assumptions did the group make in putting their plan together?
4. A spokeperson for each group should present the group's plan to the class.

A Learning Note

This exercise should illustrate that there are some problems and difficulties associated with implementing a positive reinforcement program. The evaluation of such programs is one of these difficulties.

Part Five

H. Armstrong Roberts

Three chapters make up Part Five of the text. Chapter 17 covers the history, laws and some current issues facing labor unions, including unemployment, the quality of life, membership, and resistance to unions. Chapter 18 focuses on organizing campaign issues and strategies and collective bargaining. The rights of employees in nonunionized situations are also covered in this chapter. Chapter 19 addresses employee safety and health. Such topics as the government involvement in safety and health, and new preventive health programs in firms such as Kimberly-Clark and Control Data are discussed and analyzed.

Labor Relations and Safety and Health

H. Armstrong Roberts

H. Armstrong Roberts

Chapter Seventeen

Labor Unions: History, Laws, and Issues

Learning Objectives

After studying this chapter you should be able to:
- Describe the role that unions play in the lives of over 20 million employees.

- Explain why some employees are attracted to and others resist union membership.

- Discuss how labor legislation initially encouraged the growth of labor unions.

- Define the various types of union security.

- Examine and understand the role that the National Labor Relations Board plays in labor-management relations.

Chapter Outline

Case

Tom

Stan

Hardisty Manufacturing Company (HMC) is a fairly new firm which has grown substantially in its short history. Hardisty is located in the Boston area and is a manufacturer of consumer goods. It has a volatile technology and employs about 750 persons.

The president of the company is Tom Hardisty. He used to work for the largest firm in the industry, until he had a fight with his boss, quit, and went into competition with his former employer. Several of the key executives of Hardisty were recruited from the same firm.

The last year or two have seen increases in sales for HMC. But because of extreme competitive pressures, profits have been low or nonexistent. At times, HMC has had to layoff employees. And pay and benefit increases have not kept up with inflation. Tom has been too busy trying to keep sales up and financing available to notice the lack of positive change in his own paycheck. That isn't necessarily true for all the others at HMC. Stan Goebel, the P/HRM VP, has tried to bring this up with Tom from time to time. But Tom always seems to be too busy to talk about the problem.

Then one day, Stan came rushing into Tom's office.

Stan: Tom, there are union organizers on the parking lot trying to get our employees to sign authorization cards.

Tom: Authorization cards? What are they? We engineers don't know much about unions and don't like them much either.

Stan: An authorization card is the form the organiz-ers use to get enough people to sign up to hold an election that can unionize us.

Tom: Stan, calm down. You're shaking! We have nothing to worry about. It's one happy family here. Our employees won't join a union.

Stan: Oh yeah? Then why are many of them signing the cards?

Tom: You saw some signing?

Stan: Yeah. Lots of them.

There was a pause while Tom thought for awhile.

Tom: What can we do?

Stan: Well, for one thing, we can't throw them off the parking lot. We allowed charities to solicit there. Remember, I warned you!

Tom: No. I meant, what should we do to keep the union out?

Stan: The union must get 30 percent of the employees to sign the cards. . . .

Tom: They'll never get that many. The few malcontents will sign and the rest. . . .

Stan: I've talked to enough P/HRM people who've been through this. You can't assume that. You gotta do something.

Tom: Let's talk about unions and labor relations and decide what we should do. . . .

Stan then discussed some facts of life with Tom: About labor relations, unions, contracts, law, griev-ances, and similar issues affecting Hardisty Manu-facturing Company.

This chapter is about a political and economic force in our society—the labor union. It discusses the union in the context of *labor relations*.

> Labor relations is a continuous relationship between a defined group of employees (represented by a union or association) and an employer. The relationship includes the negotiation of a written contract concerning pay, hours, and other conditions of employment and the interpretation and administration of this contract over its period of coverage.

Labor relations is a much discussed P/HRM activity. Few employers or employees get as emotionally involved over recruiting methods or career development plans, for example, as they do over labor-management relations.[1] The reason is that collective bargaining goes to the heart of employee relations problems: power. Whoever has the power to fire an employee has power over whether that employee and his or her family can survive. Whoever has the power to discipline an employee because of poor performance has the power to affect significant human needs negatively, as noted in Chapter 2. Underlying the concept of leadership in management is the need for power.

Most employers and unions have used their power fairly. The majority of employers have hired employees, given them reasonable jobs, compensated them well, respected their dignity, and retired them after rewarding careers. However, some employers have not dealt with their employees as well. They have exploited them economically and wielded many a blow to their human dignity.

Likewise most unions and associations have represented the membership well. They have fought hard and fair for improved working conditions, better wages, human dignity, and a sharing of the fruits of labor. Some, however, have been corrupt, violent, and an embarrassment to the membership. In the United States, work conditions considered unfair or exploitative have led to the development of the collective bargaining process. Employees have joined together so that, as individuals, they do not have to stand alone against the power of a General Electric, a Department of Defense, a Wayne State University, or a Barnes Hospital.

In considering collective bargaining, one focus is the big picture: national and international unions all locked in major struggles with industry or in Congress. As interesting as this is, the focus of this chapter is primarily on the effects of labor relations activities on the P/HRM function of the employer. National contracts, and especially national contracts for a multiunit organization, are the business of a few top managers, a few top union officials, some staff lawyers and support persons, and a few government officials. Very few individuals are involved in these interactions. This chapter is concerned with how the collective bargaining process affects the *day-to-day operations* of an employer and its employees.

A Diagnostic Approach to Labor Relations

Exhibit 17–1 highlights the diagnostic factors that are important in labor relations. The attitudes of employees toward unions influence whether they will join or support a union in the workplace.[2] Managerial attitudes toward unions in general and the union officials they deal with in particular also affect labor relations.

---

[1]John A. Fossum, *Labor and Relations* (Plano, Tex.: Business Publications, 1982).

[2]Arthur A. Sloane and Fred Witney, *Labor Relations* (Englewood Cliffs, N.J.: Prentice-Hall, 1981).

Exhibit 17–1 _____

Factors Affecting Labor Relations

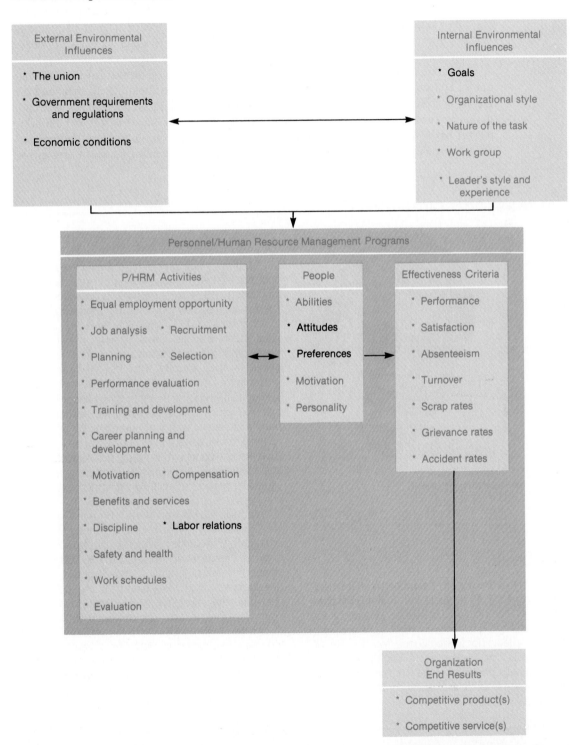

The goals of the controlling interests influence managerial attitudes and behavior toward labor relations. If management is very antiunion, the negotiation and administrative process will not proceed smoothly. The union is the other focal organization in effective collective bargaining relationships. Union officials and management interact daily and at contract time. Union and managerial attitudes toward each other affect the degree of peace and effectiveness that can exist in labor-management relations.

In addition to union requirements, two other environmental factors influence the nature of collective bargaining. Labor market conditions influence both management and the unions in their relationships. If the labor market is tight and demand for goods is strong, the union can hurt management by striking. If the demand for goods is soft and the labor market has a surplus, management has an advantage. It can sustain a strike, and perhaps even benefit economically from one. The other factor is government, which creates the

P/HRM Manager Close-Up

John L. Quigley, Jr.
Dr Pepper Company

Biography

John Quigley's degree in personnel management from Texas A&M, three years with Smith Protection Services as vice president of security operations for south Texas, and a subsequent position as assistant personnel director for Morton Foods, Inc., Division of General Mills, Inc., gave him a strong personnel generalist background when he was recruited as director of personnel for the rapidly growing Dr Pepper Company in 1967.

Job description

Mr. Quigley is vice president for human resources, coordinating all human resource and personnel functions for the company including personnel policy development, employment and recruiting, benefit administration, EEO and Affirmative Action planning, labor relations, sales training, management development, compensation and security, as well as office services support. His responsibilities have grown from a centralized manual personnel system to managing a decentralized highly responsive human resources system servicing the national company and several wholly owned domestic and international subsidiaries offering computerized support systems, personnel managers, professionals and specialists, and refined policies and programs designed to support a rapidly growing and expanding company.

In addition to his work with Dr Pepper Company, Mr. Quigley has given of himself to the personnel profession by voluntary service in the American Society for Personnel Administration, a 35,000 professional member organization. His dedication to the development of professionalism in the personnel field has taken him from ASPA district director for north Texas, to national vice chairman of the board of directors and successor to the chairmanship of the board of directors in 1982. His 12-year membership in ASPA has offered him service opportunities in behalf of growth of personnel professionalism across the continental United States as well as Hawaii, Alaska, and Mexico.

legal environment within which labor relations take place. Government boards rule on legal differences in the system, and government mediators and conciliators often help settle disputes.

Labor relations varies by the sector in which the organization operates. As will be described shortly, unions relate to managers in the business world (private sector), in government settings (public sector), and in other settings such as health, education, and voluntary organizations (third sector). Differing labor relations among the sectors are due to institutional and legal differences.

A Brief History of American Labor Unions

Unions have a long history in the United States. Even before the Declaration of Independence, skilled artisans joined together to provide members' families with financial aid in the event of illness or death.[3] Today many blue- and white-collar employees have joined together in unions. Their philosophy is the same: In joining together, there is strength. In fact, a *union* is a group of employees who have joined together to achieve present and future goals that deal with employment conditions.

The power of employees joined together is evident at the bargaining table, where union and management meet to discuss numerous issues. Many of the P/HRM decisions discussed in this book were influenced by union-management bargaining agreements. Employers in unionized organizations must often consult with union officials before taking actions that affect union members. In addition, many nonunionized companies have a workers' committee or council that managers consult before taking action. Their P/HRM policies and practices may affect employees interest in unionizing. Thus managers should be concerned with unions; they may either negotiate with union representatives at the bargaining table or face employees who want to form a union. Union objectives, organization, leadership, and attitudes are important for managers to know about.

Unions have existed in the United States since the colonial era. They originally functioned as fraternal societies providing help for members. Today, most unions are part of national organizations, many affiliated with the AFL-CIO (American Federation of Labor-Congress of Industrial Organizations).

Early Unions

Employers successfully resisted the earliest efforts to organize unions. In 1806 a court ruling made it a "conspiracy in restraint of trade" for workers to combine or exert pressure on management. In effect, unions were illegal until 1842, when the Massachusetts Supreme Court, in *Commonwealth* v. *Hunt,* decided that criminal conspiracy did not apply if unions did not use illegal tactics to achieve goals.

Even then, employers still resisted by discharging employees who joined unions. It was also easy for employers to have employees sign *yellow-dog contracts,* which promised that a prospective employee (e.g., job applicant) would not form or join a union. Employers also obtained court injunctions against strikes.

Early unions promoted social reform and free public education. Some of the more

---

[3]U.S. Department of Labor, "Brief History of the American Labor Movement," *Bulletin 1000* (Washington, D.C.: U.S. Government Printing Office, 1976), pp. 1–104.

militant groups—such as the Molly Maguires from the Pennsylvania coal mines—were considered socialist or anarchist. They were involved in rioting and bloodshed initiated by both employers and union members.

Labor Legislation

The union-management pattern of interaction is governed by state and federal laws.[4] These laws have evolved through common law and through rulings by the National Labor Relations Board and the courts. Figuratively speaking, these laws swing back and forth like a pendulum, at times favoring management and at times favoring unions.

Early Labor Law

The first government legislation affecting unions and management was the Arbitration Act of 1888. This act encouraged the voluntary settlement of labor disputes in the railroad industry. In 1926 the Railway Labor Act was passed by Congress. It provided railroad employees with the right to organize and bargain collectively with management.

In the 1930s the federal government became involved in labor disputes outside the railroad industry. The Norris-LaGuardia Act, also called the Anti-Injunction Act, was passed in 1932. The act limited the powers of federal courts to stop union picketing, boycotts, and strikes. *Injunctions,* court decrees to stop union activities, had provided employers with an easy way to hinder union activities. The Norris-LaGuardia Act also made the yellow-dog contracts unenforceable.

The Wagner Act

The National Labor Relations Act, better known as the Wagner Act, was passed in 1935. The stated purpose of the act was to encourage the growth of trade unions and restrain management from interfering with this growth. This act made the government take an active role in union-management relationships by restricting the activities of management. Five unfair labor practices specified in the Wagner Act are summarized in Exhibit 17–2.

The power to implement the Wagner Act was given to a three-person *National Labor Relations Board* (NLRB) and a staff of lawyers and other personnel responsible to the board. The board sets up elections, on request, to determine if a given group of workers wishes to have a union as a bargaining representative. The board also investigates complaints of unfair labor practices.

The Taft-Hartley Act

The Wagner Act was considered prolabor. In order to swing the pendulum back toward management in 1947, Congress passed the *Taft-Hartley Act* (also called the Labor-Management Relations Act), which amended and supplemented the Wagner Act. The Taft-Hartley Act guaranteed employee bargaining rights and specifically forbade the five unfair employer labor practices first established in the Wagner Act. But the act also specified unfair union labor practices. The union was restrained from such practices as those shown in Exhibit 17–3.

---

[4]See D. W. Twomey, *Labor Law and Legislation* (Cincinnati, O.: South-Western Publishing, 1980).

Exhibit 17–2

Employer unfair labor practices

- *To interfere with, restrain, or coerce employees in the exercise of their rights to organize* (threaten employees with loss of job if they vote for a union, grant wage increases deliberately timed to discourage employees from joining a union).
- *To dominate or interfere with the affairs of a union* (take an active part in the affairs of a union, such as a supervisor actively participating in a union, show favoritism to one union over another in an organization attempt).
- *To discriminate in regard to hiring, tenure, or any employment condition for the purpose of encouraging or discouraging membership in any union organization* (discharge an employee if he or she urges others to join a union, demote an employee for union activity).
- *To discriminate against or discharge an employee because he or she has filed charges or given testimony under the Wagner Act* (discriminate against, fire, or demote an employee because he or she gave testimony to NLRB officials or filed charges against the employer with the NLRB).
- *To refuse to bargain collectively with representatives of the employees; that is, bargain in good faith* (refuse to provide financial data, if requested by the union, when the organization pleads losses, refuses to bargain about a mandatory subject, such as hours and wages, refuse to meet with union representatives duly appointed by a certified bargaining unit).

The other major effects of the Taft-Hartley Act include the following:

- It denied supervisors legal protection in organizing their own unions.
- It provided the president of the United States, through the attorney general, the right to seek an 80-day court injunction against strikes or lockouts that may affect the nation's health.

Exhibit 17–3

Union unfair labor practices

- *To restrain or coerce employees in the exercise of their right to join or not to join a union except when an agreement is made by the employer and union that a condition of employment will be joining the union, called a union security clause authorizing a union shop* (picket as a mass and physically bar other employees from entering a company facility, act violently toward nonunion employees, threaten employees for not supporting union activities).
- *To cause an employer to discriminate against an employee other than for nonpayment of dues or initiation fees* (cause an employer to discriminate against an employee for antiunion activity, force the employer to hire only workers satisfactory to the union).
- *To refuse a bargain with an employer in good faith* (insist on negotiating illegal provisions such as the administration's prerogative to appoint supervisors, refuse to meet with the employer's representative, terminate an existing contract or strike without the appropriate notice)
- *To engage, induce, encourage, threaten, or coerce any individual to engage in strikes, refusal to work, or boycott where the objective is to:*
    Force or require any employer or self-employed person to recognize or join any labor organization or employer organization.
    Force or require an employer or self-employed person to cease using the products of or doing business with another person, or force any other employer to recognize or bargain with the union unless it has been certified by the NLRB.
    Force an employer to apply pressure to another employer to recognize a union.
    Examples are: picketing a hospital so that it will apply pressure on a subcontractor (food service, maintenance, emergency department) to recognize a union, or forcing an employer to only do business with others, such as suppliers, who have a union, or picketing by another union for recognition when a different one is already certified.
- *To charge excessive or discriminatory membership fees* (charge a higher initiation fee to employees who did not join the union until after a union-security agreement is in force)
- *To cause an employer to give payment for services not performed (featherbedding)* (force an employer to add people to the payroll when they are not needed, force payment to employees who provide no services).

- The union was forbidden to deduct union dues from members' paychecks without prior written permission.
- Employers could express their views against unions as long as they made no attempt to threaten or bribe employees.

Soon after the Taft-Hartley Act was put into practice, a number of corrupt practices in the union movement were disclosed. Investigations uncovered union leaders who had misused and stolen union membership fees and funds. It was also determined that some union leaders were involved with organized crime. The AFL expelled the entire International Brotherhood of Teamsters when the leaders failed to correct a criminal act uncovered in Senate hearings.

In 1974 Congress extended the coverage of the Taft-Hartley Act to private nonprofit hospitals and nursing homes. The extension was a major matter. Approximately 2 million employees working in about 3,300 nonprofit hospitals were affected. Before 1974 the National Labor Relations Board (NLRB) assumed jurisdiction over health care institutions. However, until the 1974 amendment, the NLRB was not authorized to handle cases in the nonprofit sector because the original law expressly excluded it from doing so.

Recognizing that hospitals supply a critical public service, the 1974 amendment established a special set of dispute-settling procedures. Unions representing hospital employees must give a 90 days' notice before terminating a labor agreement, 30 days more than Taft-Hartley requires in other industries. In addition, a hospital union may not strike or picket unless it gives 10 days' notice. This notice requirement not found in other industries, provides hospital management with the opportunity to make arrangements for the continuity of patient care.[5] There are other provisions which apply to hospitals that must be followed because of the 1974 amendment.

The Landrum-Griffin Act

In view of union corruption, Congress assumed that the individual union members were still not protected enough by the labor laws in existence. Therefore, in 1959 Congress passed the *Landrum-Griffin Act,* which is officially designated the Labor-Management Reporting and Disclosure Act. It was designed to regulate the internal affairs of unions.

This act, referred to as the bill of rights of union members, gave every union the right to: (1) nominate candidates for union office; (2) vote in union elections; and (3) attend union meetings. Union members also had the right to examine union accounts and records. In addition, the union was required to submit an annual financial report to the secretary of labor. Employers had to report any payments or loans made to unions, the officers, or members. This portion of the act was to eliminate what are called *Sweetheart contracts,* under which the union leaders and management agree to terms that work to their mutual benefit but maintain poor working conditions for other employees.

In general, labor unions were opposed to the passage of the Landrum-Griffin Act because it restricted union control over their organizations. The AFL-CIO believed it could handle any abuses through good internal management. However, the Senate Select Committee on Improper Activities in Labor and Management, headed by Senator McClellan, uncovered numerous abuses inside the union in the late 1950s. This Senate investigation weakened the prestige of unions and made it easier to pass the Landrum-Griffin Act.

---

[5]Sloan and Witney, *Labor Relations,* p. 126.

Government Employee Legislation

The second largest group of unionized employees is in the public sector. One third of all unionized public employees work for the federal government. The rest are employed primarily by local government.

There are major differences between labor law and regulation in the private and public sectors.[6] In the private sector, the law tries to get management and labor to the bargaining table as equals. In the public sector, the government defines itself as the superior through the use of the "sovereignty doctrine." The sovereignty doctrine, which has weakened in recent years, holds that the federal and state government represent the sovereign power of the people. Consequently, only the government can delegate by legislation to various organizations or by voluntarily delegating authority to them in certain areas. In addition, responsibility for negotiating with employees is complicated by the separation of powers doctrine. Some managerial responsibility lies with the executive branch, some with the legislative.

Public-sector collective bargaining is relatively new in the United States and has not been developed definitively. There is more clarity for federal employees than others. In the public sector, federal labor relations are regulated by executive orders issued by the president alone. Each new order rescinds previous orders on the same topic. In 1962, President John Kennedy issued Executive Order 10988, designed to parallel federal bargaining to private bargaining. It included a strong management-rights clause and banned strikes and the union shop.

Executive Order 11491, issued by President Richard Nixon in 1969 to update 10988, was designed to bring public bargaining even closer to that in the private sector. Under this order, the secretary of labor has the authority to determine bargaining units, to supervise procedures for union recognition, and to examine standards for unfair labor practices and rule on them.

Executive Order 11491 also created the Federal Labor Relations Council (FLRC), which review decisions of the secretary of labor, chairman of the Civil Service Commission, and director of the Office of Management and Budget. The FLRC supervises the Federal Service Impasses Panel, comprised of seven neutral members appointed by the president from outside the federal service to settle labor disputes in that sector. Executive Order 11491 also required a simple majority of employees to choose an exclusive representative union and stipulated criteria for determining the bargaining unit.

Executive Order 11838, issued by President Gerald Ford in 1975, required federal agencies to bargain with their employees on all issues unless the agency could show *compelling need* not to negotiate. All P/HRM policies became subject to negotiation. The FLRC was appointed the final arbitrator on these issues and what constitutes compelling need. Subjects for grievances were also broadened. But this order still bans union-agency shops and has a strong management-rights clause.

Labor relations regulations for public employees at state and local levels are diverse and complicated. For example, 12 states have no applicable labor laws at all for public employees. Another 20 states have such laws, and the other 18 have laws that cover certain aspects of labor relations for these employees.

For a time it was thought the answer to this confusion might be a federal law appli-

---

[6]H. B. Frazier, II, "Labor-Management Relations in the Federal Government," *Labor Law Journal*, March, 1979, pp. 130–134.

cable to state and local employees, but the Supreme Court and other federal courts have made it clear that the federal government cannot interfere with state and local employees. These rulings have also said that these government employees do not have to bargain with their employees. So the degree of public bargaining practiced and the methods used vary from state to state and city to city.

In January 1979, the executive orders were supplemented by what is called the Federal Service Labor-Management Relations Statute. The act applies to employees in federal agencies except the Postal Service (covered by the Taft-Hartley Act), the FBI, the General Accounting Office, the National Security Agency, the CIA, and agencies dealing with federal employee labor relations. Employees of the legislative and judicial branches were also excluded.

The Federal Labor Relations Authority is charged with overseeing the act in a manner similar to the National Labor Relations Board. Bargaining rights are limited under the statute. Federal employees may not bargain over wages and benefits, hiring or promotion, or classification of positions. The labor organization may not advocate a strike and unauthorized strikes may lead to decertification (the union is no longer the representative of the employee) and discipline of individual members. These steps were taken by the government under this statute when the Professional Air Traffic Controllers (PATCO) union was decertified in 1981.

In addition to federal law, the states have passed labor laws affecting certain aspects of labor relations. Normally, these laws affect strikes, picketing, and boycotts, and collective bargaining by public employees. These laws are varied across states and between employee groups within states.

The Structure and Management of Unions

The turbulent 1870s and 1880s brought growing recognition of the labor union approach to social and economic problems. These experiences helped solidify the union movement and encouraged the development of a nationwide organization.[7]

The first union federation to achieve significant size and influence was the Knights of Labor, formed around 1869. This group attracted employees and local unions from all crafts and occupational areas. In general there are two types of unions, industrial and craft. *Industrial union* members are all employees in a company or industry, regardless of occupation. *Craft union* members belong to one craft or to a closely related group of occupations. The strength of the Knights was diluted because it failed to integrate the needs and interests of skilled and unskilled, industrial and craft members.

A group of national craft unions cut their relationships with the Knights of Labor around 1886 to form the *American Federation of Labor* (AFL). They elected Samuel Gompers of the Cigar Makers' Union president. At first the AFL restricted membership to skilled tradespeople, but it began to offer membership to unskilled employees when the Congress of Industrial Organizations began to organize industrial employees.

Growth in the union movement from 1886 to 1935 was slow. The government's attitude toward union organizing was neutral, indifferent, or opposed. But with the passage of federal laws in the 1920s and 1930s that gave protection to the union organizing process, union membership began to grow (more will be said about organizing in Chapter

---

[7]A. H. Raskin, "From Sitdowns to Solidarity: Passage in the Life of American Labor," *Across the Board*, December, 1981, pp. 12–32.

18). Thus formal laws helped unions grow during their formative years. From 1933 to 1947, union membership grew from 3 million to 15 million.

In 1935 the *Congress of Industrial Organizations* (CIO) was formed by John L. Lewis, president of the United Mine Workers, in cooperation with a number of presidents of unions expelled from the AFL. The CIO was formed to organize industrial and mass-production employees. The AFL organized craft employees, such as machinists, bricklayers, and carpenters; the CIO wanted to organize craft and unskilled employees within an industry, such as assembly-line workers, machinists, and assemblers.

Competition for new union members led to bitter conflicts between the AFL and CIO, but in 1955 they merged. The structure of the present AFL-CIO is shown in Exhibit 17–4. 4. The majority of national and international labor unions now belong to the AFL-CIO, although a number of unions, representing over 4 million members, are unaffiliated. Such large and powerful unions as the Teamsters' and the United Auto Workers are not affiliated with the AFL-CIO.

How does the AFL-CIO work? Its chief governing body is the biennial convention, which sets policy. Between conventions, the executive officers, assisted by the executive council and the general board, run the AFL-CIO. Executive officers are the *president*, who interprets the constitution between meetings of the executive council and heads the union staff, and the *secretary-treasurer*, who is responsible for financial affairs. The executive council also has 33 vice presidents. It meets three times a year and sets policy

Exhibit 17–4

Structural organization of the American Federation of Labor and Congress of Industrial Organization

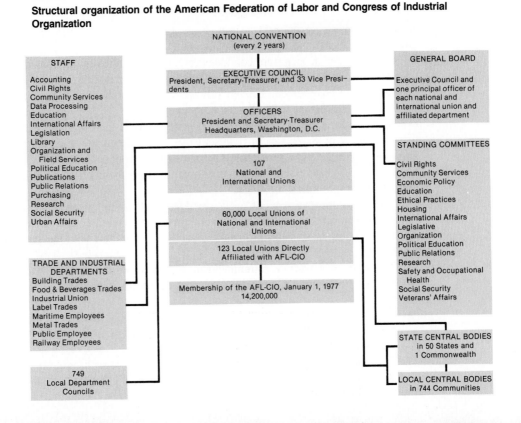

between conventions. The general board consists of the executive council and the head of each affiliated national union and department.

National headquarters provides many services to subsidiary union bodies; training for regional and local union leaders, organizing help, strike funds, and data to be used in negotiating contracts. Specialists available for consultation include lawyers, public relations specialists, and research personnel. Under the national union are regional groups of local unions which may provide office space and facilities for local unions.

Very large unions which are members of the AFL-CIO are those of the steelworkers, electrical workers, carpenters, machinists, and hotel and restaurant workers. The smallest national union—a unit in the printing trade—has 18 members.

The National Union

The constitution of the national union establishes the rules, policies, and procedures under which the local unions may be chartered and become members. Each national union exercises some control over the local unions. These controls usually deal with the collection of dues, the admission of new members by the local, and the use of union funds. The national union also provides the local unions with support for organizing campaigns, strikes, and the administration of contracts. There are over a hundred national union organizations but about 80,000 local unions.

The Local Union

The labor movement has its foundation in the local craft union. The local has direct influence over the membership. Through the local, members exercise their complaints and pay the dues that support the national union.

The activities of locals are conducted by officials elected by the members. The elected officials include a president, vice president, secretary-treasurer, business representative, and committee chairperson. Elected officials of local unions often have full-time jobs in addition to their regular union duties.

In many local unions the *business representative* is the dominant person. The major responsibilities of the business representative are to negotiate and administer the labor agreement and to settle problems that may arise in connection with the contract. The business representative also collects dues, recruits new members, coordinates social activities, and arranges union meetings.

The *union steward* represents the interests of local union members in their relations with managers on the job. In the auto industry, the steward (called a committee person) devotes full time to solving disputes that arise in connection with the union-management labor contract.

The role of a district committeeman (union steward) named Charlie Bragg, who worked in a Ford Motor Company plant, was described as follows:

> He might be called, in fact, the fixer—the man to whom workers can turn in times of trouble. . . . Unofficially, Mr. Bragg is the union to his people and often the only representative they deal with. . . .
>
> The main function of a committeeman is to settle problems right on the floor. Mr. Bragg says, "I'm a mediator, a foot-soldier out here. Without the committeeman, Ford couldn't run this plant."

. . .It is Charlie Bragg and the men like him who are fighting disciplinary actions, getting supply racks fixed, arranging days off, getting bathrooms cleaned and drinking fountains unclogged. (On the average day, Mr. Bragg handles about 20 individual problems.)

. . .His prime goal, he says, is keeping his constituents happy. But, he also must remain on working terms with their supervisors, who, he feels must regard him as tough, but flexible.[8]

It is the Charlie Braggs who are the link between the union members and management. Their actions and attitudes play a major role in the type of labor-management relationship that exists in an organization.

Managing the Union

The job of managing a union at the national or local level is challenging and time consuming. Union officials need to be dedicated, willing to work long hours, able to counsel members on personal problems, and skilled in influencing people. This combination of skills and abilities must also be obvious to members; tenure in office, especially at the local level, depends on projecting a favorable impression. Officers must run periodically for reelection. Some of the managerial problems facing union officials are member apathy, financial control, and recruitment of new members.

It is common knowledge that the majority of union members are apathetic about attending union meetings and voting on contracts or stike decisions. Thus, it is difficult for union officials to encourage members to take their union responsibiltiies more seriously.

Unions are financed through dues, fines, and initiation fees collected at the local level. However, union members resist high assessments. Union officials must convince members that, unless the union has a sound financial base, it won't have the power to secure favorable labor agreements.

The drive to organize more employees always faces union officials. Without new members, unions don't have the strength to carry out tactics to satisfy the needs, preferences, and interest of the membership. Developing effective organizing drives is the responsibility of local and national unions alike. Organizing will be discussed in more detail in Chapter 18.

Why Join a Union?

One important function of a union is to negotiate and administer the contract with the employer, which covers wages, hours, and the conditions of employment. The contract designates the formal terms of the union-management agreement in very specific language. It usually covers about two or three years. More details on contracts will be presented in Chapter 18. In addition to having a specific contract there are many other attractive features of union membership, and these appeal to different segments of the work force.

---

[8]Walter S. Mossberg, "On the Line: A Union Man at Ford, Charlie Bragg Deals in Problems, Gripes," *The Wall Street Journal*, July 26, 1973, p. 1.

First, many employees want some assurance that their jobs will exist in the future. They do not want to be fired or arbitrarily laid off because of a personality clash with a manager, an economic recession, or because of automation caused by the introduction of new technology. Unions, through collective bargaining, continually discuss and debate the issue of job security.

Second, people need to socialize and be part of a group. Unions meet these needs by bringing people with similar interests and goals. Through meetings, social events, educational programs, and common projects, unions can build a strong bond of friendship and team spirit.

Third, a safe and healthy place to work is important to employees. Unions in the United States and Canada have pushed hard for good working conditions. This well-publicized emphasis on improved working conditions appeals to employees who are considering a union.

Perhaps one of the strongest motives for joining a union is that it provides employees with a communication link to management. This link enables them to express dissatisfactions and disagreements about the job, management, and other issues. One such link is the grievance procedure detailed in the union-management contract.

Finally, compensation is an important reason for working. Employees want to receive a fair day's pay for a fair day's work and good frienge benefits. They are very concerned with receiving pay and fringe benefits that are competititve in the community.

A national survey of workers in various organizations was conducted by the University of Michigan Survey Research Center. Its focus was on how workers perceived the goals of unions. Eight-nine percent of the workers felt that unions have power to improve wages and working conditions, 87 percent believed unions improved job security, and 80 percent thought that unions can protect workers from unfair management action.[9]

A few unions have secured *guaranteed annual wages* (GAW) or guaranteed annual employment for members. The best known plans are those Procter & Gambles, Hormel, and Nunn-Bush. These plans *guarantee* regular employees a certain amount of money or hours of work. The purpose of the GAW is economic security.[10] Most companies oppose this type of guarantee, because they are concerned about continuity to pay workers when sales are down. Another breakthrough in the area of income security was a plan developed between Ford and the United Auto Workers. This plan became known as the Supplemental Unemployment Benefits (SUB) program because it supplemented unemployment benefits instead of providing a guaranteed annual income. Some companies with SUB plans are American Can, Kaiser, Reynolds, and General Motors.[11]

In summary, a major reason why unions exist is that management has not satisfied the total set of employees' needs and wants. It seems impossible for any management to continually satisfy every need and want, but some companies, such as IBM, have not been unionized. IBM has worked at making wages, salaries, fringe benefits, and other programs very attractive to employees. This concerted effort has probably been one of the main reasons why IBM employees have not unionized.

---

[9]R. P. Quinn and G. L. Staines, *The 1977 Quality of Employment Survey* (Ann Arbor, Mich.: Institute for Social Research, Survey Research Center, University of Michigan, 1979).

[10]Norma Pope and Paul A. Brinker, "Recent Developments with the Guaranteed Annual Wage: The Ford Settlement," *Labor Law Journal,* September 1968, pp. 555–62.

[11]"Lifetime Security," *Business Week,* November 14, 1977, p. 56.

Union Security

Labor unions stress the importance of security for members. Labor legislation also addresses the issue of union security. And union security is a major reason for trying to increase union membership. Unions want to increase their security by requiring all employees to join the union once it is elected as the legitimate bargaining agent.

In some elections, the union is voted in by a slim margin. In such cases, some employees obviously don't want to join the union. Different types of union "shops" have developed as a result, and they represent various degrees of union security.

Restricted Shop

When management tries to keep a union out without violating any labor laws, a *restricted shop* exists. A restricted shop is an attitude rather than a formal arrangement. Management may try to provide wages and fringe benefits that make the union and what it can offer unattractive. This is a legal effort to make the union's organizing ineffective.[12]

It is illegal to create a restricted shop by dismissing employees who want to unionize; trying to influence employees who are thinking about starting a union; or promising rewards if the union is voted down. These activities could result in legal action against management.

Open Shop

An *open shop* is one in which there is neither a union present nor a management effort to keep the union out. The employees have total freedom to decide whether or not they want a union. This type of shop is a prime target for union organizing effots.

Agency Shop

In the *agency shop*, all employees pay union dues whether or not they are members of the union. This means that no employee is a "free rider." Everyone pays dues for the services of an organized union even though some employees are not members.

Preferential Shop

In the *preferential shop*, the union is recognized, and union members are given preference in some areas. For example, when hiring new employees, union members are given preference over nonunion members. This type of preference may also be given in such areas as promotion and layoff. Many of these preferential decisions are in violation of the Taft-Hartley Act. If there is an excessive amount of preferential treatment, a closed shop may exist, which is also prohibited by the Taft-Hartley Act.

The Union Shop

The *union shop* requires the employee to join a union after being hired. An employer may hire any person, but within a period of time, that employee must join the union or lose the job. Under the Taft-Hartley Act, this period of time can be no shorter than 30 days.

---

[12]Jeff Blyskal, "Beating the UAW—Three Times," *Forbes*, March 2, 1981, pp. 37–39.

But under the Landrum-Griffin Act, this period can be shortened to seven days in the construction industry only. Most union-management labor contracts provide for the union shop.

The Taft-Hartley Act allows states to forbid union shops by passing what are called right to work laws. Under these laws, two persons doing the same job must be paid the same wages, whether or not they belong to the union. The union believes this is unfair, because the nonunionized employees pay no dues but share in the benefits won by the union. Nineteen states, located primarily in the South, the Great Plains, and the Southwest have right to work laws. Some of the larger states with these laws are Texas, Florida, Georgia, and Arizona.

Closed shop

The *closed shop* requires that a new employee be a union member when hired. The union itself provides labor to the organization. Although this type of shop is illegal, modified closed shops are found in the construction, printing, and maritime industries. For example, an ironworkers' union hall sends out union members to construction sites on request. A nonunion member has little chance to be sent from a union hall to a job, because the union's business agent makes the assignment. Union members elect the business agent, while the nonunion members have no vote.

Labor-Management Relations

The role of a labor relations manager is a very important one on the P/HRM team.[13] Surveys indicate that labor relations is the most important issue to be faced in unionized firms. Both P/HRM and operating managers are involved in labor relations. P/HRM managers or specialists are, of necessity, technical experts on labor relations who train and advise operating managers on the contract provisions. They also bargain with the union on the contract and serve as a step in the grievance process. But operation managers are the persons who make the contract work. They advice P/HRM on problem areas in the contract so they can try to improve them during the next negotiations, and they face grievances first. An overall, vital influence in labor relations is exerted by top management. Top managers' attitudes toward unions strongly influence the attitudes of P/HRM and operating managers and help determine whether union-management relations will be amiable or combative. Top managers also strongly influence the negotiating process. The bargaining philosophy and strategy they assume at the time of negotiations will help determine whether and how soon a contract will be signed, or whether impasses such as strikes, lockouts, and arbitration will occur.

Labor-Management Stereotypes

There have been a number of studies of the attitudes of how labor and management view each other. In general, they show the unflattering, dysfunctional stereotypes they have developed of one another. These stereotypes can distort the data presented during discussions about working conditions, pay, and so on. One union stereotype of a labor relations

---

[13]"The Personnel Executive's Job," *Personnel Management: Policies and Practices*, December 14, 1976.

manager is a "pretty boy," snobbish, country-club type, fawning over his boss, who could not find his way to the bathroom with a map and never worked a real day's work in his life. His job is only to cheat honest workers out of a few cents an hour to get a big bonus. Some labor relations managers, on the other hand, stereotype the union official as a loudmouth, uneducated goon who probably is stealing pension funds and no doubt beats up uncooperative workers. He will ruin the company because he does not understand the dog-eat-dog marketplace it must compete in.

These differences in perceptions between the two groups are compounded by major differences in such factors as age, education, and social class background. Furthermore, the employer organizations are hierarchical: the labor relations manager has a boss to report to. The union is peer oriented: the agreement must be approved by a vote of the members. The union leader has to be reelected to remain in office.

In sum, one of the challenges of labor relations is that on the union side of the table the representatives have more conflicts and less structure than those on the employer's side. There are conflicts within the management side, too, but usually there is an official, such as the president of the organization, who can "settle" these conflicts by a decision. This is not so on the union side.

In spite of these differences, there are many examples where the two groups are compatible and get along well. This results when both sides work hard at developing rapport. Or in some cases it is because one side has corrupted the other.

Government Officials and Others

The role players in labor relations are the employees, union officers, and labor relations executives. But others also do have an impact. The first is the government regulatory bodies that administer the labor laws. In the United States, the National Labor Relations Board (NLRB) administers the laws and regulations in the private and third sectors. Many states also have state boards to administer state labor laws.

Labor relations administrators have two major duties:

> To supervise representation elections and certify unions as bargaining
>   agents.
>
> To hear appeals of alleged violations of the laws.

Most experts believe the boards do a satisfactory job with elections. Some contend they are too slow in processing violation appeals. However, they receive a large number of complaints, and it is not an easy job. For example, in a typical month over 4,000 new cases are filed with the NLRB.[14] Some who favor the union side contend that these delays benefit management, and management deliberately takes its time and regularly appeals violation decisions. For example, cases where management is charged with firing prounion employees might take two years (with appeals and delays) to decide. By then the fired employees have other jobs or are tired of the process. Management disputes this, and the NLRB and other boards have attempted to expedite these cases.

Others with a possible impact on labor relations include customers and the general public. Customers and clients of the organization may mobilize to move the negotiation process along faster. Customers who need goods or services may exert pressure on the

---

[14]Twomey, *Labor Law and Legislation.*

employer directly to settle or lose the business. They also do this indirectly by buying elsewhere and letting the home office know it.

The general public tends to be neutral or uninterested in most labor-management incidents. Both sides try to mobilize public support through the media, however, because if the public is denied service it can bring political or other pressure to bear on the settlement. This normally happens when the public is severely affected by the loss of the goods or services.

Issues Facing Unions

To attract and retain members, unions have concentrated their efforts on issues that employees are concerned about: unemployment, social delimmas, and quality of life, as well as recruiting membership. These issues are an important part of the motivational forces influencing employees to unionize.

Unemployment

Many organizations have searched for and found technological advances that resulted in increased productivity. In many instances these advances were necessary in order for an organization to remain competitive. In some cases the technology has displaced workers, many of whom belonged to unions. For years unions resisted technological changes that displaced labor. However, as it became apparent that improvements in productivity were the only way to increase compensation, many unions changed their attitude about technology. Some unions now support technological improvement and work with management representatives to minimize the displacement of workers. They bargain for compensation for displaced workers, retraining, and relocation assistance for laid-off employees.

Early in 1982, exceptionally high unemployment was sending shock waves through the United States—in October 1982 there were about 11 million unemployed workers. Hardest hit by the jobless spiral were blue-collar workers, blacks, and teenagers. The heaviest concentration of unemployment was in the auto, steel, and construction industries clustered in factory towns in the Midwest and the industrial Northeast. These are union industries and geographical regions.[15]

Even if the economy reverses, there are experts who believe that in some industries unemployment will never fully rebound. Industries seem to be searching for ways to expand the use of computers and robots to improve quality and reduce labor costs. If this trend continues the union will have fewer blue-collar workers to attract into the membership. Fewer members could mean less political power for the union.

Social Dilemmas

Labor unions support the principle of equal rights for all people regardless of race, sex, creed, or national origin. Furthermore, like employers, unions must comply with the provisions of the 1964 Civil Rights Act. In the West and Southwest, equal opportunity for Chicano migratory workers has been a rallying point for union organizing efforts. One

---

[15] "10 Million People without Jobs—Who They Are," *U.S. News and World Report,* March 15, 1982, pp. 71–74.

dilemma that unions face, along with management, is finding enough jobs for those who are capable and willing to work.

There is a growing pool of untrained workers who are ill-equipped for jobs in high-skill occupations. Thus, the union must push hard for improved and more skill training for ill-prepared workers. However, unless the government and management are willing to support such training there is little chance that high-skill occupations will be filled or that ill-equipped workers will find jobs.

Quality of Life

Improving members' overall quality of life is an important goal of the union movement. Organized unions like the United Auto Workers have supported the national health security act, the fight against poverty, housing development, care for the aged, and a guaranteed minimum standard of living for each person in society. The union believes that such programs, which improve the life of all citizens are the responsibility of business, government, and labor.

Membership

The union membership significantly increased from 1933 to 1947. In 1933 there were only 3 million union members, accounting for about 7 percent of the total labor force; by 1947 there were *15 million* union members representing about *31* percent of the work force. The number of union members continued to increase until 1956, declined until 1963, and started to grow slowly until it reached 20 million workers in 1980, or about 20 percent of the total labor force and 28 percent of nonagricultural employment.[16]

The 10 largest unions and their membership are presented in Exhibit 17–5. The three largest unions with membership of more than a million each, are the Teamsters', Auto Workers, and the United Food and Commercial Workers. Exhibit 17–6 shows the degree of union organization in selected industries. For example, at least 75 percent of the blue-

---

Exhibit 17–5

The 10 largest unions in the United States

Union	Affiliation	Members
Teamsters, Chauffeurs, Warehousemen and Helpers of America, International Brotherhood of.	Independent	1,888,895
Automobile, Aerospace and Agricultural Implement Workers of America, International Union, United (UAW)	Independent	1,358,354
United Food and Commercial Workers	AFL–CIO	1,076,000*
Steelworkers of America, United	AFL–CIO	964,000
State, County and Municipal Employees, American Federation of	AFL–CIO	889,000
Electrical Workers, International Brotherhood of (IBEW)	AFL–CIO	825,000
Machinists and Aerospace Workers, International Association of	AFL–CIO	664,000
Carpenters and Joiners of America, United Brotherhood of	AFL–CIO	619,000
Laborers' International Union of North America	AFL–CIO	627,406
Service Employees' International Union	AFL–CIO	575,000

*Retail Clerks and Meatcutters merged in 1979 to form this union.
Source: AFL–CIO Department of Research, 1980.

---

[16]"Workers and Their Unions," *AFL-CIO American Federationist*, March 1980, pp. 5–8.

Exhibit 17–6 _____

The degree of union organization in selected industries

75 percent and over

Transportation	Paper
Contract construction	Electrical machinery
Ordnance	Transportation equipment

50 percent to less than 75 percent

Primary metals	Manufacturing
Food and kindred products	Fabricated metals
Mining	Telephone and telegraph
Apparel	Stone, clay, and glass products
Tobacco manufacturers	Federal government
Petroleum	Rubber

25 percent to less than 50 percent

Printing, publishing	Machinery
Leather	Chemicals
Furniture	Lumber
Electric, gas utilities	

Less than 25 percent

Nonmanufacturing	State government
Textile mill products	Trade
Instruments	Agriculture and fishing
Service	Finance
Local government	

collar employees in transportation are unionized, whereas less than 25 percent of local government employees are unionized.

The organizational and recruiting efforts of unions have varied according to changes in economic, social, and political conditions. New membership drives are taking place in the public sector, which includes military personnel, police, and fire fighters; among professionals, including teachers, medical personnel, athletes, and lawyers; among employees in service industries; and among agricultural workers.

Unions are very interested in attracting public employees. A 1962 executive order by President John F. Kennedy, which was strengthened by amendment in 1969 and 1971, set up a form of collective bargaining for federal government employees. As a result, public employee unions have become the fastest growing labor groups in the country.

In the past, professors, teachers, nurses, doctors, athletes, and other professionals have considered themselves about union goals, procedures, and tactics.[17] Yet these groups have recently begun to recognize union gains and adopt union strategies.

The union attempted and succeeded in organizing the 20,000 faculty members of California's huge 19-campus state university system. The California State (Cal State) system was a fertile ground for the union and they moved in. Unlike the prestigious University of California System (e.g., Berkeley, UCLA), Cal State tevolved as a collection of teacher colleges in such cities as San Jose, Chico, and Fresno.[18] Money and a slight

---

[17]Leon C. Megginson, *Personnel and Human Resources Management*

[18]"California Says Yes to Unions," *Time*, February 15, 1982, pp. 55

inferiority complex have been a lingering problem at Cal State. Also about 38 percent of the Cal State faculty were hired on a part-time or year-to-year basis. The end result of these and other problems was a vote to unionize.

Another area that unions are attempting to unionize is agriculture. These organizing efforts are especially intense in the grape, lettuce, citrus, and cotton region of California.

In addition to these new organizing efforts in industries and professions, unions are also attempting to attract white-collar, female, and black employees. In the past, white-collar employees identified more with management practices and antiunion ideals and philosophy. But now, because of boredom and frustration in many white-collar jobs, some employees have considered unionizing.

The proportion of working women who are members of labor unions is declining. However, the number of female union members is increasing. The Coalition of Labor Union Women, an alliance of blue-collar working women, was formed in 1974 to end sex discrimination in wages and hiring. It also is attempting to elect more women as union officials. With more women officials, other women might believe that unions welcome them and need their abilities and skills.

Black employees are another fast-growing segment and a target of union organizers. In 1980, there were approximately 2.5 million black trade unionists. However, blacks have not been represented in union management in proportion to their membership. Furthermore, several unions have been found guilty of discriminating against blacks. Both blacks and women are demanding more say in union decisions and will certainly acquire additional power as unions attempt to increase their membership.

Resistance to Unions

Despite well-planned and systematic organizing efforts, about 75 percent of the total labor force, or 80 million workers, still are not unionized. One reason is that many people distrust unions. Some people believe that unions stand against individualism and free enterprise. They feel that people should get ahead on their own skills and merits. They resent the union's position in favor of collectivism and the use of seniority in personnel decisions involving promotions, layoffs, and pay increases.

Many professionals resist unions because they view them as dominated by blue-collar employees. Doctors, lawyers, and professors assume that they should not be associated with blue-collar tactics and behavior. This attitude is somewhat contrary to some of the actions of such professional associations as the American Medical Association. (The major difference between an association and a union is that the association believes payment is a matter between the individual performing the service and the customer.)

Some employees resist unions because they choose to identify with management values and practices. Management typically does not support union tactics. These nonmanagers may consider their aspirations to be a part of management when they resist union organizing efforts.

The reasons for resisting union organizing efforts may also be based on historical impressions and beliefs. Some well-known union leaders have been associated with illegal acts. One report found that about 450 union officers have been convicted of serious labor-related crimes from 1973 to 1980.[19] There has also been some union-incited violence

---

[19] "Union Corruption: Worse Than Ever," *U.S. News & World Report*, September 8, 1980, pp. 33

during organizing campaigns, although such violence may have received more publicity than management-provoked violence. An accurate check of unbiased history books finds that company "thugs" were just as plentiful as union "thugs."[20]

Summary

This chapter has introduced you to labor relations, an emotionally charged P/HRM activity. It has discussed the history of labor unions, why unions appeal to some employees, some major issues facing unions, the structure and management of unions, and major labor legislation.

To summarize some of the important points covered:

1. A union is a group of employees who have joined together to achieve present and future goals that deal with employee conditions.
2. The major laws affecting labor-management relations in the United States are the Wagner Act (1935), as amended by the Taft-Hartley Act (1947), and the Landrum-Griffin Act of 1959.
3. The second largest group of unionized employees is in the public sector. In the public sector, federal labor relations are regulated by executive orders issued by the president of the United States and the Federal Service Labor-Management Relations Statute.
4. The National Labor Relations Board (NLRB) administers the laws and regulations in the private and third sector (health care and universities).
5. The contact point for the membership is the local union. Through the local, members exercise their complaints. The union steward or committeeman is the member with "on-the-job-" contact. If a union member has a complaint that deals with the labor-management contract, the steward is contacted.
6. Unions appeal to some workers for various reasons. Some of the cited reasons are job security, strength in numbers, protection against unfair management action, and the communication link to management.
7. Some of the issues that unions must face today and in the future are unemployment, equal rights for all people, improving the quality of life, attracting additional members, and some hard-core resistance to unions.

Case

Tom Hardisty and Stan Goebel had lunch after their discussion about labor relations. After lunch, Stan said: "We could follow a strategy of fighting the union to keep it out. Or we could let nature take its course and live with them."

Tom replied, "That's what you think! I'm *not* running a unionized place. I'll sell out first! You need to figure out how to keep that #*&%$ union out of HMC!"

Stan then presented a communication program and proposed increases in pay and benefits as part of the "keep the union out" strategy. He costed out the proposed changes in pay and benefits and took these to Tom.

---

[20]Raskin, "From Sitdowns to 'Solidarity'," pp. 14–18

Questions for Review and Discussion

1. What is labor relations?
2. Why do some people join, while others resist joining unions?
3. Suppose that you were working on a mass-assembly production line at American Motors, who would be your union contact person if you had a complaint?
4. Why has union membership leveled off in recent years?
5. Do you have a negative image of unions? Why?
6. Explain the impact of the Wagner Act on the growth of trade unions.
7. When would a restricted shop be considered illegal?
8. Is the Landrum-Griffin Act necessary or simply a law to harass unions?
9. Can federal employees unionize? Explain
10. A person was heard to comment, "Unions do not have to exist. Look at IBM they have been doing fine without them." What is your opinion of this comment?

Glossary

AFL-CIO   A merged group of union members consisting of individuals for the American Federation of Labor and the Congress of Industrial Organizations. Merger occurred in 1955.

Agency Shop.   A situation in which all employees pay union dues whether or not they are union members.

American Federation of Labor (AFL).   A union group devoted to improving economic and working conditions for craft employees.

Business Representative.   The local union's main person. Is responsible for negotiating and administrating the labor agreement and for settling problems that may arise in connection with the contract.

Closed Shop.   A situation in which a new employee must be a union member when hired. Popular in the construction, maritime, and printing industries.

Congress of Industrial Organizations (CIO).   Formed by John L. Lewis, president of the United Mine Workers. It was formed to organize industrial and mass-production workers and was devoted to improving the economic and working conditions.

Craft Union.   A group of individuals who belong to one craft or closely related group of occupations (e.g., carpenters, bricklayers).

Guaranteed Annual Wages.   An agreement that guarantees regular employees a certain amount of money or hours of work. Its purpose is to provide some degree of economic security.

Labor Relations.   The continuous relationship between a defined group of employees (e.g., a union or association) and an employer.

Landrum-Griffin Act.   A labor law passed in 1959 that is referred to as the bill of rights of union members. It was designed to regulate and audit the internal affairs of unions.

National Labor Relations Board.   A government regulatory body that administers labor laws and regulations in the private and third sectors.

Open Shop.   A work situation in which neither a union is present nor is there a management effort to keep the union out.

Preferential Shop.   The union is recognized and union members are given preference in some areas. These preferences are in violation of the Taft-Hartley Act.

Restricted Shop.   A practice initiated by management to keep a union out without violating labor laws. A restricted shop is an attitude rather than a formal arrangement.

Right to Work Laws.   A law that specifies that two persons doing the same job must be paid the same wages, whether or not they are union members. Nineteen states have right to work laws.

Taft-Hartley Act.   A labor amendment of the Wagner Act, passed in 1947, that guaranteed employees bargaining rights and also specified unfair labor union practices that would not be permitted.

Union.   A group of employees who have joined together to achieve present and future goals that deal with employment conditions.

Union Shop.   A situation in which an employee is required to join a union after being hired.

Union Steward.   A union representative who works at the job site to solve disputes that arise in connection with the labor-management labor contract.

Wagner Act.   A labor law passed in 1935 that was designed to encourage the growth of trade unions and restrain management from interfering with the growth.

Yellow-Dog Contracts.   A contract (now illegal) that required that a person (e.g., job applicant) would not join or form a union.

Chapter Eighteen

Organizing and Collective Bargaining

Learning Objectives

After studying this chapter, you should be able to:
- Describe what is meant by the term *organizing a bargaining unit.*

- Discuss the role of the National Labor Relations Board (NLRB) in an organizing campaign.

- Define the meaning of collective bargaining.

- Explain the steps taken before a grievance reaches the point of going to arbitration.

- Cite some examples of union-management cooperation on job-related issues.

Chapter Outline

Case

Tom and Stan met to discuss the organizing situation and the communication program. Here is a part of the conversation.

Tom The communication program looks good, Stan. We'll have personal visits with the employees to talk about the union problem. The supervisors will run some of the meetings. You and I will split up and attend as many as we can. You'll train the supervisors on why the employees shouldn't join the union. But we can't afford to add these pay and benefit increases at this time.

Stan You know the union will exploit that. Our money situation, together with the lack of security because of layoffs, puts us at a big disadvantage.

Tom I know it. But it's your job to keep the union out.

In the next days and weeks, Stan did his best. Lots of meetings were held. He also mailed letters to the employee's homes.

Who will represent or speak for whom in the collective bargaining process? *Collective bargaining* is a process by which the representatives of the organization (the employer) meet and attempt to work out a contract with representatives of the workers (the employees).[1] The employees' representative can be a union or a group of unions.

Organizing efforts at Hardisty Manufacturing (HMC) are what Tom and Stan are concerned about. The efforts at HMC are typical of thousands of others that involve a face-off between the union and management. More about the details of organizing will be presented in this chapter.

In the private, public, and third sectors of society, employees have the right to self-organization in order to collectively bargain through a *unit* of their choosing. A unit of employees is a group of two or more employees who share common employment interests and conditions and may reasonably be grouped together.[2] In determining whether a proposed unit is appropriate, the following points are considered: (1) the history of collective bargaining in the organization, and (2) the desires of the employees in the proposed unit.

This chapter will first discuss how union organizing occurs in organizations and managements' response to the organizing campaign. Next, the collective bargaining process and the administration of the labor-management contract will be discussed. Finally, the current public image of labor unions and what needs to be done about it will be discussed.

The Bargaining Unit: The Workers' Choice

A union can exist only if workers prefer to be unionized. Someone at Hardisty Manufacturing, or perhaps a group of employees, has called a union representative to come to the plant and "talk union" with the workers. The union considers the employees at Hardisty a viable unit which the union will attempt to win over. The employees who make up the bargaining unit can be decided upon jointly by labor and management, or by one or the other, but it is an important determination. Often union and management will disagree as

---

[1]John A. Fossum, *Labor Relations* (Plano, Tex.: Business Publications, 1982), p. 210. Also see A. H. Raskin, "From Sitdowns to Solidarity: Passages in the Life of American Labor," *Across the Board,* December 1981, pp. 12–32.

[2]Eugene C. Hagburg and Marvin J. Levine, *Labor Relations* (St. Paul, Minn.: West Publishing, 1978), p. 265.

to which employees or groups of employees are eligible for inclusion in a particular proposed unit. Obviously, both union and management want as much bargaining power as possible. Management may examine the make up of the proposed unit to determine if required exclusions (e.g., supervisors, security guards) have been made. If the union's proposed unit is not suitable, management may challenge the proposal and present its own proposed unit. In general, the union will seek as large a unit as possible, while management will attempt to restrict a unit's size.

The final determination by labor sector of the appropriate bargaining unit is in the hands of the following agencies and/or individual(s).

Private sector (e.g., General Motors, Xerox, U.S. Steel)—The National Labor Relations Board (NLRB).

Railway and airline sector (e.g., Illinois Central, TWA)—The National Mediation Board.

Postal sector—The National Labor Relations Board (NLRB).

Federal sector (e.g., air traffic controllers)—assistant secretary of labor for labor-management relations.

Public sector (e.g., California Highway Patrol, New York Sanitation Department)—Varies in accordance with state and local statutes.

Exhibit 18–1 represents a concise model that summarizes the union organizing and representation election process. The exhibit only applies to sectors in which the NLRB has jurisdiction. As shown, the organizing process leads to an *authorization* card campaign. This is what Tom and Stan are suddenly confronted with. It is the union's way of finding out how many workers are for unionization. The card, when signed by an employee, authorizes the union to represent that employee during negotiations. At least 30 percent of the employees in the unit must sign before the NLRB will set up an actual election. If over 50 percent of the unit employees sign up, the union may directly demand to be recognized as the representative of the unit.

When a union believes that it represents a majority of the workers but is refused managerial recognition, it can petition the NLRB to hold a *representation* election.[3] If the union receives a majority of the votes cast in the representation election, the NLRB *certifies* it as the employees' bargaining representative and contract negotiations begin. If the union does not receive a majority (51 percent) of the votes cast, it cannot represent the employees, and no new representation election can be held for the unit for a period of one year.[4]

Occasionally the NLRB conducts *decertification* elections. Here, employees who are represented by a union vote to drop the union. If a majority of the bargaining unit votes against the union, it decertifies it as the representative.

Some examples of organizing campaigns illustrate the importance of efforts to organize workers (the unions) and resistance to organizing (the management):

- DuPont employees at 14 plants rejected representation by the United Steelworkers union after an eight-year drive by the union to organize the

[handwritten margin note: May do great campaign job, but make sure your "no" votes come out!! On can become cert]

---

[3]Stephen I. Scholssberg and Frederick E. Sherman, *Organizing and the Law* (Washington, D.C.: Bureau of National Affairs, 1971).

[4]John E. Abodeely, *The NLRB and the Appropriate Bargaining Unit* (Philadelphia: Industrial Research Unit, Wharton School of Finance and Commerce, University of Pennsylvania, 1971).

Exhibit 18–1 _____

Sequence of organizing events

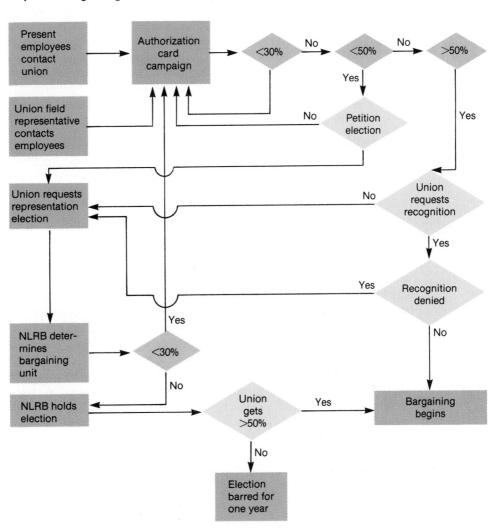

company. Six plants voted to retain their small independent locals while the others chose to remain nonunion. A total of about 11,500 workers are eligible to join the steelworkers union, and at least 93 percent turned out to vote in the representation election.[5]

- The Communication Workers recently won bargaining rights for 11,500 state-employed office workers in New Jersey.[6]

_____

[5]"Steelworkers Effort to Organize DuPont Is Turned back by Employees at 14 Plants," *The Wall Street Journal,* December 14, 1981, p. 8.

[6]"Unions on the Run," *U.S. News & World Report,* September 14, 1981, p. 61.

- The United Auto Workers have organized the Volkswagenwerk AG's Pennsylvania Rabbit factory.[7]
- J. P. Stevens & Co. denim plant in Rock Hill, South Carolina, by a vote of 433 to 299 decided not to be represented by the Amalgamated Clothing and Textile Workers Unions. This defeat occurred in the region which spawned the Hollywood movie about organizers, *Norma Rae*.[8]
- The American Federation of Teachers failed to organize 600 nurses at Fort Myers Memorial Hospital in Fort Myers, Florida, after the hospital hired consultants from Chicago; on the other hand, 200 nurses at Richmond Memorial Hospital in New York's Staten Island voted a union in.[9]

The union in the last few years have found it harder to attract new members. Unions win about 45 percent of the representation elections conducted by the NLRB. This is down from a 60 percent win rate in 1965[10]

Representation Campaigns: The Unions

The laws and executive orders covering labor relations require an employer to bargain with the representatives selected by the employees. The union's intention is to convince employees that being a member will lead to important outcomes—better wages, fairer treatment from management, job security, and better working conditions. Unions attempt to stress issues that are meaningful, current, and obvious to employees.

Do unions stress important issues? This depends on the foresight and skill of the union in determining the issues. A study of 33 representation elections found that 15 issues were raised by the union in at least half of these elections.[11] Exhibit 18–2 presents these issues and the number of elections in which each were stressed by the union. The union attempts to sell itself as a powerful force that can get the issues addressed in a way that is favorable to members. Which issues do you think the union will stress to the workers at the Hardisty plant?

Representation Campaigns: Management

Most organizations prepare some type of campaign to oppose the union move to organize workers. It is important to know that the NLRB forbids management actions to suppress the union and intimidate employees considering unionization. Neither management nor the union are permitted to engage in unfair labor practices.[12] For example, firing a union supporter or disciplining a worker that is involved in organizing efforts may be considered

---

[7]Robert L. Simison, "After Coaxing Japanese Car Makers to U.S., UAW Finds They Resist Union Organizing," *The Wall Street Journal,* August 26, 1980, p. 1.

[8]"Blue Jean Bombshell," *The Wall Street Journal,* September 1, 1981, p. 26.

[9]"Unions Move into the Office," *Business Week,* January 25, 1982, pp. 90–92.

[10]"Unions on the Run."

[11]Julius Getman, Stephen Goldberg, and Jeanne B. Herman, *Union Representation Elections: Law and Reality* (New York: Russell Sage Foundation, 1976), pp. 80–81.

[12]Edward F. Murphy, *Management vs. the Union* New York: Stein and Day, 1971), pp. 30–32.

Exhibit 18–2

Prevalent union campaign issues

Issue

Union will prevent unfairness, set up grievance procedure seniority system 27
Union will improve unsatisfactory wages 26
Union strength will provide employees with voice in wages, working conditions 26
Union, not outsider, bargains for what employees want 24
Union has obtained gains elsewhere 23
Union will improve unsatisfactory sick leave/insurance 21
Dues/initiation fees are reasonable 21
Union will improve unsatisfactory vacations/holidays 20
Union will improve unsatisfactory pensions 20
Employer promises good treatment may not continued without union 20
Employees choose union leaders 18
Employer will seek to persuade/frighten employees to vote against union 18
No strike without vote 18
Union will improve unsatisfactory working conditions 17
Employees have legal right to engage in union activity 17

Source: From *Union Representation Elections: Law and Reality,* by Julius G. Getman, Stephen B. Goldberg, and Jeanne B. Herman, © 1976 by Russell Sage Foundation. Reprinted by permission of the publisher.

---

unfair management labor practices. If these actions are not supported with facts and are related to organizing efforts, management can become involved in lawsuits.

Normally, the P/HRM department is responsible for presenting management's side of the story. Occasionally outside consultants and even experts trained in preventing organizing are used. One popular management approach is to emphasize that a union is run by outsiders. The outsider is pictured as being uninformed, uninterested, and unqualified.[13] Management attempts to communicate clearly and forcefully to the employees about the advantages of remaining nonunion. Speeches, question-and-answer sessions, bulletin board posters, personal letters to employees, and articles in the company newspaper are used to promote the nonunion advantages.

Exhibit 18–3 presents the issues covered by management in keeping employees non-

Case

Stan sat in his office and went over his program. So far, the efforts of Hardisty's management to squelch the union through communication had not been as effective as Stan had hoped. He kept hearing more and more talk about the union—in fact, his communication program seemed to have backfired in some instances, having forced many employees to think seriously about unionization for the first time. Stan himself was beginning to feel that the union was inevitable.

He got out a pencil and paper and began to write down all the reasons he could think of for remaining nonunionized. (One reason he neglected to write down, of course, was the lecture he'd get from Tom if the union ever succeeded at Hardisty.)

---

[13]James F. Rand, "Preventative Maintenance Techniques for Staying Union-Free," *Personnel Journal,* June 1980, pp. 497–99.

Exhibit 18–3 _____

Prevalent management campaign issues

Issues

Improvements not dependent on unionization	28
Wages good, equal to/better than under union contract	27
Financial costs of union dues outweigh gains	26
Union is outsider	26
Get facts before deciding, employer will provide facts and accept employee decision	25
If union wins, strike may follow	23
Loss of benefits may follow union win	22
Strikers will lose wages, lose more than gain	22
Unions not concerned with employee welfare	22
Strike may lead to loss of jobs	21
Employer has treated employees fairly/well	20
Employees should be certain to vote	18

Source: From *Union Representation Elections: Law and Reality,* by Julius G. Getman, Stephen B. Goldberg, and Jeanne B. Herman. © 1976 by Russell Sage Foundation. Reprinted by permission of the publisher.

union. The effectiveness of pointing to these kinds of issues depends to some extent on the thoroughness, clarity, and sincerity, of management's efforts.

The Role of the NLRB: Watching the Campaign

The NLRB is responsible for conducting the election and certifying the results of organizing efforts in the private and postal sectors. Often the NLRB is faced with preelection charges of one group against the other about unfair labor practices. The NLRB pays particular attention to the following areas:

Concerning the Employer

1. The NLRB makes sure that the questioning of employees about union membership is done in a fair and nonintimidating manner.
2. The NLRB checks to see if the union information provided to employees is truthful.
3. The NLRB does not allow any final presentations within 24 hours preceding the election.

Concerning the Union

1. The NLRB makes sure that no threats or intimidation are used to gain votes.
2. The NLRB guards the employees against the union's promises of special treatment for votes if the union wins.
3. No final presentations are allowed within 24 hours preceding the election.

The NLRB is a watchdog. Unfair labor practices charges can be filed by an employee, an employer, the union, or any person.[14] A formal charge requires the NLRB to officially review the claim. It is the NLRB in the private and postal sectors that guards

_____

[14]Louis Jackson and Robert Lewis, *Winning NLRB Elections* (New York: Practicing Law Institute, 1972).

against and prevents any interference in the lawful procedures to select the bargaining representative. If the interference is considered significant, an election can be set aside and rerun.

If a union legally wins an organizing election it is recognized as the bargaining representative of a unit. The NLRB requires that both the elected union and management must bargain in good faith. This requirement is spelled out in the Taft-Hartley Act as follows:

> For the purposes of this section, to bargain collectively is the performance of the mutual obligation of the employer and representative of the employees to meet at reasonable times and confer in good faith with respect to wages, hours, and other terms and conditions of employment, or the negotiation of an agreement, or any question arising thereunder, and the execution of a written contract incorporating any agreement reached if requested by either party, but such obligation does not compel either party to agree to a proposal or require the making of a concession.

If either party does not bargain in good faith, unfair labor practices can be charged. The costs, publicity, and hostility associated with not bargaining in good faith are usually too significant to disregard. Of course, good faith doesn't mean that the union or management must agree with each other about issues. This is the essence of collective bargaining—disagreement and negotiation.

Collective Bargaining

Make sure is for > 1 yr (takes 6 mos to make!) Bring in competent labor attorney.

As stated at the beginning of the chapter *collective bargaining* is a process by which the representatives of the organization meet and attempt to work out a contract with the employees' representative—the union. Collective means only that representatives are attempting to negotiate an agreement. Bargaining is the process of cajoling, debating, discussing, and threatening to bring about a favorable agreement for those being represented.

The collective bargaining process and the final agreement reached are influenced by many variables.[15] Exhibit 18–4 graphically identifies some of the variables influencing the union and management representatives. For example, the state of the economy affects collective bargaining. In a tight economy, a union push for higher wages is less likely to succeed, because it would be inflationary. The firm's representative must also consider whether the company can pay an increased wage based on current and expected economic conditions. In 1981 American Airlines, TRW, and Ford have all asked and received union agreement to give back some of the wages and fringe benefits won at the bargaining table.[16] The poor economy has been such a factor that plant after plant has been closed down because of high-labor costs. For example, employees at Ford's Sheffield, Alabama, plant had to accept a 50 percent wage and benefit cut or face a closed plant.[17]

Now, hourly workers at other car companies, as well as steelworkers, grocery clerks, and others are giving up wages and benefits to help ailing companies—and to save their

---

[15]George E. Constantino, Jr., "The Negotiator in Collective Bargaining," *Personnel Journal*, August 1975, pp. 445–47.

[16]Mark N. Doclosh, "Companies Increasingly Ask Labor to Give back Past Contract Gains," *The Wall Street Journal*, November 27, 1981, p. 1.

[17]"A Dilemma in Sheffield," *Newsweek*, December 7, 1981, p. 77.

Exhibit 18–4 _____

The forces influencing the bargaining process

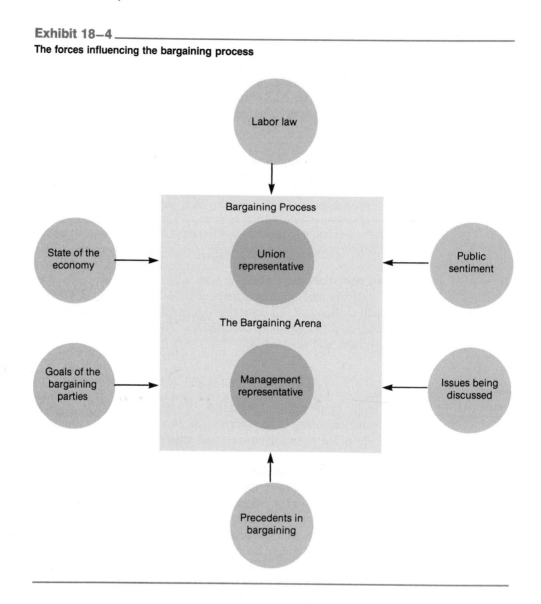

jobs. Workers at Chrysler have been doing it since 1981. Chrysler's workers were asked
to concede $1.07 billion in scheduled pay increases, cost-of-living payments and benefits.
By the time they voted on the last $622 of the concessions, Chrysler's hourly work force
had dropped to about 50,000 from about 70,000 between 1981 and 1982.[18]

In 1982, a 2½-year package of concessions was agreed to by the United Auto Workers and Ford. Under the new agreement workers gave up the equivalent of two weeks'
paid time off a year and the annual 3 percent raises. Inflation-related raises are to be
deferred for 18 months. In return, Ford agreed to expand layoff benefits, to make com-

[18]Dale D. Buss, "Auto Workers Hit Hard by Giveups, Signaling Tough Times for Labor," _The Wall Street
Journal_, January 20, 1982, p. 25.

Case

Stan wanted to know more about the union. The vote had still not been taken, but he knew from talk around the plant that the union already had an edge. He called his researchers together to see if they could find out a little about the union's past history—particularly its success or failure at the bargaining table. Jim Rogers, Stan's assistant, came to Stan with the information.

Jim: It looks pretty grim for our side, Stan, if the union wins the election. They've got a very successful team of negotiators, starting with the local union president. They've won four out of six of their negotiations so far.

Stan: And with our money problems, we can't offer our people as much as the union can. What's this local president like?

Jim: He's a young guy, 35 years old; college man. His strategy in the past has been to let management do the talking first, then he comes up with points for the union's side. And he's always armed with a lot of statistics and facts to back him up.

Stan: Well, we know his main argument will center around our refusal to increase pay and the threat of layoffs due to our financial situation.

Jim: He's got us there.

Two hours later, it was announced that Hardisty would be laying off 20 percent of its workers. Stan ran into Tom's office.

Stan: Tom, we can't lay these people off now, right in the middle of the union's campaign! We're practically handing ourselves over to the union if we do this!

Tom: Pipe down, Stan. It's your job to beat the union, but I've got to keep our heads above water, too.

Stan: I think this is the wrong move to make, Tom.

Tom: Too late now. . . it's done. Now what has your department found out about this union?

---

mitments on providing job security and on how future plant closing will be handled, and to have a profit-sharing plan. The job-security clause in this agreement has been called the wave of the future, a revolutionary step in labor-management relations.[19]

Each of the forces shown in Exhibit 18–4 involve a union and a management response. Each side of the collective bargaining table will be influenced by such factors as the economy and the environment. Unions and management are now painfully aware of how inflation, foreign competition, and the mood of a society can affect the issues being discussed at the bargaining table.

The actual process of collective bargaining involves a number of steps, such as: (1) prenegotiation; (2) selecting negotiators; (3) developing a bargaining strategy; (4) using the best tactics; and (5) reaching a formal contractual agreement.

Prenegotiation

In collective bargaining, both sides attempt to receive concessions that will help them achieve their objectives. As soon as a contract is signed by union and management, both parties begin preparing for the next collective bargaining session. Thus, the importance of careful prenegotiation preparation cannot be overemphasized.

---

[19]Robert L. Simison, "UAW Workers at Ford Endorse Concession Pact," *The Wall Street Journal*, March 1, 1982, p. 3; and Hobart Rowen, "Auto Workers, Ford Have Taken a Gutsy Step," *Houston Chronicle*, February 22, 1982, p. 6.

Data of all types are maintained by both unions and management. These data are collected over the course of the contract on the grievances filed, day-to-day complaints, contract interpretation problems, and agreements reached between the union and management in other companies. They also review how the union's agreements with other companies were reached. That is, has the union become more militant or less aggressive in recent union-management bargaining sessions? It is also important to check the background of the union negotiators. This will allow management to interpret the style and personality of the negotiators.

In the prenegotiation step, both parties typically prepare economic data and reports that can be used to help support arguments or issues raised. Particularly valuable to negotiators are Bureau of Labor Statistics' surveys on wage rates for various occupations, industries, and labor markets. In addition, cost-of-living trends and profit margins for the industry are carefully worked on and prepared.

The Negotiators

On the management side of the bargaining table may be any one of a number of people, including the P/HRM director, the executive vice president, or the company lawyer. Or management may field a team of negotiators, so that all forms of expertise are present. Typically, the team consists of a P/HRM expert, a lawyer, a manager or vice president with knowledge of the entire business organization, and an economist.

The union also uses a team approach. The union team generally consists of business agents, shop stewards, the local union president, and when the negotiation is very important, representatives from national union headquarters. When industrywide bargaining is taking place, as in the automobile industry, the chief negotiator is a representative from the national union.

The negotiating teams (union and management) meet independently before the actual bargaining sessions and plan the best strategy to use. This preparation identifies the chief spokesperson and the roles of each member of the team.

Mapping the Strategy

Because the labor agreement must be used for a long period of time, it is important to develop a winning strategy and tactics. The strategy is considered to be the plan and policies that will be pursued at the bargaining table. Tactics are the specific actions taken in the bargaining sessions. It is important to spell out the strategy and tactics because bargaining is a give-and-take process with the characteristics of a poker game, a political campaign, or a heated debate.[20]

An important issue in mapping out a strategy involves the maximum concessions that will be granted. By shifting a position during the bargaining, the other side may build up expectations that are difficult to change. By granting too much, one side may be viewed as weak. How far management or the union will go before it risks a work stoppage or lockout is considered before the sessions begin and are a part of the strategic plan.

Another part of management's strategic plan is to develop the total cost profile of the

[20]Ross Stagner and Hjalmar Rosen, *Psychology in Union-Management Relations* (Belmont, Calif.: Wadsworth, 1965); and Jeffrey Z. Rubin and Bert R. Brown, *The Social Psychology of Bargaining and Negotiation* (New York: Academic Press, 1975).

maximum concession package. That is, what will these concessions cost the company today and in the future? Will P/HRM policies or production procedures have to be changed if these concessions are granted? This form of future planning helps management determine how willing it is to take a strike. Planning for a strike is certainly difficult, but the issue should be included in strategy planning.

Tactics

Tactics are calculated actions used by both parties. Occasionally, tactics are used to mislead the other party. But they are also used to secure an agreement that is favorable to either management or the unions.

General Electric used a tactic called Boulwarism (names after the person who developed it). GE's management worked out an offer that was final and presented it to the union. No matter how heated or long negotiations became, the offer was final. The National Labor Relations Board ruled that the Boulware tactic was a failure to bargain in good faith.[21] GE appealed this decision and won in the lower courts. However, The Supreme Court informed GE that it could not give one best offer but had to start lower in order to permit the union to obtain benefits and save face with the membership.

A commonly used tactic of the union is to attempt to have management reach agreement "clause by clause." Each clause is agreed on before the next clause is discussed. This tactic focuses on separate points instead of the total package and it usually resisted by management.

Another tactic used by both sides is the attempt to wear down the other side. Long marathon sessions are used to tire out the other party. This tactic relies on fatigue to weaken the other side.

The highly skilled and effective negotiator on either side must be in complete control of his or her emotions and be somewhat of an actor. There are times when a "performance" is given to make an effective point. In order to give these performances, the person must be in control of the situation. Threats, abusive language, and tirades are considered weak tactics by both parties. Logical presentations, good manners, and calmness seem to be more effective than threatening tactics.

The Contract

Want for several (3) years for stability + save $

The union-management contract designates the formal terms of agreement. The average contract covers two or three years and varies from a few typewritten pages to more than a hundred pages, depending on the issues covered, the size of the organization, and the union.

The labor contract is divided into sections and appendexes. The sections that can be and are covered in some labor agreements are shown in Exhibit 18–5. The exhibit shows that a major part of the contract is concerned with such employment issues as wages, hours, fringe benefits, and overtime.

In general, the contract spells out the authority and responsibility of both union and management. Management rights appear in one of two forms. The first involves a statement that the control and operation of the business is the right of management except in

---

[21]Herbert R. Northrup, *Boulwarism* (Ann Arbor; Mich.: Bureau of Industrial Relations, University of Michigan, 1964).

Exhibit 18–5 _____

Content of a labor agreement

Purpose and intent of the parties	Vacations
Scope of the agreement	Seniority
Management	Safety and health
Responsibilities of the parties	Military service
Union membership and checkoff	Severance allowance
Adjustment of grievance	Savings and vacation plan
Arbitration	Supplemental unemployment benefits program
Suspension and discharge cases	S.U.B. and insurance grievances
Rates of pay	Prior agreements
Hours of work	Termination date
Overtime—Holidays	Appendices

Source: Adapted from United States Steel Corporation and the United Steelworkers Union, "Labor Agreement."

cases specified in the contract. The second is a list of all management activities that are not subject to sharing with the union. Included are such topics as planning and scheduling production, purchasing equipment, and making final hiring decisions.

The union rights spelled out in the contract involve such issues as the role the union will play in laying off members or in such areas as promotion and transfer. The union stresses seniority as a means of reducing the tendency for discrimination and favoritism in P/HRM decision making.

Administering the Contract

Day-to-day compliance with contract provisions are an important responsibility of the first-line manager, who works closely with union members. As the representative of management, the first-line manager must discipline workers, handle grievances, and prepare for such actions as strikes.

Discipline

Most contracts agree that management in a unionized firm has a right to discipline workers, providing all discipline follows legal due process.[22] If an employee or union challenges a disciplinary action, the burden of proof rests on the company. Often management will lose a case that is arbitrated (settled by an impartial third party) because improper disciplinary procedures have been followed:

Many union-management contracts specify the types of discipline and the offenses for which corrective action will be taken. Some of the infractions that are typically spelled out are:

- *Incompetence.*   Failure to perform the assigned job.
- *Misconduct.*   Insubordination, dishonesty, or violating a rule such as smoking in a restricted area.

_____
[22]"Understanding the Contract," *Personnel Journal*, August 1981, p. 612.

- *Violations of the contract.* Initiating a strike when there is no strike clause, for example.

The contract should list penalities for such infractions.[23] Inconsistent application of discipline is sometimes a problem as the discussion in Chapter 16 illustrated.

Grievances

A *grievance* is a complaint about a job that creates dissatisfaction or discomfort, whether it is valid or not. The complaint may be made by an individual or by the union.[24] It is important to note that, although the validity of the grievance may be questionable, it should be handled correctly. Even if an employee files an official grievance that seems absolutely without support, the manager should handle it according to formal contractual provisions.

Grievance procedures are usually followed in unionized companies, but they are important channels of communication in unionized and nonunionized organizations alike. In the unionized organization, the contract contains a clause covering the steps to be followed and how the grievance will be handled. The number of steps varies from contract to contract. But a labor union is not essential for establishing a procedure.

Exhibit 18–6 illustrates a four-step grievance procedure used in a unionized company.[25]

1. The employee meets with the supervisor and the union steward and presents the grievance. Most grievances are settled at this point.
2. If the grievance is not settled at step 1, there is a conference between middle management and union officials (a business agent or union committee).
3. At this point, a top-management representative and top-union officials (for example, the union president) attempt to settle the grievance.
4. Both parties (union and management) turn the grievance over to an arbitrator who makes a decision. Arbitration is usually handled by a mutually agreed-upon single individual or a panel of an odd number.

Although most grievances are handled at step 1, there are a number of important principles for managers to follow. They should (1) take every grievance seriously; (2) work with the union representative; (3) gather all information available on the grievance; (4) after weighing all the facts, provide an answer to the employee voicing the grievance; and (5) after the grievance is settled, attempt to move on to other matters.

Even though the grievance procedure shown in Exhibit 18–6 is used typically in large unionized firms (eg., AT&T, Procter & Gamble, Republic Steel), such a procedure is also needed in nonunion firms. Unfortunately, many nonunion firms do not establish grievance procedures. The lack of a grievance procedure causes frustration, antagonism, and anxiety among many employees. These feelings and attitudes are not healthy for good employee-management relations. They also can spark an interest to organize a formal bargaining representative.

---

[23]Richard Arvey and John M. Ivancevich, "Punishment in Organizations: A Review, Propositions, and Research Suggestions," *Academy of Management Review,* January 1980, pp. 123–32.

[24]Maurice S. Trotta, *Handling Grievances: A Guide for Labor and Management* (Washington, D.C.: Bureau of National Affairs, 1976), pp. 141–42.

[25]Thomas F. Gideon and Richard B. Peterson, "A Comparison of Alternate Grievance Procedures," *Employee Relations Law Journal,* Autumn 1979, pp. 222–33.

Exhibit 18–6 _____

A grievance procedure: A unionized situation

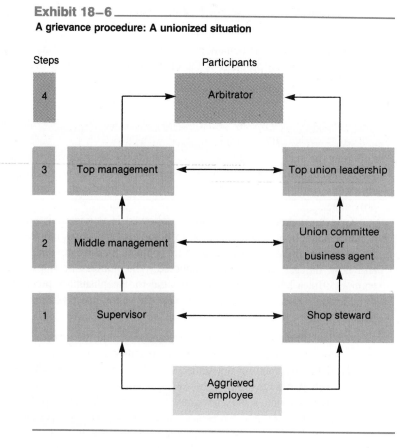

Arbitration

The grievance procedure does not always result in an acceptable solution. When a deadlock occurs, most contracts (about 96 percent) call for arbitration. *Arbitration* is a quasi-judicial process in which the parties agree to submit an unresolvable dispute to a neutral third party for binding settlement. Both parties submit their positions, and the arbitrator makes a decision.

The contract typically specifies how a dispute goes to arbitration. Normally, the case would have gone through the previous three steps in the grievance procedure (Exhibit 18–6). At the last step, for instance, if management denies the grievance or fails to modify its position sufficiently to satisfy the union, the union can request arbitration.

Procedures for selection of an arbitrator are usually written into the contract. The most typical arrangement is to use a single impartial arbitrator who hears the evidence and renders an award, or to have a tripartite board consisting of a management and a union representative and an impartial chairperson.

The arbitrators generally come from three major sources. The first group consists of attorneys who are full-time arbitrators. The second group is made up of academics who are experts in labor law, personnel/human resources management, and labor economics. The third group includes respected members of the community such as teachers and ministers.

The *award* is the decision reached by the arbitrator. It conveys the decision, a summary of the evidence, and the rationale for the decision. In preparing the award, the arbitrator must examine a number of issues:

1. Can the dispute be arbitrated?
2. Did the grievance allege an actual violation of the contract?
3. Were the grievance procedures followed in a timely manner?

If these criteria are met, the arbitrator then investigates the dispute.

The arbitrator works hard to ensure that the award draws from the framework and intent of the contract. Most contracts prohibit arbitrators from adding to or subtracting from the intent of the contract. The arbitrator must clearly show how the award fits the meaning of the contract.

Arbitration is criticized because of time delays and costs. An AFL-CIO publication reported that the average time for the filing of a grievance through the submission of an arbitration award was 223 days.[26] The time delays are presented in Exhibit 18–7.

The costs of arbitration may cause problems, especially for some unions. Although management and the union usually share equally the cost of arbitration, a financially poor union is sometimes reluctant to become involved in arbitration. This reluctance can detract from the members' respect and image of the union.

In order to expedite cases and maintain some cost control, grievants in the steel industry have the option of using a new procedure. Under this procedure, panels have been created from which arbitrators are designated to handle disputes on a rotating basis. Arbitration hearings must be held within 10 days of the appeal, and the award must be made within 48 hours after the hearing. The cases are presented by local management and union representatives rather than the "pros" or "big shots" from the union and management. Thus, instead of paying the arbitrator from $200 to $400 per day that he or she works on the case, the fee is $25 tp $75 from each party and only for the hearing day.

Arbitration in Professional Sports • Salary arbitration is a new game being played in professional baseball. Tal Smith has represented management very well in salary arbitration rulings. He believes that baseball has an inflated salary structure. Arbitration is the last resort when a player and a team cannot reach agreement on a contract.[27] Both sides present salary figures to an independent arbitrator who decides on one.

Exhibit 18–7 —————————————————————————

Arbitration time delays

	Days
Grievance date to request for panel	68
Between request for panel and panel sent out	6
Panel sent out to appointment of arbitrator	45
Appointment of arbitrator to hearing date	61
Hearing date to arbitrator award	43
Total: Grievance date to award	223

Source: John Zalusky, "Arbitration: Updating a Vital Process," *AFL-CIO American Federationist,* 83 (November 1976), p. 6.

---

[26] John Zalusky, "Arbitration: Updating a Vital Process, *American Federationist,* November 1976, p. 6.
[27] Thomas Bonk, "Smith's Job Selection Was Arbitrary Decision," *Houston Post,* March 7, 1982, p. 3C.

In the three years prior to 1982, the players won a majority of the cases. But that was before Tal Smith joined the management team. Smith represented four teams in eight arbitration hearings and won seven of them, saving the clubs a combined $1,090,000.

Overall, clubs won 14 of the 22 cases submitted to arbitration in 1982. The arbitration scorecard for 1982 is presented in Exhibit 18–8. Tal Smith is ready to provide management with his services in the years ahead as more baseball players take their salary demands to arbitration.

Strikes

A *strike* is an effort to withhold employee services so that the employer will make greater concessions at the bargaining table. The strike, or a potential strike, is a major bargaining weapon used by the union. But before a union strikes, it needs to consider the legality of striking, the members' willingness to endure the hardships of a long strike, and the employer's ability to operate the organization without union members. The greater the em-

---

Exhibit 18–8 _____

Arbitration scorecard

Decided in player's favor (8)

Player	Team	Team's figure	Player's figure	Amount player won
Larry Bradford..................................	Braves	$90,000	$130,000	$40,000
Roger Erickson...............................	Twins	105,000	160,000	55,000
Steve Trout....................................	White Sox	175,000	250,000	75,000
Mario Soto.....................................	Reds	200,000	295,000	95,000
Julio Cruz	Mariners	200,000	375,000	175,000
Willie Aikens*	Royals	275,000	375,000	100,000
Rickey Henderson	A's	350,000	535,000	185,000
Tom Hume	Reds	375,000	595,000	220,000
Total spread				945,000
Av. per case				118,125

Decided in favor of team (14)

Player	Team	Team's figure	Player's figure	Amount team won
Bobby Brown*.................................	Yankees	$90,000	$175,000	$85,000
Frank Pastore.................................	Reds	95,000	175,000	80,000
Jamie Quirk*..................................	Royals	115,000	180,000	65,000
Bob Molinaro..................................	White Sox	120,000	165,000	45,000
Don Aase	Angels	215,000	300,000	85,000
Bill Almon	White Sox	220,000	340,000	120,000
Dave Revering*	Yankees	250,000	325,000	75,000
Dave Stelb	Blue Jays	250,000	325,000	75,000
Dan Quisenberry*...........................	Royals	300,000	480,000	180,000
Ron Davis*	Yankees	300,000	575,000	275,000
Greg Minton	Giants	343,000	495,000	152,000
Bump Wills	Rangers	355,000	450,000	95,000
Carney Lansford*............................	Red Sox	440,000	650,000	210,000
Jack Morris*	Tigers	450,000	650,000	200,000
Total spread				1,742,000
Avg. per case				124,429

*Cases in which Tal Smith was involved
Courtesy of the Houston Post.

ployer's ability to operate the organization, the less chance the union will have of gaining the demands it makes.

There are a number of different types of strikes, including:

- *Economic strike.* Based on a demand for better wages or fringe benefits than the employer wants to provide.
- *Jurisdictional strike.* Exists when two unions argue over who has the right to perform a job. For example, bricklayers and ironworkers may both want to install steel rods in doorways. The rods are made a part of the brickwork and are needed to hold up heavy steel doors. If either group strikes to force the employer to grant the work to its members, a jurisdictional strike occurs. This type of strike is illegal under the Taft-Hartley Act.
- *Wildcat strike.* An unapproved strike that may suddenly occur because one union subgroup has not been satisfied by a grievance decision or by some managerial action. The union leaders do not sanction this type of strike.
- *Sitdown strike.* When employees strike but remain in the plant. Such strikes are illegal because they are an invasion of private property.

When any strike occurs, management must be able to function during the work stoppage, and the company property must be protected from strike sabotage.

Management generally views strikes with a mixture of fear and loathing. Even the threat of a strike can force concessions from management at the bargaining table, and any strike usually leaves an aftertaste that poisons labor relations for years. There does not appear to be a downward trend in the number of strikes being called in the United States. The total amount of working time lost has been low from 1974 to 1980. In 1980, 33,000 labor days (a workday) were lost to strikes, versus 48,000 labor days in 1974.[28] Strikes over noneconomic issues have been drastically reduced. In 1976 there were 1,950 strikes during the course of contracts over working conditions and union jurisdiction. In 1980 there were just 521 of these strikes.

The decline in strikes doesn't mean that the strike is not a powerful weapon available to unions. The strike will still be used even in rough economic times. Unions, however, because of economics, workers' desires, and the influx of automation (eg., robots), is less willing and able to mount strikes.[29] The government has also reduced the power of the strike weapon with the Omnibus Budget Reconciliation Act of 1981. Effective October 1, 1981, striking workers and their families were no longer eligible for food stamps.

Strikes in the public sector or by government emplpyees are troublesome for unions, management, and the government. Because of the essential nature of the work performed, the government is opposed to public employee strikes. The issue of "government sovereignty" is raised to argue against such strikes. Of course, the public employee unions like the Professional Air Traffic Controllers (PATCO) argue against this claim of the government.[30] The union argues that taking away the strike weapon reduces public employees unions to a second-class type of power.

In the summer of 1981, 12,000 air traffic controllers went on strike. President Reagan cited that the strike violated the oath taken by the controllers not to strike. The typical

---

[28]Herbert E. Meyer, "The Decline of Strikes," *Fortune,* November 2, 1981, pp. 66–70.

[29]"Hospital Staff Finds Strike Ineffective," *Dallas Morning News,* May 16, 1981, p. 21.

[30]Peter Gall and John Hoerr, "How Labor Loses from the PATCO Strike," *Business Week,* August 24, 1981, p. 35.

and usually followed practice by which a strike is "glossed over" by public employees was replaced by the president's decision to fire every striking air traffic controller. The action by President Reagan to hold public employees to the "no strike" provisions of the contract has served notice on other unionized employees in the U.S. Postal Service and in the state and local governments.[31]

If and when a union mounts a strike they usually resort to *picketing* procedures. The union hopes to shut down the company during a strike, so it may place members at plant entrances to advertise the dispute and discourage persons from entering or leaving the buildings. Peaceful persuasion through the formation of a picket line is legal, but violence is not. Picketing may also take place, without a strike, to publicize union viewpoints about an employer.

Another type of union pressure is the *boycott*. In a primary boycott, union members do not patronize the boycotted firm. This type of boycott is legal. A secondary boycott occurs when a supplier of a boycotted firm is threatened with a union strike unless it stops doing business with the boycotted company. This type of boycott is generally illegal under the Taft-Hartley Act. A special type of boycott is the *hot cargo agreement*. Under this agreement, the employer permits union members to avoid working with materials that come from employers who have been struck by a union. This type of boycott is illegal according to the Labor-Management Disclosure Act except in the construction and clothing industries.

Management's response to these union pressures may be to continue operations with a skeleton crew of managerial personnel, to shut down the plant, or to lock the employees out. The *lockout* is an effort to force the union to stop harassing the employer or to accept the conditions set by management. Lockouts are also used to prevent union work slowdowns, damage to property, or violence related to a labor dispute. Many states allow locked-out employees to draw unemployment benefits, thereby weakening the lockout. In practice the lockout is more of a threat than a widely practiced weapon of management.

Union-Management Cooperation

American labor leaders have had little use for well-intentioned schemes to make them partners with management. Thomas R. Donahue, secretary-treasurer of the AFL-CIO, states that cooperative union-management efforts have been, "the worst kind of nonsense, perpetrated either by pied pipers who promised no supervisors and no assembly lines, or romantic academics exposing European-style codetermination." Either way, says Donahue, "they set everyone's teeth on edge."[32]

Another skeptic of union-management cooperation is Ed Sadlowski. He was the youngest district director of the United Steelworkers union. In 1976, at 37 years old, he ran for the national union presidency and lost. Sadlowski made a lot of waves even within the labor union movement because he was aggressive, young, brash, and committed to

---

[31]Ibid.

[32]Charles G. Burck, "What's in It for the Unions?" *Fortune,* August 24, 1981, pp. 88–91. Also see David Lewin, "Collective Bargaining and the Quality of Work Life," *Organizational Dynamics,* Autumn 1981, pp. 37–53.

an adversary stance against management.[33] A few of the things that Sadlowski had to say were:

> There's economic blackmail today. When the Environmental Protection Agency gets on their butt about polluting the valleys and streams and air, the head of U.S. Steel says: We have to leave. Labor has been buffaloed on this score. Now they're gettin' wise. You can make steel and have clean air and still make a profit. . . . I don't expect the head of General Motors or U.S. Steel to sit down at the table and by virtue of my having supper with him give me anything I want. I'm going to demand it and take it. The sooner the laboring class—and it is a class question—realizes it, the better off they'll be.[34]

Despite the strong feelings of Donahue and Sadlowski, there is a groundswell movement in the United States toward more labor-management corporation. Unions are becoming almost as interested as management in finding innovative efforts to give more say about how they work—programs like quality circles and quality-of-work life systems that solicit ideas are become more popular.[35] Union leaders who once worried about being "management's lackeys" have been surprised to find that cooperating with management has raised their standing with members.

The Unions Take the Initiative

The United Auto Workers, the United Steelworkers of America, the Communicators Workers of America, the International Brotherhood of Electrical Workers, and the Telecommunications International Union—together representing about a fifth of the nation's organized workers—have signed national labor agreements committing themselves to plans for a better employee work life. Unions have convinced managers that many workers want to take their jobs seriously and want to be treated fairly.

Adverse economic times and foreign competition have helped the unions see that changes in relations with management were necessary. Unionized labor's share of the total work force has been declining and many of its leaders believe that labor-management cooperation might be able to reverse the decline.

During the early 1970s, the major steel companies and the United Steelworkers agreed upon a bold plan to fight the growing threat of imported steel. Joint labor-management committees sat down together to analyze and offer solutions to the problem. Lloyd McBride, now the United Steelworker's president (he defeated Ed Sadlowski) remembers the first of these meetings.

"The management guys came in and said, "Well, we want to talk about the productivity of this operation. Down in this department we could eliminate this job." The union sat there and then one representative said, 'Well that would create some problems for us. But the problems would not be so great if we could get rid of your brother-in-law down

---

[33]"Ed Sadlowski," in Studs Terkel, *American Dreams Lost & Found* (New York: Ballatine Books, 1980), pp. 260–67.

[34]Ibid., pp. 264–65.

[35]"1982 Bargaining Schedule: Labor Seeks Less," *Business Week,* December 21, 1981.

there who's not doing much. . . .' '' Confrontation, war, and adversal relations were hard to change, according to McBride. The early 1970s effort came to a halt because both parties were so locked in their previous styles of fighting against each other.[36]

At about the same time, the United Auto Workers were attempting to work with General Motors (GM) to solve productivity problems. GM had become more concerned about the lagging productivity per worker. They were aware that the traditional solutions from the top down were only somewhat successful when workers came in late or failed to report to work at all. Irving Bluestone, then director of the UAW's GM department, saw an opportunity to advance his belief that unions could cooperate with management to advance the workers' responsibilities and stature. He pushed his idea hard and in the 1973 contract negotiations, GM and the UAW signed the first national quality-of-work life agreement in the United States.

The agreement has become the model of labor-management cooperation.[37] Nowhere in it did the word ''productivity'' appear. Management would seek its rewards from work improvements in higher product quality and lower absenteeism. All the quality-of-work life programs would be strictly voluntary, and none would be used unilaterally to raise production rates or reduce human resource requirements. Labor-management work improvement committees that have been working at GM have given workers more job control and opened up communications between workers and supervisors.

Many union leaders initially feared that labor-management cooperation would undermine the collective bargaining process. After all, nothing could be further from the spirit of ''us versus them'' than mutually identifying and solving problems. Some unionists worried that management would use cooperative programs such as quality-of-work life improvements to chip away at benefits won through bargaining.

In practice, the lines between cooperation and conflict have been relatively clear.[38] Few managers or labor leaders have tried to abuse the cooperation problem-solving activities. GM and Ford are pressing for UAW wage concessions and the UAW is pushing them for more wages, more job security, and more benefits.

Cooperative efforts in autos and steel were unquestionably spurred by the crises those industries have faced. However, cooperation is also occurring in the communications industry. The Communications Workers of America and AT&T have worked out a quality-of-work life improvement program. Union members were frustrated by job pressures.[39] AT&T was pushing job performance and looking at workers closely. They even called absent workers at home to determine if they were sick and they monitored (listened to) operators on the job to see if they were efficient. The new agreement has resulted in eliminating these and other similar programs. The union is now a limited partner working on methods to improve productivity.

Opinions are still divided about whether labor-management cooperation is a threat or an aid to new organizing efforts. In some nonunion situations, management has used it to resolve problems that might have brought in a union. Yet some labor leaders believe that it is a plus for organizing efforts. Some people view the union as aggressive, hostile, and disruptive. The Telecommunications International Union has emphasized the desire to

[36]Burck, ''What's in It for the Unions?'', p. 89.

[37]Ibid.

[38]Robert E. Steiner, ''The Labor Management Cooperation Act,'' *Personnel Journal,* May 1981, pp. 344–45.

[39]Burck, ''What's in It for the Unions?''

cooperate with management. They have won 13 representative elections in Pacific Telephone Co. because workers consider them to be fair, professional, and concerned.[40]

Even in 1982, it was rare to find a union leader who would agree publically to union-management cooperation committees and forums. However, given the current economic and competitive climate, unionists—such as managers—cannot afford to overlook the possibility of more labor-management cooperation. The long-run survival of many managements and unions may depend somewhat on the degree of cooperation achieved.

The Rights of Employees in Nonunionized Situations

The rights of union members are spelled out in labor contracts. However, most employees, about 80 percent, do not belong to unions. Do these nonunionized members have working conditions, privacy, wage, grievance, and other rights?[41] There has been an emphasis among nonunionized members on their "rights of employment." There is a stead-

P/HRM Manager Close-Up

James H. Pou
University Computing
Company

Biography

James H. Pou is staff vice president of employee relations for University Computing Company. He assumed this position in 1978 after serving the company for several years as manager of compensation and benefits. He joined UCC in 1972 as a professional placement representative after spending several years in personnel assignments with the LTV Aerospace Corporation and the Continental Insurance Companies. Pou received his B.A. degree in psychology and personnel administration from the University of Texas—Austin. He served in the U.S. Army as a personnel specialist in Germany prior to completing his degree program.

Job description

James H. Pou is accountable for developing, recommending and implementing human resource objectives, policies and programs that will meet University Computing Company's present and future personnel needs. His areas of responsibility include the establishment and maintenance of compensation programs, benefit plans, and personnel policies and procedures. Most of his efforts are dedicated to the U.S. operations, however, he has some involvement with the international elements of UCC. He reports to the executive vice president and chief UCC. He directly supervises three employees and coordinates the activities of 10 other personnel people.

---

[40]Ibid.
[41]David W. Ewing, "A Bill of Rights for Employees," *Across the Board*, March 1981, pp. 42–49.

ily growing conviction that top executives have no monopoly on wisdom and understanding. Nonunion employees also want to have some say in their work destiny. The traditional view that "top management knows best" is being challenged more and more.

Privacy

The right to privacy is a part of constitutional law. However, nonunion organizations in most states give managers the right to monitor employees' conversation on company telephones without notifying the employees. Other invasions of privacy occur when an employer collects data about a worker—psychological tests, attitude surveys, and medical records. The privacy may be invaded again when the information collected is put to use. Management may use the information to make promotion decisions and answer inquiries from credit bureaus, insurance companies, and social agencies.

IBM, the most publicized nonunion organization in the United States, makes a major issue about employee rights and especially privacy.[42] At IBM:

1. Management can collect and keep in its personnel files only those facts about employees that are required by law or that are necessary to manage operations. IBM's job application forms no longer request previous addresses or information on whether the employee has relatives in the firm. Nor does it ask about prior mental problems, convictions dating back more than five years, or more recent criminal charges that have not resulted in a conviction.
2. Performance evaluations more than three years old must be weeded from an employee's personnel file.
3. Employees are entitle to know how filed information about them is being used.
4. An employee is entitled to see most of the information on file about him or her. Management may withhold some information such as a confidential discussion of an opportunity for promotion that was never given.
5. Personality and general intelligence tests are not permissible.

IBM believes that by being open and concerned about employee privacy the workers are happier. It is proud of the employees' continuing eagerness to reject unions. IBM wants its employees to feel that unions are not necessary.

Polaroid has about 14,500 nonunionized employees. The firm has a committee whose job it is to represent nonunionized employees with grievances. The grievances are presented to the committee members who are elected from the ranks.

Firing Nonunion Workers

The right of employers in private industry to fire workers not protected by a union contract is coming under close scrutiny. Court decisions in several states have awarded large settlements to employees who were judged to be fired capriciously.[43] This trend may eventually result in unprecedented job security for nonunion workers.

---

[42]Interview with Frank Cary, "IBM's Guidelines to Employee Privacy," *Harvard Business Review,* September–October 1976, pp 82–90.

[43]Section is based on "The Growing Cost of Firing Nonunion Workers," *Business Week,* April 6, 1981, pp. 95–98.

Courts in Washington and Michigan have upheld claims by nonunion workers that promises made in employee handbooks—and even orally—constitute a job contract that precludes dismissal except for "just cause." Workers in California have also won the right to seek punitive damages on top of lost wages in dismissal cases.

Estimates indicate that companies in private industry discharge about 1 million permanent employees each year without a "fair hearing." The court actions have put employers on notice to proceed cautiously. Those involved in P/HRM activities will have to pay more attention to the dismissal of workers.

A major court test on dismissal occurred in 1974, when a worker named Olga Moore successfully sued Beebe Rubber Co. after she was fired for refusing to go on a date with her foreman. More recently in 1980, a federal district court in New York ruled against a motion by Korvettes to dismiss a suit by Morton Savodnik, a 13-year employee who claimed the company dismissed him to avoid paying him a pension. The court cited the interest to protect an employee's rights.

The Shriners' Hospital for Crippled Children fired registered nurse, Juanita Vorhees. She sued the hospital claiming that "just cause" for dismissal was not supported. The Superior Court of Seattle ruled that the hospital's manual implied a "just cause" dismissal policy. The court said that the hospital had failed to demonstrate this in dismissing Vorhees. She was dismissed after a playful water fight with a patient. Her award—her job and back wages.

In another case, Wayne Pugh was fired by See Candy, Inc., of San Francisco. Pugh, the vice president and director of See's, alleged that he was fired for objecting to an arrangement whereby the firm paid a lower wage than other candy makers to seasonal union employees. This interesting case is still in court, but it is being watched because it involves a management level employee fighting the company for the rights of operating level employees.

Unfair discharge suits will probably increase in number in the 1980s. If more and more cases are won by nonunion members the union may have some organizing problems in the future.

Labor Unions and the Public Image: Some Needed Attention

The last decade has generally been a downhill slide for unions. Mainstay unions in steel, auto, transportation, and apparel have lost members.[44] Foreign competition from Japan, West Germany, and Australia keep expanding their share of a number of domestic markets and undersell many U.S. products abroad. Industry has been closing plants all across the country, but especially hard hit is the union heartland of the Northeast and Midwest. When new plants are built preference goes to right to work states or overseas locations. The only labor segment in which unions are making some gains in the government. However, cutbacks in government spending will mean fewer new jobs and fewer workers to organize.

The future of the labor movement is difficult to predict with any accuracy. However, market, economic, and public opinion data suggest that unions will not grow significantly in the next decade. Organizing nonunion workers is important but is actually a low-

---

[44]Seymour Martin Lipset and William Schneider, "Organized Labor and the Public: A Troubled Union," *Public Opinion,* August/September 1981, pp. 52–56.

priority item in union circles. There are just too many problems and roadblocks to make organizing an area of top priority. Now that inflation is taking more out of the average worker's pay envelope and plants are closing down, workers want to hold onto their jobs. Organizing, to the average union worker is not where he or she wants the union to devote energy. Saving jobs from computer-controlled robots and other technological devices is what the average union member wants his or her union leader to be fighting and negotiating for.

If any successful organizing gains are accomplished in the 1980s, they will be with new groups that are beginning to predominate the work force—engineers, programmers, and technical technicians. The union organizing efforts in these areas will be different than the traditional ones. Instead of simply passing out handbills at a plant gate informing workers about the benefits of unionization there will be a greater "Madison Avenue" touch. Television, newspaper, and carefully prepared pamphlets will be used by the unions. These campaigns will be resisted by equally as "slick" and professional management campaigns. Management will emphasize more of the individual spirit and skill theme that they claim will be dampened if a person joins a union that emphasizes collectivism and group solidarity.

In a recent Gallup Poll, it was determined that there is greater public disapproval of labor unions than at any time in the past 45 years.[45] At least part of Americans' disaffection with the union movement may be traced to their general disapproval of strikes or sick-outs by public employees such as air traffic controllers, police officers, and fire fighters. Exhibit 18–9 shows the trend in the public's disenchantment with labor unions.

Exhibit 18–9

Labor union approval: Gallup Poll 1936 to 1981

	Approve percent	Disapprove percent	No opinion percent
1981	55	35	10
1979	55	33	12
1978	59	31	10
1972	59	26	15
1967	66	23	11
1965 June	70	19	11
February	71	19	10
1963	67	23	10
1962	64	24	12
1961 May	63	22	15
February	70	18	12
1959	68	19	13
1957 September	64	18	18
February	76	14	10
1953	75	18	7
1949	62	22	16
1947	64	25	11
1941	61	30	9
1940	64	22	14
1939	68	24	8
1937	72	20	8
1936	72	20	8

[45]"Approval of Labor Unions Remains at Low," *Gallup Report,* August 1981, pp. 6–8.

If labor unions are to remain strong political and social forces in society they must stem their recent decline and negative public image. Still, the majority of Americans believe that unions do more good than harm. Most people feel that strong unions provide the only way for many workers to get a fair piece of the economic pie. The union is also viewed as a legitimate representative for workers to voice complaints and grievances.

Perhaps some of the public's growing disapproval of labor unions is directed toward the behavior of labor union leaders rather than the union's objectives. Many people still believe that labor leaders are less likely than business leaders to act in the national interest. In fact, today the public shows a greater disdain for labor leaders than they do business leaders. It is evident that corrupt and autocratic labor leader behavior is given more media publicity than corrupt and autocratic business leader behavior.[46] However, as long as union leader corruption is publicized, the image of the union movement will remain on the low end of the scale. Hopefully, union leaders who are aware of the problems poor image can cause will encourage and promote improved union leader behavior. Unless unions can improve their image, their efforts to remain a major force in society will fail.

Summary

This chapter has focused on union organizing campaigns and management resistance to them. In addition, the collective bargaining process is spelled out. Some of the important points covered include:

1. A union can exist only if workers prefer and vote to become unionized. If a union doesn't receive at least 51 percent of the votes cast in a representation election it can't serve as the employee's bargaining unit.
2. Management and the union face off and campaign against each other. Each presents their view of the situation.
3. The union and management organizing campaigns in the private sector to win over the employees is watched very closely by the National Labor Relations Board.
4. Collective bargaining is a process by which the representatives of the organization meet and attempt to work out a contract with the employees' representative—the union.
5. The steps in the collective bargaining process include:
   a. Prenegotiation.
   b. Selecting negotiators.
   c. Developing a bargaining strategy.
   d. Using the best tactics.
   e. Reaching a formal contractual agreement.
6. The day-to-day compliance with union-management contract provisions are an important responsibility of the first-line supervisor. He or she can be involved in such contract related issues as discipline procedures, grievance procedures, and strikes.
7. The grievance procedure does not always result in an acceptable solution. *Arbitration* is a quasi-judicial process in which the parties agree to submit an unresolvable dispute to a neutral third party for binding settlement.
8. The *strike* is the ultimate union weapon to encourage management to make greater

---

[46]"Union Corruption: Worse Than Ever," *U.S. News & World Report,* September 8, 1980, pp. 33–36.

concessions to the union. There appears to be a distinct trend toward fewer strikes being taken by unions.

9. The traditional adversary union-management relationship has been giving way to less antagonism and more cooperation. Adverse economic times, foreign competition, and technological advancements have created more interest in both union and management to look for areas in which to cooperate.

10. The rights of nonunion employees are very important since most workers do not belong to unions. In the areas of privacy and dismissal, the courts are becoming more involved.

11. If unions are to remain a force in society, they will have to improve their public image. Today, the public has a greater disapproval of labor unions than at any time in the past 45 years.

Questions for Review and Discussion

1. It is claimed that the P/HRM department plays a major role that influences whether employees vote to organize into a union. What do you think about this claim?

Case

The results of the union versus management vote were counted at Hardisty Manufacturing Company. The union had gotten 30 percent of the employees to sign authorization cards. And the NLRB had stepped in to schedule the unionization election. Shortly after the NLRB examiner left, Tom called Stan into his office.

Tom: How could we lose this election? Why do I have a P/HRM manager if he can't beat the union?

Stan: It's not over yet. They still have to get a majority. But Tom, we've got to start thinking about a strategy. . .the tactics we'll use. . .this problem isn't going to just "go away". . .we've got to face it. I've been in contact with some professional negotiators who've agreed to speak for us, in case the union wins.

Tom: Is that necessary?

Stan: I think it is. There's a lot going against us. We were really hurt by the pay item. You told me we had to lay people off to cut costs, but the layoffs came in the middle of the union's organizing campaign. A lot of people felt threatened. When people get threatened, they join unions.

Tom: See here, I'm tired of excuses. Just do your job and shut out that union! Hire whoever you have to. And I promise you, we'll have no more layoffs. We just had to keep our heads above water, that's all, so we had to lay off some workers. But no more. I'll help you in any way I can. By the way, how's that communication program coming along?

Between then and the election, both sides campaigned, but Stan felt that the management's efforts weren't as organized or as effective as the union's. At the last minute, Tom called back the workers who had been laid off; the votes looked close. But when the representative votes were counted, the union had won. HMC challenged the votes of several persons, but in the end, the NLRB declared the union as the bargaining agent, and negotiation began.

One week later, Stan quit. Tom had refused to talk to him since the election. After the experience, both men felt hostile toward unions, but Stan blamed Tom more than anything. He felt that Hardisty's whole antiunion campaign had been mismanaged from the start.

2. Do negotiators at a bargaining table have to possess some acting abilities? Explain.
3. Should employees have a right to privacy while on the job? Why?
4. Why would an agency like the NLRB be needed to supervise and oversee representation elections?
5. In what areas should union and management be more willing to cooperate?
6. What are some of the typical delays in the grievance to arbitration process?
7. Should public employees such as air traffic controllers be permitted to strike? Why?
8. Why has the public image of unions been on the decline?

Glossary

Arbitration. A quasi-judicial process in which the parties agree to submit the unresolvable dispute to a neutral third party for binding settlement.

Boycott. A primary boycott finds union members not patronizing the boycotted firm. In a secondary boycott a supplier of a boycotted firm is threatened with a union strike unless it stops doing business with the firm. This type of boycott is illegal under the Taft-Hartley Act.

Collective Bargaining. The process by which the representatives of the organization meet and attempt to work out a contract with representatives of the union.

Decertification Election. Employees who are represented by a union vote to drop the union. If they vote to drop the union it is referred to as decertification.

Grievance. A complaint about a job that creates dissatisfaction or discomfort for the worker.

Hot Cargo Agreement. The employer permits union members to avoid working with materials that come from employers who have been struck by a union. This type of boycott is illegal.

Lockout. A management response to union pressures in which a skeleton crew of managerial personnel is used to maintain a workplace and the total plant is basically closed to employees.

Representation Election. A vote to determine if a particular group will represent the workers in collective bargaining.

Strike. An effort by employees to withhold their services from an employer in order to get greater concessions at the collective bargaining table.

Chapter Nineteen

Employee Safety and Health

Learning Objectives

After studying this chapter you should be able to:
- Define what is meant by safety hazards, health hazards, health, and stress

- Describe both union and management attitudes about OSHA

- Explain how environmental and person stressors interact to cause stress

- Discuss why preventive health programs are growing in popularity

- Illustrate when OSHA requires an organization to report and record an illness, injury, or death

Chapter Outline

Case

Clint

The ambulance had just pulled away from Lysander Manufacturing. It was headed for a Denver hospital, carrying Dale Silas. Dale had been badly hurt; there was already talk that he might be disabled for the rest of his life.

Clint Woodley, the plant manager, wondered if there was anything he could have done to prevent Dale's injury. It was not the first injury this year at Lysander. Clint decided to visit his friend, Bob Undine, who operated a similar plant in a nearby town. He called Bob and arranged to have lunch the next day.

At lunch, Clint explained how upset he was about Dale's injury. Dale had been with Lysander for 15 years—longer than Clint had been. He had a wife and five children to support. The word from the hospital was not very good.

Bob: Well, Clint, sometimes accidents happen. You know our business is dangerous. And sometimes the men are not following the safety rules. What is your safety record over the last 10 years?

Clint: I don't really know. We've only got records since OSHA (Occupational Safety and Health Act) came in. But the P/HRM guy, Otto Richmond, handles that paperwork. When our people are hired, we tell them to be safe. The supervisors are supposed to handle that.

Bob: You mean you don't have a safety unit?

Clint: No.

Bob: Then you probably don't do accident research, safety design and prevention, safety inspections, or safety training either, do you?

Clint: No. We do fill out the OSHA paperwork. Luckily, we've never been inspected by OSHA.

Bob: Well, then, maybe you ought to be upset about Dale. You aren't doing all you could to protect your employees. And if you don't do it, maybe OSHA will make you.

Clint: I don't want that. Can I come back with you and see how you run your plant?

Bob: Sure.

This chapter covers some of the main points that Bob and his safety executive, Mary Lou Vaugh, explained to Clint.

> *Safety hazards* are those aspects of the work environment which have the potential of immediate and sometimes violent harm to an employee. Examples are loss of hearing, eyesight, or body parts; cuts, sprains, bruises, broken bones; burns and electric shock.
>
> *Health hazards* are those aspects of the work environment which slowly and cumulatively (and often irreversibly) lead to deterioration of an employee's health. Examples are cancer, poisoning, and respiratory diseases as well as depression, loss of temper, and other psychological disorders. Typical causes include physical and biological hazards, toxic and cancer-causing dusts and chemicals, and stressful working conditions.

How many safety and health hazards exist in workplaces today? On the average, 1 employee in 10 is killed or injured at work *each year*. But some occupations (such as dock workers) have many more injuries per year than others (e.g., file clerks), so the odds for some workers are worse than 1 in 10 each year.

Statistics on safety and health hazards are debated. The official statistics indicate that about 400,000 persons per year contract an occupational disease, and deaths from this cause average 100,000 per year. But Ashford who prepared a report for the Ford Foundation cites data to indicate this figure is too low and argues that many occupationally contrasted diseases are not reported as being caused by work.[1]

Reports indicate there are about 14,000 accidental deaths at work a year (nearly 55 a day, or 7 people every working hour) and about 6 million reported accidents.[2] The Occupational Safety and Health Administration (OSHA) places work-related deaths at about 9,000 per year. All agencies do not report the same figures. Note the use of the verb "reported." A number of studies indicate that perhaps as few as half of all occupational accidents are reported.

Accidents and illnesses are not evenly distributed among employers in the United States. Employees facing serious health and safety dangers include fire fighters, miners, construction and transportation workers, roofing and sheet metal workers, recreational vehicle manufacturers, lumber and woodworkers, and blue-collar and first line supervisors in manufacturing and agriculture. A few white-collar jobs are relatively dangerous: dentists and hospital operating room personnel, beauticians, and X-ray technicians.

All accidents and diseases are tragic to the employees involved, of course. There is pain at the time of the accident, and there can be psychological problems later. In addition to pain, suffering, and death, there are also direct measurable costs to both employee and employer. About 43 million workdays were lost in the United States because of health-related absenteeism in 1979.[3] This may mean direct costs of workers' compensation and indirect costs of lost productivity for the enterprise. The average company's workers' compensation for disability payments is 1 percent of payroll, and the indirect costs are estimated to be five times greater. These indirect costs include cost of wages paid the injured employee, damage to plant and equipment, costs of replacement employees, and time costs for supervisors and personnel people investigating and reporting the accident or illness. Both because of the humanitarian desire of management to reduce suffering and because of the huge direct and indirect costs of accidents, deaths, and illnesses, the effective enterprise tries hard to create safe and healthy conditions at work.

An unsafe or unhealthy work environment can also affect an employee's ability and motivation to work. As noted in Chapter 2, security/preservation is one of the most fundamental needs people have. Poor safety and health conditions are likely to endanger fulfillment of the security needs of employees.

Until recently, the typical response to concern about health and safety was to compensate the victims of job-related accidents with worker's compensation and similar insurance schemes. This chapter will discuss both the compensation approaches and the programs designed to prevent accidents, health hazards, and deaths at work.

---

[1] Nicholas Asford, *Crises in the Workplace: Occupational Disease and Injury: A Report to the Ford Foundation* (Cambridge, Mass.: Mit Press, 1976). Chaps. 1, 3.

[2] Arthur B Shostak, *Blue-Collar Stress* (Reading, Mass.: Addison-Wesley Publishing, 1980).

[3] U.S. Department of Labor, Bureau of Labor Statistics, *Occupational Injuries and Illness in 1979: Summary* (Washington, D.C.: U.S. Government Printing Office, March 1981).

A Diagnostic Approach to Safety and Health

The environmental factors important to health and safety are highlighted in Exhibit 19–1. Probably the most crucial factor is the nature of the task, especially as it is affected by the technology and working conditions of the organizational environment. For instance, health and safety problems are a lot more serious for coal miners—whose working conditions require them to breath coal dust in the air—than for typists. An X-ray technician has a much greater chance of getting cancer as a result of working conditions than does an elementary school teacher. Some examples of potential job hazards are presented in Exhibit 19–2.

A second vital factor is employee attitudes toward health and safety; they can vary from concern for safety and cooperation regarding safety programs, to apathy. If employees are apathetic about it, the best employer safety program and the most stringent safety inspection by the government or the safety specialists in the P/HRM department will not be successful in improving safety and health conditions.

A third factor affecting health and safety on the job is government. Federal and state governments have attempted to legislate conditions to improve safety and health for some years.[4] Some government programs currently in operation will be discussed later. However, perhaps the most publicity about government involvement has been the accident that closed down the Three Mile Island nuclear plant in 1979. This accident led to the discovery of dangers at other nuclear plants.[5] As a result, the Nuclear Regulatory Commission identified dozens of improvements—ranging from new equipment to better operation training—for the country's 72 operating nuclear reactors.

A fourth factor is the trade unions. Many unions have been very concerned about the safety and health of their employees and have pressured employers in collective bargaining for better programs. Some unions have taken extraordinary steps to protect their members' health and safety. For example, the Teamsters' Union hired a nationally known occupational health expert to investigate unexplained illnesses at the Robert Shaw Controls Company plant in Ohio. The United Rubber Workers' contract calls for a study of the effects of benzene on employees. The Oil, Chemical and Atomic Workers Union has been subsidizing medical student interns and residents to study occupational health conditions in plants where their members work. Unions also have used their political power to get legislation passed to improve the safety and health of members.

A fifth factor is management's goals. Some socially responsible managers and owners had active safety programs long before the laws required them. They made safety and health an important strategic goal and implemented it with significant safety considerations designed into the enterprise's layout. The safety program included safety statistics, contests, and training sessions. Other managers, not so safety conscious, did little other than what was required by law. Thus managerial attitudes play a large part in the significance of the health and safety program of the enterprise.

The final factor affecting health and safety programs is economic conditions. We would accept the worst possible assumptions about human nature if we believed that any employer *knowingly* would choose to provide dangerous working conditions or would

---

[4] Robert E. Harvey, "Industry Faces Costly Remedies for Occupational Illness," *Iron Age,* October 14, 1981, pp. 67–21.

[5] John R. Emshwiller, "Many Nuclear-Plant Perils Remain Three Years after Three Mile Island," *The Wall Street Journal,* February 26, 1982, p.23.

Exhibit 19–1 _____

Factors Affecting Safety and Health

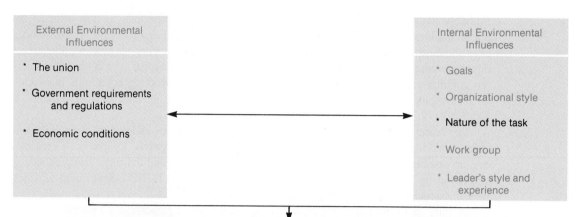

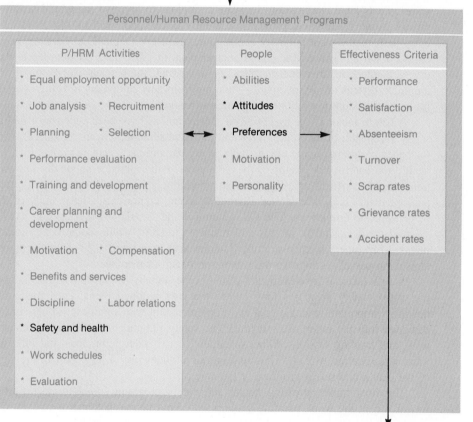

Exhibit 19–2 _____

Examples of job and safety hazards

Occupation	Potential hazard	Possible outcome
Textile workers	Cotton dust	Brown lung or byssinosis (a debilitating lung disease)
	Noise	Temporary or permanent hearing loss
	Chemical exposures	
	Aniline-based dyes	Bladder cancer and liver damage
	Formaldehyde	Dermatitis, allergic lung disease, possibly cancer
	Furfuraldehyde	Dermatitis, respiratory irritation, fatigue, headache, tremors, numbness of the tongue
	Moving machine parts without barriers	Loss of fingers or hands
Hospital workers	Infectious diseases	
	Hepatitis	Liver damage
	Herpes simplex virus	Painful skin lesions
	Chemical exposures	
	Anesthetic gases	Spontaneous abortions
	Metallic mercury	Poisoning of nervous system and kidneys
	Inorganic acids and alkalis	Irritation to respiratory tract and skin
	Physical hazards	
	Ionizing radiation	Burns, birth defects, cancer
	Microwave radiation	Sterility, harm to eyes, possibly increases risk of cataracts
	UV light	Burning or sensitization of skin, skin cancer, cataracts
	Safety hazards	
	Lifting or carrying	Back pain or permanent back injury
	Puncture wounds from syringes	Infections
Welders	Infrared and visible light radiation	Burns, headache, fatigue, eye damage
	UV radiation	Burns, skin tumors, eye damage
	Chemical exposures	
	Carbon monoxide	Cardiovascular disease
	Acetylene	Asphyxiation, fire, explosion
	Metallic oxides	Contact dermatitis, eye irritation, respiratory irritation, metal fume fever (symptoms similar to the flue), possible kidney damage
	Phosphine	Lethal at even low doses; irritating to eyes, nose, skin; acts as anesthetic
Clerical workers	Improperly designed chairs and work stations; lack of movement	Backache, aggravation of hemorrhoids, varicose veins, and other blood-circulation conditions, eyestrain
	Noise	Hearing impairment, stress reactions
	Chemical exposures	
	Ozone from copy machines	Irritation of eyes, nose, throat; respiratory damage
	Benzene and toluene in rubber cement and "cleaners"	Benzene is associated with several blood diseases (including leukemia) and toluene may cause intoxication
	Methanol and ammonia in duplicating machine solvents	Irritation to eyes, nose, and throat

refuse to provide reasonable safeguards for employees. But there is a lack of knowledge about the consequences of some dangerous working conditions, and even when there is such knowledge, economic conditions can prevent employers from doing all they might wish. The risks of being a uranium miner are well known: 10 to 11 percent will die of cancer within 10 years. As long as there are no alternative methods and as long as there is a need for uranium, some employees will be risking shorter lives in these jobs. Engineers and scientists are constantly at work to determine the dangers and to prevent or mitigate the consequences. But the costs of some of the prevention programs are such that the enterprise may find them prohibitive, and may consider the programs economically infeasible.

Who Is Involved with Safety and Health?

As with other P/HRM functions, the success of a safety and health program requires the support and cooperation of operating and P/HRM managers. But it is more complicated than that. In some organizations, safety is a separate function of its own, though both operating managers and staff still have their parts to play to protect employees.

Top management must support safety and health with an adequate budget. They must give it psychological support also. Acting on safety reports is another way top managers

P/HRM Manager Close-Up

William J. Danos
New Wales Chemicals, Inc.

Biography

William J. Danos, safety engineer of New Wales Cemicals, Inc., was graduated from Louisiana State University, Baton Rouge, with a degree in chemical

engineering. He has had extensive training in the safety field, including the Industrial Hygiene Training Course (National Safety Council) and the Industrial Facilities Protection Program (Ft. Gordon, Georgia). Danos entered the safety field in 1959 as safety supervisor at Allied Chemical Corporation, Baton Rouge Works. Since that time he has held positions such as safety engineer for Boh Brothers Construction Company and safety supervisor for Uniroyal, Inc.

In addition, Danos was editor of *The Chemical Treat,* a magazine at Allied Chemical. He is a certified safety trainer and has served as national safety and health chairman for ASPA.

Job description

As safety engineer at New Wales Chemicals, William J. Danos is responsible for total loss-control programs. This includes such areas as safety on the job, security, fire prevention, medical attention, and workers' compensation.

can be involved in these efforts. Without this support, the safety and health effort is hampered. Some organizations have responded to the environmental problems which can increase accidents, deaths, and disabilities by placing the responsibility for employee health and safety with the chief executive officer of the organization; the hospital administrator, the agency administrator, the company president. This is the approach taken by most smaller organizations that have health and safety threats, or middle-sized organizations with few health or safety threats. Operating managers also are responsible, since accidents and injuries will take place, and health hazards will exist, in the work unit. They must be aware of health and safety considerations and cooperate with the specialists who can help them reduce accidents and occupational illness. In larger and some medium-sized organizations, there is a safety unit in the P/HRM department. This chapter will illustrate what a safety and health specialist does.

The success of the safety program rests primarily on how well employees and supervisors cooperate with safety rules and regulations. Often this relationship is formalized in the creation of a safety committee consisting of the safety specialist, representative employees, and managers.

Usually there are two levels of safety committees. At the policy level is the committee made up of major division heads; this committee sets safety policy and rules, investigates major hazards, and has budget responsibility. At the departmental level, both supervisors and managers are members. Safety committees are concerned with the organization's entire safety program: inspection, design, record-keeping, training, and motivation programs. The more people who can be involved through the committees, the more likely is the program to be successful. Finally, the government inspector plays a role in keeping the organization on its toes regarding the safety of the employees.

Employee health and safety is a mature P/HRM function—Stage IV, as described in Exhibit 1–7 (Chapter 1). Many studies have been made of it, especially by engineers and psychologists.

Causes of Work Accidents and Work-Related Illnesses

Work accidents and work-related illnesses have many causes. The major causes of occupational accidents are:

- The task to be done.
- The working conditions.
- The nature of the employees.

Some examples of causes in the task and working conditions area include poorly designed or inadequately repaired machines, lack of protective equipment, and the presence of dangerous chemicals or gases. Other working conditions that contribute to accidents include excessive work hours leading to employee fatigue, noise, lack of proper lighting, boredom, and horseplay and fighting at work. The National Institute for Occupational Safety and Health (NIOSH) should find out more about the causes of accidents and occupational health hazards.

There are data to indicate that some employees have more accidents than the average. Such a person is said to be an accident repeater. These studies indicate that employees who (1) are under 30 years of age, (2) lack psychomotor and perceptual skills, (3) are impulsive, and (4) are easily bored are more likely to have accidents than others.[6] Although some believe accident proneness can be measured by a set of attitude or motivational instruments, most experts who have examined the data carefully do not believe that attitudinal-motivational "causes" of accidents are a significant influence on accident rates. We need to know much more about accident proneness before such serious actions as attempting to screen out the "accident prone" person are implemented.

Organization Responses to Safety and Health

The safety department or unit and the safety committee can take three approaches to improving the safety of working conditions:

- Prevention and design.
- Inspection and research.
- Training and motivation.

Bob Undine's plant mentioned at the beginning of this chapter has taken all three approaches.

Safety Design and Preventive Approaches

Numerous preventive measures have been adopted by organizations in attempts to improve their safety records. One is to design more safety into the workplace through safety engineering. Engineers have helped through the study of human-factors engineering, which seeks to make jobs more comfortable, less confusing, and less fatiguing. This can keep employees more alert and less open to accidents.

Safety engineers design safety into the workplace with the analytical design approach. This total design approach analyzes all factors involved in the job. Included are such factors as speed of the assembly line, stresses in the work, and job design. On the basis of this analysis, steps are taken to improve safety precautions. Protective guards are designed for machinery and equipment. Color coding warns of dangerous areas. Standard safety colors, which should be taught in safety classes, include gray for machinery and red where the area presents danger of fire. Other dangers may be highlighted by bright orange paint.

Protective clothing and devices are also supplied for employees working in hazardous job situations. these can include:

Head protection, principally with helmets

Eye and face protection, with goggles, face shields, and spectacles.

Hearing protection, with muffs and inserts.

Respiratory protection, with air-purifying devices such as filter respirators and gas masks, and air-supplying devices.

Hand protection, with gloves.

Foot and leg protection, with safety shoes, boots, guards, and leggings.

---

[6]Bureau of Labor Statistics. *Injury Rates by Industry* (Washington, D.C.: U.S. Government Printing Office, 1978).

Body protection, with garments such as suits, aprons, jackets, and coveralls.

Belts and lifelines to prevent those working in high places from falling.

The few studies on the effectiveness of these preventive design measures indicate that they do reduce accidents.[7]

Well-designed rest periods increase safety and productivity, as do clearly understood rules and regulations. These rules should be developed from analysis of equipment and conditions such as flammability. No smoking areas and hard hat areas where safety helmets are required for all employees and visitors are examples. Effective selection and placement of employees can also improve safety. It makes sense, for example, to assign the physically handicapped where their handicaps cannot add to the possibility of accidents.

Inspection, Reporting, and Accident Research

A second activity of safety departments or specialists is to inspect the workplace with the goal of reducing accidents and illnesses. The safety specialist is looking for a number of things, including answers to these questions:

Are safety rules being observed? How many near misses were there?

Are safety guards, protective equipment, and so on being used?

Are there potential hazards in the workplace that safety redesign could improve?

Are there potential occupational health hazards?

A related activity is to investigate accidents or "close calls" to determine the facts for insurance purposes. More important, such investigations also can determine preventive measures that should be taken in the future. Following an accident requiring more than first aid treatment, the safety specialist, P/HRM specialist, or manager must *investigate* and report the facts to the government and insurance companies. These data are also used to analyze the causes of accidents, with a view to preventing possible recurrences.

Reporting of accidents and occupational illnesses is an important part of the safety specialist's job. Usually, the report is filled out by the injured employee's supervisor and checked by the safety specialist. The supervisor compiles the report because he or she usually is present when the accident occurs. And doing so requires the supervisor to think about safety in the unit and what can be done to prevent similar accidents.

At regular intervals during the work year, safety and personnel specialists carry out *accident research;* that is, systematic evaluation of the evidence concerning accidents and health hazards. Data for this research should be gathered from both external and internal sources. Safety and health journals point out recent findings which should stimulate the safety specialist to look for hazardous conditions at the workplace. Reports from the National Institute of Occupational Safety and Health, a research organization created by OSHA legislation, also provide important data inputs for research. Data developed at the workplace will include accident reports, inspection reports by government and the organization's safety specialists, and recommendations of the safety committees.

---

[7]James Gardner, "Employee Safety." in *Handbook of Modern Personnel Administration,* ed. Joseph Famularo (New York: McGraw-Hill, 1978), Chap. 48

Accident research often involves computation of organizational accident rates. These are compared to industry and national figures to determine the organization's relative safety performance. Several statistics are computed. Accident frequency rate is computed as follows per million labor-hours of work:

$$\text{Frequency rate} = \frac{\text{Number of accidents} \times 1,000,000}{\text{Number of work hours in the period}}$$

The accidents used in this computation are those causing the worker to lose work time.

The second statistic is the accident severity rate. This is computed as follows:

$$\text{Accident severity rate} = \frac{\text{Number of workdays lost} \times 1,000,000}{\text{Number of work hours in the period}}$$

OSHA suggests reporting accidents as number of injuries per 100 full-time employees per year, as a simpler approach. The formula is:

$$\frac{\text{Number of illnesses and injuries}}{\text{Total hours worked by all employees for the year}} \times 200,000$$

The base equals the number of workers employed (100 full-time equivalent) working full time(for example, 40 hours per week and for 50 weeks if vacation is 2 weeks).

The organization's statistics should be compared with the industry's statistics and government statistics (from the Department of Labor and OSHA). Most studies find that although effective accident research should be very complex, in reality it is unsophisticated and unscientific.

Safety Training and Motivation Programs

The third approach organizations take to safety is training and motivation programs. Safety training usually is part of the orientation program. It also takes place during the employee's career. This training is usually voluntary, but some is required by government agencies. Studies of the effectiveness of such training are mixed. Some studies indicate that some methods, such as job instruction training (JIT) and accident simulations, are more effective than others. Others contend that the employees' perception that management really believes in safety training accounts for its success.[8] A few studies find that the programs make employees more *aware* of safety, but not necessarily safer in their behavior. Nevertheless, effectively developed safety training programs can help provide a safer environment for all employees.

Safety specialists have also tried to improve safety conditions and accident statistics by various motivation devices such as contests and communication programs. These are intended to reinforce safety training. One device is to place posters around the workplace with slogans such as "A Safe Worker Is a Happy Worker."Posters are available from the National Safety Council or can be prepared for the enterprise. Communication programs also include items in company publications and safety booklets, and billboards. The billboard in front of Bob Undine's plant, for example, reads:

---

[8]Roger Dunbar, "Manager's Influence on Subordinate's Thinking about Safety," *Academy of Management Journal,* June 1975, pp. 364–69.

> Welcome to American Manufacturing Company
>
> A Good Place to Work
> A Safe Place to Work
>
> We have had no accidents for
> <u>182</u> days

Sometimes safety communications are tied into a safety contest. If lower accidents result over a period, an award is given. The little research that has been done on safety communications and contests is mixed. Some believe they are useful. Others contend they have no effect or produce undesirable side effects, such as failure to report accidents or a large number of accidents once the contest is over or has been lost.[9]

In general, too little is known scientifically at this point to recommend use or reduction of safety motivation programs. One example of the needed research is a study which examined the conditions under which safety motivation and education programs were effective in a shelving manufacturing company. It found that:

- There are safety-conscious people and others who are unaware of safety. The safety-conscious people were influenced by safety posters.
- Safety booklets were influential to the safety-conscious employees when their work group was also safety-conscious.
- Five-minute safety talks by supervisors were effective when the work group was safety-conscious and when the supervisor was safety-conscious.
- Safety training was effective on the safety-conscious employee when the supervisor and top management were safety-conscious.
- Safety inspections were effective when the work group and supervisor were safety-conscious.

Government Responses to Safety and Health Programs

Although many organizations (such as Bob Undine's) have done a good job of safeguarding the safety and health of their employees, with little or no supervision from government sources, others (as Clint Woodley's) have not. This has led governments to become involved in holding the organization responsible for prevention of accidents, disabilities, illnesses, and deaths related to the tasks workers perform and the conditions under which they work.

Prior to passage of the Occupational Safety and Health Act in 1970, the feeling was that private organizations had not done enough to assure safe and healthy working conditions. The federal law in effect, the Walsh-Healy Act, was thought to be too weak or inadequately enforced, and state programs were incomplete, diverse, and lacked authority. The basic requirements of OSHA are presented in Exhibit 19–3.

Lobbying by unions and employees led to the passage of several federal laws related

---

[9]Robert McKelvey et al., ''Performance Efficiency and Injury Avoidance as a Function of Positive and Negative Incentives,'' *Journal of Safety Research*, June 1973, pp. 90–96.

Exhibit 19–3 _____

Job safety and health protection requirements per OSHA

The Occupational Safety and Health Act of 1970 provides job safety and health protection for workers through the promotion of safe and healthful working conditions throughout the nation. Requirements of the Act include the following:

Employers:

Each employer must furnish to each of his employees employment and a place of employment free from recognized hazards that are causing or are likely to cause death or serious harm to his employees; and shall comply with occupational safety and health standards issued under the Act.

Employees:

Each employee shall comply with all occupational safety and health standards, rules, regulations, and orders issued under the Act that apply to his own actions and conduct on the job. The Occupational Safety and Health Administration (OSHA) of the Department of Labor has the primary responsibility for administering the Act. OSHA issues occupational safety and health standards, and its Compliance Safety and Health Officers conduct jobsite inspections to ensure compliance with the Act

Inspection:

The Act requires that a representative of the employer and a representative authorized by the employees be given an opportunity to accompany the OSHA inspector for the purpose of aiding the inspection. Where there is no authorized employee representative, the OSHA Compliance Officer must consult with a reasonable number of employees concerning safety and health conditions in the workplace.

Complaint:

Employees or their representatives have the right to file a complaint with the nearest OSHA office requesting an inspection if they believe unsafe or unhealthful conditions exist in their workplace. OSHA will withhold, on request, names of employees complaining. The Act provides that employees may not be discharged or discriminated against in any way for filing safety and health complaints or otherwise exercising their rights under the Act. An employee who believes he has been discriminated against may file a complaint with the nearest OSHA office within thirty days of the alleged discrimination.

Citation:

If upon inspection OSHA believes an employer has violated the Act, a citation alleging such violations will be issued to the employer. Each citation will specify a time period within which the alleged violation must be corrected. The OSHA citation must be prominently displayed at or near the place of alleged violation for three days, or until it is corrected, whichever is later, to warn employees of dangers that may exist there.

Proposed Penalty:

The Act provides for mandatory penalties against employers of up to $1,000 for each serious violation and for optional penalties of up to $1,000 for each nonserious violation. Penalties of up to $1,000 per day may be proposed for failure to correct violations within the proposed time period. Also, any employer who willfully or repeatedly violates the Act may be assessed penalties of up to $10,000 for each such violation. Criminal penalties are also provided in the Act. Any willful violation resulting in death of an employee, upon conviction, is punishable by a fine of more more than $10,000 or by imprisonment for not more than six months, or by both. Conviction of an employer after a first conviction doubles these maximum penalties.

Voluntary Activity:

While providing penalties for violations, the Act also encourages efforts by labor and management, before an OSHA inspection, to reduce injuries and illnesses arising out of employment. The Department of Labor encourages employers and employees to reduce workplace hazards voluntarily and to develop and improve safety and health programs in all workplaces and industries. Such cooperative action would initially focus on the identification and elimination of hazards that could cause death, injury, or illness to employees and supervisors. There are many public and private organizations that can provide information and assistance in this effort, if requested.

Source: *OSHA Bulletin.*

to specific occupations, such as the Coal Mine Health and Safety Act of 1969 and the related Black Lung Benefits Act of 1972. The movement for federal supervision of health and safety programs culminated in passage of the Occupational Safety and Health Act which is administered by the Occupational Safety and Health Administration of the Department of Labor. To conduct research and develop safety and health standards, the act created the National Institute of Occupational Safety and Health (NIOSH).

OSHA, the product of three years of bitter legislative lobbying, was designed to remedy safety problems on the job. The compromise law that was enacted initially received wide support. Its purpose was to provide employment "free from recognized hazards" to employees. OSHA provisions originally applied to 4.1 million businesses and 57 million employees in almost every organization engaged in interstate commerce.[10]

OSHA has been enforced by federal inspectors or in partnership with state safety and health agencies. It encourages the states to assume responsibility for developing and administering occupational and health laws and carrying out their own statistical programs. Before being granted full authority for its programs, a state must go through three steps. First, the state plan must have the preliminary approval of OSHA. Second, the state promises to take "developmental steps" to do certain things at certain times, such as adjusting legislation, hiring inspectors, and providing for an industrial hygiene laboratory. OSHA monitors the state plan for three years, and if the state fulfills these obligations, the third step is a trial period at full-enforcement levels for at least a year. At the end of this intensive evaluation period, a final decision is made by OSHA on the qualifications of the state program.

If OSHA and the employer fail to provide safe working conditions, employees as individuals or their unions can seek injunctions against the employer to force it to do so or submit to an inspection of the workplace. The employer cannot discriminate against an employee who takes these actions. OSHA has many requirements, but the three that most directly affect most employers are:

> Meeting safety standards set by OSHA.
>
> Submitting to OSHA inspections.
>
> Keeping records and reporting accidents and illnesses.

OSHA Safety Standards

OSHA has established safety standards, defined as those "practices, means, operations, or processes, reasonably necessary to provide safe . . . employment." The standards can affect any aspect of the workplace; new standards were established or proposed, for example, for such factors as lead, mercury, silica, benzene, talc dust, cotton dust, noise, and general health hazards. The standards may be industrywide or apply only to a specific enterprise.

The secretary of labor revises, modifies, or revokes existing standards or creates new ones on his own initiative or on the basis of petitions from interested parties (employees or unions). The National Institute of Occupational Safety and Health in the Department of Health and Human Services (HHS) is responsible for doing research from which standards are developed and for training those involved to implement them. Federal or national consensus standards (such as those of the National Fire Protection Association) have

---

[10] "Will Reform Be the Death of OSHA," *Nation's Business*, April 1980, pp. 55–58.

also become OSHA standards. And temporary emergency standards can be created for imminent danger. Employers may be granted temporary variances by showing inability to comply with a standard within the time allowed, if they have a plan to protect employees against the hazard.

The employer is responsible for knowing what these standards are and abiding by them. This is not easy. The *initial* standards were published in The Federal Register in 350 pages of small print, and interpretations of the standards are issued yearly *by volume.* One recent annual volume was 780 pages long! OSHA officers work with compliance operations manuals two inches thick. Even the *checklist* which summarizes the general industry standards is 11 pages long and lists 80 items. The responsible manager is subject to thousands of pages of such standards. If they are not met, an organization can be shut down, and the responsible manager can be fined or jailed for not meeting OSHA's standards.

OSHA Inspections

see p 599 bottom

To make sure the law is obeyed, OSHA inspectors visit places of employment, on their own schedules or on invitation of an employer, union, or employee. An employee who requests an inspection need not be identified to the employer. If the employer is found guilty of a violation, the penalties include (1) willful or repeated violations, $10,000 per violation; (2) citation for serious violation, $1,000 each; (3) citation for less serious violation, up to $1,000 discretionary; (4) failure to correct cited violation, $1,000 per day; (5) willful violation causing death, up to $10,000 or up to six months in jail; (6) falsification of statements or records, up to $10,000 and/or six months in jail. For example, NL Industries was fined $500,000 and Newport News Shipyard was fined $786,000.

Even if not prepared Smile bring em in & look for poster

A Supreme Court decision ruled that employers can bar OSHA job safety inspectors from their workplaces if the inspectors don't have a search warrant.[11] But these warrants have been made easier to obtain. They can be issued by a court in advance without notifying the employer, so the surprise element of the inspection can be maintained.

OSHA inspectors examine the premises for compliance and the records for accuracy. They categorize a violation as imminent danger (in which case they can close the place down), serious (which calls for a major fine), nonserious (fine up to $1,000) or de mini-

© 1978 by NEA, Inc. Reprinted by permission of NEA.

[11]"Justices to Hear Test of Job Unit's Safety Checks," *The Wall Street Journal,* April 19, 1977, p. 14.

mus (small—a notification is given, but no fine). Atlas Roofing (Georgia) and Frank Irey (Pennsylvania) argued that fining without court action violated the Seventh Amendment, but the Supreme Court supported OSHA unanimously.[12] The employer has the right to appeal fines or citations within OSHA (up to the level of the OSHA Review Commission) or in the courts.

OSHA Record-Keeping and Reporting

The third major OSHA requirement is that the employer keep standardized records of illnesses and injuries and calculate accident ratios. These are shown to OSHA compliance officers who ask to see them. The form used is illustrated in Exhibit 19–4. Accidents and

Exhibit 19–4

OSHA injury and illness reporting form

VIII. Injury and Illness Summary (covering calendar year 1977)

Instructions:
- This section may be completed by copying data from OSHA Form No. 102 "Summary, Occupational Injuries and Illnesses," which you are required to complete and post in your establishment.
- Leave Section VIII blank if there were no recordable injuries or illnesses during 1977.
- Code 30 — Add all occupational illnesses (Code 21 + 22 + 23 + 24 + 25 + 26 + 29) and enter on this line for each column (3) through (8).
- Code 31 — Add occupational injuries (Code 10) and the sum of all occupational illnesses (Code 30) and enter on this line for each column (3) through (8).

Code (1)	Category (2)	Fatalities (deaths) (3)	Lost workday cases			Nonfatal cases without lost workdays*	
			Number of cases (4)	Number of cases involving permanent transfer to another job or termination of employment (5)	Number of lost workdays (6)	Number of cases (7)	Number of cases involving transfer to another job or termination of employment (8)
10	Occupational injuries						
21	Occupational skin diseases or disorders						
22	Dust diseases of the lungs (pneumoconioses)						
23	Respiratory conditions due to toxic agents						
24	Poisoning (systemic effects of toxic materials)						
25	Disorders due to physical agents (other than toxic materials)						
26	Disorders due to repeated trauma						
29	All other occupational illnesses						
30	Sum of all occupational illnesses (Add Codes 21 through 29)						
31	Total of all occupational injuries and illnesses (Add Codes 10 + 30)						

*Nonfatal cases without lost workdays—Cases resulting in: Medical treatment beyond first aid, diagnosis of occupational illness, loss of consciousness, restriction of work or motion, or transfer to another job (without lost workdays).

Comments: _____

_____

IX.   Report prepared by: _____ Date: _____

Title: _____ Area code and phone: _____

---

[12]"Justices Uphold Right of Job Safety Unit to Set Penalties without Going to Court," *The Wall Street Journal*, March 24, 1977.

illnesses that must be reported are those that result in deaths, disabilities that cause the employee to miss work, and medical care injuries that require treatment by a physician.

An OSHA guide to when to report and record an illness, injury, or death is shown in Exhibit 19–5. Injuries or illnesses that require only first aid and involve no loss of work time need not be reported. Employers go to great lengths to categorize incidents as "minor injuries," trying to treat them through first aid and keeping the employee on the job (even a make-work job), to avoid reporting them. To do so might lead to an OSHA inspection or raise their workers' compensation insurance rates. The employer must also report accident frequency and severity rates. The firm must also post OSHA Form 102 in a prominent place at work. It is a summary of the injuries and illnesses report.

Some Consequences of OSHA: Management's View

Most managers generally agree that OSHA has had a very rocky history.[13] They believe it has fallen far short of its promise. Let's examine some of the areas toward which managerial criticism is pointed. *Nonqualified inspectors*

Safety Standards • The general conclusion of most managers is that the agency's standards, more than 10 years after the law was passed, are still unreadable, arbitrary, overly specific, too oriented toward trivia, too costly to implement, and unworkable. An example of the trivia in the OSHA standards appears in a publication on ranch safety. It suggested

Exhibit 19–5 _____

Guide for reporting and recording accidents, illnesses, and deaths

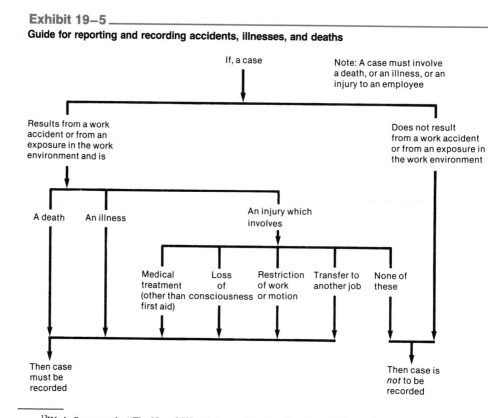

[13]Wade Swormstedt, "The New OSHA," *Screen Printing*, December 1981, pp. 58–63, 117–18.

to ranchers that "since dangerous gases come from manure pits, you should be careful not to fall into manure pits." We don't suppose many ranchers willingly fall into them, with or without dangerous gases.

A more critical condition than the poor quality of the standards is the fact that many of them originally were not in written form. In the first five years, only three new sets of standards were written. Many others are still in the process. OSHA has difficulty writing standards for existing technology, but it *really* has problems with new technologies where no standards exist. It is very difficult to adjust old standards to new technologies. Managers believe that what is needed is a whole new strategy for standard setting and enforcement.[14]

In the same way, OSHA did not try to inspect all industries equally but created priorities based upon known hazardous occupations, but managers feel all standards should not have equal emphasis. In the standards already set, the readability should be improved. More importantly, the agency should categorize the subparts of the standards into categories based on likelihood of accident or illness. These categories might be:

Most important. To be enforced at once and fully.

Of average importance. To be enforced later and in the spirit, not the letter, of the regulation.

Desirable. To be enforced when the most important standards and those of average importance are in full compliance.

If the standards were publicized to highlight these weights, employers could live with OSHA a bit more easily.

OSHA Inspections • OSHA does not inspect each industry with equal frequency. Initially, they set up five target industries to be inspected often because of their high rates of accidents: roof and sheet metal work; meat packing; miscellaneous transportation (mobile homes), and lumber and wood products. Later foundries and casting and metal-stamping industries were added to the target industries list. Target health hazard industries are those involving asbestos, carbon monoxide, cotton dust, lead, and silica.

Appealing Violations • An employer who wishes to appeal a violation citation can do so within OSHA, through the Occupational Safety and Health Review Commission, or through the federal courts. Generally speaking neither management nor labor has been happy with the inspections, one side claiming too few, the other too many. The Supreme Court decision regarding the need for search warrants is a result. Because of a shortage of inspectors and this Court ruling and because OSHA recognizes that it cannot enforce the law without the employers' help, the agency has begun to emphasize voluntary compliance. This consists of educational programs and "dry run" inspections in which the employer is advised of hazards but is given a chance to correct them before a citation is issued. President Reagan used in his campaign in 1980 the rules of OSHA to point out the excesses of government involvement in business. Since he took office in January 1981, the number of OSHA inspectors have been cut to about 1,100.[15] Likewise, the inspections being carried out were cut by 21 percent since President Reagan has been in office (now about 21,000 inspections a year).

---

[14]Ibid.

[15]"A Deregulation Report Card," *Newsweek,* January 11, 1982, pp. 50–53.

Consequences of Record-Keeping and Reporting • Few managers would quarrel with the need to keep adequate records on accidents and health and to calculate accident ratios. It seems reasonable for them to be recorded and reported in a standardized way, for ease in summarizing. But OSHA has been severely criticized by managers for the amount of paperwork required and the frequent changes in it.

Final Management Thoughts on OSHA

So far, there is only impressionistic managerial evidence on OSHA. Ashford, who had great hopes for OSHA, concluded his Ford Foundation report by saying ''The OSHA Act has failed thus far to live up to its potential for reducing job injury and disease.'' General Motors pointed out that although it was spending $15 per car to implement OSHA, and although in the first five years of OSHA the company has been inspected 614 times, received 258 citations, and spent $29 million to fulfill the requirements (and 11 million *worker-years* to get in compliance) ''there was no correlation between meeting OSHA's regulations and reduction of accidents.''[16]

Ultimately, whether OSHA succeeds or fails depends on a decrease in the number and severity of accidents and the incidence of occupational disease in the working population. OSHA's annual reports are phrased in bureaucratic ''success'' terms such as increases in numbers of inspections, pamphlets printed, and dollars of research spent. Until it can show that the *costs* of enforcement are exceeded by *benefits* in terms of reduced accidents and fewer disease victims, we shall have to wait and see whether the program should be called a success or a bureaucratic nightmare.

Management feels that an important factor is not presently covered in OSHA's approach: the worker's responsibility for his or her own health and safety. All the responsibility is placed on *management*. For example, if employees wish to skip medical tests to determine if they are developing an occupational disease, OSHA has ruled they can. If an employee refuses to cooperate in safety matters and an OSHA inspector finds a violation, the *company* is held responsible. For example, there are many instances of employees refusing to wear the safety equipment recommended by OSHA. If the inspector sees this, he *fines the company*. All the company can do is discipline (or possibly fire) the employee.

What can the operating manager or P/HRM specialist do to help keep the enterprise in compliance with OSHA? The P/HRM specialist should know the standards that apply to the organization and check to see that they are being met. P/HRM is also responsible for keeping OSHA records up to date and filing them on time. The operating manager must know the standards that apply to her or his unit or department and see that the unit meets the standards.

As citizens, all managers should see to it that OSHA is effective at the organization. But they can also write their representatives to improve it so that:

Standards are understandable and focus on important items.

Advisory inspections are permitted.

Records and reports are minimized and efficient.

---

[16]Ashford, *Crises in the Workplace*.

Some Consequences of OSHA: Union's Views

As would be expected, the union's view of OSHA is more favorable than management's. The union believes that the passage of OSHA and its history clearly demonstrate the need for a federal role in safety and health.[17] The identification of hazards is a task of such proportion that it can only be accomplished with the resources and authority of the federal government.

The union believes that OSHA has clearly made great strides despite managerial resistance. Fatalities have decreased 10 percent since OSHA, meaning that the lives of thousands of workers have been saved. Similarly, thousands of workers have been spared serious injuries, with a 15 percent overall decline in total injuries during OSHA's lifetime.

OSHA Regulations and Worker Involvement • OSHA has provided workers access to the employer's records of illnesses and injuries. Consequently, many employers have encouraged the participation of workers in the enforcement process. Where effective, local union safety and health committees have been established to deal with problems at the plant level. Armed with training and education, and backed by their international unions, these local committees are having an impact on making the workplace safer and healthier. Health and safety is now the fastest growing among union programs. Each year, under OSHA's New Directions program, more than 20,000 workers are trained in recognition and control of hazards, more than half through union programs.

Justice Is Too Slow • Everytime a major standard to improve safety and health is proposed, management resists. They use every political and legal avenue to block standards. Management consultants are hired to argue against the standard's validity. Who suffers? The workers, say the unions, Their argument is that the courts take too long to make rulings.

The estimated time of standards development for changes in safety and health conditions is 2½ to 3 years. Judicial stays may add one or more years delay. For example, the Coke Oven standard, subject of a Steelworkers union petition for regulation in 1971, was still pending in 1982 before the U.S. Supreme Court.

OSHA Enforcement Differences • The OSHA staff is still too thin in numbers to do the job. A major purpose of the law was to achieve a nationwide, uniform, strong enforcement program. Despite the intent, enforcement is still somewhat unsystematic. There are differences in enforcement aggressiveness from area to area in the country. The union would like to see more aggressive enforcement across the country. Unfortunately, the cutbacks in staff and funding under the Reagan administration are considered to be reasons why enforcement variability will probably become even greater.

Union leaders like the United Auto Workers' Douglas Frazer have stated, "There seems to be a policy of weakening health standards to suit the interests of industry, rather than safeguarding worker's health and safety as a primary mission."[18] Frazer believes that the Reagan initiated changes will be a setback. Cuts in staff, budgets, and less interest in

---

[17]Section is largely based on Lane Kirkland, "OSHA: A 10-Year Success Story," *AFL-CIO American Federationist,* July 1980, pp. 1–4.

[18]Swormstedt, "The New OSHA," p. 61.

safety and health suggest that there will be less enforcement of OSHA. This according to union leaders means a return to more severe, more frequent, and more costly accidents and illnesses.

Some Jobs Are Still Not Adequately Covered • There are still extremely dangerous jobs not covered by OSHA standards. Grain elevator and mill workers are not covered by a specific OSHA standard. Grain handlers face each day the threat of sudden death in an explosion or the development of an eventually incapacitating illness arising from their chronic exposures to grain dust and pesticides.[19] Grain elevator explosions are not a new occurrence. Exhibit 19–6 lists some of the more tragic dust explosions.

Unions believe that rural locations, unorganized workers, small facilities together with the political power of agribusiness management groups—who regard any regulation as overregulation—have served to perpetuate the hazards in the grain industry. Only recently have grain elevator workers received a degree of public attention, probably due to explosions like those listed in Exhibit 19–6.

The safety and health problems in grain elevators will not be significantly improved until OSHA standards are set. The problem, as mentioned above, is delay after delay. Setting standards and moving through the courts is a lengthy process. The union wants everyone to think about grain workers and others, who, even today as we move into the mid-1980s, work in filthy, dangerous, and life-threatening jobs daily.

Final Union Thoughts on OSHA

The union believes that OSHA has resulted in better informed employees, increased union involvement in safety and health, and better working conditions. These are all positive contributions. However, the union is still not satisfied that OSHA has achieved everything that it should. Workers are still needlessly being killed and subjected to work-related conditions and procedures that are detrimental to their quality of life.

Unions now are fearful that the progress made under OSHA will be lost without support from President Reagan. His actions during 1981 indicate that OSHA will not be

Exhibit 19–6 _____

An alarming safety scorecard

Dust explosions		Deaths	Injuries
Zilwaukee, Michigan	January 22, 1976	5	13
Houston, Texas	February 22, 1976	9	7
Delevan, Minnesota	August 19, 1976	2	3
Chicago, Illinois	August 4, 1977	2	3
Tupelo, Mississippi	December 22, 1977	4	15
Westwego, Louisiana	December 22, 1977	36	9
Galveston, Texas	December 27, 1977	18	23
Liberty, Missouri	January 19, 1978	3	6
Savage, Minnesota	October 3, 1978	3	2
Lexington, Nebraska	January 23, 1979	1	1

Source: Harbrant, Robert F., Enforcement: A Dangerous Job with No Standards to Cover It, *AFL-CIO American Federationist,* July 1980, p. 15.

---

[19] Robert F. Harbant, "A Dangerous Job with No Standards to Cover It," *AFL-CIO American Federationist,* July 1980, pp. 15–16.

a top priority and that deregulation will be the rule rather than the exception.[20] This could mean fewer inspections, less aggressive enforcement, and less management interest in improving the safety and health conditons.

Health Programs

What is meant by the word health? While "the absence of disease" is one way of defining health, it is more informative to define it as "a state of physical, mental, and social well-being."[21] This definition points to the relationships among body, mind, and social patterns. An employee's health can be harmed through disease, accident, or stress. Managers now realize that they must be concerned about the general health of employees, and this includes psychological well-being. A competent manager or operator who is depressed and has low self-esteem is as nonproductive as a manager or operator who was injured and is hospitalized.

Today more and more organizations such as Control Data, IBM, Prudential, Tenneco, and Kimberly-Clark have initiated what are called *preventive health programs*.[22] One objective of these programs is to achieve a higher level of employee "wellness" and to decrease health impairment costs by providing a program that is medically valid and responsive to workers needs.

Preventive Health: Kimberly-Clark and Control Data

In order to examine a preventive health program in action, the Kimberly-Clark's program will be discussed. Kimberly-Clark was selected because its program is highly publicized, respected by its employees, and is being evaluated for its effects on cost, productivity, and well-being.[23] In 1977, Kimberly-Clark initiated its preventive health program, which consists of collecting information and samples from an employee to conduct medical history and health risk profile, medical tests of urine, blood, hearing, eyesight, extremity flexibility, and so on, exercise testing by treadmill or bicycle ergometer, health profile analysis by a physician, and recommendations to improve health. The company has constructed a 32,000 square foot exercise facility that can be used to follow through on many of the physician's health improvement recommendations.

The health screening at Kimberly-Clark has identified cases of hypertension, obesity, high cholesterol, cancer, ulcers, and high risk for heart attack. Cancer was detected in eight employees. Also several employees required surgery for heart problems detected in the program.

Kimberly-Clark believes that they are investing in the long run with their preventive health program. Identifying health problems, improving wellness, and being concerned

---

[20]"A Deregulation Report Card," p. 52.

[21]Gloria C. Gordon and Mary Sue Henifin, "Health and Safety, Job Stress, and Shift Work," in *Making Organizations Human and Productive,* ed. H. Meltzer and Walter R. Nord (New York: John Wiley & Sons, 1981), p. 322.

[22]John M. Ivancevich and Michael T. Matteson, "Optimizing Human Resources: A Case for Preventive Health and Stress Management," *Organizational Dynamics,* Autumn 1980, pp. 4–25.

[23]Robert E. Dedmon and Mary Katherine Kubiak, "The Medical Director's Role in Industry," *Personnel Administrator,* September 1981, pp. 59–64.

about employees are reasons why Kimberly-Clark is willing to invest so much in their preventive health program.

A program similar to Kimberly-Clark's is used by Control Data Corporation (CDC). The CDC Stay Well program was initiated in 1980.[24] It is offered as a free corporate benefit to CDC's 57,000 U.S.-based employees and their spouses. There were 27,000 CDC employees in the program in 1981 and the company hoped to significantly increase that number by the end of 1983.

For employees and their spouses, the CDC program consists of an orientation session a health screening exam, a group interpretation session, and a series of courses that teach the skills necessary to change health-related behavior. CDC has a very strict confidentiality policy. No one at the company has access to any individual data except physicians who review the data. Individual participants decide whether they will share the information with their personal physicians. Each employee can decide what courses of action will be taken after hearing and seeing the CDC physician's analysis of his or her health risk profile.

CDC is conducting an evaluation of the effects, if any, of the program on health-related attitudes. The firm is also studying the consequences of those changes on the health of employees and in the company in terms of health care costs, worker productivity, absenteeism, and turnover. A three-year analysis of data is being conducted so that modifications and improvements can be made.

Kimberly-Clark, Control Data, and hundreds of other organizations believe that preventive health programs make good sense. It is estimated that $18–$25 billion is lost each year through nonmanagerial employee absenteeism, hospitalization, or death.[25] If these costs can even be cut by as little as 5 percent through preventive health programs they would be a significant bargain. Preventive health is an idea whose time has come to many corporations.

Stress Management

Stress is a common experience that is a part of life. However, the concept of stress is a very difficult one to pin down in specific terms. There are experts who think of stress as the pressures in the world that produce emotional discomfort. Others feel that emotional discomfort is the stress that is caused by pressure or conditions that are called stressors. Still others view stress in terms of physiological or body reactions: blood pressure, heart rate, or hormone levels.[26] Instead of entering another interpretation of stress will be defined as a *person's physical, chemical, and mental reactions to stressors or stimuli in the environment—the boss, co-workers, P/HRM policies,* and so on. Stress occurs whenever environmental forces (stimuli) throw the bodily and mental functions of a person out of equilibrium.

Stress has typically been cast in terms of negative reactions. Of course, it can also be

---

[24]Murray P. Naditch, "Wellness Program Reaps Healthy Benefits for Sponsoring Employer," *Risk Management,* October 1981, pp. 21–24.

[25]This is a conservative estimate. Some experts estimate this figure to actually be closer to $100 billion. See John M. Ivancevich and Michael T. Matteson, *Stress and Work: A Managerial Perspective* (Glenview, Ill.: Scott, Foresman, 1980), pp. 18–19.

[26]For various interpretations of stress, see Tom Cox, *Stress* (Baltimore: University Park Press, 1978); Hans Selye, *The Stress of Life* (New York: McGraw-Hill, 1976); and K. Albrecht, *Stress and the Manager* (Englewood Cliffs, N.J.: Prentice-Hall, 1979).

good for a person. Stress is what helps a person complete a report on time or generate a good, quick problem-solving procedure. In this chapter we acknowledge the positive aspects of stress—life without stress is death—but our main attention will be on the negative aspects of stress.

Stress and Disease • Job-related stress has been associated with a vast array of diseases such as coronary heart disease, hypertension, peptic ulcers, colitis, and various psychological problems such as anxiety and depression. Research has shown that stress affects the endocrine system, the cardiovascular system, the muscular system, and the emotions directly.[27] It also has a general arousal influence on the entire body.

The stress and disease linkage continues to be studied and is of interest to managers. A person that is emotionally troubled and depressed because of stress is often unable to function on the job and may even create problems for other workers if he or she attempts to work. In general, psychological job stress reactions are not severe psychoses. They are, however, frustrating; they do reduce a person's desire to work; they do cause feelings of fatigue. Thus, although many experts are concerned about the stress-coronary heart disease association there is also the possible stress-psychological reaction association.

"You need a good rest — can you just wheel without dealing for a while?"

Reprinted by permission The Wall Street Journal.

[27]For example, see J. G. Bruhn and S. Wolf, *The Roseto Story: An Anatomy of Health* (Norman, Okla.: University of Oklahoma Press, 1979); and K. R. Pelletier, *Mind as Healer, Mind as Slayer* (New York: Delacorte Press, 1977); and H. Weiner, *Psychobiology and Human Disease* (New York: Elsevier, North-Holland, 1977).

The Person/Environment Fit • Changes in the work and personal environment are inevitable. Too often managers underestimate how changes can throw a person off kilter. A person that does not feel comfortable with his or her work environment is in what psychologists refer to as in a state of disequilibrium. The person (skills, abilities, goals) does not fit with the work environment (boss, co-workers, compensation system). The costs of the lack of fit in person/environment can be many: subjective (feeling fatigued), behavioral (accident prone), cognitive (a mental block), physiological (elevated blood pressure), and/or organizational (higher absence rate).[28]

Research studies point out that these five levels of stress caused by disequilibrium or lack of fit are costly. The costs to an organization are found in premature deaths of employees, higher rates of accidents, performance inefficiencies, increased turnover, increased disability payments, and in many other areas.[29]

One way to attack the stress cost problem is to identify the stressors that contribute to it. Exhibit 19–7 is presented to show some of the major person and environmental stressors that lead to stress and dysfunctional consequences. This managerial model illustrates that stress is caused by the interaction of people with their environment. It is a person's perception of a work situation that can make a stressor stressful. This is what is portrayed in Exhibit 19–7. Covering each detail of Exhibit 19–7 is beyond the scope of this book. Consequently, only a few of the stressors will be examined.

Overload • A person's workload can cause stress. Workload can relate to the quantity of the work (quantitative) or the quality (qualitative) of the activity to be completed (mental requirements). Underload can create problems as well as overload. Being overloaded can cause a person to work long hours to stay even which can result in fatigue and more accidents. On the other hand, boredom can set in if a person is underloaded. A bored worker often avoids work by staying at home more frequently. The worker that is bored and stays at home often mopes around. The result—a lack of adequate exercise to maintain a healthy body.[30] It is a vicious circle.

Role Conflict • How a person behaves in a given job depends on many factors. A combination of the expectations and demands an employee places upon him or herself and those of co-workers results in a set of forces called role pressures. When a situation arises in which two or more role pressures are in conflict with one another, role conflict exists. Role conflict exists whenever compliance with one set of pressures makes compliance with one set of pressures makes compliance with another set difficult, objectionable, or impossible.

Researchers have found that conflict is associated with job dissatisfaction and anxiety.[31] It has also been linked to heart disease, elevated blood pressure, and excessive eating. Role conflict seems to undermine a peaceful work state and this leads to physiological and psychological changes.

---

[28]Marilyn J. Davidson and Cary L. Cooper, "A Model of Occupational Stress," *Journal of Occupational Medicine,* August 1981, pp. 564–74.

[29]Cox, *Stress.*

[30]Michael J. Smith, "Recognition and Control of Psychosocial Job Stress," *Professional Safety,* August 1981, pp. 20–26.

[31]S. M. Sales and J. House, "Job Dissatisfaction as a Possible Risk Factor in Coronary Heart Disease," *Journal of Chronic Disease,* 1971, pp. 861–73.

Exhibit 19–7

A managerial model for examining job stress

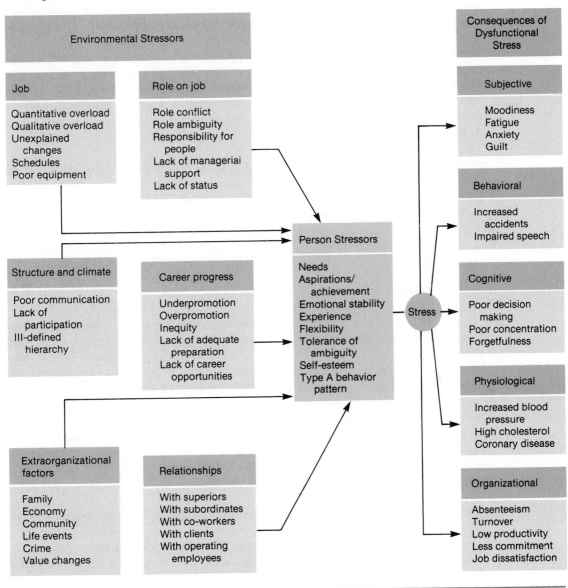

Life Events • Holmes and Rahe have studied how life events can contribute to a stressful life.[32] Based on their research they developed a numerical value for each life event, ranking the events in order of magnitude. After developing the scoring system, the medical histories and life events scores of patients were reviewed. It was found that patients who

---

[32]T. H. Holmes and R. H. Rahe, "The Social Readjustment Rating Scale," _Journal of Psychosomatic Medicine,_ 1967, pp. 213–18.

had a high score on what the researchers called the Social Readjustment Rating Scale (SRRS) were more likely to contract illness following the events. The SRRS is presented in Exhibit 19–8. People with scores of over 300 were very likely to contract some form of stress-related illness, such as ulcers, migrane headaches, colitis, and heart disease, in the near future.

The work of Holmes and Rahe with the SRRS points out the connection between life changes (stressors) and a lowered resistance to fight illness. This connection is illustrated by such information that 10 times as many widows and widowers die during the first year after the death of a spouse as nonwidowed individuals in a similar age-group. Also the illness rate for divorced persons during the first year after the divorce is 12 times higher than for married persons.

A Person Stressor: Type A Behavior Pattern • In the 1950s two cardiologists, Friedman and Rosenman, began to look at the way a person's behavior pattern can be used to predict the incidence of coronary heart disease.[33] What they discovered was called the Type A behavior pattern. It is defined as:

> . . . an action-emotion complex that can be observed in any person who is aggressively involved in a chronic, incessant struggle to achieve more and more in less and less time, and if required to do so, against the opposing efforts of other things or other persons.

The hard-core Type A person is hard-driving, competitive, has a sense of time urgency, and is chronically impatient with delays. (The opposite of the Type A is the Type B person.) Research has linked Type A-ness with coronary heart disease. Type A men have been found to experience 6½ times the incidence of heart disease than Type B-ness.[34] Also the Type A person has higher blood pressure than the Type B.

There is little doubt that Type A behavior is associated in some ways to a number of diseases. The precise role it plays, however, is not clear. It is incorrect to definitely associate Type A with stress. Yet there is likely to be more stress experienced by Type As. Type As tend to create stress for themselves by constantly exposing themselves to stressors that the Type B avoids like work overload, handling too many projects, and always rushing to finish one job just to start a new job.

Pinpointing Worker Stress • There are a number of methods available to managers for identifying stress within themselves and employees. The precise identification of negative stress should be left to the professional. A well-trained behavioral scientist, physician, or counselor can use psychological tests, in-depth interviews, or medical history forms and medical tests to uncover stress problems.

The nonprofessional involved in pinpointing stress problems at work is the manager. He or she can also do some diagnosis. First, the manager should look for sudden, unexplained changes in mood, tensions, and loss of temper episodes. Second, when an efficient worker becomes sloppy or when a prompt worker becomes late this signifies changes in behavior. This can be a signal that the person is experiencing stress.

---

[33]M. Friedman and R. Rosenman, *Type A Behavior and Your Heart* (New York: Alfred A. Knopf, 1974).

[34]R. Rosenman, M. Friedman, R. Straus, C. Jenkins, S. Zyzanski, and M. Wurm, "Coronary Heart Disease in the Western Collaborative Group Study: A Follow-Up Experience of 4½ years," *Journal of Chronic Disease,* 1970, pp. 173–90.

Exhibit 19–8 _____

The social readjustment rating scale*

Instructions: Check off each of these life events that has happened to you during the previous year. Total the associated points. A score of 150 or less means a relatively low amount of life change and a low susceptibility to stress-induced health breakdown. A score of 150 to 300 points implies about a 50 percent chance of a major health breakdown in the next two years. A score above 300 raises the odds to about 80 percent, according to the Holmes-Rahe statistical preduction model.

	Life events	*Mean value*
1.	Death of spouse	100
2.	Divorce	73
3.	Marital separation from mate	65
4.	Detention in jail or other institution	63
5.	Death of a close family member	63
6.	Major personal injury or illness	53
7.	Marriage	50
8.	Being fired at work	47
9.	Marital reconciliation with mate	45
10.	Retirement from work	45
11.	Major change in the health or behavior of a family member	44
12.	Pregnancy	40
13.	Sexual difficulties	39
14.	Gaining a new family member (e.g., through birth, adoption, oldster moving in, etc.)	39
15.	Major business readjustment (e.g., merger, reorganization, bankruptcy, etc.)	39
16.	Major change in financial state (e.g., a lot worse off or a lot better off than usual)	38
17.	Death of a close friend	37
18.	Changing to a different line of work	36
19.	Major change in the number of arguments with spouse (e.g., either a lot more or a lot less than usual regarding child rearing, personal habits, etc.)	35
20.	Taking on a mortgage greater than $10,000 (e.g., purchasing a home, business, etc.)	31
21.	Foreclosure on a mortgage or loan	30
22.	Major change in responsibilities at work (e.g., promotion, demotion, lateral transfer)	29
23.	Son or daughter leaving home (e.g., marriage, attending college, etc.)	29
24.	In-law troubles	29
25.	Outstanding personal achievement	28
26.	Wife beginning or ceasing work outside the home	26
27.	Beginning or ceasing formal schooling	26
28.	Major change in living conditions (e.g., building a new home, remodeling, deterioration of home or neighborhood)	25
29.	Revision of personal habits (dress, manners, associations, etc.)	24
30.	Troubles with the boss	23
31.	Major change in working hours or conditions	20
32.	Change in residence	20
33.	Changing to a new school	20
34.	Major change in usual type and/or amount of recreation	19
35.	Major change in church activities (e.g., a lot more or a lot less than usual)	19
36.	Major change in social activities (e.g., clubs, dancing, movies, visiting, etc.)	18
37.	Taking on a mortgage or loan less than $10,000 (e.g., purchasing a car, TV, freezer, etc.)	17
38.	Major change in sleeping habits (a lot more or a lot less sleep, or change in part of day when asleep)	16
39.	Major change in number of family get-togethers (e.g., a lot more or a lot less than usual)	15
40.	Major change in eating habits (a lot more or a lot less food intake, or very different meal hours or surroundings)	15
41.	Vacation	13
42.	Christmas	12
43.	Minor violations of the law (e.g., traffic tickets, jaywalking, disturbing the peace, etc.)	11

Source: Reprinted with permission from *Journal of Psychosomatic Research*, vol. 11, no. 2, T. H. Holmes and R. H. Rahe, The Social Readjustment Rating Scale, pp. 213–18. Copyright 1967, Pergamon Press, Ltd.

Coping with Stress • As implied above stress in life is inevitable. However, when it hurts the person, co-workers, or the organization it must be addressed. There are two ways to cope with stress. The first is to eliminate the source of what we call the stressor(s) that is causing the stress. This means changing policies, the structure, the work requirements, or whatever is necessary. The second approach is to deal with the stress individually or organizationally.

Individual stress coping programs include meditation, biofeedback, training, exercise, diet, and even prayer. These programs work for some people. They help the person feel better, relax, and regenerate energy. A few coping programs are briefly mentioned in Exhibit 19–9.

There are also organizational stress coping programs. In fact, some would call the Kimberly-Clark and Control Data approach a stress management program. Experts in organizations can use their knowledge about stress and employee health to develop and implement organizationally sponsored stress coping workshops and seminars.[35] In addition, these experts can recommend structural, job, and policy changes that can eventually improve the well-being of employees.

The P/HRM department has a role to play in stress coping programs. It can provide specialists, facilities, monitoring or evaluation, and other important resources. Organiza-

---

Exhibit 19–9 _____

Stress coping methods: A few samples

Planning: Much stress in personal and work life can be managed by planning. Take some time to assess your personal and career goals. At work, set aisde some time to plan tomorrows's activities. How do they relate to your goals or your company's goals?

Physical exercise: Regular exercise can contribute to the physical health of the individual, and it can also help the person overcome stress, both as an outlet and as physical conditioning. Of course, you should consult a physician before embarking on a strenuous exercise program.

Diet: Prolonged stress can deplete your body's supply of infection-fighting vitamins, leaving you susceptible to disease. Also, eating habits change under stress. The manager, up against a deadline, might well work through lunch or arrive late at dinner and unwind by downing a double scotch. During stressful periods, maintaining a good diet is essential.

Biofeedback: This therapeutic technique is used in the treatment of migraine headaches, high blood pressure, muscle tension, and other stress-related problems. It involves the monitoring of one or more body functions with electronic devices that signal the user with tones, clicks, or lights. For example, people can learn to control brain waves, pulse rate, blood pressure, and the temperature in their hands and feet.

Meditation or relaxation: Emerging from Far Eastern philosophies, these techniques include meditation, transcendental meditation, yoga, and Zen. The Americanization of meditation, which was popularized in Herbert Bensen's book *The Relaxation Response,* has a person sit in a comfortable chair in a quiet area with subdued lighting. The person closes his or her eyes, takes a deep breath, and exhales. Each time the person exhales, he or she repeats a single word or mantra. Repeating this single word helps to eliminate distracting thoughts. This process takes approximately 20 minutes, although some individuals can achieve a refreshing relaxation in just a few moments.

Variations include tensing and relaxing muscles until relaxation of the entire body is reached. Others recommend thinking of a favorite vacation spot—a deserted beach or a calm lake—recalling all the sights and sounds.

Psychotherapy: A wide variety of interpersonal techniques are used that usually involve intensive one-to-one work with a professional therapist.

Psychoanalysis: This is a form of psychotherapy during which the therapist takes the patient into the depths of his or her personality to examine the root causes of abnormal behavior.

---

[35]Michael T. Matteson and John M. Ivancevich, *Managing Job Stress and Health* (New York: Macmillan, 1982).

"There's a fine line between meditating and snoozing."
Reprinted by permission The Wall Street Journal.

tions such as IBM, Tenneco, Control Data, Shell, and Prudential already have P/HRM employees performing such duties as setting up exercise classes, initiating fitness programs, and providing diet counseling. We expect more and more organizations to become concerned about and involved with stress management as we moved toward the 1990s.

Workers' Compensation and Disability Programs

Disability programs are designed to help workers who are ill or injured and cannot work (see Chapter 15). Employees show little preference for them. Although before his accident Dale Silas was probably not too interested in workers' compensation, he is now. He's also interested in Lysander's health insurance plan.

There are three programs in the United States for private- and third-sector employees. One is federal. The social security system is called OASDI, and the "DI" stands for disability insurance. A person who is totally disabled and unable to work can receive a small payment, perhaps $60 a week, from social security until age 65. As with other social security programs, this is financed by employer and employee payroll contributions.

The second program is the state-run workers' compensation, financed by employer payments. It pays for permanent partial, total partial, or total disability arising out of the employment situation. Requirements, payments, and procedures vary somewhat from state to state. Workers' compensation systems are compulsory in most states. For federal government employees, the Federal Employees Compensation Act of 1949 (last amended in 1974) provides for payments for accidents and injuries paralleling workers' compensation.

The compensation comes in two forms: monetary reimbursement, and payment of medical expenses. The amount of compensation is based on fixed schedules of minimum and maximum payments. Disability payments are often based on formulas of the employee's earnings, modified by economic conditions such as the number of dependents. There is usually a week's waiting period prior to the payment of the compensation and fixed compensation for permanent losses (such as $200 for loss of a finger).

The employee receives workers' compensation no matter whose fault an accident is. Payment is made for physical impairments and for neuroses which may result from a physical loss. The employer must also pay compensation for diseases which result from occupations (such as black lung disease in mining) and for the results of undue stress laid on employees, such as hernias resulting from lifting heavy materials. Both workers' compensation laws and OSHA require the employer to keep detailed accident and death records.

The employer pays the entire cost of workers' compensation, usually by participating in private insurance plans or state-run schemes or by self-insurance. The improvement of safety conditions at the work site can lead to lower insurance costs if accidents decline as a result.

The cost of workers' compensation varies by industry and type of work. For example, in a recent year, the average firm devoted less than 1 percent of its total compensation to workers' compensation. This varied from 1.5 percent for nonoffice, nonmanufacturing jobs to a low of 0.03 percent for office employees. But workers' compensation claims went from $3.9 to over $20 billion from 1972 to 1981.[36]

In some states, if the employee will receive social security disability payments, workers' compensation is adjusted so that a joint maximum (for example, $80 per week) is not exceeded.

Criticism of workers' compensation programs centers on the fact that the systems were designed to prevent hardship but not to discourage return to work or rehabilitation of the injured worker. The National Commission on State Workers' Compensation was very critical of state workers' compensation plans. It found that the benefits are too low, and too many employers have inadequate accident prevention programs. The commission made 80 specific recommendations to the states which, if not actuated, should be legislated by Congress.

The third program under which employees receive workers' compensation is private disability insurance provided by employers. About two thirds of the companies surveyed provide accident and sickness insurance to their employees (usually for blue-collar workers). A variation for white-collar workers is sick pay-salary continuance insurance. About 85 percent of the companies surveyed have this. These plans pay wages or salaries to employees with short-term disabilities. Generally they supplement workers' compensation. Long-term disability pay or pensions for employees was also being offered by 74 percent of companies surveyed for managers, 62 percent for white-collar employees, and 28 percent for blue-collar workers. This insurance is designed to supplement government programs and bring total compensation up to a more livable level. Luckily for Dale Silas, Lysander does have disability coverage.

Evaluation of Safety and Health Programs

Health and (especially) safety programs have begun to receive more attention in recent years. The consequences of inadequate programs are measurable: increased workers' compensation payments, larger insurance costs, fines from OSHA, and union pressures. A safety management program requires these steps.

Establishment of indicator systems (for example, accident statistics).
Development of effective reporting systems.
Development of rules and procedures.
Rewarding supervisors for effective management of the safety function.

Top-management support is needed, and proper design of jobs and worker-machine interactions is necessary, but probably the key is participation by employees.

---

[36]Berkeley Rice, "Can Companies Kill?" *Psychology Today,* June 1981, pp. 80–85.

A health and safety program can be evaluated fairly directly in a cost/benefits sense. The costs of safety specialists, new safety devices, and other measures can be calculated. Reductions in accidents, lowered insurance costs, and lowered fines can be weighed against these costs. Studies evaluating safety and health programs show that safety is cost effective.

In one study, 54 respondents were interviewed and received questionnaires from 86 more in the chemical, paper, and wood-product industries in Texas.[37] It was determined that the most cost-effective safety programs were *not* the most expensive ones. They were programs which combined a number of safety approaches: safety rules, off-the-job safety, safety training, safety orientation, safety meetings, medical facilities and staff, and strong top-management participation and support of the safety program. Engineering and nonengineering approaches were used, but the emphasis was on the engineering aspects of safety. Cost/benefits studies for health and safety programs can be very helpful in analyzing and improving them.

Summary

Effective safety and health programs can exist in all organizations. The nature of the safety program varies, of course, as the diagnostic approach emphasizes. Some clues to this are given in the statements below:

1. Safety hazards are those aspects of the work environment which have the potential of immediate and sometimes violent harm to an employee.
2. Health hazards are those aspects of the work environment which slowly and cumulatively lead to deterioration of an employee's health.
3. Support from top management and unions for health and safety programs helps assure their effectiveness.
4. The major causes of occupational accidents are the task to be done, the working conditions, and the employee.
5. Organizational responses to health and safety challenges include:

    a. Safety design and preventive approaches.
    b. Inspection, reporting, and accident research.
    c. Safety training and motivation programs.
    d. Auditing safety programs.
    e. Health programs for employees.

6. The Occupational Safety and Health Act was the culmination of the movement for federal supervision of health and safety programs. It has requirements such as:
    a. Meeting safety standards set by OSHA.
    b. Submitting to OSHA inspections.
    c. Keeping records and reporting accidents and illnesses.

7. Today more and more organizations have initiated preventive health programs. These are designed to improve the health and well-being of employees.
8. Stress can play a major role in the health of employees. Thus, more firms are now

---

[37]Foster Rinefort, "A New Look at Occupational Safety," *Personnel Administrator*, November 1977, pp. 29–36.

concerned about understanding and managing stress. Individual- and organizational-based stress management programs are being used.

9. Workers' compensation and disability programs are designed to help workers who are ill or injured and cannot work.

Exhibit 19–10 provided recommendations on health and safety for the model organizations described in Exhibit 1–7 (Chapter 1).

Questions for Review and Discussion

1. How do top managers, operating executives, employees, union officials, safety committees, and safety specialists interact to make the workplace healthy and safe?
2. Why do organizations set up safety and health programs?
3. Why should organizations be concerned about the consequences of occupational stress?
4. Explain what is done in a preventive health program.
5. What are some major causes of accidents and work-related illnesses?
6. Describe the programs organizations have to prevent accidents and illnesses. Which are most effective? Least effective?
7. Why did the U.S. government legislate in the occupational safety and health area?
8. What legal requirements must an organization follow in the health and safety area?

Exhibit 19–10 _____

Recommendations on health and safety for model organizations

Type of organization	Formal safety department	Safety as duty of P/HRM specialist	Formal health department	Arrangement with health team	Preventive health programs	Stress management programs (organizations)
1. Large size, low complexity, high stability	X		X			X
2. Medium size, low complexity, high stability	X			X		X
3. Small size, low complexity, high stability		X		X		
4. Medium size, moderate complexity, moderate stability	X			X	X	X
5. Large size, high complexity, low stability	X		X		X	X
6. Medium size, high complexity, low stability	X			X	X	X
7. Small size, high complexity, low stability				X	X	

Case

After the visit to Bob's plant, Clint returned to his own. He did not feel good, thinking that maybe a safety unit could have prevented Dale's accident. That night, he drove to Denver to visit Dale in the hospital. There was good news: Dale would not be totally disabled. He would be handicapped, but he would be able to work about half the time after his recuperation.

Clint had taken the time to check with Otto Richmond of the P/HRM department about the company's disability plan and workers' compensation. He could tell Dale that between the two plans his compensation would be kept up at its normal level.

Clint I feel very upset though, Dale. Maybe, just maybe, your accident needn't have happened. So

I'm hiring a safety specialist as soon as possible to try to avoid similar accidents in the future.

Dale I'm glad you are. But it was my fault too. I've been at Lysander a long time. I know I shouldn't have done that with the machine. I just got sloppy.

Clint The best news I've gotten in a long time is that you'll be back. Will you help me with the safety program?

Dale I'm a living witness of what can happen if you're not safety conscious. You can bet I'll be behind the safety program.

In the years that followed, Lysander's safety record improved. The improvement was at least partly due to the new safety program Clint installed.

9. Evaluate the relative success or failure of OSHA, the U.S. health and safety agency. What can be done to improve its future operations?
10. What is workers' compensation? Why does it exist? What does it do?

Glossary

Accident Research. The systematic evaluation of the evidence concerning accidents and health hazards.

Health. The state of physical, mental, and social well-being.

Health Hazards. Those aspects of the work environment which slowly and cumulatively (and often irreversibly) lead to deterioration of an employee's health.

Life Events. The changes in a person's life that can contribute to stress.

Occupational Safety and Health Act (1970). An act designed to protect the safety and health of employees. According to this act, employers are responsible for providing workplaces free from hazards to safety and health.

Occupational Safety and Health Administration (OSHA). The government agency responsible for carrying out and administering the Occupational Safety and Health Act.

Preventive Programs. A program instituted within an organization to achieve a high level of employee wellness and to decrease health impairment costs. Programs typically involve health screening exams, stress testing, and physician recommendations.

Safety Hazards. Those aspects of the work environment which have the potential of immediate and sometimes violent harm to an employee.

Stress. A person's physical, chemical, and mental reactions to stressors or stimuli in the environment—the boss, co-workers, P/HRM policies, and so on

Type A Behavior Pattern. An action-emotion complex that can be observed in a person who is aggressive, in a struggle against time, competitive, and chronically impatient.

Part Five

Labor Relations and Safety and Health Cases and Exercises

APPLICATION CASE V–1
Modern Management, Inc.: Union Busters with Briefcases

APPLICATION CASE V–2
DuPont: A Leader in Safety and Health

EXERCISE V
Union-Management Contract Negotiations

APPLICATION CASE V–1

Modern Management, Inc.: Union Busters With Briefcases*

In the old days they used billy clubs and brass knuckles. However, today's union busters go by the name "labor relations consultants."—but they're still out to stop unions from organizing employees. Union "busters" give private counseling on specific company policies, advising management how to circumvent union organizing efforts.

Herbert Melnick operates Modern Management, Inc., of Bannockburn, Illinois. His firm has 70 consultants engaged in helping firms avoid unionization. The consultants are paid over $700 plus expenses per day. The firm in 1981 had a 93 percent success rate. Today there are about 1,000 firms like Modern Management and another 1,500 independent practitioners in the union-busting business. Their specialization is called by critics psychological manipulation of the workers' attitudes in the workplace.

Nonunion companies want to prevent unionization. Management of a unionized shop wants to decertify the union. These goals are within the purview of Modern Management and other union busters. Are they successful? In the NLRB representation elections lost by unions, over 90 percent involve labor relations consultants.

In March 1981, the House Subcommittee on Labor Management Relations issued a report on labor relations consultants. A key recommendation was that the Department of Labor should be more diligent in enforcing the reporting requirements for consultants under the Landrum-Griffin Act. "Virtually every union is required to and does report its activities under the provisions of the Act," the report says. "It is inequitable that the Department does not require consultants, even in instances when they are clearly running management's antiunion campaign, to disclose their involvement."

Some of the situations that led to the call for tighter controls involved PPG Industries, St. Francis Hospital (Milwaukee, Wis.), and Humana Corporation. Listed below are brief descriptions of these situations:

PPG Industries

The law firm representing PPG Industries' Lexington, N.C., plant reportedly trumped up an alienation of affection suit filed in May 1979, against Teamsters' organizer Pat Suporta to discredit her. Suporta had helped win an election at the plant in July 1978. Even after the suit was withdrawn in June 1979, PPG attempted (but failed) to use it as new evidence to get the NLRB to overturn IBT certification. The company's law firm is Hogg, Allen, Ryce, Norton & Blue in Coral Gables, Fla. In a separate incident, PPG fired employee, Terri Drake, in March 1979, four days after she was identified as a union supporter. She and many others on the in-plant committee were blacklisted and couldn't get jobs in the Lexington area. The company also was found to have bugged an employees' cafeteria.

---

*Case is based on "Union Busters," *Viewpoint,* Spring 1981, pp. 6–7.

St. Francis Hospital

In the first NLRB complaint directly against a labor consultant, the board charges that Modern Management, Inc., "independently violated the National Labor Relations Act by its having complete control and use of supervisory personnel at St. Francis Hospital in a systematic and antiunion campaign." The tactics included, the complaint says, "illegal interrogations, promises of benefits, promises of improved conditions of employment and threats of reprisal against employees for engaging in union activities." The St. Francis Federation of Nurses and Health Professionals, American Federation of Teachers, lost an October 1979 election by a vote of 100 to 95. NLRB set aside the election in July 1980.

Humana Corp.

Lloyd Laudermilch, a member of Operating Engineers Local 501 in Las Vegas, Nev., was coached by management at Sunrise Hospital, its parent company, Humana Corp., and its consultants, West Coast Industrial Relations, on how to initiate, gather support for, and file a decertification petition with NLRB. This is a clear violation of the law, which forbids an employer from discussing a decertification petition with employees. Laudermilch was asked—but refused—to sign an affidavit saying that he had never talked to any management people about filing the petition. For his efforts Laudermilch was promised a better job: busting unions at other hospitals owned by Humana. Fortunately he kept the union informed of his activities and the decert effort failed.

Questions for Thought

1. Should union busters like Modern Management be permitted to stop union organizing efforts?
2. Why would union busting be a popular tactic among organizations?
3. Are union busters like Modern Management worth $700 a day plus expenses for each labor relations consultant? Why?

APPLICATION CASE V–2

DuPont: A Leader in Safety and Health*

At DuPont, a company whose origins are in gunpowder, safety is very important. The DuPont plant in Kinston, North Carolina, has a record of more than 66 million hours worked without a disabling injury. The hours started accumulating in 1964. The record went until 1977 when a worker slipped on an icy sidewalk outside the plant and sustained a head injury. If the Kinston plant had incurred injuries at the same rate as an average chemical plant of similar size, it would have experienced 366 injuries.

The story of Kinston is a classic one that shows that safety pays. Visitors to the plant are greeted by a large sign bragging about safety. This is the case throughout DuPont plants. The founder of the corporation Eleuthere Irene duPont was a French immigrant who was an assistant to a chemist in France. At a time when most U.S. firms took few precautions to control accidents, fire, explosions, or employee injuries, Mr. DuPont was ahead of his time. He designed his gunpowder mills to minimize the potential damage in the event of an explosion.

Each plant—located on the banks of the Brandywine Creek near Wilmington, Delaware—was built with three heavy stone walls. The fourth wall was made of light wood and faced the stream. In the event of an explosion, the risk was limited to one building; the force would vent itself by blowing the roof and wooden wall toward the water.

Today DuPont, which has more than 130,000 employees at more than 140 manufacturing sites worldwide, produces more than 1,700 products. DuPont is known as a safety leader and trend setter in 30 countries. In 1980, DuPont's U.S. lost workday incidence rate was .039 injuries per 200,000 hours, representing a total of 40 injuries for a population of 106,000 employees. This means that the company's workers' compensation costs would be 68 times higher if its safety performance were no better than that of the rest of the U.S. industry. The motto at DuPont is to use plant safety statistics to determine how well managers are performing.

The first step for new employees at the Kinston plant is to sign up at the payroll department. The second step is to pick up personal safety gear. Employees attend a 30-minute safety meeting once each month. DuPont considers this so important that it pays its shift workers overtime for their attendance at these meetings.

The Kinston plant manager and his superintendents, about 10 in all, serve as the central safety committee; they meet each morning at the plant. Safety isn't the only topic the committee covers, but it is always first on the agenda. Each superintendent has a safety committee in his department. Production employees serve with supervisors on these committees.

As safety inspections are made so regularly, it is a safe assumption that, at almost any given time, an inspection is taking place somewhere in the plant. Each week the plant manager visits some area of the plant to make a safety inspection; each member of the central committee is also responsible for one inspection each week.

Bulletin boards throughout work areas have safety messages and posters. Videotaped safety presentations are shown to employees in the lunchroom. Off-the-job risks such as

---

*Adapted from John Teresko, "The Safest Plant in the World," *Industry Week*, October 5, 1981, pp. 45–47.

winter road hazards, home safety, firearms, and sports and fitness are also shown on videotapes.

DuPont has a history of being safety and health leaders. In 1818, a DuPont plant explosion killed 40 employees. DuPont pensioned the widows and gave them houses to live in and undertook the education and medical care expenses of the children. In 1915, the company hired a full-time medical director. Records show that now DuPont has approximately 73 full-time physicians, 58 part-time physicians, 150 physicians on a fee-for-service basis, and 202 full-time nurses. Also to safeguard the health of employees who work with DuPont chemical products, the company in 1935 established the Haskell Laboratory for Toxicology & Industrial Medicine. In 1982 it had about 280 employees.

About the time OSHA came into existence, DuPont began to market its in-house expertise in safety management. DuPont's annual sales of "how to" expertise and equipment totals about $36 million. These sales have helped DuPont's image as a safety and health leader and its balance sheet.

Behind DuPont's internal safety performance and its success in merchandising its expertise is an appreciation of the high cost of work-related accidents. DuPont estimates that the average cost to a company of a lost-time injury incident is between $10,000 and $11,000. Additional costs of workers compensation, and lost-time injuries constitute a profit drain amoutning to an estimated average of 4 percent of total profits.

Questions for Thought

1. What do you think about DuPont's use of safety statistics in the appraisal of managers' performance?
2. Since DuPont has such a successful history in safety and health management do you feel it is possible to attain a zero-risk accident and injury goal? Why?
3. Do you feel that DuPont is a good model for other firms involved in manufacturing or working with dangerous products? Why?

EXERCISE V

Union-Management Contract Negotiations

Objective. To permit individuals to become involved in labor-management contract negotiations in a role-playing session.

Set up the Exercise

1. Groups (even number of groups must be formed) of four to eight people will form. Half of the groups will be union teams and the other half will be management teams.
2. Read the description of the Dana Lou Corporation of Hamilton, Ohio.

3. Review and discuss in groups the four bargaining issues and the data collected on competitors (15 minutes).
4. The instructor will provide the union team(s), the "union negotiators" instructions; and the management team(s), the "management negotiations" instructions.
5. Groups face off against each other (one management team versus one union team). The negotiator represents the team's position.
6. Individuals should answer the exercise questions after the negotiations—section 8 of the setup instructions.

Dana Lou Corporation

Dana Lou Corporation is a medium-sized company with about 1,100 employees in Hamilton, Ohio, a suburb of Cincinnati. It competes in the electronic repair parts industry and is slightly larger than most of its main competitors. The firm's success (profitability and growth) has been attributed to a dedicated work force that takes great pride in their work.

In 1964, the Communications Workers of America (CWA) organized the plant. Since then labor-management relations have been good and there has only been two days lost to a strike in 1972. Labor and management both feel that the cooperation between them is much better than is found in other firms of the same size in the area.

The current labor-management contract expires in three weeks. Representatives from the union and management have been negotiating a number of bargaining issues for the last three days, but there seems to be little agreement.

The Bargaining Issues

1. Republic National Medical and Dental Insurance Protection
   Present contract: Dana Lou pays 50 percent of premiums for all full-time employees.
   New contract issues: The CWA wants Dana Lou to pay the full premium; management wants to hold the line.
   In terms of costs, the data look like this

Percent of premium paid	Dana Lou contribution	
0	0	
25	$ 55,000	
50	110,000	Present contribution
75	$165,000	
100	220,000	

2. Preventive health director, staff, and participation
   Present contract: Dana Lou has two part-time physicians and two full-time nurses (cost is $66,000 per year).
   New contract issues: The CWA wants a full-time fitness director, a full-time physician, counselors for alcohol and drug abuse problems, and partial payment for employee use of YMCA and YWCA exercise facilities (estimated increase over present arrangements, $108,000).

3. Vacation benefits

   Present contract: One-week full pay for the first year, two weeks for employees with 2 to 10 years of service, and three weeks for employees with over 10 years.

   New contract issues: CWA wants all employees with 15 or more years of service to have four weeks of full-paid vacation. Management wants no change in present program.

4. Wage increases for skilled quality inspectors

   Present contract: Inspectors rate is $5.95 per hour; inspector apprentices, $4.30.

   New contract issues: CWA want an increase of $0.50 per hour for the plant's 95 inspectors and a $0.40 per hour increase for the plant's 25 inspector apprentices. Management wants to hold the line on salary increases because they believe that layoffs will have to occur.

   Unions proposal would cost Dana Lou 95 × $0.05 = *$47.50* and 25 × $0.40 = *$10.00* or *$57.50* per hour.

Competitor Data (Hamilton, Ohio, Survey)

Company contribution	Blue Fox Corp.	Wintex, Inc.	Lafley Mfg.
To medical and dental insurance	100%	50%	50%
Preventive health director.................	No	No	No
Payment of physical fitness fees for employees	Yes	No	Yes
Vacation benefits.......................	3 weeks all employees after 1 year; 1 week in first year	2 weeks all employees until 10 years of service and then 3 weeks	2 weeks all employees for first 5 years and then 3 weeks
Wage rates inspectors	$5.80	$5.97	$5.93
Inspector apprentices	$4.45	$4.50	$4.20

The Negotiations

7. One member from each of the two groups facing each other will negotiate the four issues. The rest of the group must remain *totally* quiet during the negotiations. The negotiators should *role play* for exactly 20 minutes. At the end of this time they are to record the agreement points reached.

Final Agreements

Medical and dental protection _____

_____

Preventive health director/Staff and participation _____

_____

Vacation benefits _____

_____

Wage increases _____

_____

8. Each individual is to analyze the negotiations:
   How successful were the negotiators? _____

   Would you have negotiated differently? How? _____

   _____

   Were the negotiations prepared? _____

A Learning Note

This exercise will illustrate how difficult discussing issues can be when people have a fixed attitude or position.

Part Six

H. Armstrong Roberts

A person's work schedule can have an impact on his or her work behavior and performance as well as affect activities outside of work. An entire chapter is therefore devoted to work scheduling. The emphasis in Chapter 20 is on flexitime, part-time, job sharing, and compressed workweek schedules. Where, why, and how these newer types of schedules are used is covered. In Chapter 21 the methods required to examine the impact of the P/HRM function are examined. Measurement of the costs and benefits of the P/HRM function is an important practice occurring in an increasing number of organizations. This final chapter takes one last look at P/HRM managers as they enter the mid-1980s.

Work Scheduling and Evaluation

Department of Labor

H. Armstrong Roberts

Chapter Twenty

Work Scheduling

Learning Objectives

After studying this chapter, you should be able to:
- Define what is meant by the traditional workweek, flexitime, permanent part-time employment, job sharing, and the compressed workweek.

- Describe the involvement of P/HRM in work scheduling.

- Explain why fatigue may be an especially troublesome problem with the compressed workweek.

- Discuss the employee benefits derived from flexitime, part-time, and job-sharing schedules.

- Distinguish between permanent and temporary part-time employment.

Chapter Outline

Case

Amanda Wilson

The turnover of registered nurses at La Grange Community Hospital in La Grange, Illinois, had become an epidemic. The hospital, located in a suburb of Chicago, employed over 450 nurses. Amanda Wilson was hired about six months ago as the hospital administrator. She noticed that the turnover at La Grange Community was higher than any other hospital of similar size in the area. Amanda assigned Jack Quenton a P/HRM in-house (hospital employed) researcher to examine the problem. Jack worked on the problem for about three months.

Last week Jack submitted a report to Amanda. The report was based on a review of the hospital's P/HRM programs, what other hospitals in the area were doing in terms of P/HRM programs, and exit interviews Jack had conducted with 30 nurses who had quit La Grange Community recently. As Amanda worked her way through the thorough report she was especially astonished by the exit interview data. It showed that most of the "leavers"—the nurses who had quit— wanted a more flexible working schedule. They had objected to the standard eight-hour shifts.

The report recommended that La Grange Community immediately undertake a pilot experiment of instituting a flexitime working schedule in the medical-surgical wards. The experiment would run for one year and then decisions about schedules in other units such as maternity, emergency, operating room, and intensive care would be made.

Amanda asked Jack to provide her with more details on nontraditional work schedules like flexitime. She wanted to see what others had done and whether flexitime could be used in nursing. The details Jack presented to Amanda are similar to the material covered in this chapter.

Despite a growing number of experiments to change the length and arrangement of the five-day, 40-hour workweek it has remained a fixture in industry for over 40 years. Since 1940, the workweek has been relatively stable, despite a growing feeling that many people would derive more satisfaction from an increase in leisure time. The traditional work schedule remains: (1) five days, 40 hours; (2) from 9:00 A.M. to 5:00 P.M.; (3) Monday–Friday; and (4) with a standard lunch hour and a few coffee breaks daily.

From about 1970, however, industry, government, education, and health care institutions have become interested in new kinds of work schedules. This chapter will examine a few of the newer schedules, namely flexitime (in which employees vary their starting and stopping time), part-time, work sharing (in which two workers share the job; e.g., one works the morning, the other works the afternoon), and compressed workweeks (working less than five days; e.g., a four-day, 10-hour day schedule). P/HRM departments are naturally involved in the decision making that goes into work scheduling. Specifically, P/HRM specialists aid management in examining, implementing, and evaluating alternative work schedules. These P/HRM activities are extremely important in devising work schedules that contribute to improved morale, increased productivity, and enhanced leisure time gratification.

Breaking the traditional patterns of work scheduling for the sake of change is not the reason why newer work schedules are being considered by more and more organizations. They are being given serious consideration because in a number of experiments and settings they have been associated with improved end results—satisfaction, performance, and morale. This chapter will examine not only work scheduling, but also the kind of impact they are having on people and organizations. Ten years ago, the work schedules presented in this chapter were a German import—foreign, different, and of questionable value. Today, about 9.5 million full-time workers in the United States enjoy flexible work schedules and compressed workweeks, and an additional 11.8 million workers hold voluntary, permanent part-time jobs.[1] This constitutes about 20 percent of the entire labor force in the United States.

The Changing Work Environment

Changes and questioning about work schedules are occurring at an accelerated rate in organizations. In this chapter our focus is on work scheduling changes and questions that have been raised about scheduling practices. A few of these questions are:

- Most Americans work a 9-to-5 schedule, five days a week. Since 1940 this has been the predominant pattern. Is this what workers really want?
- The standard five-day, 40-hour a week work schedule offers organizations consistency, ease of administration, and predictability. What does it offer the worker?
- Many workers report dissatisfaction with their jobs. Is a major contributing cause the lockstep work schedules they have?
- Most workers pour into cities and towns to their jobs, lemminglike, at the same time every morning, and then leave together every evening. The result is clogged roads, jammed public transportation, and frayed nerves. Is there any way that this type of clogging and jamming can be reduced?[2]

These facts of everyday living pose interesting challenges to P/HRM specialists. The challenges and questions raised will be addressed by examining actual company use of new work schedules. Their answers will indicate that the work environment of the 1980s is demanding changes in the traditional work schedules. The changes of expectations itself place a premium on improved management of organizational time and resources.

Workers' expectations about the job, the organization, and the family unit are different from those of a generation ago. Today many workers are requesting jobs that have security, provide an acceptable level of earnings and fringe benefits, but also provide more autonomy, responsibility, and opportunity for self-development. The work ethic still exists, but there is now a request for increased self-dignity.

More and more workers claim that they would like to exchange some work time for

---

[1]*New Work Schedules for a Changing Society* (Scarsdale, New York: Work in America Institute, 1981) p. 3.

[2]Stanley D. Nollen, "What Is Happening to Flexitime, Flexitour, Gliding Time, the Variable Day, and Permanent Part-Time Employment? and the Four-Day Week?" *Across the Board*, April 1980, p. 6.

more personal time. By personal time they mean time for leisure, family, household tasks, and education. Time to develop hobbies and to enjoy the fruits of hard work.

Family structures have changed dramatically in the past 10 years. The "traditional family" of husband (breadwinner), wife (homemaker), and two children—has all but vanished. Only 7 percent of all family units fit this model.[3] In many families both husband and wife work, there are also more single-parent families, and a large number of single people. Many of these trends create the potential for conflict between work (the job) and home (the family, leisure time).

Productivity pressures, increased competition, and a concern about treating people more fairly have also encouraged many employers to examine new work schedules. The concept of viewing workers as assets in accounting terms is gaining acceptance in more organizations.

Another change is the employer's concern over energy and transportation problems. Despite increases in the fuel efficiency of smaller cars, the cost and time to commute by car from home to work and back is a continuing problem. Employers are responding to this problem by encouraging car pooling, offering van-pooling programs, and encouraging public transportation authorities to increase and improve their service.

Energy consumption and conservation are now regular agenda issues discussed by organizations. Ways to contain costs of heating, cooling, lighting, and operating offices and plants are constantly being examined. This examination includes paying attention to the impact of work schedules on energy costs.

A Diagnostic Approach to Work Scheduling

Exhibit 20–1 examines how work scheduling is affected by various factors in the environment. Work scheduling decision makers must pay attention to external environment influences. The union in some cases has resisted changes in work scheduling. Unions have a disdain for tampering with overtime laws. It took the union time, patience, argument, and lobbying to gain the 8-hour day and the 40-hour week. Overtime work at a premium pay is something the union is fearful of losing with the move toward more part-time employment and compressed workweeks.

Government legislation affects work schedules. In fact the Walsh-Healy Public Contracts Act of 1936 and the Fair Labor Standards Act of 1938 were passed to reduce hours of work and encourage the spreading of work among unemployed people.

Economic conditions also play a role in work scheduling. Downturns, stagflation, and other conditions have resulted in an increase in part-timers and a decrease in the number of hours worked by full-time employees.

The goals of management also play a major role in work scheduling. Management may feel that work schedules can affect morale, satisfaction, and productivity, and if so managers would be inclined to experiment with scheduling. On the other hand, management may want a schedule that is easy to administer; in that case it is best to stay with the traditional work schedule.

The attitudes, preferences, and motivation of workers also are important. Some workers prefer a work schedule that is different than their traditional one. However, other workers may not prefer a nontraditional work schedule. Determining these preferences,

[3] *New Work Schedules for a Changing Society,* p. 20.

Exhibit 20–1

Factors affecting the work scheduling decisions

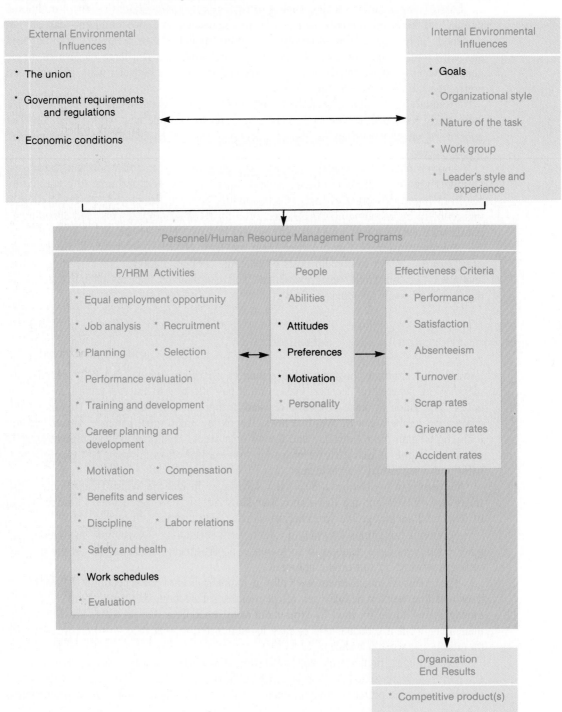

attitudes, and motivations about work schedules are the responsibility of line managers and P/HRM specialists. Implementing a changed work schedule without diagnosing what workers want and think is likely to be a costly, frustrating mistake.

Legislation: The Government

Unions have displayed some positive interest in some of the new work schedules, but they are concerned about violations of the law. The union wants to protect its members from the exploitation that is possible through some of the new work schedules. Most collective bargaining agreements require premium pay (usually time and a half) after eight hours of work in a day. In fact the Fair Labor Standards Act requires overtime pay after 40 hours a week for employees in interstate commerce and public administration.

Many compressed workweek schedules call for 9, 10, 11, or 12 hours of work a day. If employers had to pay overtime rates for the extra hours they would be uneconomical. Flexitime with fixed workdays of eight hours or less are no problem with labor unions. But when the flexitime schedule permits variable length days (8½, 9, 10 hours), the union often raises the issues of exploitation and the law.

P/HRM specialists must consult and be knowledgeable about four federal statutes when considering changes in work schedules. The Fair Labor Standards Act of 1938 has already been presented. The Walsh-Healy Public Contracts Act requires overtime pay after eight hours a day for employees working on federal contracts of more than $10,000.[4] The Contract Work Hours and Safety Standards Act requires overtime pay after eight hours on federal construction contracts. The Federal Pay Act is applied to all nonexempt federal workers. It requires overtime pay after 8 hours a day or 40 hours a week. These laws exempt many supervisory and professional employees who have been able to be placed on new work schedules. Many blue-collar workers would like to have the same scheduling opportunities, but are hemmed in by the very laws that have protected them for years.

Several unions have been able to accept changes in traditional work schedules without giving up the protection of the law. Local 21 of the International Federation of Professional and Technical Employees, at the request of its members, negotiated flexitime agreements in California. About 1,000 union members, all white-collar employees, were covered. The agreement was that: (1) the contract contain explicit language about worker's protection and provide an appropriate grievance procedure for overtime disputes, and (2) the employees must be held accountable for meeting their time requirements. One contract with Almeda County set up an 80-hour pay period rather than a 40-hour week or 8-hour day.[5]

Of course, even in situations that are nonunion the law must be followed regarding work scheduling. One challenge of the 1980s is to increase the flexibility of new work scheduling alternatives without violating the law. Building in such flexibility will require more cooperation and agreement between labor and management. Agreement can only occur if the details and specifics of each work scheduling alternative are clearly understood.

---

[4]Richard I. Henderson, *Compensation Management* (Reston, Va.: Reston Publishing, 1979), pp. 435–36.

[5]Stanley Nollen and Virginia Hider Martin, *Alternative Work Schedules* (New York: AMACOM, 1978).

Flexitime

Flexible work hours (flexitime for short) means that employees are able to select their starting and quitting times within limits set by management.[6] A flexible schedule can differ in a number of ways: (1) daily versus periodic choice of starting and quitting time; (2) variable versus constant length of workday (crediting and debiting hours is allowed); and (3) core time—the management imposed requirement of hours when all employees must be on the job. The different types of flexitime going from the least to the most flexible are:

Flexitour   Requires employees to select specific starting and quitting time, and work on the schedule for a specified period like a week or month. The work period is usually eight hours.

Gliding time   Variation in starting and quitting time is permitted, but workday total is usually eight hours.

Variable day   Credit and debit of work hours is permitted (e.g., an employee can work 10 hours one day and 6 hours on another day), as long as the total hours worked are even at the end of the week (40) or month (160).

Maniflex   Credit and debit hours are permitted, and a core time is not required on all days. The core may be 10:00 A.M. until 2:00 P.M. Monday and Friday only.

Flexiplace   This means that an employee can change the location of work as well as the hours—working at home, at satellite locations, and so on would be examples.

As of 1980, the U.S. Bureau of Labor Statistics estimated that about 11.9 percent of all full-time nonfarm wage and salary workers were on flexible work schedules. This means about 7.6 million workers.[7] There are also many professionals, sales personnel, professors, and managers who set their own work hours informally who are not counted in the flexitime statistics. Exhibit 20–2 presents a breakdown of flexitime by occupations and by industries.

The usage of flexitime work scheduling has more than doubled from 1974 to 1980 from 3.2 percent to 8.1 percent (adjusted to omit professionals, managers, and sales personnel). Exhibit 20–3 shows the increase of flexitime work scheduling between August 1974 and May 1980.

Many types of jobs have converted to flexitime: they include bank tellers, accounting departments, engineers, keypunch operators, laboratory technicians, nurses, data processing, nonexempt production workers, and insurance clerks and claim examiners. A directory of the users of flexitime has even been published.[8]

Flexitime is difficult to implement in production units with assembly lines and multiple shifts. In such units it is impossible to have workers coming and going since work

---

[6]Many interesting examples of flexitime scheduling can be found in Stanley Nollen, *New work Schedules in Practice: Managing Time in a Changing Society* (New York: Van Nostrand Reinhold, 1981).

[7]U.S. Department of Labor, U.S. Bureau of Labor Statistics, ''Ten Million Americans Work Flexible Schedules, 2 Million Work Full Time in Three to Four-and-a-Half Days,'' *news release,* (Washington, D.C.: Office of Information, February 24, 1981).

[8]*Alternative Work Schedule Directory* (Washington, D.C.: National Council on Alternative Work Patterns, 1978)

Exhibit 20–2 _____

Usage of flexitime in the United States by occupation and industry, 1980 (full-time nonfarm wage and salary workers)

Occupation and industry	Number (000)	Percent
All occupations	7,638	11.9
Professional and technical workers	1,914	15.8
Managers and administrators	1,622	20.2
Sales workers	878	26.5
Clerical workers	1,296	9.8
Craft workers	753	7.4
Operatives, except transport equipment	387	4.4
Transport equipment operatives	388	14.3
Laborers	214	7.3
Service workers	569	8.7
Occupations excluding professional and technical workers, managers and administrators, and sales workers	3,608	8.1
All industries	7,922	11.9
Mining	83	10.6
Construction	439	10.1
Manufacturing	1,516	7.9
Transportation and public utilities	620	11.7
Wholesale and retail trade	1,633	4.7
Finance, insurance, and real estate	725	17.1
Professional services	1,555	11.4
Other services	696	16.9
Federal public administration, except postal	404	24.9
Postal service	47	7.6
State public administration	125	14.4
Local public administration	148	8.9

Source: U.S. Bureau of Labor Statistics, news release, February 24, 1981.

pace is largely machine controlled. Also, it is difficult to arrange flexitime for receptionists, retail sales clerks, bus drivers, or nurses (e.g., operating room or intensive care units). In these cases, the job must be continuously covered and this limits the type of work scheduling.

In flexitime system there are two major time periods—core time and flexible time. During the core time period all employees in a unit or group must be at work. The flexible time period is the hours within which the employee is free to choose whether or not to be on the job. There is also, of course, the requirement that during a day a required number of hours must be worked. A typical flexitime schedule is shown in Exhibit 20–4 for Verser Engineering and Construction Co., a medium-sized firm that has used this schedule since 1977.

Some Benefits of Flexitime

The reported success rates of flexitime programs is impressive. Half or more of all user firms report dollar and cents improvements. Increased productivity, lower unit labor costs, and improved morale have been attributed to flexitime.[9] There are also benefits in less

_____

[9]Stanley D. Nollen, "Does Flexitime Improve Productivity?" _Harvard Business Review,_ September 1979, pp. 12, 16–18, 22.

Exhibit 20–3

Growth in usage of flexitime in the United States

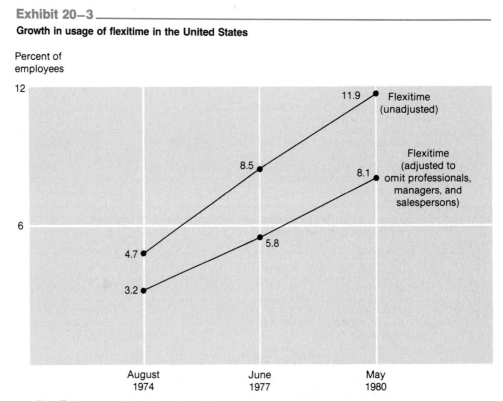

Percent of
employees

Note: Estimates are obtained from three different surveys whose methodology, coverage, and reliability differ.
Source: For flexitime data, for 1980: U.S. Bureau of Labor Statistics, news release, February 24, 1981; for 1977:
Stanley D. Nollen and Virginia H. Martin *Alternative Work Schedules, Part 1: Flexitime* (New York: AMACOM, 1978);
Work in America Institute; for 1974: calculated by Stanley D. Nollen from data by Virginia H. Martin.

paid absence and idle time, increased morale, and less overtime pay (because of less
absence and higher productivity).[10]

One might ask, why are there productivity gains? Flexitime apparently increases the
effective quantity of labor input. For example, if a car breaks down on the way to work,

Exhibit 20–4

Verser's flexitime schedule (total for workday must be eight hours)

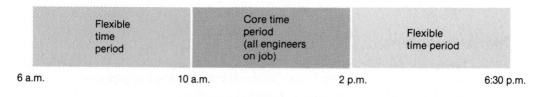

[10]C. W. Proehl, Jr., "A Survey of the Empirical Literature on Flexible Work Hours: Character and Consequences of a Major Innovation," *Academy of Management Review*, October 1978, pp. 837–53.

the worker can stay later to make up the lost time. The firm gets more hours of work and, therefore, more productivity for the same cost. Also because many workers like flexitime, an employer may have an easier time recruiting workers that prefer this type of work schedule. Again because of the match between work schedule and worker preference there is likely to be less absenteeism and turnover which means lower costs and better productivity.

There is another potential benefit of flexitime in that the schedule could be matched with the person's biological clock. Some of us are morning people—we are more productive in the A.M. Others are afternoon or early evening people. Flexitime permits employers in many cases to set up work schedules that optimizes worker productivity and takes advantage of the workers' biological clocks.

Some Problems of Flexitime

Productivity gains, morale improvements, cost containment—it sounds so attractive that we may wonder why every organization doesn't have flexitime work schedules. The reason is that flexitime can cause some major problems. Supervisors have to change their procedures and even work harder at the outset of implementing flexitime schedules. Consequently, many supervisors drag their feet and resist flexitime.

There is also the increased cost in some organizations of heating and cooling buildings for longer workdays. The regular day is from 9:00 A.M. to 5:00 P.M. A flexitime schedule may require the building or plant to be open from 6:00 A.M. to 7:30 P.M. The result is more energy expenses.

There is also the problem of using flexitime in only some jobs. While some workers are on flexitime there are employees who are not able to have this kind of work schedule. What can happen is antagonism and jealousy across occupations between the ''haves'' and the ''have nots.''

The publicity given flexitime in the popular press and management literature has been overwhelmingly positive, yet there remain workers who do not prefer flexitime. How can they say no when everyone around them is saying yes? This a question that is not easy to answer. However, it points out that the assumption that everyone wants to go on a flexitime schedule may not be correct. What is a benefit to one worker may be a threat or inconvenience to another.

Managing Flexitime

There are a number of guidelines for successfully managing flexitime work schedules. Top-management support is essential. Flexitime transfers some control over work from managers to workers. The top-management team must actively support this shifting of control. A climate of trust in the judgment of workers about their schedules is important. For example, if an honor system for checking in is used, before flexitime is implemented it would be a display of low trust if a formal sign-in, sign-out system is used after flexitime has been implemented. Top management has to encourage all levels of management to be supportive and trusting with flexitime schedules.

Another important guideline is to help the first-line supervisor. The job of this level supervisor gets more difficult with flexitime because he or she must: (1) still generate results, (2) balance the work schedules, (3) provide workers with some scheduling flexibility, and (4) plan further into the future. Thus, the first-line supervisor has fewer decisions to make about individual schedules, but still has responsibility to do the job. This responsibility is especially crucial in planning and coordinating activities.

A third management guideline is that supervisors should be trained to meet their new responsibilities and problems. The training should focus on what flexitime is, the supervisors' responsibilities, what research indicates about flexitime schedules, and some of the pitfalls to avoid. The supervisor needs to understand a few important points that can be presented in training. They are:

- Work schedule choices, responsibility, and authority need to be clearly communicated to workers.
- The design of flexitime schedules must be understood—core hours (when everyone must be present), day length, timekeeping methods, disciplinary procedures.
- Jobs may have to be redesigned in order for flexitime to work. Training could cover job redesign approaches.

The fourth management guideline is that flexitime, like other work scheduling programs, should be evaluated. The schedule should be evaluted in terms of productivity, morale, energy costs, and the overall climate of the organization. A cost/benefit framework can be used to examine the effects of flexitime. It may also be worthwhile from a public goodwill standpoint to include in the evaluation an analysis of flexitime's impact on transportation efficiency. Cities such as Boston, Chicago, Seattle, and Ottawa are examining the impact of flexitime work scheduling on commuting time, traffic congestion, and energy conservation.

In Ottawa the number of federal employees who started work during the heavist 30-minute peak rush-hour period dropped from 78 to 40 percent after flexitime was implemented. In Toronto, after a year of citywide flexitime, almost half of the downtown employees on flexitime schedules elected to travel outside the peak rush hour in the morning.[11]

Including a transportation analysis as part of the flexitime analysis can be important not only for city governments, but also for organizations. Those firms that take into consideration the impact of flexitime on transporation patterns and congestion can derive public relations benefits. For example, they could by using flexitime where possible help the entire city or area run more smoothly. In the future, citizens could associate social responsibility and flexitime scheduling when considering what an organization is doing for the community.

Part-Time Employment

Part-time work includes all work demanding less than full time. The U.S. government counts people who work less than 35 hours a week as part-timers. For federal employees, 32 hours a week is the dividing line between full- and part-time work. Today about 22 million workers are considered part-timers. This is about 22 percent of the American labor force.[12]

Two thirds of all part-timers are adult women. The next largest component, 25 per-

---

[11]Nollen, "New Work Schedules in Practice," p. 23.

[12]Clark Kerr and Jerome M. Rosow, *Work in America* (New York: Van Nostrand Rheinhold, 1979), p. 170.

cent, are teenagers. Part-time employment is especially prevalent in the fast-food industry, insurance, and banks. For example, 90 percent of the 250,000 employees of McDonald's fast-food restaurants are part-timers.[13]

There are several kinds of part-time employees:

Permanent part-time employment   The job and the workers are expected to be part time for a long time on a regular basis.

Job sharing   Two or more part-timers share one job. The workers are part time, but the job is full time.

Work sharing   A temporary reduction in working hours chosen by a group of employees during economic hard times. This is an alternative to being laid off.[14]

Temporary part-time employment   The worker is on a job only a short time (e.g., Kelly girls).

Phased retirement   Part-time employment selected by employees who are gradually changing from full-time to retired status.

Permanent part-time employment is quite common in wholesale and retail trade industries as well as in service industries. Although it is common, it is still largely unnoticed. Part-time employment works especially well where there are specific jobs to complete, independent projects such as in insurance claims, and where the workload has a predictable cycle such as in banking traffic. On the other hand, part-time employment is not well suited for managerial jobs or where the work flow requires a worker to be continuously available.

An example of staffing an organization with a part-time work force is found at Control Data Corporation. The company wanted to allow mothers needing supplemental income the opportunity to work. A part-time work schedule was established. Control Data opened a bindery that would collate, bind, and mail computer manuals and documents to customers.[15]

The bindery runs from 6:00 A.M. to 10:00 P.M. with employees, mostly minority women from an economically depressed area of St. Paul, Minnesota, choosing a three-, four-, or six-hour shift. The choices were designed to fit the workers' needs. The plant employs female heads of households, handicapped people who cannot work full time, and students. Workers are compensated the same hourly rate as full-time workers in comparable jobs at other Control Data plants and fringe benefits are prorated proportionate to hours worked.

Supervisors work standard eight-hour shifts. However, it should be mentioned that almost all of the supervisors started as part-timers. As their home situations and career plans changed they expressed interest and converted to full-time work when it was available.

The productivity per capita in this part-time staffed plant is much higher than at other plants of the firm. Profits are up and employees appear to be committed and dedicated. Management also believes that there is less worker fatigue because of the shorter shifts.

---

[13]Ibid.

[14]Fred Best, *Work Sharing: Policy Options and Assessments* (Kalamazoo, Mich.: Upjohn Institute for Employment Research, 1980).

[15]A. R. Cohen and H. Gadon, *Alternative Work Schedules: Integrating Individual and Organizational Needs* (Reading, Mass.: Addison-Wesley Publishing, 1979), pp. 100–01.

Some Benefits of Permanent Part-Time Employment and Job Sharing

Permanent part-time employment succeeds when it is used for a specific operating purpose. For example, when Occidental Life Insurance Company's business grew, management decided that it needed more than a single eight-hour day shift of claims examiners, keypunch operators, and record clerks to process business. There was not enough work for a whole eight-hour second shift. The answer was to establish a part-time minishift that worked from 5 P.M. until 10 P.M.[16]

When Massachusetts Mutual Life Insurance Company had trouble recruiting full-time office employees, they established job sharing. One employee worked from 9 A.M. to 2 P.M. (usually a mother with children in school) and the other worker came in from 2:00 P.M. to 5 P.M. (usually a student from a local college).

The main employer benefits of part-time and job-sharing scheduling are reduced labor cost, including less overtime. In addition, productivity is often higher, absenteeism and tardiness are lower, and (except for students) turnover is lower.[17] There is also the possibility that with part-timers there is less job fatigue caused by working on tedious, repetitive jobs. Thus, performance is better because workers complete jobs in shorter time spans.[18]

Some Problems with Part-Time Scheduling

A number of problems are associated with part-time employment. Management must examine and work out a plan to balance fringe benefits paid to part- and full-time employees. Not all fringe benefits can be prorated to time actually worked. This results in feelings of inequity by both part- and full-timers.

Although most part-timers have paid vacations, only about half get any group health or life insurance or pension plans. A major stumbling block is the health insurance (vacations and pensions can be more easily prorated). Companies are faced with paying $600 to $1,000 annually for health insurance for part-timers. Prorating of health insurance premiums payments means that the insurance company agreement will have to fit part- and full-time employees. This is extremely difficult to work out on a equitable prorated basis.

One solution to the health insurance problem is to allow employees to select their mix of fringe benefits. This is called a *cafeteria* benefit program. Full- and part-time employees could choose from among the fringe benefits the ones they wanted. The company's contribution to the cafeteria selection could be based on time worked (full or part).

Labor unions pose another problem in part-time scheduling. Permanent part-time employment has been referred to as, "Another piece of bread in this dry sandwich of alternative work schedules."[19] Unions are reluctant to support part-time employment because it increases the competition for jobs during periods of high unemployment. The full-time

---

[16]Nollen, "What Is Happening?" p. 14.

[17]Ibid, p. 14.

[18]Ethel B. Jones and James E. Long, "Part-Week Work and Human Capital Investment by Married Women," *Journal of Human Resources,* Fall 1979, p. 18.

[19]John Zalusky, "Alternative Work Schedules: A Labor Union View," *Journal of the College and University Personnel Association,* Summer 1977, p. 42.

employee more than the part-timer is a union member. Thus, union opposition is largely based on protecting the interests of its members.

There is also the belief that part-time workers are not interested in advancement opportunities. This is a stereotype that comes from part-time employment's association with low-level jobs, and the fact that women and students hold most part-time jobs. There are also some who feel that part-time work is not worthy or masculine. Among all permanent part-time workers, 70 percent are women. These stereotypes are difficult to overcome. The work ethic for decades has encouraged people to work full time. This cultural barrier and the stereotypes held are slowly being overcome by the positive contributions being made by part-time employees. Only through part-time or job-sharing schedules can many people work, earn an income, and make productive inputs into society. This message is slowly beginning to find its way into society.

Managing Part-Time Employment and Job Sharing

A managerial concern of part-time employment and job sharing is their potentially high-labor costs. Some labor costs are fixed per employee. Since part-time employees work fewer hours than full-time employees, their hourly cost can be higher. Managers with the aid and guidance of P/HRM specialists must develop a fringe benefit program that is fair to part-time and job-sharing employees. Unless this is done, the stereotypes and negative reactions directed toward part-time employment and job sharing will continue.

Effectively managing various P/HRM activities is also important in controlling costs for part-time and job-sharing work scheduling. Recruitment costs can be high for part-time employment because more people have to be recruited or regular recruitment methods are not suited to find part-timers. These costs may be more managable if compensation for present part-timers and job sharers is attractive enough to retain them as employees. There are also specialized part-time and job-sharing placement companies that may be able to provide services to the organization.

Supervision of part-timers can be costly. The part-time employee is not on the job as much as the full-time employee. Thus, if self-starting, self-motivated part-timers can be attracted the costs of supervision can be reduced or at least controlled within acceptable limits.

It also makes sense in terms of P/HRM to treat part-time and job-sharing employees as important human resources. Fair treatment, equitable compensation, and opportunities for job-involved decision making are important steps in making part time and job sharing acceptable and attractive types of work schedules.

Job sharing presents a number of special kind of management problems: (1) matching the workers as partners and then with the job; (2) encouraging and rewarding cooperative work efforts; (3) deciding the specific work schedule; and (4) encouraging communication between partners. If employers initiate job sharing it is very important for the organization to thoroughly analyze the jobs and the prospective partners. The employer's role and involvement are especially important in determining work schedules and creating a supportive atmosphere for the job sharers to work in as a team. Even when job-sharing arrangements are initiated by workers there is a distinct need to maintain open communication and cooperation. Instead of balancing the needs and preferences of a single employee and the job, management must in job sharing balance the needs and preferences of two employees and the job.

Compressed Workweeks

The compressed workweek (CWW) is a work schedule in which a trade is made between the number of hours worked per day, and the number of days worked per week, in order to work the standard length hours.[20] The CWW can be: (1) four days of 10 hours each—4/40; (2) three-day workweeks often about 12 hours each day—3/36; (3) four-and-one-half-day workweeks with four nine-hour periods and one four-hour day; and (4) a work weekend of two 12-hour days, paid at premium rates.

In 1980, about 2.7 percent of all full-time, nonfarm wage and salary workers, or about 1.8 million workers, were on CWWs. Exhibit 20–5 indicates that the CWW had leveled off between 1976–79, but 1979–80 witnessed some growth.[21]

Some Benefits of Compressed Workweeks

The regular utilization of facilities is a benefit of the CWW. There are fewer start-ups if a four- or three-day schedule is used. However, if a business plant, office, or facility must be open at least five days the CWW causes some job coverage problems.[22] In situations where employers are able to cut utility and overhead costs by closing on the fifth day the CWW offers cost savings.

There have been a few research studies that indicate that the morale of CWW workers is higher and paid absences lower than workers under standard work schedules.[23] In a quasi-experimental study in a manufacturing facility a 25-month period investigation was conducted. The study examined satisfaction, absenteeism, and performance of 4/40 workers versus 5/40 workers. At the 13-month period of the study, workers on the 4/40 work schedule were more satisfied with job conditions, experienced less anxiety-stress, and performed better than did the comparison 5/40 workers. However, these benefits were not found at the 25-month data point.[24] It was concluded that the 4/40 may have a short-term impact, but that long- term benefits, must be questionned and examined more closely.

The traditional 5/40 workweek has been under attack in the nursing profession. Because nursing care of hospitalized patients is a seven-day, 24-hour responsibility, nursing has not been one area of CWW popularity. This lack of popularity seems to be changing. The list of hospitals using CWWs is increasing yearly. The CWW schedules for nurses include a 7/70 at Valley Medical Center in Fresno, California, a 7/56 at Baptist Medical Center—Monclair in Birmingham, Alabama, a 2/16 weekend plan at Women's Hospital in Houston, and a 4/40 at University Hospital in Seattle.[25]

The evaluation of these nurse work-scheduling programs has been conducted by in-

[20]Simcha Ronen and Sophia B. Primps, "The Compressed Work Week as Organizational Change: Behavioral and Attitudinal Outcomes," *Academy of Management Journal,* January 1981, p. 61.

[21]U.S. Department of Labor, Bureau of Labor Statistics, news release (Washington, D.C.: Office of Information, February 24, 1981).

[22]*New Work Schedule For A Changing Society, op. cit.,* p. 54.

[23]L. W. Foster, J. C. Latack, and L. J. Reindl, "Effects and Promises of the Shortened Work Week." Paper presented at the 39th annual meeting of Academy of Management, Atlanta, Georgia, 1979.

[24]For the 13-month study, see John M. Ivancevich, "Effects of the Shorter Workweek on Selected Satisfaction and Performance Measures," *Journal of Applied Psychology,* 1974, pp. 717–21; for the 25-month study, see John M. Ivancevich and Herbert L. Lyon. "The Shortened Workweek: A Field Experiment," *Journal of Applied Psychology,* February 1977, pp. 34–37.

[25]Elmina M. Price, "Seven Days on and Seven Days off," *American Journal of Nursing,* June 1981, pp. 1142–43, and "The Demise of the Traditional 5-40 Workweek?" *American Journal of Nursing,* June 1981, pp. 1138–41.

Exhibit 20–5 _____

Growth of compressed workweeks

Percent of all nonfarm wage
and salary workers who
work full time

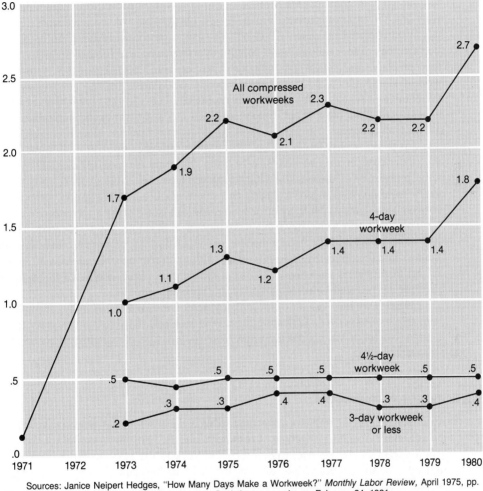

Sources: Janice Neipert Hedges, "How Many Days Make a Workweek?" *Monthly Labor Review,* April 1975, pp. 29–36. U.S. Department of Labor, Bureau of Labor Statistics, news release, February 24, 1981.

house researchers. The results suggest lower staff turnover, reduced overtime, less absenteeism, and improved nurse job satisfaction. There are a number of critics who remain unconvinced about the impact of the CWW. Some feel that nurses on flexitime schedules tend to stand out as an elite group and this will eventually decrease morale. There is also the issue of fatigue. Nurses working more than eight hours are prone to more errors. An error in nursing can be a life or death matter.[26]

_____

[26]Suzanne LaViolette, "Shortage Spurs Flurry of Flexitime Experiments," *Modern Health Care,* March 1981, p. 42.

Some Problems with Compressed Workweeks

Labor laws and union contracts often specifically address the issue of working more than eight hours a day. Overtime rates usually have to be paid for a more than eight-hour workday. Collective bargaining has to specifically cover this issue.

One union agreed to a 3/36 plan for 400 full-time employees of the Meredith Corporation printing plant in Des Moines, Iowa. It was decided in labor-management discussions that the printing presses cannot be run on the basis of five-day workweeks. They had to be operated all seven days, but this would be too demanding on employees and their families. The solution was to assign a fourth crew where there were previously three. The company also created two 12-hour shifts per day. This allowed the continuous operation of the presses. One crew works Monday-Wednesday and the other workers Thursday-Saturday. Sunday work is alternatively divided between the crews. The Sunday work is paid at double time. This system is given credit for production improvement, and absenteeism decreases.[27]

A problem with CWWs is that fatigue often affects performance. Working 10-, 11-, or 12-hour days in any job can be very tiring. Not only can performance suffer, but there is the probability of increased accident frequency. A tired worker often inadvertently becomes more lax with regard to health and safety practices. A mistake of a machine operator can cause injury, while an error by a nurse can cause serious problems.

The CWW does not have the flexibility of a flexitime work schedule. The person who must work a compressed schedule may find that his or her life and personal time become more complicated. Those workers with child-rearing obligations may have a special set of problems working a 3/36 or 4/40 schedule. They may have to be away from home during times that their children are not in school.

Unlike flexitime and part-time employment, the CWW does not give workers any more freedom of choice. Preferring the CWW schedule in order to stay away from work in larger blocks of time is not a positive vote for this type of schedule. It is more of a job avoidance vote.

Managing Compressed Workweeks

An important part of implementing the CWW is the matching of workers' schedules with the necessary operating schedule. Customers, clients, and others dealing with an organization expect timely service. When a person goes to the store to purchase a product in midday, on say a Friday, she expects the store to be open for business. Management needs to carefully work out a coverage plan when using CWW schedules.

There is also the need to pay close managerial attention to the fatigue associated with longer workdays. Fatigue is a serious problem as each study reporting on the impact of the CWW has shown.[28] Not only can fatigue result in a decrease in effectiveness, it can be harmful to the tired worker, co-workers, and even commuters who will be on the road with the worker. It is management's responsibility to examine more closely the consequences of the longer workday on fatigue. There may well be an increase in legal action brought by workers who claim that the CWW and especially the fatigue caused by it

---

[27]"Union Agreement Gives Workers 3-day Week, 4-day Weekends," *Management Review,* January 1981, p. 31.

[28]Ronen and Primps, "The Compressed Workweek," p. 71.

precipitated family, personal, and job-related problems. Certainly management would be implicated in such cases.

Work Scheduling: A Look Ahead

Each of the work schedules covered in this chapter were virtually unheard of in the 1970s in the United States or Canada. Today they are each growing in importance. Indications are that at least flexitime and part-time employment will become ever more popular in the 1980s and 1990s.

Flexitime

Flexitime schedules are already found in most industries. One expert predicts that it will soon become as commonplace as the standard nine to five routine.[29] The reason for flexitime's continued and increased popularity are these:

- Workers like the scheduling flexibility that it provides them and the self-management aspects of it. It permits workers greater ease of balancing work schedules with outside-of-work activities.
- Flexitime can be used in numerous work settings with most occupations.
- Managers like flexitime because it provides benefits to a company at a reasonable cost.
- The record of keeping flexitime programs is impressive. Few managers opt to discontinue its use. This U.S. and Canadian loyalty to flexitime once it is in place is supported by the situation in Europe where 30 percent of German and Swiss work forces are on flexitime.[30]
- Flexitime is able to work well with a variety of managerial programs designed to improve performance and reduce the number of boring, monotonous, and repetitive jobs. Job enrichment, team building, job rotation, and job redesign can all work in conjunction with flexitime schedules.

Predictions are always risky but it seems reasonable to state that flexitime schedules will continue to be a popular work schedule. Perhaps as many as 25 percent of all non-farm workers will be on flexitime schedules by 1993. Currently, about 12 percent are on flexitime schedules.

Part-Time Employment

There are sets of opposing forces that cloud up the view of part-time employment in the next decade. Some of these opposing forces are:

- Labor unions generally have resisted the expansion of part-time employment.
- There is a labor surplus and the need for part-timers is reduced by such an excess of people.
- Service industries continue to grow and this means that the need for part-timers will increase.

---

[29]Nollen, "What Is Happening?", p. 17.

[30]Robert T. Golembiewski, Ronald G. Fox, and Carl W. Proehl, Jr., "Flexitime: The Supervisor's Verdict," *The Wharton Magazine,* Summer 1980, pp. 43–44.

P/HRM Manager Close-Up

Richard W. Hucke
Roy F. Weston, Inc.

location (domestic and foreign) and training and development. He is a graduate of Bryant College holding a degree in business administration, a member of the American Society of Personnel Administrators and past officer of the Monmouth/ Ocean County, N.J. Industrial Relations Association. Mr. Hucke has taught college courses on OSHA and has developed and conducted management level seminars on the various aspects of human resources.

Biography

Richard W. Hucke became vice president, Human Resources Division for Roy F. Weston, Inc., when he joined the firm in 1977. Mr. Hucke has over 15 years experience in all aspects of human resources including both domestic and foreign recruiting, labor relations and negotiations, safety and health management, affirmative action/equal employment opportunities administration, salary administration, re-

Job description

Mr. Hucke has total responsibility for ensuring the corporation functions from an innovative and progressive human resources vantage by maintaining state of the art knowledge of the various functions of his group.

Specific functions include the maintenance and expansion of a highly professional, technically oriented staff, development and implementation of corporate policy, identification and method selection of the corporations training and development needs.

Mr. Hucke reports directly to Mr. Roy F. Weston, president and CEO of the corporation, and has a staff of six including a compensation specialist, services administrator, and a technical recruiter.

- The demographics of the country are changing. There will be fewer young and more middle-aged people. This translates into less demand for part-time workers.
- Fringe benefits are higher in cost for part-timers. Even if cafeteria plans are used some employers remain reluctant to employ part-timers.
- Masculine values are not compatible with the image of part-time work, nor is the traditional work ethic. It will take time for more people to recognize that challenging work is important, but that doing challenging and hard work is not equivalent to long hours of work.

These conflicting set of forces suggest that part-time employment work schedules will not show a significant increase in the next decade. It should, however, continue along with job sharing to be an alternative work schedule though not a mainstream one such as flexitime.

*Views about Human Resources at Weston—
Richard W. Hucke*

The efficiency with which any organization can be operated will depend to a considerable measure upon how effectively its personnel can be managed and utilized. Since the activities of most organizations today are becoming more and more complex in nature, the managers in these organizations are required to have greater technical competency than was formerly the case. In addition to this greater technical competency, they must possess a better understanding of human behavior and of the processes by which personnel can be managed effectively. Every manager, therefore, must be able to work effectively with people and to resolve satisfactorily the many and varied problems that the management of these people may entail. Effective personnel management requires the development of a program that will permit employees to be selected and trained for those jobs that are most appropriate to their developed abilitites. Moreover, it requires that employees be motivated to exert their maximum efforts, that their performances be evaluated properly for results, and that they be remunerated on the basis of their contributions to the organization.

Fortunately, a growing body of knowledge relating to human behavior and to management systems and processes is being accumulated from experience and research which can be of assistance to the manager in developing better relations with subordinates. Human resources management is able to borrow from many of the more basic disciplines and to apply the contributions of these disciplines to the improvement of the personnel program.

There are certain basic processes to be performed, general principles and rules to be observed, as well as tools, techniques, and methods to be utilized in the management of personnel in any organization regardless of its type, purpose, or the qualifications of its personnel. Since all organizations must operate with and through people, the management of such organizations basically is a process of managing people. Any manager or supervisor who is responsible for the work of others in an organization therefore must engage in personnel management and in the various processes, such as training, motivating, and counseling, that this responsibility entails. The primary function of human resources is to provide managers with services and assistance that they may require in managing subordinates more effectively and in accordance with established personnel policies and procedures, to establish and maintain productive application of sound management processes for human resources of the corporation, including sensitivity to the strong input of human considerations to professional capability. Result areas to be considered for such processes are productivity, capability, compliance, cost, dignity, and order.

Compressed Workweek

There are two future possibilities for the CWW. First, it will remain a possible work schedule for select organizations and individuals. As discussed, CWWs are difficult to implement in many settings. The CWW also has little impact on the worker's desire to manage his or her life more and on the quality of work life. The shorter week may be valued by many, but with it comes a tiring, longer workday. These and other kind of limitations will hold down the increased use of the CWW. Thus, the CWW will probably not grow in popularity in the next decade.

On the other hand, a renewed energy crisis could increase the use of CWWs. Two of the advantages of the CWW are (1) the energy savings caused by plant and office closings, and (2) the reduction in worker commuting to and from work. If an energy crisis occurs it might be anticipated that the federal government would mandate shorter workweeks in many industries.

Summary

A major change occurring in the workplace is the willingness of union leaders, managers, and workers to experiment with various work schedules. Today the traditional five-day, 40 hour workweek is followed by most people. However, this chapter shows that P/HRM specialists and managers are becoming more and more involved with nontraditional work schedules. The main points about these newer kinds of work schedules are as follows:

1. The work environment, workers' scheduling preferences, and expectations, and demographics are changing, Now people are beginning to question the economic, social, and personal value of working a five-day, 40-hour, Monday-Friday schedule. These questions and many experiments indicate that there are alternatives.
2. Flexitime is the most popular alternative to the traditional work schedule. It allows employees to select their starting and quitting times within limits set by management.
3. Flexitime schedules can differ on many dimensions—for example, variable versus constant length of workday, when the worker must be present, and even the location of where the work takes place.
4. The latest statistics (1980) indicate that 11.9 percent of all full-time wage and salary workers are on flexible schedules. It seems reasonable to predict that by 1993 about 25 percent of these workers will have flexitime schedules.
5. Part-time employment means working less than 35 hours a week in private industry and less than 32 hours a week in the federal government. Twenty-two million Americans, mostly women and teenagers, are part-time employees.
6. Part-time employment is prevalent in fast foods, insurance, and banking.

Case

Amanda

Amanda finished her reading on the subject of new work schedules and was interested in flexitime. She believed that it could work in some units, but was still skeptical about the use in other units. For example, in intensive care full-time coverage is important and vital. She also wondered whether providing scheduling alternatives for some nurses and not others would increase the turnover rate even more. Despite these concerns she was willing to experiment with flexitime on a limited basis. She called in Jack Quenton, the P/HRM manager, the supervisor of nursing, and two nursing supervisors to start the process of setting up the experiment.

7. Job sharing is a form of part-time employment in which two or more part-timers share full-time jobs. This is especially convenient for employees with special personal challenges such as child rearing or going to school while working.

8. The compressed workweek (CWW) is a schedule in which a trade is made between the number of hours worked per day and the number of days worked per week. Thus, instead of five-day 40-hour (5/40) schedule, people may work 4/40, 3/36, 7/70, and so forth.

9. The CWW work schedule isn't growing in numbers such as flexitime and part-time employment. About 1.8 million workers are now on CWW schedules.

10. Fatigue is a potential problem of management concern of the CWW. Managerial responsibilities for safety, health, and effective performance require careful evaluation of the fatigue issue before CWWs are adopted.

Questions for Review and Discussion

1. Would job sharing be a solution to problems of layoffs in the steel and automobile industry? Why?
2. Why is evaluation of any type of work schedule important to management?
3. Why would a young worker prefer to work part time?
4. Does working part time pose a threat to the cultural tradition of being employed full time? Explain.
5. Is it practical for flexitime to be used in an intensive care unit for nurses at La Grange Community Hospital? Why?
6. What is the value of the compressed workweek to society in times of an energy crunch?
7. Why does the traditional five-day, 40-hour workweek still remain the predominant work schedule in the United States and Canada?
8. Why would managerial support be so important at the start of using a flexitime schedule?

Glossary

Compressed Workweek (CWW). A work schedule in which a trade is made between the number of hours worked per day, and the number of days worked per week, in order to work the standard length hours–four days, 10 hours each day or three days, 12 hours each day are examples of the CWW schedule.

Core Work Time. A period of time in a flexitime work schedule in which all employees in a particular unit or group must be at work.

Flexitime Work Schedules. A work schedule in which the employee is able to select his or her starting and quitting times within limits set by management.

Flexible Work Time. A period of time in a flexitime work schedule in which the employee is free to choose whether or not to be on the job.

Job Sharing. A situation in which two or more part-timers share one job. The workers are part time, but the job is full time.

Part-Time Employment A job in which a person works less than 35 hours a week. For federal employees, 32 hours a week is the dividing line between full- and part-time work.

Chapter Twenty One

Evaluating the P/HRM Function

Learning Objectives

After studying this chapter, you should be able to:

- Define what is meant by the evaluation of the P/HRM function.

- Describe the difference between functional and dysfunctional turnover.

- Explain why P/HRM managers must have diagnostic skills.

- Discuss why science is needed to examine P/HRM programs.

Chapter Outline

Case

Emily

Denton

The setting is a massive conference room. The top managers of General Products, a large manufacturing company in Seattle, are participating in the annual planning meeting. Each functional vice president presents the department's budget for next year, after a review of the past year's accomplishments.

After Emily Park, vice president for marketing, completes her budget request, her advertising budget for the next year is cut, with the explanation that "profits are down at the plant."

Denton Major, vice president for P/HRM and organization planning, speaks next.

Denton: Well, folks, I'm not going to take much of your time. It's been a long day. You know what we do for the company. We hire, train, and pay the employees, provide benefits, counsel, help with discipline, EEO, and so on. P/HRM is not asking for any major increases. My budget is simply last

year's budget adjusted upward 9 percent for inflation. Any questions?

Emily: Wait a minute, Denton. My budget just got cut. Here you come asking for 9 percent more than last year. I suppose we have to have a P/HRM department. But why shouldn't my advertising budget be increased and your budget cut? After all, advertising brings in customers and helps us make money. What *specifically* does P/HRM do for our profit and loss statement? How *specifically* does P/HRM help us reach our goals of growth and profitability?

Emily has unknowingly pointed out what purpose a personnel audit serves. If Denton had been systematically evaluating the P/HRM department, he would have some answers ready. And it looks like he will need some good ones, or the P/HRM budget and activities could well be cut.

Evaluation of the P/HRM function (the personnel audit) is a systematic, formal experience designed to measure the costs and benefits of the total P/HRM program and to compare its efficiency and effectiveness with the organization's past performance, the performance of comparable effective enterprises, and the enterprise's objectives.

Evaluation of P/HRM is performed for these purposes:

- To justify P/HRM's existence and budget.
- To improve the P/HRM function by providing a means to decide when to drop activities and when to add them.
- To provide feedback from employees and operating managers on P/HRM effectiveness.
- To help P/HRM do its part to achieve the organization's objectives.

Top management's part in the personnel audit is to insist that all aspects of the organization be evaluated and to establish the general philosophy of evaluation. The P/HRM department is often involved in designing the audit. In part the data for the audit arise from the cost/benefit studies of the P/HRM activities as described in Chapters 3–20. The operating manager's role is to help gather the data and to help evaluate the P/HRM function in the same way it evaluates other functions and users of resources in the organization.[1]

Evaluation of the P/HRM function is a Stage II activity—many researchers have advocated its implementation, but only a few good empirical studies of effective and ineffective ways of evaluating or auditing P/HRM activity have been done.

A Diagnostic Approach to Evaluation of the P/HRM Function

Exhibit 21–1 shows the factors in the diagnostic model which affect evaluation of the P/HRM function in an organization. The major factors in determining whether evaluation takes place are the orientation or attitudes of the controlling interests toward evaluation and the organization's style.

Some managers feel formal evaluations of the function are very useful. Others do not favor them.[2] Formal evaluation programs of functions are more likely to be conducted in some types of organizations than others. Larger organizations that are labor intensive and geographically dispersed probably have some type of evaluation for most functional departments, including P/HRM. Such programs are also more likely when economic conditions are bad, particularly for profit-oriented organizations, because they can establish the cost effectiveness of such functions.

Approaches to Evaluation of the P/HRM Function

Once it has been decided that it is useful to evaluate the effectiveness of the P/HRM function and the organization's use of human resources, the next issue is how it should be done and what measures or criteria of effectiveness should be used. The criteria can be grouped as follows:

1. Performance measures.
    a. Overall P/HRM performance; for example, the unit labor costs per unit of output.
    b. P/HRM department costs and performance—the cost per employee of P/HRM programs.
2. Employee satisfaction measures.
    a. Employees' satisfaction with their jobs.
    b. Employees' satisfaction with P/HRM activites such as training, pay, benefits, and career development.
3. Indirect measures of employee performance.
    a. Employee turnover—rate of quits as a percentage of the labor force and by units over time.
    b. Absenteeism—rate of voluntary absences of the labor force and by units over time.

---

[1]Vytenis P. Kuraitis, "The Personnel Audit," *Personnel Administrator,* November 1981, pp. 29–34; and Albert S. King, "A Programmatic Procedure for Evaluating Personnel Policies," *Personnel Administrator,* September 1982, pp. 82–95.

[2]Jac Fitz-Enz, "Quantifying the Human Resources Function," *Personnel,* March–April 1980, pp. 41–52.

Exhibit 21–1 _____
Factors affecting the evaluation of the P/HRM function

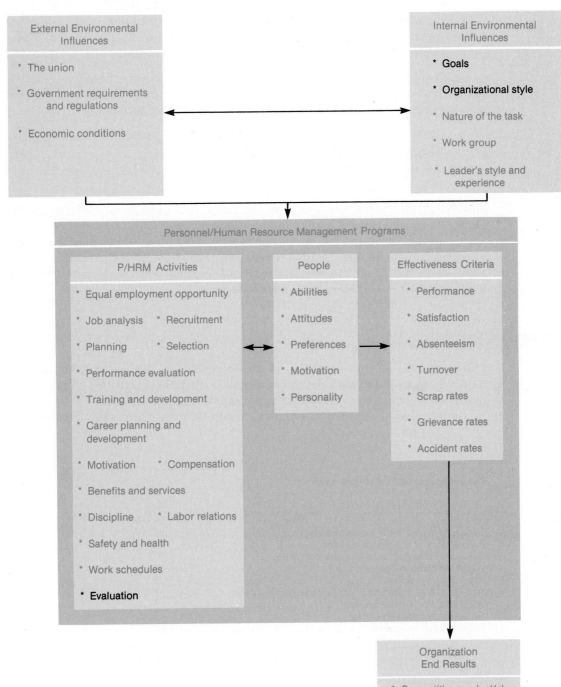

c. Scrap rates (e.g., poor quality output that must be scrapped).

d. Other measures of quality.

e. Rates of employee request for transfer.

f. Number of grievances per unit and in total labor force over time.

g. Safety and accident rates.

h. Number of improvement suggestions per employee over time.

Each of these measures or some combination of them measures the efficiency and/or effectiveness of the P/HRM effort. To make P/HRM worthwhile, it is necessary for the organization to measure its achievements against specific goals, such as:

Reduce labor costs by 3 percent this year.

Reduce absenteeism by 2 percent this year.

Increase the satisfaction index by 5 percent compared to last year's attitude survey results.

These goals are set relative to past trends, current achievements of relevant other organizations, or higher aspiration level of today's managers.

Once these criteria are set, the next decision is to determine which of the approaches to evaluation is to be used. A BNA survey indicated which approaches are being most used (see Exhibit 21–2).[3] In this chapter we will examine some of the most frequently used approaches to evaluation of the P/HRM function.

Evaluation by Checklist

One approach is to copy the practices of other organizations. This is usually implemented by developing a checklist of the model organization's P/HRM activities. Checklists are also used by consultants to analyze an organization's P/HRM function.

In the checklist approach to evaluation, the P/HRM department or a consultant pre-

Exhibit 21–2 _____

Personnel evaluation methods used

	All companies	Larger	Smaller
Evaluating departmental results against goals	33%*	37%	23%
Periodic audit of policies, procedures.	25	25	26
Surveys, meetings, discussions, and interviews.	20	19	23
Analysis of turnover figures	16	15	19
Analysis of grievances	8	9	10
Analysis of cost of performing various personnel functions	6	7	5
Analysis of training effectiveness	5	5	5
Analysis of accident frequency	5	6	4
Feedback from managers	5	5	5

*Includes 7 percent of companies specifying an MBO program for the personnel department.
Source: _Labor Policy and Practice—Personnel_ (Washington, D.C.: Bureau of National Affairs, 1975).

_____

[3] Bureau of National Affairs, _Employee Absenteeism and Turnover_, Personnel Policies Forum, Survey 106 (Washington, D.C.: U.S. Government Printing Office, May 1974).

pares a list of important P/HRM activities to be performed. The checklist usually requires the analyst to check *yes* or *no* columns beside the listed activity. The checklist may also include items designed to determine if existing P/HRM policies are being followed. The items on the checklist are usually grouped by P/HRM activity area, such as employment planning or safety and health.

Although a checklist is better than a totally informal approach, it still is a rather simple approach to evaluation. And even though checklists provide a format that is relatively easy to record and prepare, scoring interpretation is quite difficult. Three nos in one group of items may not equal three others. Some of the policies are more important than others. Ignoring EEOC or OSHA rules is a lot more negative than the absence of a Christmas party, for example.

Statistical Approaches to Evaluation

The most frequently used formal evaluation methods are those that examine the work organization's employment statistics and analyze them. The statistical approach can be much more sophisticated than checklists. The statistics gathered are compared to the unit's own past performance or to some other yardstick of measurement. Of course, quantitative factors alone never explain or evaluate anything by themselves. The *reasons* for the statistics are the important thing; statistics only indicate where to begin to look for evaluation problems.

The raw data of such reports are interesting themselves, and they can provide some input to evaluation. Most organizations that perform evaluation, however, analyze these data by the use of ratios and similar comparative methods. Exhibit 21–3 provides a list of such ratios and similar analytical methods. Once these and similar ratios are computed for an organization, they can be compared to similar organizations' ratios.[4]

The statistical approaches used most frequently consider turnover, absenteeism, grievances, attitude surveys and other measures of effectiveness, and statistical analysis of the P/HRM department itself. Because of the widespread organizational review of these statistics they were selected for inclusion in this chapter.

Evaluation of Turnover

Turnover is the net result of the exit of some employees and entrance of others to the work organization. Turnover can be quite costly to an employer. One estimate is that it costs American industry $11 billion a year. The cost of replacing a single nonmanagement employee has been estimated at over $2,500.[5] The costs of turnover include: increased costs for social security and unemployment compensation; terminal vacations; severance pay; underutilized facilities until the replacement is hired; employment costs, such as recruiting ads and expenses, interview time, test costs, computer record costs, and moving expenses; and administration costs of notification and payroll changes. Obviously there is

---

[4]P. M. Mirvis and E. E. Lawler, III, "Measuring the Financial Impact of Employee Attitudes," *Journal of Applied Psychology,* February 1977, pp. 1–8.

[5]Joseph Augustine, "Personnel Turnover," in *Handbook of Modern Personnel Administration,* ed. Joseph Famularo (New York: McGraw-Hill, 1972) chap. 62.

Exhibit 21–3 _____

P/HRM evaluation ratios

Effectiveness ratios
 Ratio of number of employees to total output—in general.
 Sales in dollars per employee for the whole company or by organizational unit (business).
 Output in units per employee hour worked for the entire organizational unit.
 Scrap loss per unit of the organization.
 Payroll costs by unit per employee grade.

Accident ratios
 Frequency of accident rate for the organization as a whole or by unit.
 Number of lost-time accidents.
 Compensation paid per 1,000 hours worked for accidents.
 Accidents by type.
 Accidents classified by type of injury to each part of the body.
 Average cost of accident by part of the body involved.

Organizational labor relations ratios
 Number of grievances filed.
 Number of arbitration awards lost.

Turnover and absenteeism ratios
 Attendance, tardiness, and overtime comparisons by organizational unit as a measure of how well an
  operation is handling employees.
 Employee turnover by unit and for the organization.

Employment ratios
 Vacations granted as a percentage of employees eligible.
 Sick-leave days granted as a percentage of labor-days worked.
 Military leaves granted per 100 employees.
 Jury duty leaves granted per 100 employees.
 Maternity leaves granted per 100 employees.
 Educational leaves granted per 100 employees.
 Personal leaves granted per 100 employees.
 Employment distribution by chronological age.
 Employment distribution by length of service with organization.
 Employment distribution by sex, race, national origin, religion.
 Managerial distribution by chronological age, sex, race, national origin, religion.
 Average age of work force.
 Average age of managerial work force.

also a loss of productivity until the new employee reaches the performance level of the one who left the job.

Average monthly turnover rates for the January–September 1981 period were 1.4 percent of the work force in the Bureau of National Affairs' survey. The bar graphs in Exhibit 21–4 show turnover averages by size of firm or industry, and region of the country.[6]

All turnover is not a net loss, however. Employees who are not contributing to organizational effectiveness should be retrained or dehired. The employer has no control over some turnovers: A student's husband or wife, for example, may work until graduation and then move away.

_____

[6]The BNA data is based on the BNA's Personnel Policies Forum and/or the American Society for Personnel Administration, Bureau of National Affairs, *Job Absence and Turnover*, December 17, 1981.

Exhibit 21–4

Average monthly turnover rates: January–September 1981

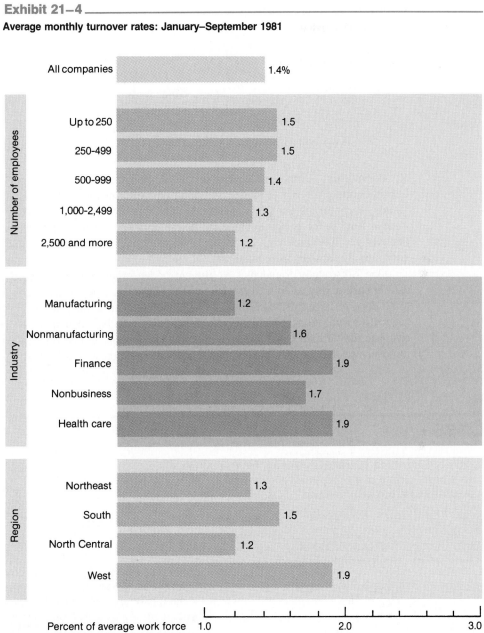

There are several quantitative methods for computing turnover. Some of the traditional formulations are:

$$\text{Separation rate} = \frac{\text{Number of separations during the month}}{\text{Total number of employees at midmonth}} \times 100 \qquad (1)$$

$$\text{Quit rate} = \frac{\text{Total quits}}{\text{Average working force}} \times 100 \qquad (2)$$

$$\text{Avoidable turnover} = \frac{\text{Total separations} - \text{Unavoidables}}{\text{Average work force}} \times 100 \qquad (3)$$

Formula (1) is the most general and is the one recommended by the Department of Labor. Formula (2) tries to isolate a difficult type of turnover, and formula (3) is the most refined. It eliminates quits by those groups that can be expected to leave: part-timers and women leaving for maternity reasons. These data can be refined further by computing turnover per 100 employees by length of employment, by job classification, by job category, and by each organizational unit.

One BNA study found that 57 percent of the organizations surveyed computed the data in such a way as to analyze turnover by department or division. This is more likely to be done in large businesses and nonmanufacturing firms than in other types of organizations. Organizations which include all employees in the calculation (67 percent) could calculate the differences in turnover by employee groups. In one recent year, the average turnover was 4.2 percent, but the rate in one organization was as high as 38 percent.[7]

Case

Denton applied some quantitative formulas to acquire a better picture of the General Products turnover situation. Here is what he found:

$$\text{Separation rate} = \frac{\text{Average for last six months}}{\text{Total number of employees at mid-month}} \times 100$$

$$= \frac{397}{9,000} \times 100$$

$$= 4.4\%$$

$$\text{Quit rate} = \frac{\text{Total quits}}{\text{Average working force}} \times 100$$

$$= \frac{318}{8,750} \times 100$$

$$= 3.6\%$$

$$\text{Avoidable turnover} = \frac{\text{Total separations} - \text{Unavoidables}}{\text{Average work force}} \times 100$$

$$= \frac{397 - 94}{8,750} \times 100$$

$$= 3.5\%$$

He looked at these figures and compared them to figures that he had on two of the main competitors in the Seattle area. He found that General Products' rates were significantly lower than the competitors. This data would help him build a case for P/HRM's contribution to General Products the next time he had to fight for budget dollars.

---

[7]Bureau of National Affairs, *Employee Absenteeism and Turnover.*

One way employers analyze the turnover rate is to compare the organization's rate with those of other organizations. Various sources publish average turnover rates quarterly or yearly. These include agencies such as the government labor departments, the Administrative Management Society, and BNA's quarterly reports on turnover and absenteeism. Another approach is to analyze the enterprise's turnover by comparing the differences in rates by employee classifications or departments.

Most theories of turnover maintain that employees leave their jobs when their needs are not being satisfied at their present place of work *and* an alternative job becomes available which the employees believe will satisfy more of their needs. These theories have not received a great deal of support, but they seem plausible.

Recent work has questioned the assumption that turnover is always a bad thing for an organization. One organizational researcher, Dalton has suggested that levels of turnover are often overstated.[8] He suggests that some turnover is beneficial or functional. This is the case when a person wants to leave the organization and the management is unconcerned about the loss. This lack of concern may be due to the poor evaluation of the person's performance or a lack of ability. If researchers add this type of turnover to what is called dysfunctional turnover the number of leavers is overstated. Dysfunctional turnover occurs when a person leaves an organization and the firm wants to retain the person.

Dalton contends that the traditional analysis of turnover (especially formulas [1] and [2] above) disregards the organizational benefits of functional turnover. Even with functional turnover there are some costs—recruitment, training, and a portion of the administrative overhead.[9] Consequently, P/HRM researchers should consider separating dysfunctional and functional turnover.

Analysis of a large number of studies examining the interrelationships between turnover and absenteeism shows that, in general, these factors are intercorrelated.[10] That is, if turnover is high, absenteeism is also likely to be high. These studies also found that both were caused by the same factors. In general, employees first exhibited high absenteeism, and this led to high turnover. Thus absenteeism and turnover are not alternative methods of showing dissatisfaction. Rather, high absenteeism is a sign that high turnover is likely in the future.

Overall, organizations try to reduce turnover by a number of methods: better employee selection, orientation, communication, supervisor training, incentive awards, and data analyses. In addition, many organizations have tried to determine why their turnover takes place. One method is to interview employees just before they leave the enterprise to try to determine why they are leaving. This is called an exit interview. Some find exit interviews unreliable and not useful. Others contend that, properly done, they are reliable enough for these purposes. Problems can arise when exiting employees give partial reasons for leaving because they need references from the employer or might want to be reemployed at a future date.

Other methods which have been tried to reduce turnover, besides exit interviews, include telephone or in-person interviews a few weeks after termination. These would

---

[8]D. R. Dalton, "Turnover and Absenteeism: Measures of Personnel Effectiveness," in *Applied Readings in Personnel and Human Resource Management,* ed. R. J. Schuler, J. M. McFillen, and D. R. Dalton (St. Paul, Minn.: West Publishing, 1981).

[9]D. R. Dalton, D. M. Krackhardt, and L. W. Porter, "Functional Turnover: An Empirical Assessment," *Journal of Applied Psychology,* December 1981, pp. 716–21.

[10]R. M. Steers and S. R. Rhodes, "A New Look at Absenteeism," *Personnel,* November–December 1980, pp. 60–65; and Dalton, "Turnover and Absenteeism."

seem to have the same flaws as exit interviews, but little data are available on the reliability of these methods. Another approach being tried is to give employees a questionnaire as they are exiting and ask them to complete it and mail it back a month or so later. This gives the employee some protection and would appear to be a much better approach than the others. Organizations using this method find a rather low percentage of employees complete the questionnaires, however. No reliability data appear to be available on these questionnaires.

In summary, turnover needs to be examined and monitored since it involves the most important resource of an organization. The firm needs to know who is leaving, why they are leaving, and whether any effort on their part can slowdown turnover. These are questions that can be answered if a thorough evaluation of a turnover program is implemented.

Evaluation of Absences

A second measure used to evaluate the P/HRM function is absenteeism rates.

> Absenteeism is the failure of employees to report for work when they are scheduled to work.

> Tardiness is partial absenteeism, in that employees report late to work.

Absenteeism is undesirable because of its costs and the operating problems it causes.[11] Absenteeism's costs to the organization include the costs of benefits, which continue even when workers are absent, so benefit costs are higher per unit of output. Overtime pay also may be necessary for the worker who is doing the job for the missing worker. Facilities may be underutilized and productivity may drop because of reduced output due to understaffing. There also may be increased break-in costs for replacements, substandard production, the need for more help from supervisors and peers, and increased inspection costs.

It is estimated that 400 million workdays are lost per year in the United States because of absenteeism. This is about 5.1 days per employee.[12] In many industries, absenteeism runs as high as 10 to 20 percent of the work force on any given day. Combining the average number of workdays lost per year with an estimate of the daily cost of nonmanagerial absenteeism per worker $66, including wages, fringe benefits, and loss in productivity, yields an annual cost of about $26.4 billion.[13]

How is absenteeism computed? The standard formula used by over 70 percent of those who compute absenteeism is:[14]

$$\frac{\text{Number of employee days lost through job absence in the period}}{\text{Average number of employees} \times \text{Number of work days}} \times 100.$$

[11]P. M. Muchinsky and P. C. Morrow, "A Multidisciplinary Model of Voluntary Employee Turnover," *Journal of Vocational Behavior,* December 1980, pp. 263–90.

[12]S. F. Yolles, D. A. Carone, and L. W. Krinsky, *Absenteeism in Industry* (Springfield, Ill.: Charles C Thomas, 1975).

[13]R. M. Steers and S. R. Rhodes. "Major Influences on Attendance: A Process Model," *Journal of Applied Psychology,* August 1978, p. 391.

[14]Bureau National Affairs, *Employee Absenteeism and Turnover,* p. 12.

Most others use a variation of this formula, such as

$$\frac{\text{Total hours of absence}}{\text{Total hours worked (or scheduled)}} \times 100$$

Of 136 enterprises surveyed by BNA, about 40 percent calculated absenteeism rates, usually for all employees, and most often monthly (54 percent) or annually (40 percent). Of those calculating absenteeism, 70 percent did so by department or division. Most also separated out long-term absences from short-term ones.

Current research raises questions about the use of absence rates, especially aggregate measures of absenteeism, to evaluate the P/HRM function. Some observers suggest abandoning the measure. It appears that it is more useful to pursue research designed to identify absence-prone persons, work groups, working conditions, and communities with a view to designing strategies to reduce absenteeism.

One example is a study by Behrend and Pocock of 1,200 men employed at a General Motors plant in Scotland. One of the major conclusions of this study was that overall absence ratios, although of some use, are open to serious misinterpretation.[15] For example, the "average" employee in their study experienced three absences per year, totaling about 18 days. But the range was from employees who were not absent 1 day in six years to several who were absent 600 days over the six-year period. The authors convincingly demonstrate that it makes much more sense to classify employees into categories of absence proneness. When this approach is used, management can focus on workers with higher absence rates. Remedial action can then be taken to improve health if the cause appears to be illness, or by counseling, discipline, and so on if health is not a factor.

Evaluation of Complaints and Grievances

A complaint is a statement (in written or oral form) of dissatisfaction or criticism by an employee to a manager.

A grievance is a complaint which has been presented formally and in writing to a management or union official.

Chapter 18 discussed what grievances are and how they are processed. The complaint-grievance rate and the severity of the grievances is another way to evaluate the P/HRM function. Of course, not all complaints or grievances relate to P/HRM issues. They can be about equipment, machinery, and other matters, too. And the grievance rate can be related to the militancy of the union or the imminence to contract negotiations. Nevertheless, an increase in the rate and severity of complaints and grievances can indicate dissatisfaction, which in turn might lead to increases in absenteeism and turnover. Both factors indicate how successful the P/HRM department is in securing productivity and satisfaction for the employee. Statistical analyses of complaints and grievances have not been done as scientifically as for turnover and absenteeism.

Evaluation Using Attitude and Opinion Surveys

Another indicator of employee and managerial evaluation of the P/HRM program is obtained through the use of attitude or opinion surveys.

---

[15]Hilde Behrend and Stuart Pocock, "Absence and the Individual: A Six-Year Study in One Organization," *International Labour Review*, November–December 1976, pp. 311–27.

> An attitude or opinion survey is a set of written instruments completed by employees (usually anonymously) expressing their reactions to employer policies and practices.

Effective attitude surveys are designed with precise goals in mind. The questions and items used are designed professionally and are tested on a sample of employees for reliability and validity prior to administration. Several other administrative factors may affect the validity. One is whether the employees feel that the employer is sincerely interested in knowing the truth and will act wherever possible to follow up on their suggestions.

The survey may include many P/HRM activities, job satisfaction, and other aspects of the organization's operations. Usually after the results of the survey are in, they are analyzed and fed back to the employee units. Organizations use attitude surveys to help evaluate the effectiveness of the total P/HRM program, or parts of it, such as pay, benefits, or training.

About 30 percent of organizations (mostly the larger and medium-sized ones) conduct regular attitude surveys. They are usually conducted on a yearly basis.[16] The organization itself can design the surveys, but approaches developed by consultants and similar services are also available. The survey develops a "snapshot view" of employee attitudes by unit and total organization. Typical topics surveyed are given in Exhibit 21–5.

One vital factor in the usefulness of attitude surveys is maintaining confidentiality of the data provided by employees. To assure reliability and validity of the data as far as possible, it has become typical to assure anonymity by questioning groups of employees together. Often the information is gathered by an outside consultant such as a university professor.

A typical survey is handled as follows. The P/HRM department contacts a consultant

Exhibit 21–5 _____

Attitudes covered in many surveys

Attitudes toward working conditions and the job	_Attitudes toward compensation and rewards_	_Attitudes toward supervisor_	_Attitudes toward the employer_
Physical working conditions	Salaries	Communication abilities	P/HRM policies
Work scheduling and planning	Benefits	Qualifications and abilities	Communications
Work assignments and worker abilities	Promotions	Supervisory style	General reputation in community
Job demands	Status and recognition		Reputation nationally
Job security			Attitudes toward future unionization
Hours of work			
Safety on the job			
Interpersonal relations at work			
Adequacy of training by employer			

---

[16]"Personnel Policies: Research and Evaluation" (ASPA-BNA Survey No. 37), *Bulletin to Management,* March 22, 1979, p. 6.

to administer the survey. The consultant first works with P/HRM in developing the data-gathering approach. Design of these questionnaires or interview schedules is an important technical project. It should be done by professionals in P/HRM or with expertise in surveying. Typically, the consultant works with the P/HRM department and a sample of operating managers and employees in developing the survey. Finally, the consultant gathers the data and processes it or sends it to a computer service center for processing. No one from the employing organization sees the actual data or questionnaires completed by the employees.

In preparation for the attitude survey, employees receive a letter explaining the purpose of the study (such as to improve working conditions). The letter also explains the safeguards for the employees that will be provided, such as the use of consultants. If a questionnaire is used, the employees complete them in homogeneous groups (exempt or nonexempt, for example).

The two principle methods used to gather data are interviews and questionnaires. Sometimes both are used by an organization. Surveys indicate that almost two thirds of the employers use questionnaires alone, less than 10 percent use only interviews, and the rest use a combination of both.[17] Studies suggest that information is more reliable and complete if interviews are used. Usually the interviews follow the structured approach. If questionnaires are used, three approaches are followed: yes, no, or don't know answers; open-ended essay questions; or structured questions with multiple-choice answers. An example of the latter is given in Exhibit 21–6.

After the data is gathered, they are analyzed. Present responses are compared to past ones to see if the trends are positive or negative. Responses from different subunits are compared to see if some are more favorable than others.

Overall indications lead to management actions of one type or another. Policies are revised, enforced, or created, and the results are communicated to the employees. The attitude survey tends to generate expectations on the part of employees. Thus, management needs to be sure that some feedback and action follows the survey. Failure to do something often results in future resistance to surveys and to a feeling that any survey is ritualistic and not useful, as both managers and researchers have found.[18]

Quality of Work Life Survey • For a number of years Graphic Controls Corporation (Buffalo, New York) has worked with the Institute for Social Research (ISR) at the University of Michigan.[19] The ISR serves as an outside research group that surveys the quality of work life in the corporation and prepares a report of its findings. Graphic Controls contacted the ISR seeking help to learn more about the attitudes of its employees.

The first survey was administered in 1975 and the data obtained was used to make a number of decisions. The decisions involved P/HRM policies concerning working conditions, fringe benefits, development of skills, and improvement in the overall quality of work life (environment, supervision, opportunities). In addition to the survey data Graphic Controls reviewed annually safety records, employment, and promotion.

---

[17]*Ibid.*

[18]R. B. Dunham and F. J. Smith, *Organization Surveys* (Glenview, Ill.: Scott, Foresman, 1979); and Paul R. Lees-Haley and Cheryl E. Lees-Haley, "Attitude Survey Norms: A Dangerous Ally," *Personnel Administrator,* October 1982, pp. 51–56.

[19]Edward E. Lawler, Phillip Mirvis, William M. H. Clarkson, and Lyman Randall, "How Graphic Control Assesses the Human Side of the Corporation," *Management Review,* October 1981, pp. 54–63.

Exhibit 21–6 _____

Attitude survey (partial sample)

INSTRUCTIONS

This is a survey of the ideas and opinions of Baker Company salaried employees. WHAT YOU SAY IN THIS QUESTIONNAIRE IS COMPLETELY CONFIDENTIAL. We do not want to know who you are. We do want to know, however, how employees with different interests, experience, and doing different kinds of work, feel about their jobs and Baker.

This is not a test. There are no right or wrong answers. Whether the results of this survey give a true picture of the Baker Company depends on whether each of you answers each of the questions in the way you really feel. The usefulness of this survey in making Baker a better place to work depends on the honesty and care with which you answer the questions.

Your answers will be compiled with many others and summarized to prepare a _report_ for Baker. Your identity will always be protected. We do not need your name, only your impressions. Your written comments will be put in typewritten form so that your handwriting will not even be seen by anyone at Baker.

Please complete each of the six parts of the survey so that all of your impressions can be recorded. Remember your honest impressions are all that we are asking for.

PART I: THE JOB AND CONDITIONS

The statements below are related to certain aspects of your job at Baker. Please circle the response number that best describes how you feel about the statement.

1 = Strongly disagree 2 = Disagree 3 = Undecided 4 = Agree 5 = Strongly agree

Pay	Strongly disagree	Disagree	Undecided	Agree	Strongly Agree
My pay is all right for the kind of work I do.....................	1	2	3	4	5
I make as much money as most of my friends....................	1	2	3	4	5
My pay allows me to keep up with the cost of living..............	1	2	3	4	5
I am satisfied with the pay I receive for my job	1	2	3	4	5
Most employees at Baker get paid at least what they deserve......	1	2	3	4	5
I understand how my salary is determined	1	2	3	4	5
What changes, if any, should be made with the Baker pay system? _____					

_____
_____

Fringe benefits					
Our major fringe benefit plan provides excellent coverage.....	1	2	3	4	5
I understand what our fringe benefits at Baker are..........	1	2	3	4	5
I am satisfied with our fringe benefit plan.......................	1	2	3	4	5
What, if anything, should be done with the Baker fringe benefit plants? _____					

_____
_____

In 1977, Graphic Controls management decided to make the survey and analysis a part of the company's annual report. William Clarkson, the firm's chief executive officer, explains Graphic's interest in surveying and going public like this:

> Psychological research tells us that a key human need is to know where one stands and how one rates. A good manager has measurements for key areas of the business. A quality-of-work life audit provides valid data for one of the cornerstones that make a business successful—the human resources of the organization. For managers and for employees, it provides data about human resources and organization climate and lets them know how they and the corporation are performing in the days ahead.[20]

The ISR researchers and Graphic Controls agreed that the data collected in the survey could be made public. This is a unique agreement. Usually researchers turn data over to management. Often, if it doesn't look favorable little is heard about it again. The Graphic Controls audit data was made available to anyone, present or prospective employees, interested in learning about the characteristics of the firm—the quality of work life.

Highlights of the report are presented in Exhibit 21–7. Readers of the report were invited to request a summary document that included information on a more detailed and complete analysis of the audit.

In 1977 the audit measurements occurred in a new context. Following the 1977 audit, the company had been acquired by the Times Mirror and had made a number of major P/HRM policy changes. These major changes are reflected in declines in employee ratings of pay and satisfaction and increases in turnover. On the positive side there are a number of trends. Employment of women and minorities, identified as a concern in the 1977 survey, increased dramatically in 1979.

Despite the apparent success of attitude surveys in firms such as Graphic Controls, there are a number of factors for P/HRM specialists in attitude surveys and management to consider. Attitude surveys such as the Graphics Controls audit are expensive. There is the expense of administering the survey, auditing P/HRM department records, the fees of researchers or maintaining an in-house survey team, and the productive time lost when managers and employees meet to complete the surveys and interpret the results. In times of inflation, high unemployment, and sluggish productivity, managements often reduce expenditures on "people programs" as Graphic Controls.

Recall William Clarkson's view about Graphic Controls reasons for conducting the audit. He makes a lot of sense. Organizations need to continually monitor their humen assets. Research indicates that reliable and valid surveys can and often do result in cost savings in reduced absenteeism and turnover. Surveys can also provide an "early warning signal of problem areas."[21]

Compliance Methods of Evaluation

In the compliance approach to evaluation of the P/HRM function, the main concern is the extent to which personnel procedures reflecting the law or company policy are being followed in the organization. Attempts are then made to determine where changes are needed.

---

[20]Ibid., p. 56.
[21]Ibid., p. 63.

Exhibit 21–7 _____

A Report from the
Institute for Social Research
on the Quality of Work Life
In Graphic Controls Corporation

The health of a corporation is determined not only by its financial results, but also by its relationship with its people. Over the past few years, Graphic Controls has been working with the Institute for Social Research of the University of Michigan to measure wages, working conditions, safety, and other things that make up people's lives at work. This is the first report of the *quality of work* life in the corporation.

This report covers the period from 1975 through 1977. To prepare it, the Institute reviewed corporate records and various employment practices. In addition, employees from all United States locations had the opportunity to complete two confidential surveys about their experiences at work and their satisfaction on the job.

What constitutes a good quality of work life differs for every corporation and for every person. Because it is impossible to measure all of the things that contribute to the quality of work life in a corporation, we have concentrated on the *basic elements* that are common to most of them. Accordingly, we reviewed corporate records and calculated rates for accidents, wage increases, female and minority employment, and promotions.

The relationship between a corporation and its people can also be measured in the way working life is satisfying to employees and contributes to their well-being. We, therefore, asked employees to report their *satisfaction* with pay, fringe benefits,

job security, their chances to develop their skills and abilities, and other aspects of work life in Graphic Controls. We also recorded their rates of absenteeism and turnover. Lastly, we asked employees to report their involvement in community affairs, their satisfaction with their lives, and their outlook toward the future.

On the facing page is a summary of the Institute's findings. More complete information on our review of jobs, supervision, and the opportunities employees had to express ideas, air grievances, and participate in decisions is available from Lyman Randall, Human Resources Group, Graphic Controls Corporation.

We hope you find this report interesting and informative. It represents our efforts to provide an accurate and reliable picture of the quality of work life in Graphic Controls. In essence, it is an audit of the human side of the corporation. There is no bottom line in this report. Instead, there are a number of measures that account for some part of people's lives at work. The reader is, therefore, encouraged to weigh each of them when coming to conclusion about the quality of work life in Graphic Controls.

Edward E. Lawler III   Philip H. Mirvis
Institute for Social Research

The Survey Results

The basic elements of good quality of work life are a *safe work environment, equitable wages, equal employment opportunities, and opportunities for advancement.*

Highlights:

	1975	*1976*	*1977*
OSHA accidents	2.5%	2.0%	1.7%

One study describes how First National City Bank (New York), one of America's largest banks, performs this audit. The first step is to identify 18 crucial personnel areas it wishes to audit. Then the bank randomly chooses branch banks (eliminating recently reorganized banks) to be studied. The audit procedure followed is diagrammed in Exhibit 21–8. The review is conducted by the Personnel Practices Review Unit (six personnel reviewers, an operations manager, and clerical support), which reviews all branches every other year.[22] The bank believes that this audit has substantially improved its P/HRM effectiveness.

_____

[22]Paul Sheibar, ''Personnel Practices Review: A Personnel Audit Activity,'' *Personnel Journal,* March 1974, pp. 211–17.

A smaller percentage of the work force suffered serious injuries on the job in 1976 and 1977. The great majority of employees also said they were safe from physical danger at work. Some 8 percent reported that dangerous or unhealthy conditions were a problem for them.

	1975	1976	1977
Wages		*	*

*Increased beyond inflation rate

Wages per hour increased the past two years. Overall, 62 percent of the work force felt that their wages were fair in comparison to those paid by other organizations in the area. 72 percent said their wages were sufficient to meet monthly expenses.

	1975	1976	1977
Female employment	30.5%	32.0%	34.3%
Minority employment	7.5	8.7	8.6

Female employment increased the past two years. Overall, 72% of the female employees reported they were treated fairly on the job. The percentage of minority employees increased in 1976 but not in 1977. Overall, 84 percent of the minority employees said they were treated fairly on the job.

	1975	1976	1977
Promotions	7.0%	11.1%	10.9%

The percentage of employees promoted increased in 1976 but not in 1977. 61 percent of the employees said they were satisfied with their chances for advancement.

The relationship between a corporation and its people can also be measured in the way working life is *satisfying* to employees and *contributes to their well-being on—and off—the job.*

	Percent satisfied		
Satisfaction	1975	1976–77	Differ-ence
Pay	69.9%	71.0%	1.1%
Fringe benefits	69.0	89.5	20.5
Job security	76.8	76.1	−0.7
Working conditions	71.2	77.2	6.0
Co-Worker relations	88.2	89.1	0.9
Accomplishments	80.5	77.7	−2.8
Chances to develop skills	72.4	74.6	2.2
Overall job satisfaction	93.7	90.2	−3.5

Most employees were satisfied with their working lives in both 1975 and 1976–77. During this time, there was a significant increase in satisfaction with fringe benefits and a small increase in satisfaction with working conditions. Other changes were insignificant. Overall job satisfaction is higher than that recorded in Gallup polls and the Institute's own survey of the national work force.

Absenteeism and Turnover?
Absenteeism went from 3.5 percent to 2.8 percent of the scheduled work hours during the three year period. Turnover was reduced from 12.7 percent to 9.3 percent of the work force from 1975 to 1976. In 1977, it increased to 12.9 percent. Counting the loss of Business Forms Division employees, 33.3 percent of the work force left in 1977.

Work and the Quality of Life:
Working life contributes, in some measure, to the quality of life. Overall, 95 percent of the employees expressed satisfaction with their lives. 57 percent of the work force were members of community, church, or social organizations and the vast majority reported voting in local and national elections. 70 percent of the employees said their jobs today were preparing them with the training and experience they need for their jobs in the future. Nationally, fewer workers feel as optimistic about their employment future.

P/HRM Research: Final Comments

The purposes of P/HRM research are to find solutions for human resources problems, to aid in evaluation of the P/HRM function, and to extend the knowledge of human resources to all those concerned. This activity is performed by universities, consultants, independent research institutes, and/or employers. The employers who perform their own P/HRM research include AT&T, IBM, and General Electric. Sometimes P/HRM research is attached to units other than P/HRM departments, such as research and development groups. One study asked P/HRM researchers to estimate how they spent their time. They reported that they spent 20 percent consulting with line managers, 15 percent running their department, 9 percent on self-development, and 55 percent on research. Of this, 13 percent was

Exhibit 21-8

Personnel compliance audit process at Citibank

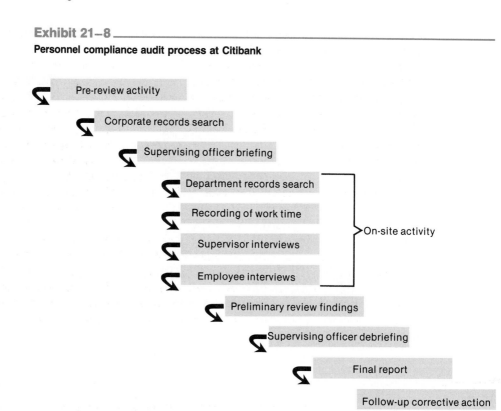

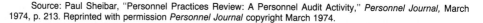

Source: Paul Sheibar, ''Personnel Practices Review: A Personnel Audit Activity,'' *Personnel Journal,* March 1974, p. 213. Reprinted with permission *Personnel Journal* copyright March 1974.

spent analyzing P/HRM statistics, 15 percent studying improved means of employment, 16 percent on improving the organization climate, and 11 percent studying training and development.[23]

Much of the research the P/HRM department does is descriptive. Studies show that most departments use surveys, historical studies, and case studies.[24] Few have tried experimenting with various approaches to P/HRM.

Some time ago, Cohen and Nagel (1934) suggested that there were four basic ways of knowing. These are tenacity, intuition, authority, and science. Managers and P/HRM researchers use all these techniques. Managers use *tenacity* when they form a belief about a P/HRM issue (e.g., if a worker is paid more productivity will increase). This belief continues to be held even if research shows it to be incorrect. Managers use *intuition* on P/HRM matters when they feel an answer to be obvious or when they have a hunch on how to solve a problem. *Authority* is used when managers seek answers or methods or

---

[23]John Hinrichs, ''Characteristics of the Personnel Research Functions,'' *Personnel Journal,* August 1969, pp. 597–604.

[24]Max Wortman, Jr., ''Corporated Industrial Relations Research: Dream or Reality?'' *Academy of Management Journal,* June 1966, pp. 127–35.

programs from an expert or consultant. Asking a performance appraisal expert to implement what he or she feels is best is using authority.

Science in P/HRM as presented in this book is used to solve, diagnose, and evaluate problems. In contrast to tenacity, intuition, and authority, science aims at obtaining answers, charting the way by using information and knowledge that is objective. The meaning of "objectivity" in this sense is that the knowledge about absenteeism, turnover, or safety and health ratios is certifiable, independent of individual opinion. It means that the research data was obtained by the use of the scientific method of inquiry. In other words, the scientific approach to P/HRM research involves using some rigorous standards of science in an attempt to minimize subjectivity and maximize objectivity.

The use of the scientific approach to P/HRM research consists of four stages: (1) observation of the situation in the real world; (2) formulation of explanations of the situation using induction; (3) generation of predictions about the situation using deduction; and (4) verification of the predictions using scientific methods. This approach to P/HRM research is shown in Exhibit 21–9. If there is anything that will enhance the prestige and influence of the P/HRM function in organizations, it is the use of more science and rigorous research to study and understand the kinds of P/HRM programs covered in Chapters 4–20. By using more P/HRM research managers can reduce the risks of relying too heavily on opinions or prejudices about people, programs, environmental forces, and the future.

Summary

Any function as important as the effective use of human resources needs to be evaluated. The difficulty in evaluating the results of the P/HRM function is that effectiveness has multiple causes, and it is difficult to separate out how much of the effectiveness results

Exhibit 21–9

Four stages of the scientific approach to P/HRM research

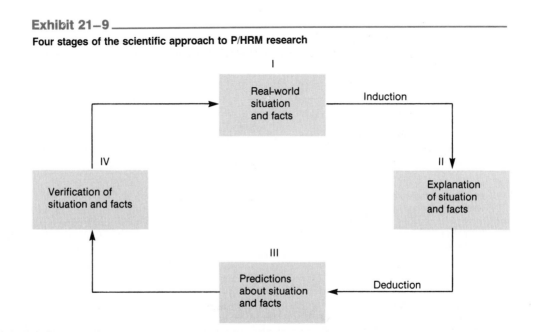

from each cause. Here is a list of some of the major statements in the evaluation section of Chapter 21 to use as a guideline.

1. Evaluation of the P/HRM function is a systematic, formal experience designed to measure the costs and benefits of the total P/HRM program and to compare its efficiency and effectiveness with the enterprise's past performance, the performance of comparable effective organizations, and the firm's objectives.
2. This evaluation is performed to
    a. Justify P/HRM existence and budget.
    b. Improve the P/HRM function by providing a means to decide when to drop activities and when to add them.
    c. Provide feedback from employees and operating managers on P/HRM's effectiveness.
    d. Help P/HRM to do its part to achieve the objectives of the organization.
3. Evaluation of the P/HRM function can be done by one or a combination of the following means:
    a. Checklist.
    b. Statistical approaches, including evaluation of turnover, absenteeism, and complaints and grievances, and the use of attitude and opinion surveys.
    c. Compliance methods of evaluation.

Exhibit 21–10 provides recommendations for the model organizations on P/HRM audits and evaluation and research.

Exhibit 21–10 _____

Recommendations for model organizations on research and evaluation of the P/HRM function

Type of organization	Checklist	Statistical	Compliance	Performed by			
				Organization	Consultant	Organization and consultant	P/HRM research department
1. Large size, low complexity, high stability			X	X			X
2. Medium size, low complexity, high stability		X	X			X	
3. Small size, low complexity, high stability	X				X		
4. Medium size, moderate complexity, moderate stability		X	X			X	
5. Large size, high complexity, low stability			X	X			X
6. Medium size, high complexity, low stability	X					X	
7. Small size, high complexity, low stability							

Case

The setting is again the conference room at General Products. The time is the next annual planning meeting. Last year, because Denton Major was not in a position to justify his budget for P/HRM he was not awarded the 9 percent increase he asked for. In fact, P/HRM was cut by the same percentage figure as the marketing department was. If he could help it, that wouldn't happen again. Emily Park, vice president for marketing, had struck at his weak flank. In the past year, he had examined the P/HRM audit approaches.

In evaluation, use of a checklist or copying other organizations appeared useful and easy. Compliance methods appeared useful, as did attitude surveys. Statistical approaches, especially evaluation of turnover, also appeared to be helpful.

As Denton waited, he was confident of the results of his budget request this year. Eventually, his time came to present his request.

Denton The P/HRM department has a report that is included in your packet of materials. You'll note that we have the results of our compliance audit. The company is substantially in compliance with government regulations. This was not true a year ago. But we set that as an objective and reached it.

From the checklist, attitude survey, and compliance items, we came up with qualitative and quantitative targets for our P/HRM program. Our major targets were to reduce costly turnover and improve the cost effectiveness of our compensation program.

Next year's objectives are given on page 10 of the report. You'll also note our cost/benefit studies justify the shift of funds among our P/HRM programs and the justification for an 8 percent increase in our budget.

Henry The budget for P/HRM is well documented and appears reasonable.

Emily A big improvement from last year's presentation, Denton.

Denton's budget was approved.

The P/HRM Manager: A Last Look

This book has been designed to help you view the P/HRM function in action and to see the full range of activities and programs conducted by employees in this function. Some readers may already work in P/HRM or will work in such a department in the future. Certainly most readers will be involved in their careers with human resource issues, problems, and challenges. We have attempted to always be realistic and to show P/HRM in all its glory and power as well as in a condition of being overworked and even uncertain. There is nothing unique to P/HRM to being overloaded and uncertain. We all experience these conditions occasionally. In viewing the P/HRM professional and the activities he or she conducts, the book relied on a number of mechanisms.

The Diagnostic Approach • It was shown that the effective P/HRM manager is a diagnostician who observes the various aspects of the organization's environment. She or he considers the size, structure, goals, and style of the organization, and the nature of the employee, the tasks, the work group, and the leader. The diagnostic manager realizes that the P/HRM policies of the organization must be congruent with all these factors, and others, if P/HRM is to do its part to contribute to organization effectiveness.

Model Organizations • This mechanism was used in many chapters to focus attention specifically on how P/HRM activities are performed differently in different types of organizations. This is certainly true of the many different kinds of organizations in the private, public, and third sectors.

The Role of the Top Manager and Operating Manager • Top managers and operating managers have important parts to play in the P/HRM process. Successful P/HRM managers know how to relate to these persons and to present P/HRM programs to them in the language and thought processes of operating and top managers. How is this done?

The P/HRM Manager in Action

The P/HRM manager portrayed in this book manages by objectives and works at showing how P/HRM contributes to organizational goals. Few organizations exist solely to hire and develop people. They exist to reach goals such as producing goods to satisfy customers while achieving a profit, or curing patients at reasonable cost, or improving the education of teenage children in a community.

The P/HRM manager of the 1980s must not only be a diagnostician, but a researcher and a futurist as well. As this chapter illustrates, research of P/HRM programs is essential.

P/HRM Manager Close-Up

David A. Miron
Owens-Illinois

Biography

David A. Miron is director of human resource management for Owens-Illinois. He holds a bachelor's degree from St. Joseph's University in Philadelphia, a master's degree in foreign service from Georgetown University and a doctoral degree in education from Harvard University where he specialized in organizational behavior and human motivation. In ad-

dition, he was a fellow in the President's Educational Program in Systematic Analysis sponsored by The White House at the University of Maryland's Graduate School of Economics.

Prior to joining Owens-Illinois in August 1979, David A. Miron was vice president of McBer and Company, a management consulting organization in Boston specializing in human resource development. As part of his consulting at McBer, he worked on executive development issues at Honeywell, Travelers Insurance Company, Mead Corporation, IBM, General Electric, Wickes, and the U.S. State Department. David Miron speaks Spanish and he has taught at the Italian government's Institute for Professional Administration. He has also led seminars in Brazil for Promon and in Colombia for Celanese. Prior to joining McBer and Company, he was director of planning for the U.S. Peace Corps with responsibility for developing a five-year planning process in each of the 60 country operations.

Job description

Mr. Miron is responsible for management development, organization development, and human resource systems at Owens-Illinois.

Without adequate research, important planning, evaluation, rewards, industrial relations, and other P/HRM programs will have to be run on the basis of hunches and intuition.

As a futurist, the P/HRM manager must develop a profile of the people in society. In the United States and Canada a wealth of statistics are available to help develop future recruitment, selection, development, and employment growth plans. Some of the statistics that are used and scrutinized are birthrates, changing family patterns, education levels, and age patterns. These statistics need to be consulted so that organizations can better cope with the people available for employment. Today we know that lifestyles are changing, the average U.S. and Canadian citizen is growing older and is more educated.

The P/HRM manager is part of the team that makes the key decisions, the strategic decisions such as: Are we going to grow? In what direction are we going to grow? Are we going to merge with another organization? What's the future going to be if our plans work out?

Each of these strategic decisions has important implications for P/HRM managers. And the P/HRM department can provide important counsel about the human resources affecting these decisions. P/HRM can only have the impact it should have if its leadership is well trained to do the job and if it can convey to top management a goal-oriented attitude when seeking additional funds to do its job.

The P/HRM manager who is part of the top-management team will be reporting what programs have been phased out, with appropriate savings, and what programs have been kept, and the savings and improvements resulting from them. Specific budget justifications will be made for proposed additions and specific measurable results that will help the enterprise reach its goals will be proposed. Further, the P/HRM manager will be able to show how to achieve these results. Managers who are used to making decisions this way will know that this executive team makes the *real* decisions that affect personnel.

In the smaller organization, the executive responsible for P/HRM and other functions should begin to consider P/HRM decisions in the same hardnosed way he or she does other decisions. Resources are scarce, and human resources are the most precious to conserve and develop.

Many explanations for U.S. and other western country economic woes have been advanced. In the United States the culprits include inadequate investment in new plants, overregulation from the government, and excessive taxation. No doubt these are contributors to many problems. Perhaps a closer look at P/HRM activities and programs, is also needed to get to the core of the nation's problems—inflation, lagging productivity, an unfavorable trade balance. P/HRM experts can help attack problems involving human attitudes and behavior. This is the overriding challenge of P/HRM as a field of study and research.

The implications of changing values in society, economic woes, and the general malaise and societal pessimism are being recognized by P/HRM practitioners. They are aware that a single plan or program (e.g., selection, training, performance appraisal) will not work every time, for all workers, in all organizations. Also they know that managing workers now require plans and programs appropriate for the 1980s. The traditional way to pay workers, schedule work, evaluate performance, select employees, compensate workers, enforce discipline, improve worker safety and health, and so forth will most likely change drastically in the future. These changes will require proactive P/HRM programs that will, at first, be difficult to initiate, sustain, and evaluate. Yet, the heart of P/HRM is people: only in this century have we seen the awakening of organizations to this most important asset. In effect, the P/HRM manager of the future will play a major part in the dynamic, increasingly, fast-paced world of tomorrow. Such a set of challenges is not for the faint-hearted. We happen to believe that there are many P/HRM specialists and people interested in P/HRM who are willing to accept such a set of challenges.

Questions for Review and Discussion

1. What is a personnel audit?
2. Why are P/HRM activities and functions evaluated by some organizations?
3. Why do some experts feel that the level of turnover in organizations has been overstated?
4. Compare and contrast the statistical indicators of P/HRM evaluation. Which are the best indicators? How are they measured?
5. Why must a P/HRM manager be a diagnostician and also look into the future?
6. What challenges lie ahead for the P/HRM manager?

Glossary

Absenteeism.   The failure of employees to report to work when they are scheduled to do so.

Attitude Survey.   A set of written instruments completed by employees expressing their reactions to employer policies and practices.

Part Six

Work Scheduling and Evaluation Cases and Exercise

APPLICATION CASE VI–1

Henrico County, Virginia's Police Department Experiment with the Compressed Workweek*

In July 1981, Henrico County, Virginia, implemented a 4/40 workweek for its police division. Under the system, each officer would work four consecutive 10-hour days, as opposed to the seven consecutive 8-hour days he or she had previously worked before receiving any time off. Officers complained that they were physically and mentally fatigued when they had to work seven consecutive days before getting time off. Consequently, the police division suffered from a relatively high turnover and absenteeism rate under the 7/56 schedule.

The chief of police appointed a four-member committee to look at the problems and complaints about the 7/56 schedule. He wanted the committee to develop a plan that would (1) provide more days off and time off on weekends; (2) increase the total officers available during peak hours; (3) decrease the response time to calls; and (4) reduce officer fatigue and absenteeism.

The committee examined a number of alternative work schedules. They found that other police departments around the United States were using variations of a four-day, 10 hour a day schedule. These other departments found that a majority of their officers preferred the 4/40 schedule. The Henrico County police committee decided to recommend a 4-day, 10 hour a day schedule with a rotating cycle. Each officer would work four days, then have three days off; four days, three off; and four days, two off. It was necessary to have one cycle of two days in order that the days off would rotate each month. The rotating schedule allowed officers to have up to 33 weekends off per year, as opposed to the 12 allotted under the 7/56 schedule.

Three months after the 4/40 rotating schedule was implemented, an attitude survey was used to acquire officer reactions. Of the officers contacted, 79 percent felt that the 4/40 rotating schedule increased officer safety; 67 percent felt it increased work satisfaction; 96 percent believed it increased the availability of officers during peak hours of call for service; and 57 percent felt it improved their family life.

Six months after implementing the new work schedule, sick leave records indicated a 18.2 percent decline compared to the same period last year. Also officer productivity increased. Felony arrests increased 42.5 percent, misdemeanor arrests increased 69.5 percent, drunk driving arrests increased 75.4 percent and other traffic-related arrests increased 38.9 percent. The only noticeable flaws with the new system involved the transfer of information between shifts and the high levels of reported fatigue. The officers complained that in the 4/40 arrangement less time is taken to trade information. After working for 10 hours the officers are anxious to get away from work as soon as their shift is over. Fatigue is still as nagging a problem as it was with the 7/56 schedule. There is some fear that the fatigue problem may result in tragic consequences for some officers in the future.

The four-person committee is ready to meet again in about four weeks to examine the 4/40 rotating schedule. They are thinking about (1) continuing the schedule as is, (2)

---

*Case is based on Robert H. Crowder, Jr., "The Four-Day, Ten-Hour Workweek," *Personnel Journal*, January 1982, pp. 26–28.

making some modifications, or (3) dropping the 4/40 and returning to the 7/56 work schedule. There is some sentiment among officers for each of these options.

Questions for Thought

1. Are the three-month and six-month evaluations sufficient to conclude that the Henrico County, 4/40 plan is a success? Why?
2. At this point what option seems to be best for the police officers? Why?
3. Should an employer such as Henrico County be concerned about the family time of its employees? Why?

APPLICATION CASE VI–2

IBM's Method of Tracking Productivity*

For several years, IBM has been using the common staffing system (CSS) to measure the productivity of its indirect work force. It covers the indirect work force in 37 of 39 equipment manufacturing plants throughout the world and another 26,000 people in IBM organizations in Europe and Japan. P/HRM experts and managers in IBM wanted to improve the productivity of the indirect work force. This meant that research, evaluation, and analysis were needed to tackle the workload measurement problem. Consequently, an IBM task force (industrial engineers, managers, P/HRM specialists) was appointed to develop:

1. A productivity measurement system.
2. A system that enables comparisons and tracking of trends over time.
3. A system to measure workload in meaningful terms.

In general, each IBM plant performs similar job tasks to manufacture products. How the tasks are described by plant managers, however, and how they are organized, differed from plant to plant. Therefore, the task force first prepared descriptions for all tasks which they called activities. For example, the CSS activity called procurement engineering is the task of identifying manufacturing requirements, maintaining cost estimates, and so forth, for parts IBM purchases from a vendor. This activity may be located in the procurement function at one plant, the industrial engineering function at another plant, or in manufacturing engineering at a third. In the CSS plan, this activity is identified as part of the

---

*Case is based and modified from Kenneth A. Charon and James D. Schlumpf, "IBM's Common Staffing System," *Management Review,* August 1981, pp. 8–14.

"manufacturing engineering" functional responsibility. CSS standardizes the different organizational arrangements by assigning activities to "model functions."

For each activity the task force identified the factors that cause indirect work. They are called indicators. The activities are the "input" in productivity measures and the indicators are the "output."

For example, "indirect plant population" is an indicator of the need for secretarial services. As one changes so does the other. Exhibit VI–1 shows five model functions, a typical activity for each function, and a typical indicator for the activity. Eventually the task force identified about 140 activities and about 60 work-causing indicators in each of the CSS applications (manufacturing and nonmanufacturing). Obviously, an indicator can be related to more than one activity. Total labor force, for instance, is the work-causing indicator for the activity of salary administration within the P/HRM function and also for the activity of safety administration within the facilities services function.

Once each year every manufacturing location inputs via a terminal into a computer data base the number of people in each of the activities and the quantities of each of the indicators at the plant. The computer is programmed to analyze this data mathematically. A productivity ratio of people per unit of indicator for each activity at each plant is calculated.

These ratios are used by P/HRM and management for measuring the productivity at each plant since the previous year's survey. For example, a plant might report that it has 100 secretaries and an employee population of 1,000. The productivity ratio for this plant is 0.1. The questions then asked at IBM are: (1) Is this good or bad? (2) Can it be improved? (3) How does it compare to last year?

The questions are partially answered by computer-generated graphs. Exhibit VI–2 and VI–3 are such graphs. The overall average productivity ratio is expressed by the diagonal line. Exhibit VI–3 shows an average number of secretaries at a location the size of plant A to be 90. Thus, plant A's comparison index score is 1.11. This indicates that plant A management and P/HRM should be able to improve this index by 11 percent.

In addition to the graphs, managers receive reports for the average of each activity in each of IBM's plants. Summaries of these analyses for activity, function, county, and business unit are provided for managerial action and follow-up. The P/HRM department uses the CSS for three purposes: productivity comparisons, human resource planning, and productivity tracking. The IBM managers through the CSS program have established a common dictionary of terminology. This encourages conversation between managers, plant, and countries.

The IBM effort in the CSS program is based on the P/HRM department and management's belief that the primary factors affecting productivity are universal and everyone's

Exhibit VI–1 _____

Typical examples of functions, activities, and indicators

Functions	Activities	Indicators
General services	Secretarial services	Indirect labor force
P/HRM	Salary administration	Total labor force
Finance	Vendor Billing	Purchasing dollars
Information systems	Computer operations	Installed equipment
Quality assurance	Cost estimating	Value added dollars

Exhibit VI–2

A productivity ratio: Average plant

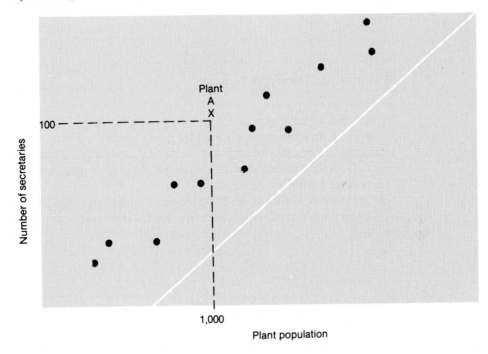

Plant
A
X

100

Number of secretaries

1,000

Plant population

Exhibit VI–3

A productivity ratio: Norm index

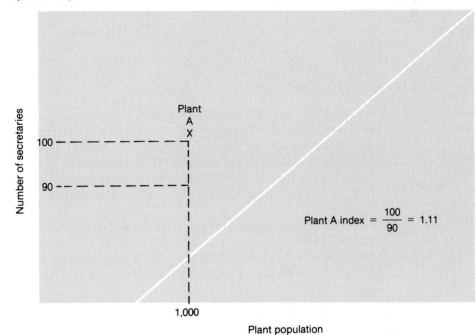

Plant
A
X

100

90

Number of secretaries

Plant A index $= \dfrac{100}{90} = 1.11$

1,000

Plant population

business. By collecting data, analyzing it, and feeding it back to plant managers and P/HRM representatives, IBM top management believes it can do a better job of pinpointing successes or failures of plants within various countries.

Questions for Thought

1. Currently IBM is using the CSS to address actual results. How could the P/HRM department use it for longer time planning?
2. Suppose that a productivity ratio of an IBM plant is better than average, say 0.87 for secretaries? Does this mean that the plant is operating at the best possible level? Why?
3. Do you feel that there would be problems in defining some jobs in engineering making it difficult to use the CSS? Explain.

EXERCISE VI

Evaluating the Productivity Contributions of P/HRM

Objective. To consider the reasons why there is a lack of substantive research on the impact of P/HRM activities on organizational productivity.

Set up the Exercise

1. Individuals are to first read the following reasons cited by some people why P/HRM contributions to productivity are not well researched (5–10 minutes):
   a. P/HRM departments are small. To conduct good research on P/HRM productivity contributions requires people and time that is not available.
   b. There is a general lack of performance data available to measure P/HRM's impact.
   c. Little is expected in most organizations in terms of P/HRM contributions to productivity.
   d. P/HRM experts themselves are not motivated to evaluate their department's contributions.
   e. More research than the literature suggests is being conducted by P/HRM departments. However, there is a reluctance to share findings with competitors and the public.

2. After individually reviewing these five expert opinions form groups of four to eight to

discuss the accuracy of the claims. For those opinions which the group considers inaccurate or fairly inaccurate develop a solution (20 to 30 minutes).
3. A group representative will present the group's solutions to the entire class. These solutions can be discussed in the entire class (10 to 15 minutes).

A Learning Note

This exercise will point out some of the reasons why the impact of P/HRM on organizational productivity has not been clearly communicated.

Name Index

681

Subject Index

Set Linotron 202 in 10½ point Times Roman, leaded 1½ points, and 9 point Helvetica light, leaded 2 points. Part numbers are 36 point and part titles are 24 point Helvetica Heavy. Chapter numbers are 30 point and chapter titles are 24 point Helvetica Heavy. The size of the type area is 36 by 50 picas.